D1826995

PARKER SCHOOL OF FOREIGN AND COMPARATIVE LAW

COLUMBIA UNIVERSITY

COMMERCIAL ARBITRATION: AN INTERNATIONAL BIBLIOGRAPHY

Transnational Juris Publication, Inc.
Irvington-on-Hudson, NY — USA
Kluwer Law & Taxation Publishers
Deventer — The Netherlands

Published by:

Transnational Juris Publications, Inc.
One Bridge Street
Irvington-on-Hudson, NY 10533
914/591/4288 Fax 914/591/2688

and

Kluwer Law & Taxation Publishers
Staverentraat 32015
7400 GA Deventer
The Netherlands
31 (0) 5700 47261 Fax 31 (0) 5700 22244

ISBN 1-56425-002-4   Transnational Juris
ISBN 906544 7113   Kluwer Law & Taxation

Library of Congress Cataloging-in-Publication Data

Commercial arbitration : international bibliography / Parker School of
    Foreign and Comparative Law, Columbia University.
            p. cm.
Includes bibliographical references.
ISBN 1-56425-002-4 : $185.00
    1. Arbitration and award, International -- Bibliography. I. Parker
School of Foreign and Comparative Law.
K2400.A12C66 1992
016.341.5'22--dc20   92-23736
                                                             CIP

Manufactured in the United States of America

PARKER SCHOOL OF FOREIGN AND COMPARATIVE LAW

COMMERCIAL ARBITRATION

AN INTERNATIONAL BIBLIOGRAPHY

PART ONE

SUBJECT-MATTER BIBLIOGRAPHY

14.   THE ARBITRAL PROCESS

15.   ARBITRATION PROCEDURE

16.   INTERIM MEASURES OF PROTECTION

17.   AWARDS

PART TWO

COUNTRY-BY-COUNTRY BIBLIOGRAPHY

PREFACE

The task of the Parker School of Foreign and Comparative Law is to promote the study and teaching of foreign and comparative law. To that end, it sponsors, and provides financial support for, all courses in foreign and comparative law at the Columbia Law School. The Parker School is also, and since its inception has been, engaged in promoting publications in foreign and comparative law. From an early time, it has realized that well conceived bibliographies are among the more important tools of the student of foreign and comparative law. The Szladits Bibliography on Foreign and Comparative Law, conceived and begun by Professor Charles Szladits and now continued by Professor Vratislav Pechota, has been one of the universally acclaimed works pioneered by the Parker School.

In recent times, the Parker School has concentrated its research and publication efforts on the fields of international arbitration and legal developments in the countries of the former East-European bloc. Its efforts in the field of international arbitration have led to the publication of the *World Arbitration Reporter*, a multi-volume comprehensive work on laws and institutions dealing with arbitration around the world. It is the sponsor of *The American Review of International Arbitration,* the only publication of its kind in the United States and one of the leading publications on this subject in the world. In 1989, the Parker School also commenced the publication of its *Guide to International Arbitration and Arbitrators,* which, in addition to the rules of the principal arbitration institutions, lists the names of some five hundred practitioners of the art of arbitration. A second edition was published in 1992 and contains some thousand names. In 1990, the Parker School published *International Commercial Arbitration and the Courts,* an international source work, containing references to international agreements, laws, court decisions, and publications on the relationship between courts and arbitrators.

The work presented here is of more universal scope. It contains bibliographies of publications all over the world relating to commercial arbitration. It is not limited to, but includes, publications in English. It should prove an invaluable tool to anyone who seeks information on any subject relating to arbitration anywhere in the world. It is contemplated that this bibliography will be updated periodically in new editions.

Professor Vratislav Pechota is primarily responsible for this volume. It could not have been published without the patient and diligent efforts of Shirley Yeh in the preparation of the manuscript. The Parker School is greatly indebted to both.

Hans Smit
Stanley H. Fuld
Professor of Law,
Director, Parker School of
Foreign and Comparative Law

INTRODUCTION

Commercial arbitration in the contemporary world is a profoundly international process. It involves the use of a diverse range of rules and procedures that often transcends the confines of the national legal order. Both the parties and the arbitrators must be aware of the transnational dimension of the arbitral process, and of its repercussions for their case.

Serious inquiry into the salient features of the arbitral process in general, as well as careful preparation for the conduct of an arbitration in a specific case, require consideration and analysis of relevant sources. Mastering these sources is a formidable task. In addition to statutory materials and applicable rules, there is a vast assortment of books and articles describing, analyzing, and summarizing the arbitration laws and practices of the countries of the world and providing insights into particular aspects of the arbitral process.

The amount of literature dealing with commercial arbitration has grown substantially during the last two decades. About five thousand books and articles have been published worldwide during that period. No single academic or arbitral institution can possibly possess this wealth of literature. Yet it is important to know that it exists.

The Parker School of Foreign and Comparative Law at Columbia University has compiled a comprehensive international bibliography on commercial arbitration. The desire to make this compilation available to a wider professional audience prompted the preparation of this bibliographical guide. The extent of the literature and the number and variety of the law reviews, professional journals, yearbooks, symposia volumes, and other periodicals and non-periodical editions now available imposes practical limits to bibliographical inquiry undertaken by individual researchers. This volume seeks to assist in finding relevant titles among the voluminous arbitration literature.

The compilation of a bibliography as large as this requires considerable time and effort. Each entry must be carefully evaluated and classified. In classifying the entries, we adhered generally to the categorization used by the UNCITRAL Model Law on International Commercial Arbitration and the UNCITRAL Arbitration Rules. In addition, our classification covers various sources of arbitration law, as well as topics needed for conceptual analysis.

The books and articles described are arranged both according to the subject matter and geographically. As a consequence, the volume has been divided into two main parts: the subject matter bibliography and the country-by-country bibliography. The subject-matter bibliography arranges the entries into twenty principal headings:

Commercial arbitration in general;
Sources of arbitration law;
International arbitration institutions and rules;
National arbitration institutions and rules;
The nature of arbitral adjudication;
Dispute;
Parties;
Agreement to arbitrate;
Arbitration and third parties;
Multi-party arbitration;
Arbitrators and arbitral tribunals;
Authority of the arbitral tribunal;
Applicable law;
The arbitral process;
Arbitration procedure;
Interim measures of protection;
Awards;
Costs;
Arbitration and the courts; and
Recognition and enforcement of arbitral awards.

The country-by-country bibliography includes books and articles on arbitration law and practice in over one hundred regions and countries of the world.

Every effort has been made to make the bibliography as accurate, complete, and easy to use as possible. Inevitably, some users may disagree with the classification given to a particular entry. As a general rule, entries overlapping several areas are listed under the more general subject area.

It is hoped that this bibliography will be useful both as a guide to books and articles on specific topics and a guide to the law and practice of particular countries.

ABBREVIATIONS

AALCC Q. Bull. - Quarterly Bulletin of the Asian-African Legal Consultative
   Committee (IND)
A.B.A. J. - American Bar Association Journal (USA)
Adel. L. Rev. - Adelaide Law Review (AUS)
Afr. L. Rep. - African Law Reports (NIG)
AktG - Die Aktiengesellschaft (FRG)
Alb. L. Rev. - Albany Law Review (USA)
All E.R. Ann. Rev. - All England Reports Annual Review (UK)
Alta. L. Rev. - Alberta Law Review (CAN)
Am. Bus. L.J. - American Business Law Journal (USA)
Am. J. Comp. L. - American Journal of Comparative Law (USA)
Am. J. Int'l L. - American Journal of International Law (USA)
Am. J. Leg. History - American Journal of Legal History (USA)
Am. Rev. Int'l Arb. - American Review of International Arbitration (USA)
Am. Soc. Int'l L. Proc. - Proceedings of the American Society for International
   Law (USA)
Am. U.L. Rev. - American University Law Review (USA)
Am. U.J. Int'l L. & Pol'y - The American University Journal of International
   Law and Policy (USA)
Anglo-Am. L .Rev. - Anglo-American Law Review (USA)
Ann. Français Droit Int'l - Annuaire Français de Droit International (FRA)
Ann. Jur. Que. - Annuaire de Jurisprudence du Québec (CAN)
Ann. Suisse Droit Int'l - Annuaire Suisse de Droit International (SWI)
Antitrust & Trade Reg. Rep. (BNA) - Bureau of National Affairs
Antitrust and Trade Regulation Reporter (USA)
Anuario Der. Int'l - Anuario de Derecho Internacional (SPA)
Anuario Der. Mar. - Anuario de Derecho Maritimo (SPA)
Arab L.Q. - Arab Law Quarterly (UK)
Arb. Int'l - Arbitration International (UK)
Arbitration - Arbitration: The Journal of the Chartered Institute of Arbitrators
   (UK)
Arb. J. - Arbitration Journal (USA)
Austl. Bus. L. Rev. - Australian Business Law Review (AUS)
Austl. L.J. - Australian Law Journal (AUS)
Austl. L.R. - Australian Law Reports (AUS)
AWD - Aussenwirtschaftsdienst des Betriebs-Berater (FRG)
BB - Der Betriebs-Berater (FRG)
B.C. Int'l & Comp. L. Rev. - Boston College International and Comparative
   Law Review (USA)
BJM - Basler Juristische Mitteilungen (SWI)
Bol. A. Esp. Arb. - Boletín de la Asociación Española del Arbitraje (SPA)
Brit. Y.B. Int'l L. - British Year Book of International Law (UK)
Brooklyn J. Int'l L. - Brooklyn Journal of International Law (USA)
B.U. Int'l L.J. - Boston University International Law Journal (USA)

B.U. L. Rev. - Boston University Law Review (USA)
Bull. Czechoslovak L. - Bulletin of Czechoslovak Law (CZE)
Bull. Japan Shipping Exch. - Bulletin of the Japan Shipping Exchange (JAP)
Bull. Swiss Arb. A. - Bulletin of the Swiss Arbitration Association (SWI)
Bus. L. Rev. - Business Law Review (UK)
Bus. Law. - The Business Lawyer (USA)
B.Y.U. L. Rev. - Brigham Young University Law Review (USA)
Cal. W. Int'l L.J. - California Western International Law Journal (USA)
Calcutta L.J. - Calcutta Law Journal (IND)
Calif. L. Rev. - California Law Review (USA)
Can. Arb. J. - Canadian Arbitration Journal (CAN)
Can. B. Rev. - Canadian Bar Review (CAN)
Can. Bus. L.J. - Canadian Business Law Journal (CAN)
Can. Y.B. Int'l L. - Canadian Year Book of International Law (CAN)
Cardozo L. Rev. - Cardozo Law Review (USA)
Caribbean L. & Bus. - Caribbean Laws and Business (BAR)
Case W. Res. J. Int'l L. - Case Western Reserve Journal of International
        Law (USA)
Cath. U.L. Rev. - Catholic University Law Review (USA)
Chulalongkorn L. Rev. - Chulalongkorn Law Review (THA)
Civil Just. Q. - Civil Justice Quarterly (UK)
Colum. J. Transnat'l L. - Columbia Journal of Transnational Law (USA)
Colum. L. Rev. - Columbia Law Review (USA)
Com. L.J. - Commercial Law Journal (USA)
Common Mkt. L. Rev. - Common Market Law Review (NET)
Commonwealth L. Bull. - Commonwealth Law Bulletin (UK)
Comp. & Int'l L.J. Southern Afr. - The Comparative and International Law
        Journal of Southern Africa (RSA)
Company L.J. - Company Law Journal (IND)
Conn. J. Int'l L. - Connecticut Journal of International Law (USA)
Conn. L. Rev. - Connecticut Law Review (USA)
Cornell Int'l L.J. - Cornell International Law Journal (USA)
Cornell L.Q. - Cornell Law Quarterly (USA)
Cornell L. Rev. - Cornell Law Review (USA)
Creighton L. Rev. - Creighton Law Review (USA)
Cumb. L. Rev. - Cumberland Law Review (USA)
Dalloz - Recueil Dalloz-Sirey (FRA)
Delhi L. Rev. - Delhi Law Review (IND)
Den. J. Int'l L. & Pol'y - Denver Journal of International Law and Policy
        (USA)
Dick. J. Int'l L. - Dickinson Journal of International Law (USA)
Dir. Mar. - Diritto Maritimo (ITA)
DJ - Deutsche Justiz (FRG)
DJZ - Deutsche Juristen Zeitung (FRG)
Droit et Pratique du Com. Int'l - Droit et Pratique du Commerce Interna-
        tional/International Trade Law and Practice (FRA)

Droit Mar. Français - Droit Maritime Français (FRA)

Duke L.J. - Duke Law Journal (USA)

Duq. L. Rev. - Duquesne Law Review (USA)

East Afr. L.J. - East African Law Journal (KEN)

East Asian Exec. Rep. - East Asian Executive Report (USA)

Emory J. Int'l Disp. Res. - Emory Journal of International Dispute
    Resolution (USA)

Europ. Transport L. - European Transport Law (BEL)

Fed. L. Rev. - Federal Law Review (AUS)

Fordham Int'l L.J. - Fordham International Law Journal (USA)

Fordham L. Rev. - Fordham Law Review (USA)

Fordham Urb. L.J. - Fordham Urban Law Journal (USA)

Ga. J. Int'l & Comp. L. - Georgia Journal of International and Comparative
    Law (USA)

Geo. Wash. J. Int'l L. & Econ. - George Washington Journal of International
    Law and Economics (USA)

Geo. Wash. L. Rev. - George Washington Law Review (USA)

German Y.B. Int'l L. - German Yearbook of International Law (FRG)

GRUR Int'l - Gewerblicher Rechtsschutz und Urheberrecht, Internationaler
    Teil (FRG)

Harv. Int'l L.J. - Harvard International Law Journal (USA)

Harv. L. Rev. - Harvard Law Review (USA)

Harv. J. L. & Pub. Pol'y - Harvard Journal of Law and Public Policy (USA)

Hastings Int'l & Comp. L. Rev. - Hastings International and Comparative Law
    Review (USA)

Hastings L.J. - Hastings Law Journal (USA)

Holdsworth L. Rev. - Holdsworth Law Review (UK)

Hong Kong L.J. - Hong Kong Law Journal (HKG)

Houston J. Int'l L. - Houston Journal of International Law (USA)

Houston L. Rev. - Houston Law Review (USA)

I.C.A. Arb. Q. - Indian Council of Arbitration, Arbitration Quarterly (IND)

ICCA Int'l Arb. Congress: Proceedings - International Council for Commercial
    Arbitration, International Arbitration Congress: Proceedings

ICSID Rev. - Foreign Investment L.J. — ICSID Review - Foreign
Investment Law Journal (UN)

Idaho L. Rev. - Idaho Law Review (USA)

I.L.M. - International Legal Materials (USA)

Indian J. Int'l L. - Indian Journal of International Law (IND)

Indian J. Leg. Studies - Indian Journal of Legal Studies (IND)

Int'l & Comp. L.Q. - International and Comparative Law Quarterly (UK)

Int'l Arb. Rep. - International Arbitration Report (USA)

Int'l Bus. Law. - International Business Lawyer (UK)

Int'l Bus. L.J. - International Business Law Journal/Revue de Droit des
    Affaires Internationales (FRA)]

Int'l Constr. L. Rev. - International Construction Law Review (UK)

Int'l Contr. - International Contract (SWI)

Int'l Fin. L. Rev. - International Financial Law Review (UK)
Int'l Handbook Com. Arb. - International Handbook on Commercial
    Arbitration (NET)
Int'l J. Leg. Info. - International Journal of Legal Information (USA)
Int'l Law. - International Lawyer (USA)
Int'l Litigation Q. - International Litigation Quarterly (USA)
Int'l Tax & Bus. Law. - International Tax and Business Lawyer (USA)
Int'l Trade L. & Prac. - International Trade Law and Practice/Droit et pratique
    du commerce international (FRA)
Int'l Trade L.J. - International Trade Law Journal (USA)
Int'l Y.B. Civil & Com. Arb. - International Year Book on Civil and Commer-
    cial Arbitration (USA)
Iowa L. Rev. - Iowa Law Review (USA)
IPRax - Praxis des Internationalen Privat- und Verfahrensrechts (FRG)
Italian Y.B. Int'l L. - Italian Yearbook of International Law (ITA)
Jahrbuch Schiedsgerichtsbarkeit - JahrbuchfürdiePraxisder
    Schiedsgerichtsbarkeit (FRG)
Japanese Ann. Int'l L. - Japanese Annual of International Law (JAP)
JBl. - Juristische Blätter (AST)
J. Afr. L. - Journal of African Law (UK)
J. Bus. L. - Journal of Business Law (UK)
JCAA Quarterly - Quarterly of the Japan Commercial Arbitration
    Association (JAP)
J. Comp. Bus. & Cap. Market L. - Journal of Comparative Business and
    Capital Market Law (NET)
J. Contemp. L. - Journal of Contemporary Law (USA)
J. Corp. L. - Journal of Corporation Law (USA)
J. Droit Int'l (Clunet) - Journal de Droit International (Clunet) (FRA)
JdT - Journal des Tribunaux (SWI)
J. Energy & Nat. Resources L. - Journal of Energy and Natural Resources
    Law (USA)
J. Ind. L. Inst. - Journal of the Indian Law Institute (IND)
J. Int'l Arb. - Journal of International Arbitration (SWI)
J. Int'l L. & Econ. - Journal of International Law and Economics (continued by
    George Washington Journal of International Law and Economics)
    (USA)
J. L. & Com. - Journal of Law and Commerce (USA)
J. Mar. L. & Com. - Journal of Maritime Law and Commerce (USA)
J. Marshall L. Rev. - John Marshall Law Review (USA)
J. Pat. Off. Soc'y - Journal of the Patent Office Society (USA)
JR - Juristische Rundschau (FRG)
JT - Journal des Tribunaux (BEL)
Jurispr. Arg. - Jurisprudencia Argentina (ARG)
J. World Trade L. - Journal of World Trade Law (UK)
JZ - Juristenzeitung (FRG)
Korean J. Comp. L. - Korean Journal of Comparative Law (KOR)

KTS - Konkurs-, Treuhand- und Schiedsgerichtswesen (FRG)
L. & Int'l Aff. - Law & International Affairs (BAN)
L. & Pol'y Int'l Bus. - Law and Policy in International Business (USA)
La. L. Rev. - Louisiana Law Review (USA)
Law. Am. - Lawyer of the Americas (USA)
Law & Contemp. Probs. - Law and Contemporary Problems (USA)
Law & Hist. Rev. - Law and History Review (USA)
Lloyd's Arb. Rep. - Lloyd's Arbitration Reports (UK)
Lloyd's Mar. & Com. L.Q. - Lloyd's Maritime and Commercial Law
        Quarterly (UK)
Loy. L.A. Int'l & Comp. L.J. - Loyola of Los Angeles International and
        Comparative Law Review (USA)
Loy. L.A. L. Rev. - Loyola of Los Angeles Law Review (USA)
Loy. U. Chi. L.J. - Loyola University of Chicago Law Journal (USA)
L.Q. Rev. - Law Quarterly Review (UK)
L. Soc'y Gazette - Law Society Gazette (CAN)
Malaya L. Rev. - Malaya Law Review (SIN)
Malayan L.J. - Malayan Law Journal (MAL)
Management Int'l J. - Management International Journal (USA)
Mar. Law. - Maritime Lawyer (USA)
Md. J. Int'l L. & Trade - Maryland Journal of International Law and
        Trade (USA)
MDR - Monatsschrift für Deutsches Recht (FRG)
Melbourne U.L. Rev. - Melbourne University Law Review (AUS)
Miami L.Q. - Miami Law Quarterly (USA)
Mich. J. Int'l L. - Michigan Journal of International Law (USA)
Mich. L. Rev. - Michigan Law Review (USA)
Mich. Y.B. Int'l Legal Stud. - Michigan Yearbook of International Legal
        Studies (USA)
Middle E. Exec. Rep. - Middle East Executive Reports (USA)
Minn. L. Rev. - Minnesota Law Review (USA)
Mo. J. Disp. Res. - Missouri Journal of Dispute Resolution (USA)
Mod. L. Rev. - The Modern Law Review (UK)
N.C.J. Int'l L. & Com. Reg. - North Carolina Journal of International Law and
        Commercial Regulation (USA)
N.C. L. Rev. - North Carolina Law Review (USA)
Neth. Int'l L. Rev. - Netherlands International Law Review (NET)
Neth. Y.B. Int'l L. - Netherlands Yearbook of International Law (NET)
New L.J. - New Law Journal (UK)
NJW - Neue Juristische Wochenschrift (FRG)
N. Ky. L. Rev. - Northern Kentucky Law Review (USA)
Nordic J. Int'l L. - Nordic Journal of International Law (DEN)
Notre Dame Int'l & Comp. L.J. - Notre Dame International and Comparative
        Law Journal (USA)
Nw. J. Int'l L. & Bus. - Northwestern Journal of International Law and
        Business (USA)

N.Y.L.J. - New York Law Journal (USA)
N.Y. L. Sch. J. Int'l & Comp. L. - New York Law School Journal of International and Comparative Law (USA)
N.Y.U. J. Int'l L. & Pol. - New York University Journal of International Law and Politics (USA)
N.Y.U.L.J.- New York University Law Journal (USA)
N.Y.U. L. Rev. - New York University Law Review (USA)
Ohio St. J. Disp. Res. - Ohio State Journal on Dispute Resolution (USA)
ÖJZ - Österreichische Juristen-Zeitung (AST)
Osaka U. L. Rev. - Osaka University Law Review (JAP)
Pace L. Rev. - Pace Law Review (USA)
Pat., Trademark & Copyright J. (BNA) - Bureau of National Affairs Patent, Trademark and Copyright Journal (USA)
Pepperdine L. Rev. - Pepperdine Law Review (USA)
Philippine L.J. - Philippine Law Journal (PHI)
Polish Y.B. Int'l L. - Polish Yearbook of International Law (POL)
Pub. Cont. L.J. - Public Contract Law Journal (USA)
Queensl. Inst. Tech. L.J. - Queensland Institute of Technology Law Journal (AUS)
Queensl. L. Soc'y J. - Queensland Law Society Journal (AUS)
Rabels Z. - Rabels Zeitschrift für ausländisches öffentliches Recht und Völkerrecht (FRG)
Rassegna dell'Arb. - Rassegna dell'Arbitrato (ITA)
Recueil des Cours - Académie de droit international de la Haye, Recueil des Cours (NET)
Rev. Arb. - Revue de l'arbitrage (FRA)
Rev. Barreau - Revue du Barreau (CAN)
Rev. Corte Esp. Arb. - Revista de la Corte Española de Arbitraje (SPA)Rev.
Crit. Droit Int'l Privé - Revue critique de droit international privé (FRA)
Rev. Droit Com. Belge - Revue du droit commercial belge (BEL)
Rev. Droit Int'l & Droit Comp. - Revue de droit international et de droit comparé (BEL)
Rev. Droit Jud. - Revue de Droit Judiciare (CAN)
Rev. Egyptienne Droit Int'l - Revue égyptienne de droit international (EGY)
Rev. Esp. Der. Int'l - Revista Española de Derecho Internacional (SPA)
Rev. Ghana L. - Review of Ghana Law (GHA)
Rev. Hellénique Droit Int'l - Revue hellénique de droit international (GRE)
Rev. Int'l Bus. L. - Review of International Business Law (CAN)
Rev. Int'l Droit Comp. - Revue internationale de droit comparé (FRA)
Rev. Soc. L. - Review of Socialist Law (NET)
Rev. Trib. - Revista dos Tribunais (BRA)
Rev. Trim. Jurispr. - Revista Trimestrial de Jurisprudencia (BRA)
Riv. Dir. Int'le - Rivista di diritto internazionale (ITA)
Riv. Dir. Int'le Priv. & Proc. - Rivista di diritto internazionale privato e processuale (ITA)
Riv. Dir. Proc. - Rivista di diritto processuale (ITA)

Riv. Trim. Dir. & Proc. Civ. - Rivista trimestrale di diritto e procedura civile (ITA)

RIW - Recht der internationalen Wirtschaft (FRG)

Rutgers L. Rev. - Rutgers Law Review (USA)

S.A. Mercantile L.J. - South African Mercantile Journal (RSA)

Schweiz. Jahrbuch Int'les Recht - Schweizerisches Jahrbuch für internationales Recht (SWI)

S. Cal. L. Rev. - Southern California Law Review (USA)

S.C. L. Rev. - South Carolina Law Review (USA)

Sec. L. Rev. - Securities Law Review (USA)

S.G.P. - Sovetskoe Gosudarstvo i Pravo (SOV)

SJZ - Schweizerische Juristen-Zeitung (SWI)

Solicitors' J. - Solicitors' Journal (UK)

South Afr. L.J. - South African Law Journal (RSA)

South Afr. Y.B. Int'l L. - South African Yearbook of International Law (RSA)

Soviet Stat. & Dec. - Soviet Statutes and Decisions (USA)

Soviet Y.B. Mar. L. - Soviet Yearbook of Maritime Law (SOV)

Soviet Y.B. Int'l L. - Sovietskii Ezhegodnik Mezhdunarodnogo Prava/ Soviet Yearbook of International Law (SOV)

Sri Lanka J. Int'l L. - Sri Lanka Journal of International Law (SLA)

Stan. J. Int'l L. - Stanford Journal of International Law (USA)

Stan. J. Int'l Stud. - Stanford Journal of International Studies (USA)

Stan. L. Rev. - Stanford Law Review (USA)

St. John's L. Rev. - St. John's Law Review (USA)

St. Louis U. L.J. - St. Louis University Law Journal (USA)

Stet. L. Rev. - Stetson Law Review (USA)

Suff. U.L. Rev. - Suffolk University Law Review (USA)

Suff. Transnat'l L.J. - Suffolk Transnational Law Journal (USA)

Sw. U. L. Rev. - Southwestern University Law Review (USA)

Swiss Rev. Int'l Competition L. - Swiss Review of International Competition Law (SWI)

Syracuse J. Int'l L. & Com. - Syracuse Journal of International Law and Commerce (USA)

Tex. Int'l L.J. - Texas International Law Journal (USA)

Tort & Ins. L.J. - Tort and Insurance Law Journal (USA)

Touro L. Rev. - Touro Law Review (USA)

Transnat'l Law. - Transnational Lawyer (USA)

Trent L.J. - Trent Law Journal (UK)

Trial Lawyers Q. - Trial Lawyers Quarterly (USA)

Tul. L. Rev. - Tulane Law Review (USA)

Tul. Mar. L.J. - Tulane Maritime Law Journal (USA)

U. Balt. L. Rev. - University of Baltimore Law Review (USA)

U. B.C. L. Rev. - University of British Columbia Law Review (CAN)

U.C.L.A. Pac. Basin L.J. - University of California Los Angeles Pacific Basin Law Journal (USA)

U. Fla. L. Rev. - University of Florida Law Review (USA)

U. Ghana L.J. - University of Ghana Law Journal (GHA)

U. Miami Inter-Am. L. Rev. - University of Miami Inter- American Law Review (USA)

U. Miami L. Rev. - University of Miami Law Review (USA)

U. Minn. L. Rev. - University of Minnesota Law Review (USA)

UNCITRAL Y.B. - UNCITRAL Yearbook (UN)

U. Pa. J. Int'l Bus. L. - University of Pennsylvania Journal of International Business Law (USA)

U. Pa. L. Rev. - University of Pennsylvania Law Review (USA)

U. Pitt. L. Rev. - University of Pittsburgh Law Review (USA)

U. Rich. L. Rev. - University of Richmond Law Review (USA)

U. Tol. L. Rev. - University of Toledo Review (USA)

Va. J. Int'l L. - Virginia Journal of International Law (USA)

Va. L. Rev. - Virginia Law Review (USA)

Vand. J. Transnat'l L. - Vanderbilt Journal of Transnational Law (USA)

Vand. L. Rev. - Vanderbilt Law Review (USA)

VersR - Versicherungs Recht (FRG)

W.A.R. - World Arbitration Reporter (USA)

Wash. & Lee L. Rev. - Washington & Lee Law Review (USA)

Washburn L.J. - Washburn Law Journal (USA)

Wash. L. Rev. - Washington Law Review and State Bar Journal (USA)

Wash. U.L.Q. - Washington University Law Quarterly (USA)

West's Int'l L. Bull. - West's International Law Bulletin (USA)

Whittier L. Rev. - Whittier Law Review (USA)

Willamette L. Rev. - Willamette Law Review (USA)

Wis. Int'l L.J. - Wisconsin International Law Journal (USA)

World Arb. & Med. Rep. - World Arbitration & Mediation Report (UK)

Yale J. World Pub. Ord. - Yale Journal of World Public Order (USA)

Yale L.J. - Yale Law Journal (USA)

Yale L. Rev. - Yale Law Review (USA)

Yale Stud. World Pub. Ord. - Yale Studies in World Public Order (Continued by Yale Journal of World Public Order/ The Yale Journal of International Law) (USA)

Y.B. Com. Arb. - Yearbook Commercial Arbitration (NET)

Y.B. Mar. L. - Yearbook Maritime Law (NET)

Y.B. Swed. & Int'l Arb. - Yearbook of Swedish and International Arbitration (SWE)

ZIP - Zeitschrift für Wirtschaftsrecht und Insolvenzpraxis (FRG)

ZRV - Zeitschrift für Rechtsvergleichung (AST)

ZSR - Zeitschrift für schweizerisches Recht/Revue de droit suisse (SWI)

ZZP - Zeitschrift für Zivilprozess (FRG)

PART ONE

SUBJECT-MATTER
BIBLIOGRAPHY

1. COMMERCIAL ARBITRATION IN GENERAL

1.01 COMMERCIAL ARBITRATION - DOMESTIC AND INTERNATIONAL

Aksen, International Arbitration: Its Time Has Arrived, 14 *Case W. Res. J. Int'l L.* 247 (1982)

————, The Need to Utilize International Arbitration, 17 *Vand. J. Transnat'l L.* 11 (1984)

Allison, Arbitration of Private Antitrust Claims in International Trade: A Study in the Subordination of National Interests to the Demands of a World Market, 18 *N.Y.U. J. Int'l L. & Pol.* 361 (1986)

Antaki, A Critical Evaluation of International Commercial Arbitration, in *Resolving International Business Disputes through Arbitration: Materials of the Conference in Toronto,* Jan. 19 & 20, 1987

Aramburú Menchaca, Reflexiones sobre el arbitraje comercial internacional, in 2 *Estudios de Derecho internacional en homenaje a Miaja de la Muela* 981 (1972)

Bagner, Enforcement of International Commercial Contracts by Arbitration: Recent Developments, 14 *Case W. Res. J. Int'l L.* 573 (1982)

Balladore Pallieri, L'arbitrage privé dans les rapports internationaux, 51 *Recueil des Cours* 291 (1935-I)

Berger, K., Internationale Wirtschaftsschiedsgerichtsbarkeit. Verfahrens- und materiellrechtliche Grundprobleme im *Spiegel moderner Schiedsgesetze und Schiedspraxis* (Berlin 1992)

Bernini, L'arbitrato internazionale, 19 *Rassegna dell'Arb.* 133 (1979)

Bernini, G., *Lezioni di diritto dell'arbitrato* (Bologna 1992)

Böckstiegel, Arbitragem e Tribunais, in *Boletim de Estudos Juridicos do Investimento Internacional* (Sao Paulo, IOB) 3-14 (No. 9, 1979)

Boyd, Innovation and Reform in the Law of Arbitration, 51 *Arbitration* 440 (1985)

Bratus, Arbitration and International Economic Cooperation Towards Industrial, Scientific and Technical Development, in *ICCA, Fourth Int'l Arb. Congress: Proceedings* 89 (1972)

Broderick, The Future of Arbitration in the Settlement of International Commercial Disputes, 2 *Notre Dame Int'l & Comp. L.J.* 171 (1984)

Brower, Ch.N. & Marks, L.R., *International Commercial Arbitration. Materials of a Conference* (New York 1983)

Brown, L.F., ed., *The International Arbitration Kit: A Compilation of Basic and Frequently Requested Documents.* (3rd ed. New York 1986)

Carabiber, L'évolution de l'arbitrage commercial international, 99 *Recueil des Cours* 119 (1960-I)

Carbonneau, Arbitral Adjudication: A Comparative Assessment of its Remedial and Substantive Status in Transnational Commerce, 19 *Tex. Int'l L.J.* 33 (1984)

Carbonneau, T., ed., *Resolving Transnational Disputes Through Arbitration.* Sixth Sokol Colloquium (Charlottesville, VA 1984)

Chafic, Quelques réfléxions sur la philosophie de l'arbitrage commercial, in *Euro-Arab Arbitration II* 17 (F. Kemicha ed. 1989)

Charfi, L'expérience tunisienne en matière d'arbitrage international, in *Centre d'Etudes, Les Entreprises Tunisiennes et l'Arbitrage Commercial International* 209 (1983)

Coulson, A New Look at International Commercial Arbitration, 14 *Case W. Res. J. Int'l L.* 359 (1982)

Cremades, Arbitration and Business, in *ICCA, Sixth Int'l Arb. Congress: Proceedings* 77 (1978)

⸻, The Impact of International Arbitration on the Development of Business Law, 31 *Am. J. Comp. L.* 533 (1983)

⸻, Ventajas del arbitraje en el comercio internacional, in *El Arbitraje Comercial Internacional* 81 (Mexico 1983)

David, L'avenir de l'arbitrage, in *Liber Amicorum for Martin Domke* 56 (P. Sanders ed. 1967)

Davison, Arbitration - Its Future - Its Prospects, 51 *Arbitration* 225 (1985)

Delaume, Transnational Commercial Arbitration, in *Digest of Commercial Laws of the World* (L. Nelson ed. issue May 1980)

————, *Transnational Contracts, Applicable Law and Settlement of Disputes: A Study in Conflict Avoidance* (Dobbs Ferry, NY 1975)

De Vries, International Commercial Arbitration: A Transnational View, 1 *J. Int'l Arb.* 7 (1984)

Domke, Arbitration, in *Nationalism and Multinational Enterprise. Legal, Economic and Managerial Aspects* 233 (H. Hahlo, J. Smith & B. Wright eds. 1973)

————, New Aspects of East-West Trade Arbitration, in *A.I.A., Essays in Memoriam Eugenio Minoli* 121 (Turin 1974)

————, Promotion of Diffusion of International Commercial Arbitration, in *ICCA, 3rd Int'l Arb. Congress: Proceedings* 353 (1969)

Domke & Glossner, The Present State of the Law Regarding International Commercial Arbitration, in *The Present State of International Law and Other Essays Written in Honour of the Centenary Celebration of the ILA* 1873-1973 307 (M. Bos ed. 1973)

Ehrenhaft, Effective International Commercial Arbitration, 9 *Law & Pol'y Int'l Bus.* 1191 (1977)

Fadlallah, La spécificité de l'Arbitrage Commercial International, in *Euro-Arab Arbitration III* 21 (F. Kemicha ed. 1991)

Fink, L'arbitrage socialiste dans le commerce Est-Ouest, 1 *Droit et Pratique du Commerce Int'l* 367 (1975)

Fouchard, Quand un arbitrage est-il international, 1970 *Rev. Arb.* 59

Garcini, Développement de l'arbitrage commercial, in *ICCA, Fifth Int'l Arb. Congress: Proceedings* C IIIb 1-8 (1975)

Gebrehana, T., *Arbitration: An Element of International Law* (Stockholm 1985)

Glossner, International Commercial Arbitration, *Int'l Bus. Law.* 9 (November 1983)

————, Sociological Aspects of International Commercial Arbitration, in *The Art of Arbitration* 143 (J. Schultsz & A. van den Berg eds. 1982)

Graziadei, Internationalization of National Arbitration, in *A.I.A., Essays in Memoriam Eugenio Minoli* 225 (Turin 1974)

Haight, International Arbitration, 14 *Case W. Res. J. Int'l L.* 253 (1982)

Hellwig, Nationale und internationale Schiedsgerichtsbarkeit, 30 *RIW* 421 (1984)

Higgins, Brown & Roach, Pitfalls in International Commercial Arbitration, 35 *Bus. Law.* 1035 (1980)

Holtzmann, Arbitration: An Indispensable Aid to Multinational Enterprises, 10 J. *Int'l L. & Econ.* 337 (1975)

————, International Commercial Dispute Settlement: Developments of a Decade, in *Essays in International Law. Thirtieth Anniversary Commemorative Volume* 95 (New Delhi 1987)

Hoyle, Arbitration, 6 *Bus. L. Rev.* 335 (1985) and 7 *Bus. L. Rev.* 37 (1986)

International Chamber of Commerce, *International Arbitration, Sixty Years of ICC Arbitration: A Look at the Future* (Paris 1984)

Jakubowski, Reflections on the Philosophy of International Commercial Arbitration and Conciliation, in *The Art of Arbitration* 175 (J. Schultsz & A. van den Berg eds. 1982)

Katona, Problems of Arbitration in International Trade, 23 *Acta Juridica* (Budapest) 57 (Nos. 1-2, 1981)

Kerr, Commercial Dispute Resolution: The Changing Scene, in *Liber Amicorum for The Rt. Hon. Lord Wilberforce* 111 (M. Bos & I. Brownlie eds. 1987)

Krishnamurthi, Arbitration and International Co-operation Towards Industrial, Scientific and Technical Development, in *ICCA, Fourth Int'l Arb. Congress: Proceedings* 113 (1972)

————, The International Arbitration Movement, in *A.I.A., Essays in Memoriam Eugenio Minoli* 281 (Turin 1974)

Lalive, International Arbitration - Teaching and Research, in *Contemporary Problems in Int'l Arbitration* 16 (J.D.M. Lew ed 1986)

6

———, L'importance de l'arbitrage commercial international, in *First Int'l Commercial Arbitration Conference: Proceedings* 15 (N. Antaki & A. Prujiner eds. 1986)

———, Problèmes relatifs à l'arbitrage international commercial, 120 *Recueil des Cours* 569 (1967-II)

———, Problèmes specifique de l'arbitrage international, 1980 *Rev. Arb.* 341

Lew, Nationality of International Commercial Arbitration, 5 *Bus. L. Rev.* 318 (1984)

Lew, J., ed., *Contemporary Problems in International Arbitration* (London 1986)

Lookofsky, J., *Transnational Litigation and Commercial Arbitration. A Comparative Analysis of American, European, and International Law* (Ardsley-on-Hudson, NY and Copenhagen 1992)

McClelland, International Arbitration: A Practical Guide to the System for the Litigation of Transnational Commercial Disputes, 17 *Va. J. Int'l L.* 729 (1977)

———, International Arbitration: A Practical Guide for the Effective Use of the System for Litigation of Transnational Commercial Disputes, 12 *Int'l Law.* 83 (1978)

McClendon, Alternate Methods of Dispute Settlement, 17 *Houston L. Rev.* 979 (1980)

Mackie, K.J., ed., *A Handbook of Dispute Resolution: ADR in Action* (London 1991)

Martin & Hunter, International Commercial Arbitration, *Int'l Bus. Law.* 5 (Nov. 1983)

Melis & Strohbach, East-West Arbitration, 7 *Y.B. Com. Arb.* 395 (1982)

Menchaca, Reflexiones sobre el arbitraje commercial internacional, in 2 *Estudios de derecho internacional: Homenaje al Profesor Miaja de la Muela* 995 (Madrid 1979)

Mendes, Canada: A New Forum to Develop the Cultural Psychology of International Commercial Arbitration, 3 *J. Int'l Arb.* 71 (No. 3, 1986)

Mentschikoff, Commercial Arbitration, 61 *Colum. L. Rev.* 846 (1961)

Minoli, Sviluppi desiderabili del diritto che regola l'arbitrato concernente affari internazionali, 8 *Rassegna dell'Arb.* 1 (1968)

Motulsky, L'évolution récente en matière d'arbitrage international, 1959 *Rev. Arb.* 3

Mustill, Sir Michael J. & S. C. Boyd, *The Law and Practice of Commercial Arbitration in England* (2nd ed. 1989)

Noriega Velasco, Arbitration and International Co-operation for the Industrial Increase of Underdeveloped Countries, in *ICCA, Fourth Int'l Arb. Congress: Proceedings* 748 (1972)

Nussbaum, Problems of International Arbitration, in 1 *Int'l Y.B. Civil & Com. Arb.* 1 (A. Nussbaum ed. 1928)

Note, Arbitral Adjudication: A Comparative Assessment of its Remedial and Substantive Status in Transnational Commerce, 10 *Tex. Int'l L.J.* 33 (1984)

Oppetit, Les Etats et l'arbitrage international: esquisse de systématisation, 1985 *Rev. Arb.* 493

Palkhivala, Arbitration vs. Litigation, 2 *Lex et Juris - The Law Magazine* 26 (No. 1, 1987)

Park, The Influence of National Legal Systems on International Commercial Arbitration: Recent Developments in English Arbitration Law, in *Resolving Transnational Disputes Through International Arbitration* 80 (T. Carbonneau, ed. 1980)

Paulsson, Le Tier Monde dans l'arbitrage commercial international, 1983 *Rev. Arb.* 3

————, The Extent of Independence of International Arbitration from the Law of the Situs, in *Contemporary Problems in Int'l Arbitration* 141 (J.D.M. Lew ed. 1986)

Pearson, The Spreading of International Commercial Arbitration, in *ICCA, Third Int'l Arb. Congress: Proceedings* 307 (1969)

Perlman & Nelson, New Approaches to the Resolution of International Commercial Disputes, 17 *Int'l Law.* 215 (1983)

Phillips, Arbitration: The Revolution of the 80's, 52 *Arbitration* 75 (1986)

Rajski, La tendence à la codification progressive du droit commercial international, *Colliard Collection* 321 (Paris 1984)

Reymond, L'evoluzione del diritto comune dell'arbitrato internazionale: esperienze e prospettive, 39 *Riv. Trim. Dir. & Proc. Civ.* 120 (1985)

Rinker, The Future of Arbitration in Latin America: A Study of its Regional Development, 8 *Case W. Res. J. Int'l L.* 480 (1976)

Rogers, An Overview of the International Arbitration Scene, 53 *Arbitration* 239 (1987)

Rubino-Sammartano, International and Foreign Arbitration, 5 J. *Int'l Arb.* 85 (No. 3, 1988)

Rundstein, L'arbitrage international en matière privée, 23 *Recueil des Cours* 331 (1928-III)

Sanchez Dominguez, Arbitraje y conciliación en el comercio internacional, in *El Arbitraje en el Derecho Latinoamericano y Español* 527 (L. Perret & U. Montoya Alberti eds. 1989)

Sanders, Arbitration (Including Recognition and Enforcement of Awards), 27 *Neth. Int'l L. Rev.* 392 (1980)

———, Aspects de l'arbitrage international, 53 *Rev. Droit Int'l & Droit Comp.* 129 (1976)

———, International Commercial Arbitration, 20 *Neth. Int'l L. Rev.* 37 (1973)

———, International Commercial Arbitration, in *A.I.A., Essays in Memoriam Eugenio Minoli* 467 (Turin 1974)

———, Trends in the Field of International Commercial Arbitration, 145 *Recueil des Cours* 205 (1975-II)

Santos Belandro, R., *Arbitraje comercial internacional: tendencias y perspectivas* (Montevideo 1988)

Schneider, Multi-Fora Disputes, 6 *Arb. Int'l* 101 (1990)

Seide, K., ed., *A Dictionary of Arbitration and Its Terms* (Dobbs Ferry, NY 1970)

Smedresman, Conflict of Laws in International Commercial Arbitration: A Survey of Recent Developments, 7 *Calif. W. Int'l L.J.* 263 (1977)

Smit, The Future of International Commercial Arbitration, 2 *West's Int'l L. Bull.* 5 (Issue 4, Fall 1984)

————, The Future of International Commercial Arbitration: A Single Transnational Institution? 25 *Colum. J. Transnat'l L.* 9 (1986)

Smit, Th. E. Carbonneau Resolving Transnational Disputes Through International Arbitration, The Sixth Sokol Colloquium (book review), 34 *AJCL* 395 (1986)

Stein & Wotman, International Commercial Arbitration in the 1980's: A Comparison of the Major Systems and Rules, 38 *Bus. Law.* 1685 (1983)

Steyn, Methods of Conducting International Commercial Arbitrations: A Re-Examination, in *Second Bermuda Int'l Arb. Conference: A Collection of Papers* (Hamilton, Bermuda, April 19-22, 1983)

Straus, Why International Commercial Arbitration Is Lagging in Latin America: Problems and Cures, 33 *Arb. J.* 21 (1978)

————, The Growing Consensus on International Commercial Arbitration, 68 *Amer. J. Int'l L.* 709 (1974)

Tindall, International Commercial Arbitration, 7 *Am. Bus. L. J.* 65 (1969)

van Houtte, International Arbitration and National Adjudication, in 4 *Hague-Zagreb Essays on the Law of International Trade* 321 (C. Voskuil & J. Wade eds. 1981)

Wetter, Methods of Settling International Commercial Disputes, 3 *Int'l Arb. Rep.* 21 (No. 5, 1988)

Wilner, Acceptance of Arbitration by Developing Countries, in *Resolving Transnational Disputes Through International Arbitration* 283 (Th. Carbonneau ed. 1984)

Yates, Arbitration or Court Litigation for Private International Dispute Resolution: The Lesser of Two Evils, in *Resolving Transnational Disputes Through International Arbitration* 224 (Th. Carbonneau ed. 1984)

1.02 HISTORY OF COMMERCIAL ARBITRATION

Abrahams, The Origins of Arbitration in Britain, 54 *Arbitration* 263 (1988)

Aiken, New Netherlands Arbitration in the 17th Century, 29 *Arb. J.* (n.s.) 145 (1945)

Aylwin Azocar, P., *El juicio arbitral* (Santiago de Chile 1958)

Bignardi, A., *Controversiae Agrorum e arbitrati internazionali,* Milano: Giuffre (1984)

Boyd, Innovation and Reform in the Law of Arbitration, 51 *Arbitration* 440 (1985)

Bressler, Arbitration and the Courts in Jewish Law, 9 *Journal of Halacha and Contemporary Society* 105 (1985)

Carabiber, L'évolution de l'arbitrage commercial international, 99 *Recueil des Cours* 119 (1960-I)

Carbonneau, Etude historique et comparée de l'arbitrage: vers un droit materiel de l'arbitrage commercial international fondé sur la motivation des sentences, 36 *Rev. Int'l Droit Comp.* 727 (1984)

Comish, Arbitration at Common Law before the First (English) Arbitration Act 1698, 56 *Arbitration* 194 (1990)

David, Arbitrage du 19e et arbitrage du 20e siècle, in *Mélanges René Savatier* 219 (Paris 1963)

Davison, Arbitration — Its Future — Its Prospects, 50 *Arbitration* 147 (Nov. 1984) and 51 *Arbitration* 225 (Feb. 1985)

Domke & Keller, Western Hemisphere System of Commercial Arbitration, 6 *Univ. Toronto L.J.* 308 (1946)

Glossner, Arbitration — A Glance into History, in *ICC, Hommage a Frederic Eisemann* 19 (1978)

Hammond, Arbitration in Ancient Greece, 1 *Arbitration Int'l* 188 (1985)

Hunter, Arbitration Procedure in England: Past, Present and Future, 1 *Arb. Int'l* 82 (1985)

11

Jones, History of Commercial Arbitration in England and the United States, in *International Trade Arbitration* 127 (M. Domke, ed. 1958)

————, Three Centuries of Commercial Arbitration in New York: A Brief Survey, 1956 *Wash. U.L.Q.* 193

Kassis A., *Problèmes de base de l'arbitrage en droit comparé et en droit international. Vol. 1: Arbitrage juridictionnel et arbitrage contractuel* (Paris 1987)

Kellor, F., *American Arbitration* (New York 1948)

Krause, H., *Die geschichtliche Entwicklung des Schiedsgerichtswesens in Deutschland* (Berlin 1930)

Lane, The Role of the Legislature and the Courts in the Development of the Arbitration Process, 52 *Arbitration* 195 (1986)

Lorenzen, Commercial Arbitration — International and Interstate Aspects, 43 *Yale L.J.* 716 (1934)

Magdelain, Aspects arbitraux de la justice civile archaique à Rome, 27 *Revue Int'l des Droits de l'Antiquité* 205 (1980)

Matray, Quelques problèmes de l'arbitrage commercial international (doctrine et jurisprudence), in *L'Arbitrage* 289 (L. Matray & G. de Leval eds. 1989)

Miller, Avoiding Legal Judgment: The Submission of Disputes to Arbitration in Medieval Iceland, 28 *Am. J. Leg. History* 95 (1984)

Moglen, Commercial Arbitration in the Eighteenth Century: Searching for the Transformation of American Law, 93 *Yale L.J.* 135 (1983)

Monnier, Le rôle de la Suisse dans l'histoire de l'arbitrage de droit international privé, in *Recueil de Travaux Suisses* 3 (C. Reymond & E. Bucher eds. 1984)

Mustill, Arbitration: History and Background, 6 *J. Int'l Arb.* 44 (No. 2, 1989)

Nagel, Anmerkungen zu einigen hanseatischen Schiedsklauseln, in *Festschrift für Karl Heinz Schwab* 367 (P. Gottwald & H. Prütting eds. 1990)

Phillips, The History of Arbitration, 47 *Arbitration* 16 (1981); also 1 *Com. Arbitrator* 12 (No. 3, June 1982)

Phillips, J.F., *Arbitration: Law, Practice and Precedents* (Cambridge 1988)

Powell, Settlement of Disputes by Arbitration in Fifteenth-Century England, 2 *Law & Hist. Rev.* 21 (1984)

Puchta, W. H., *Das Institut der Schiedsrichter, nach seinem heutigen Gebrauche und seiner Brauchbarkeit fur Abkürzung und Verminderung der Prozesse betrachtet von* (Erlangen 1832)

Report on the Evidence and Reasons of the Award between Johannis Orlandos & Andreas Luriottis, Greek Deputies, of the One Part, and Le Roy, Bayard & Co., and G.G. & S. Howland, of the Other Part., By the Arbitrators. New York, printed by W.E. Dean, 1826.

Rundstein, L'arbitrage international en matière privée, 23 *Recueil des Cours* 331 (1928-III)

Stein, Arbitration under Roman Law, 41 *Arbitration* 203 (1974)

Steyn, Arbitration and the Courts: Arbitration Systems in England and Wales and Recent Changes in Arbitration Law, 46 *Arbitration* 146 (1980)

von Mehren, From Vynior's Case to Mitsubishi: The Future of Arbitration and Public Law, 12 *Brooklyn J. Int'l L.* 583 (1986)

Wenger, W., *Zum obligationenrechtlichen Schiedsverfahren im schweizerischen Recht: Eine rechtsvergleichende und historische Studie* (Basel 1968)

Wolaver, The Historical Background of Commercial Arbitration, 83 *U. Pa. L. Rev.* 132 (1933)

1.03 TREATISES AND FESTSCHRIFTEN

Abova, T.E., *Arbitrazhnyi protsess v SSSR: poniatie, osnovnye printsipy* (Moscow 1985)

Associazione Italiana per l'Arbitrato, *Commercial Arbitration - Essays in Memoriam Eugenio Minoli* (Turin 1974)

Berger, K., Internationale Wirtschaftsschiedsgerichtsbarkeit. Verfahrens-und materiellrechtliche Grundprobleme im Spiegel moderner Schiedsgesetze und Schiedspraxis (Berlin 1992)

Bernini, G., *Lezioni di diritto dell'arbitato* (Bologna 1992)

Blegvad, B.-M., P. Bolding & O. Lando, *Arbitration as a Means of Solving Conflicts* (Copenhagen 1973)

Böckstiegel, K.-H., ed., *Recht und Praxis der Schiedsgerichtsbarkeit der Internationalen Handelskammer* (Cologne 1986)

———, ed., *Schiedsgerichtsbarkeit in Frankreich* (Cologne 1983)

Böckstiegel, K.-H. & O. Glossner, eds., *Festschrift für Arthur Bülow zum 80. Geburtstag* (Cologne 1981)

Briseño Sierra, H., *El arbitraje en el derecho privado* (Mexico 1963)

———, *El arbitraje comercial: doctrina y legislación* (Mexico 1979)

Bucher, A., *Die neue internationale Schiedsgerichtsbarkeit in der Schweiz* (Basel 1989)

———, *Le nouvel arbitrage international en Suisse. Théorie et pratique de droit* (Basel 1988)

Bucher, A. & P.-Y., Tschanz, *International Arbitration in Switzerland* (Basel 1989)

Carabiber, C., *L'arbitrage international de droit privé* (Paris 1960)

Chillón Medina, J. M. & J. F. Merino Merchán, *Tratado de arbitraje privado interno e internacional* (Madrid 1978)

Cohn, E.J., M. Domke & F. Eisemann, eds., *Handbook of Institutional Arbitration in International Trade* (Amsterdam 1977)

14

Cremades, B. M., *Arbitraje Comercial Internacional* (2nd ed. 1984)

――――, *Arbitration in Spain* (London/Madrid/Cologne 1991)

David, David on Arbitration in the International Trade. A Book Review, in *The Art of Arbitration* 89 (J. Schultsz & A. van den Berg eds. 1982)

David, R., *Arbitration in International Trade* (Deventer 1985)

――――, *L'arbitrage dans le commerce international* (Paris 1982)

Domke, Bibliography of International Commercial Arbitration, in *ICCA, 3rd Int'l Arb'n Congress: Proceedings* 409 (1969)

――――, *Domke on Commercial Arbitration (The Law and Practice of Commercial Arbitration).* Rev. ed. by Gabriel M. Wilner (Wilmette, Ill. 1984)

――――, ed., *International Trade Arbitration: A Road to World-Wide Cooperation* (New York 1958)

El-Ahdab, A. H., *Arbitration with the Arab Countries* (Deventer 1990)

――――, *L'arbitrage dans les pays arabes* (Paris 1988)

Farani, M., *Law of Arbitration* (Lahore 1979)

Fellhauer, H. & H., Strohbach, eds., *Handbuch der internationalen Handelsschiedsgerichtsbarkeit* (Berlin 1969)

Fouchard, P., L'arbitrage commercial international, in *Bibliothèque de droit international privé,* vol. II (Paris 1965)

Ginnings, A.T., *Arbitration: A Practical Guide* (Aldershot 1984)

Glossner, O., J. Bredow & M. Bühler, *Das Schiedsgericht in der Praxis.* 3rd (rev. ed. Heidelberg 1990)

Goldstajn, A. & S. Triva, *Medunarodna trgovacka arbitraza* (Zagreb 1987)

Habscheid, W. & K. H. Schwab, eds., *Beiträge zum internationalen Verfahrensrecht und zur Schiedsgerichtsbarkeit. Festschrift für Heinrich Nagel zum* 75. Geburtstag (Münster 1987)

Henn, G., *Schiedsverfahrensrecht: ein Handbuch* (Heidelberg 1986)

Hunter, R.L.C., *The Law of Arbitration in Scotland* (Edinburgh 1987)

International Chamber of Commerce, *Hommage à Fréderic Eisemann, Liber Amicorum* (Paris 1978)

Jarrosson, C., *La notion d'arbitrage* (Paris 1987)

Karmali, A.E., *International Commercial Arbitration* (Bombay 1974)

Krause, H. & F. Bozenhardt, *Internationale Handelsschiedsgerichtsbarkeit* (Stuttgart 1990)

Lalive, P., J.-F. Poudret & C. Reymond, *Le droit de l'arbitrage interne et international en Suisse* (Lausanne 1989)

Lebedev, S., *Mezhdunarodnyi torgovyi arbitrazh* (Moscow 1965)

Lee, E., *Encyclopedia of Arbitration Law* (London 1984)

————, *Encyclopedia of International Commercial Arbitration* (London 1986)

Lookofsky, J., *Transnational Litigatin and Commercial Arbitration. A Comparative Analysis of American, European, and International Law* (Ardsley-on-Hudson, NY and Copenhagen 1992)

Marshall, E., *Gill: The Law of Arbitration* (3rd ed., London 1983)

Matray, L. & G. de Leval, eds., *L'Arbitrage. Travaux offerts au professeur Albert Fettweis* (Brussels 1989)

Monroy Cabra, M.G., *Arbitraje Comercial* (Bogota 1982)

Montoya Alberti, U., *El arbitraje comercial* (Lima 1988)

Moreau, B. & T. Bernard, *Droit interne et droit international de l'arbitrage* (2nd ed. 1985)

Mustill, Sir Michael J. & S. C. Boyd, *The Law and Practice of Commercial Arbitration in England* (2nd ed. 1989)

Ramos Mendez, F., *Arbitraje y Proceso Internacional* (Barcelona 1987)

Redfern, A. & M. Hunter, *Law and Practice of International Commercial Arbitration* (2nd ed. 1991)

Robert, J. & B. Morceau, *L'arbitrage - droit interne, droit international privé* (5th ed. Paris 1983)

16

Rubino-Sammartano, M., *L'arbitrato internazionale* (Padua 1989)

————— , International Arbitration Law (Deventer 1990)

Russell, F., *Russell on the Law of Arbitration* (20th ed. by A. Walton & M. Vitoria 1982)

Saleh, S., *Commercial Arbitration in the Arab Middle East* (London 1984)

Sanders, P., ed., *International Arbitration - Liber Amicorum for Martin Domke* (The Hague 1967)

Schizzerotto, G., *Dell'arbitrato* (3rd ed. Milan 1988)

Schlosser, P., *Das Recht der internationalen privaten Schiedsgerichtsbarkeit* (2nd rev. ed. Tübingen 1989)

Schmitthoff, C., *International Commercial Arbitration* (3 volumes), (Dobbs Ferry, N Y 1975)

Schottelius, D.J., *Die internationale Schiedsgerichtsbarkeit: eine Studie über die Bildung eines internationalen Schiedsgerichtssystem* (Cologne 1957)

————— , *Die kaufmannische Schiedsgerichtsbarkeit* (Bremen 1953)

Schultsz, J.C. & A.J. van den Berg, eds., *The Art of Arbitration. Essays on International Arbitration. Liber Amicorum Pieter Sanders 12 September 1912-1982* (Deventer 1982)

Schütze, R., D. Tscherning & W(alter) Wais, *Handbuch des Schiedsverfahrens. Praxis der deutschen und internationalen Schiedsgerichtsbarkeit* (2nd ed. Berlin 1990)

Simpson, J. & H. Fox, *International Arbitration - Law and Practice* (1959)

Storme M. & B. Demeulenaere, *International Commercial Arbitration in Belgium: A Handbook* (Deventer 1989)

Strohbach, H., *Handbuch der internationalen Handelsschiedsgerichtsbarkeit* (Berlin 1990)

Tyan, E., *Le droit de l'arbitrage* (Beyrouth 1972)

Tyczka, M., *Arbitraz i postepowanie arbitrazove*, (3rd ed. Warsaw 1985) van den Berg, A. J., R. van Delden & H.J. Snijders, *Arbitragerecht* (Zwolle 1988)

Wetter, J.G., *The International Arbitral Process: Public and Private,* volumes I - V (Dobbs Ferry, NY 1979)

1.04 PERIODICALS

American Arbitration Association, *Arbitration Journal* (New York 1945-)

American Arbitration Association, *Arbitration and the Law*, 1981 (published annually), (New York 1982-)

American Arbitration Association, *Arbitration Times* (New York)

American Arbitration Association, *Lawyers' Arbitration Letter's* (New York)

Arbitration Institute of the Stockholm Chamber of Commerce, Swedish and International Arbitration. *Yearbook of the Arbitration Institute of the Stockholm Chamber of Commerce* (Stockholm 1982-)

Arbitration Materials (J. Werner, publisher and general editor), (Geneva 1989-)

Arbitrator's Institute of Canada, Inc., *Canadian Arbitration Journal* (Toronto)

Association Suisse de l'Arbitrage, *Bulletin de 'Association Suisse de l'Arbitrage* (Geneva 1983-)

Associazione Italiana per l'Arbitrato, *Rassegna dell'Arbitrato* (Rome 1960-)

BNA International Inc., *World Arbitration & Mediation Report* (London 1990-)

British Columbia International Arbitration Centre, *Arbitration Canada* (Vancouver 1987-)

Canadian Arbitration, *Conciliation and Amicable Composition Centre, Inter-American Arbitration* (L. Kos-Rabcewicz-Zubkowski editor-in-chief), (Ottawa)

Chartered Institute of Arbitrators, *Arbitration* (London)

Comité Français de l'Arbitrage, *Revue de l'Arbitrage* (Paris)

Consejo Superior de Cámaras de Comercio, *Industria y Navegación de España, Revista de la Corte Española de Arbitraje* (Madrid)

German Institute of Arbitration, *DIS-Mitteilungen* (Cologne 1988-)

Indian Council of Arbitration, *ICA Arbitration Quarterly* (New Delhi)

19

Institute of Arbitrators Australia, *The Arbitrator* (Melbourne 1981-)

Institute for Transnational Arbitration, *News and Notes from the Institute for Transnational Arbitration* (Houston, TX)

International Centre for Settlement of Investment Disputes, *ICSID Review-Foreign Investment Law Journal* (Washington 1986-)

International Centre for Settlement of Investment Disputes, *News from ICSID* (Washington)

International Chamber of Commerce, *ICC International Court of Arbitration Bulletin/Bulletin de la Cour Internationale d' Arbitrage de la CCI* (Paris 1990-)

International Council for Commercial Arbitration, *Yearbook Commercial Arbitration* (P. Sanders gen. editor 1976-1985, A.J. van den Berg gen. editor since 1986), (Deventer 1976-)

Japan Commercial Arbitration Association, *Japan Commercial Arbitration Journal* (Tokyo)

Japan Shipping Exchange, Inc., *Bulletin of the Japan Shipping Exchange* (Tokyo 19..-)

Journal of International Arbitration (J. Werner, publisher and general editor), (Geneva 1984-)

Jahrbuch für die Praxis der Schiedsgerichtsbarkeit (edited by O. Glossner), (Heidelberg 1988-)

Lloyd's of London Press, Inc., *Lloyd's Arbitration Reports* (London 1988-)

London Court of International Arbitration, *Arbitration International* (London 1985-)

Mealey Publications, *International Arbitration Report* (Wayne, PA 1985)

Mediterranean and Middle East Institute of Arbitration, *Mediterranean and Middle East Arbitration Quarterly* (Nicosia 1987-)

Nussbaum, A., ed., *International Year Book on Civil and Commercial Arbitration* (New York 1928-)

————, ed., *Internationales Jahrbuch fur Schiedsgerichtswesen*, 4 vols. (Berlin 1926-1934)

Parker School of Foreign and Comparative Law, *American Review of International Arbitration* (Ardsley-on-Hudson, NY 1990-)

Sanders, P., ed., *Union international des avocats: Arbitrage commercial international,* 3 vols. (The Hague 1951, 1960, 1965)

Society of Maritime Arbitrators, Inc., *The Arbitrator* (New York)

Stichting Tijdschrift voor Arbitrage, *Tijdschrift voor Arbitrage* (A.J. van den Berg, editor-in-chief), (The Hague)

The Korean Commercial Arbitration Board, *Journal of Commercial Arbitration* (in Korean), (Seoul)

Young Lawyers International Association, *International Arbitration Gazette* (Brussels 1984-)

1.05 BIBLIOGRAPHIES

Everard Goodman, Bibliography of Recent Publications on Arbitration, 6 *Y.B. Com. Arb.* 253 (1981)

Goldman & Routh, Bibliography on Arbitration and Litigation in East Asian-United States Transactions, 15 *Int'l Law.* 149 (1981)

Hiramoto, A Path to Resources on International Commercial Arbitration 1980-1986, 4 *Int'l Tax & Bus. Law.* 297 (1986)

Jarvis, An Annotated Bibliography of English-Language Materials on Maritime Arbitration, 14 *Tul. Mar. L.J.* 49 (1989)

Zagorin, Bibliography of Books and Articles on International Commercial Arbitration, 17 *Int'l J. Leg. Info.* 233 (1989)

Ziadé, Selective Bibliography on Arbitration and Arab Countries, 3 *ICSID Rev. - Foreign Investment L.J.* 423 (1988)

———, Selective Bibliography on the Iran-United States Claims Tribunal, 2 *ICSID Rev. - Foreign Investment L.J.* 534 (1987)

2. SOURCES OF ARBITRATION LAW

2.01 SOURCES IN GENERAL

Abbot, Latin America and International Arbitration Conventions: The Quandary of Non-Ratification, 17 *Harv. Int'l L.J.* 131 (1976)

Associazione Italiana per l'Arbitrato, *Convenzioni internazionali concernenti l'Italia in materia di arbitrato* (Rome 1981)

Associazione Italiana per l'Arbitrato, *Multilateral Conventions and Other Instruments on Arbitration* (Rome 1974)

Broches, Promotion of Improvement of Conventions on Arbitration, in *ICCA, Third Int'l Arb. Congress: Proceedings* 325 (1969)

Chillón Medina, J. M. & J. F. Merino Merchán, *Tratado de arbitraje privado interno e internacional* (Madrid 1978)

di Blase, Gli ammodernamienti alla disciplina italiana dell'arbitrato e le convenzioni internazionali, 66 *Riv. Dir. Int'le* 859 (1983)

Gentinetta, Das Verhältnis des Europäischen Übereinkommens über die internationale Handelsschiedsgerichtsbarkeit von 1961 zu anderen multilateralen Abkommen auf dem Gebiet der privaten Schiedsgerichtsbarkeit, 25 *Ann. Suisse Droit Int'l* 149 (1968)

Indonesian Board of Arbitration, *Arbitration in Indonesia and International Conventions on Arbitration* (Jakarta 1978)

Krishnamurthi, Some Thoughts on a New Convention on International Arbitration, in *The Art of Arbitration* 207 (J. Schultsz & A. van den Berg eds. 1982)

Lanfranchi, Le convenzioni internazionali multilaterali in materia di arbitrato, 3 *Riv. Dir. Int'le Priv. & Proc.* 195 (1967)

Lee, E., *Encyclopedia of International Commercial Arbitration* (London 1986)

Nussbaum, Staatsverträge im Bereich des Schiedsgerichtswesen als Prufstein internationaler Privatrechtsregelung, 4 *Archiv für Volkerrecht* 385 (1954)

Parker School of Foreign and Comparative Law, *International Commercial Arbitration and the Courts* (Dobbs Ferry, NY 1990)

Paulsson, International Commercial Arbitrations, in *Handbook of Arbitration Practice* 333 (R. Bernstein ed. 1987)

Punzi, L'efficacia del lodo arbitrale nelle convenzioni internazionali e nell'ordinamento interno, 25 *Rassegna dell'Arb.* 305 (1985)

Remiro Brotons, A., *Ejecución de sentencias arbitrales extranjeras. Los convenios internacionales y su aplicación en España* (Madrid 1980)

Robert, Interprétation par voie d'arbitrage des traités internationaux, 1968 *Rev. Arb.* 46

Schwebel, S.M., *International Arbitration: Three Salient Problems* (Cambridge 1987)

Siqueiros, Arbitral Autonomy and National Sovereign Authority in Latin America, in *Lex Mercatoria and Arbitration* 183 (Th. Carbonneau ed. 1990)

United Nations, International Commercial Arbitration, Report by Ion Nestor, Special Rapporteur, UN Doc. A/CN.9/64 (1972), reprinted in 3 *UNCITRAL Y.B.* 193 (1972)

2.02 GENEVA PROTOCOL ON ARBITRATION CLAUSES 1923

Balladore Pallieri, L'arbitrage privé dans les rapports internationaux, 51 *Recueil des Cours* 291 (1935-I)

Briseño Sierra, El arbitraje privado internacional, in *El Arbitraje Comercial Internacional* 29 (Mexico 1983)

Gaja, Problems of Applicability of International Conventions on Commercial Arbitration, in *A.I.A., Essays in Memoriam Eugenio Minoli* 191 (Turin 1974)

Greminger, H. -W., *Die Genfer Abkommen von 1923 und 1927 über die internationale private Schiedsgerichtsbarkeit* (Winterthur 1957)

Hossain, International Commercial Arbitration, State Succession and the Commonwealth, 36 *Brit. Y.B. Int'l L.* 370 (1960)

Ledoux, La Convention de New York et la Convention européenne sur l'arbitrage international et les concessions de vente en Belgique, 91 *JT* 305 (1976)

Mezger, Zur Auslegung und Bewertung der Genfer Schiedsabkommen von 1923 und 1927, 24 *Rabels Z.* 222 (1959)

Monroy Cabra, M.G., *Arbitraje Comercial* (Bogota 1982)

Nussbaum, Problems of International Arbitration, in 1 *Int'l Y.B. Civil & Com. Arb.* 1 (A. Nussbaum ed. 1928)

————, Treaties on Commercial Arbitration—A Test of International Private-Law Legislation, 56 *Harv. L. Rev.* 219 (1942)

Pechota, Geneva Protocol on Arbitration Clauses, 1923, in 1 *W.A.R.* 1 (H. Smit & V. Pechota eds. 1986, 1987)

Renggli, P., *Die Grenzen der Parteifreiheit im internationalen privatrechtlichen Schiedsverfahren, unter besonderer Berücksichtigung des Genferprotokolls von 1923* (Bern 1955)

Samtleben, Arbitragem comercial no direito internacional privado Brazileiro, in *Estudos em Homenagem ao Prof. Doutor A. Ferrer-Correia* 691 (Coimbra 1986)

van den Berg, A. J., *The New York Arbitration Convention of 1958* (Deventer 1981)

2.03 GENEVA CONVENTION ON EXECUTION
OF FOREIGN AWARDS 1927

Angell, Spain's Attitude to Arbitration, *Int'l Fin. L. Rev.* 23 (June 1984)

Balladore Pallieri, L'arbitrage privé dans les rapports internationaux, 51 *Recueil des Cours* 291 (1935-I)

Briseño Sierra, El arbitraje privado internacional, in *El Arbitraje Comercial Internacional* 29 (Mexico 1983)

Cremades, The Enforcement of British Arbitral Awards in Spain, 45 *Arbitration* 30 and 97 (1979)

Deshpande, Enforcement of Foreign Awards in India, U.K. and U.S.A., 4 *J. Int'l Arb.* 41 (No. 1, 1987)

Gaja, Problems of Applicability of International Conventions on Commercial Arbitration, in *A.I.A., Essays in Memoriam Eugenio Minoli* 191 (Turin 1974)

Greminger, H.-W., *Die Genfer Abkommen von 1923 und 1927 über die internationale private Schiedsgerichtsbarkeit* (Winterthur 1957)

Hossain, International Commercial Arbitration, State Succession and the Commonwealth, 36 *Brit. Y.B. Int'l L.* 370 (1960)

Ledoux, La Convention de New York et la Convention européenne sur l'arbitrage international et les concessions de vente en Belgique, 91 *JT* 305 (1976)

Lorenzen, Commercial Arbitration — Enforcement of Foreign Awards, 45 *Yale L.J.* 39 (1935)

Mezger, Zur Auslegung und Bewertung der Genfer Schiedsabkommen von 1923 und 1927, 24 *Rabels Z.* 222 (1959)

Nussbaum, Problems of International Arbitration, in 1 *Int'l Y.B. Civil & Com. Arb.* 1 (A. Nussbaum ed. 1928)

——, Treaties on Commercial Arbitration — A Test of International Private-Law Legislation, 56 *Harv. L. Rev.* 219 (1942)

Pechota, Geneva Convention on the Execution of Foreign Arbitral Awards, 1927, in 1 *W.A.R.* 11 (H. Smit & V. Pechota eds. 1986, 1987)

Punzi, L'efficacia del lodo arbitrale nelle convenzioni internazionali e nell'ordinamento interno, 25 *Rassegna dell'Arb.* 305 (1985)

Remiro Brotons, A., *Ejecución de sentencias arbitrales extranjeras. Los convenios internacionales y su aplicación en España* (Madrid 1980)

Sornarajah, The Enforcement of Foreign Arbitral Awards in Singapore, 1988 *Malayan L.J.* l x x x v i

van den Berg, A. J., *The New York Arbitration Convention of 1958* (Deventer 1981)

2.04 NEW YORK CONVENTION ON RECOGNITION AND ENFORCEMENT OF FOREIGN ARBITRAL AWARDS 1958

Achebe, The United Nations Convention on the Recognition and Enforcement of Foreign Arbitral Awards of June 10, 1958: Implications for United States Investors in Nigeria, 9 *Tex. Int'l L.J.* 157 (1974)

————, United Nations Arbitration Convention: Implications for Nigeria, 8 *J. World Trade L.* 240 (1974)

Agyemang, African Courts, the Settlement of Investment Disputes and the Enforcement of Awards, 33 *J. Afr. L.* 31 (1989)

Aksen, American Arbitration Accession Arrives in the Age of Aquarius: United States Implements United Nations Convention on the Recognition and Enforcement of Foreign Arbitral Awards, 3 *Sw. U. L. Rev.* 1 (1971); also in *A.A.A., New Strategies for Peaceful Resolution of Int'l Business Disputes* 37 (1971)

————, The Application of the New York Convention by the United States, 4 *Y.B. Com. Arb.* 341 (1979)

Aksen & Dorman, Application of the New York Convention by United States Courts: A Twenty Year Review, 2 *Am. Rev. Int'l Arb.* 65 (1991)

Al-Hejailan, Arab Middle East and the New York Convention, in *First International Commercial Arbitration Conference: Proceedings* 262 (N. Antaki & A. Prujiner eds. 1986)

Allison, Arbitration of Private Antitrust Claims in International Trade: A Study in the Subordination of National Interests to the Demands of a World Market, 18 *N.Y.U. J. Int'l L. & Pol.* 361 (1986)

Alvarez, The Role of Arbitration in Canada — New Perspectives, 21 *U. B.C. L. Rev.* 247 (1987)

American Arbitration Association, *New Strategies for Peaceful Resolution of International Business Disputes* (Dobbs Ferry, NY 1971)

Angell, Spain's Attitude to Arbitration, *Int'l Fin. L. Rev.* 23 (June 1984)

Bakshi, Foreign Forum for Enforcing Awards, 1987 (1) *Company L.J.* 16

Barclay, Enforcement of Arbitration Awards, 41 *Arbitration* 194 (1974)

28

Bateson, The 1958 Convention on Foreign Arbitral Awards, 1958 *J. Bus. L.* 393

Baxi, Goodbye to Unification? The Indian Supreme Court and the United Nations Arbitration Convention, 15 *J. Ind. L. Inst.* 353 (1973)

Béguin, Le droit français de l'arbitrage international et la Convention de New York du 10 juin 1958, in *First International Commercial Arbitration Conference: Proceedings* 218 (N. Antaki & A. Prujiner eds. 1986)

Berglin, The Application in United States Courts of the Public Policy Provisions of the Convention on the Recognition and Enforcement of Foreign Arbitral Awards, 4 *Dick. J. Int'l L.* 167 (1986)

Bernini, The Enforcement of Arbitration Awards, 47 *Arbitration* 99 (1981)

———, The Enforcement of Foreign Arbitral Awards by National Judiciaries: A Trial of the New York Convention's Ambit and Workability, in *The Art of Arbitration* 51 (J. Schultsz & A. van den Berg eds. 1982)

Bertheau, T. R., *Das New Yorker Abkommen vom 10.6.1958 über die Anerkennung und Vollstreckung ausländischer Schiedssprüche* (Winterthur 1965)

Block, Le droit belge de l'arbitrage et la Convention de New York du 10 juin 1958, in *L'Arbitrage* 129 (L. Matray & G. de Leval eds. 1989)

Bombau & Zivy, Influence of the 1958 New York Convention on Recognition and Enforcement of Foreign Arbitral Awards in Argentina, 1990 *Int'l Bus. L.J.* 815

Booysen, The Municipal Enforcement of Arbitration Awards against States in Terms of Arbitration Conventions, with Special Reference to the New York Convention — Does International Law Provide for a Municipal Law Concept of an Arbitrable Act of State? 12 *South Afr. Y.B. Int'l L.* 73 (1986-1987)

Booysen, H., *The Application of the New York Convention to Arbitration to which a State is a Party* (Saarbrücken 1987)

Bredin, La Convention de New York du 10 juin 1958 pour la reconnaissance et l'exécution des sentences arbitrales étrangères, 87 *J. Droit Int'l (Clunet)* 1003 (1960)

Briseño Sierra, El arbitraje privado internacional, in *El Arbitraje Comercial Internacional* 29 (Mexico 1983)

Brody, An Argument for Pre-award Attachment in International Arbitration Under the New York Convention, 18 *Cornell Int'l L.J.* 99 (1985)

Brower & Tupman, Court-Ordered Provisional Measures Under the New York Convention, 80 *Am. J. Int'l L.* 24 (1986)

Brown, Enforcement of Foreign Arbitral Awards — the United Nations Convention on the Recognition and Enforcement of Foreign Arbitral Awards, 14 *Ga. J. Int'l & Comp. L.* 217 (1984)

Bucher, A., *Die neue internationale Schiedsgerichtsbarkeit in der Schweiz* (Basel 1989)

―――, *Le nouvel arbitrage international en Suisse. Théorie et pratique de droit* (Basel 1988)

Bucher, A. & P.-Y. Tschanz, *International Arbitration in Switzerland* (Basel 1989)

Bülow, La convention des parties relative à la procedure d'arbitrage visée a l'Art. V, par.1, litt. d) de la Convention de New York, in *A.I.A., Essays in Memoriam Eugenio Minoli* 81 (Turin 1974)

Carbonneau, American and Other National Variations on the Theme of International Commercial Arbitration, 18 *Ga. J. Int'l & Comp. L.* 143 (1988)

Carpi, L'esecutorietà della sentenza arbitrale secondo la Convenzione di New York, 43 *Riv. Dir. Proc.* 386 (1988); also in *Arbitrato nazionale e internazionale: interpretazione es esecuzione del lodo* 31 (G. Carli ed. 1989)

Chiasson, Canada: No Man's Land No More, *3 J. Int'l Arb.* 67 (No. 2, 1986)

Cole, Public Policy Exception to the New York Convention on the Recognition and Enforcement of Arbitral Awards, 1 *Ohio St. J. Dis. Res.* 365 (1986)

Contini, International Commercial Arbitration — the United Nations Convention on the Recognition and Enforcement of Foreign Arbitral Awards, 8 *Am. J. Comp. L.* 283 (1959)

Cremades, Is Exclusion of Concurrent Courts' Jurisdiction over Conservatory Measures to Be Introduced through a Revision of the Convention?, 6 *J. Int'l Arb.* 105 (No. 3, 1989)

―――, The Enforcement of British Arbitral Awards in Spain, 45 *Arbitration* 30 and 97 (1979)

Comment, United Nations Foreign Arbitral Awards Convention: United States Accession, 2 *Cal. W. Int'l L.J.* 69 (1971)

30

de Bruin, De 'affaire C,' 1989 *Tijdschrift voor Arbitrage* 1

Deshpande, Enforcement of Foreign Awards in India, U.K. and U.S.A., 4 *J. Int'l Arb.* 41 (No. 1, 1987)

―――, Jurisdiction over 'Foreign' and 'Domestic' Awards in the New York Convention 1958, 7 *Arb. Int'l* 123 (1991)

Domke, The United Nations Conference on International Commercial Arbitration, 53 *Am. J. Int'l L.* 414 (1959)

―――, The United States Implementation of the United Nations Arbitral Convention, 19 *Am. J. Comp. L.* 575 (1971)

Ebb, At the End of a Long Trail: How the Bombay High Court Strengthened International Arbitration in India, 44 *Arb. J.* 28 (No. 2, 1989)

―――, Developing Views on What Constitutes a 'Foreign Arbitration Agreement' and a 'Foreign Award' under the New York Convention, 1 *Am. Rev. Int'l Arb.* 364 (1990)

El-Hakim, Should the Key Terms Award, Commercial and Binding Be Defined in the New York Convention? 6 *J. Int'l Arb.* 161 (No. 1, 1989)

Eyzaguirre Echeverria, Arbitration in Latin America: The Experience of the Inter-American Commercial Arbitration Commission, 4 *Int'l Tax & Bus. Law.* 288 (1986)

Ferrante, About the Nature (National or A-National, Contractual or Jurisdictional) of ICC Awards Under the New York Convention, in *The Art of Arbitration* 129 (J. Schultsz & A. van den Berg eds. 1982)

Fois, Primi orientamenti giurisprudenziali in Italia circa l'interpretazione della Convenzione di New York sull'Arbitrato, 12 *Riv. Dir. Int'le Priv. & Proc.* 299 (1976)

Gaja, Problems of Applicability of International Conventions on Commercial Arbitration, in *A.I.A., Essays in Memoriam Eugenio Minoli* 191 (Turin 1974)

Gaja, G., ed., *The New York Convention* (Dobbs Ferry, NY 1979)

Giardina, Court Decisions in Italy Interpreting and Implementing the New York Convention, 7 *J. Int'l Arb.* 77 (No. 2, 1990)

―――, L'applicazione in Italia della Convenzione di New York sull'Arbitrato, 7 *Riv. Dir. Int'le Priv. & Proc.* 268 (1971)

Ginsburgs, G., *The Soviet Union and International Cooperation in Legal Matters. Part I: Recognition of Arbitral Agreements and Execution of Foreign Commercial Arbitral Awards* (Dordrecht 1988)

Glossner, Das Übereinkommen von New York über die Anerkennung und Vollstreckung ausländischer Schiedsprüche von 1958 - ein Fazit, in *Recht über See. Festschrift für Wilhelm Stödter* 47 (H. Ipsen ed. 1979)

————, The New York Convention on the Recognition and Enforcement of Foreign Arbitral Awards — Some Thoughts After 30 Years — 1958-1988, in *Arbitration in Settlement of International Commercial Disputes Involving the Far East and Arbitration in Combined Transportation* 275 (P. Sanders ed. 1989)

Goldring, The 1958 United Nations Convention on Recognition and Enforcement of Foreign Arbitral Awards and the Australian Constitution, 5 *Fed. L. Rev.* 203 (1972-73)

Graham, International Commercial Arbitration: The Developing Canadian Profile, in *UNCITRAL Arbitration Model in Canada* 77 (R. Paterson & B. Thompson eds. 1987)

————, The New York Convention of 1958: A Canadian Perspective, in *First International Commercial Arbitration Conference: Proceedings* 185 (N. Antaki & A. Prujiner eds. 1986)

Grigera Naón, Argentinien nach der Ratifizierung des New Yorker Abkommens über die Anerkennung und Vollstreckung von ausländischen Schiedssprüchen von 1958, 2 *Jahrbuch Schiedsgerichtsbarkeit* 111 (1988)

————, Ratification by Argentina of the 1958 New York Convention on Recognition and Enforcement of Foreign Arbitral Awards, 6 *J. Int'l Arb.* 121 (No. 3, 1989)

Haight, G., *Convention on the Recognition and Enforcement of Foreign Arbitral Awards. Summary Analysis of Record of United Nations Conference,* May/June 1958 (New York 1958)

Heller, Zur Vollstreckung eines jugoslawischen Schiedsspruches in Österreich, 9 *IPRax* 315 (1989)

Holquín Holquín, El concepto de orden público en la Convención de Nueva York y otros comentarios, in *Alternativas a la justicia institucional: arbitraje, conciliación* 131 (Bogota 1988)

Holmes, Pre-award Attachment Under the UN Convention on the Recognition and Enforcement of Foreign Arbitral Awards, 21 *Va. J. Int'l L.* 785 (1981)

Hornick, Indonesia — Foreign Arbitral Awards Not Enforceable, 7 *East Asian Exec. Rep.* 11 (No. 11, 1985)

Hosoi, Practical Aspects of the Recognition and Enforcement in Japan of Foreign Arbitration Awards Under the 1958 New York Convention, 10 *Bull. Japan Shipping Exch.* 31 (No. 10, March 1984)

International Chamber of Commerce, *International Commercial Arbitration and the Convention of New York* (Paris 1960)

Iwasaki, Application of New York Convention by Japanese Courts, 10 *Bull. Japan Shipping Exch.* 1 (1984)

Jarvin, Is Exclusion of Concurrent Courts' Jurisdiction over Conservatory Measures to Be Introduced by a Revision of the Convention? 6 *J. Int'l Arb.* 171 (No. 1, 1989)

Kassis A., *Problèmes de base de l'arbitrage en droit comparé et en droit international. Vol. 1: Arbitrage juridictionnel et arbitrage contractuel* (Paris 1987)

Keutgen & Huys, L'arbitrage et la Convention de New York, 91 *JT* 232 (1976)

Kimbrough, Viabilité générale de l'arbitrage à Singapour: l'accession a la Convention de New York comble la dernière lacune, 1986 *Int'l Bus. L.J.* 783

Klein, La Convention de New York pour la reconnaissance et l'exécution des sentences arbitrales étrangères, 57 *SJZ* 229 and 247 (1961)

Lalonde, The New Environment for Commercial Arbitration in Canada, 1 *Rev. Int'l Bus.* L. 31 (1987); also in 1988 *Int'l Bus. L. J.* 963

Ledoux, La Convention de New York et la Convention européenne sur l'arbitrage international et les concessions de vente en Belgique, 91 *JT* 305 (1976)

Lessing, Sauer-Getriebe K.G. v. White Hydraulics, Inc. — Applicability of the Federal Arbitration Act to International Commercial Arbitration, 2 *Int'l Tax & Bus. Law.* 331 (1984)

Love, Arbitration: the Convention on the Recognition and Enforcement of Foreign Arbitral Awards, as Implemented by U.S. Law, Applies to Arbitration Awards Involving Wholly Foreign Interests and Rendered in the United States, 15 *J. Mar. L. & Com.* 134 (1984)

Lucchesi, Zur Frage der Anerkennung und Vollstreckung des 'lodo irrituale' (= formfreien Schiedssprüches) ausserhalb Italiens, 24 *ZRV* 1 (1983)

Lüer, German Court Decisions Interpreting and Implementing the New York Convention, 7 *J. Int'l Arb.* 127 (No. 1, 1990)

Luzzatto, Accordi internazionali e diritto interno in materia di arbitrato: la Convenzione di New York del 1958, 4 *Riv. Dir. Int'le Priv. & Proc.* 24 (1968)

————, Arbitrato irrituale italiano e Convenzione di New York, 21 *Rassegna dell'Arb.* 105 (1981)

McClendon, Enforcement of Foreign Arbitral Awards in the United States, 4 *Nw. J. Int'l L. & Bus.* 58 (1982)

McLaughlin & Genevro, Enforcement of Arbitral Awards Under the New York Convention - Practice in U.S.Courts, 3 *Int'l Tax & Bus. Law.* 249 (1986)

McMahon, Implementation of U.N. Convention on Foreign Arbitral Awards in the U.S., in *A.A.A., New Strategies for Peaceful Resolution of Int'l Business Disputes* 75 (1971); also in 2 *J. Mar. L. & Com.* 735 (1971)

Maier, H.J., *Europäisches Übereinkommen über die internationale Handelsschiedsgerichtsbarkeit und UN Übereinkommen über die Anerkennung und Vollstreckung ausländischer Schiedssprüche* (Cologne 1966)

Martinez, Recognition and Enforcement on International Arbitral Awards under the United Nations Convention of 1958: The "Refusal" Provisions, 24 *Int'l Law.* 487 (1990)

Melis, Enforcement of Arbitral Awards in Eastern Europe, in *Contemporary Problems in International Arbitration* 332 (J.D.M. Lew ed. 1986)

Mendes & Binavince, Canada and the New York Convention on Foreign Arbitral Awards, 1984 *Can. Arb. J.* 2 (Spring 1984)

Mendes, Canada: A New Forum to Develop the Cultural Psychology of International Commercial Arbitration, 3 *J. Int'l Arb.* 71 (No. 3, 1986)

Minoli, L'Italia et la Convenzione di New York per il ricinoscimento e l'esecuzione delle sentenze arbitrali straniere, 42 *Riv. Dir. Int'le* 102 (1959)

————, L'Italie et la Convention de New York pour la reconnaissance et l'exécution des sentences arbitrales étrangères, in *Liber Amicorum for Martin Domke* 199 (P. Sanders ed. 1967)

————, La nuova Convenzione per il riconoscimento e l'esecuzione delle sentenze arbitrali stranieri, 12 *Riv. Trim. Dir. & Proc. Civ.* 954 (1958)

Mirabelli, The Application of the New York Convention by the Italian Courts, 4 *Y.B. Com. Arb.* 362 (1979)

Mirabito, The United Nations Convention on the Recognition and Enforcement of Foreign Arbitral Awards: The First Four Years, 5 *Ga. J. Int'l & Comp. L.* 471 (1975)

Mok Young-Joon, The Principle of Reciprocity in the United Nations Convention on the Recognition and Enforcement of Foreign Arbitral Awards of 1958, 21 *Case W. Res. J. Int'l L.* 123 (1989)

Morera, Consequences de l'entrée en vigueur en Italie de la Convention de New York du 10 juin 1958 sur le régime des arbitrages étrangers, in *A.I.A., Essays in Memoriam Eugenio Minoli* 337 (Turin 1974)

Morviducci, La forma de la clausola compromissoria secondo la Convenzione di New York del 1958, 56 *Riv. Dir. Int'le* 732 (1973)

Moussali, Arbitrage International: Syrie, 1991 *Int'l Bus. L.J.* 401

Narayan, The United Nations Convention on International Commercial Arbitration 1958, 1960 *Indian J. Int'l L.* 33

Nariman, Foreign Arbitral Awards in India: Problems, Pitfalls, and Progress, 6 *J. Int'l Arb.* 25 (No. 1, 1989)

Nattier, International Commercial Arbitration in Latin America: Enforcement of Arbitral Agreements and Awards, 21 *Tex. Int'l L. J.* 397 (1986)

Neuteufel, Art. XXIX EGEO und das New Yorker Übereinkommen über die Anerkennung und Vollstreckung ausländischer Schiedssprüche, 1984 *O JZ* 320

Nicotina, Oggetto e limiti dell'accertamento giudiciale nel giudicio do delibazione di lodo estero secondo la Convenzione di New York, 25 *Rassegna dell'Arb.* 129 (1985)

Note, Application of the Convention on the Recognition and Enforcement of Foreign Arbitral Awards: Mitsubishi Motor Corp. v. Soler Chrysler-Plymouth, Inc., 8 *Fordham Int'l L.J.* 194 (1984)

————, Enforcement of Foreign Arbitral Awards under the United Nations Convention of 1958: A Survey of Recent Federal Case Law. Notes and Comments, 11 *Md. J. Int'l L. & Trade* 13 (1987)

————, The Validity of the Foreign Sovereign Immunity Defense in Suits Under the Convention on the Recognition and Enforcement of Foreign Arbitral Awards, 7 *Fordham Int'l L. J.* 321 (1983-84)

Oppetit, Le refus d'exécution d'une sentence arbitrale étrangère dans le cadre de la Convention de New York, 1971 *Rev. Arb.* 97

Palmer, Mitsubishi: the Erosion of the New York Convention and International Arbitration, 1984 *Wis. Int'l L.J.* 151 (Symposium)

Parker School of Foreign and Comparative Law, *International Commercial Arbitration and the Courts* (Dobbs Ferry, NY 1990)

Parker School of Foreign and Comparative Law, *The 1989 Guide to International Arbitration and Arbitrators* (Dobbs Ferry, NY 1989)

Patchett, K.W., *Recognition of Commercial Judgments and Awards in the Commonwealth* (London 1984)

Patkos, The United Nations Convention of 1958 on the Recognition and Enforcement of Foreign Arbitral Awards in the Light of the Greek Civil Procedure Code of 1971, 25 *Rev. Hellénique Droit Int'l* 295 (1972)

Paulsson, The Contribution of English and American Legislation, in *Euro-Arab Arbitration III* 104 (F. Kemicha ed. 1991)

Pechota, New York Convention on the Recognition and Enforcement of Foreign Arbitral Awards, in 1 *W.A.R.* 23.0 (H. Smit & V. Pechota eds. 1986, 1987)

Pisar, The United Nations Convention on Foreign Arbitral Awards, 1959 *J. Bus. L.* 219; reprinted in 33 *S. Cal. L. Rev.* 14 (1959)

Pointet, P.J., *La Convention de New York sur l'exécution des sentences arbitrales étrangères* (Zurich 1958)

Poudret, Challenge and Enforcement of Arbitral Awards in Switzerland, 4 *Arb. Int'l* 278 (1988)

————, La clause arbitrale par référence selon la Convention de New York et l'art. 6 du Concordat sur l'arbitrage, in *Mélanges Guy Flattet* 523 (Lausanne 1985)

Punzi, L'efficacia del lodo arbitrale nelle convenzioni internazionali e nell'ordinamento interno, 25 *Rassegna dell'Arb.* 305 (1985)

Quigley, Accession by the United States to the United Nations Convention on the Recognition and Enforcement of Foreign Arbitral Awards, 70 *Yale L.J.* 1049 (1961)

————, Convention on Foreign Arbitral Awards, 58 *A.B.A. J.* 821 (1972)

Rached, S., *At-Takhim fi Al-llakat Ad-Dawliyat Al-Khassat [Arbitration in Private International Law Relations] - Vol.1 [Arbitration Convention]*, (Cairo 1984)

Ramos Mendez, First Applications by the Spanish Supreme Court of the New York Convention of June 10, 1958 to the Exequatur of Foreign Arbitral Awards, 10 *Int'l Trade L. & Prac.* 95 (1984)

Recchia, An Italian Approach to International Conventions on Arbitration, in *A.I.A., Essays in Memoriam Eugenio Minoli* 393 (Turin 1974)

————, Nuove prospettive dell'arbitrato commerciale in Italia, 23 *Rassegna dell'Arb.* 41 (1983)

Remiro Brotons, A., *Ejecución de sentencias arbitrales extranjeras. Los convenios internacionales y su aplicación en España* (Madrid 1980)

Ricci, Problemi sulla recezione all'estero dei lodi rituali italiani, 41 *Riv. Dir. Proc.* 117 (1986)

Riccomagno, Recognition and Enforcement of Foreign Arbitral Awards in Italy under the New York Convention of 1958, 1 *Y.B. Mar. L.* 119 (1984)

Richard, Enforcement of Foreign Arbitral Awards under the United Nations Convention of 1958: A Survey of Recent Federal Case Law, 11 *Md. J. Int'l L. & Trade* 13 (1987)

Robert, La Convention de New York du 10 juin 1958 pour la reconnaissance et l'exécution des sentences arbitrales étrangères, 1958 *Rev. Arb.* 70

Rubino-Sammartano, An International Arbitral Court of Appeal as an Alternative to Long Attacks and Recognition Proceedings, 6 *J. Int'l Arb.* 180 (No. 1, 1989)

Report, Canada and the United Nations Convention on Arbitral Awards, 9 *Can. Arb. J.* 2 (No. 1, 1984)

Sajko, The New York Arbitration Convention of 1958 from the Yugoslav Point of View: Selected Issues, in *Essays on International Commercial Arbitration* 199 (P. Sarcevic ed. 1989)

Sanders, A Twenty Year's Review of the Convention on the Recognition and Enforcement of Foreign Arbitral Awards, 13 *Int'l Law.* 269 (1979); reprinted in *Arbitration and the Licensing Process* 3 (R. Goldscheider & M. de Haas eds. 1984)

———, International Commercial Arbitration - How to Improve Its Functioning? 46 *Arbitration* 9 (1980)

———, New York Convention on the Recognition and Enforcement of Foreign Arbitral Awards, 6 *Neth. Int'l L. Rev.* 43 (1959)

———, Trends in the Field of International Commercial Arbitration, 145 *Recueil des Cours* 205 (1975-II)

Sandrock & Hentzen, Enforcing Foreign Arbitral Awards in the Federal Republic of Germany: The Example of a United States Award, 2 *Transnat'l Law.* 49 (1989)

Santos, International Commercial Arbitration, in *Commercial Arbitration* 122 (J. Ricalde ed. 1983)

Schwartz, La forme écrite de l'art. II, al. 2 de la Convention de New York pour la reconnaissance et l'exécution des sentences arbitrales étrangères du 10 juin 1958, 64 *SJZ* 49 (1968)

Schwebel, S.M., *International Arbitration: Three Salient Problems* (Cambridge 1987)

Sedlacek, Das Vereinte Nationen-Übereinkommen vom 10. Juni 1958 über die Anerkennung und Vollstreckung ausländischer Schiedssprüche, 3 *ZRV* 23 (1962)

Sidel & Mao Tong, China: Recognition and Enforcement of Foreign Arbitral Awards under the N.Y. Convention, 10 *East Asian Exec. Rep.* 14 (No. 5, 1988)

Siqueiros, Panórama actual del arbitraje comercial internacional, in *El Arbitraje Comercial Internacional* 135 (Mexico 1983)

Smit, A-National Arbitration, 63 *Tul. L. Rev.* 629 (1989)

Smith, Determining the Arbitrability of International Antitrust Disputes, 8 *J. Comp. Bus. & Cap. Market L.* 197 (1986)

Sornarajah, The Enforcement of Foreign Arbitral Awards in Singapore, 1988 *Malayan L.J.* lxxxvi

Somarajah, M., *International Commercial Arbitration: The Problem of State Contracts* (Singapore 1990)

Springer, The U.N. Convention on Recognition and Enforcement of Foreign Arbitral Awards, 3 *Int'l Law.* 320 (1969); also in *A.A.A., New Strategies for Peaceful Resolution of Int'l Business Disputes* 25 (1971)

Sultan, The United Nations Arbitration Convention and United States Policy, 53 *Am. J. Int'l L.* 807 (1959)

Swisher, International Commercial Arbitration under the United Nations Convention and the Amended Federal Arbitration Statute, 47 *Wash. L. Rev.* 441 (1972)

Trammer, Konwencja o uznawaniu i wykonywaniu zagranicznych orzeczen arbitrazowych, 16 *Panstwo i Prawo* 738 (No. 11, 1961)

Trooboff & Goldstein, Foreign Arbitral Awards and the 1958 New York Convention: Experience to Date in the United States Courts, 17 *Va. J. Int'l L.* 469 (1977)

Tschanz, Le droit américain et la Convention de New York, in *First International Commercial Arbitration Conference: Proceedings* 249 (N. Antaki & A. Prujiner eds. 1986)

Tupman, Staying Enforcement of Arbitral Awards under the New York Convention, 3 *Arb. Int'l* 223 (1987)

Tupman & Brower, Court-Ordered Provisional Measures under the New York Convention, 80 *Am. J. Int'l L.* 24 (1986)

Ünal, The New York Convention and the Recognition and Enforcement of Foreign Arbitral Awards in Turkish Law, 7 *J. Int'l Arb.* 55 (No. 4, 1990)

United Nations, Study on the Application and Interpretation of the Convention on the Recognition and Enforcement of Foreign Arbitral Awards: Report of the Secretary-General, UN Doc. A/CN.9/168 (1979); reprinted in 10 *UNCITRAL Y.B.* 100 (1979)

Uwanno & Sathirathai, Introduction to the Thai Legal System. [Section c) International Commercial Arbitration], 4 *Chulalongkorn L. Rev.* 39, 105 (1985-1986)

van den Berg, Consolidated Arbitrations and the 1958 New York Arbitration Convention, 2 *Arb. Int'l* 367 (1986)

————, Does the New York Arbitration Convention of 1958 Apply Retroactively? 1 *Arb. Int'l* 103 (1985)

————, Non-Domestic Arbitral Awards under the 1958 New York Convention, 2 *Arb. Int'l* 191 (1986)

————, Recent Enforcement Problems under the New York and ICSID Conventions, 5 *Arb. Int'l* 2 (1989)

————, Should an International Arbitrator Apply the New York Arbitration Convention of 1958? in *The Art of Arbitration* 39 (J. Schultsz & A. van den Berg eds. 1982)

————, Some Recent Problems in the Practice of Enforcement under the New York and ICSID Conventions, in *Arbitration and the Courts: Fifth ICSID/AAA/ ICC Colloquium* (Washington 1987)

————, Some Recent Problems in the Practice of Enforcement under the New York and ICSID Conventions, 2 *ICSID Rev. - Foreign Investment L.J.* 439 (1987)

————, The New York Arbitration Convention of 1958 and the Arab Countries, in *First Euro-Arab Arb. Conference: Proceedings* 54 (F. Kemicha ed. 1987)

————, The New York Arbitration Convention 1958 and the Panama Convention of 1975, 5 *Arb. Int'l* 214 (1989)

————, When Is an Arbitral Award Non-Domestic Under the New York Convention of 1958? 6 *Pace L. Rev.* 25 (1985)

van den Berg, A. J., *The New York Arbitration Convention of 1958* (Deventer 1981)

Vigoriti, Recent Developments in the Recognition and Execution of Foreign Judgments and Arbitral Awards in Italy, 6 *Civil Just. Q.* 248 (1987)

von Preuschen, Die Vollstreckung ausländischer Schiedssprüche in Japan nach dem Inkrafttreten des UN-Übereinkommens, 10 *AWD* 112 (1964)

Wackenhuth, Die Schriftform für Schiedsvereinbarungen nach dem UN-Übereinkommen und Allgemeine Geschäftsbedingungen, 99 *ZZP* 445 (1986)

Walter, Das Schiedsverfahren im deutsch-italienischen Rechtsverkehr, 28 *RIW* 693 (1982)

Wenger, Zur Anwendbarkeit des New Yorker Übereinkommen über die Anerkennung und Vollstreckung ausländischer Schiedssprüche auf einem 'freien' Schiedsspruch (lodo irrituale) des italianischen Rechts, 2 *IPRax* 135 (1982)

Werner, Should the New York Convention be Revised to Provide for Court Intervention in Arbitral Proceedings? 6 *J. Int'l Arb.* 113 (No. 3, 1989)

Wysocka, B., *Uznawanie i wykonywanie zagranicznych orzeczen arbitrazowych w Polsce* (Warsaw 1987)

2.05 EUROPEAN CONVENTION ON INTERNATIONAL COMMERCIAL ARBITRATION 1961

Barclay, Rules for the Settlement of International Disputes, 42 *Arbitration* 31 (1975)

Benjamin, The European Convention on International Commercial Arbitration, 37 *Brit. Y.B. Int'l L.* 478 (1961)

————, The Work of the Economic Commission for Europe in the Field of International Commercial Arbitration, 7 *Int'l & Comp. L.Q.* 22 (1958)

Booysen, The Municipal Enforcement of Arbitration Awards against States in Terms of Arbitration Conventions, with Special Reference to the New York Convention — Does International Law Provide for a Municipal Law Concept of an Arbitrable Act of State? 12 *South Afr. Y.B. Int'l L.* 73 (1986-1987)

Briseño Sierra, El arbitraje privado internacional, in *El Arbitraje Comercial Internacional* 29 (Mexico 1983)

Bülow, Europäisches Übereinkommen über die internationale Handelsschiedsgerichtsbarkeit, 1961 *AWD* 144

Chipev, Organizatsia na arbitrazha spored Evropeiskata konventsia na vnshotrgovski arbitrazh, 1983 *Vaprosy na mezhdunarodnoto chastno pravo (Sofia)* 203

Cremades, Evolution récente du droit espagnol en matière d'arbitrage, 1988 *Rev. Arb.* 223

Donner, Evropská úmluva o mezinárodní obchodní arbitrázi, 5 *Casopis pro mezinárodní právo* 332 (1961)

Garnefsky, Das Europäische Übereinkommen über die internationale Handelsschiedsgerichtsbarkeit und das Sowjetrecht, 9 *Osteuroparecht* 14 (1963)

Gentinetta, Das Verhältnis des Europäischen Übereinkommens über die internationale Handelsschiedsgerichtsbarkeit von 1961 zu anderen multilateralen Abkommen auf dem Gebiet der privaten Schiedsgerichtsbarkeit, 25 *Ann. Suisse Droit Int'l* 149 (1968)

Ginsburgs, G., *The Soviet Union and International Cooperation in Legal Matters. Part I: Recognition of Arbitral Agreements and Execution of Foreign Commercial Arbitral Awards* (Dordrecht 1988)

Golsong, L'arrangement relatif a l'application de la Convention Européenne sur l'Arbitrage Commercial International, 8 *Ann. Français Droit Int'l* 741 (1962)

Hascher, European Convention on International Commercial Arbitration of 1961: Commentary, 15 *Y.B. Com. Arb.* 624 (1990)

Klein, Das Europäische Übereinkommen über die internationale Handelsschiedsgerichtsbarkeit, 76 *ZZP* 342 (1963)

————, La Convention européenne sur l'arbitrage commercial international, 51 *Rev. Crit. Droit Int'l Privé* 621 (1962)

Kopelmanas, La place de la Convention européenne sur l'arbitrage commercial international du 21 avril 1961 dans l'évolution du droit international de l'arbitrage, 7 *Ann. Français Droit Int'l* 331 (1961)

Lando, The Law Applicable to the Merits of the Dispute, in *Essays on International Commercial Arbitration* 129 (P. Sarcevic ed. 1989)

————, The Law Applicable to the Merits of the Dispute, in *Contemporary Problems in International Arbitration* 101 (J.D.M. Lew ed. 1986)

Luzzatto, La Convenzione di Ginevra del 1961, 7 *Riv. Dir. Int'le Priv. & Proc.* 47 (1971)

Maier, H.J., *Europäisches Übereinkommen über die internationale Handelsschiedsgerichtsbarkeit und UN Übereinkommen über die Anerkennung und Vollstreckung ausländischer Schiedssprüche* (Cologne 1966)

Mezger, Compétence-compétence des arbitres et indépendence de la Convention arbitrale dans la Convention dite Européenne sur l'Arbitrage Commercial International de 1961, in *A.I.A., Essays in Memoriam Eugenio Minoli* 315 (Turin 1974)

————, Das Europäische Übereinkommen über die internationale Handelsschiedsgerichtsbarkeit, 29 *Rabels Z.* 231 (1965)

Monaco, Le droit applicable au fond du litige dans la convention sur l'arbitrage commercial international, 9 *Nederlands Tijtschrift voor Int'l Ret* 331 (1962)

Paulsson, May a State Invoke Its Internal Law to Repudiate Consent to International Commercial Arbitration? Reflections on the Benteler v. Belgium Preliminary Award, 2 *Arb. Int'l* 90 (1986)

Pechota, European Convention on International Commercial Arbitration, 1961, in 1 *W.A.R.* 163 (H. Smit & V. Pechota eds. 1986, 1987)

Pointet, La Convention de Genève sur l'Arbitrage Commercial International/The Geneva Convention on International Commercial Arbitration, in 3 *Arbitrage International Commercial/International Commercial Arbitration* 262 (P. Sanders ed. 1965)

Pointet, P.J., *La Convention européenne sur l'arbitrage commercial international* (Zurich 1961)

Recchia, An Italian Approach to International Conventions on Arbitration, in *A.I.A., Essays in Memoriam Eugenio Minoli* 393 (Turin 1974)

Santos, International Commercial Arbitration, in *Commercial Arbitration* 122 (J. Ricalde ed. 1983)

Sarre, European Commercial Arbitration, 1961 *J. Bus. L.* 352

Sawczuk, M., ed., *Odrebnosci krajowe miedzynarodowego arbitrazu handlowego — Les particularités nationales de l'arbitrage commercial international* (Lublin 1987)

Schlosser, Quelles nouvelles de l'arbitrage Outre-Rhin? 1987 *Rev. Arb.* 293

Schwebel, S. M., *International Arbitration: Three Salient Problems* (Cambridge 1987)

Trolle, Geneve-Konventionen af 1961 om Handelsvoldgift, 1961 *Ugeskrift for Retsvaesen* 203

van den Berg, A. J., *The New York Arbitration Convention of 1958* (Deventer 1981)

van Heukelom, Het Europese Verdrag inzake Internationale Handels arbitrage van 21 April 1961, 1961 *Arbitrale Rechtspraak* 161

2.06 WASHINGTON CONVENTION ON SETTLEMENT OF INVESTMENT DISPUTES 1965

Agyemang, African Courts, the Settlement of Investment Disputes and the Enforcement of Awards, 33 *J. Afr. L.* 31 (1989)

Aksen, G. & R. von Mehren, eds., *International Arbitration Between Private Parties and Governments* (New York 1982)

Albrecht, Some Legal Questions Concerning the Convention on the Settlement of Investment Disputes between States and Nationals of Other States, 12 *St. Louis U.L.J.* 679 (1968)

Amadio, M., *Le contentieux international de l'investissement privé et la Convention de la Banque Mondiale du 18 mars 1965* (Paris 1967)

Amerasinghe, Jurisdiction Ratione Personae under the Convention on the Settlement of Investment Disputes between States and Nationals of Other States, 47 *Brit. Y.B. Int'l L.* 227 (1974)

Bernardini, P., *L'arbitrato internazionale* (Milan 1987)

Blumereau, L'adhésion de l'Arabie Saoudite à la Convention CIRDI: ouverture à l'arbitrage international, 7 *Droit et Pratique du Com. Int'l* 726 (1981)

Booysen, The Municipal Enforcement of Arbitration Awards against States in Terms of Arbitration Conventions, with Special Reference to the New York Convention — Does International Law Provide for a Municipal Law Concept of an Arbitrable Act of State? 12 *South Afr. Y.B. Int'l L.* 73 (1986-1987)

Briseño Sierra, El arbitraje privado internacional, in *El Arbitraje Comercial Internacional* 29 (Mexico 1983)

Broches, Awards Rendered Pursuant to the ICSID Convention: Binding Force, Finality, Recognition, Enforcement, Execution, 2 *ICSID Rev. - Foreign Investment L.J.* 287 (1987)

————, The Convention on the Settlement of Investment Disputes between States and Nationals of Other States, 136 *Recueil des Cours* 333 (1972-II)

————, The Convention on the Settlement of Investment Disputes between States and Nationals of Other States: Applicable Law and Default Procedure, in *Liber Amicorum for Martin Domke* 12 (P. Sanders ed. 1967)

45

Buffenstein, Foreign Investment Arbitration and Joint Ventures, 5 *N.C.J. Int'l L. & Com. Reg.* 191 (1980)

Chantikul, The Convention on the Settlement of Investment Disputes between States and Nationals of Other States, 1 *Chulalongkorn L. Rev.* 48 (1982)

Cherian, A Proposal to Amend Article 14(1) (Qualifications of Arbitrators) of the World Bank Convention on the Settlement of Investment Disputes Between States and Nationals of Other States, in *ICCA, Fifth Int'l Arb. Congress: Proceedings C Ig* 1-4 (1975)

Cherian, J., *Investment Contracts and Arbitration. The World Bank Convention on the Settlement of Investment Disputes* (Leiden 1975)

Chong Su Yun, The Convention on the Settlement of Investment Disputes — Commentary and Forecast, 11 *Malaya L. Rev.* 287 (1969)

Coll, United States Enforcement of Arbitral Awards Against Sovereign States: Implications of the ICSID Convention, 17 *Harv. J. Int'l L.* 401 (1976)

de Berranger, L'article 52 de la Convention de Washington du 18 mars 1965 et les premiers enseignements de sa pratique, 1988 *Rev. Arb.* 95

Delaume, Arbitration with Governments: Domestic and International, 17 *Int'l Law.* 687 (1983)

————, Foreign Sovereign Immunity: Impact on Arbitration, 38 *Arb. J.* 34 (No. 2, 1983)

————, La Convention pour le règlement des différends relatifs aux investissements entre Etats et ressortissants d'autres Etats, 93 *J. Droit Int'l (Clunet)* 26 (1966)

————, State Contracts and Transnational Arbitration, 75 *Am. J. Int'l L.* 784 (1981)

Delaume, G., *Transnational Contracts, Applicable Law and Settlement of Disputes: A Study in Conflict Avoidance* (Dobbs Ferry, NY 1975)

Farley, Commentary: The Convention on the Settlement of Investment Disputes between States and Nationals of Other States, 5 *Duq. L. Rev.* 19 (1966)

Feuerle, International Arbitration and Choice of Law Under Art. 42 of the Convention on the Settlement of Investment Disputes, 4 *Yale Stud. World Pub. Ord.* 89 (1977)

Fischer, Die schiedsgerichtliche Beilegung von privaten Investitions-streitigkeiten im Lichte der Weltbankkonvention vom 18. März 1965, 1 *Verfassung und Recht in Übersee* 262 (1968)

Goldman, Le droit applicable selon la Convention de la B.I.R.D., du 18 mars 1965, pour le règlement des différends relatifs aux investissements entre Etats et ressortissants d'autre Etats, in *Investissements étrangers et arbitrage entre Etats et personnes privées* 133 (Paris 1969)

Gonzalez & Padilla, The International Centre for the Settlement of Investment Disputes: An Assessment from the Philippine Perspective, 59 *Philippine L.J.* 222 (1984)

Lattanzi, Convenzione de Washington sulle controversie relative ad investimenti e invalidità delle sentenze arbitrali, 70 *Riv. Dir. Int'le* 521 (1987)

Lauterpacht, The World Bank Convention on the Settlement of International Investment Disputes, in *Recueil d'Etudes de Droit International en Hommage à Paul Guggenheim* 642 (Geneva 1968)

Masood, Law Applicable in Arbitration of Investment Disputes under the World Bank Convention, 15 *J. Ind. L. Inst.* 311 (1973)

Monroy Cabra, M.G., *Arbitraje Comercial* (Bogota 1982)

Note, Confidentiality in ICSID Arbitration After AMCO ASIA CORP. v. INDONESIA: Watchword or White Elephant? 10 *Fordham Int'l L. J.* 93 (1986)

O'Hare, The Convention on the Settlement of Investment Disputes, 6 *Stan. J. Int'l Studies* 146 (1972)

Pirrung, J, *Die Schiedsgerichtsbarkeit nach dem Weltbankübereinkommen für Investitionsstreitigkeiten* (Berlin 1972)

Rodley, Some Aspects of the World Bank Convention on the Settlement of Investment Disputes, 1966 *Canadian Y.B. Int'l L.* 43

Roulet, La Convention du 18 mars 1965 pour le règlement des différends relatifs aux investissements entre Etats et ressortissants d'autres Etats, 22 *Ann. Suisse Droit Int'l* 121 (1965)

Sacerdoti, La Convenzione di Washington del 1965 per la soluzione delle controversie tra Stati e nazionali di altri Stati en materia di investimenti, 5 *Riv. Dir. Int'le Priv. & Proc.* 614 (1969)

————, La Convenzione di Washington del 1965: bilancio di un ventennio del'ICSID, 23 *Riv. Dir. Int'le Priv. & Proc.* 13 (1987)

Shifman, Convention on the Settlement of Investment Disputes between States and Nationals of Other States, 1965, in 1 *W.A.R.* 71 (H. Smit & V. Pechota eds. 1986, 1987)

Sprague, A Courageous Course for Latin America: Urging the Ratification of the ICSID, 5 *Houston J. Int'l L.* 157 (1982)

Sutherland, The World Bank Convention on the Settlement of Investment Disputes, 28 *Int'l & Comp.L.Q.* 367 (1979)

Szasz, The Investment Disputes Convention and Latin America, 11 *Va. J. Int'l L.* 256 (1971)

Tita, Gli arbitrati predisposti dalle convenzioni ICSID e MIGA e la suroga assicurativa, 23 *Riv. Dir. Int'le Priv. & Proc.* 497 (1987)

van den Berg, Recent Enforcement Problems under the New York and ICSID Conventions, 5 *Arb. Int'l* 2 (1989)

————, Some Recent Problems in the Practice of Enforcement under the New York and ICSID Conventions, in *Arbitration and the Courts: Fifth ICSID/AAA/ ICC Colloquium* (Washington 1987)

————, Some Recent Problems in the Practice of Enforcement under the New York and ICSID Conventions, 2 *ICSID Rev. - Foreign Investment L.J.* 439 (1987)

van den Berg, A. J., *The New York Arbitration Convention of 1958* (Deventer 1981)

Vitanyi, Quelques refléxions sur la Convention pour le règlement des différends relatifs aux investissements entre Etats et ressortissants d'autres Etats, 47/48 *Annuaire de l'Association des Auditeurs et Anciens Auditeurs de l'Académie de Droit Int'l de la Haye 139 (1977-78); also in New Directions in International Law: Essays in Honour of Wolfgang Abendroth* 193 (Frankfurt 1982)

2.07 EUROPEAN CONVENTION PROVIDING A UNIFORM LAW ON ARBITRATION 1966

Arnold, Das Europäische Übereinkommen vom 20. Januar 1966 zur Einführung eines einheitlichen Gesetzes über die Schiedsgerichtsbarkeit, 1967 *NJW* 142

Barclay, Arbitration in the Common Market, 39 *Arbitration* 73 (1972)

————, Rules for the Settlement of International Disputes, 42 *Arbitration* 31 (1975)

Council of Europe, *Explanatory Report on the European Convention Providing a Uniform Law on Arbitration* (Strasbourg 1967)

Granzow, J., *Das UNCITRAL-Modellgesetz über die internazionale Handelsschiedsgerichtsbarkeit von 1985* (Munich 1988)

Jenard, Projet de Convention Européenne portant loi uniforme en matière d'arbitrage/Draft European Convention Providing a Uniform Law on Arbitration, 3 *Arbitrage International Commercial/International Commercial Arbitration* 370 (P. Sanders ed., 1965)

Krüger, The Council of Europe and Unification of Private Law, 16 *Am. J. Comp. L.* 127 (1968)

Ledoux, La Convention de New York et la Convention européenne sur l'arbitrage international et les concessions de vente en Belgique, 91 *JT* 305 (1976)

Sanders, Harmonization of Arbitration Laws. A Model Law? in *Festschrift für Arthur Bülow* 185 (K.-H. Böckstiegel & O. Glossner eds. 1981)

Schwebel, S.M., *International Arbitration: Three Salient Problems* (Cambridge 1987)

Shifman, European Convention Providing a Uniform Law on Arbitration, 1966, in 1 *W.A.R.* 190 (H. Smit & V. Pechota eds. 1986, 1987)

2.08 MOSCOW CONVENTION ON SETTLEMENT BY ARBITRATION OF CIVIL LAW DISPUTES 1972

Butler, W., *Soviet Commercial Arbitration* (Dobbs Ferry and Paris 1989)

Capatina, L'arbitrage du commerce extérieur selon la Convention de Moscou de 1972, 102 *J. Droit Int'l (Clunet)* 503 (1975)

Ginsburgs, G., *The Soviet Union and International Cooperation in Legal Matters. Part I: Recognition of Arbitral Agreements and Execution of Foreign Commercial Arbitral Awards* (Dordrecht 1988)

Hanak, Arbitration in Socialist Countries, 44 *Arbitration* 180 (1978)

————, Arbitration in Socialist Countries, in *ICCA, Sixth Int'l Arb. Congress: Proceedings* 49 (1978)

Jakubowski, La Convention de Moscou du 29 mai 1972 sur le règlement des litiges par voies d'arbitrage, 1973 *Rev. Arb.* 59

Khlestova, I.O., *Arbitrazh vo vneshneekonomicheskikh otnosheniakh stran-chlenov SEV* (Moscow 1980)

Labedzki, Rezim prawny orzeczen arbitrazowych objetych konwencja moskiewska z 1972 r., 38 *Panstwo i Prawo* 59 (No. 7, July 1983)

Lebedev, International Commercial Arbitration in the Socialist Countries Members of the CMEA, 158 *Recueil des Cours* 87 (1977-V)

————, ed., *Handbook on Foreign Trade Arbitration in the CMEA Member Countries* (Moscow 1983)

Melis, Enforcement of Arbitral Awards in Eastern Europe, in *Contemporary Problems in International Arbitration* 332 (J.D.M. Lew ed. 1986)

Pechota, International Economic Arbitration in the USSR and Eastern Europe, 8 *N.Y. L. Sch. J. Int'l & Comp. L.* 377 (1987)

————, Moscow Convention on Settlement by Arbitration of Civil Law Disputes Resulting from Economic, Scientific, and Technical Cooperation, 1972, in 1 *W.A.R.* 217.1 (H. Smit & V. Pechota eds. 1986, 1987)

Pozdnyakov, Commercial Arbitration in CMEA Member Countries, 4 *Int'l Tax & Bus. Law.* 272 (1986)

Stalev, L'arbitrage économique internationale dans les pays-membres du CAEM après la Convention de Moscou de 1972, in *Problèmes juridiques de l'intégration économique socialiste* (Sofia 1977)

Strohbach, General Introduction on Arbitration in CMEA Countries, in *International Handbook on Commercial Arbitration* (A.J. van den Berg gen. ed. 1984,1986)

————, On the Setting Aside of Arbitration Awards, in *ICC, Hommage à Frederic Eisemann* 77 (1978)

Trammer, La Convention de Moscou sur l'arbitrage du 26 mai 1972, in *A.I.A., Essays in Memorian Eugenio Minoli* 517 (Turin 1974)

Ustor, Arbitration in CMEA Countries, 14 *Communicazioni e studi dell'Istituto di Diritto Internazionale e Straniero della Università di Milano* 957 (1975)

van den Berg, A. J., *The New York Arbitration Convention of 1958* (Deventer 1981)

Wysocka, B., *Uznawanie i wykonywanie zagranicznych orzeczen arbitrazowych w Polsce* (Warsaw 1987)

2.09 INTER-AMERICAN CONVENTION ON INTERNATIONAL COMMERCIAL ARBITRATION 1975

Abbot, Latin America and International Arbitration Conventions: The Quandary of Non-Ratification, 17 *Harv. Int'l L.J.* 131 (1976)

Benetti Salgar, La Convención de Panamá sobre Arbitraje Comercial Internacional, in *Alternativas a la justicia institucional: arbitraje, conciliación* 139 (Bogota 1988)

Boutin, De la teoria de la doble personalidad del Estado y el arbitraje internacional en el nuevo Código Judicial Panameño, in *El Arbitraje en el Derecho Latinoamericano y Español* 459 (L. Perret & U. Montoya Alberti eds. 1989)

Caminos, The Inter-American Convention on International Commercial Arbitration, 3 *ICSID Rev. - Foreign Investment L.J.* 107 (1988)

Eyzaguirre Echeverria, Arbitration in Latin America: The Experience of the Inter-American Commercial Arbitration Commission, 4 *Int'l Tax & Bus. Law.* 288 (1986)

Eyzaguirre Echeverria & Siqueiros, Arbitration in Latin America, in *Arbitration in Settlement of International Commercial Disputes Involving the Far East and Arbitration in Combined Transportation* 81 (P. Sanders ed. 1989)

Fouchard, La Convention interaméricain sur l'arbitrage commercial international (Panama, 20 janvier 1975), 1977 *Rev. Arb.* 203

Garro, Inter-American Convention on International Commercial Arbitration, 1975, in 1 *W.A.R.* 255.1 (H. Smit & V. Pechota eds. 1986, 1987)

Kos-Rabcewicz-Zubkowski, Les conventions interaméricaines sur l'arbitrage commercial et la Commission interaméricaine d'arbitrage commercial, 1983 *Rev. Arb.* 411

―――――, Panamerykanskie konwencje dotyczace arbitrazu handlowego, 44 *Panstwo i Prawo* 84 (No. 3, 1989)

Leich, The Inter-American Convention on International Commercial Arbitration, 75 *Am. J. Int'l L.* 982 (1981)

Lowry, The United States Joins the Inter-American Arbitration Convention, 7 *J. Int'l Arb.* 84 (No. 3, 1990)

Norberg, General Introduction to Inter-American Commercial Arbitration, 3 *Y.B. Com. Arb.* 1 (1978) and 8 *Y.B. Com. Arb.* 77 (1983)

————, Inter-American Commercial Arbitration Revisited, 7 *Law. Am.* 275 (1975)

————, Inter-American Commercial Arbitration: Unicorn or Beast of Burden? 5 *Pace L. Rev.* 607 (1985)

————, Inter-American Convention on International Commercial Arbitration, in *ICCA, Sixth Int'l Arb. Congress: Proceedings* 451 (1978)

————, Recent Developments in Inter-American Commercial Arbitration, 13 *Case W. Res. J. Int'l L.* 107 (1981)

————, Recent Developments in Inter-American Commercial Arbitration, 12 *Nw. J. Int'l L. & Bus.* 86 (1991)

————, U.S. Ratification and Implementation of the Inter-American Convention: A Commentary, 1 *Am. Rev. Int'l Arb.* 588 (1990)

————, United States Implements Inter-American Convention on Commercial Arbitration? 45 *Arb. J.* 23 (No. 4, 1990)

Norberg C., *Inter-American Commercial Arbitration* (Dobbs Ferry and Paris 1989)

Note, The Inter-American Convention on International Commercial Arbitration, 9 *Law. Amer.* 43 (1977)

Pitti G., Ambito de aplicación del Convenio Interamericano sobre Arbitraje Comercial Internacional, in *El Arbitraje en el Derecho Latinoamericano y Español* 473 (L. Perrot & U. Montoya Alberti eds. 1989)

Trigueros & Vasquez Pando, La Convención Interamericana sobre Arbitraje Comercial Internacional, 8 *Revista de Investigaciones Jurídicas* 289 (1984)

van den Berg, The New York Arbitration Convention 1958 and the Panama Convention of 1975, 5 *Arb. Int'l* 214 (1989)

van den Berg, A.J., *The New York Arbitration Convention of 1958* (Deventer 1981)

2.10 UN CONVENTION ON CARRIAGE OF GOODS BY SEA (HAMBURG RULES) 1978

Astle, W.E., *The Hamburg Rules* (London 1981)

Bernini, Links Between Arbitrators and the Courts, 44 *Arbitration* 77 (1978)

Carbone & Luzzatto, Arbitration Clauses, Carriage by Sea and Uniform Law, in *Studies on the Revision of the Brussels Convention on Bills of Lading* 353 (Genoa 1974); also in 76 *Dir. Maritimo* 253 (1974)

Dias, United Nations Convention on the Carriage of Goods by Sea, 1978 ('Hamburg Rules'), in 1 *W.A.R.* 108 (H. Smit & V. Pechota eds. 1986, 1987)

Healy, Arbitration (Il seminario di Buenos Aires sulle Regole di Amburgo), 85 *Dir. Maritimo* 742 (1983)

Jackson, The Hague-Visby Rules and Forum, Arbitration and Choice of Law Clauses, 1980 *Lloyd's Mar. & Com. L.Q.* 159 (1980)

Keane, Waiver of Maritime Arbitration, 8 *J. Mar. L. & Com.* 195 (1977)

Kheifets, Recognition and Enforcement of Foreign Court Judgments and Arbitral Awards in Maritime Disputes, 1985 *Soviet Y.B. Mar. L.* 87

Lebedev, 'Combined Transport' Disputes in Soviet Arbitration Practice, in *Arbitration in Settlement of International Commercial Disputes Involving the Far East and Arbitration in Combined Transportation* 347 (P. Sanders ed. 1989)

Lüddeke, Ch., *A Guide to the Hamburg Rules: An Industry Report* (London 1991)

McCormack, Arbitration in Combined Transportations — A Rare Bird, in *Arbitration in Settlement of International Commercial Disputes Involving the Far East and Arbitration in Combined Transportation* 325 (P. Sanders ed. 1989)

Malpica de Lamadrid, El arbitraje internacional y el derecho maritimo, in *El Arbitraje Comercial Internacional* 413 (Mexico 1983)

Mankabady, S., ed., *The Hamburg Rules and the Carriage of Goods by Sea: Collected Papers and Documents* (Groningen 1983)

O'Hare, Cargo Dispute Resolution and the Hamburg Rules, 29 *Int'l & Comp. L.Q.* 219 (1980)

Ray, La responsibilidad de transportistas en las reglas de Hamburgo y la solución arbitral de controversias, in *El Arbitraje Comercial Internacional* 461 (Mexico 1983)

Selvig, E., *The Hamburg Rules—The Convention on Carriage of Goods by Sea,* 1978 (Oslo 1978)

Tetley, Arbitration Clauses in Ocean Bills of Lading, 2 *Y.B. Mar. L.* 51 (1985-1986)

————, The Hamburg Rules: A Commentary, 1979 *Lloyd's Mar. & Com. L.Q.* 1 (1979)

Wilner, The Revised Hague Rules on Bills of Lading, 32 *Arb. J.* 35 (1977)

2.11 INTER-AMERICAN CONVENTION ON VALIDITY OF FOREIGN AWARDS 1979

Eyzaguirre Echeverria, Arbitration in Latin America: The Experience of the Inter-American Commercial Arbitration Commission, 4 *Int'l Tax & Bus. Law.* 288 (1986)

Eyzaguirre Echeverria & Siqueiros, Arbitration in Latin America, in *Arbitration in Settlement of International Commercial Disputes Involving the Far East and Arbitration in Combined Transportation* 81 (P. Sanders ed. 1989)

Garro, The Inter-American Convention on Extraterritorial Validity of Foreign Judgments and Arbitral Awards, 1979, in 1 *W.A.R.* 265.0 (H. Smit & V. Pechota eds. 1986, 1987)

Kos-Rabcewicz-Zubkowski, Les conventions interaméricaines sur l'arbitrage commercial et la Commission interaméricaine d'arbitrage commercial, 1983 *Rev. Arb.* 411

————, Panamerykanskie konwencje dotyczace arbitrazu handlowego, 44 *Panstwo i Prawo* 84 (No. 3, 1989)

Levin, International Commercial Arbitration: Domestic Recognition and Enforcement of the Inter-American Convention on International Arbitration, 10 *Syracuse J. Int'l L. & Com.* 169 (1983)

Norberg, General Introduction to Inter-American Commercial Arbitration, 3 *Y.B. Com. Arb.* 1 (1978) and 8 *Y.B. Com. Arb.* 77 (1983)

————, Inter-American Commercial Arbitration: Unicorn or Beast of Burden? 5 *Pace L. Rev.* 607 (1985)

————, Recent Developments in Inter-American Commercial Arbitration, 13 *Case W. Res. J. Int'l L.* 107 (1981)

Norberg C., *Inter-American Commercial Arbitration* (Dobbs Ferry and Paris 1989)

2.12 UNCITRAL MODEL LAW ON INTERNATIONAL COMMERCIAL ARBITRATION 1985

Ajibola, Arbitration in Developing Countries, 54 *Arbitration* 132 (1988)

Al-Baharna, International Commercial Arbitration in Perspective, 3 *Arab L.Q.* 3 (1988)

Alvarez, The Role of Arbitration in Canada — New Perspectives, 21 *U. B.C. L. Rev.* 247 (1987)

Bernini, Recent Legislations and International Unification of the Law on Arbitration, in *First International Commercial Arbitration Conference: Proceedings* 315 (N. Antaki & A. Prujiner eds. 1986)

Blessing, International Arbitration Procedures, 17 *Int'l Bus. Law.* 408 and 451 (1989)

————, The Major Western and Soviet Arbitration Rules: A Comparison of the Rules of UNCITRAL, UNCITRAL Model Law, LCIA, ICC, AAA and the Rules of the USSR Chamber of Commerce and Industry, 6 *J. Int'l Arb.* 7 (No. 3, 1989)

Böckstiegel, Das UNCITRAL-Modell-Gesetz für die internationale Wirtschaftsschiedsgerichtsbarkeit, 30 *RIW* 670 (1984)

Bonell, Le Nazione Unite e l'arbitrato commerciale internazionale, 18 *Riv. Dir. Int'le Priv. & Proc.* 269 (1982)

————, Una nuova disciplina modello sull'arbitrato commerciale internazionale, 1987 *Diritto del Commercio Internazionale* 3

Boyd, The UNCITRAL Model Law on International Commercial Arbitration: Commentary, in *First International Commercial Arbitration Conference: Proceedings* 393 (N. Antaki & A. Prujiner eds. 1986)

Brazil, Resolution of Trade Disputes in the Asian Pacific Region, 10 *Adel. L. Rev.* 49 (1985)

Brierley, Quebec's New (1986) Arbitration Law, 13 *Can. Bus. L.J.* 58 (1987)

Briseño Sierra, La formación de la litis en la Ley Modelo sobre Arbitraje Comercial de la UNCITRAL, in *Alternativas a la justicia institucional: arbitraje, conciliación* 171 (Bogota 1988)

Broches, A Model Law on International Commercial Arbitration: A Progress Report on the Work Undertaken within the UN Commission on International Trade Law (UNCITRAL), 18 *Geo. Wash. J. Int'l L. & Econ.* 79 (1984)

————, Commentary on the UNCITRAL Model Law, in *Int'l Handbook Com. Arb.* (A. van den Berg gen. ed. 1984), Suppl. 11, Jan. 1990

————, The 1985 UNCITRAL Model Law on International Commercial Arbitration: An Exercise in International Legislation, 18 *Neth. Y.B. Int'l L.* 3 (1987)

Broches A., *Commentary on the UNCITRAL Model Law on International Commercial Arbitration* (Deventer 1990)

Bühler, Staatsgerichtliche Aufhebungskontrolle am Schiedsort? Zur Reform Belgiens, 7 *IPRax* 253 (1987)

Calavros, C., *Das UNCITRAL-Modellgesetz über die internationale Handelsschiedsgerichtsbarkeit* (Bielefeld 1988)

Chafic, L'impact de la Loi-type dans le monde arabe: le projet égyptien, in *Euro-Arab Arbitration III* 186 (F. Kemicha ed. 1991)

Chiasson, Canada: No Man's Land No More, 3 *J. Int'l Arb.* 67 (No. 2, 1986)

Chiasson & Lalonde, Recent Canadian Legislation on Arbitration, 2 *Arb. Int'l* 370 (1986)

Coelho Bento Suares & Moura Ramos, Arbitragem comercial internacional: analise da lei-modelo da CNUDCI de 1985, 1985 *Documentaçao e Direito Comparado* 231 (No. 21)

————, Arbitragem comercial internacional: analise da lei-modelo da CNUDCI de 1985 e das disposicoes pertinentes do direito portugues, in *Contratos internacionais: compra e venda, clausulas penais, arbitragem* 315 (Coimbra 1986)

Cohen, International Commercial Arbitration: A Comparative Analysis of the United States System and the UNCITRAL Model Law, 12 *Brooklyn J. Int'l L.* 703 (1986)

Craig, The Uses and Abuses of Appeal from International Arbitration Awards, in *Private Investors Abroad— Problems and Solutions in International Business in 1987* 14.1 (J. Moss ed. 1987)

————, Uses and Abuses of Appeal from Awards, 4 *Arb. Int'l* 174 (1988)

Croft, Australia Adopts the UNCITRAL Model Law, 5 *Arb. Int'l* 189 (1989)

Davenport, The UNCITRAL Model Law on International Commercial Arbitration: the User's Choice, 4 *Arb. Int'l* 69 (1988)

Davidson, F., *International Commercial Arbitration: Scotland and the UNCITRAL Model Law* (Edinburgh 1991)

Davies, The Draft Arbitration Law in Egypt, 3 *Arab L.Q.* 119 (1988)

Dervaird, Lord, Scotland and the UNCITRAL Model Law. The Report to the Lord Advocate of the Scottish Advisory Committee on Arbitration Law, 6 *Arb. Int'l* 63 (1990)

Deshpande, International Commercial Arbitration: Uniformity of Jurisdiction, 5 *J. Int'l Arb.* 115 (No. 2, 1988)

Deutsches Institut für Schiedsgerichtswesen e.V., *Übernahme des UNCITRAL Modellgesetz über die internationale Handelsschiedsgerichtsbarkeit in das deutsche Recht* (Cologne 1989)

Dore, I.I., *Arbitration and Conciliation Under the UNCITRAL Rules: A Textual Analysis* (Dordrecht 1986)

————, *Theory and Practice of Multiparty Commercial Arbitration, With Special Reference to the UNCITRAL Framework* (London 1990)

Erecinski, Problems in the Administration of Evidence Arising from the Rules of the International Commercial Arbitration, 17 *Polish Y.B. Int'l L.* 41 (1988)

Esplugues & McNerney, Aproximación a la nueva ley modelo de UNCITRAL sobre arbitraje comercial internacional, 3 *Rev. Corte Esp. Arb.* 11 (1986)

Evans, Some Thoughts on Adoption of the UNCITRAL Model Law, 53 *Arbitration* 121 (1987)

Finlay, An Overview of Commercial Arbitration in Australia, 4 *J. Int'l Arb.* 103 (No. 4, 1987)

Fischer-Zernin & Junker, Between Scylla and Charybdis: Fact Gathering in German Arbitration, 4 J. *Int'l Arb.* 9 (No. 2, 1987)

Fleischhauer, International Arbitration Report: UNCITRAL Model Law on International Commercial Arbitration, 41 *Arb. J.* 17 (No. 1, March 1986)

――――, The Contribution of UNCITRAL in the Field of Commercial Arbitration, in *Essays on International Law. Thirtieth Anniversary Commemorative Volume* 16 (New Delhi 1987)

Fouchard, La Loi-type de la C.N.U.D.C.I. sur l'arbitrage commercial international, 114 *J. Droit Int'l (Clunet)* 861 (1987)

Franke, A Model Law on International Commercial Arbitration, 1984 *Y.B. Swed. & Int'l Arb.* 54

Gaillard, The UNCITRAL Model Law and Recent Statutes on International Arbitration in Europe and North America, 2 *ICSID Rev. - Foreign Investment L.J.* 424 (1987)

Garro, El arbitraje en América Central y la Ley modelo propuesta por la Comisión de las Naciones Unidas para el Derecho Mercantil Internacional (UNCITRAL), in *A.B.A., Conferencia sobre Arbitraje Comercial y Laboral, San Salvador,* 7-12 Diciembre 1987

――――, The UNCITRAL Model Law and the 1988 Spanish Arbitration Act: Models for Reform in Central America, 1 *Am. Rev. Int'l Arb.* 201 (1990)

――――, The UNCITRAL Model Law and the 1988 Spanish Arbitration Act: Models for Reform in Central America, in *Commercial and Labor Arbitration in Central America* 23 (A. Garro ed. 1991)

Goodman, UNCITRAL Model Law on International and Commercial Arbitration: Divergent Approaches in England and Scotland: A Question of Appeal? 18 *Int'l Bus. Law.* 250 (1990)

Graham, International Commercial Arbitration: The Developing Canadian Profile, in *UNCITRAL Arbitration Model in Canada* 77 (R. Paterson & B. Thompson eds. 1987)

Grigera Naón, La ley modelo de la CNUDMI sobre arbitraje comercial internacional y el derecho argentino, 1989-*A La Ley* 1021

Herrmann, For an UNCITRAL Model Restatement of Arbitration Law in the United Kingdom, 4 *Arb. Int'l* 62 (1988)

――――, Introductory Note on the UNCITRAL Model Law on International Commercial Arbitration, 1985 *Revue de Droit Uniforme/Uniform Law Review* 285 (No. 1)

————, Overcoming Regional Differences: Arbitral Practice, Comparative Law and the Approximation of Laws, in *Arbitration in Settlement of International Commercial Disputes Involving the Far East and Arbitration in Combined Transportation* 291 (P. Sanders ed. 1989)

————, Presentation of the UNCITRAL Model Law, in *Euro-Arab Arbitration III* 165 (F. Kemicha ed 1991)

————, The British Columbia Enactment of the UNCITRAL Model Law, in *UNCITRAL Arbitration Model in Canada* 65 (R. Paterson & B. Thompson eds. 1987)

————, The Role of the Courts under the UNCITRAL Model Law Script, in *Contemporary Problems in Int'l Arbitration* 164 (J.D.M. Lew ed. 1986)

————, The UNCITRAL Model Law — Its Background, Salient Features, and Purposes, 1 *Arb. Int'l* 6 and 81 (1985)

————, The UNCITRAL Model Law on International Commercial Arbitration: Introduction and General Provisions, in *Essays on International Commercial Arbitration* 3 (P. Sarcevic ed. 1989)

————, The UNCITRAL Model Law on International Commercial Arbitration — Its Salient Features and Prospects, in *First Int'l Commercial Arbitration Conference: Proceedings* 351 (N. Antaki & A. Prujiner eds. 1986)

————, UNCITRAL Adopts Model Law on International Commercial Arbitration, 2 *Arb. Int'l* 2 (No. 1, January 1986)

————, UNCITRAL's Work Toward a Model Law on International Commercial Disputes, 4 *Pace L. Rev.* 537 (1984)

Hoellering, The UNCITRAL Model Law on International Commercial Arbitration, 20 *Int'l Law.* 327 (1986)

Holtzmann, International Commercial Dispute Settlement: Developments of a Decade, in *Essays in International Law. Thirtieth Anniversary Commemorative Volume* 95 (New Delhi 1987)

Holtzmann, H. & J. Neuhaus, *A Guide to the UNCITRAL Model Law on International Commercial Arbitration: Legislative History and Commentary* (Deventer 1989)

Hunter, Impact of the UNCITRAL Model Law in the Non-Arab World, in *Euro-Arab Arbitration III* 180 (F. Kemicha ed. 1991)

————, International Commercial Arbitration: The UNCITRAL Model Law, 12 *Int'l Bus. Law.* 189 (1984)

————, The UNCITRAL Model Law, 13 *Int'l Bus. Law.* 399 (1985)

————, UNCITRAL—Proposed Model Law on International Commercial Arbitration, 49 *Arbitration* 83 (1983)

————, UNCITRAL Model Law — Which Road Should London Take? 49 *Arbitration* 288 (1984)

Husslein-Stich, G., *Das UNCITRAL-Modelgesetz über die internationale Handelsschiedsgerichtsbarkeit* (Cologne 1990)

Jarvin, La loi-type de la C.N.U.D.C.I. sur l'arbitrage commercial international, 1986 *Rev. Arb.* 509

————, The Sources and Limits of the Arbitrator's Powers, 2 *Arb. Int'l* 140 (1986)

Kaplan, Hong Kong and the UNCITRAL Model Law, 54 *Arbitration* 173 (1988)

————, The Hong Kong Arbitration Ordinance and UNCITRAL Model Law, 57 *Arbitration* 110 (1991)

Kavass, I.L. & A. Liivak, comps., *UNCITRAL Model Law on International Commercial Arbitration: A Documentary History* (Buffalo, NY 1985)

Kerr, Arbitration and the Courts —— the UNCITRAL Model Law, 50 *Arbitration* 3 (1984)

————, Arbitration and the Courts: the UNCITRAL Model Law, 34 *Int'l & Comp. L.Q.* 1 (1985)

Kolkey, Towards Adoption of the UNCITRAL Model Law: Reflections on the U.S. Statutory Framework for International Commercial Arbitration, 1 *Am. Rev. Int'l Arb.* 491 (1990)

Kornblum, Übernahme des UNCITRAL-Modellgesetzes in das deutsche Schiedsverfahrensrecht, 1 *Jahrbuch Schiedsgerichtsbarkeit* 34 (1987)

Kos-Rabcewicz-Zubkowski, International Arbitration Laws in Canada: Adaptation of UNCITRAL Model Law on International Commercial Arbitration, 5 *J. Int'l Arb.* 43 (No. 3, 1988)

————, L'adaptation de la loi-type de la C.N.U.D.C.I. dans les provinces de common law au Canada, 1989 *Rev. Arb.* 37

Lalonde, The New Environment for Commercial Arbitration in Canada, 1 *Rev. Int'l Bus. L.* 31 (1987); also in 1988 *Int'l Bus. L. J.* 963

Lew, The Unification of the Law on International Commercial Arbitration, 5 *Bus. L. Rev.* 145 (1984)

Lionnet, The UNCITRAL Model Law: A German Perspective, 6 *Arb. Int'l* 343 (1990)

Lorcher, Schiedsgerichtsbarkeit: Übernahme des UNCITRAL-Modellgesetzes? 20 *Zeitschrift für Rechtspolitik* 230 (1987)

Lucio, The UNCITRAL Model Law on International Commercial Arbitration, 17 *U. Miami Inter-Am. L. Rev.* 313 (1986)

McNerney & Esplugues, International Commercial Arbitration: The UNCITRAL Model Law, 9 *B. C. Int'l & Comp. L. Rev.* 47 (1986)

Mendes, Canada: A New Forum to Develop the Cultural Psychology of International Commercial Arbitration, 3 *J. Int'l Arb.* 71 (No. 3, 1986)

Monroy Cabra, Comentarios al texto de una ley modelo sobre arbitraje comercial internacional de UNCITRAL, 58 *Revista de la Cámara de Comercio de Bogotá* 155 (1985)

————, Comentarios al texto de una Ley Modelo sobre Arbitraje Comercial Internacional de UNCITRAL, in *Alternativas a la justicia institucional: arbitraje, conciliación* 155 (Bogota 1988)

Mora Rojas, The UNCITRAL Model Law on International Commercial Arbitration, in *Commercial and Labor Arbitration in Central America* 203 (A. Garro ed. 1991)

Mustill, A New Arbitration Act for the United Kingdom? The Response of the Departmental Advisory Committee to the UNCITRAL Model Law, 6 *Arb. Int'l* 3 (1990)

Najar & Polkinghorne, Australia's Adoption of the UNCITRAL Model Law, 4 *Int'l Arb. Rep.* 21 (No. 3, 1989)

Neill, New Zealand and the UNCITRAL Model Law, 6 *Arb. Int'l* 271 (1990)

New York State Bar Association, The UNCITRAL Model Law on International Commercial Arbitration: A Report, 23 *N.Y.U. J. Int'l L. & Pol.* 87 (1990)

Nöcker, Das neue Schiedsverfahrenrecht in Kanada, 34 *RIW* 363 (1988)

——, Gesetzgebungstechnische Aspekte bei einer Übernahme des UNCITRAL-Modellgesetzes, 36 *RIW* 28 (1990)

Nöcker, T., *Das Recht der Schiedsgerichtsbarkeit in Kanada* (Heidelberg 1988)

Note, The UNCITRAL Model Law — Lex Facit Arbitrum, 2 *Arb. Int'l* 241 (1986)

Paes de Barros Leaes, Lei-modelo de arbitragem comercial internacional, 24(60) *Revista de direito mercantil industrial, economico e financeiro (Sao Paulo)* 66 (Oct.-Dec. 1985)

Park, Discovery, 51 *Arbitration* 352 (1985)

Paterson, International Commercial Arbitration Act: An Overview, in *UNCITRAL Arbitration Model in Canada* 113 (R. Paterson & B. Thompson eds. 1987)

Paterson R. & B. Thompson eds., UNCITRAL Arbitration Model in Canada. *Canadian International Commercial Arbitration Legislation* (Toronto 1987)

Paulsson, Report on the UNCITRAL Model Law on International Commercial Arbitration as Adopted in Vienna on 21 June 1985, 52 *Arbitration* 98 (1986)

Phillips, Arbitration: The Revolution of the 80's, 52 *Arbitration* 75 (1986)

Potter, International Commercial Arbitration in the United States: Considering Whether to Adopt UNCITRAL's Model Law, 10 *Mich. J. Int'l L.* 912 (1989)

Rashed, The UNCITRAL Model Law and Recent Developments in Egypt, 3 *ICSID Rev. - Foreign Investment L.J.* 126 (1988)

Real, UNCITRAL-Modellgesetz über die internationale Handelsschiedsgerichtsbarkeit, 89 *Zeitschrift für vergleichende Rechtswissenschaft* 407 (1990)

Report to the Washington Foreign Law Society on the UNCITRAL Model Law on International Commercial Arbitration, 3 *Ohio St. J. Dis. Res.* 303 (1988)

Reymond, The Report of the Mustill Committee: A Foreign View, 106 *L.Q. Rev.* 431 (1990)

Rivkin & Kellner, In Support of the F.A.A.: An Argument Against U.S. Adoption of the UNCITRAL Model Law, 1 *Am. Rev. Int'l Arb.* 535 (1990)

Rogers, The UNCITRAL Model Law: An Australian Perspective, 6 *Arb. Int'l* 348 (1990)

Romeu-Matta, New Developments in International Commercial Arbitration: A Comparative Survey of New State Statutes and the UNCITRAL Model Law, 1 *Am. Rev. Int'l Arb.* 140 (1990)

Rubino-Sammartano, A Civil Law Approach to the UNCITRAL Model Law and to Arbitral Rules of Evidence, 51 *Arbitration* 278 (1985)

————, La legge uniforme arbitrale delle Nazioni Unite, in embrione, e le rules of evidence arbitrali, 39 *Foro Padano* 97 (1984)

Sanders, P., ed., *UNCITRAL's Project for a Model Law on International Commercial Arbitration. Proceedings of the ICCA Interim Meeting, May 9-12, 1984, Lausanne* (Deventer 1984)

Sarcevic, The Setting Aside and Enforcement of Arbitral Awards under the UNCITRAL Model Law, in *Essays on International Commercial Arbitration* 177 (P. Sarcevic ed. 1989)

Sarcevic, P., ed., *Essays on International Commercial Arbitration* (London/Dordrecht 1989)

Saxby, A User's Perspective of the UNCITRAL Model Law, 2 *Arb. Int'l* 164 (1986)

Schwab, Das UNCITRAL-Model Law und das deutsche Recht, in *Beiträge zum internationalen Verfahrensrecht und zur Schiedsgerichtsbarkeit. Festschrift für Heinrich Nagel* 427 (W. Habscheid & K. Schwab eds. 1987)

Schwebel, S.M., *International Arbitration: Three Salient Problems* (Cambridge 1987)

Semple, The UNCITRAL Model Law and the United Kingdom, 56 *Arbitration* 95 (1990)

Shifman, Developments in Adoption of the 1985 UNCITRAL Model Law on International Commercial Arbitration, 1 *Am. Rev. Int'l Arb.* 281 (1990)

————, UNCITRAL Model Law on International Commercial Arbitration, in 1 *W.A.R.* 135.2 (H. Smit & V. Pechota eds. 1986, 1987)

Sornarajah, The UNCITRAL Model Law: A Third World Viewpoint, 6 *J. Int'l Arb.* 7 (No. 4, 1989)

Strohbach, Mustergesetz über die internationale Handelsschiedsgerichts-barkeit: UNCITRAL-Modelgesetz 1985, 1987 *Recht im Aussenhandel* (No. 93) at I-III (German text of the Model Law appended)

Sutton, Hong Kong Enacts the UNCITRAL Model Law, 6 *Arb. Int'l* 358 (1990)

Szasz, Introduction to the Model Law of UNCITRAL on International Commercial Arbitration, 24 *Rassegna dell'Arb.* 5 (1984)

Thieffry, UNCITRAL contre les Anglais, l'avenir de la loi-type de la CNUDCI pour la promotion de l'arbitrage international, 1986 *G.P.*, No. 90 a 91, at 2

Thompson, The Marriage of the UNCITRAL Model Arbitration Law and the UNCITRAL Arbitration Rules, in *UNCITRAL Arbitration Model in Canada* 143 (R. Paterson & B. Thompson eds. 1987)

Triva, Pocetak arbitraznog postupka. Uoci prihvacanja UNCITRAL-ovog model-zakona o medunarodnoj trgovackoj arbitrazi i mogucnosti da ga SFR Jugoslavija inkorporira u svoj pravni sistem, 35 *Zbornik Pravnog Fakulteta u Zagrebu* 195 (1985)

Ungar, The Enforcement of Arbitral Awards Under UNCITRAL's Model Law on International Commercial Arbitration, 25 *Colum. J. Transnat'l L.* 717 (1987)

United Nations, Analytical Commentary on Draft Text of a Model Law on International Commercial Arbitration: Report of the Secretary-General, UN Doc. A/CN.9/264 (1985), reprinted in 16 *UNCITRAL Y.B.* 104 (1985)

————, Analytical Compilation of Comments by Governments and International Organizations on the Draft Text of a Model Law on International Commercial Arbitration: Report of the Secretary-General, UN Doc. A/CN.9/263 and Add. 1-3 (1985); also in 16 *UNCITRAL Y.B.* 53 (1985)

Walder-Bohner, Das UNCITRAL-Model Law und die Bestimmungen über die Internationale Schiedsbarkeit im schweizerischen IPR-Gesetz: Vergleich anhand einiger Beispiele, in *Law in East and West: On the Occasion of the 30th Anniversary of the Institute of Comparative Law, Waseda University* 727 (Tokyo 1988)

Weiss, The Status of the UNCITRAL Model Law on International Commercial Arbitration vis-a-vis the International Chamber of Commerce (ICC), London Court of International Arbitration and UNCITRAL Arbitration Rules: Conflict or Complement? 13 *Syracuse J. Int'l L. & Com.* 367 (1986)

Wetter, The Mustill Commitee Report on the UNCITRAL Model Law, 6 *Arb. Int'l* 268 (1990)

2.13 BILATERAL TREATIES

American Arbitration Association, *New Strategies for Peaceful Resolution of International Business Disputes* (Dobbs Ferry, NY 1971)

Associazione Italiana per l'Arbitrato, *Convenzioni internazionali concernenti l'Italia in materia di arbitrato* (Rome 1981)

Audit, Les 'Accords' d'Alger du 19 janvier 1981 tendant au règlement des différends entre les Etats-Unis et l'Iran, 108 *J. Droit Int'l (Clunet)* 713 (1981)

Broches, Bilateral Investment Protection Treaties and Arbitration of Investment Disputes, in *The Art of Arbitration* 63 (J. Schultsz & A. van den Berg eds. 1982)

Butler, W., *Arbitration in the Soviet Union* (Dobbs Ferry 1989)

Capatina, O., *Litigio arbitral de comercio exterior* (Havana 1985)

Chillón Medina, J. M. & J. F. Merino Merchán, *Tratado de arbitraje privado interno e internacional* (Madrid 1978)

Cremades, Evolution récente du droit espagnol en matière d'arbitrage, 1988 *Rev. Arb.* 223

―――, La reconnaissance en Espagne des décisions judiciaires et des actes authentiques français, 1975 *Rev. Crit. Droit Int'l Privé* 355 and 595

―――, The Enforcement of British Arbitral Awards in Spain, 45 *Arbitration* 30 and 97 (1979)

Cremades, B. M., *Panorámica Española del arbitraje comercial internacional* (Madrid 1975)

Doi, International Commercial Arbitration in Japan, in *Liber Amicorum for Martin Domke* 65 (P. Sanders ed. 1967)

El-Ahdab, A. H., *Arbitration with the Arab Countries* (Deventer 1990)

―――, *L'arbitrage dans les pays arabes* (Paris 1988)

Fellhauer, H. & H. Strohbach, eds., *Handbuch der international en Handelsschiedsgerichtsbarkeit* (Berlin 1969)

Gallins, Bilateral Investment Protection Treaties, 2 *J. Energy & Nat. Resources L.* 77 (1984)

Gann, The U.S. Bilateral Investment Treaty Program, 21 *Stanford J. Int'l L.* 373 (1985)

Ginsburgs, Recognition of Arbitration Agreements in Post-war Soviet Bilateral Treaty Practice, 11 *Rev. Soc. L.* 13 (1985)

Ginsburgs, G., *The Soviet Union and International Cooperation in Legal Matters. Part I: Recognition of Arbitral Agreements and Execution of Foreign Commercial Arbitral Awards* (Dordrecht 1988)

Goldstajn, A. & S. Triva, *Medunarodna trgovacka arbitraza* (Zagreb 1987)

Golsong, Dispute Settlement in Recently Negotiated Bilateral Investment Treaties — The Reference to the ICSID Additional Facility, in *Realism in Law-Making: Essays on International Law in Honour of Willem Riphagen* 35 (A. Bos & H. Siblezs eds. 1986)

Gonzales Soria, J., *La intervención judicial en el arbitraje. Recursos jurisdiccionales y ejecución judicial del laudo arbitral* (Madrid 1988)

Gonzalez Campos, El Convenio entre España y Francia de 28 de mayo de 1969 sobre reconocimiento y ejecución de decisiones extranjeras, in *2 Estudios de Derecho internacional público y privado. Homenaje al Profesor Sela* 993 (1970)

Gudgeon, Arbitration Provisions of U.S. Bilateral Investment Treaties, in *International Investment Disputes: Avoidance and Settlement* 41 (S. Rubin & R. Nelson eds. 1985)

Indonesian Board of Arbitration, *Arbitration in Indonesia and International Conventions on Arbitration* (Jakarta 1978)

Julliard, Les conventions bilatérales d'investissement conclues par la France, 106 *J. Droit Int'l (Clunet)* 274 (1979)

Kerameus, Arbitrage international et ordre juridique hellénique, 1987 *Rev. Arb.* 35

Krüger, Probleme des algerischen internationalen Vertrags- und Schiedsrecht, in *Vertragspraxis und Streiterledigung im Wirtschaftsverkehr mit arabischen Staaten* 17 (K.-H. Böckstiegel ed. 1981)

————, Probleme des saudi-arabischen internationalen Vertrags- und Schiedsrecht, in *Vertragspraxis und Streiterledigung im Wirtschaftsverkehr mit arabischen Staaten* 61 (K.-H. Böckstiegel ed. 1981)

Ledoux, La Convention de New York et la Convention européenne sur l'arbitrage international et les concessions de vente en Belgique, 91 *JT* 305 (1976)

Luthge, J., *Die Kollisionsrechtliche Funktion der Schiedsgerichtsvereinbarung* (Bonn 1975)

McLaughlin & Genevro, Enforcement of Arbitral Awards Under the New York Convention — Practice in U.S. Courts, 3 *Int'l Tax & Bus. Law.* 249 (1986)

Majoros, Exécution de décisions étrangères et procédure d'exéquatur en Europe de l'Est: Tour d'horizon avec des références de droit comparé, in *Le Juriste Suisse Face au Droit et aux Jugements Etrangers: Ouverture ou Repli?* 135 (F. Knoepfler ed. 1988)

Migliorino, La surroga dello stato all'investitore privato indennizzato negli accordi bilaterali sugli investimenti, 22 *Riv. Dir. Int'le Priv. & Proc.* 275 (1986)

Mordiglia, Enforcement of Foreign Arbitration Awards in Italy, in 2 *Fifth Int'l Congress of Maritime Arbitrators* (New York 1981)

Morton, United States-Soviet Commercial Arbitration under the 1972 Trade Agreement, 7 *Case W. Res. J. Int'l L.* 121 (1974)

Nussbaum, Staatsverträge im Bereich des Schiedsgerichtswesen als Prufstein internationaler Privatrechtsregelung, 4 *Archiv für Volkerrecht* 385 (1954)

————, Treaties on Commercial Arbitration — A Test of International Private-Law Legislation, 56 *Harv. L. Rev.* 219 (1942)

Note, Commercial Dispute Resolution between the United States and the People's Republic of China: Problems and Prospects, 7 *Suff. Transnat'l L.J.* 329 (1983)

Paulsson, International Commercial Arbitrations, in *Handbook of Arbitration Practice* 333 (R. Bernstein ed. 1987)

Peter, Settlement of Investment Disputes, 5 *J. Int'l Arb.* 131 (No. 1, 1988)

Pogany, Bilateral Investment Treaties: Some Recent Examples, 2 *ICSID Rev. - Foreign Investment L.J.* 457 (1987)

Razumov, Arbitration Treaties between the USSR and Countries in the Far East, in *Arbitration in Settlement of International Commercial Disputes Involving the Far East and Arbitration in Combined Transportation* 145 (P. Sanders ed. 1989)

Rechberger, Das Anerkennungs- und Vollstreckungsabkommen zwischen Österreich und dem Fürstentum Liechtenstein, 16 *ZRV* 122 (1975)

Ruiloba Santana, El Convenio hispano-francés de 28 de mayo de 1969 sobre reconocimiento y ejecución de sentencias extranjeras y actas autenticas en materia civil y mercantil, 23 *Rev. Esp. Der. Int'l* 42 (1970)

Sachs, Das bilaterale französisch-algerische Schiedsabkommen vom 27. März 1983 — Ein Muster auch für andere Staaten?, 6 *IPRax* 309 (1986)

————, The New U.S. Bilateral Investment Treaties, 2 *Int'l Tax & Bus. Law.* 192 (1984)

Sacks, Arbitration of Disputes Between the People's Republic of China and U.S. Corporations, in *Arbitration and the Licensing Process* 5-83 (R. Goldscheider & M. de Haas eds. 1984-)

Sandrock & Hentzen, Enforcing Foreign Arbitral Awards in the Federal Republic of Germany: The Example of a United States Award, 2 *Transnat'l Law.* 49 (1989)

Schütze, R., D. Tscherning & W. Wais, *Handbuch des Schiedsverfahrens. Praxis der deutschen und internationalen Schiedsgerichtsbarkeit* (2nd ed. Berlin 1990)

Sitaru, Reglementari procedurale si de fond privind arbitrajul comercial international in acordurile bilaterale incheiate de Republica Socialista Romania, 40 *Revista Romana de Drept* 19 (August 1984)

Solveni, Dichiarazione di efficacia in Italia di lodi arbitrali inglesi convertiti in sentenze della High Court of Justice ai sensi della Sez. 26 dell'Arbitration Act, 1950, 88 *Dir. Mar.* 451 (1986)

Storme M. & B. Demeulenaere, *International Commercial Arbitration in Belgium: A Handbook* (Deventer 1989)

Strohbach, The CMEA Countries, in *Arbitration in Settlement of International Commercial Disputes Involving the Far East and Arbitration in Combined Transportation* 133 (P. Sanders ed. 1989)

Timmermans, The USSR Maritime Arbitration Commission, 1987 *Lloyd's Mar. & Com. L.Q.* 350 and 468

Tyan, E., *Le droit de l'arbitrage* (Beyrouth 1972)

United Nations Centre on Transnational Corporations, *Bilateral Investment Treaties* (New York 1988)

Uwanno & Sathirathai, Introduction to the Thai Legal System [Section c) International Commercial Arbitration], 4 *Chulalongkorn L. Rev.* 39, 105 (1985-1986)

van den Berg, A. J., *The New York Arbitration Convention of 1958* (Deventer 1981)

Vulliemin, J. -M., *Jugement et sentence arbitrale: étude de droit international privé et de droit comparé* (2nd ed. Lausanne 1990)

Walker, Commercial Arbitration in United States Treaties, 11 *Arb. J.* 68 (1956)

2.14 NATIONAL LEGISLATION

Abhod, Iran: National Report, 4 *Y.B. Com. Arb.* 81 (1979)

Abrahamson, Ireland: National Report, 9 *Y.B. Com. Arb.* 3 (1984)

Abromson, The English Arbitration Act of 1979: A Symbiotic Relationship Between the Courts and Arbitration Tribunals, 5 *Suffolk Transnat'l L.J.* 7 (1980)

Abu Zayyad, Kuwait: National Report, 4 *Y.B. Com. Arb.* 139 (1979)

Agarwal, R.G., ed., *S.C. Das's The Arbitration Act: Act X of 1940.* 4th ed. (Allahabad 1978)

Ahdab, L'arbitrage en Arabie Saoudite, 1981 *Rev. Arb.* 234

Allison, Arbitration of Private Antitrust Claims in International Trade: A Study in the Subordination of National Interests to the Demands of a World Market, 18 *N.Y.U.J. Int'l L. & Pol.* 361 (1986)

Al-Mukhtar, Arbitration in Iraq — Its Practical Problems — Opinions and Suggestions, 50 *Arbitration* 171 (Nov. 1984)

Alvarez, La nouvelle législation canadienne sur l'arbitrage commercial international, 1986 *Rev. Arb.* 529

American Arbitration Association, *New Strategies for Peaceful Resolution of International Business Disputes* (Dobbs Ferry, NY 1971)

Amin, S.H., *Middle East Legal Systems* (Glasgow 1985)

Amoussou-Guenou, La réforme de l'arbitrage en République fédérale du Nigéria, 1989 *Rev. Arb.* 445

Aramburú Menchaca, Commercial Arbitration in Peru, in *Arbitration in Settlement of International Commercial Disputes Involving the Far East and Arbitration in Combined Transportation* 111 (P. Sanders ed. 1989)

————, International Commercial Arbitration in the Andean Pact (Observations for a Community Regime), in *The Art of Arbitration* 27 (J. Schultsz & A. van den Berg eds. 1982)

————, Peru: National Report, 3 *Y.B. Com. Arb.* 116 (1978)

Arroyo Martinez, I., *Legislación arbitral* (Madrid 1989)

Asa'ad, *Commercial Arbitration and Legal System in Kuwait* (Kuwait 1978)

Ascarelli, Arbitration under Italian Law, 1 *Int'l Y. B. Civil & Com. Arb.* 79 (1928)

Atanda, The Nigerian Arbitration and Conciliation Decree, 1988, 1 *Am. Rev. Int'l Arb.* 452 (1990)

Atwood, Issues in Federal State Relations Under the Federal Arbitration Act, 37 *Univ. Fla. L. Rev.* 61 (1985)

Audit, A National Codification of International Commercial Arbitration: The French Decree of May 12, 1981, in *Resolving Transnational Disputes through International Arbitration* 117 (T. Carbonneau ed. 1984)

Ayarragaray, C., *Naturaleza del Proceso Arbitral* (Buenos Aires 1970)

Barclay, Arbitration in Latin America, 43 *Arbitration* 105 (1977)

Basu, N.D., *The Arbitration Act, 1940* (8th. ed. Calcutta 1982)

Bauer, Some Suggested Changes to the U.S. Arbitration Act, in 1 *Fifth Int'l Congress of Maritime Arbitrators* (New York 1981)

Baumbach, A. & K.H. Schwab, eds., *Schiedsgerichtsbarkeit. Systematischer Kommentar* (Munich 1960)

Béguin, Le droit français de l'arbitrage international et la Convention de New York du 10 juin 1958, in *First International Commercial Arbitration Conference: Proceedings* 218 (N. Antaki & A. Prujiner eds. 1986)

Bellet & Mezger, L'arbitrage international dans le nouveau code de procédure civile, 70 *Rev. Crit. Droit Int'l Privé* 611 (1981)

Benjamin, The Developing Nations and Certain Legislative Obstacles in the Field of International Commercial Arbitration, in *Liber Amicorum for Martin Domke* 1 (P. Sanders ed. 1967)

Berger, K., *Internationale Wirtschaftsschiedsgerichtsbarkeit. Verfahrens- und materellrechtliche Grundprobleme im Spiegel moderner Schiedsgesetze und Schiedspraxis* (Berlin 1992)

Bernardini, P., *L'arbitrato internazionale* (Milan 1987)

Bernini, Domestic and International Arbitration in Italy after the Legislative Reform, 5 *Pace L. Rev.* 543 (1985)

————, La legge 9 Febbraio 1983 N.28 e la modifica dell'arbitrato: prospettive internazionali, 24 *Rassegna dell'Arb.* 193 (1984)

Bernini, G., *Lezioni di diritto dell'arbitrato* (Bologna 1992)

Bischoff, Arbitration Act 1979: cinq ans après, 37 *Droit Mar. Français* 179 (1985)

Blessing, Das neue Internationale Schiedsgerichtsrecht der Schweiz — Ein Fortschritt oder ein Rückschritt? in *Die Internationale Schiedsgerichtsbarkeit in der Schweiz* 13 (K.-H. Böckstiegel ed. 1989)

————, The New International Arbitration Law in Switzerland: A Significant Step towards Liberalism, 5 *J. Int'l Arb.* 9 (No. 2, 1988)

Blom, Conflict of Laws Aspects of the International Commercial Arbitration Act, in *UNCITRAL Arbitration Model in Canada* 127 (R. Paterson & B. Thompson eds. 1987)

Böckstiegel, K.-H., ed., *Handelsschiedsgerichtsbarkeit in England und in der Bundesrepublik Deutschland/Commercial Arbitration in the Federal Republic of Germany and in England* (Cologne 1987)

————, ed., *Schiedsgerichtsbarkeit im deutsch-amerikanischen Wirtschaftverkehr/Arbitration in US-German Business Relations* (Cologne 1985)

Bourdin, La convention d'arbitrage international en droit français depuis le Décret du 12 mai 1981, in *Droit et pratique de l'arbitrage international en France* 11 (Y. Derains ed. 1984)

Boyd, The Role of National Law and the National Courts in England, in *Contemporary Problems in International Arbitration* 149 (J.D.M. Lew ed. 1986)

Braun, A., ed., *L'arbitrage/Het scheidsgerecht* (Brussels 1983)

Brierley, Quebec Arbitration Law: A New Era Begins, 40 *Arb. J.* 20 (No. 3, 1985)

————, Quebec's New (1986) Arbitration Law, 13 *Can. Bus. L.J.* 58 (1987)

Briguglio, La disciplina spagnola dell'arbitrato e le recenti modifiche introdotte dalla Ley del 6 agosto 1984 — qualche riflessione comparatistica, 25 *Rassegna dell'Arb.* 259 (1985)

————, La riforma dell'arbitrato, 35 *Giustizia Civile* 415 (1985)

Briseño Sierra, Mexico: National Report, 3 *Y.B. Com. Arb.* 94 (1978)

—————, H., *El arbitraje comercial: doctrina y legislación* (Mexico 1979)

Bronzini, Arbitrato, recenti innovazione legislative. Problemi e soluzione, 61 *Nuovo Diritto* 161 (1984)

Bucher, Das Kapitel 11 des IPR-Gesetzes über die internationale Schiedsgerichtsbarkeit, in *Beiträge zum neuen IPR des Sachen-, Schuld- und Gesellschaftsrechts. Festschrift für Professor Rudolf Moser* 193 (Zurich 1987)

—————, Arbitration under the ICC-Rules in Switzerland and the Concordat, in *Recueil de Travaux Suisses* 127 (C. Reymond & E. Bucher eds. 1984)

—————, Die Regeln betreffend Schiedsgerichtsbarkeit im neuen IPRG und deren verfassungsrechtlicher Hintergrund, in *Die schweizerische Rechtsordnung in ihren internationalen Bezügen* 265 (G. Jenni & W. Kälin eds. 1988)

Bucher, A., *Die neue internationale Schiedsgerichtsbarkeit in der Schweiz* (Basel 1989)

—————, *Le nouvel arbitrage international en Suisse. Théorie et pratique de droit* (Basel 1988)

Bucher, A. & P.-Y. Tschanz, *International Arbitration in Switzerland* (Basel 1989)

Budin, La nouvelle loi suisse sur l'arbitrage international, 1988 *Rev. Arb.* 51

Bühler, Das neue niederländische Gesetz für Schiedsgerichtsbarkeit, 33 *RIW* 901 (1987)

—————, Staatsgerichtliche Aufhebungskontrolle am Schiedsort? Zur Reform Belgiens, 7 *IPRax* 253 (1987)

Bühring-Uhle, Das neue spanische Schiedsgerichtsbarkeit-Gesetz, 88 *Zeitschrift für vergleichende Rechtswissenschaft* 287 (1989)

Bulgarian Chamber of Commerce and Industry, *International Commercial Arbitration in Bulgaria* (Sofia 1989)

Burckhardt, T., *Zum Anwendungsbereich des interkantonalen Konkordats über die Schiedsgerichtsbarkeit vom 27. März 1969* (Basel 1982)

Buzghaia, Libya: National Report, 4 *Y.B. Com. Arb.* 148 (1979)

Caldwell, A Practitioner's Guide to the New Hong Kong Arbitration Ordinance, 6 *Int'l Arb. Rep.* 22 (No. 2, 1991)

Capatina, Admissibilité de l'arbitrage occasionnel de commerce extérieur en droit roumain, *Revue roumain d'études internationales* 411 (No. 4, 1981)

Carbonneau, American and Other National Variations on the Theme of International Commercial Arbitration, 18 *Ga. J. Int'l & Comp. L.* 143 (1988)

————, The Reform of the French Procedural Law on Arbitration: An Analytical Commentary on the Decree of May 14, 1980, 4 *Hastings Int'l & Comp. L. Rev.* 273 (1981)

Carpi, Gli aspetti processuali della riforma dell'arbitrato, 38 *Riv. Trim. Dir. & Proc. Civ.* 47 (1984)

Chafik, Egypt: National Report, 4 *Y.B. Com. Arb.* 44 (1979)

Chatterjee, The Djibouti Code of International Arbitration, 4 *J. Int'l Arb.* 57 (No. 1, 1987)

Chiasson & Lalonde, Recent Canadian Legislation on Arbitration, 2 *Arb. Int'l* 370 (1986)

Chillón Medina & Merino Merchán, The Arbitration Object in Spanish Law, in *ICCA, Sixth Int'l Arb. Congress: Proceedings* 249 (1978)

Chillón Medina, J. M. & J. F. Merino Merchán, *Tratado de arbitraje privado interno e internacional* (Madrid 1978)

Cho Dong-Won, Republic of Korea: National Report, 7 *Y.B. Com. Arb.* 16 (1982)

Clark & Lange, Recent Changes in English Arbitration Practice Widen Opportunities for More Effective International Arbitrations, 35 *Bus. Law.* 1621 (1980)

Coelho Bento Suares & Moura Ramos, Arbitragem comercial internacional: analise da lei-modelo da CNUDCI de 1985 e das disposicoes pertinentes do direito portugues, in *Contratos internacionais: compra e venda, clausulas penais, arbitragem* 315 (Coimbra 1986)

Cohen & Dayton, The New Federal Arbitration Law, 12 *Va. L. Rev.* 265 (1926)

Conrick, Where the Kings Writ Does Not Run: The Origins and Effect of the Arbitration Act 1979, 1 *Queensland Inst. Tech. L.J.* 1 (1985)

Costabel, Fundamental Changes in Italian Arbitration Law, 1983 *Lloyd's Mar. & Com. L.Q.* 440

Coulson, Commercial Arbitration in the United States, 51 *Arbitration* 367 (May 1985)

Craig, Park & Paulsson, French Codification of a Legal Framework for International Commercial Arbitration, 13 *L. & Pol'y Int'l Bus.* 727 (1981)

―――, French Codification of Legal Framework for International Arbitration, 7 *Y.B. Com. Arb.* 407 (1982)

Cremades, Arbitration in Spain, in *Arbitration in Settlement of International Commercial Disputes Involving the Far East and Arbitration in Combined Transportation* 255 (P. Sanders ed. 1989)

―――, España estrena nueva Ley de arbitraje, 5 *Rev. Corte Esp. Arb.* 9 (1988-89)

―――, L'Espagne étrenne une nouvelle loi sur l'arbitrage, 1989 *Rev. Arb.* 189

―――, The New Spanish Law of Arbitration, 6 *J. Int'l Arb.* 35 (No. 2, 1989)

Cremades, B.M., *Panorámica Española del Arbitraje Comercial Internacional* (Madrid 1975)

Croft, International Commercial Arbitration: Developments in the State of Victoria, Australia, in *UNCITRAL Arbitration Model in Canada* 35 (R. Paterson & B. Thompson eds. 1987)

Comment, Judicial Implementation of the United Kingdom Arbitration Act, 1979: Pioneer Shipping v. B.T.P. Tioxide (The Nema), 24 *Harv. Int'l L.J.* 103 (1983)

―――, Preemption of State Law under the Federal Arbitration Act, 15 *U. Balt. L. Rev.* 129 (1985)

Dahl & Garro, Cuba's System of International Commercial Arbitration: A Convergence of Soviet and Latin American Trends, 15 *Law. Amer.* 441 (1984)

D'Aloisio, International Arbitration: Arbitration (Foreign Awards and Agreements) Act, 1974 (CTH), 5 *Austl. Bus. L. Rev.* 295 (1977)

Dashdondog, Mongolia: National Report, 1 *Y.B. Com. Arb.* 63 (1976)

David, Principes directeurs de la législation en matière d'arbitrage commercial international, in *ICCA, Third Int'l Arb. Congress: Proceedings* 299 (1969)

Davidson, International Commercial Arbitration Law in Canada, 12 *Nw. J. Int'l L. & Bus.* 97 (1991)

Davies, The Draft Arbitration Law in Egypt, 3 *Arab L.Q.* 119 (1988)

de Boisséson, M., *Le droit français de l'arbitrage: interne et international* (Paris 1990)

de Groot, Arbitration in the Netherlands: Background to the Arbitration Act 1986, 1 *Int'l Company & Com. L. Rev.* 191 (1990)

de la Guardia, Panama: National Report, 3 *Y.B. Com. Arb.* 106 (1978)

Delaume, International Arbitration under French Law: The Decree of May 12, 1981, 37 *Arb. J.* 38 (No. 3, 1982); reprinted in *Arbitration and the Licensing Process* 5 (R. Goldscheider & M. de Haas eds. 1984-)

Delvolvé, J.-L., ed., *Arbitration in France. The French Law of National and International Arbitration*. Trilingual edition: French, English, German (Deventer 1982)

de Magalhaes J. & L.O. Batista, *Arbitragem comercial* (Rio de Janeiro 1986)

Deodato, G. & G. Migliorisi, eds., *Codice dell'arbitrato* (Milan 1989)

Derains, France: National Report, 6 *Y.B. Com. Arb.* 1 (1981) and 7 *Y.B. Com. Arb.* 35 (1982)

———, Le code djiboutien de l'arbitrage international, 1984 *Rev. Arb.* 465

Dermine, L., *L'arbitrage commercial en Belgique: Commentaire de la loi du 4 juillet 1972* (Brussels 1975)

de Speville, Arbitration in Hong Kong: The Arbitration Ordinance 1963-1982, 1 *Arb. Int'l* 109 (1985)

Dias Rubio, Colombia: National Report, 3 *Y.B. Com. Arb.* 58 (1978)

di Blase, Gli ammodernamienti alla disciplina italiana dell'arbitrato e le convenzioni internazionali, 66 *Riv. Dir. Int'l e* 859 (1983)

Dilger, Arbitration, Enforcement of Foreign Judgments and Arbitration Awards, Clauses on the Choice of Law, and Agreements on Jurisdiction of the in Egypt, Saudi Arabia and the Gulf States, in *International Bar Association: Proceedings of the Seminar on Middle East Law* 35 (1981)

Doi, International Commercial Arbitration in Japan, in *Liber Amicorum for Martin Domke* 65 (P. Sanders ed. 1967)

————, Japan: National Report, 4 *Y.B. Com. Arb.* 115 (1979)

Donaldson, Commercial Arbitrations – 1979 and After, 11 *Int'l Bus. Law.* 189 (1983); 48 *Arbitration* 259 (1983)

————, Commercial Arbitration — 1979 and After, in *International Commercial and Maritime Arbitration* 1 (F.D. Rose ed. 1988)

————, The 1979 Arbitration Act, 45 *Arbitration* 147 (1979)

Donner, Czechoslovakia: National Report, 1 *Y.B. Com. Arb.* 30 (1976)

Donnini, Su alcuni aspetti della riforma dell'arbitrato: in particolare la riconoscibilità del lodo all'estero, 25 *Rassegna dell'Arb.* 283 (1985)

Dorter, J. & G. Widmer, *Arbitration (Commercial) in Australia— Law and Practice* (Sydney 1979)

Duintjer Tebbens, A Facelift for Dutch Arbitration Law, 34 *Neth. Int'l L. Rev.* 141 (1987)

Dutois, B., F. Knoepfler, P. Lalive & P. Mercier, eds., *Répertoire de droit international privé suisse. Volume I: Le contrat international/L'arbitrage international* (Berne 1982)

Eckhoff, Norway: National Report, 5 *Y.B. Com. Arb.* 97 (1980); 7 *Y.B. Com. Arb.* 64 (1982); 11 *Y.B. Com. Arb.* 87 (1986)

El-Ahbar, L'arbitrage en Arabie saoudite sous le régime de la nouvelle loi de 1983 et de son décret d'application de 1985, 1986 *Rev. Arb.* 541

————, Arbitration in Saudi Arabia under the New Arbitration Act, 1983 and Its Implementation Rules of 1985 - Part One, 3 *J.Int'l Arb.* 27 (No.3, 1986) and 3 *J. Int'l Arb.* 23 (No.4, 1986)

El-Ahdab, A. H., *Arbitration with the Arab Countries* (Deventer 1990)

————, *L'arbitrage dans les pays arabes* (Paris 1988)

El-Hakim, Syria: National Report, 7 *Y.B. Com. Arb.* 35 (1982)

Elland & Goldsmith, The Arbitration Act 1979, 6 *Int'l L. & Prac.* 63 (1980)

Evans & Ellis, International Commercial Arbitration: A Comparison of Legal Regimes, 8 *Tex. Int'l L.J.* 17 (1973)

Eyzaguirre Echeverria, Chile: National Report, 3 *Y.B. Com. Arb.* 45 (1978)

Eyzaguirre Echeverria, R., *El arbitraje comercial en la legislación chilena y su regulación international* (Santiago de Chile 1981)

Farani, M., *The Arbitration Laws* (3rd ed. Lahore 1977)

Fasching, H. W., *Schiedsgericht und Schiedsverfahren im österreichischen und internationalen Rechte* (Vienna 1973)

Feldman, Waiver of Foreign Sovereign Immunity by Agreement to Arbitrate: Legislation Proposed by the American Bar Association, 40 *Arb. J.* 24 (No. 1, 1985)

Fellhauer, H. & H. Strohbach, eds., *Handbuch der internationalen Handelsschiedsgerichtsbarkeit* (Berlin 1969)

Ferland, Ph., *L'arbitrage conventionnel* (Montreal 1983)

Fernandez del Castillo, El arbitraje comercial en la legislación de México, 9 *Boletín del Instituto de Derecho Comparado de México* 55 (1956)

Fernández Rozas, El largo camino hacia la Ley 36/1988 de Arbitraje, 5 *Rev. Corte Esp. Arb.* 29 (1988-89)

Fernández Rozas, J., *Legislación sobre arbitraje interno e internacional* (Madrid 1990)

Foster, C.A., *The Law and Practice of Commercial Arbitration in North Carolina* (Durham 1986)

Fouchard, L'arbitrage commercial et la législation, in *Mélanges P. Roblot 63* (1983)

————, L'arbitrage international après le Décret du 12 mai 1981, 109 *J. Droit Int'l (Clunet)* 374 (1982

Fournier, Costa Rica: National Report, 3 *Y.B. Com. Arb.* 70 (1978)

Foustoucos, L'arbitrage international en Grèce, 1987 *Rev. Arb.* 23

Foustoucos, A.C., *L'arbitrage (interne et international) en droit privé hellénique* (Paris 1976)

Gabaldon, F., *El arbitraje en el Código de procedimiento civi*l (Caracas 1987)

Gaillard, The UNCITRAL Model Law and Recent Statutes on International Arbitration in Europe and North America, 2 *ICSID Rev. - Foreign Investment L.J.* 424 (1987)

Garcini, Cuba: National Report, 1 *Y.B. Com. Arb.* 27 (1976)

Garvey & Heffelfinger, Towards Federalizing U.S. International Commercial Arbitration Law, 25 *Int'l Law.* 209 (1991)

Gastambide, International Arbitration Under the French Decree of 12 May 1981, 48 *Arbitration* 45 (1982)

Glossner, O., *Commercial Arbitration in the Federal Republic of Germany* (Deventer 1984)

Golbert, International Arbitration Law Proposed for California, in *Arbitration & the Law: AAA General Counsel's Annual Report 1987-88* 262 (1988)

Golbert & Kolkey, California's Adoption of a Code for International Commercial Arbitration and Conciliation, 10 *Loy. L.A. Int'l & Comp. L.J.* 583 (1988)

————, California's New International Arbitration and Conciliation Code, 11 *L.A. Law.* 46 (No. 8, 1988)

Goldman, La nouvelle réglementation française de l'arbitrage international, in *The Art of Arbitration* 153 (J. Schultsz & A. van den Berg eds. 1982)

Goldring, Australia: National Report, 2 *Y.B. Com. Arb.* 3 (1977); 9 *Y.B. Com. Arb.* 39 (1984) and 14 *Y.B. Com. Arb.* 488 (1989)

————, Australian Law and International Commercial Arbitration, 15 *Col. J. Transnat'l L.* 216 (1976)

Goldstajn, International Commercial Arbitration and Municipal Arbitration Legislation, in *ICCA, Third Int'l Arb. Congress: Proceedings* 453 (1969)

————, Yugoslavia: National Report, 1 *Y.B. Com. Arb.* 106 (1976); 8 *Y.B. Com. Arb.* 81 (1983); 10 *Y.B. Com. Arb.* 3 (1985)

Golob, Arbitral Tribunals According to the Draft of the Polish Code of Civil Procedure, 1 *Int'l Y.B. Civil & Com. Arb.* 128 (A. Nussbaum ed. 1928)

Gomez de la Torre, Aspectos comerciales y procesuales del sistema ecuatoriano de derecho internacional privado, 6 *Anuario Ecuatoriano de Derecho Int'l* 83 (Nos. 8-9 y 10, Años 1976-1980)

Goossen, Chinese Contract Law and the New Civil Code, 8 *East Asian Exec. Rep.* 9 (No. 7, July 1986)

Grade, The Annulment of Arbitral Awards in Belgium, 5 *Int'l Fin. L. Rev.* 35 (No. 11, 1986)

Graham, International Commercial Arbitration: The Developing Canadian Profile, in *UNCITRAL Arbitration Model in Canada* 77 (R. Paterson & B. Thompson eds. 1987)

Grasso, La nuova disciplina dell'arbitrato alla luce della legge 9 febbraio 1983, N.28, 25 *Rassegna dell'Arb.* 27 (1985)

Grieg & Kaplan, Hong Kong: National Report, 11 *Y.B. Comm. Arb.* 3 (1986)

Grigera Naón, El arbitraje comercial en el derecho argentino interno e internacional privado, 1982 *Revista de derecho mercantil* 115

Grigera Naón & Samtleben, Schiedsgerichtsbarkeit in Argentinien, 29 *RIW* 721 (1983)

Grunsky, W., D. Leipold, W. Munzberg, P. Schlosser & E. Schumann, *Stein-Jonas Kommentar zur Zivilprozessordnung. Paragraphs 1044 - 1048. EG ZPO* (20th rev. ed. Tübingen 1987)

Habscheid, Das neue schweizerische Recht des internationalen Schiedsverfahrens, 48 *KTS* 177 (1987)

————, Das schweizerische Schiedskonkordat, der Entwurf zu einem Bundesgesetz über das Internationale Privatrecht und die internationale Schiedsgerichtsbarkeit, in *Beiträge zum internationalen Verfahrensrecht und zur Schiedsgerichtsbarkeit. Festschrift für Heinrich Nagel* 70 (W. Habscheid & K. Schwab eds. 1987)

————, Il concordato svizzero sull'arbitrato e l'arbitrato internazionale, 40 *Riv. Trim. Dir. & Proc. Civ.* 1197 (1986)

Hacking, Where We Are Now: Trends and Developments since the Arbitration Act, 2 *J. Int. Arb.* 7 (No. 4, 1985)

Hahn, D., *L'arbitrage commercial international en Suisse face aux règles de concurrence de la CEE* (Geneva 1985)

Hanna, The Commercial Arbitration Bill 1984, 3 *The Arbitrator* 77 (1984)

Hassan & Samie, International Commercial Arbitration in Pakistan, 33 *Arb. J.* 41 (1978)

Hejailan, Saudi Arabia: National Report, 4 *Y.B. Com. Arb.* 162 (1979)

Herrmann, The British Columbia Enactment of the UNCITRAL Model Law, in *UNCITRAL Arbitration Model in Canada* 65 (R. Paterson & B. Thompson eds. 1987)

Hirschman, The Second Arbitration Trilogy: The Federalization of Arbitration Law, 71 *Va. L. Rev.* 1305 (1985)

Hitters, Posibilidad de prorrogar la jurisdicción en favor de tribunales o arbitros extrajeros. Limitaciones, 1984-III *Jurispr. Arg.* 763

Hoellering, Provisions of U.S. Law on Arbitration Agreements, in *Arbitration & the Law: AAA General Counsel's Annual Report 1987-88* 170 (1988)

Holtzmann, Powers of Arbitrators under United States Law to Fill "Gaps" Arising under Long-Term Commercial Contracts, in *ICCA, Fifth Int'l Arb. Congress: Proceedings* C IVh 1-17 (1975)

Hornick, Indonesia — Foreign Arbitral Awards Not Enforceable, 7 *East Asian Exec. Rep.* 11 (No. 11, 1985)

Hoyle, An Introductory View of Arbitration in Egypt, 50 *Arbitration* 166 (Nov. 1984)

Hrivnak, Czechoslovak Regulations Governing Arbitration in International Trade, 24 *Bull. Czechoslovak L.* 19 (1985)

Hunter, Arbitration Procedure in England: Past, Present and Future, 1 *Arb. Int'l* 82 (1985)

Impallomeni, Une modification au Code de procédure civile en Italie: les nouvelles règles sur l'arbitrage, 9 *Int'l Trade L. & Prac.* 599 (1983)

Inglis, Some Points of Difference Between the Scots and English Laws of Arbitration, 43 *Arbitration* 72 (1977)

International Chamber of Commerce, *Arbitration Law in Europe* (Paris 1981)

———, *Commercial Arbitration and the Law Throughout the World/ L'Arbitrage Commercial et la Loi dans les différents pays* (Basel 1949, 1964)

Jacobs, South Africa: National Report II, 9 *Y.B. Com. Arb.* 50 (1984)

Jacobs, M.S., *The Law of Arbitration in South Africa* (Cape Town 1977)

Jaffer & Osmany, Pakistan: National Report, 5 *Y.B. Com. Arb.* 114 (1980) and 7 *Y.B. Com. Arb.* 66 (1982)

Jakubowski & Wisniewski, Poland: National Report, 1 *Y.B. Com. Arb.* 64 (1976)

Jalili, Arbitration in Saudi Arabia, 50 *Arbitration* 163 (Nov. 1984)

Jambu-Merlin, The New French Arbitration Act, in 1 *Fifth Int'l Congress of Maritime Arbitrators* (New York 1981)

Jarvin, Canada's Determined Move Towards International Commercial Arbitration, 3 *J. Int'l Arb.* 111 (No. 3, 1986)

———, London As a Place for International Arbitration: Some Observations in Light of the Arbitration Act 1979 and the Bank Mellat v. Helleniki Techniki case, 1 *J. Int'l Arb.* 59 (1984)

Jen Tsien-Hsin & Liu Shao-Shan, People's Republic of China: National Report, 3 *Y.B. Com. Arb.* 153 (1978)

Jimenez Salazar, Ecuador: National Report, 3 *Y.B. Com. Arb.* 76 (1978)

Jokela, Finland: National Report, 5 *Y.B. Com. Arb.* 41 (1980)

Jolidon, P., *Commentaire du Concordat suisse sur l'arbitrage* (Berne 1984)

Kang Seok Jeon, Non-Judicial Dispute Resolution Procedures in the Republic of Korea with an Emphasis on Arbitration, 14 *Korean J. Comp. L.* 31 (1986)

Kaplan, Arbitration in Hong Kong, 3 *J. Int'l Arb.* 7 (No. 4, 1986); also 52 *Arbitration* 12 (Feb. 1986)

Karrer, Switzerland's New Law is Modern, Liberal and Pragmatic, 3 *Int'l Arb. Rep.* 21 (1988)

Kassis, Particularités et problèmes de l'arbitrage dans les droits des pays arabes, 63 *Rev. Droit Int'l & Droit Comp.* 7 (1986)

Kassis, A., *Problèmes de base de l'arbitrage en droit comparé et en droit international. Vol. 1: Arbitrage juridictionnel et arbitrage contractuel* (Paris 1987)

Kelmann, Arbitration under Soviet Law, in *Int'l Y.B. Civil & Com. Arb.* 145 (A. Nussbaum ed. 1928)

Kennedy-Grant, New Zealand: National Report, 8 *Y.B. Com. Arb.* 34 (1983); 11 *Y.B. Com. Arb.* 83 (1986)

Kerr, The Arbitration Act 1979, 43 *Mod. Law Rev.* 45 (1980)

Klein, Internationales Schiedsverfahren und nationale Rechtsordnungen, 24 *Schweiz. Jahrbuch Int'les Recht* 87 (1967)

Knoepfler & Schweizer, L'arbitrage international et des voies de recours: à propos du projet de Loi fédérale sur le DIP, in *Mélanges Guy Flattet* 491 (Lausanne 1985)

Koral, La nouvelle loi turque sur le droit international privé et la procédure internationale et le principe de la reciprocité dans l'arbitrage, 1983 *Rev. Arb.* 47

Kos-Rabcewicz-Zubkowski, Arbitration in the Code of Civil Procedure of Quebec, 8 *Rassegna dell'Arb.* 85 (1968); also 2 *La Revue Juridique Themis* 143 (1968)

———, International Arbitration Laws in Canada: Adaptation of UNCITRAL Model Law on International Commercial Arbitration, 5 *J. Int'l Arb.* 43 (No. 3, 1988)

———, International Arbitration Laws in Canada: Recent Legislation (Ontario and Saskatchewan), 5 *J. Int'l Arb.* 164 (No. 4, 1988)

———, International Commercial Arbitration in the Common Law Provinces of Canada, 44 *Arb. J.* 14 (No. 3, 1989)

Kos-Rabcewicz-Zubkowski, L., *Commercial and Civil Law Arbitration in Canada* (Ottawa 1978)

Kotora, New Rules of Arbitration Proceedings and Recognition and Enforcement of Foreign Awards and Judicial Decisions in Czechoslovakia, 7 *Diritto negli Scambi Int'li* 225 (1968)

Krilyszyn & Bajons, Zur Internationalisierung des österreichischen Schiedsrecht, 1 *Jahrbuch Schiedsgerichtsbarkeit* 234 (1987)

Krishnamurthi, India: National Report, 2 *Y.B. Com. Arb.* 31 (1977); 11 *Y.B. Com. Arb.* 73 (1986)

Lalive, The New Swiss Law on International Arbitration, 4 *Arb. Int'l* 2 (1988)

Lalive & Gaillard, Le nouveau droit de l'arbitrage international en Suisse, 116 *J. Droit Int'l (Clunet)* 905 (1989)

Lalive, P., J.-F. Poudret & C. Reymond, *Le droit de l'arbitrage interne et international en Suisse* (Lausanne 1989)

Lalonde, The New Environment for Commercial Arbitration in Canada, 1 *Rev. Int'l Bus. L.* 31 (1987); also in 1988 *Int'l Bus. L. J.* 963

Lando, Danisches Schiedsrecht nach dem Schiedsgerichtsbarkeitsgesetz von 1972, *Zeitschrift für das gesamte Handels- und Gesellschaftsrecht* 517 (1972)

Lanz, R., *Das Konkordat über die Schiedsgerichtsbarkeit vom 27. März 1969* (Zurich 1971)

Lécuyer-Thieffry, Les nouvelles lois des Etats américans sur l'arbitrage international, 1989 *Rev. Arb.* 43

Lee, E., *Encyclopedia of International Commercial Arbitration* (London 1986)

Legras de Grandcourt, Evolution contemporaine des législations européennes, in *Euro-Arab Arbitration III* 119 (F. Kemicha ed. 1991)

Lerrick, A. & Q. J. Mian, *Saudi Arabia Business and Labour Law: Its Interpretation and Application. Chapter 3 - Arbitration* (2nd ed., London 1987)

Leung, The Arbitration (Amendment) Ordinance (1982) of Hong Kong, 48 *Arbitration* 92 (1982)

——, The Hong Kong Arbitration Ordinance 1982, 1985 *J. Bus. L.* 423 (1985)

Level, La procédure arbitrale, in *Droit et pratique de l'arbitrage international en France 51* (Y. Derains ed. Paris 1984)

Lew, J., *Applicable Law in International Commercial Arbitration. A Study in Commercial Arbitration Awards* (Dobbs Ferry, NY 1978)

Liemen, Schiedsgerichtsbarkeit und Vollstreckung von Schiedssprüchen im Iran, 24 *RIW* 780 (1978)

Liew Song-kun, Commercial Arbitration in Korea with Special Reference to the UNCITRAL Rules, 5 *Korean J. Comp. L.* 69 (1977)

————, Commercial Arbitration in Korea with Special Reference to the UNCITRAL Rules, in Business Laws in Korea 905 (Kim Chan-Jin ed., 2nd ed. 1988)

Lois Caballe, Comentarios a la Ley 36/1988, de 5 de diciembre, de Arbitraje, 46 *Revista General de Derecho* 7789 (1989)

Longo, Towards a "Common Core" of Legal Rules on Commercial Arbitration, 59 *Austl. L.J.* 407 (1985)

Loumiet, United States: Florida International Arbitration Act. Introductory Note, 26 *I.L.M.* 949 (1987)

Loumiet, O'Naghten & Swan, Proposed Florida International Arbitration Act, 16 *U. Miami Inter-Am. L. Rev.* 591 (1985)

Luzzatto, International Commercial Arbitration and the Municipal Law of States, 157 *Recueil des Cours* 9 (1977-IV)

McClendon, State International Arbitration Laws: Are They Needed or Desirable? 1 *Am. Rev. Int'l Arb.* 245 (1990)

McClendon, J.S. & R.E. Everard Goodman, *International Commercial Arbitration in New York* (Ardsley-on-Hudson, NY 1986)

Malamud, Argentina: National Report, 3 *Y.B. Com. Arb.* 17 (1978) and 8 *Y.B. Com. Arb.* 65 (1983)

Malamud, J., *El Arbitraje Comercial y el Nuevo Código de Procedimientos* (Buenos Aires 1968)

Mann, Some Recent Developments in English Law of Arbitration, in *Inter Nationes. Festschrift für Stefan Riesenfeld* (E. Jayme, G. Kegel & M. Lutter eds. 1983)

Marotta Rangel, Brazil: National Report, 3 *Y.B. Com. Arb.* 31 (1978) and 7 *Y.B. Com. Arb.* 57 (1982)

Marriott, Arbitration Law Reform, 6 *Int'l Arb. Rep.* 25 (No. 5, 1991)

Marshall, The Law of Arbitration — A Difference between Scotts and English, 15 *Juridical Review* 115 (1970)

Matray, Belgium: National Report, 5 *Y.B. Com. Arb.* 1 (1980); 11 *Y.B. Com. Arb.* 57 (1986)

Mechri, L'arbitrage en Tunisie, 16 *Rassegna dell'Arb.* 3 (1976)

————, Les insuffisances du Code de procédure civile et commerciale et les modifications qui s'imposent, in *Centre d'Etudes, Les Entreprises Tunisiennes et l'Arbitrage Commercial International* 365 (1983)

Melis, Zur Neuorderung der Bestimmungen über die Schiedsgerichtsbarkeit in der österreichischen Zivilprozessordnung, in *Festschrift für Arthur Bülow* 129 (K.-H. Böckstiegel & O. Glossner eds. 1981)

Melis, W., *A Guide to Commercial Arbitration in Austria* (Vienna 1983)

Mellman, Seeking Its Place in the Sun: Florida's Emerging Role in International Commercial Arbitration, 19 *U. Miami Inter-Am. L. Rev.* 363 (1987-88)

Mendes, Canada: A New Forum to Develop the Cultural Psychology of International Commercial Arbitration, 3 *J. Int'l Arb.* 71 (No. 3, 1986)

Meneu, La legislación y la práctica española del arbitraje mercantil, in *ICCA, Third Int'l Arb. Congress: Proceedings* 501 (1969)

Merchant & Merchant, The Law Relating to Recognition and Enforcement of Foreign Arbitral Agreements and Awards in the United States of America and India, in *ICCA, Fifth Int'l Arb. Congress: Proceedings* C Im 1-10 (1975)

Mezger, Das französische Dekret vom 14. Mai 1980 und die organisierte Schiedsgerichtsbarkeit, in *Festschrift für Arthur Bülow* 141 (K.-H. Böckstiegel & O. Glossner eds. 1981)

Minakov, A.I., *Arbitrazhnye soglashenia i praktika rassmotreniya vneshneekonomicheskikh sporov* (Moscow 1985)

Mittelstein, Law and Practice of Arbitral Tribunals in Germany, in 1 *Int'l Y.B. Civil & Com. Arb.* 33 (1928)

Mokal, S. M. I. K., *The Arbitration Act, 1940 (X of 1940): With Commentary* (4th ed., Lahore 1986)

Montesano, Negozio e processo nel nuovo arbitrato, 39 *Riv. Dir. Proc.* 214 (1984)

Morgan & Redmont, Arbitration in the Channel Islands, *Int'l Bus. Law.* 275 (1985)

Morris, The Problem of Uniform Arbitration Legislation in Canada, 13 *Arb. J.* 103 (1958)

Mustill, A New Arbitration Act for the United Kingdom? The Response of the Departmental Advisory Committee to the UNCITRAL Model Law, 6 *Arb. Int'l* 3 (1990)

————, Domestic Arbitration Law — Proposals for Consolidation Amendment and Development, 56 *Arbitration* 82 (1990)

————, Transnational Arbitration and English Law, in *International Commercial and Maritime Arbitration* 15 (F.D. Rose ed. 1988)

————, Vers une nouvelle loi anglaise sur l'arbitrage, 1991 *Rev. Arb.* 383

Mustill, Sir Michael J. & S. C. Boyd, *The Law and Practice of Commercial Arbitration in England* (2nd ed. 1989)

Nattier, International Commercial Arbitration in Latin America: Enforcement of Arbitral Agreements and Awards, 21 *Tex. Int'l L. J.* 397 (1986)

Nestor, Romania: National Report, 1 *Y.B. Com. Arb.* 77 (1976)

Newman & Burrows, New York Law Revision Changes Attachment Picture, 1 *Int'l Arb. Rep.* 301 (1986)

Neuroud & Park, Predestination and Swiss Arbitration Law: Geneva's Application of the Intercantonal Concordat, 2 *B. U. Int'l L.J.* 1 (1983)

Nicotina, Il regime dell'arbitrato in Italia dopo la legge 9 febbraio 1983 No. 28, 25 *Rassegna dell'Arb.* 291 (1985)

Nilsson, Problems of Sovereign Immunity under the Swedish Law of Arbitration, 1982 *Y.B. Swed. & Int'l Arb.* 41

Nöcker, T., *Das Recht der Schiedsgerichtsbarkeit in Kanada* (Heidelberg 1988)

Nöcker & Hentzen, The New Legislation on Arbitration in Canada, 22 *Int'l Law*. 829(1988)

Nomura, Some Aspects of the Use of Commercial Arbitration by Japanese Corporations, 33 *Osaka U. L. Rev.* 47 (March 1986); also in *East and West: Legal Philosophies in Japan* 50 (M. Yasaki ed. 1987)

Note, Saudi Arabia: Arbitration Rules Introduced, *Int'l Fin. L. Rev.* 42 (Nov. 1985)

O'Connor, The Rise (or Is It Demise) of Arbitration in Kenya, 53 *Arbitration* 61(1987)

Ochoa Bunsow, A., *El derecho applicable en el arbitraje comercial international* (Mexico 1980)

Ogawa, Proposed Draft of Japan's New Arbitration Law, 7 *J. Int'l Arb.* 33 (No. 2, 1990)

————, The New Thai Arbitration Act of 1987, 6 *J. Int'l Arb.* 97 (No. 3, 1989)

Ottolenghi, Arbitration Institutions in Israel, 38 *Arb. J.* 53 (No. 3, 1983)

————, Israel: National Report, 2 *Y.B. Com. Arb.* 47 (1977); 11 *Y.B. Com. Arb.* 79 (1986)

Overby, Arbitrability of Disputes under the Federal Arbitration Act, 71 *Iowa L. Rev.* 1137 (1986)

Oyekunle, Nigeria: National Report, 2 *Y.B. Com. Arb.* 66 (1977)

Paez, Ley de arbitraje comercial, *Revista de Derecho* 69 (No. 1, 1964)

Panchaud, Une législation en matière d'arbitrage: le projet de Concordat des Cantons suisses, 1969, in *ICCA, Third Int'l Arb. Congress: Proceedings* 539 (1969)

Park, Judicial Supervision of Transnational Commercial Arbitration: The English Arbitration Act of 1979, 21 *Harv. Int'l L.J.* 87 (1980)

————, The Influence of National Legal Systems on International Commercial Arbitration: Recent Developments in English Arbitration Law, in *Resolving Transnational Disputes Through International Arbitration* 80 (T. Carbonneau ed. 1980)

Parker School of Foreign and Comparative Law, *International Commercial Arbitration and the Courts* (Dobbs Ferry 1990)

Parra Aranguren, Venezuela: National Report, 3 *Y.B. Com. Arb.* 133 (1978)

Paterson, International Commercial Arbitration Act: An Overview, in *UNCITRAL Arbitration Model in Canada* 113 (R. Paterson & B. Thompson eds. 1987)

Paterson R. & B. Thompson, eds., *UNCITRAL Arbitration Model in Canada. Canadian International Commercial Arbitration Legislation* (Toronto 1987)

Patkos, The United Nations Convention of 1958 on the Recognition and Enforcement of Foreign Arbitral Awards in the Light of the Greek Civil Procedure Code of 1971, 25 *Rev. Hellénique Droit Int'l* 295 (1972)

Paulsson, Arbitration Unbound in Belgium, 2 *Arb. Int'l* 68 (1986)

——, La réforme de la loi de l'arbitrage de Hong Kong, 1984 *Rev. Arb.* 325

Pereira Barrocas, Necessidade de uma nova ordem judicial a arbitragem, 45 *Revista da Ordem dos Advogados* 433 (1985)

Perrot, La réforme du droit de l'arbitrage: l'application à l'arbitrage des règles de nouveau Code de procédure civile, 1980 *Rev. Arb.* 642

Pestalozzi, Arbitration and Its New Prospects in Brazil, 4 *J. Int'l Arb.* 131 (No. 3, 1987)

Piaggi, El arbitraje international y la realidad argentina, *La Ley*, Apr. 6, 1983, at 1

Plehn, International Arbitration in Spain: A New Institution versus an Old Law, 20 *Int'l Law.* 247 (1986)

Pomerleau, L'arbitrage interprovincial et international au Canada: aspects constitutionnel et législatif, 1985 *Rev. Arb.* 373 (1985)

Poudret, La clause arbitrale par référence selon la Convention de New York et l'art.6 du Concordat sur l'arbitrage, in *Mélanges Guy Flattet* 523 (Lausanne 1985)

Poudret, J.-F. & A. Würzburger, *Code de procédure civile vaudois et concordat sur l'arbitrage, annoté et commenté* (2nd ed. Lausanne 1980)

Poudret, Reymond & Würzburger, L'application du concordat intercantonal sur l'arbitrage par le tribunal cantonal vaudois, 1981 *JdT* 67 (1981)

Prujiner, Les nouvelles règles de l'arbitrage au Québec, 1987 *Rev. Arb.* 425 (1987)

Ramos Mendez, Les clauses d'arbitrage international et leur validité selon le droit espagnol, 1982 *Rev. Arb.* 147

————, Vereinbarkeit eines Schiedsverfahrens nach der VglSchO der IHK mit einem Schiedsverfahren nach dem spanischen Gesetz von 1953, in *Festschrift für Walther J. Habscheid* 239 (W. Lindacher, D. Pfaff et al. eds. 1989)

Rashed, The UNCITRAL Model Law and Recent Developments in Egypt, 3 *ICSID Rev. - Foreign Investment L.J.* 126 (1988)

Recchia, La nouvelle loi italienne sur l'arbitrage, 1984 *Rev. Arb.* 65

————, Nuove prospettive dell'arbitrato commerciale in Italia, 23 *Rassegna dell'Arb.* 41 (1983)

Recent Developments: The Federal Arbitration Act, 1986 *Mo. J. Disp. Res.* 143

Recent Developments: The Uniform Arbitration Act, 1986 *Mo. J. Disp. Res.* 169

Recent Developments: The Uniform Arbitration Act, 1987 *Mo. J. Disp. Res.* 177

Redmond, Arbitration in the Channel Islands, 2 *J. Int'l Arb.* 45 (No. 4, 1985); also in 52 *Arbitration* 181 (1986)

Reymond, Das Zusammenwirken von Kapitel XII des Bundesgesetzes über das Internationale Privatrecht mit dem kantonalen Recht, in *Die Internationale Schiedsgerichtsbarkeit in der Schweiz* 113 (K.-H. Böckstiegel ed. 1989)

————, International Arbitration in Switzerland: First Experiences with the New Act, 1 *Am. Rev. Int'l Arb.* 303 (1990)

————, The New Swiss Uniform Arbitration Act and International Commercial Arbitration, 7 *Ga. J. Int'l & Comp. L.* 85 (1977)

Ricci, Modificazioni della disciplina dell'Arbitrato (Legge 9 febbraio 1983, n.28), 1983 *Nuove Leggi Civili Commentate* 733

Robert, L'arbitrage en matière internationale. Commentaire du décret No. 81-500 du 12 mai 1981, 1981 *Recueil Dalloz Sirey* 209

Robert, J. & T. Carbonneau, *The French Law of Arbitration* (New York 1983)

Roberts, The Development of Arbitration in Hong Kong, 50 *Arbitration* 27 (1984)

Romeu-Matta, New Developments in International Commercial Arbitration: A Comparative Survey of New State Statutes and the UNCITRAL Model Law, 1 *Am. Rev. Int'l Arb.* 140 (1990)

Rothstein, Recognizing and Enforcing Arbitral Agreements and Awards Against Foreign States: The Mathias Amendments to the Foreign Sovereign Immunities Act and Title 9, 1 *Emory J. Int'l Disp. Res.* 101 (1986)

Ruede, T. & R. Hadenfeldt, *Schweizerisches Schiedsgerichtsrecht* (Zurich 1980)

Ruiz, Spain: New Arbitration Law, 55 *Arbitration* 281 (1989)

Sacks, Arbitration in Connecticut: Issues in Judicial Intervention Under the Connecticut Arbitration Statutes, 17 *Conn. L. Rev.* 387 (1985)

Sajko, The New York Arbitration Convention of 1958 from the Yugoslav Point of View: Selected Issues, in *Essays on International Commercial Arbitration* 199 (P. Sarcevic ed. 1989)

Saleh, The Settlement of Disputes in the Arab World: Arbitration and Other Methods, 1 *Arab Law Q.* 198 (1986); reprinted in 4 *Int'l Tax & Bus. Law.* 280 (1986)

Samtleben, Arbitragem comercial no direito internacional privado Brazileiro, in *Estudos em Homenagem ao Prof. Doutor A. Ferrer-Correia* 691 (Coimbra 1986)

———, Arbitragem no Brazil, 77 *Revista da Faculdade de Direito, Universidade de Sao Paulo* 185 (1982)

———, Länderbericht Kuba, in *Die Aussenhandelsschiedsgerichtsbarkeit der sozialistischen Länder* 274 (D. Pfaff ed. 1973)

———, Schiedsgerichtsbarkeit in Brasilien, 27 *RIW* 376 (1981)

———, Schiedsgerichtsbarkeit in Chile, 29 *RIW* 167 (1983)

————, Schiedsgerichtsbarkeit in den Andenpaktstaaten, 30 *RIW* 600 (1984)

Samuel, A Critical Look at the Reform of Swiss Arbitration Law, 7 *Arb. Int'l* 27 (1991)

————, The 1979 Arbitration Act —Judicial Review of Arbitration Awards on the Merits in England, 2 *J. Int. Arb.* 53 (No. 4, 1985)

————, The New Swiss Private International Law Act, 37 *Int'l & Comp. L.Q.* 681 (1988)

Sanders, A New Arbitration Law for the Netherlands, 4 *Pace L. Rev.* 581 (1984)

————, International Commercial Arbitration — How to Improve Its Functioning? 46 *Arbitration* 9 (1980)

————, Netherlands: National Report, 6 *Y.B. Com. Arb.* 60 (1981)

————, The Dutch Arbitration Act of 1986, 1987 *J. Bus. L.* 321 & 403

————, The New Dutch Arbitration Act, 3 *Arb. Int'l* 194 (1987)

————, The New Dutch Arbitration Act, 27 *Rassegna dell'Arb.* 27 (1987)

————, The New Dutch Arbitration Act, 14 *N. Ky. L. Rev.* 41 (1987)

————, The New Dutch Arbitration Act, 1987 *Int'l Bus. L.J.* 539

————, The New Dutch Arbitration Act, in *AAA, Arbitration & the Law, 1986* 162 (1987)

————, Observations sur la loi britannique sur l'arbitrage ('Arbitration Act 1979'), 19 *Rassegna dell'Arb.* 155 (1979)

Sanders, P., *Het nieuwe arbitragerecht* (Deventer 1987)

Sanders, P., ed., *International Handbook on Commercial Arbitration: National Reports, Basic Legal Texts* (Deventer 1984)

Sanders, P. & A. van den Berg, eds., *The Netherlands Arbitration Act 1986: Text and Notes, English, Français, Deutsch* (Deventer 1987)

Sandrock, Das Gesetz zur Neuregelung des Internationalen Privatrechts und die internationale Schiedsgerichtsbarkeit, 33 *RIW Beilage* 2 zu Heft 5/1987 (1987)

————, Die Bedeutung des Gesetzes zur Neuregelung des Internationalen Privatrechts für die Unternehmenspraxis, 32 *RIW* 841 (1986)

Sareika, Rechtsprechung zum kanadischen Recht der Schiedsgerichtsbarkeit, 22 *RIW* 261 (1976)

Sauvepanne, Die Schiedsgerichtsbarkeit in der Benelux, 7 *Jahrbuch für internationales Recht* 86 (1956)

Schaeffer, South Africa: National Report I, 2 *Y.B. Com. Arb.* 76 (1977)

Schlosser, Notwendige Reformen des deutschen Rechts der Schiedsgerichtsbarkeit, 1987 *Zeitschrift für Wirtschaftsrecht und Insolvenzpraxis* 492

————, Quelles nouvelles de l'arbitrage Outre-Rhin? 1987 *Rev. Arb.* 293

————, What is International in the Legal Basis of International Arbitration? 1985 *Comp. L. Rev.* 113 (No. 1/1985) and 85 (No. 2/1985)

Schmitthoff, Arbitration — the Next Step in the United Kingdom, 4 *Arb. Int'l* 67 (1988)

Schneider & Patocchi, The New Swiss Law on International Arbitration, 55 *Arbitration* 268 (1989)

Schnyder, Intertemporalrecht und internationale Schiedsgerichtsbarkeit im neuen IPR-Gesetz in der Schweiz, 10 *IPRax* 60 (1990)

Schnyder, A. K., *Das neue IPR-Gesetz* (Zurich 1988)

Schultsz, Ein neues Schiedsgerichtsgesetz für die Nederlande, 7 *IPRax* 383 (1987)

————, Les nouvelles dispositions de la législation néederlandaise en matière d'arbitage, 1988 *Rev. Arb.* 209

————, The Bill on Applicability of Dutch Law to Awards Rendered by the Iran-United States Claims Tribunal, in *Legislation in the Netherlands and International Arbitration* 32 (1986)

Schultsz, J.C. & S.L. Buruma, eds., *Legislation in the Netherlands and International Arbitration. Internationale Arbitrage* (Deventer 1986)

Schütze, Die Neuordnung der Aussenhandelsschiedsgerichtsbarkeit in der Tschechoslowakei, 12 *Jahrbuch für Ostrecht* 95 (1975)

Schwab, K. H. & G. Walter, *Schiedsgerichtsbarkeit: Systematische Kommentar zu den Vorschriftender Zivilprozessordnung, des Arbeitsgerichtsgesetzes, der Staatsverträge und der Kostengesetze über das privatrechtliche Schiedsgerichtsvefahren* (4th ed. Munich 1990)

Scotford, Commercial Arbitration: New South Wales Commercial Arbitration Bill 1984, 1985 *Lloyd's Mar. & Com. L.Q.* 136

Sebestyen, Hungary: National Report, 1 *Y.B. Com. Arb.* 53 (1976)

Sedlacek, V., *Arbitration in Czechoslovak Foreign Trade* (Prague 1982)

Seppala, French Domestic Arbitration Law, 16 *Int'l Law.* 749 (1982)

Shenton & Toland, London as a Venue for International Arbitration: The Arbitration Act, 1979, 12 *L. & Pol'y Int'l Bus.* 643 (1980)

Simmonds, K., B. Hill & S. Jarvin, eds., *Commercial Arbitration Law in Asia and the Pacific* (Paris & Dobbs Ferry, NY 1987)

Singh, S.D., *The Law of Arbitration* (8th ed. Lucknow 1980)

Singhania & Co., *International Commercial Arbitration Law, Procedures and Facilities in India* (New Delhi 1985)

Sipkov, The Law of Foreign Trade in the People's Republic of Bulgaria, 37 *Law & Contemp. Prob.* 485 (1972)

Smedresman, The Arbitration Act, 1979, 11 *J. Mar. L. & Com.* 319 (1980)

Stalev, Bulgaria: National Report, 1 *Y.B. Com. Arb.* 18 (1976); 7 *Y.B. Com. Arb.* 60 (1982); 11 *Y.B. Com. Arb.* 61 (1986)

————, Das neue bulgarische Gesetz über die internationale Handelsschiedsgerichtsbarkeit, 2 *Jahrbuch Schiedsgerichtsbarkeit* 208 (1988)

Stastny, M. & S. Hanak, *Act 98/1963 Relating to Arbitration in International Trade and to Enforcement of Awards: A Commentary* (Prague 1984)

Steyn, Arbitration and the Courts: Arbitration Systems in England and Wales and Recent Changes in Arbitration Law, 46 *Arbitration* 146 (1980)

————, Arbitration Law Reform: Towards a New Arbitration Act, 6 *Int'l Arb. Rep.* 27 (No. 4, 1991)

97

————, England: National Report, 8 *Y.B. Com. Arb.* 3 (1983)

————, Towards a New English Arbitration Act, 7 *Arb. Int'l* 17 (1991)

Steyn & Marriott, Towards a New Arbitration Act, 57 *Arbitration* 14 (1991)

Storme, Aspects importants du droit arbitral belge, 53 *Rev. Droit Int'l & Droit Comp.* 116 (1976)

Storme, M. & B. Demeulenaere, *International Commercial Arbitration in Belgium: A Handbook* (Deventer 1989)

Strohbach, German Democratic Republic: National Report, 1 *Y.B. Com. Arb.* 40 (1976)

————, International Commercial Arbitration in the GDR, *Law and Legislation in the German Democratic Republic* 26 (Nos. 1-2/1984)

Sturges, Commercial Arbitration in the United States of America, in 1 *Int'l Y.B. Civil & Com. Arb.* 165 (A. Nussbaum ed. 1928)

Subekti, Indonesia: National Report, 5 *Y.B. Com. Arb.* 84 (1980) and 7 *Y.B. Com. Arb.* 63 (1982)

Sundaraswamy, Law of Arbitration in India, 20 *Arbitration Q.* 3 (1985)

Suratgar, Arbitration in the Iranian Legal System, 20 *Arb. J.* 143 (1965)

Sutton, Hong Kong Enacts the UNCITRAL Model Law, 6 *Arb. Int'l* 358 (1990)

Swisher, International Commercial Arbitration under the United Nations Convention and the Amended Federal Arbitration Statute, 47 *Wash. L. Rev.* 441 (1972)

Taliadoros, Arbitration Between Private Persons in Greek Law, 9 *Int'l Trade L. & Prac.* 604 (1983)

Tedeschi, Commercial Arbitration in Australia, 15 *Rassegna dell'Arb.* 117 (1975)

Thomas, An Appraisal of the Arbitration Act 1979, 1981 *Lloyd's Mar. & Com. L.Q.* 199

————, Arbitration in England: The Current Issues, 4 *Arb. Int'l* 75 (1988)

————, International Commercial Arbitration Agreements and the Enforcement of Foreign Arbitral Awards — A Commentary on the Arbitration Act 1975, 1981 *Lloyd's Mar. & Com. L.Q.* 17

Thuilleaux, La loi de 1986 sur l'arbitrage au Québec, au regard de la loi française sur l'arbitrage, 1988 *Int'l Bus. L.J.* 905

Triebel & Lange, Reform des englischen Schiedsgerichtsrechts, 26 *RIW* 616 (1980)

Triva, Pocetak arbitraznog postupka. Uoci prihvacanja UNCITRAL-ovog model-zakona o medunarodnoj trgovackoj arbitrazi i mogucnosti da ga SFR Jugoslavija inkorporira u svoj pravni system, 35 *Zbornik Pravnog Fakulteta u Zagrebu* 195 (1985)

Trolle, Denmark: National Report, 5 *Y.B. Com. Arb.* 28 (1980)

Tschanz, International Arbitration in the United States: The Need for a New Act, 3 *Arb. Int'l* 309 (1987)

————, Le nouveau droit suisse de l'arbitrage international, 1988 *Int'l Bus. L.J.* 437

Turner, C., *Yorston, Fortescue & Turner Australian Mercantile Law.* 17th ed. Chapter 25: Commercial Arbitration and Awards (Sydney 1985)

Uwanno & Sathirathai, Introduction to the Thai Legal System. [Section c) International Commercial Arbitration], 4 *Chulalongkorn L. Rev.* 39, 105 (1985-1986)

van den Berg, Saudi Arabia: National Report, 9 *Y.B. Com. Arb.* 7 (1984)

Vanderelst, Increasing the Appeal of Belgium as an International Arbitration Forum? The Belgian Law of March 27, 1985 Concerning the Annulment of Arbitral Awards, 3 *J. Int'l Arb.* 77 (No. 2, 1986)

van Houtte, La loi belge du 27 mars 1985 sur l'arbitrage international, 1986 *Rev. Arb.* 29

van Praag, Arbitral Tribunals for Civil and Commercial Disputes Under the Law of the Netherlands, 1 *Int'l Y.B. Civil & Com. Arb.* 99 (1928)

Vellekoop, The New Arbitration Law in the Netherlands, 6 *Int'l Fin. L. Rev.* 16 (No. 5, May 1987)

Verde, G., ed., *L'arbitrato secondo la legge 28/1983* (Naples 1985) von Hoffmann, Anmerkungen zum neuen Internationalen Schiedsrecht der Schweiz, in *Die Internationale Schiedsgerichtsbarkeit in der Schweiz* 147 (K.-H. Böckstiegel ed. 1989)

————, Die Novellierung des deutschen Schiedsverfahrensrechts von 1986, 6 *IPRax* 337 (1986)

Walder-Bohner, Das UNCITRAL-Model Law und die Bestimmungen über die Internationale Schiedsbarkeit im schweizerischen IPR-Gesetz: Vergleich anhand einiger Beispiele, in *Law in East and West: On the Occasion of the 30th Anniversary of the Institute of Comparative Law, Waseda University* 727 (Tokyo 1988)

————, Die neuen Zürcher Bestimmungen über die Schiedsgerichtsbarkeit im Lichte des Konkordats, 72 *SJZ* 249 (1976)

————, Frage der Anfechtung von Schiedsgerichtsentscheiden durch Rechtsmittel (Ein Gegenvorschlag zum Entwurf des Bundesrates über das Internationale Privatrecht), 79 *SJZ* 356 (1983)

Walder-Bohner, H.U., *Das schweizerische Konkordat über die Schiedsgerichtsbarkeit* (Zurich 1982)

Walter, Die internationale Schiedsgerichtsbarkeit in der Schweiz — Offene Fragen zu Kap. 12 des IPR-Gesetzes, 1990 *Zeitschrift des Berner Juristenvereins* 161 (No. 4)

Wehli, Arbitral Tribunals under Austrian Law, 1 *Int'l Y.B. Civil & Com. Arb.* 114 (1928)

Wehrli, D., *Rechtsprechung zum Schweizerischen Konkordat über die Schiedsgerichtsbarkeit* (Zurich 1985)

Weiss, Arbitral Tribunals in the Czechoslovak Republic, 1 *Int'l Y.B. Civil & Com. Arb.* 161 (A. Nussbaum ed. 1928)

Wetter, Salient Features of Swedish Arbitration Clauses, 1983 *Y.B. Swed. & Int'l Arb.* 33

Wickremesinghe, K.D.P., *Civil Procedure in Ceylon (Ch. 24 - Reference to Arbitration),* (Colombo 1971)

Wiget, Über das Verhältniss der Schiedsgerichtsordnungen ICC, UNCITRAL, ECE zum Zürcher Schiedsgerichtsrecht, 75 *SJZ* 17 (1979)

Williams, Law Reform, Hong Kong Arbitration, 10 *Int'l Bus.L.* 317 (1982)

Wright, California's International Commercial Arbitration Act: New Procedures for the Arbitration and Conciliation of International Commercial Disputes, 17 *Int'l Bus. Law.* 45 (1989)

Yamulki, Iraq: National Report, 4 *Y.B. Com. Arb.* 104 (1979)

Ziadé, Lebanon: International Arbitration Provisions of the Code of Civil Procedure, 27 *I.L.M.* 1022 (1988)

2.15 JUDICIAL DECISIONS

Adams, Arbitration, 1985 *All ER Ann. Rev.* 13

―――, Arbitration, 1986 *All ER Ann. Rev.* 11

Aksen, El arbitraje comercial internacional entre gobiernos, in *El Arbitraje Comercial Internacional* 511 (Mexico 1983)

―――, The Application of the New York Convention by the United States, 4 *Y.B. Com. Arb.* 341 (1979)

Allison, Arbitration of Private Antitrust Claims in International Trade: A Study in the Subordination of National Interests to the Demands of a World Market, 18 *N.Y.U. J. Int'l L. & Pol.* 361 (1986)

Bajons, Zur Nationalität internationaler Schiedssachen: der Fall "Norsolor" vor den österreichischen Gerichten, in *Festschrift für Winfried Kralik* 3 (Vienna 1986)

Bakshi, Arbitration Agreement: A Very Important Judgment, 1985(1) *Company L.J.* 195

Barron, Court-Ordered Consolidation of Arbitration Proceedings in the United States, 4 *J. Int'l Arb.* 81 (No. 1, 1987)

Bates, Commercial Arbitration and the Courts in Australia: Signs and Change, 1987 *J. Bus. L.* 527; also in 54 *Arbitration* 160 (1988)

Bebr, Arbitration Tribunals and Article 177 of the EEC Treaty, 22 *Common Mkt. L. Rev.* 489 (1985)

Bedell, Harrison & Harvey, The McMahon Mandate: Compulsory Arbitration of Securities and RICO Claims, 19 *Loy. U. Chi. L.J.* 1 (1987)

Bellet, The Evolution of French Judicial Views on International Arbitration, 34 *Arb. J.* 28 (No. 1, 1979)

Bentil, Judicial Intervention and International Commercial Arbitration, 130 *Solicitors' J.* 191 (1986)

―――, Making England a More Attractive Venue for International Commercial Arbitration by Less Judicial Oversight, 5 *J. Int'l Arb.* 49 (No. 1, 1988)

Bernini & van den Berg, The Enforcement of Arbitral Award Against a State; The Problem of Immunity from Execution, in *Contemporary Problems in Int'l Arbitration* 359 (J.D.M. Lew ed. 1986)

Bingham, Reasons and Reasons for Reasons: Differences Between a Court Judgment and an Arbitration Award, 4 *Arb. Int'l* 141 (1988)

Branson & Wallace, Court-Ordered Consolidated Arbitrations in the United States: Recent Authority Assures Parties the Choice, 5 *J. Int'l Arb.* 89 (No. 1, 1988)

Brierley, Quebec Arbitration Law: A New Era Begins, 40 *Arb. J.* 20 (No. 3, 1985)

Bucher, A., *Die neue internationale Schiedsgerichtsbarkeit in der Schweiz* (Basel 1989)

————, *Le nouvel arbitrage international en Suisse. Théorie et pratique de droit* (Basel 1988)

Bucher, A. & P.-Y. Tschanz, *International Arbitration in Switzerland* (Basel 1989)

Byrne, The Effect of RICO on Maritime Arbitration, 12 *Tul. Mar. L.J.* 77 (1987)

Carbonneau, American and Other National Variations on the Theme of International Commercial Arbitration, 18 *Ga. J. Int'l & Comp. L.* 143 (1988)

————, L'arbitrage en droit américain, 1988 *Rev. Arb.* 3

————, Mitsubishi: The Folly of Quixotic Internationalism, 2 *Arb. Int'l* 116 (1986)

————, The Elaboration of a French Court Doctrine on International Commercial Arbitration: A Study in Liberal Civilian Judicial Creativity, 55 *Tul. L. Rev.* 1 (1980)

————, The Exuberant Pathway to Quixotic Internationalism: Assessing the Folly of Mitsubishi, 19 *Vand. J. Transnat'l L.* 265 (1986)

————, The French Jurisprudence on International Commercial Arbitration, in *Resolving Transnational Disputes Through International Arbitration* 146 (T. Carbonneau ed. 1984)

103

Cloud, Mitsubishi and the Arbitrability of Antitrust Claims: Did the Supreme Court Throw the Baby Out with the Bathwater? 18 *L. & Pol'y Int'l Bus.* 341 (1986)

Collins, The Law Governing the Agreement and Procedure in International Commercial Arbitration in England, in *Contemporary Problems in International Arbitration* 126 (J.D.M. Lew ed. 1986)

Cremades, Les effets de la clause d'arbitrage dans la jurisprudence espagnole récente, in *The Art of Arbitration* 83 (J. Schultsz & A. van den Berg eds. 1982)

————, The Enforcement of British Arbitral Awards in Spain, 45 *Arbitration* 30 and 97 (1979)

Comment, Arbitration and Antitrust: A Leg Up for International Arbitration [Mitsubishi Motors Corp. v. Soler Chrysler-Plymouth, Inc., 105 *S. Ct.* 3346 (1985)], 25 *Washburn L.J.* 536 (1986)

————, Arbitration and Intellectual Property: A Survey of Arbitration in Patent, Trademark and Copyright Cases, 48 *Alb. L. Rev.* 797 (1984)

————, Enforcing International Commercial Arbitration Agreements — Post-Mitsubishi Motors Corp. v. Soler Chrysler-Plymouth, Inc., 36 *Am. U.L. Rev.* 57 (1986)

————, Judicial Implementation of the United Kingdom Arbitration Act, 1979: Pioneer Shipping v. B.T.P. Tioxide (The Nema), 24 *Harv. Int'l L.J.* 103 (1983)

————, Transnational Contractual Disputes: Antitrust Joins Securities Law Claims as Arbitrable Subject Matter, 12 *Brooklyn J. Int'l L.* 731 (1986)

Davenport, Stale Arbitrations — Again, 104 *L.Q. Rev.* 493 (1988)

Davidson, F., *International Commercial Arbitration: Scotland and the UNCITRAL Model Law* (Edinburgh 1991)

de Bruin, De 'affaire C,' 1989 *Tijdschrift voor Arbitrage* 1

de Grandcourt, Les interférences du contentieux arbitral et des contentieux adjacents, in *First Euro-Arab Arbitration Conference: Proceedings* 224 (F. Kemicha ed. 1987)

Deitrick, The Conflicting Policies Between Arbitration and Bankruptcy, 40 *Bus. Law.* 33 (1984)

Delaume, Judicial Decisions Related to Sovereign Immunity and Transnational Arbitration, 2 *ICSID Rev. - Foreign Investment L.J.* 403 (1987)

————, L'arbitrage transnational et les tribunaux américains, 108 *J. Droit Int'l (Clunet)* 788 (1981)

————, SEEE v. Yugoslavia: Epitaph or Interlude? 4 *J. Int'l Arb.* 25 (No. 3, 1987)

De Ly, Judicial Review of Decisions of the I.C.C. Court of International Arbitration, 7 *J. Int'l Arb.* 153 (No. 1, 1990)

Derains, L'obligation de minimiser le dommage dans la jurisprudence arbitrale, 1987 *Int'l Bus. L.J.* 375

Deshpande, International Commercial Arbitration and Domestic Courts in India, 2 *J. Int'l Arb.* 45 (No. 1, 1985)

————, Judicial Interpretation of Commercial Arbitration, 16 *Indian Council of Arbitration Q.* 3 (No. 1, March-April 1981)

Diamond, 1983 California Court of Appeal Survey: Arbitration, 6 *Whittier L. Rev.* 207 (1984)

Doi, The Effect of an Arbitration Clause in a Voidable Contract: Separability Doctrine Adopted by the Supreme Court of Japan, in *Law in East and West/ Recht in Ost und West* 609 (Tokyo 1988)

Donaldson, Mitsubishi and Antitrust Arbitration — It's All the Japanese You Need to Know, 1986 *Brigham Young Univ. L. Rev.* 219 (1986)

Durovic, Uloga arbitraze u stvaranju medunarodnog privrednog prava, 1986 *Jugoslovenska Revija za Medunarodno Pravo* 204 (summary in French at 216)

Engelhardt, Aus der neueren Rechtsprechung zur Schiedsgerichtsbarkeit, 42 *JZ* 227 (1987)

Fiotto, The United States Arbitration Act and Preliminary Injunctions: A New Interpretation of an Old Statute, 66 *B. U. L. Rev.* 1041 (1986)

Forsyth, Enforcement of Arbitral Awards, Choice of Law in Contract, Characterization and a New Attitude to Private International Law, 104 *South Afr. L.J.* 4 (1987)

Fouchard, Les institutions permanentes d'arbitrage devant le juge étatique (à propos d'une jurisprudence récente), 1987 *Rev. Arb.* 225

Fox, Mitsubishi v. Soler and Its Impact on International Commercial Arbitration, 19 *J. World Trade L.* 579 (1985)

————, Preemption of State Law under the Federal Arbitration Act, 15 *Baltimore L. Rev.* 129 (1985)

Furnish, Commercial Arbitration Agreements and the Uniform Commercial Code, 67 *Calif. L. Rev.* 317 (1979)

Gaillard, L'affaire SOFIDIF ou les difficultés de l'arbitrage multipartite (à propos de l'arrêt rendu par la Cour d'Appel de Paris le 19 décembre 1986), 1987 *Rev. Arb.* 275

————, The Enforcement of ICSID Awards in France: The Decision of the Paris Court of Appeal in the SOABI Case, 5 *ICSID Rev. - Foreign Investment L.J.* 69 (1990)

Glossner, Eine zentrale Gerichtsinstanz für internationale Schiedsverfahren in der Bundesrepublik Deutschland? 32 *RIW* 214 (1986)

Gonzales Soria, J., *La intervención judicial en el arbitraje. Recursos jurisdiccionales y ejecución judicial del laudo arbitral* (Madrid 1988)

Hermann, Disputes Between States and Foreign Companies, in *Contemporary Problems in Int'l Arbitration* 250 (J.D.M. Lew ed. 1986)

Hiramoto, A Path to Resources on International Commercial Arbitration 1980-1986, 4 *Int'l Tax & Bus. Law.* 297 (1986)

Hoellering, Shearson/American Express v. McMahon: Broadened Domain of Arbitration in U.S.A., 4 *J. Int'l Arb.* 153 (No. 3, 1987)

Hurlburt, Setting Aside Private Non-labour Arbitration Awards for Errors of Law — Some Recent Decisions, 26 *Alta. L. Rev.* 345 (1988)

Jaffe, The Judicial Trend Toward Finality of Commercial Arbitral Awards in England, 24 *Tex. Int'l L.J.* 67 (1989)

Jarvin, Arbitrability of Antitrust Disputes: The Mitsubishi v. Soler Case, 25 *Swiss Rev. Int'l Competition L.* 53 (Oct. 1985)

————, Skiljeforfarande och konkurrenslagstiftning; nagra anmarkningar till Mitsubishimalet [Arbitration and Antitrust Law: Some Remarks on the Mitsubishi Case], 1986 *Tidskrift utgiven av Juridiska Foreningen i Finland* 219

Jones, Arbitration from the Viewpoint of the Practicing Attorney: An Analysis of Arbitration Cases Decided by the New York State Court of Appeals from January, 1973 to September, 1985, 14 *Fordham Urb. L.J.* 523 (1985-86)

Kaplan, N., J. Spruce & T. Cheng, *Hong Kong Arbitration: Cases and Materials* (Singapore/Hong Kong 1991)

Kaufmann-Kohler, Specificity of International Arbitration — Its Increasing Role in Case Law Illustrated by Geneva Court Practice on Application for Stays Imposed on Arbitral Awards, in *Recueil de Travaux Suisses* 297 (C. Reymond & E. Bucher eds. 1984)

Kerameus, Arbitrage international et ordre juridique hellénique, 1987 *Rev. Arb.* 35

Koslow, The Arbitrator's Power to Award Punitive Damages in International Contract Actions, 19 *N.Y.U. J. Int'l L. & Pol.* 203 (1986)

Kos-Rabcewicz-Zubkowski, Absolute Lack of Jurisdiction of Courts When an Undertaking to Arbitrate is Stipulated in a Contract, 24 *Inter-American Bar Association Conference: Proceedings* 143 (Panama, Feb. 4-10, 1984)

Kropholler, J., ed., *Die deutsche Rechtsprechung auf dem Gebiete des Internationalen Privatrechts im Jahre 1981, 1982, 1983, 1984, 1985* (Tübingen 1984, 1985, 1986, 1987)

La China, L'arbitrato interno e internazionale, 42 *Riv. Trim. Dir. & Proc. Civ.* 1387 (1988)

Lake & Dana, Judicial Review of Awards of the Iran-United States Claims Tribunal: Are the Tribunal's Awards Dutch? 16 *L. & Pol'y Int'l Bus.* 755 (1984)

Ledoux, La Convention de New York et la Convention européenne sur l'arbitrage international et les concessions de vente en Belgique, 91 *JT* 305 (1976)

Lessing, Sauer-Getriebe K.G. v. White Hydraulics, Inc. — Applicability of the Federal Arbitration Act to International Commercial Arbitration, 2 *Int'l Tax & Bus. Law.* 331 (1984)

Lipner, International Antitrust Law: To Arbitrate or Not to Arbitrate, 19 *Geo. Wash. J. Int'l L. & Econ.* 395 (1985)

Lowenfeld, Singapore and the Local Bar: Aberration or Ill Omen? 5 *J. Int'l Arb.* 71 (No. 3, 1988)

————, The Mitsubishi Case: Another View, 2 *Arb. Int'l* 178 (1986)

McClendon, Subject-Matter Arbitrability in International Cases: Mitsubishi Motors Closes the Circle, 11 *N.C. J. Int'l L. & Com. Reg.* 81 (1986)

McGrath, Son of Mitsubishi — Arbitration of Domestic Antitrust Disputes, 12 *Brooklyn J. Int'l L.* 693 (1986)

McKellar, To Consolidate or Not to Consolidate: A Study of Federal Court Decisions, 44 *Arb. J.* 15 (No. 4, 1989)

McPherson, Arbitration, Valuation and Certainty of Terms, 60 *Austl. L.J.* 8 (1986)

Majoros, Das Kollisionsrecht der Konventionskonflikte etabliert sich: Die Regel der maximalen Wirksamkeit in der doctrine des schweizerischen Bundesgerichts (Entscheidung Denysiana v. 14 Marz 1984), in *Festschrift für Karl H. Neumayer* 431 (W. Barfuss; B. Dutois, H. Forkel, U. Immenga & F. Majoros eds. 1985)

Miller, Consolidation in Hong Kong — the Shui On Case, 3 *Arb. Int'l* 87 (No. 1, 1987)

Mordiglia, Enforcement of Foreign Arbitration Awards in Italy, in 2 *Fifth Int'l Congress of Maritime Arbitrators* (New York 1981)

Mustill, Sir Michael J. & S. C. Boyd, *The Law and Practice of Commercial Arbitration in England* (2nd ed. 1989)

Nelson, The Arbitrability of Securities Disputes between Brokers and Customers — Phillips v. Merrill Lynch, Pierce, Fenner & Smith, Inc., 20 *Creighton L. Rev.* 1009 (1987)

Nomura, Some Aspects of the Use of Commercial Arbitration by Japanese Corporations, 33 *Osaka Univ. L. Rev.* 47 (March 1986); also in *East and West: Legal Philosophies in Japan* 50 (M. Yasaki ed. 1987)

Note, Application of the Convention on the Recognition and Enforcement of Foreign Arbitral Awards: Mitsubishi Motor Corp. v. Soler Chrysler-Plymouth, Inc., 8 *Fordham Int'l L.J.* 194 (1984)

———, Authority of United States Bankruptcy Courts to Stay International Arbitral Proceedings, 11 *Fordham Int'l L.J.* 148 (1987)

———, Challenge of Arbitrators: Is an Institutional Decision Final? 2 *Arb. Int'l* 261 (1986)

————, Enforcement of Foreign Arbitral Awards under the United Nations Convention of 1958: A Survey of Recent Federal Case Law. Notes and Comments, 11 *Md. J. Int'l L. & Trade* 13 (1987)

————, Transnational Antitrust Claims are Nonarbitrable under the Federal Arbitration Act and Art. II (1) of the Convention on the Recognition and Enforcement of Foreign Arbitral Awards: Mitsubishi v. Soler Chrysler-Plymouth, 17 *Vand. J. Transnat'l L.* 741 (1984)

O'Connell, Arbitration and Forum Selection Clauses in International Business: The Supreme Court Takes on Internationalist View, 43 *Fordham L. Rev.* 424 (1974)

Oppetit, Arbitrage juridictionnel et arbitrage contractuel: à propos d'une jurisprudence récente, 1977 *Rev. Arb.* 317

————, Le refus d'exécution d'une sentence arbitrale étrangère dans le cadre de la Convention de New York, 1971 *Rev. Arb.* 97

Park, Private Adjudicators and the Public Interest: The Expanding Scope of International Arbitration, 12 *Brooklyn J. Int'l L.* 629 (1986)

Parker School of Foreign and Comparative Law, *International Commercial Arbitration and the Courts* (Dobbs Ferry 1990)

Parnass, International Arbitration and the Comity of Error: Mitsubishi Motors Corp. v. Soler Chrysler-Plymouth, Inc., 19 *Conn. L. Rev.* 435 (1987)

Parris, J., *Casebook of Arbitration Law* (London 1976)

Poncet, Challenges to the Jurisdiction of International Arbitrators: An Important Decision of the Swiss Supreme Court, 50 *Arbitration* 156 (1984)

Poser, Arbitrability of International Securities Disputes, 12 *Brooklyn J. Int'l L.* 675 (1986)

Poudret, Jurisprudence du Tribunal cantonal vaudois en matière d'arbitrage interne et international (1980-1987), 136 *JdT* 1 (No. 1, 1988)

————, Refléxions à propos de la recevabilité du recours en réforme ou en nulité au Tribunal fédérale en matière d'arbitrage, 106 *ZSR* 765 (1987)

Punzi, Sull'inammissibilità dell'impugnazione immediata con le azioni c.d. negoziali del lodo arbitrale non dichiarato esecutivo, 26 *Rassegna dell'Arb.* 183 (1986)

Raeschke-Kessler, Die neuere Rechtsprechung des Bundesgerichtshofs zur Schiedsgerichtsbarkeit, 1 *Jahrbuch Schiedsgerichtsbarkeit* 201 (1987)

――――, Die neuere Rechtsprechung zur Schiedsgerichtsbarkeit, 2 *Jahrbuch Schiedsgerichtsbarkeit* 225 (1988)

――――, Neuere Entwicklungen im Bereich der Internationalen Schiedsgerichtsbarkeit, 41 *NJW* 3041 (1988)

Recent Developments: The Uniform Arbitration Act, 1986 *Mo. J. Disp. Res.* 169

Recent Developments: The Uniform Arbitration Act, 1987 *Mo. J. Disp. Res.* 177

Redfern, International Commercial Arbitration. Jurisdiction Denied: the Pyramid Collapses, 1986 *J. Bus. L.* 15

Rendon, Graniel & Zivy, Jurisprudence méxicaine: la validité de la clause arbitrale internationale, 1987 *Int'l Bus. L.J.* 629

Riccomagno, Recognition and Enforcement of Foreign Arbitral Awards in Italy under the New York Convention of 1958, 1 *Y.B. Mar. L.* 119 (1984)

Richard, Enforcement of Foreign Arbitral Awards under the United Nations Convention of 1958: A Survey of Recent Federal Case Law, 11 *Md. J. Int'l L. & Trade* 13 (1987)

Rogers, Forum Non Conveniens in Arbitration, 4 *Arb. Int'l* 240 (1988)

Samtleben, Arbitragem comercial no direito internacional privado Brazileiro, in *Estudos em Homenagem ao Prof. Doutor A. Ferrer-Correia* 691 (Coimbra 1986)

――――, Arbitration in Brazil, 18 *U. Miami Inter-Am. L. Rev.* 1 (1986)

Samuel, Developments in English Arbitration Law since the 1984 Antaios Decision, 5 *J. Int'l Arb.* 9 (No. 3, 1988)

Saravalle, Arbitrato internazionale e leggi antitrust: il caso Mitsubishi, 22 *Riv. Dir. Int'le Priv. & Proc.* 597 (1986)

Schlosser, Deutsche und französische Rechtsprechung zur Schiedsgerichtbarkeit 1988, 2 *Jahrbuch Schiedsgerichtsbarkeit* 241 (1988)

――――, Quelles nouvelles de l'arbitrage Outre-Rhin? 1987 *Rev. Arb.* 293

Schmidt, Präklusion und Einlassung auf die schiedsgerichtliche Verhandlung zur Hauptsache — Vertragsdenken und Prozessdenken in der jüngeren Praxis, in *Beiträge zum internationalen Verfahrensrecht und zur Schiedsgerichtsbarkeit. Festschrift für Heinrich Nagel* 373 (W. Habscheid & K. Schwab eds. 1987)

Schmitthoff, C., *Schmitthoff's Export Trade. The Law and Practice of International Trade* (8th ed. 1986)

Seidl-Hohenveldern, Austrian Public Policy and the Enforcement of Foreign Arbitral Awards, 4 *Arb. Int'l* 322 (1988)

Sethu, Abandonment in Contract, 1987 *Malayan L.J.* xli

Smit, Mitsubishi: It Is Not What It Seems to Be, 4 *J. Int'l Arb.* 7 (No. 3, 1987)

Smith, Determining the Arbitrability of International Antitrust Disputes, 8 *J. Comp. Bus. & Cap. Market L.* 197 (1986)

Sopata, Mitsubishi Motors Corp. v. Soler Chrysler-Plymouth, Inc.: International Arbitration and Antitrust Claims, 7 *Nw. J. Int'l L. & Bus.* 595 (1986)

Stanton, The Court of Appeal of Paris and Lack of Arbitral Jurisdiction, 2 *Arb. Int'l* 220 (1986)

Steyn, Arbitration and the Courts: Arbitration Systems in England and Wales and Recent Changes in Arbitration Law, 46 *Arbitration* 146 (1980)

Stipanowich, Punitive Damages in Arbitration: Garrity v. Lyle Stuart, Inc. Reconsidered, 66 *B. U. L. Rev.* 953 (1986)

Sujan, M.A., *The Law Relating to Government Arbitration* (New Delhi 1985)

Sweeney, Judicial Review of Arbitral Proceedings, in 2 *Fifth Int'l Congress of Maritime Arbitrators* (New York 1981)

Taylor, The Arbitrability of Federal Securities Claims: *Wilko's* Swan Song, 42 *U. Miami L. Rev.* 203 (1987)

Thomas, Commercial Arbitration: The Curial Law of Arbitration Proceedings, 1984 *Lloyd's Mar. & Com. L.Q.* 491 (1984)

————, The Antaios: The Nema Guidelines Reconsidered, 1985 *J. Bus. L.* 200

Trappe, Progress and Future Improvements in Arbitration, 42 *Arbitration* 98 (1975)

Tschanz, Le droit américain et la Convention de New York, in *First International Commercial Arbitration Conference: Proceedings* 249 (N. Antaki & A. Prujiner eds. 1986)

Tueller, Problems of Arbitration of International Contract Disputes and Recognition and Enforcement of Foreign Judgments in the Federal Republic of Germany: A Recent Decision of the Bundesgerichtshof, 17 *Stan. J. Int'l L.* 207 (1981)

Tupman, Challenge and Disqualification of Arbitrators in International Commercial Arbitration, 38 *Int'l & Comp. L.Q.* 26 (1989)

————, Staying Enforcement of Arbitral Awards under the New York Convention, 3 *Arb. Int'l* 223 (1987)

van den Berg, Some Recent Problems in the Practice of Enforcement under the New York and ICSID Conventions, in *Arbitration and the Courts: Fifth ICSID/AAA/ICC Colloquium* (Washington 1987)

————, When Is an Arbitral Award Non-Domestic Under the New York Convention of 1958? 6 *Pace L. Rev.* 25 (1985)

van den Berg, A. J., *The New York Arbitration Convention of 1958* (Deventer 1981)

Veeder, Multi-Party Disputes: Consolidation under English Law, 2 *Arb. Int'l* 310 (1986)

Victor & Bialos, The Arbitration of International Antitrust Claims: A Bold Supreme Court Experiment in Alternative Dispute Resolution, in *Fordham Corporate Law Institute: Annual Proceedings: Antitrust & Trade Policy in the U.S. and the European Community* 184 (New York 1986)

Vigoriti, Corte d'Appello Firenze e l'impugnazione del lodo arbitrale (1987-1989), 30 *Rassegna del'Arb.* 33 (1990)

von Mehren, From Vynior's Case to Mitsubishi: The Future of Arbitration and Public Law, 12 *Brooklyn J. Int'l L.* 583 (1986)

————, International Commercial Arbitration: The Contribution of the French Jurisprudence, 46 *La. L. Rev.* 1045 (1986)

Vulliemin, Jurisprudenzia suiza en materia de arbitraje comercial internacional, 5 *Rev. Corte Esp. Arb.* 255 (1986)

Walsh, Arbitration in International Commercial Transactions: Mitsubishi Motors Corp. v. Soler Chrysler-Plymouth, Inc. and Its Aftermath, 13 *Syracuse J. Int'l L. & Com.* 200 (1986)

Weitbrecht, US-Antitrustrecht vor internationalen Handelsschiedsgerichten (zu Mitsubishi Motors Corp. v. Soler Chrysler-Plymouth, Inc., U.S. Supreme Court, Entscheidung von 2. Juli 1985, -U.S.-, 105 S. Ct. 3346), 6 *IPRax* 313 (1986)

Wenger, Internationale Schiedsverfahren in der Schweiz. Beständigkeit und Fortentwicklung in der neueren Rechtssprechung (zu Cour de Justice de Genève vom 6.5.1983 und 3.6.1983), 1985 *Praxis des int'len Privat- und Verfahrensrechts* 54 (No. 1)

Wenger & Huber, Neue Enscheide des schweizerischen Bundesgericht zum Recht der internationalen Schiedsgerichtsbarkeit gemäss IPR-Gesetz, 11 *IPRax* 87 (1991)

Werner, A Swiss Comment on Mitsubishi, 3 *J. Int'l Arb.* 81 (No. 4, 1986)

Wetter, The Importance of Having a Connection, 3 *Arb. Int'l* 329 (1987)

Zdravkovic, Certains cas de la jurisprudence yougoslave et étrangère sur l'exécution des sentences arbitrales étrangères, in *ICCA, Fifth Int'l Arb. Congress: Proceedings C Izi* 1-16 (1975)

2.16 ARBITRAL DECISIONS

Alt, Neue Schiedssprüche zum Recht der Verstaatlichung, 35 *Österreich. Zeitschrift für Öffentliches & Völkerrecht* 265 (1985)

Audit, L'affaire Noc c/ Libyan Sun Oil Company, 1991 *Rev. Arb.* 263

Ballantyne, European Experience and Perception of Arbitration with Arab Countries, in *First Euro-Arab Arb. Conference: Proceedings* 160 (F. Kemicha ed. 1987)

Barinova, I.I., *Kommentarii sudebnoi i arbitrazhnoi praktiki po morskim delam* (Moscow 1988)

Bell, Resolution of International Trade Disputes: An Analysis of the Soviet Foreign Trade Arbitration Commission's Decisions Concerning the Doctrine of Force Majeure as an Excuse to the Performance of Private International Trade Agreements, 10 *Md. J. Int'l L. & Trade* 135 (1986)

Bernini & van den Berg, The Enforcement of Arbitral Award Against a State: The Problem of Immunity from Execution, in *Contemporary Problems in Int'l Arbitration* 359 (J.D.M. Lew ed. 1986)

Branson & Wallace, Awarding Interest in International Commercial Arbitration: Establishing a Uniform Approach, 28 *Va. J. Int'l L.* 919 (1988)

Bühring-Uhle, The IBM-Fujitsu Arbitration: A Landmark in Innovative Dispute Resolution, 2 *Am. Rev. Int'l Arb.* 113 (1991)

Cafani Panico, Clausola compromissoria e capacità delle persone giuridiche, 24 *Diritto Comunitario e degli Scambi Internazionali* 480 (1985)

Cahier, The Strengths and Weaknesses of International Arbitration Involving a State as a Party, in *Contemporary Problems in Int'l Arbitration* 241 (J.D.M. Lew ed. 1986)

Carbonneau, Etude historique et comparée de l'arbitrage: vers un droit matériel de l'arbitrage commercial international fondé sur la motivation des sentences, 36 *Rev. Int'le Droit Comp.* 727 (1984)

Carver & Hossain, An Arbitration Case Study: The Dispute That Never Was, 5 *ICSID Rev. - Foreign Investment L.J.* 311 (1990)

Catranis, Probleme der Nationalisierung ausländischer Unternehmen vor internationalen Schiedsgerichten: die Libyschen Schiedsfälle, 28 *RIW* 19 (1982)

China Maritime Arbitration Commission, *Selection of Awards and Conciliation Statements* (1984-1988), (Beijing 1989)

Cohen-Jonathan, L'arbitrage Texaco-Calasiatic contre le gouvernement Libyen: sentence au fond du 19 janvier 1977, 23 *Ann. Français Droit Int'l* 452 (1977)

Cohen, M.M., ed., *Index and Digest of the Award Service of the Society of Maritime Arbitrators,* Volumes 3A & 3B (New York 1986)

Coussirat-Coustère, V. & P. M. Eisemann, *Répertoire de la jurisprudence arbitrale internationale/Repertory of International Arbitral Jurisprudence.* Volume I: 1794-1918 (Dordrecht 1989)

Delaume, ICSID Tribunals and Provisional Measures — A Review of the Cases, 1 *ICSID Review - Foreign Investment L.J.* 392 (1986)

Derman, Nationalization and the Protective Arbitration Clause, 5 *J. Int'l Arb.* 131 (No. 4, 1988)

Dong Yougan, Arbitration Cases Concerning the Responsibilities of the Party Failing to Fulfil the Contractual Obligations, *China Patents & Trademarks* 99 (No. 3, 1985)

―――, Arbitration Cases Handled by the Foreign Economic and Trade Arbitration Commission, *China Patents and Trademarks* 101 (No. 1, 1987)

El-Kosheri & Riad, The Changing Roles in the Arbitration Process (with Regard to the Applicable Law Governing the New Generation of the Petroleum Agreements), 1 *Arab Law Q.* 475 (1986); also in *First Euro-Arab Arb. Conference: Proceedings* 253 (F. Kemicha ed. 1987)

Ferrante, Proposals for Developing an Arbitral Jurisprudence, in *ICCA, Third Int'l Arb. Congress: Proceedings* 427 (1969)

Fouchard, L'arbitrage ELF Aquitaine Iran c/ National Iranian Oil Company: une nouvelle contribution au droit international de l'arbitrage, 1984 *Rev. Arb.* 333

Friedland, ICSID's Emerging Jurisprudence, 19 *N.Y.U. J. Int'l L. & Pol.* 33 (1986)

―――, Provisional Measures in ICSID Arbitration, 2 *Arb. Int'l* 335 (1986)

Gaillard, Centre International pour le Règlement des Différends relatifs aux Investissements (C.I.R.D.): Chronique des sentences arbitrales, 114 *J. Droit Int'l (Clunet)* 135 (1987)

————, The Enforcement of ICSID Awards in France: The Decision of the Paris Court of Appeal in the SOABI Case, 5 *ICSID Rev. - Foreign Investment L.J.* 69 (1990)

Glossner, Schiedsverfahren oder Zivilprozessverfahren: Der Macao Sardine Case. The Rt. Hon. Lord Justice Kerr, 1 *Jahrbuch Schiedsgerichtsbarkeit* 251 (1987)

Goldman, L'arbitre, les conflits des lois et la *lex mercatoria*, in *First Int'l Commercial Arbitration Conference: Proceedings* 104 (N. Antaki & A. Prujiner eds. 1986)

Gruss, Enteignung und Aufhebung von Erdölkonzessionen: der Schiedsspruch im libyschen Erdölstreit, 39 *Zeitschrift für ausländisches öffentliches Recht & Völkerrecht* 782 (1979)

Harmathy, Arbitrage en Hongrie (Contrat de commission), 27 *Acta Juridica Academiae Sci. Hungaricae* 295 (1985)

Hiramoto, A Path to Resources on International Commercial Arbitration 1980-1986, 4 *Int'l Tax & Bus. Law.* 297 (1986)

International Chamber of Commerce, *L'apport de la jurisprudence arbitrale. Seminaire des 7 et 8 avril 1986* (Paris 1986)

Jarvin, Aus der Praxis des ICC Schiedsgerichtshofes, in *Recht und Praxis der Schiedsgerichtsbarkeit der Internationalen Handelskammer* 7 (K.-H. Böckstiegel ed. 1986)

————, I.C.C. Court of Arbitration Case Note, 3 *Int'l Constr. L. Rev.* 277 (1986)

————, I.C.C. Court of Arbitration Case Notes, 3 *Int'l Constr. L. Rev.* 470 (1986)

Jarvin, S. & Y. Derains, *Collection of ICC Arbitral Awards/Recueil des sentences arbitrales de la CII, 1974-1985* (Paris & Deventer 1990)

Kahn, Contrats d'Etat et nationalisation: les apports de la sentence arbitrale du 24 mars 1982, 109 *J. Droit Int'l* (Clunet) 844 (1982)

Kasalova, E., T. Donner, J. Hrivnak & M. Stastny, *Thirty Years of the Arbitration Court of the Czechoslovak Chamber of Commerce and Industry in Prague* (Prague 1981)

Kerr, Arbitration v. Litigation. The Macao Sardine Case, 15 *Int'l Bus. Law.* 152 (1987); 3 *Arb. Int'l* 79 (No. 1, 1987).

Krafzik, B., *Die Spruchpraxis der Hanseatischen Schiedsgerichte* (Berlin 1974)

Lake & Dana, Judicial Review of Awards of the Iran-United States Claims Tribunal: Are the Tribunal's Awards Dutch? 16 *L. & Pol'y Int'l Bus.* 755 (1984)

Lalive, Contracts Between a State or a State Agency and a Foreign Company: Theory and Practice: Choice of Law in a New Arbitration Case, 13 *Int'l & Comp. L.Q.* 987 (1964)

Lesguillons, Pratique arbitrale concernant la "force majeure" et la "frustration", 27 *Diritto Comunitario e degli Scambi Internazionali* 773 (1988)

Mann, The AMINOIL Arbitration, 54 *Brit. Y.B. Int'l L.* 313 (1983)

Maslov, Awards of the Maritime Arbitration Commission, 6 *Ga. J. Int'l & Comp. L.* 529 (1976)

Medalie, The Libyan Producers' Agreement Arbitration: Developing Innovative Procedures in a Complex Multiparty Arbitration, 7 *J. Int'l Arb.* 7 (No. 2, 1990)

Minakov, A.I., *Arbitrazhnye soglashenia i praktika rassmotreniya vneshneekonomicheskikh sporov* (Moscow 1985)

Nomura, Some Aspects of the Use of Commercial Arbitration by Japanese Corporations, 33 *Osaka Univ. L. Rev.* 47 (March 1986); also in *East and West: Legal Philosophies in Japan* 50 (M. Yasaki ed. 1987)

Note, Arbitration under the Auspices of the ICSID: Implications of the Decision on Jurisdiction in Alcoa Minerals of Jamaica, Inc. v. Government of Jamaica, 17 *Harv. Int'l L.J.* 90 (1976)

―――, Confidentiality in ICSID Arbitration After AMCO ASIA CORP. v. INDONESIA: Watchword or White Elephant? 10 *Fordham Int'l L. J.* 93 (1986)

Orlov, Arbitration Procedure in East-West Trade, 55 *Nordic J. Int'l L.* 310 (1986)

Pajardi, P., *L'arbitrato. Col massimario completo comentato della giurisprudenza di legittimità e di merito dal 1980 al 1988* (Milan 1990)

Pellonpää, & Fitzmaurice, Taking of Property in the Practice of the Iran-United States Claims Tribunal, 19 *Neth. Y.B. Int'l L.* 53 (1988)

Popov, K., *Praktika na Arbitrazhniia sud pri Bulgarskata Turgovsko-promishlena palata, 1981-1985g.* (Sofia 1987)

Praendl, Measure of Damages in International Commercial Arbitration, 23 *Stan. J. Int'l L.* 263 (1987)

Rabinovich, The Procedure for Signing Transactions with Soviet Foreign Trade Organizations, 22 *Int'l Law.* 143 (1988)

Raeschke-Kessler & Bühler, Aufsicht über den Schiedsrichter durch den ICC-Schiedsgerichtshof (Paris) und rechtliches Gehör der Parteien, 8 *ZIP* 1157 (1987)

Rambaud, L'annulation des sentences Klöckner et Amco, 32 *Ann. Français Droit Int'l* 259 (1986)

Rand, Hornick & Friedland, ICSID's Emerging Jurisprudence: The Scope of ICSID's Jurisdiction, 19 *N.Y.U. J. Int'l L. & Pol.* 33 (1986)

Redfern, The Arbitration Between the Government of Kuwait and Aminoil, 55 *Brit. Y.B. Int'l L.* 65 (1984)

Report on the Evidence and Reasons of the Award between Johannis Orlandos & Andreas Luriottis, Greek Deputies, of the One Part, and Le Roy, Bayard & Co., and G.G. & S. Howland, of the Other Part, By the Arbitrators. New York, printed by W.E. Dean, 1826.

Robert, Observations sur une sentence arbitrale internationale: sentence rendue le 3 juillet 1958 par la Commision Arbitrale du Commerce Extérieur à Moscou dans le litige "Arbitrage petrolier Israel-Soirets," 1960 *Rev. Arb.* 76 & 92 (text of the award)

Schmidt, Arbitration under the Auspices of the International Centre for Settlement of Investment Disputes (ICSID): Implications of the Decision on Jurisdiction in Alcoa Minerals of Jamaica, 17 *Harv. Int'l L. Rev.* 90 (1976)

Schwebel, S. M., *International Arbitration: Three Salient Problems* (Cambridge 1987)

Seppala, The Pyramids of Egypt Case, 2 *Int'l Constr. L. Rev.* 180

Shifman, Maritime International Nominees Establishment v. Republic of Guinea: Effect on U.S. Jurisdiction of an Agreement by a Foreign Sovereign to Arbitrate before the ICSID, 16 *J. Int'l L. & Econ.* 451 (1982)

Smit, The Carte Blanche Case, 1 *Am. Rev. Int'l Arb.* 172 (1990)

Sornarajah, M., *International Commercial Arbitration: The Problem of State Contracts* (Singapore 1990)

Stewart, The Iran-United States Claims Tribunal: A Review of Developments 1983-84, 16 *L. & Pol'y Int'l Bus.* 677 (1984)

Stewart & Sherman, Developments at the Iran-U.S. Claims Tribunal: 1981-1983, 24 *Va. J. Int'l L.* 1 (1984)

Stork, The Use of Arbitration in Copyright Disputes: IBM v. Fujitsu, 3 *High Technology L.J.* 241 (1988)

Straatmann, K. & P. Ulmer, eds., *Handelsrechtliche Schiedsgerichts-Praxis. Sammlung von Schiedssprüchen unter Einschuss von Urteilen und Texten zur Schiedsgerichtsbarkeit,* 2 vols. (Cologne 1975)

Taliadoros, Arbitral Award Given in Athens: SA Industrielle et Commerciale Aluminium de Grece v. The Public Enterprise for Electricity of Greece, 15 *Int'l Bus. Law.* 360 (1987)

Tanimoto, Necessity of Establishing of Custom and of Arbitration Award Based on the Custom, in *ICCA, Fourth Int'l Arb. Congress: Proceedings* 826 (1972)

Tesón, State Contracts and Oil Expropriations: The Aminoil-Kuwait Arbitration, 24 *Va. J. Int'l L.* 323 (1984)

Timmermann, F.H., ed., *Rechtssprechung kaufmännischer Schiedsgerichte: Sammlung von Schiedssprüchen unter Einschluss von Urteilen und Texten zur Schiedsgerichtsbarkeit.* Vol. 4, (Baden-Baden 1988) [Continuation of K. Straatmann & P. Ulmer, eds., Handelsrechtliche Schiedsgerichts-Praxis]

Tschanz, Contributions of the Aminoil Award to the Law of State Contract, 18 *Int'l Law.* 245 (1984)

Tupman, Case Studies in the Jurisdiction of the International Centre for Settlement of Investment Disputes, 35 *Int'l & Comp. L. Q.* 813 (1986)

USSR Chamber of Commerce and Industry, *Collected Arbitration Cases* (Moscow 1972-)

Varma, Petroleum Concessions in International Arbitration: Texaco Overseas Petroleum Company v. Libyan Arab Republic, 18 *Colum. J. Transnat'l L.* 259 (1979)

von Mehren & Kourides, International Arbitration Between States and Foreign Private Parties: The Libyan Nationalization Case, 75 *Am. J. Int'l L.* 476 (1981)

————, The Libyan Nationalizations: TOPCO/CALASIATIC v. Libyan Arbitration, 12 *Natural Resources Law.* 419 (1979)

White, Expropriation of the Libyan Oil Concessions: Two Conflicting International Arbitrations, 30 *Int'l & Comp. L.Q.* 1 (1981)

Wilkinson, Judicial Review of Foreign Arbitral Awards on Antitrust Matters After Mitsubishi Motors, 26 *Colum. J. Transnat'l L.* 407 (1988)

Wisniewski, Awards of the Court of Arbitration at the Polish Chamber of Foreign Trade in Warsaw, 10 *Polish Y.B. Int'l L.* 269 (1980)

————, Awards of the Court of Arbitration at the Polish Chamber of Foreign Trade, 15 *Polish Y.B. Int'l L.* 301 (1986)

————, Awards of the Court of Arbitration at the Polish Chamber of Foreign Trade, 16 *Polish Y.B. Int'l L.* 191 (1987)

————, Awards of the Court of Arbitration at the Polish Chamber of Foreign Trade in Warsaw, 17 *Polish Y.B. Int'l L.* 251 (1988)

————, The Practice of the Court of Arbitration at the Polish Chamber of Foreign Trade: Major Trends and Problems as Illustrated by Chosen Awards, 1989 *Int'l Bus. L.J.* 1011

3. INTERNATIONAL ARBITRATION INSTITUTIONS AND RULES

3.01 INTERNATIONAL ARBITRATION INSTITUTIONS AND RULES GENERALLY

Alcala Zamora, En torno a la internacionalización del arbitraje de derecho privado: dificultades a superar, in *ICCA, Third Int'l Arb. Congress: Proceedings* 369(1969)

Atallah, The Arab Regional Arbitration Centres, in *First Euro-Arab Arb. Conference: Proceedings* 66 (F. Kemicha ed. 1987)

Carbonneau, Arbitral Adjudication: A Comparative Assessment of Its Remedial and Substantive Status in Transnational Commerce, 19 *Tex. Int'l L.J.* 33 (1984)

Delaume, L'arbitrage transnational et les tribunaux nationaux, 111 *J. Droit Int'l (Clunet)* 521 (1984)

Franks, An Approach to the Development of Model Rules of International Commercial Arbitration through an International Arbitration Commission, in *ICCA, Fifth Int'l Arb. Congress: Proceedings* C Ic 1-5 (1975)

Graving, The International Commercial Arbitration Institutions: How Good a Job Are They Doing? 4 *Am. U.J. Int'l L. & Pol'y* 319 (1989)

Haddad, The Amman Convention of 1987 on Commercial Arbitration, 1 *Am. Rev. Int'l Arb.* 132 (1990)

————, Inter-Arab Conventions on Commercial Arbitration, in *Euro-Arab Arbitration III* 48 (F. Kemicha ed. 1991)

Katona, Ad hoc Arbitration Rules: Similarities and Differences. A Comparative Review, 3 *Questions of Int'l Law: Hungarian Perspectives* 93 (H. Bokor-Szegö ed. 1986)

Kos-Rabcewicz-Zubkowski, L. & P.L. Davidson, *Commercial Arbitration Institutions: An International Directory and Guide* (New York 1986)

Lew, The Internationalisation of Arbitration — The Answer to Unification, in *ICCA,—— Fifth Int'l Arb. Congress: Proceedings* C In 1-18 (1975)

Matray, La fondation de Francarbi, 1991 *Rev. Arb.* 132

Schütze, R., D. Tscherning & W. Wais, *Handbuch des Schiedsverfahrens. Praxis der deutschen und internationalen Schiedsgerichtsbarkeit* (2nd ed. Berlin 1990)

3.02 INTER-AMERICAN COMMERCIAL ARBITRATION COMMISSION

Briseño Sierra, El arbitraje comercial en México y las leyes-tipo internacionales, 1 *Rev. Corte Esp. Arb.* 67 (1984)

Domke, Inter-American Commercial Arbitration, 4 *Miami L.Q.* 425 (1950)

Eyzaguirre Echeverria, Arbitration in Latin America: The Experience of the Inter-American Commercial Arbitration Commission, 4 *Int'l Tax & Bus. Law.* 288 (1986)

Eyzaguirre Echeverria & Siqueiros, Arbitration in Latin America, in *Arbitration in Settlement of International Commercial Disputes Involving the Far East and Arbitration in Combined Transportation* 81 (P. Sanders ed. 1989)

Goldman, Arbitration and Transfer of Technology in Latin America, in *Arbitration and the Licensing Process* 5-29 (R. Goldscheider & M. de Haas eds. 1984-)

Kos-Rabcewicz-Zubkowski, L'arbitrage de la Commission Interaméricaine d'Arbitrage Commercial, in *First Int'l Commercial Arbitration Conference: Proceedings* 87 (N. Antaki & A. Prujiner, eds. 1986)

―――, Les conventions interaméricaines sur l'arbitrage commercial et la Commission interaméricaine d'arbitrage commercial, 1983 *Rev. Arb.* 411

―――, Panamerykanskie konwencje dotyczace arbitrazu handlowego, 44 *Panstwo i Prawo* 84 (No. 3, 1989)

Kos-Rabcewicz-Zubkowski, L. & P.L. Davidson, *Commercial Arbitration Institutions: An International Directory and Guide* (New York 1986)

Malpica de Lamadrid, El arbitraje internacional y el derecho marítimo, in *El Arbitraje Comercial Internacional* 413 (Mexico 1983)

Norberg, General Introduction to Inter-American Commercial Arbitration, in *Int'l Handbook Com. Arb.* (A. van den Berg, gen. ed. 1984), Suppl. 12, January 1991

―――, Institutional Arbitration in New York: The Inter-American Commercial Arbitration Commission, 3 *Forum New York* 4 (No. 1, 1986)

―――, Inter-American Commercial Arbitration, 1 *Law. Am.* 25 (1969)

————, Inter-American Commercial Arbitration Revisited, 7 *Law. Am.* 275 (1975)

————, Inter-American Commercial Arbitration: Unicorn or Beast of Burden? 5 *Pace L. Rev.* 607 (1985)

————, Recent Developments in Inter-American Commercial Arbitration, 13 *Case W. Res. J. Int'l L.* 107 (1981)

————, Recent Developments in Inter-American Commercial Arbitration, 12 *Nw. J. Int'l L. & Bus.* 86 (1991)

Norberg C., *Inter-American Commercial Arbitration* (Dobbs Ferry and Paris 1989)

Shifman, UNCITRAL Rules as Adopted by the Inter-American Commercial Arbitration Commission, in 3 *W.A.R.* 3205 (H. Smit & V. Pechota eds. 1987)

Siqueiros, Panórama actual del arbitraje comercial internacional, in *El Arbitraje Comercial Internacional* 135 (Mexico 1983)

Trigueros & Vasquez Pando, La Convención Interamericana sobre Arbitraje Comercial Internacional, 8 *Revista de Investigaciones Jurídicas* 289 (1984)

3.03 INTERNATIONAL CENTRE FOR THE SETTLEMENT OF INVESTMENT DISPUTES

Agyemang, African States and ICSID Arbitration, 21 *Comp. & Int'l L.J. Southern Afr.* 177 (1988)

Aksen, G. & R. von Mehren, eds., *International Arbitration Between Private Parties and Governments* (New York 1982)

Amerasinghe, The ICSID and Development through the Multinational Corporation, 9 *Vand. J. Transnat'l L.* 793 (1976)

————, Dispute Settlement Machinery in Relations Between States and Multinational Enterprises — with Particular Reference to the ICSID, 11 *Int'l Law.* 45 (1977)

————, How to Use the International Centre for Settlement of Investment Disputes by Reference to Its Model Clauses, 13 *Indian J. Int'l L.* 530 (1973)

————, Jurisdiction Ratione Personae under the Convention on the Settlement of Investment Disputes between States and Nationals of Other States, 47 *Brit. Y.B. Int'l L.* 227 (1974)

————, Submissions to the Jurisdiction of the International Centre for Settlement of Investment Disputes, 5 *J. Mar. L. & Com.* 211 (1974)

————, The International Centre for Settlement of Investment Disputes and Development through the Multinational Corporations, 9 *Vand. J. Transnat'l L.* 793 (1976)

————, The Jurisdiction of the International Centre for Settlement of Investment Disputes, 19 *Indian J. Int'l L.* 166 (1979)

Baker & Ryans, The International Centre for Settlement of Investment Disputes (ICSID), 10. *J. World Trade L.* 65 (1976)

Baker & Yoder, ICSID Arbitration and the U.S. Multilateral Corporation: An Alternative Dispute Resolution Method in International Business, 5 *J. Int'l Arb.* 81 (No. 4, 1988)

Bernardini, Considérations pratiques sur le règlement des différends relatifs aux investissements: le point de vue des utilisateurs, 21 *Rassegna dell'Arb.* 7 (1981)

————, Le prime esperienze arbitrali del Centro Internazionale per il Regolamento delle Controversie relative ad investimenti, 17 *Riv. Dir. Int'le Priv. & Proc.* 29 (1981)

Bliesener, La compétence du CIRDI dans la pratique arbitrale, 68 *Rev. Droit Int'l & Droit Comp.* 95 (1991)

Branson & Tupman, Selecting an Arbitral Forum: A Guide to Cost-Effective International Arbitration, 24 *Va. J. Int'l L.* 917 (1984)

Broches, Arbitration Clauses and Institutional Arbitration-ICSID: A Special Case, in *A.I.A., Essays in Memoriam Eugenio Minoli* 69 (Turin 1974)

————, Arbitration of Investment Disputes, 1984(1) *Malayan L.J.* at lxxiii

————, Awards Rendered Pursuant to the ICSID Convention: Binding Force, Finality, Recognition, Enforcement, Execution, 2 *ICSID Rev. - Foreign Investment L.J.* 287 (1987)

————, Bilateral Investment Protection Treaties and Arbitration of Investment Disputes, in *The Art of Arbitration* 63 (J. Schultsz & A. van den Berg, eds. 1982)

————, L'évolution du C.I.R.D.I., 1979 *Rev. Arb.* 323

————, Settlement of Disputes Arising out of Investment in Developing Countries, 11 *Int'l Bus. Law.* 206 (1984)

————, The Additional Facility of the ICSID, 4 *Y.B. Com. Arb.* 373 (1979)

————, The Experience of the International Centre for Settlement of Investment Disputes, in *International Investment Disputes* 75 (S. Rubun & R. Nelson eds. 1985)

————, The International Centre for Settlement of Investment Disputes, in *Handbook of Institutional Arbitration in International Trade* 1 (E. Cohn, M. Domke & F. Eisemann eds. 1977)

Buffenstein, Foreign Investment Arbitration and Joint Ventures, 5 *N.C.J. Int'l L. & Com. Reg.* 191 (1980)

Cherian, J., *Investment Contracts and Arbitration. The World Bank Convention on the Settlement of Investment Disputes* (Leiden 1975)

Chong Su Yun, The Convention on the Settlement of Investment Disputes — Commentary and Forecast, 11 *Malaya L. Rev.* 287 (1969)

Chukwumerije, ICSID Arbitration and Sovereign Immunity, 19 *Anglo-Am. L. Rev.* 166 (1990)

de Bérranger, L'article 52 de la Convention de Washington du 18 mars 1965 et les premiers enseignements de sa pratique, 1988 *Rev. Arb.* 95

Delaume, Arbitration with Governments: Domestic and International, 17 *Int'l Law.* 687 (1983)

————, Foreign Sovereign Immunity: Impact on Arbitration, 38 *Arb. J.* 34 (No. 2, 1983)

————, ICSID Arbitration, in *Contemporary Problems in International Arbitration* 23 (J.D.M. Lew ed. 1986)

————, ICSID Arbitration Proceedings, 4 *Int'l Tax & Bus. Law.* 218 (1986)

————, ICSID Arbitration Proceedings: Practical Aspects, 5 *Pace L. Rev.* 563 (1985)

————, ICSID Arbitration and the Courts, 77 *Am. J. Int'l L.* 784 (1983)

————, ICSID Arbitration in Practice, 2 *Int'l Tax & Bus. Law.* 58 (1984)

————, ICSID Arbitration: Practical Considerations, 1 *J. Int'l Arb.* 101 (No. 2, 1984)

————, ICSID and the Transnational Financial Community, 1 *ICSID Rev.-Foreign Investment L.J.* 237 (1986)

————, ICSID Tribunals and Provisional Measures — A Review of the Cases, 1 *ICSID Rev. - Foreign Investment L.J.* 392 (1986)

————, Judicial Decisions Related to Sovereign Immunity and Transnational Arbitration, 2 *ICSID* Rev. - *Foreign Investment L.J.* 403 (1987)

————, Le Centre International pour le Règlement des Différends Relatifs aux Investissements (CIRDI), 109 *J. Droit Int'l (Clunet)* 775 (1982)

————, Le CIRDI et l'immunité des Etats, 1983 *Rev. Arb.* 143

————, Les clauses CIRDI et les procédures s'y rapportant, 22 *Rassegna dell'Arb.* 17 (1982)

————, Sovereign Immunity and International Arbitration, 3 *Arb. Int'l* 28 (No. 1, 1987)

————, Sovereign Immunity and Transnational Arbitration, in *Contemporary Problems in Int'l Arbitration* 313 (J.D.M. Lew ed. 1986)

————, State Contracts and Transnational Arbitration, 75 *Am. J. Int'l L.* 784 (1981)

Delaume, G., *Transnational Contracts, Applicable Law and Settlement of Disputes: A Study in Conflict Avoidance* (Dobbs Ferry, NY 1975)

Derman, Nationalization and the Protective Arbitration Clause, 5 *J. Int'l Arb.* 131 (No. 4, 1988)

Feldman, The Annulment Proceedings and the Finality of ICSID Arbitral Awards, 2 *ICSID Rev. - Foreign Investment L.J.* 85 (1987)

Forrestal, Examples of and Reasons for Increased Use of International Arbitration, in *International Arbitration between Private Parties and Governments* 15 (G. Aksen & R. von Mehren eds. 1982)

Friedland, ICSID and Court-Ordered Provisional Remedies: An Update, 4 *Arb. Int'l* 161 (1988)

————, ICSID's Emerging Jurisprudence, 19 *N.Y.U. J. Int'l L. & Pol.* 33 (1986)

————, Provisional Measures in ICSID Arbitration, 2 *Arb. Int'l* 335 (1986)

Gaillard, Centre International pour le Règlement des Différends relatifs aux Investissements (C.I.R.D.): Chronique des sentences arbitrales, 114 *J. Droit Int'l (Clunet)* 135 (1987)

————, Quelques obsérvations sur la rédaction des clauses d'arbitrage CIRDI, 97 *Penant* 291 (1987)

————, Some Notes on the Drafting of ICSID Arbitration Clauses, 3 *ICSID Rev. - Foreign Investment L.J.* 136 (1988)

————, The Enforcement of ICSID Awards in France: The Decision of the Paris Court of Appeal in the SOABI Case, 5 *ICSID Rev. - Foreign Investment L.J.* 69 (1990)

Giardina, L'esecuzione delle sentenze CIRDI, 22 *Rassegna dell'Arb.* 69 (1982)

————, L'exécution des sentences du Centre international pour le règlement des différends relatifs aux investissements, 71 *Rev. Crit. Droit Int'l Privé* 273 (1982)

————, La legge regolatrice dei contratti di investimento nel sistema ICSID, 18 *Riv. Dir. Int'le Priv. & Proc.* 677 (1982)

————, The International Center for Settlement of Investment Disputes between States and Nationals of Other States (ICSID), in *Essays on International Commercial Arbitration* 214 (P. Sarcevic ed. 1989)

Golsong, Dispute Settlement in Recently Negotiated Bilateral Investment Treaties — The Reference to the ICSID Additional Facility, in *Realism in Law-Making: Essays on International Law in Honour of Willem Riphagen* 35 (A. Bos & H. Siblezs eds. 1986)

————, Schwächung des Schiedsdispositifs bei Investitionsstreitigkeiten. Das ICSID-Annulierungsverfahren und seine mögliche Fortentwicklung, in *Festschrift für Walther J. Habscheid* 113 (W. Lindacher, D. Pfaff et al. eds. 1989)

Gonzalez & Padilla, The International Centre for the Settlement of Investment Disputes: An Assessment from the Philippine Perspective, 59 *Philippine L.J.* 222 (1984)

Gopal, International Centre on the Settlement of Investment Disputes, 14 *Case W. Res. J. Int'l L.* 591 (1982)

————, Rules of the International Centre for Settlement of Investment Disputes, 1982 *Malayan L.J.* cxviii

Hahn, Die Anerkennung und Vollstreckung von ICSID-Schiedssprüchen in Frankreich, 37 *RIW* 459 (1991)

Kemby, International Centre for the Settlement of Investment Disputes (ICSID), in 4 *Modern Legal Systems Cyclopedia* 699 (K. R. Redden gen. ed. 1984)

Kos-Rabcewicz-Zubkowski, L. & P.L. Davidson, *Commercial Arbitration Institutions: An International Directory and Guide* (New York 1986)

Lalive, Some Threats to International Investment Arbitration, 1 *ICSID Rev. - Foreign Investment L.J.* 26 (1986)

————, The First 'World Bank' Arbitration (Holiday Inns v. Morocco) — Some Legal Problems, 51 *Brit. Y.B. Int'l L.* 123 (1980)

Lattanzi, Convenzione de Washington sulle controversie relative ad investimenti e invalidità delle sentenze arbitrali, 70 *Riv. Dir. Int'le* 521 (1987)

Leahy & Orentlicher, Enforcement of Arbitral Awards Issued by the Additional Facility of the International Centre for Settlement of Investment Disputes (ICSID), 2 *J. Int'l Arb.* 15 (No. 3, 1985)

Lelewer, International Commercial Arbitration as a Model for Resolving Treaty Disputes, 21 *N.Y.U. J. Int'l L. & Pol.* 379 (1989)

Lerner, Profiles of Selected Arbitral Agencies and Comparison of Their Rules and the UNCITRAL Arbitration Rules, in *Arbitration and the Licensing Process* 2-3 (R. Goldscheider & M. de Haas eds. 1984-)

Marchais, Judicial Attitudes Towards Decisions Taken by Arbitral Institutions — Current Trends — the Experience of ICSID, in *Arbitration and the Courts: Fifth ICSID/AAA/ICC Colloquium* (Washington 1987)

————, Mésures provisoires et autonomie du système d'arbitrage CIRDI, 14 *Droit et Pratique du Com. Int'l* 275 (1988)

————, Setting up the Initial Procedural Framework in ICSID Arbitration, 5 *News from ICSID* 5 (No. 1, Winter 1988)

Masood, Provisional Measures of Protection in Arbitration under the World Bank Convention, 1 *Delhi L. Rev.* 138 (1972)

Migliorino, La surroga dello stato all'investitore privato indennizzato negli accordi bilaterali sugli investimenti, 22 *Riv. Dir. Int'le Priv. & Proc.* 275 (1986)

Niggemann, The ICSID Klöckner v. Cameroon Award: The Dissenting Opinion, 1 *J. Int'l Arb.* 331 (1984)

————, Die dritte Annulierung eines ICSID-Schiedsspruches — Die Entscheidung in Sachen Mine v. Guinea, 11 *IPRax* 77 (1991)

————, Zuständigkeitsprobleme der Weltbankschiedsgerichtsbarkeit im Licht der bisherigen Schiedsverfahren, 5 *IPRax* 185 (1985)

Note, Arbitration under the Auspices of the ICSID: Implications of the Decision on Jurisdiction in Alcoa Minerals of Jamaica, Inc. v. Government of Jamaica, 17 *Harv. Int'l L.J.* 90 (1976)

————, Confidentiality in ICSID Arbitration After AMCO Asia Corp. v. Indonesia: Watchword or White Elephant? 10 *Fordham Int'l L. J.* 93 (1986)

O'Keefe, The International Centre for Settlement of Investment Disputes, *Yearbook of World Affairs* 286 (1980)

O'Neill, American Legal Developments in Commercial Arbitration Involving Foreign States and State Enterprises, 6 *J. Int'l Arb.* 117 (No. 1, 1989)

Ott, R., *Die Beilegung von Investitionsstreitigkeiten durch Schiedsgerichte: Die Praxis von ICSID* (Bern 1983)

Ouakrat, La pratique du CIRDI, 13 *Droit et Pratique du Com. Int'l* 273 (1987)

Parra, The International Centre for the Settlement of Investment Disputes and Immunity of Arbitrators, in *The Immunity of Arbitrators* 105 (J.D.M. Lew ed. 1990)

Paulsson, Les obligations des partenaires dans un accord de développement économique: la sentence arbitrale Cameroun c/ Klöckner, 1984 *Rev. Arb.* 19

————, The ICSID Klöckner v. Cameroon Award: The Duties of Partners in North-South Economic Development Agreements, 1 *J. Int'l Arb.* 145 (1984)

Pirrung, J., *Die Schiedsgerichtsbarkeit nach dem Weltbankübereinkommen für Investitionsstreitigkeiten* (Berlin 1972)

Pirrwitz, Annulment of Arbitral Awards Under Article 52 of the Washington Convention on the Settlement of Investment Disputes Between States and Nationals of Other States, 23 *Tex. Int'l L.J.* 73 (1988)

Rambaud, Deux arbitrages C.I.R.D.I., 30 *Ann. Français Droit Int'l* 391 (1984)

————, L'annulation des sentences Klöckner et Amco, 32 *Ann. Français de Droit Int'l* 259 (1986)

————, Note sur l'extension du 'système CIRDI' 29 *Ann. Français Droit Int'l* 290 (1983)

————, Premiers enseignements des arbitrages du CIRDI, 28 *Ann. Français Droit Int'l* 471 (1982)

Rand, Hornick & Friedland, ICSID's Emerging Jurisprudence: The Scope of ICSID's Jurisdiction, 19 *N.Y.U. J. Int'l L. & Pol.* 33 (1986)

Razafindralambo, Le CIRDI: point de vue des Etats du Tiers-Monde, 22 *Rassegna dell'Arb.* 57 (1982)

Redfern, ICSID - Losing Its Appeal? 3 *Arb. Int'l* 98 (1987)

131

Regli, J.-P., *Contrats d'Etat et arbitrage entre Etats et personnes privées* (Geneva 1983)

Reisman, The Breakdown of the Control Mechanism in ICSID Arbitration, 1989 *Duke L.J.* 739 (1989)

Ruiz del Rio, Arbitration Clauses in International Loans, 4 *J. Int'l Arb.* 45 (No. 3, 1987)

Ryans & Baker, The International Centre for Settlement of Investment Disputes (ICSID), 10 *J. World Trade L.* 65 (1976)

Sacerdoti, La convenzione di Washington del 1965: bilancio di un ventennio del'ICSID, 23 *Riv. Dir. Int'le Priv. & Proc.* 13 (1987)

Schatz, The Effect of the Annulment Decisions in AMCO v. Indonesia and Klöckner v. Cameroon on the Future of the International Centre for the Settlement of Investment Disputes, 3 *Am. U. J. Int'l L. & Pol'y* 481 (1988)

Schlechtriem, Zur Überprufbarkeit von ICSID-Schiedssprüchen: Die Aufhebungsentscheidung im Falle Klöckner/Kamerun, 6 *IPRax* 69 (1986)

Schmidt, Arbitration under the Auspices of the International Centre for Settlement of Investment Disputes (ICSID): Implications of the Decision on Jurisdiction in Alcoa Minerals of Jamaica, 17 *Harv. Int'l L. Rev.* 90 (1976)

Shifman, Maritime International Nominees Establishment v. Republic of Guinea: Effect on U.S. Jurisdiction of an Agreement by a Foreign Sovereign to Arbitrate before the ICSID, 16 *J. Int'l L. & Econ.* 451 (1982)

———, The Rules of the International Centre for Settlement of Investment Disputes, in 3 *W.A.R.* 3387 (H. Smit & V. Pechota eds. 1987)

Shihata, Le CIRDI et les pays en voie de développement et plus particulièrement les pays arabes, in *First Euro-Arab Arb. Conference: Proceedings* 89 (F. Kemicha ed. 1987)

———, Obstacles Facing International Arbitration, 4 *Int'l Tax & Bus. Law.* 209 (1986)

———, The Role of ICSID and the Projected Multilateral Investment Guarantee Agency (MIGA), 41 *Aussenwirtschaft* 105 (1986)

———, The Settlement of Disputes Regarding Foreign Investment: The Role of the World Bank, with Particular Reference to ICSID and MIGA, 1 *Am. U.J. Int'l L. & Pol'y* 97 (1986); also 1 *Arab Law Q.* 265 (1986)

————, Towards a Greater Depolitization of Investment Disputes: The Roles of ICSID and MIGA, 1 *ICSID Rev. - Foreign Investment L.J.* 1 (1986)

Sinagra, A., *L'arbitrato commerciale internazionale nel sistema del CIRDI ed i suoi recenti sviluppi* (Padova 1984)

Soley, ICSID Implementation: An Effective Alternative to International Conflict, 19 *Int'l Law.* 521 (1985)

Szasz, Using the New International Centre for Settlement of Investment Disputes, 7 *East Afr. L.J.* 128 (1971)

Toop, S., *Mixed International Arbitration: Studies in Arbitration Between States and Private Persons* (Cambridge 1990)

Toriello, The Additional Facility of the International Centre for Settlement of Investment Disputes, 4 *Italian Y.B. Int'l L.* 59 (1978-79)

Tupman, Case Studies in the Jurisdiction of the International Centre for Settlement of Investment Disputes, 35 *Int'l & Comp. L. Q.* 813 (1986)

————, Challenge and Disqualification of Arbitrators in International Commercial Arbitration, 38 *Int'l & Comp. L.Q.* 26 (1989)

United Nations Centre on Transnational Corporations, *Bilateral Investment Treaties* (New York 1988) [United Nations Publication Sales No. E.88.II.A.1]

Vitanyi, Quelques refléxions sur la Convention pour le règlement des différends relatifs aux investissements entre Etats et ressortissants d'autres Etats, 47/48 *Annuaire de l'Association des Auditeurs et Anciens Auditeurs de l'Académie de Droit Int'l de la Haye* 139 (1977-78)

————, Quelques refléxions sur la Convention pour le règlement des différends relatifs aux investissements entre Etats et ressortissants d'autres Etats, in *New Directions in International Law: Essays in Honour of Wolfgang Abendroth* 193 (Frankfurt 1982)

Vuylstehe, Foreign Investment Protection and ICSID Arbitration, 4 *Ga. J. Int'l & Comp. L.* 343 (1974)

3.04 INTERNATIONAL CHAMBER OF COMMERCE

Aden, Auslegung und Revisibilität ausländischer AGB am Beispiel der Schiedsverfahrensordnung der Internationalen Handelskammer, 35 *RIW* 607 (1989)

————, Der Verfahrensverstoss des Schiedsgerichtsinstituts: Überlegungen zur Änderung der ICC-Schiedsgerichtsordnung zum 1.1.1988, 34 *RIW* 757 (1988)

Aden, M., *Internationale Handelsschiedsgerichtsbarkeit. Kommentar zu den Verfahrensordnungen* (Heidelberg 1988)

Arnaldez, Un centre international: La Chambre de Commerce Internationale, 1990 *Rev. Arb.* 249

Arnaldez & Jakande, Les amendments apportés au Règlement d'arbitrage de la Chambre de commerce internationale (C.C.I.), 1988 *Rev. Arb.* 67

Arnaldez & Schäfer, Le règlement de référé pré-arbitrale de la Chambre de commerce internationale, 1990 *Rev. Arb.* 835

Bannicke, International Chamber of Commerce Court of Arbitration, 23 *Alta. L. Rev.* 51 (1985)

Barclay, Rules for the Settlement of International Disputes, 42 *Arbitration* 31 (1975)

Bentil, Judicial Intervention and International Commercial Arbitration, 130 *Solicitors' J.* 191 (1986)

Beyly, The Manager and Arbitration, 3 *J. Int'l Arb.* 7 (No. 1, 1986)

Blessing, International Arbitration Procedures, 17 *Int'l Bus. Law.* 408 and 451 (1989)

————, The Major Western and Soviet Arbitration Rules: A Comparison of the Rules of UNCITRAL, UNCITRAL Model Law, LCIA, ICC, AAA and the Rules of the USSR Chamber of Commerce and Industry, 6 *J. Int'l Arb.* 7 (No. 3, 1989)

Böckstiegel, Arbitration of Disputes Between States and Private Enterprises in the International Chamber of Commerce, 59 *Am. J. Int'l L.* 579 (1965)

————, The New Arbitration Rules of the International Chamber of Commerce, in *Internationales Recht und Witschaftsordnung.Festschrift für F.A. Mann* 575 (Munich 1977)

Böckstiegel, K.-H., ed., *Recht und Praxis der Schiedsgerichtsbarkeit der Internationalen Handelskammer* (Cologne 1986)

Bond, The 1986 Reform of ICC's Practice Relating to Costs and Payments, 2 *Arb. Int'l* 358 (1986)

————, Neuregelung der Kostenfestsetzung und Zahlungsweise in ICC-Schiedsverfahren, 7 *IPRax* 58 (1987)

————, Arbitration of International Commercial Disputes under the Auspices of the International Chamber of Commerce, 4 *Int'l J. Technology Management* 489 (1989)

————, How to Draft an Arbitration Clause, 6 *J. Int'l Arb.* 65 (No. 2, 1989)

————, ICC Arbitration in Theory and Practice, 26 *Rassegna dell'Arb.* 141 (1986)

————, ICC Terms of Reference Rule Saves Time and Money While Promoting Common Understanding, 6 *Int'l Arb. Rep.* 33 (No. 8, 1991)

————, Recent Developments in International Chamber of Commerce (ICC) Arbitration, 1 *Int'l Q.* 113 (1989)

————, The International Arbitrator: From the Perspective of the ICC International Court of Arbitration, 12 *Nw. J. Int'l L. & Bus.* 1 (1991)

————, The New Swiss Law on International Arbitration and the Arbitral Institutions, 1989 *Int'l Bus. L.J.* 785

————, The Present Status of the International Court of Arbitration of the ICC: A Comment on an Appraisal, 1 *Am. Rev. Int'l Arb.* 108 (1990)

————, The Selection of ICC Arbitrators and the Requirement of Independence, 4 *Arb. Int'l* 300 (1988)

Branson & Tupman, Selecting an Arbitral Forum: A Guide to Cost-Effective International Arbitration, 24 *Va. J. Int'l L.* 917 (1984)

Branson & Wallace, Awarding Interest in International Commercial Arbitration: Establishing a Uniform Approach, 28 *Va. J. Int'l L.* 919 (1988)

Bredow, Vergleichs- und Schiedsgerichtsordnung der Internationalen Handelskammer, 1 *Jahrbuch Schiedsgerichtsbarkeit* 138 (1987)

Bredow & Bühler, Zur Änderung der Schiedsgerichtsordnung der Internationalen Handelskammer, 8 *IPRax* 69 (1988)

Briguglio, Die Schiedsrichterablehnung im italienischen Recht und nach den Regeln der ICC-Schiedsordnung, 2 *Jahrbuch Schiedsgerichtsbarkeit* 23 (1988)

Briseño Sierra, El arbitraje privado internacional, in *El Arbitraje Comercial Internacional* 29 (Mexico 1983)

Bucher, Arbitration under the ICC-Rules in Switzerland and the Concordat, in *Recueil de Travaux Suisses* 127 (C. Reymond & E. Bucher 1984)

Bühler, Grundsätze und Praxis des Kostenrechts im ICC-Schiedsverfahren, 87 *Zeitschrift für vergleichende Rechtswissenschaft* 431 (1988)

―――, Technical Expertise: An Additional Means for Preventing or Settling Commercial Disputes, 6 *J. Int'l Arb.* 135 (No. 1, 1989)

Carbonneau & Firestone, Transnational Law-Making: Assessing the Impact of the Vienna Convention and the Viability of Arbitral Adjudication, 1 *Emory J. Int'l Disp. Res.* 51 (1986)

Chillón Medina, J. M. & J. F. Merino Merchán, *Tratado de arbitraje privado interno e internacional* (Madrid 1978)

Cohn, The Rules of Arbitration of the International Chamber of Commerce, 14 *Int'l & Comp. L.Q.* 132 (1965)

Craig, International Ambition and National Restraints in ICC Arbitration, 1 *Arb. Int'l* 49 (1985)

Craig, W.L., W. Park & J. Paulsson, *International Chamber of Commerce Arbitration* (Dobbs Ferry, NY 1990)

Cremades, Modifications au règlement de la Cour d'arbitrage de la Chambre de Commerce Internationale, 1987 *Gaz. Pal. 2, doctr.* 764

Cremades, B. M., *Panorámica Española del Arbitraje Comercial Internacional* (Madrid 1975)

Dallal, Appointment of an Arbitrator under ICC Rules in Jordan, 2 *Int'l Constr. L. Rev.* 177 (1985) de Bournonville, Au sujet des demandes incidents en matière d'arbitrage, in *L'arbitrage* 55 (L. Matray & G. de Leval eds. 1989)

de Hancock, The ICC Court of Arbitration: The Institution and Its Procedures, 1 *J. Int'l Arb.* 21 (1984)

De Ly, Judicial Review of Decisions of the ICC Court of International Arbitration, 7 *J. Int'l Arb.* 153 (No. 1, 1990)

Derains, International Chamber of Commerce Arbitration, 5 *Pace L. Rev.* 591 (1985)

————, L'expérience de la Cour d'arbitrage de la Chambre de commerce internationale en matière de propriété industrielle, 1977 *Rev. Arb.* 40

————, Las características del arbitraje de la Cámara de Comercio Internacional y sus reglas, in *El Arbitraje Comercial Internacional* 251 (Mexico 1983)

————, Les arbitrages de la C.C.I. et les pays en developpement, in *Centre d'Etudes, Les Entreprises Tunisiennes et l'Arbitrage Commercial International* 15 (1983)

————, Mesures dilatoires en matière d'arbitrage et moyens de s'y opposer, in *Festschrift für Arthur Bülow* 31 (K.-H. Böckstiegel & O. Glossner eds. 1981)

————, New Trends in the Practical Application of the ICC Rules of Arbitration, 3 *Nw. .J. Int'l L.& Bus.* 39 (1981)

————, The Future of ICC Arbitration, 14 *J. Int'l L. & Econ.* 437 (1980)

————, The International Chamber of Commerce Continuing Education of Lawyers and Arbitrators, 5 *Y.B. Com. Arb.* 301 (1980)

Ebb, At the End of a Long Trail: How the Bombay High Court Strengthened International Arbitration in India, 44 *Arb. J.* 28 (No. 2, 1989)

Edwards, Arbitration Under the Rules of the International Chamber of Commerce, 2 *Arbitrator* 45 (1983)

Eisemann, Conciliation As a Means of Settlement of International Business Disputes: The UNCITRAL Rules as Compared with the ICC System, in *The Art of Arbitration* 121 (J. Schultsz & A. van den Berg eds. 1982)

————, The Court of Arbitration: Outline of Its Changes from Inception to the Present Day, in *ICC, 60 Years of ICC Arbitration* 391 (1984)

El-Ahdab, A. H., *Arbitration with the Arab Countries* (Deventer 1990)

————, *L'arbitrage dans les pays arabes* (Paris 1988)

Erecinski, Problems in the Administration of Evidence Arising from the Rules of the International Commercial Arbitration, 17 *Polish Y.B. Int'l L.* 41 (1988)

Ferrante, About the Nature (National or A-National, Contractual or Juris-dictional) of ICC Awards Under the New York Convention, in *The Art of Arbitration* 129 (J. Schultsz & A. van den Berg eds. 1982)

Fouchard, Le règlement d'arbitrage, 106 *J. Droit Int'l (Clunet)* 816 (1979)

Freear, Practice and Procedure under the ICC-CMI International Maritime Arbitration Rules, 1 *Fifth Int'l Congress of Maritime Arbitrators* (New York 1981)

Gaudet, The International Chamber of Commerce Court of Arbitration, 4 *Int'l Tax & Bus. Law.* 213 (1986)

————, Die ICC-Schiedsgerichtsbarkeit, in *Recht und Praxis der Schiedsgerichtsbarkeit der Internationalen Handelskammer* 1 (K.-H. Böckstiegel ed. 1986)

————, Overcoming Regional Differences, 5 *J. Int'l Arb.* 67 (No. 4, 1988); also in *Arbitration in Settlement of International Commercial Disputes Involving the Far East and Arbitration in Combined Transportation* 301 (P. Sanders ed. 1989)

Glossner, Der Einfluss der Internationalen Handelskammer (ICC) auf die moderne Schiedsgerichtsbarkeit, 30 *RIW* 15 (1984)

————, Le règlement de conciliation et d'arbitrage de la Chambre de Commerce Internationale: quelques aspects pratiques de son développement, in *ICCA, Fourth Int'l Arb. Congress: Proceedings* 703 (1972)

————, The Conduct of ICC Arbitration Proceedings, in *Contemporary Problems in International Arbitration* 210 (J.D.M. Lew ed. 1986)

————, The Rules of Conciliation and Arbitration of the International Chamber of Commerce, in *A.I.A., Essays in Memoriam Eugenio Minoli* 219 (Turin 1974)

————, Zur Bedeutung der Internationalen Handelskammer für die Rechtsfortbildung, in *Rechtsfortbildung durch internationale Schiedsgerichtsbarkeit* 83 (K.-H. Böckstiegel ed. 1981)

Goekjian, ICC Arbitration from a Practitioner's Perspective, 14 *J. Int'l L. & Econ.* 407 (1980)

Goldman, International Arbitration in Europe, in *IBA, Soviet Foreign Trade Reforms & East/West Arbitration* 217 (1988)

Goldsmith, How to Draft Terms of Reference, 3 *Arb. Int'l* 298 (1987)

Hacking (The Lord), A New Competition—Rivals for Centres of Arbitration, 45 *Arbitration* 166 (1979)

Hanak, The Experience of Socialist Lawyers in Arbitration Held in Non-Socialist Countries on Litigations Between Businessmen from East and West, 10 *Int'l Bus. Law.* 145 (1982)

Holtzmann & Bernini, Hypothetical Case for Use in a Comparative Study of Arbitration Practice in Various Legal Systems, in *Comparative Arbitration Practice and Public Policy in Arbitration* 19 (P. Sanders ed. 1987)

International Chamber of Commerce, *International Arbitration, Sixty Years of ICC Arbitration: A Look at the Future* (Paris 1984)

——, *Multi-party Arbitration* (Paris 1991)

——, *The Arbitral Process and the Independence of Arbitrators/La procédure arbitrale et l'indépendence des arbitres* (Paris 1991)

Jarvin, An International Chamber of Commerce Perspective, in *UNCITRAL Arbitration Model in Canada* 55 (R. Paterson & B. Thompson eds. 1987)

——, Änderungen der Vergleichs- und Schiedsgerichtsordnung der Internationalen Handelskammer (ICC Paris), 1 *Jahrbuch Schiedsgerichtsbarkeit* 140 (1987)

——, Arbitrating International Disputes, in 3 *The Law and Business of Licensing: Licensing in the 1980s* 2G-217 (R. Goldscheider & T. Arnold eds. 1987)

——, Aus der Praxis des ICC Schiedsgerichtshofes, in *Recht und Praxis der Schiedsgerichtsbarkeit der Internationalen Handelskammer* 7 (K.-H. Böckstiegel ed. 1986)

——, Choosing the Place of Arbitration: Where Do We Stand? 16 *Int'l Bus. Law.* 417 (1988)

————, Construction Disputes under the International Chamber of Commerce (ICC) Court of Arbitration Rules, 2 *Int'l Constr. L. Rev.* 139 (1985)

————, Die Erfahrung der ICC mit technischen Gutachten, in *Der komplexe Langzeitvertrag/The Complex Long-Term Contract* 551 (F. Nicklisch ed. 1987)

————, ICC Court of Arbitration Case Note, 3 *Int'l Constr. L. Rev.* 277 (1986)

————, ICC Court of Arbitration Case Notes, 3 *Int'l Constr. L. Rev.* 470 (1986)

————, International Chamber of Commerce Court of Arbitration, 3 *Int'l Constr. L. Rev.* 67 (1985)

————, L'arbitrage commercial dans les relations Est-West, 10 *Int'l Trade L. & Prac.* 117 (1984)

————, La Cour d'Arbitrage de la Chambre de Commerce Internationale, in *First Int'l Commercial Arbitration Conference: Proceedings* 67 (N. Antaki & A. Prujiner eds. 1986)

————, Settling International Business Disputes: Recent Developments, *Int'l Fin. L. Rev.* 16 (No. 2, Feb. 1984)

————, The Enforcement of ICC Arbitral Award, 1988 *Int'l Bus. L.J.* 241

————, The ICC Court of Arbitration—Recent Developments and Experience Related to Arab Countries, 1 *Arab L.Q.* 280 (1986)

————, The Place of Arbitration, 1990 *Y.B. Swed. & Int'l Arb.* 85

————, The Sources and Limits of the Arbitrator's Powers, 2 *Arb. Int'l* 140 (1986)

————, The Sources and Limits of the Arbitrator's Powers, in *Contemporary Problems in Int'l Arbitration* 50 (J.D.M. Lew ed. 1986)

Jarvin, S. & Y. Derains, *Collection of ICC Arbitral Awards/Recueil des sentences arbitrales de la CII, 1974-1985* (Paris & Deventer 1990)

Kassis, The Questionable Validity of Arbitration and Awards under the Rules of the International Chambre of Commerce, 6 *J. Int'l Arb.* 79 (No. 2, 1989)

Kassis, A., *Refléxions sur le Règlement d'arbitrage de la Chambre de commerce internationale: les déviations de l'arbitrage institutionel* (Paris 1988)

Kos-Rabcewicz-Zubkowski, L. & P.L. Davidson, *Commercial Arbitration Institutions: An International Directory and Guide* (New York 1986)

Kreindler, A Defendant's Initial 'Rights and Duties' in an ICC Arbitration, 10 *Int'l Fin. L. Rev.* 29 (No. 8, 1991)

————, A Defendant's Initial 'Rights and Duties' in International Arbitration on the Basis of the ICC Rules, 6 *Int'l Arb. Rep.* 32 (No. 9, 1991)

Laman, Industrial Contract: Important Considerations in Preparation for International Commercial Arbitration, in *Commercial Arbitration* 57 (J. Ricalde ed. 1983)

Lécuyer-Thieffry, Examination of ICC's New Pre-Arbitral Referee Procedure, 1 *World Arb. & Med. Rep.* 13 (No. 1, 1990)

Lerner, Profiles of Selected Arbitral Agencies and Comparison of Their Rules and the UNCITRAL Arbitration Rules, in *Arbitration and the Licensing Process* 2-3 (R. Goldscheider & M. de Haas eds. 1984-)

Loquin, L'examen du projet de sentence par l'institution et la sentence au deuxième degré, 1990 *Rev. Arb.* 427

McClelland, Toward a More Mature System of International Commercial Arbitration: The Establishment of Uniform Rules of Procedure and the Elimination of the Conflict of Laws Questions, 5 *N.C.J. Int'l L. & Com. Reg.* 169 (1980)

Melis, Force Majeur and Hardship Clauses in International Commercial Contracts in View of the Practice of the ICC Court of Arbitration, 1 *J. Int'l Arb. 213 (No. 3, 1984)*

Migeal, ICC-CMI Arbitration Rules, in *Fifth International Congress of Maritime Arbitrators* (New York 1981)

Nerz, Vor- und Nachteile eines Schiedsverfahrens nach der Schiedsgerichtsordnung der Internationalen Handelskammer, 36 *RIW* 350 (1990)

Nicklisch, Terms of Reference: Sinn und Zweck der Terms of Reference, Technik der Abfassung, 34 *RIW* 763 (1988)

Note, Challenge of Arbitrators: Is an Institutional Decision Final? 2 *Arb. Int'l* 261 (1986)

Parker School of Foreign and Comparative Law, *The 1989 Guide to International Arbitration and Arbitrators* (Dobbs Ferry 1989)

Paulsson, A Better Mousetrap: 1990 ICC Rules for a Pre-arbitral Referee Procedure, 18 *Int'l Bus. Law*. 214 (1990)

————, Arbitration under the Rules of the International Chamber of Commerce, in *Resolving Transnational Disputes Through International Arbitration* 235 (Th. Carbonneau ed. 1984)

————, La Lex mercatoria dans l'arbitrage C.C.I., 1990 *Rev. Arb*. 55

————, The Contemporary Role of ICC Arbitration in Resolving International Business Disputes, 9 *Int'l Trade L. & Prac*. 323 (1983)

————, Vicarious Hypochondria and Institutional Arbitration, 6 *Arb. Int'l* 226 (1990)

————, Vicarious Hypochondria and Institutional Arbitration, 1990 *Y.B. Swed. & Int'l Arb*. 96

Pineus, ICC/CMI Arbitration Rules, 14 *Europ. Transport. L*. 839 (1979)

Plantey, The International Court of Arbitration of the International Chamber of Commerce in the New Economic Trends, in *Eastern Bloc Joint Ventures* 146 (D. Winter ed. 1990)

Prujiner, La gestion des arbitrages commerciaux internationaux: l'exemple de la Cour d'arbitrage de la CCI, 115 *J. Droit Int'l (Clunet)* 662 (1988)

Raeschke-Kessler & Bühler, Aufsicht über den Schiedsrichter durch den ICC-Schiedsgerichtshof (Paris) und rechtliches Gehör der Parteien, 8 *ZIP 1157* (1987)

Ramos Mendez, Vereinbarkeit eines Schiedsverfahrens nach der VglSchO der IHK mit einem Schiedsverfahren nach dem spanischen Gesetz von 1953, in *Festschrift für Walther J. Habscheid* 239 (W. Lindacher, D. Pfaff et al. eds. 1989)

Reiner, Schiedsgerichtshof der Internationalen Handelskammer: Änderungen der Schiedsordnung und neue Vergleichsordnung, 1990 *JBl.* 80

Reiner, A., *Handbuch der ICC-Schiedsgerichtsbarkeit. Die Verfahrensordnung des Schiedsgerichtshofes der Internationalen Handelskammer* (Vienna 1989)

Rhodes & Sloan, The Pitfalls of International Commercial Arbitration, 17 *Vand. J. Transnat'l L*. 19 (1984)

Robert, Le nouveau Règlement de conciliation et d'arbitrage de la Chambre de commerce internationale, 1976 *Rev. Arb*. 83

Rubino-Sammartano, Nazionalità degli arbitrati e regolamento della Camera di Commercio Internazionale, 20 *Rassegna dell'Arb*. 179 (1980)

Sacerdoti, Il diritto dell'arbitrato commerciale internazionale nei nuovi regolamenti della Camera del Commercio Internazionale e dell'UNCITRAL, 12 *Riv. Dir. Int'le Priv. & Proc.* 222 (1976)

————, The New Arbitration Rules of ICC and UNCITRAL, 11 *J. World Trade L.* 248 (1977)

Sandrock, Die Terms of Reference und die Grenzen ihrer Präklusionswirkungen. Ein Rechtsinstitut der Verfahrensordnung des Schiedsgerichtshofes der Internationalen Handelskammer in Paris und seine Geheimnisse, 33 *RIW* 649 (1987)

Schlosser, Party-Appointed Arbitrators and Multiple Defendants Having Conflicting Interests, in *Law in East and West/Recht in Ost und West* 739 (Tokyo 1988)

Schollenberger, International Commercial Arbitration in Europe, in 1A *The Law of Transnational Business Transactions* 19-1 (V.P. Nanda ed. 1988)

Schwab, Die Schiedsgerichtsbarkeit der Internationalen Handelskammer aus der Sicht des deutschen Rechts, in *Festschrift für Winfried Kralik* 317 (Vienna 1986)

Schwebel, S.M., *International Arbitration: Three Salient Problems* (Cambridge 1987)

Seppala & Gogek, Multi-Party Arbitration under ICC Rules, 9 *Int'l Fin. L. Rev.* 32 (No. 11, 1989)

Shifman, The Rules of the Court of Arbitration of the International Chamber of Commerce, in 3 *W.A.R.* 3643 (H. Smit & V. Pechota eds. 1987)

Smit, De eerste ICC-arbitrage in Venezuela, 1988 *Tijdschrift voor Arbitrage* 173

————, Provisional Relief in International Arbitration: The ICC and Other Proposed Rules, 1 *Am. Rev. Int'l Arb.* 388 (1990)

————, Substance and Procedure in International Arbitration, 65 *Tul. L. Rev.* 1309 (1991)

————, The Future of International Commercial Arbitration: A Single Transnational Institution? 25 *Colum. J. Transnat'l L.* 9 (1986)

Smith, Impartiality of the Party-Appointed Arbitrator, 6 *Arb. Int'l* 320 (1990)

Stevenson, An Introduction to ICC Arbitration, 14 *J. Int'l L. & Econ.* 381 (1980)

Stoedter, The International Maritime Arbitration Rules (ICC-CMI), 8 *Int'l Bus. Law.* 302 (1980)

Thompson, International Chamber of Commerce — Arbitration Disputes Arising under International Construction Contracts, 5 *Int'l Bus. Law.* 225 (1977)

————, The Court of Arbitration of the International Chamber of Commerce, in *Handbook of Institutional Arbitration in International Trade* 17 (E. Cohn, M. Domke & F. Eisenmann eds. 1977)

Toop, S., *Mixed International Arbitration: Studies in Arbitration Between States and Private Persons* (Cambridge 1990)

Triebel, The ICC Rules of Conciliation and Arbitration of 1988, 3 *Int'l Arb. Rep.* 19 (No. 4, 1988)

————, Kleine Reform der Verfahrensordnung des Schiedsgerichtshofes der Internationalen Handelskammer, 22 *NJW* 1403 (1989)

Tupman, Challenge and Disqualification of Arbitrators in International Commercial Arbitration, 38 *Int'l & Comp. L.Q.* 26 (1989)

van den Hoven, Commercial Disputes and Their Settlement, a Factor in Business Planning, in *ICC, 60 Years of ICC Arbitration* 35 (1984)

von Hoffmann, Mehrparteienschiedsgerichtsbarkeit und Internationale Handelskammer, in *Beiträge zum internationalen Verfahrensrecht und zur Schiedsgerichtsbarkeit. Festschrift für Heinrich Nagel* 112 (W. Habscheid & K. Schwab eds. 1987)

Wackenhuth, Die (unterbliebene) Einrede der Unzuständigkeit des Schiedsgerichts nach ausgewählten Schiedsgerichtsordnungen, 32 *RIW* 11 (1986)

Weiss, The Status of the UNCITRAL Model Law on International Commercial Arbitration vis-a-vis the International Chamber of Commerce (ICC), London Court of International Arbitration and UNCITRAL Arbitration Rules: Conflict or Complement? 13 *Syracuse J. Int'l L. & Com.* 367 (1986)

Werner, Remuneration of Arbitrators by the International Chamber of Commerce, 5 *J. Int'l Arb.* 135 (No. 3, 1988)

144

Wetter, The Present Status of the International Court of Arbitration of the ICC: An Appraisal, 1 *Am. Rev. Int'l Arb.* 91 (1990)

Wiget, Über das Verhältniss der Schiedsgerichtsordnungen ICC, UNCITRAL, ECE zum Zürcher Schiedsgerichtsrecht, 75 *SJZ* 17 (1979)

Wortley, Quelques devéloppements modernes qui touchent les controverses entre les particuliers et les Etats et les entités étatiques, in *Liber Amicorum for Martin Domke* 348 (P. Sanders ed. 1967)

3.05 IRAN-UNITED STATES CLAIMS TRIBUNAL

Aksen, The Iran-U.S. Claims Tribunal and the UNCITRAL Arbitration Rules — An Early Comment, in *The Art of Arbitration* 1 (J. Schultsz & A. van den Berg eds. 1982)

Amin, Iran-United States Claims Settlement, 1983 *Lloyd's Mar. & Com. L.Q.* 248

Audit, Le Tribunal des Différends Irano-Americains (1981-1984), 112 *J. Droit Int'l (Clunet)* 791 (1985)

————, Les 'Accords' d'Alger du 19 janvier 1981 tendant au règlement des différends entre les Etats-Unis et l'Iran, 108 *J. Droit Int'l (Clunet)* 713 (1981)

Baker & Davis, Arbitral Proceedings Under the UNCITRAL Rules: The Experience of the Iran-United States Claims Tribunal, 23 *Geo. Wash. J. Int'l L. & Econ.* 267 (1989)

————, Establishment of an Arbitral Tribunal under the UNCITRAL Rules: The Experience of the Iran-United States Claims Tribunal, 23 *Int'l Law.* 81 (1989)

Belland, The Iran-United States Claims Tribunal: Some Reflections on Trying a Claim, 1 *J. Int'l Arb.* 237 (No. 3, 1984)

Bellet, Symposium on the Iran-United States Claims Tribunal: Foreword, 16 *L. & Pol'y Int'l Bus.* 667 (1984)

Belman, Owen & Lowenfeld, The U.S.-Iranian Hostage Settlement, 75 *Am. Soc. Int'l L. Proc.* 236 (1981)

Berglin, The Iranian Forum Clause Decisions of the Iran-United States Claims Tribunal, 3 *Arb. Int'l* 46 (No. 1, 1987)

————, Treaty Interpretation and the Impact of Contractual Choice of Forum Clauses on the Jurisdiction of International Tribunals: The Iranian Forum Clause Decisions of the Iran-United States Claims Tribunal, 21 *Tex. Int'l L.J.* 39 (1985)

Bernardini, P., *L'arbitrato internazionale* (Milan 1987)

Böckstiegel, A Special Arbitration Convention: The Algiers Declarations Creating the Iran-United States Claims Tribunal and Their Application, in *First Euro-Arab Arb. Conference: Proceedings* 78 (F. Kemicha ed. 1987)

————, Applying the UNCITRAL Rules: The Experience of the Iran-United States Claims Tribunal, 4 *Int'l Tax & Bus. Law.* 266 (1986)

————, Practice of International Dispute Settlement — Thoughts after Resigning as President of the Iran-United States Claims Tribunal, in *Liber Amicorum Honouring Nicolas Mateesco Matte* 17 (G.R. Baccelli ed. 1989)

————, Zur Bedeutung des Iran-United States Claims Tribunal für die Entwicklung des internationalen Rechts, in *Festschrift der Rechtswissenschaftlichen Fakultät zur 600-Jahr-Feier der Universität zu Köln* (Cologne 1988)

Borris, Die UNCITRAL-Schiedsregeln in der Praxis des Iran-United States Claims Tribunal, 2 *Jahrbuch Schiedsgerichtsbarkeit* 3 (1988)

Branson, Continuous Ownership of a Claim: A Hard Case at the Iran-United States Claims Tribunal Makes Bad Law, 3 *Arb. Int'l* 164 (1987)

Caron, Interim Measures of Protection: Theory and Practice in Light of the Iran-United States Claims Tribunal, 46 *Zeitschrift für ausländisches öffentliches Recht und Völkerrecht* 465 (1986)

————, The Nature of the Iran-United States Claims Tribunal and the Evolving Structure of International Dispute Resolution, 84 *Am. J. Int'l L.* 104 (1990)

Crook, Applicable Law in International Arbitration: The Iran-U.S. Claims Tribunal Experience, 83 *Am. J. Int'l L.* 278 (1989)

Cutler, Negotiating the Iranian Settlement, 67 *A.B.A. J.* 996 (1981)

Doumbia-Henry, The Limits of the Jurisdiction of the Iran-US Claims Tribunal: A Response to Mr. Branson, 4 *Arb. Int'l* 228 (1988)

Fox, States and the Undertaking to Arbitrate, 37 *Int'l & Comp. L.Q.* 1 (1988)

Gold, The Iran-United States Claims Tribunal and the Articles of Agreement of the International Monetary Fund, 18 *Geo. Wash. J. Int'l L. & Econ.* 537 (1985)

Hardenberg, The Awards of the Iran-US Claims Tribunal Seen in Connection with the Law of the Netherlands, 12 *Int'l Bus. Law.* 337 (1984)

Hoffman, The Iranian Asset Negotiations, 17 *Vand. J. Transnat'l L.* 47 (1984)

Holtzmann, Some Lessons of the Iran-United States Claims Tribunal, in *Private Investors Abroad— Problems and Solutions in International Business in 1987* 16.1 (J. Ross ed. 1987)

Jones, The Iran-United States Claims Tribunal: Private Rights and State Responsibility, 24 *Va. J. Int'l L.* 259 (1984)

Khalilian, Controversial Theory of Frustration Before Iran-United States Claims Tribunal, 7 *J. Int'l Arb.* 5 (No. 3, 1990)

Khan, R., *The Iran-United States Claims Tribunal. Controversies, Cases and Contribution* (Dordrecht 1990)

Labouz, Le Tribunal des Différends Irano-Américains, *Cahier du C.E.D.I.N., Centre de Droit International de Nanterre* (No. 1, 1984)

Lagergren, Iran-United States Claims Tribunal, in *Realism in Law-Making: Essays on International Law in Honour of Willem Riphagen* 113 (A. Bos & H. Siblesz eds. 1986)

Lake & Dana, Judicial Review of Awards of the Iran-United States Claims Tribunal: Are the Tribunal's Awards Dutch? 16 *L. & Pol'y Int'l Bus.* 755 (1984)

Lauterpacht, The Iran-United States Claims Tribunal — An Assessment, in *Private Investors Abroad: Problems and Solutions in International Business* 213 (M. Landwehr ed. 1982)

Leurent, Problèmes soulevés par les demandes des double nationaux devant le Tribunal des différends irano-américains, 74 *Rev. Crit. Droit Int'l Privé* 273 & 477 (1985)

Lewis, What Goes Around Comes Around: Can Iran Enforce Awards of the Iran-U.S. Claims Tribunal in the United States? 26 *Colum. J. Transnat'l L.* 515 (1988)

Lillich, R.B., ed., *The Iran-United States Claims Tribunal 1981-1983* (Charlottesville, VA 1984)

Lombard, Arbitration Has Worked at Exxon, 42 *Arb. J.* 3 (No. 1, 1987)

Lowenfeld, The U.S.-Iranian Dispute Settlement Accords: An Arbitrator Looks at the Prospects for Arbitration, 36 *Arb. J.* 1 (No. 3, 1981)

———, The Iran-U.S. Claims Tribunal: An Interim Appraisal, 38 *Arb. J.* 14 (Dec. 1983)

148

McCabe, Arbitral Discovery and the Iran-United States Claims Tribunal Experience, 20 *Int'l Law*. 499 (1986)

McLaughlin & Teclaff, The Iranian Hostage Agreement: A Legal Analysis, 4 *Fordham Int'l L.J.* 223 (1981)

Malloy, The Iran Crisis: Law under Pressure, 1984 *Wis. Int'l L.J.* 15 (Symposium)

Mosk, Lessons from The Hague — An Update on the Iran-United States Claims Tribunal, 14 *Pepperdine L. Rev.* 819 (1987)

————, The Role of Party-Appointed Arbitrators in International Arbitration: The Experience of the Iran-United States Claims Tribunal, 1 *Transnat'l Law*. 253 (1988)

Norton & Collins, Reflections on the Iranian Hostage Settlement, 67 *A.B.A. J.* 428 (1981)

Note, Changed Circumstances and the Iranian Claims Arbitration: Applications to Forum Selection Clauses and Frustration of Contract, 16 *Geo. Wash. J. Int'l L. & Econ.* 335 (1982)

————, Iranian Hostage Agreement under International and U.S. Law, 81 *Colum. L. Rev.* 822 (1981)

————, Settlement of the Iranian Hostage Crisis: An Exercise of Constitutional and Statutory Prerogative in Foreign Affairs, 13 *N.Y.U. J. Int'l L. & Pol.* 993 (1981)

————, U.S.-Iran Hostage Agreement: A Study in Presidential Power, 15 *Cornell Int'l L.J.* 1619 (1982)

Pellonpää & Fitzmaurice, Taking of Property in the Practice of the Iran-United States Claims Tribunal, 19 *Neth. Y.B. Int'l L.* 53 (1988)

Pirrie, S. & J. Arnold, eds., *Iran-United States Claims Tribunal Reports* (Cambridge 1983-)

Przetacznik & Pechota, UNCITRAL Rules as Applied by the Iran-United States Claims Tribunal, In 3 *W.A.R.* 3222 (H. Smit & V. Pechota eds. 1987)

Rubino-Sammartano M., *International Arbitration Law* (Deventer 1990)

Sandrock, Das Haager Iranisch-USamerikanische Schiedsgericht: keine nachahmenswerte Institution? 29 *Archiv des Völkerrechts* 104 (1991)

Schultsz, The Bill on Applicability of Dutch Law to Awards Rendered by the Iran-United States Claims Tribunal, in *Legislation in the Netherlands and International Arbitration* 32 (1986)

Seidl-Hohenveldern, L'évaluations des dommages dans les arbitrages transnationaux, 33 *Ann. Français de Droit Int'l* 7 (1987)

————, Le réglement du contentieux irano-américain par les accords d'Alger du 19 janvier 1981, in *Le droit des relations économiques internationales: Etudes offertes à Berthold Goldman* 343 (Paris 1983)

Selby & Steward, Practical Aspects of Arbitrating Claims before the Iran-United States Claims Tribunal, 18 *Int'l Law. 211* (1984)

Shirazi, Iran-U.S. Claims Tribunal: An Unfair International Award on the Basis of Unjust Enrichment, 5 *J. Int'l Arb.* 111 (No. 3, 1988)

Stein, Jurisprudence and Jurists' Prudence: The Iranian Forum Clause Decisions of the Iranian-U.S. Claims Tribunal, 78 *Am. J. Int'l L.* 1 (1984)

Stern, A propos d'une décision du Tribunal des différends irano-américains, 28 *Ann. Français Droit Int'l* 425 (1982)

————, Changements de circonstances et clauses d'élection de for devant le Tribunal des différends irano-américains, 29 *Ann. Français Droit Int'l* 313 (1983)

————, Les questions de nationalité des personnes physiques et de nationalité et de contrôle des personnes morales devant le Tribunal des différends irano-américains, 30 *Ann. Français Droit Int'l* 425 (1984)

Stewart, The Iran-United States Claims Tribunal: A Review of Developments 1983-84, 16 *L. & Pol'y Int'l Bus.* 677 (1984)

Stewart & Sherman, Developments at the Iran-U.S. Claims Tribunal: 1981-1983, 24 *Va. J. Int'l L.* 1 (1984)

Straus, The Practice of the Iran-U.S. Claims Tribunal in Receiving Evidence from Parties and from Experts, 3 *J. Int'l Arb.* 57 (No. 3, 1986)

Suy, Settling U.S. Claims Against Iran through Arbitration, 29 *Am. J. Comp. L.* 523 (1981)

Swanson, Iran-U.S. Claims Tribunal: A Policy Analysis of the Expropriation Cases, 18 *Case W. Res. J. Int'l L.* 307 (1986)

Toop, S., *Mixed International Arbitration: Studies in Arbitration Between States and Private Persons* (Cambridge 1990)

van den Berg, Proposed Dutch Law on the Iran-U.S. Claims Settlement Declaration, 12 *Int'l Bus. Law.* 341 (1984)

van Hof, J., *Commentary on the UNCITRAL Arbitration Rules. The Application by the Iran-U.S. Claims Tribunal* (Deventer 1991)

von Mehren, The Iran-U.S.A. Arbitral Tribunal, 31 *Am. J. Comp. L.* 713 (1983)

Westberg, Contract Excuse in International Business Transactions: Awards of the Iran-United States Claims Tribunal, 4 *ICSID Rev. - Foreign Investment L.J.* 215 (1989)

————, The Applicable Law Issue in International Business Transactions with Government Parties: Ruling of the Iran-United States Claims Tribunal, 2 *ICSID Rev. - Foreign Investment L.J.* 473 (1987)

————, Compensation in Cases of Expropriation and Nationalization: Awards of the Iran-United States Claims Tribunal, 5 *ICSID Rev. - Foreign Investment L.J.* 256 (1990)

Westberg, J., *International Business Transactions Involving Government Parties — Awards of the Iran-United States Claims Tribunal* (Washington 1991)

Wühler, Zur Bedeutung des Iran-United States Claims Tribunal für die Rechtsfortbildung, in *Rechtsfortbild und durch Internationale Schiedsgerichtsbarkeit* 93 (K.-H. Böckstiegel ed. 1989)

Ziade, Selective Bibliography on the Iran-United States Claims Tribunal, 2 *ICSID Rev. - Foreign Investment L.J.* 534 (1987)

3.06 MULTILATERAL INVESTMENT GUARANTEE AGENCY

Alsop, The World Bank's Multilateral Investment Guarantee Agency, 25 *Colum. J. Transnat'l L.* 101 (1986)

Chatterjee, The Convention Establishing the Multilateral Investment Guarantee Agency, 36 *Int'l & Comp. L.Q.* 76 (1987)

Delaume, The Proper Law of State Contracts and the Lex Mercatoria: A Reappraisal, 3 *ICSID Rev. - Foreign Investment L.J.* 79 (1988)

Ebenroth, C.-Th. & J. Karl, *Die Multilaterale Investitionsgarantie-Agentur. Kommentar zum MIGA-Übereinkommen* (Heidelberg 1989)

Gramlich, Das Übereinkommen zur Errichtung einer 'Multilateral Investment Guarantee Agency': Grenzüberschreitender Investitionsschutz und Entwicklungszusammenarbeit Hand in Hand? 38 *Österr. Z. öffentl. Recht & Völkerrecht* 1 (1987)

Peter, Settlement of Investment Disputes, 5 *J. Int'l Arb.* 131 (No. 1, 1988)

Shihata, The Role of ICSID and the Projected Multilateral Investment Guarantee Agency (MIGA), 41 *Aussenwirtschaft* 105 (1986)

————, The Settlement of Disputes Regarding Foreign Investment: The Role of the World Bank, with Particular Reference to ICSID and MIGA, 1 *Am. U.J. Int'l L. & Pol'y* 97 (1986); also *1 Arab L. Q.* 265 (1986)

————, Towards a Greater Depolitization of Investment Disputes: The Roles of ICSID and MIGA, 1 *ICSID Review - Foreign Investment L.J.* 1 (1986)

Shihata, I., *MIGA and Foreign Investment: Origins, Operations, Policies and Basic Documents of the Multilateral Investment Guarantee Agency* (Dordrecht 1988)

Stern, T., *Die Multilaterale Investitionsgarantie-Agentur (MIGA). Ein neues versicherungsrechtliches Instrument zur Verbesserung des Schutzes deutscher Investitionen im Ausland* (Cologne 1990)

Tita, Gli arbitrati predisposti dalle convenzioni ICSID e MIGA e la suroga assicurativa, 23 *Riv. Dir. Int'le Priv. & Proc.* 497 (1987)

Touscoz, L'Agence Multilaterale de Garantie des Investissements, 13 *Droit et Pratique du Com. Int'l* 311 (1987)

————, Le règlement des différends dans la Convention instituant l'Agence Multilatérale de Garantie des Investissement (A.M.G.I.): un devéloppement de l'arbitrage international et du droit des investissements internationaux, 1988 *Rev. Arb.* 629

————, Les opérations de garantie de l'Agence Multilatérale de Garantie des Investissements (A.M.G.I.), 114 *J. Droit Int'l (Clunet)* 901 (1987)

Voss, The Multilateral Investment Guarantee Agency: Status, Mandate, Concept, Features, Implications, 21 *J. World Trade L.* 5 (No. 4, 1987)

3.07 OECD INTERNATIONAL ENERGY AGENCY

Dorman, Rules of the International Energy Agency Dispute Settlement Centre, in 3 *W.A.R.* 3542 (H. Smit & V. Pechota eds. 1987)

3.08 PERMANENT COURT OF ARBITRATION AT THE HAGUE

Przetacznik, The Permanent Court of Arbitration at the Hague: The Rules of Arbitration and Conciliation for Settlement of International Disputes between Two Parties of Which One Is a State, in 3 *W.A.R.* 3524 (H. Smit & V. Pechota eds. 1987)

Schwebel, S.M., *International Arbitration: Three Salient Problems* (Cambridge 1987)

Wortley, Quelques devéloppements modernes qui touchent les controverses entre les particuliers et les Etats et les entités étatiques, in *Liber Amicorum for Martin Domke 348* (P. Sanders ed. 1967)

3.09 REGIONAL CENTRE FOR COMMERCIAL ARBITRATION CAIRO

Aboul Enein, Arbitration under the Auspices of the Cairo Regional Centre, 4 *Int'l Tax & Bus. Law.* 256 (1986)

————, Arbitration under the Auspices of the Cairo Regional Centre for Commercial Arbitration (An AALCC Centre), 2 *J. Int'L Arb.* 23 (No. 4, 1985)

Atallah, The Arab Regional Arbitration Centres, in *First Euro-Arab Arb. Conference: Proceedings* 66 (F. Kemicha ed. 1987)

Davies, Arbitration Centre for Cairo, 3 *Int'l Fin. L. Rev.* 41 (No. 6, 1984)

Dorman, UNCITRAL Rules as Applied by the Regional Centre for Commercial Arbitration at Cairo, in 3 *W.A.R.* 3198 (H. Smit & V. Pechota eds. 1987)

El-Ahdab, A. H., *Arbitration with the Arab Countries* (Deventer 1990)

————, *L'arbitrage dans les pays arabes* (Paris 1988)

Khafagui, Centre d'Arbitrage Commercial International au Caire, 76 *L'Egypte Contemporaine* 5 (1985)

————, Regional Center for Arbitration at Cairo, 76 *L'Egypte Contemporaine* 321 (1985)

Kos-Rabcewicz-Zubkowski, L. & Davidson, P.L., *Commercial Arbitration Institutions: An International Directory and Guide* (New York 1986)

Sen, AALCC Dispute Settlement and the UNCITRAL Arbitration Rules, 4 *Int'l Tax & Bus. Law.* 247 (1986)

Wall, The Asian-African Legal Consultative Committee and International Commercial Arbitration, 17 *Can. Y.B. Int'l L.* 324 (1979)

Ziadé, Selective Bibliography on Arbitration and Arab Countries, 3 *ICSID Rev. -Foreign Investment L.J.* 423 (1988)

3.10 REGIONAL CENTRE FOR COMMERCIAL ARBITRATION KUALA LUMPUR

Broches, Arbitration of Investment Disputes, 1984(1) *Malayan L.J.* at lxxiii

Dorman, UNCITRAL Rules as Applied by the Regional Centre for Arbitration at Kuala Lumpur, in 3 *W.A.R.* 3186 (H. Smit & V. Pechota eds. 1987)

Kos-Rabcewicz-Zubkowski, L. & P.L. Davidson, *Commercial Arbitration Institutions: An International Directory and Guide* (New York 1986)

Lim, Commercial Arbitration and the Kuala Lumpur Regional Arbitration Centre, in *Arbitration in Settlement of International Commercial Disputes Involving the Far East and Arbitration in Combined Transportation* 57 (P. Sanders ed. 1989)

————, Malaysia Offers Regional Centre for Arbitration in Kuala Lumpur, 0 *World Arb. & Med. Rep.* 11 (1989)

————, The Kuala Lumpur Regional Arbitration Centre, 3 *ICSID Rev. - Foreign Investment L.J.* 118 (1988)

Note, Arbitration Centre at Kuala Lumpur, 13 *J. World Trade L.* 88 (1979)

Sen, AALCC Dispute Settlement and the UNCITRAL Arbitration Rules, 4 *Int'l Tax & Bus. Law.* 247 (1986)

Wall, The Asian-African Legal Consultative Committee and International Commercial Arbitration, 17 *Can. Y.B. Int'l L.* 324 (1979)

3.11 UNCITRAL ARBITRATION RULES

Aden, M., *Internationale Handelsschiedsgerichtsbarkeit. Kommentar zu den Verfahrensordnungen* (Heidelberg 1988)

Agarwal, Rules of Procedure in International Arbitrations with Special Reference to Model Rules Drafted by UNCITRAL, in *ICCA, Fifth Int'l Arb. Congress: Proceedings* C Ir 1-6 (1975)

Aksen, The Iran-U.S. Claims Tribunal and the UNCITRAL Arbitration Rules — An Early Comment, in *The Art of Arbitration* 1 (J. Schultsz & A. van den Berg eds. 1982)

Baker & Davis, Arbitral Proceedings under the UNCITRAL Rules: The Experience of the Iran-United States Claims Tribunal, 23 *Geo. Wash. J. Int'l L. & Econ.* 267 (1989)

———, Establishment of an Arbitral Tribunal under the UNCITRAL Rules: The Experience of the Iran-United States Claims Tribunal, 23 *Int'l Law.* 81 (1989)

Barclay, Unadministered Arbitration and the UNCITRAL Draft Rules Pertaining to It, in *ICCA, Fifth Int'l Arb. Congress: Proceedings* C Ih 1-9 (1975)

Blessing, International Arbitration Procedures, 17 *Int'l Bus. Law.* 408 and 451 (1989)

———, The Major Western and Soviet Arbitration Rules: A Comparison of the Rules of UNCITRAL, UNCITRAL Model Law, LCIA, ICC, AAA and the Rules of the USSR Chamber of Commerce and Industry, 6 *J. Int'l Arb.* 7 (No. 3, 1989)

Böckstiegel, Applying the UNCITRAL Rules: The Experience of the Iran-United States Claims Tribunal, 4 *Int'l Tax & Bus. Law.* 266 (1986)

———, Die UNCITRAL Verfahrensordnung für Wirtschaftsschieds-gerichtsbarkeit und das anwendbare nationale Recht, 28 *RIW* 706 (1982)

———, The Relevance of National Arbitration Law for Arbitration under the UNCITRAL Rules, 1 *J. Int'l Arb.* 223 (No. 3, 1984)

Borris, Die UNCITRAL-Schiedsregeln in der Praxis des Iran-United States Claims Tribunal, 2 *Jahrbuch Schiedsgerichtsbarkeit* 3 (1988)

Branson & Tupman, Selecting an Arbitral Forum: A Guide to Cost-Effective International Arbitration, 24 *Va. J. Int'l L.* 917 (1984)

Briseño Sierra, UNCITRAL Arbitration Rules, in *ICCA, Fifth Int'l Arb. Congress: Proceedings* C Iy 1-3 (1975)

Dietz, Introduction: Development of the UNCITRAL Arbitration Rules, 27 *Am. J. Comp. L.* 449 (1979)

Dore, I.I., *Arbitration and Conciliation Under the UNCITRAL Rules: A Textual Analysis* (Dordrecht 1986)

Erecinski, Problems in the Administration of Evidence Arising from the Rules of the International Commercial Arbitration, 17 *Polish Y.B. Int'l L.* 41 (1988)

Fleischhauer, The Contribution of UNCITRAL in the Field of Commercial Arbitration, in *Essays on International Law. Thirtieth Anniversary Commemorative Volume 16* (New Delhi 1987)

Fouchard, Le règlement d'arbitrage, 106 *J. Droit Int'l (Clunet)* 816 (1979)

Gionea, Les efforts pour la réglementation et l'unification de la procédure arbitrale sur le plan international, 1 *Le Nuove Frontiere del Diritto e il Problema dell'Unificazione* 451 (1979)

Glossner, Die UNCITRAL Schiedsregeln zwischen Privatrecht und Völkerrecht, 27 *RIW* 300 (1981)

————, Die UNCITRAL-Schiedsordnung in der Praxis, 24 *RIW* 141 (1978)

Greenwell, UNCITRAL Arbitration Rules, in *Australian Academy of Sciences, Meeting on International Trade Law* 325 (Canberra 1977)

Hoffman, The Iranian Asset Negotiations, 17 *Vand. J. Transnat'l L.* 47 (1984)

Holtzmann, The Desirability of Including More Specific Provisions Concerning Place of Arbitration in the Model Clause in the UNCITRAL Rules, in *ICCA, Fifth Int'l Arb. Congress: Proceedings* C Iv 1-3 (1975)

Hunter, UNCITRAL and Construction Industry Arbitration, 2 *Int'l Constr. L. Rev.* 165 (1985)

Jenard, Le règlement d'arbitrage de la Commission des Nations Unies pour le Droit Commercial International, 54 *Rev. Droit Int'l & Droit Comp.* 201 (1977)

Kitagawa, Applicable Law of the UNCITRAL Rules, in *ICCA, Fifth Int'l Arb. Congress: Proceedings* C Ik 1-6 (1975)

Lando, The Law Applicable to the Merits of the Dispute, 2 *Arb. Int'l* 104 (1986)

Leahy & Pierce, Sanctions to Control Party Misbehavior in International Arbitration, 26 *Va. J. Int'l L.* 291 (1986)

Lerner, Profiles of Selected Arbitral Agencies and Comparison of Their Rules and the UNCITRAL Arbitration Rules, in *Arbitration and the Licensing Process* 2-3 (R. Goldscheider & M. de Haas eds. 1984-)

Liew, Commercial Arbitration in Korea with Special Reference to the UNCITRAL Rules, 5 *Korean J. Comp. L.* 69 (1977)

―――, Commercial Arbitration in Korea with Special Reference to the UNCITRAL Rules, in *Business Laws in Korea* 905 (Kim Chan-Jin ed. 2nd ed. 1988)

McClelland, Toward a More Mature System of International Commercial Arbitration: The Establishment of Uniform Rules of Procedure and the Elimination of the Conflict of Laws Questions, 5 *N.C.J. Int'l L. & Com. Reg.* 169 (1980)

Melis, Arbitration and the Courts, 51 *Arbitration* 453 (1985)

Norwegian Group of the International Bar Association, *International Commercial Arbitration in Action: Papers from a Conference in Oslo in 1982* (Oslo 1983)

Oyekunle, Savremeni problemi spljnotrgovinske arbitraze u svetlosti rada UNCITRAL, in *Spoljnotrgovinska arbitraza* (J. Vilus ed. 1982)

Parker School of Foreign and Comparative Law, *The 1989 Guide to International Arbitration and Arbitrators* (Dobbs Ferry 1989)

Pechota, UNCITRAL Arbitration Rules, in 3 *W.A.R.* 3083 (H. Smit & V. Pechota eds. 1987)

Philip, The Significance of the Place of Arbitration in International Arbitration, 1985 *Y.B. Swedish & Int'l Arb.* 37 (1985)

Pirrung, Die Schiedsverfahrensordnung der UNCITRAL, 23 *RIW* 513 (1977)

Rao, Some Suggestions for Amendment in Draft UNCITRAL Arbitration Rules, in *ICCA, Fifth Int'l Arb. Congress: Proceedings* C Iu 1-3 (1975)

Rauh, K., *Die Schieds- und Schlichtungsordnungen der UNCITRAL* (Cologne 1983)

Rhodes & Sloan, The Pitfalls of International Commercial Arbitration, 17 *Vand. J. Transnat'l L.* 19 (1984)

Sacerdoti, Il diritto dell'arbitrato commerciale internazionale nei nuovi regolamenti della Camera del Commercio Internazionale e dell'UNCITRAL, 12 *Riv. Dir. Int'le Priv. & Proc.* 222 (1976)

————, The New Arbitration Rules of ICC and UNCITRAL, 11 *J. World Trade L.* 248 (1977)

Samuels, The Soviet Position on International Arbitration: A Wealth of Choices or Choices for the Wealthy, 26 *Va. J. Int'l L.* 417 (1986)

Sanders, Aspects de l'arbitrage international, 53 *Rev. Droit Int'l & Droit Comp.* 129 (1976)

————, Commentary on UNCITRAL Arbitration Rules, 2 *Y.B. Com. Arb.* 172 (1977)

————, International Commercial Arbitration — How to Improve Its Functioning? 46 *Arbitration* 9 (1980)

————, Model Rules for International Commercial Arbitration: UNCITRAL Arbitration Rules, in *ICCA, Fifth Int'l Arb. Congress: Proceedings* C Ia 1-17 (1975)
————, Procedures and Practices under the UNCITRAL Rules, 27 *Am. J. Comp. L.* 453 (1979)

————, Règlement d'arbitrage de la CNUDCI, 4 *Int'l Trade L. & Prac.* 269 (1978)

Santos, International Commercial Arbitration, in *Commercial Arbitration* 122 (J. Ricalde ed. 1983)

Schollenberger, International Commercial Arbitration in Europe, in 1A *The Law of Transnational Business Transactions* 19-1 (V.P. Nanda ed. 1988)

Schwebel, S.M., *International Arbitration: Three Salient Problems* (Cambridge 1987)

Sekolec, J., *Arbitrazna pravila UNCITRAL* (Ljubljana 1983)

Sen, AALCC Dispute Settlement and the UNCITRAL Arbitration Rules, 4 *Int'l Tax & Bus. Law.* 247 (1986)

Smit, The Future of International Commercial Arbitration: A Single Transnational Institution?, 25 *Colum. J. Transnat'l L.* 9 (1986)

Steyn, Methods of Conducting International Commercial Arbitrations: A Re-Examination, in *Second Bermuda Int'l Arb. Conference: A Collection of Papers* (Hamilton, Bermuda, April 19-22, 1983)

Straus, Pieter Sanders and the UNCITRAL Rules, in *The Art of Arbitration* 301 (J. Schultsz & A. van den Berg eds. 1982)

Subramanian, Development of Model Rules for Arbitration — An Overview, in *ICCA, Fifth Int'l Arb. Congress: Proceedings* C Id 1-3 (1975)

Sundaram, Comments on UNCITRAL Arbitration Rules, in *ICCA, Fifth Int'l Arb. Congress: Proceedings* C IIg 1-2 (1975)

Thompson, The UNCITRAL Arbitration Rules, 17 *Harv. Int'l L.J.* 141 (1976)

———, The Marriage of the UNCITRAL Model Arbitration Law and the UNCITRAL Arbitration Rules, in *UNCITRAL Arbitration Model in Canada* 143 (R. Paterson & B. Thompson eds. 1987)

United Nations, International Commercial Arbitration, Report by Ion Nestor, Special Rapporteur, UN Doc. A/CN.9/64 (1972), reprinted in 3 *UNCITRAL Y.B.* 193 (1972)

van Hof, J., *Commentary on the UNCITRAL Arbitration Rules. The Application by the Iran-U.S. Claims Tribunal* (Deventer 1991)

von Hoffmann, UNCITRAL Rules für internationale Schiedsverfahren, 22 *RIW* 1 (1976)

Wackenhuth, Die (unterbliebene) Einrede der Unzuständigkeit des Schiedsgerichts nach ausgewählten Schiedsgerichtsordnungen, 32 *RIW* 11 (1986)

Weiss, The Status of the UNCITRAL Model Law on International Commercial Arbitration vis-a-vis the International Chamber of Commerce (ICC), London Court of International Arbitration and UNCITRAL Arbitration Rules: Conflict or Complement? 13 *Syracuse J. Int'l L. & Com.* 367 (1986)

Wiget, Über das Verhältniss der Schiedsgerichtsordnungen ICC, UNCITRAL, ECE zum Zürcher Schiedsgerichtsrecht, 75 *SJZ* 17 (1979)

Won Kap Lee, Model Rules for International Commercial Arbitration, in *ICCA, Fifth Int'l Arb. Congress: Proceedings* C If 1-4 (1975)

3.12 UN ECONOMIC COMMISSIONS

Aden, M., *Internationale Handelsschiedsgerichtsbarkeit. Kommentar zu den Verfahrensordnungen* (Heidelberg 1988)

Arnold, Die Schiedsgerichtsordnung der Wirtschaftskommission für Europa der Vereinten Nationen, 1967 *AWD* 179

Benjamin, The Work of the Economic Commission for Europe in the Field of International Commercial Arbitration, 7 *Int'l & Comp. L.Q.* 22 (1958)

Cohn, The Rules of Arbitration of the United Nations Economic Commission for Europe, 16 *Int'l & Comp. L.Q.* 946 (1967)

Domke, The Bangkok Conference on Commercial Arbitration, 17 *Arb. J.* 23 (1962)

Dorman, Arbitration Rules of the United Nations Economic Commission for Europe, in 3 *W.A.R.* 3323 (H. Smit & V. Pechota eds. 1987)

———, UN/ECE Arbitration Rules for Certain Categories of Perishable Agricultural Products, in 3 *W.A.R.* 3358 (H. Smit & V. Pechota eds. 1987)

———, United Nations Economic and Social Commission for Asia and the Pacific (ESCAP) — Rules for International Commercial Arbitration, in 3 *W.A.R.* 3347 (H. Smit & V. Pechota eds. 1987)

Indian Council of Arbitration, *International Seminar on Commercial Arbitration* (18-19 March 1968), (New Delhi 1968)

Kos-Rabcewicz-Zubkowski, L. & P.L. Davidson, *Commercial Arbitration Institutions: An International Directory and Guide* (New York 1986)

Sanders, ECAFE Rules for International Commercial Arbitration, in *Liber Amicorum for Martin Domke* 252 (P. Sanders ed. 1967)

Schwebel, S.M., *International Arbitration: Three Salient Problems* (Cambridge 1987)

Siqueiros, Panórama actual del arbitraje comercial internacional, in *El Arbitraje Comercial Internacional* 135 (Mexico 1983)

Wackenhuth, Die (unterbliebene) Einrede der Unzuständigkeit des Schiedsgerichts nach ausgewählten Schiedsgerichtsordnungen, 32 *RIW* 11 (1986)

Wiget, Über das Verhältniss der Schiedsgerichtsordnungen ICC, UNCITRAL, ECE zum Zürcher Schiedsgerichtsrecht, 75 *SJZ* 17 (1979)

3.13 OTHER INTERNATIONAL INSTITUTIONS AND RULES

Anderson & Rugman, The Canada-U.S. Free Trade Agreement: A Legal and Economic Analysis of the Dispute Settlement Mechanism, 6 *J. Int'l Arb.* 65 (No. 4, 1989)

Arellano Garcia, Bases para la creación de una organización internacional de arbitraje comercial, in *El Arbitraje Comercial Internacional* 205 (Mexico 1983)

Beaumont, The Rules of Conciliation, Arbitration and Expertise of the Euro-Arab Chambers of Commerce, 2 *Int'l Constr. L. Rev.* 392 (1985)

Chartier, Centre d'Arbitrage de la Chambre Officielle Franco-Allemande de Commerce et d'Industrie, 1986 *Rev. Arb.* 291

Comment, The International Court of Arbitration for Maritime and Inland Navigation in Gdynia, 1961 *Bull. Czechoslovak L.* 69

Derains, Clauses et procédures d'arbitrage internationales dans le pays arabes, in *First Euro-Arab Arbitration Conference: Proceedings* 150 (F. Kemicha ed. 1987)

El-Ahbar, Le Centre arabe d'arbitrage commercial à Rabat, 1989 *Rev. Arb.* 631

Gaillard, Euro-Arab Chambers of Commerce: Rules of Conciliation, Arbitration and Expertise, Introductory Note, 24 *I.L.M.* 1119 (1985)

Goodman-Everard, De wereld contra Irak: een monsterprocedure, maar niet de 'mother of all arbitrations,' 1991 *Tijdschrift voor Arbitrage* 155

Groos, L'arbitrage de la Chambre Officielle Franco-Allemande de Commerce et d'Industrie, 1986 *Int'l Bus.* L.J. 205

————, Schiedsgerichtsbarkeit im deutsch-französischen Wirtschaftsverkehr, 33 *RIW* 343 (1987)

Groos, Langer & Sandrock, Die Schiedsgerichtsbarkeit der Offiziellen Deutsch-Französischen Industrie- und Handelskammer, 40 *BB*, Annex 14 (No. 32, 1985)

Groos, Langer, Sandrock & Dorman, Rules of the Official Franco-German Chamber of Commerce and Industry, in 3 *W.A.R.* 3742 (H. Smit & V. Pechota eds. 1987)

Habib-Deloncle, Le Règlement de conciliation, d'arbitrage et d'expertise des chambres de commerce euro-arabes, 1983 *Rev. Arb.* 239

Hangarter, Die Schiedsgerichtsbarkeit der Handelskammer Deutschland-Schweiz, 1 *Jahrbuch Schiedsgerichtsbarkeit* 169 (1987)

————, Die Schiedsgerichtsbarkeit der Handelskammer Deutschland-Schweiz, in *Die Internationale Schiedsgerichtsbarkeit in der Schweiz* 189 (K.-H. Böckstiegel ed. 1989)

Maktouf, Euro-Arab Arbitration Rules, 6 *Middle E. Exec. Rep.* 15 (No. 1, 1983)

Mebroukine, Le Règlement d'arbitrage algéro-français du 27 mars 1983, 1986 *Rev. Arb.* 191

Nanowski, Z., *Z problematyki miedzynarodowego arbitrazu handlowego v Polsce* (Warsaw 1982?)

Pechota, UNCITRAL Rules as Applied in Arbitrations under the Optional Clause for Use in Contracts in USSR-United States Trade, 1977, in 3 *W.A.R.* 3313 (H. Smit & V. Pechota eds. 1987)

Przetacznik & Pechota, Rules of the International Court of Arbitration for Marine and Inland Navigation at Gdynia, In 3 *W.A.R.* 3728 (H. Smit & V. Pechota eds. 1987)

Rattray, Feasibility of a Caribbean Arbitration Centre, 1 *Caribbean L. & Bus.* 91 (No. 3, 1989)

Rigault, Arbitrage de la Chambre Officielle Franco-Allemande de Commerce et d'Industrie, 1986 *Cah. Jurid. & Fisc.* 297

Samuel & Gearhart, Sporting Arbitration and the International Olympic Committee's Court of Arbitration for Sport, 6 *J. Int'l Arb.* 39 (No. 4, 1989)

Sandrock, Die Entscheidung von Streitigkeiten durch Schiedsgerichte, in *Französisches Vertragsrecht für deutsche Exporteure* 54 (C. Witz & T.M. Bopp eds. 1989)

Shifman, Rules of the Euro-Arab Chambers of Commerce, in 3 *W.A.R.* 3711 (H. Smit & V. Pechota eds. 1987)

Spedding, Interpretation of Art. 132 of the Lome II Convention. Arbitration or Court Proceeding, 12 *Int'l Bus. Law.* 382 (1984)

Stewart & Pechota, Franco-Algerian Agreement on the Settlement by Arbitration of Disputes Arising from Commercial Contracts, 1983, in 3 *W.A.R.* 3630 (H. Smit & V. Pechota eds. 1987)

Strohbach, Legal Aspects of Arbitration under the International Court of Arbitration for Marine and Inland Navigation [Gdynia Arbitration Court], in *A.I.A, Essays in Memoriam Eugenio Minoli* 495 (Turin 1974)

Szurski, Basic Information on Polish Law and Practice Concerning International Commercial Arbitration, in *Arbitration in Settlement of International Commercial Disputes Involving the Far East and Arbitration in Combined Transportation* 149 (P. Sanders ed. 1989)

von Breitenstein, Eine neue Arbitrage-Institution: Das COFACI-Schiedszentrum in Paris, 39 *NJW* 1402 (1986)

Ziadé, Selective Bibliography on Arbitration and Arab Countries, 3 *ICSID Rev. -Foreign Investment L.J.* 423 (1988)

3.14 INTERNATIONAL COUNCIL FOR COMMERCIAL ARBITRATION

Bernini, The Future of ICCA: Some Perspectives, 12 *Y.B. Com. Arb.* xvii (1987)

ICCA, Travaux du Congrès International de l'Arbitrage. Paris, 11-13 Mai 1961, 1961 *Rev. Arb.* 37-161

ICCA, Travaux du 2e Congrès International de l'Arbitrage. Rotterdam, 6-9 Juillet 1966, 1966 *Rev. Arb.* 1-157

ICCA, Coopération entre organismes d'arbitrage/Co-operation among Arbitration Organizations. *Third International Arbitration Congress, Venice, 6-8 October 1969* (Milan 1970), also published in 1969 *Rev. Arb.* (No. 4)

ICCA, *Collection of the Fourth International Congress on Arbitration Materials. Moscow, 3-6 October 1972* (Moscow 1974)

ICCA, *The Fifth International Arbitration Congress, 7-10 January 1975, New Delhi: Proceedings* (New Delhi 1976)

ICCA, *Sixth International Arbitration Congress. Mexico City, March 13-16, 1978* (Mexico 1980)

ICCA, *Seventh International Arbitration Congress, Hamburg, June 7-11, 1982. ICCA Congress Series No. 1* (Deventer 1983)

Sanders, P., ed., *Comparative Arbitration Practice and Public Policy in Arbitration. ICCA Eighth Int'l Arbitration Congress* (New York, 6-9 May 1986), (Deventer 1987)

————, ed., *Arbitration in Settlement of International Commercial Disputes Involving the Far East and Arbitration in Combined Transportation: ICCA Ninth Int'l Arb. Congress* (Tokyo, 31 May - 3 June 1988), (Deventer 1989)

Sanders, Aspects de l'arbitrage international, 53 *Rev. Droit Int'l & Droit Comp.* 129 (1976)

Vigrass, The Role of Institutions in Arbitration, in *Handbook of Arbitration Practice* 367 (R. Bernstein ed. 1987)

3.15 PROPOSALS TO CREATE AN INTERNATIONAL ARBITRATION SYSTEM

Caron, The Nature of the Iran-United States Claims Tribunal and the Evolving Structure of International Dispute Resolution, 84 *Am. J. Int'l L.* 104 (1990)

Franks, An Approach to the Development of Model Rules of International Commercial Arbitration through an International Arbitration Commission, in *ICCA, Fifth Int'l Arb. Congress: Proceedings* C Ic 1-5 (1975)

Jakubowski, On Creation of the International Organization of Commercial Arbitration, in *ICCA, Fourth Int'l Arb. Congress: Proceedings* 730 (1972)

McClelland, Toward a More Mature System of International Commercial Arbitration: The Establishment of Uniform Rules of Procedure and the Elimination of the Conflict of Laws Questions, 5 *N.C.J. Int'l L. & Com. Reg.* 169 (1980)

Rubino-Sammartano, An International Arbitral Court of Appeal as an Alternative to Long Attacks and Recognition Proceedings, 6 *J. Int'l Arb.* 180 (No. 1, 1989)

Smit, The Future of International Commercial Arbitration: A Single Transnational Institution? 25 *Colum. J. Transnat'l L.* 9 (1986)

Straus, A Network of Arbitration Associations, in *A.I.A., Essays in Memoriam Eugenio Minoli* 487 (Turin 1974)

4. NATIONAL ARBITRATION INSTITUTIONS AND RULES

4.01 NATIONAL INSTITUTIONS AND RULES GENERALLY

Aden, M., *Internationale Handelsschiedsgerichtsbarkeit. Kommentar zu den Verfahrensordnungen* (Heidelberg 1988)

Blessing, International Arbitration Procedures, 17 *Int'l Bus. Law.* 408 and 451 (1989)

Böckstiegel, K.-H., ed., *Handelsschiedsgerichtsbarkeit in England und in der Bundesrepublik Deutschland/Commercial Arbitration in the Federal Republic of Germany and in England* (Cologne 1987)

————, ed., *Schiedsgerichtsbarkeit im deutsch-amerikanischen Wirtschaftverkehr/Arbitration in US-German Business Relations* (Cologne 1985)

Chillón Medina, J. M. & J. F. Merino Merchán, *Tratado de arbitraje privado interno e internacional* (Madrid 1978)

Clow & Stewart, International Arbitration: Storming the Citadel, 9 *Int'l Fin. L. Rev.* 10 (No. 3, 1990)

Erecinski, Problems in the Administration of Evidence Arising from the Rules of the International Commercial Arbitration, 17 *Polish Y.B. Int'l L.* 41 (1988)

Fouchard, Les institutions permanentes d'arbitrage devant le juge étatique (à propos d'une jurisprudence récente), 1987 *Rev. Arb.* 225

————, Typologie des institutions d'arbitrage, 1990 *Rev. Arb.* 281

Fowler et al., A Survey of Arbitral Forums, 5 *N.C. J. Int'l L. & Com. Reg.* 219 (1980)

Glossner, O., *Commercial Arbitration in the Federal Republic of Germany* (Deventer 1984)

Graving, The International Commercial Arbitration Institutions: How Good a Job Are They Doing? 4 *Am. U.J. Int'l L. & Pol'y* 319 (1989)

Grzybowski, Arbitral Tribunals for Foreign Trade in Socialist Countries, 37 *Law & Contemp. Probs.* 592 (1972)

Hacking (The Lord), A New Competition — Rivals for Centres of Arbitration, 45 *Arbitration* 166 (1979)

Hanak, The Experience of Socialist Lawyers in Arbitration Held in Non-Socialist Countries on Litigations Between Businessmen from East and West, 10 *Int'l Bus. Law.* 145 (1982)

Hiramoto, A Path to Resources on International Commercial Arbitration 1980-1986, 4 *Int'l Tax & Bus. Law.* 297 (1986)

Hudson, General Average Adjustment and Arbitration in the People's Republic of China, 1976 *Lloyd's Mar. & Com. L.Q.* 135

ICCA, Seventh International Arbitration Congress, Hamburg, June 7-11, 1982. *ICCA Congress Series No. 1* (Deventer 1983)

Katona, Ad hoc Arbitration Rules: Similarities and Differences. A Comparative Review, 3 *Questions of Int'l Law: Hungarian Perspectives* 93 (H. Bokor-Szegö ed. 1986)

Kemicha, F., ed., *Euro-Arab Arbitration II/Arbitrage Euro-Arabe II* (London 1989)

Keutgen, Les règlements d'arbitrage, in *L'arbitrage* 45 (L. Matray & G. de Leval eds. 1989)

Kopelmanas, Le rôle des règlements d'arbitrage dans le développement des procédures arbitrales applicables au règlement de litiges commerciaux à caractère international, 21 *Ann. Français Droit Int'l* 294 (1975)

Kornmeier, Die Verfahrensordnungen in der internationalen Schiedsgerichtsbarkeit, 26 *RIW* 381 (1980)

Kos-Rabcewicz-Zubkowski, L. & P.L Davidson, *Commercial Arbitration Institutions: An International Directory and Guide* (New York 1986)

Lebedev, Institutional Arbitrations of General and Specialized Jurisdiction and Some Notes on International Cooperation, in *ICCA, 4th Int'l Arb. Congress: Proc.* 784 (1972)

Lebedev, S., ed., *Handbook on Foreign Trade Arbitration in the CMEA Member Countries* (Moscow 1983)

Lee, E., *Encyclopedia of International Commercial Arbitration* (London 1986)

Melis, Taak en verantwoordelijkheid van arbitrage-instituten, 1988 *Tijdschrift voor Arbitrage*

Park & Hill, International Arbitration, in *Modern Legal Systems Cyclopedia* 873 (K.R. Redden gen. ed. 1984)

Paulsson, Arbitral Institutions Adapt, 6 *Int'l Arb. Rep.* 23 (No. 6, 1991)

Robert, Principes directeurs des règlements d'arbitrage applicable aux affaires commerciales internationales, in *ICCA, Third Int'l Arb. Congress: Proceedings* 279 (1969)

Strohbach, The CMEA Countries, in *Arbitration in Settlement of International Commercial Disputes Involving the Far East and Arbitration in Combined Transportation* 133 (P. Sanders ed. 1989)

Wetter, J.G., *The International Arbitral Process: Public and Private, volumes I - V* (Dobbs Ferry, NY 1979)

173

4.02 AMERICAN ARBITRATION ASSOCIATION

American Arbitration Association, *Lawyers' Arbitration Letters*, (Ardsley-on-Hudson, NY 1990)

Blessing, International Arbitration Procedures, 17 *Int'l Bus. Law.* 408 and 451 (1989)

————, The Major Western and Soviet Arbitration Rules: A Comparison of the Rules of UNCITRAL, UNCITRAL Model Law, LCIA, ICC, AAA and the Rules of the USSR Chamber of Commerce and Industry, 6 *J. Int'l Arb.* 7 (No. 3, 1989)

Coulson, American Arbitration Association and Immunity of Arbitrators, in *The Immunity of Arbitrators* 97 (J.D.M. Lew ed. 1990)

————, Commercial Arbitration in the United States, 51 *Arbitration* 367 (May 1985)

————, Do We Know How Arbitration Panels Decide? 6 *J. Int'l Arb.* 7 (No. 2, 1989)

————, International Commercial Arbitration in the United States of America, in *Arbitration in Settlement of International Commercial Disputes Involving the Far East and Arbitration in Combined Transportation* 161 (P. Sanders ed. 1989)

————, The Future Growth of Institutional Administration in International Commercial Arbitration, in *The Art of Arbitration* 73 (J. Schultsz & A. van den Berg eds. 1982)

Coulson, R., *Business Arbitration — What You Need to Know* (Rev. 3rd ed. 1987)

Cox, The Selection Process and the Appointment of Arbitrators, 46 *Arb. J.* 28 (No. 2, 1991); also in *Commercial Arbitration for the 1990s* (R. Medalie ed. 1991)

Eckstrom, L., *Licensing in Foreign and Domestic Operations. Volume I,* Chapter 7: Arbitration (by Steven Z. Szczepanski), (New York 1972, updated 1987)

Friedland, Arbitration under the AAA's Rules, 6 *Arb. Int'l* 301 (1990)

Friedman, Multidoor Courthouse Procedures of the AAA, *Arbitration & the Law 1986: AAA General Counsel's Annual Report* 24 (1987)

————, Arbitrating Your Case under the Securities Arbitration Rules of the American Arbitration Association, *Arbitration & the Law 1987-88: AAA General Counsel's Annual Report* 92 (1988)

————, Arbitrating Your Case under the Securities Rules of the American Arbitration Association, 43 *Arb. J.* 23 (No. 2, 1988)

Furnish, Commercial Arbitration Agreements and the Uniform Commercial Code, 67 *Calif. L. Rev.* 317 (1979)

Hoellering, Arbitration of Patent Disputes, in *Arbitration & the Law: AAA General Counsel's Annual Report 1987-88* 163 (1988)

————, International Commercial Arbitration: United States Perspective, in *UNCITRAL Arbitration Model in Canada* 17 (R. Paterson & B. Thompson, eds. 1987)

————, Is a New Practice Emerging from the Experience of the American Arbitration Association? 4 *Int'l Tax & Bus Law.* 230 (1986)

————, The New International Arbitration Rules of the American Arbitration Association, *New York Law Journal,* Feb. 14, 1991; also in *Arbitration & the Law: AAA General Counsel's Annual Report 1990-91* 236 (1991)

————, The American Arbitration Association, in *First International Commercial Arbitration Conference: Proceedings* 81 (N. Antaki & A. Prujiner, eds. 1986)

Hoellering & Shifman, American Arbitration Association, in 4A *W.A.R.* 5647 (H. Smit & V. Pechota eds. 1989)

Hoeniger, Tools to Tailor AAA for Large, Complex Matters, 44 *Arb. J.* 15 (1989)

Holtzmann, Five Ways the American Arbitration Association Can Assist in Resolving Disputes in Trade with the Soviet Union, in *IBA, Soviet Foreign Trade Reforms & East/West Arbitration* 155 (1988)

————, United States of America: The American Arbitration Association, in *Handbook of Institutional Arbitration in International Trade* 249 (E. Cohn, M. Domke & F. Eisemann eds. 1977)

International Chamber of Commerce, *The Arbitral Process and the Independence of Arbitrators/La procédure arbitrale et l'indépendence des arbitres* (Paris 1991)

Kellor, F., *American Arbitration* (New York 1948)

Kos-Rabcewicz-Zubkowski, L. & P.L. Davidson, *Commercial Arbitration Institutions: An International Directory and Guide* (New York 1986)

Kritzer & Anderson, The Arbitration Alternative: A Comparative Analysis of Case Processing Time, Disposition Mode, and Cost in the American Arbitration Association and the Courts, 8 *Just. Sys. J.* 6 (1983)

Lécuyer-Thieffry, C. & P. Thieffry, *Le règlement des litiges civils et commerciaux avec les Etats-Unis* (Paris 1986)

Leloczky, East-West Arbitration: A Practitioner's Viewpoint from Hungary, 4 *Arb. Int'l* 266 (1988)

McClelland, Toward a More Mature System of International Commercial Arbitration: The Establishment of Uniform Rules of Procedure and the Elimination of the Conflict of Laws Questions, 5 *N.C.J. Int'l L. & Com. Reg.* 169 (1980)

Meade, Arbitration Overview: The AAA's Role in Domestic and International Arbitration, 1 *J. Int'l Arb.* 263 (1984)

Parker School of Foreign and Comparative Law, *The 1989 Guide to International Arbitration and Arbitrators* (Dobbs Ferry 1989)

Peterson, C. & C. McCarthy, *Arbitration Strategy and Technique* (Charlottesville, VA 1986)

Rhodes & Sloan, The Pitfalls of International Commercial Arbitration, 17 *Vand. J. Transnat'l L.* 19 (1984)

Smit, The Future of International Commercial Arbitration: A Single Transnational Institution? 25 *Colum. J. Transnat'l L.* 9 (1986)

Smit, The New International Arbitration Rules of the A.A.A., 2 *Am. Rev. Int'l Arb.* 1 (1991)

Smith, Impartiality of the Party-Appointed Arbitrator, 6 *Arb. Int'l* 320 (1990)

4.03 ARBITRATION INSTITUTE OF THE STOCKHOLM CHAMBER OF COMMERCE

Alley, International Arbitration: The Alternative of the Stockholm Chamber of Commerce, 22 *Int'l Law.* 837 (1988)

Arbitration Institute of the Stockholm Chamber of Commerce, *Arbitration in Sweden* (2nd rev. ed. 1984)

Arkin, New Opportunities for Arbitration in East/West Trade, 3 *Transnat'l Law.* 495 (1990)

Coulson, Soviet-American Contract Arbitration, 1983 *Y.B. Swed. & Int'l Arb.* 20

Franke, International Arbitration in Sweden, 76 *Am. Soc. Int'l L. Proc.* 166 (1982)

———, International Arbitration in Sweden, 2 *Int'l Constr. L. Rev.* 159 (1985)

———, SCC Arbitration Goes Further International, 3 *Int'l Arb. Rep.* 22 (No. 3, 1988)

———, Special Features of Arbitration in Stockholm, 49 *Arbitration* 99 (Aug. 1983)

———, The Arbitration Institute of the Stockholm Chamber of Commerce, 1982 *Y.B. Swed. & Int'l Arb.* 6

———, The Arbitration Institute of the Stockholm Chamber of Commerce, 1990 *Y.B. Swed. & Int'l Arb.* 14

Hanak, The Experience of Socialist Lawyers in Arbitration Held in Non-Socialist Countries on Litigations Between Businessmen from East and West, 10 *Int'l Bus. Law.* 145 (1982)

Hjerner, Sweden: The Stockholm Arbitration Institute, in *Handbook of Institutional Arbitration* 187 (E. Cohn, M. Domke & F. Eisemann eds. 1977)

Hobér, Profile: Stockholm Chamber of Commerce, 2 *Int'l Arb. Rep.* 161 (1987)

Holtzmann, Five Ways the American Arbitration Association Can Assist in Resolving Disputes in Trade with the Soviet Union, in *IBA, Soviet Foreign Trade Reforms & East/West Arbitration* 155 (1988)

Kos-Rabcewicz-Zubkowski, L. & P.L. Davidson, *Commercial Arbitration Institutions: An International Directory and Guide* (New York 1986)

Maggs, Reglament Arbitrazhnogo Instituta Stokgol'mskoi Torgovoi Palaty, 4 *Arb. Int'l* 331 (1988)

Norwegian Group of the International Bar Association, *International Commercial Arbitration in Action: Papers from a Conference in Oslo in 1982* (Oslo 1983)

Parker School of Foreign and Comparative Law, *The 1989 Guide to International Arbitration and Arbitrators* (Dobbs Ferry 1989)

Wetter, Institutional Arbitration in Sweden: A Guide to the 1988 Rules of the Arbitration Institute of the Stockholm Chamber of Commerce, 43 *Arb. J.* 5 (No. 2, 1988)

Wetter & Shifman, The Arbitration Institute of the Stockholm Chamber of Commerce, in 4A *W.A.R.* 5339 (H. Smit & V. Pechota eds. 1989)

4.04 ASSOCIAZIONE ITALIANA PER L'ARBITRATO

Deodato, G. & Migliorisi, G., eds., *Codice dell'arbitrato* (Milan 1989)

Gambardella & Carbone, Développement de l'arbitrage commercial en Italie: le rôle des Chambres de Commerce et la coopération entre organismes d'arbitrage au niveau national, in *ICCA, Third Int'l Arb. Congress: Proceedings* 431 (1969)

Kos-Rabcewicz-Zubkowski, L. & P.L. Davidson, *Commercial Arbitration Institutions: An International Directory and Guide* (New York 1986)

Longo, Arbitres et Cour d'Arbitrage dans les procédures de l'Association Italienne pour l'Arbitrage, in *A.I.A., Essays in Memoriam Eugenio Minoli* 293 (Turin 1974)

Parker School of Foreign and Comparative Law, *The 1989 Guide to International Arbitration and Arbitrators* (Dobbs Ferry 1989)

Recchia, Commentaire du nouveau Règlement de l'Association italienne pour l'arbitrage, 1988 *Rev. Arb.* 390

———, Italy: Associazione Italiana per l'Arbitrato, in *Handbook of Institutional Arbitration in International Trade* 101 (E. Cohn, M. Domke & F. Eisemann eds. 1977)

———, Le nouveau Règlement d'arbitrage de l'Association italienne pour l'arbitrage, 1979 *Rev. Arb.* 217

Reviglio, Arbitration and the Enterprise: An Italian Perspective, 44 *Arb. J.* 45 (No. 1, 1989)

Sacerdoti, Italian Arbitration Association, in 4 *W.A.R.* 4807 (H. Smit & V. Pechota eds. 1980)

179

4.05 COURT OF ARBITRATION AT THE RUSSIAN CHAMBER OF COMMERCE AND INDUSTRY

Bell, Resolution of International Trade Disputes: An Analysis of the Soviet Foreign Trade Arbitration Commission's Decisions Concerning the Doctrine of Force Majeure as an Excuse to the Performance of Private International Trade Agreements, 10 *Md. J. Int'l L. & Trade* 135 (1986)

Berman, Force Majeure and the Denial of an Export License under Soviet Law: A Comment on Jordan Investments Ltd. v. Soiuznefteksport, 73 *Harv. L. Rev.* 1128 (1960)

Blessing, International Arbitration Procedures, 17 *Int'l Bus. Law.* 408 and 451 (1989)

————, The Major Western and Soviet Arbitration Rules: A Comparison of the Rules of UNCITRAL, UNCITRAL Model Law, LCIA, ICC, AAA and the Rules of the USSR Chamber of Commerce and Industry, 6 *J. Int'l Arb.* 7 (No. 3, 1989)

Butler, W., *Arbitration in the Soviet Union* (Dobbs Ferry 1989)

————, *Soviet Commercial Arbitration* (Dobbs Ferry and Paris 1989)

————, ed., *Soviet Commercial and Maritime Arbitration* (Dobbs Ferry, NY 1980-)

Chew, A Procedural and Substantive Analysis of Fairness of Chinese and Soviet Foreign Trade Arbitrations, 21 *Tex. Int'l L.J.* 291 (1986)

Hanotiau, L'arbitrage commercial dans les relations belgo-soviétiques, 1983 *JT* 462

Hascher, Actualité de l'arbitrage international en U.R.S.S., 1988 *Rev. Arb.* 237

Hobér, Arbitration in Moscow, 3 *Arb. Int'l* 119 (1987)

Hobér, K., *Joint Ventures in the Soviet Union.* Chapter XII: Dispute Resolution and Applicable Law (Dobbs Ferry 1989)

Kabatov, Arbitration in the USSR: New Statute and Rules of the Arbitration Court at the USSR Chamber of Commerce and Industry, in *IBA, Soviet Foreign Trade Reforms & East/West Arbitration* 119 (1988); also in 5 *Arb. Int'l* 45 (1989)

————, Kompetentsia Vneshnetorgovoi Arbitrazhnoi Kommissii, 1983 *S.G.P.* 55 (No. 2)

Kheifets, Jurisdictions of Permanent USSR Arbitration Courts Distinguished, in *ICCA, Fifth Int'l Arb. Congress: Proceedings* C Izb 1-4 (1975)

Kotlarchuk, Has the U.S.S.R. Foreign Trade Commission Reached the Age of Aquarius with the Newly Revised Arbitration Statute of 1975? 11 *Int'l Law.* 467 (1977)

Kuss, Neuere Entwicklungen und Perspektiven der Ost-West-Schiedsgerichtsbarkeit, 33 *RIW* 584 (1987)

Larkin, The Effect of the Commission on International Trade Arbitration in the Soviet Union, 33 *Geo. Wash. L. Rev.* 728 (1965)

Lebedev, Application of Law by the Maritime Arbitration Commission in Settling Disputes, 6 *Ga. J. Int'l & Comp. L.* 519 (1976)

————, Union of Soviet Socialist Republics: The Foreign Trade Arbitration Commission of the U.S.S.R. Chamber of Commerce and Industry, in *Handbook of Institutional Arbitration in International Trade* 273 (E. Cohn, M. Domke & F. Eisemann eds. 1977)

Lebedev S., *Mezhdunarodnyi kommercheskii arbitrazh: kompetentsia arbitrov i soglashenie stran* (Moscow 1988)

————, *Mezhdunarodnyi torgovyi arbitrazh* (Moscow 1965)

————, ed., *Handbook on Foreign Trade Arbitration in the CMEA Member Countries* (Moscow 1983)

Leff, The Foreign Trade Arbitration Commission of the USSR and the West, 24 *Arb. J.* 1 (1969); also in *A.A.A., New Strategies* 143 (1971)

Minakov, Practice of the Foreign Trade Arbitration Commission of the USSR Chamber of Commerce and Industry, 24 *Soviet Stat. & Dec.* 63 (No. 4, 1988)

Monroy Cabra, M.G., *Arbitraje Comercial* (Bogota 1982)

Morton, United States-Soviet Commercial Arbitration Under the 1972 Trade Agreement, 7 *Case W. Res. J. Int'l L.* 121 (1974)

Orlov, Arbitration Procedure in East-West Trade, 55 *Nordic J. Int'l L.* 310 (1986)

Parker School of Foreign and Comparative Law, *The 1989 Guide to International Arbitration and Arbitrators* (Dobbs Ferry 1989)

Pechota, An Outline of Recent Changes in Soviet Domestic and International Arbitration, 1 *Am. Rev. Int'l Arb.* 154 (1990)

————, International Economic Arbitration in the USSR and Eastern Europe, 8 *N.Y. L. Sch. J. Int'l & Comp. L.* 377 (1987)

————, The Court of Arbitration at the USSR Chamber of Commerce and Industry, in 4A *W.A.R.* 5439 (H. Smit & V. Pechota eds. 1989)

Pisar, The Communist System of Foreign Trade Adjudication, 72 *Harv. L. Rev.* 1409 (1959)

Pisar, S., *Coexistence & Commerce,* Chapters 20 - 24 (New York 1970)

Pozdnyakov, 50 *let Vneshnetorgovoi arbitrazhnoi komissii, Vneshniaya Torgovlya* 39 (No. 7, 1982)

————, Commercial Arbitration in CMEA Member Countries, 4 *Int'l Tax & Bus. Law.* 272 (1986)

————, Decree of the Presidium of the USSR Supreme Soviet, December 14, 1987, on Arbitration Court at the USSR Chamber of Commerce and Industry, Moscow, 2 *Jahrbuch Schiedsgerichtsbarkeit* 181 (1988)

Rabinovich, The Procedure for Signing Transactions with Soviet Foreign Trade Organizations, 22 *Int'l Law.* 143 (1988)

Ramzaitsev, Deiatel'nost' Vneshnetorgovoi Arbitrazhnoi Komissii v Moskve v 1957 godu, 1958 *Soviet Y.B. Int'l L.* 463

————, Deiatel'nost' Vneshnetorgovoi Arbitrazhnoi Komissii v Moskve v 1958 i 1959 gg., 1960 *Soviet Y.B. Int'l L.* 346

————, La jurisprudence en matière de droit international privé de la Commission arbitrale soviétique pour le commerce extérieur, 1958 *Rev. Crit. Droit Int'l Privé* 459

————, The Law Applied by Arbitral Tribunals, in *The Sources of the Law of International Trade* 138 (C. Schmitthoff ed. 1964)

Ramzaitsev, D.F., *Vneshnetorgovyi arbitrazh v SSSR* (Moscow 1952)

Razumov, Arbitration Treaties between the USSR and Countries in the Far East, in *Arbitration in Settlement of International Commercial Disputes Involving the Far East and Arbitration in Combined Transportation* 145 (P. Sanders ed. 1989)

————, *Deiatelnost Vneshnetorgovoi Arbitrazhnoi Komissii, Informatsionnyi Sbornik Torgovoi Palaty SSSR* (1982)

Robert, Observations sur une sentence arbitrale internationale: sentence rendue le 3 juillet 1958 par la Commission Arbitrale du Commerce Extérieur à Moscou dans le litige "Arbitrage petrolier Israel-Soirets," 1960 *Rev. Arb.* 76 & 92 (text of the award)

Samuels, The Soviet Position on International Arbitration: A Wealth of Choices or Choices for the Wealthy, 26 *Va. J. Int'l L.* 417 (1986)

Schmidt, L'interprétation des contrats internationaux par la Commission Arbitrale du Commerce Extérieur de l'URSS, 1985 *Int'l Bus. L.J.* 239

Semmler, The Case for FTAC Arbitration of Disputes Between Soviet Enterprises and American Firms, 14 *Colum. J. Transnat'l L.* 302 (1975)

Timmermans, The New Statute on the Arbitration Court at the USSR Chamber of Commerce and Industry, 5 *J. Int'l Arb.* 97 (No. 3, 1988)

Usenko, The USSR Chamber of Commerce and Industry, in *ICCA, Fourth Int'l Arb. Congress: Proceedings* 361 (1972)

Waehler, J.P., *Die Aussenhandels- und Seeschiedsgerichtsbarkeit in der UdSSR* (Berlin 1974)

4.06 JAPAN COMMERCIAL ARBITRATION ASSOCIATION

Akroyd, The Role of Arbitration in Japanese Foreign Trade, 44 *Arbitration* 136 (1978)

Chave, Profile: The Japan Commercial Arbitration Association, 2 *Int'l Arb. Rep.* 96 (1987)

Doi, International Commercial Arbitration in Japan, in *Liber Amicorum for Martin Domke* 65 (P. Sanders ed. 1967)

Hattori, International Commercial Arbitration Practised by the Japan Commercial Arbitration Association, in *ICCA, Third Int'l Arb. Congress: Proceedings* 459 (1969)

Kakinuki, Dispute Resolution in Japan: Choosing the Right Alternative, 9 *East Asian Exec. Rep.* 7 (No. 11, 1987)

Kitagawa, Contractual Autonomy in International Commercial Arbitration Including a Japanese Perspective, in *Liber Amicorum for Martin Domke* 133 (P. Sanders ed. 1967)

Kitagawa & Fukushima, Japan: The Japan Commercial Arbitration Association, in *Handbook of Institutional Arbitration in International Trade* 115 (E. Cohn, M. Domke & F. Eisemann eds. 1977)

Kos-Rabcewicz-Zubkowski, L. & P.L. Davidson, *Commercial Arbitration Institutions: An International Directory and Guide* (New York 1986)

Nomura, Some Aspects of the Use of Commercial Arbitration by Japanese Corporations, 33 *Osaka Univ. L. Rev.* 47 (March 1986); also in *East and West: Legal Philosophies in Japan* 50 (M. Yasaki ed. 1987)

Parker School of Foreign and Comparative Law, *The 1989 Guide to International Arbitration and Arbitrators* (Dobbs Ferry 1989)

Sawada, International Commercial Arbitration — Practice of Arbitral Institutions in Japan, 30 *Japanese Ann. Int'l L.* 69 (1987)

————, Practice of Arbitral Institutions in Japan, 4 *Arb. Int'l* 120 (1988)

Shifman, Japan Commercial Arbitration Association, in 4 *W.A.R.* 4913 (H. Smit & V. Pechota eds. 1989)

Sono, The Japanese Experience, in *UNCITRAL Arbitration Model in Canada* 25 (R. Paterson & B. Thompson eds. 1987)

Taniguchi, Commercial Arbitration in Japan, in *Arbitration in Settlement of International Commercial Disputes Involving the Far East and Arbitration in Combined Transportation* 29 (P. Sanders ed. 1989)

4.07 LONDON COURT OF INTERNATIONAL ARBITRATION

Blessing, The Major Western and Soviet Arbitration Rules: A Comparison of the Rules of UNCITRAL, UNCITRAL Model Law, LCIA, ICC, AAA and the Rules of the USSR Chamber of Commerce and Industry, 6 *J. Int'l Arb.* 7 (No. 3, 1989)

Clark & Lange, Recent Changes in English Arbitration Practice Widen Opportunities for More Effective International Arbitrations, 35 *Bus. Law.* 1621 (1980)

de Hauteclocque, Renouveau et croissance de la London Court of International Arbitration, 17 *Droit et Pratique du Com. Int'l* 170 (1991)

El-Ahdab, A. H., *Arbitration with the Arab Countries* (Deventer 1990)

————, *L'arbitrage dans les pays arabes* (Paris 1988)

Erecinski, Problems in the Administration of Evidence Arising from the Rules of the International Commercial Arbitration, 17 *Polish Y.B. Int'l L.* 41 (1988)

Hacking (The Lord), A New Competition — Rivals for Centres of Arbitration, 45 *Arbitration* 166 (1979)

Hallgarten, International Commercial Arbitration in London, in *IBA, Soviet Foreign Trade Reforms & East/West Arbitration* 181 (1988)

Hanak, The Experience of Socialist Lawyers in Arbitration Held in Non-Socialist Countries on Litigations Between Businessmen from East and West, 10 *Int'l Bus. Law.* 145 (1982)

Hunter & Paulsson, A Commentary on the 1985 Rules of the London Court of International Arbitration, 50 *Arbitration* 333 (May 1985); also in 10 *Y.B. Com. Arb.* 167 (1985)

Kos-Rabcewicz-Zubkowski, L. & P.L. Davidson, *Commercial Arbitration Institutions: An International Directory and Guide* (New York 1986)

Lebedev, Reglament Mezhdunarodnogo kommercheskogo arbitrazha: angliiskaia model', 1991 *S.G.P.* 84 (No. 5, 1991)

Norwegian Group of the International Bar Association, *International Commercial Arbitration in Action: Papers from a Conference in Oslo in 1982* (Oslo 1983)

Parker School of Foreign and Comparative Law, *The 1989 Guide to International Arbitration and Arbitrators* (Dobbs Ferry 1989)

Salans, The 1985 Rules of the London Court of International Arbitration, 2 *Arb. Int'l* 40 (No. 1, Jan. 1986)

Schollenberger, International Commercial Arbitration in Europe, in 1A *The Law of Transnational Business Transactions* 19-1 (V.P. Nanda ed. 1988)

Schwebel, S.M., *International Arbitration: Three Salient Problems* (Cambridge 1987)

Shifman, The London Court of International Arbitration, in 4A *W.A.R.* 5561 (H. Smit & V. Pechota eds. 1989)

Sieghart, International Arbitration Rules of the London Court of Arbitration, 47 *Arbitration* 130 (1981)

Slade, London Court of International Arbitration, in *First International Commercial Arbitration Conference: Proceedings* 75 (N. Antaki & A. Prujiner eds. 1986)

Smith, Impartiality of the Party-Appointed Arbitrator, 6 *Arb. Int'l* 320 (1990)

Steyn, Methods of Conducting International Commercial Arbitrations: A Re-Examination, in *Second Bermuda Int'l Arbitration Conference: A Collection of Papers* (Hamilton, Bermuda, April 19-22, 1983)

Vigrass, Arbitration Services in the United Kingdom Relevant to Anglo-German Business Relations, in *Handelsschiedsgerichtsbarkeit in England und in der Bundesrepublik Deutschland* 143 (K.-H. Böckstiegel ed. 1987)

————, Arbitration and Administrative Services, 47 *Arbitration* 27 (1981)

————, Arbitration in London, 45 *Arbitration* 104 (1979)

————, The Role of Institutions in Arbitration, in *Handbook of Arbitration Practice* 367 (R. Bernstein ed. 1987)

Wall, United Kingdom: The London Court of Arbitration, in *Handbook of Institutional Arbitration in International Trade* 225 (E. Cohn, M. Domke & F. Eisemann eds. 1977)

Weiss, The Status of the UNCITRAL Model Law on International Commercial Arbitration vis-a-vis the International Chamber of Commerce (ICC), London Court of International Arbitration and UNCITRAL Arbitration Rules: Conflict or Complement? 13 *Syracuse J. Int'l L. & Com.* 367 (1986)

4.08 NETHERLANDS ARBITRATION INSTITUTE

Kos-Rabcewicz-Zubkowski, L. & P.L. Davidson, *Commercial Arbitration Institutions: An International Directory and Guide* (New York 1986)

Netherlands Arbitration Institute (adapted by Bette E. Shifman), in 4A *W.A.R.* 4989 (H. Smit & V. Pechota eds. 1989)

Parker School of Foreign and Comparative Law, *The 1989 Guide to International Arbitration and Arbitrators* (Dobbs Ferry 1989)

van den Berg, Twintig vragen aan het NAI Secretariaat, 1988 *Tijdschrift voor Arbitrage* 151

van Marwijk Kooy, The Netherlands: The Netherlands Arbitration Institute, in *Handbook of Institutional Arbitration in International Trade* 133 (E. Cohn, M. Domke & F. Eisemann eds. 1977)

4.09 SPANISH COURT OF ARBITRATION

Cobos, L'arbitrage en Espagne et le Règlement du Centre espagnol d'arbitrage, 1980 *Rev. Arb.* 64

Cremades, B.M. & E.G. Cabiedes, *Litigating in Spain. Considerations for Foreign Practitioners, Including International Judicial Assistance, Enforcement of Foreign Judgments, Bankruptcy, Arbitration and Other Civil Proceedings in Spain* (Deventer 1989)

Löber, Spanischer Schiedsgerichtshof errichtet: Corte Española de Arbitraje, 4 *IPRax* 112 (1984)

Pechota, Spanish Court of Arbitration, in 4A *W.A.R.* 5275 (H. Smit & V. Pechota eds. 1989)

Plehn, International Arbitration in Spain: A New Institution versus an Old Law, 20 *Int'l Law.* 247 (1986)

Roca Aymar, La Corte Española de Arbitraje y el comercio exterior, 1 *Rev. Corte Esp. Arb.* 265 (1984)

Verdera y Tuells, International Commercial Arbitration and the Spanish Court of Arbitration, 3 *J. Int'l Arb.* 47 (No. 1, 1986)

4.10 OTHER NATIONAL INSTITUTIONS

Ackermann, Die Rechtsprechung des Schiedsgerichtes bei der Kammer für Aussenhandel der DDR, 33 *RIW* 499 (1987)

Addamo, La funzione della Camera Arbitrale Italiana per il Commercio delle Pelle, 25 *Rassegna dell'Arb.* 145 (1985)

————, I cinquant'anni della Camera Arbitrale Italiana delle Pelli, 26 *Rassegna dell'Arb.* 128 (1986)

Addamo, R. R., *Manuale dell'arbitrate commerciale e dell'arbitro* (Milan 1987)

Aden, M., *Internationale Handelsschiedsgerichtsbarkeit. Kommentar zu den Verfahrensordnungen* (Heidelberg 1988)

Alvarez, The Role of Arbitration in Canada — New Perspectives, 21 *U. B.C. L.Rev.* 247 (1987)

Antaki, A Critical Evaluation of International Commercial Arbitration, in *Resolving International Business Disputes through Arbitration: Materials of the Conference in Toronto, Jan. 19 & 20, 1987*

Arkin, New Opportunities for Arbitration in East/West Trade, 3 *Transnat'l Law.* 495 (1990)

Azzali, Chamber of Arbitration of Milan, 8 *Int'l Constr. L. Rev.*

Bachmann, Switzerland: The Court of Arbitration of the Zurich Chamber of Commerce, in *Handbook of Institutional Arbitration in International Trade* 203 (E. Cohn, M. Domke & F. Eisemann eds. 1977)

Barinova, I.I., *Kommentarii sudebnoi i arbitrazhnoi praktiki po morskim delam* (Moscow 1988)

Bauer, Maritime Arbitration in New York, 8 *Int'l Bus. Law.* 306 (1980)

Bellhouse, Singapore: International Arbitration Center Established, 3 *Asia Law & Practice* 31 (No. 9, 1991)

Böshagen, Aus der Arbeit des Deutschen Ausschusses für Schiedsgerichtswesen, in *Festschrift für Arthur Bülow* 17 (K.-H. Böckstiegel & O. Glossner eds. 1981)

191

Briseño Sierra, El arbitraje comercial en México y las leyes-tipo internacionales, 1 *Rev. Corte Esp. Arb.* 67 (1984)

Broedermann, China and Admiralty — An Introduction to Chinese Maritime Law and U.S.-Chinese Shipping Relations, 15 *J. Mar. L. & Com.* 539, 562 (1984)

Bulgarian Chamber of Commerce and Industry, *International Commercial Arbitration in Bulgaria* (Sofia 1989)

Capatina, Les charactéristiques de la Commission d'arbitrage pour les litiges de commerce extérieur de Bucarest, *Annuaire de l'URSS et des pays socialistes européens* 89 (Strasbourg 1974)

Capatina, O., *Litigio arbitral de comercio exterior* (Havana 1985)

Chapman, FOSFA International Arbitration, 2 *Arb. Int'l* 323 (1986)

Chew, A Procedural and Substantive Analysis of Fairness of Chinese and Soviet Foreign Trade Arbitrations, 21 *Tex. Int'l L.J.* 291 (1986)

China Maritime Arbitration Commission, *Selection of Awards and Conciliation Statements* (1984-1988), (Beijing 1989)

Cleveland, How to Save Maritime Arbitration in New York (A Modest Proposal), in 2 *Fifth Int'l Congress of Maritime Arbitrators* (New York 1981)

Cohen, M.M., ed., *Index and Digest of the Award Service of the Society of Maritime Arbitrators,* Volumes 3A & 3B (New York 1986)

Croft, International Commercial Arbitration: Developments in the State of Victoria, Australia, in *UNCITRAL Arbitration Model in Canada* 35 (R. Paterson & B. Thompson eds. 1987)

Cuth, The Arbitration Court of the Czechoslovak Chamber of Commerce and Industry, 21 *Bull. Czechoslovak L.* 94 (No. 2, 1982)

Dahl & Garro, Cuba's System of International Commercial Arbitration: A Convergence of Soviet and Latin American Trends, 15 *Law. Am.* 441 (1984)

Davies, A View of London Maritime Arbitration, 52 *Arbitration* 150 (1986)

de Bournonville, Au sujet des demandes incidents en matière d'arbitrage, in *L'arbitrage* 55 (L. Matray & G. de Leval eds. 1989)

de Fina, Arbitration Law Reforms, International Facilities and Rules, Australian Development, 52 *Arbitration* 158 (1986)

Deodato, G. & Migliorisi, G., eds., *Codice dell'arbitrato* (Milan 1989)

Djurovic, Foreign Trade Court of Arbitration at the Economic Chamber of Yugoslavia: An Institution of Self-Management Judiciary, 10 *Yugoslav L.* 25 (1983)

Dong Yougan, Arbitration Cases Concerning the Responsibilities of the Party Failing to Fulfill the Contractual Obligations, *China Patents & Trademarks* 99 (No. 3, 1985)

————, Arbitration Cases Handled by the Foreign Economic and Trade Arbitration Commission, *China Patents and Trademarks* 101 (No. 1, 1987)

du Pontavice, Un centre spécialisé: La Chambre Arbitrale Maritime de Paris, 1990 *Rev. Arb.* 239

El-Ahdab, A. H., *Arbitration with the Arab Countries* (Deventer 1990)

————, *L'arbitrage dans les pays arabes* (Paris 1988)

Erecinski, Problems in the Administration of Evidence Arising from the Rules of the International Commercial Arbitration, 17 *Polish Y.B. Int'l L.* 41 (1988)

Ester Ledesma, Eficacia del laudo arbitral, in *El Arbitraje en el Derecho Latinoamericano y Español* 99 (L. Perret & U. Montoya Alberti eds. 1989)

Fabro, Les institutions chinoises d'arbitrage commercial international, 1977 *Rev. Arb.* 377

Farago, Decisions of the Hungarian Chamber of Commerce in COMECON Arbitrations, 14 *Int'l & Comp. L.Q.* 1124 (1965)

Fellhauer, H. & H. Strohbach, eds., *Handbuch der internationalen Handelsschiedsgerichtsbarkeit* (Berlin 1969)

Filipescu, I. & A. Dragos Sitaru, *Dreptul international privat. Spete si solutii din practica judiciara arbitrala pentru comertul exterior* (Bucharest 1986)

Fischer-Zernin & Junker, Arbitration and Mediation: Synthesis or Antithesis? 5 *J. Int'l Arb.* 22 (No. 1, 1988)

————, Between Scylla and Charybdis: Fact Gathering in German Arbitration, 4 *J. Int'l Arb.* 9 (No. 2, 1987)

Foustoucos, Les institutions d'arbitrage commercial en Grèce, in *ICCA, Sixth Int'l Arb. Congress: Proceedings* 121 (1978)

————, Une novelle institution permanente d'arbitrage en Grèce, 1978 *Rev. Arb.* 418

Georgiev, Le règlement de la Cour d'arbitrage près de la Chambre de commerce et d'industrie de Bulgarie, 1980 *Rev. Arb.* 44

Goldstajn, A. & S. Triva, *Medunarodna trgovacka arbitraza* (Zagreb 1987)

Goyeneche & Caivano, El arbitraje en el comercio de granos, 1985-II *Jurispr. Arg.* 807

Hanak, The Experience of Socialist Lawyers in Arbitration Held in Non-Socialist Countries on Litigations Between Businessmen from East and West, 10 *Int'l Bus. Law.* 145 (1982)

Hanotiau, L'arbitrage commercial dans les relations belgo-soviétiques, 1983 *JT* 462

Harmathy, Arbitrage en Hongrie (Contrat de commission), 27 *Acta Juridica Academiae Sci. Hungaricae* 295 (1985)

Hobér, Arbitration in Moscow, 3 *Arb. Int'l* 119 (1987)

Huys, M., Centre belge pour l'Etude et la Pratique de l'Arbitrage National et International CEPANI: Schiedsordnung, 1 *Jahrbuch Schiedsgerichtsbarkeit* 176 (1987)

Indonesian Board of Arbitration, *Arbitration in Indonesia and International Conventions on Arbitration* (Jakarta 1978)

Iwasaki, Survey of Maritime Arbitration in New York, 15 *J. Mar. L. & Com.* 69 (1984)

Jakubowski, The Settlement of Foreign Trade Disputes in Poland, 11 *Int'l & Comp. L.Q.* 806 (1962)

Jakubowski, J., *Permanent Arbitration Courts for Foreign Trade in Poland* (Warsaw 1962)

Jakubowski & Wisniewski, Poland: The Court of Arbitration at the Polish Chamber of Foreign Trade, in *Handbook of Institutional Arbitration in International Trade* 147 (E. Cohn, M. Domke & F. Eisemann eds. 1977)

Jarvis, Problems with and Solutions for New York Maritime Arbitration, 1986 *Lloyd's Mar. & Com. L.Q.* 535

Jarvis & Mellman, A Comment of the Rules of the Maritime Arbitration Board of Miami, 19 *J. Mar. L. & Com.* 463 (1988)

Johnson, Commodity Trade Arbitration, in *Handbook of Arbitration Practice* 189 (R. Bernstein ed. 1987)

Johnson, D., *International Commodity Arbitration* (London 1991)

Kang Seok Jeon, Non-Judicial Dispute Resolution Procedures in the Republic of Korea with an Emphasis on Arbitration, 14 *Korean J. Comp. L.* 31 (1986)

Kaplan, Arbitration in Hong Kong, 3 *J. Int'l Arb.* 7 (No. 4, 1986); also 52 *Arbitration* 12 (Feb. 1986)

———, Modern International Arbitration: A Hong Kong Viewpoint, 53 *Arbitration* 225 (1987)

Karrer, Arbitration Procedure in Switzerland: Zurich and Geneva Compared, 2 *Int'l Contr.* 49 (1981)

Kasalova, E., T. Donner, J. Hrivnak & M. Stastny, *Thirty Years of the Arbitration Court of the Czechoslovak Chamber of Commerce and Industry in Prague* (Prague 1981)

Kessler, J., *Schiedsgerichtsvertrag und Schiedsverfahren* (Munich 1970)

Kheifets, O pravilakh proizvodstva del v Morskoi arbitrazhnoi komissii, 1988 *Khozaistvo i Pravo* 60 (No. 3)

———, On the Changes in the Procedure of the Hearing of Cases in the Maritime Arbitration Commission at the USSR Chamber of Commerce and Industry, 1984 *Soviet Y.B. Mar. L.* 113

Kleckner, Foreign Trade Arbitration in Romania, 5 *N.Y.U. J. Int'l L. & Pol.* 233 (1972)

Korean Commercial Arbitration Board, *Guide to Arbitration Practice in Korea* (Seoul 1990)

Kos-Rabcewicz-Zubkowski, L. & P.L. Davidson, *Commercial Arbitration Institutions: An International Directory and Guide* (New York 1986)

Kotora, New Rules of Arbitration Proceedings and Recognition and Enforcement of Foreign Awards and Judicial Decisions in Czechoslovakia, 7 *Diritto negli Scambi Int'li* 225 (1968)

Krafzik, B., *Die Spruchpraxis der Hanseatischen Schiedsgerichte* (Berlin 1974)

Krilyszyn & Bajons, Zur Internationalisierung des österreichischen Schiedsrecht, 1 *Jahrbuch Schiedsgerichtsbarkeit* 234 (1987)

Krishnamurthi, India: The Indian Council of Arbitration, in *Handbook of Institutional Arbitration in International Trade* 83 (E. Cohn, M. Domke & F. Eisemann eds. 1977)

Kuss, Neuere Entwicklungen und Perspektiven der Ost-West-Schiedsgerichtsbarkeit, 33 *RIW* 584 (1987)

Kuster, Zurich, siège d'arbitrage international, 1982 *Rev. Arb.* 3

Lalonde, The New Environment for Commercial Arbitration in Canada, 1 *Rev. Int'l Bus. L.* 31 (1987); also in 1988 *Int'l Bus. L. J.* 963

Lebedev, Application of Law by the Maritime Arbitration Commission in Settling Disputes, 44 *Arbitration* 18 (1977)

———, Commentary on the Statute of the Maritime Arbitration Commission at the USSR Chamber of Commerce and Industry, 7 *Y.B. Com. Arb.* 249 (1982)

———, La Commission d'arbitrage maritime près de la Chambre de commerce de l'URSS, 1971 *Rev. Arb.* 137

———, Morskoi Arbitrazh v SSSR, 1971 *Soviet Y.B. Int'l L.* 226

Lebedev, S. N., *Morskaia Arbitrazhnaia Komissia* (Moscow 1972)

Lebedev, S., ed., *Handbook on Foreign Trade Arbitration in the CMEA Member Countries* (Moscow 1983)

Lee, How to Settle Commercial Disputes in China, 4 *Int'l Fin. L. Rev.* 33 (No. 2, 1985)

Le Fur, Un centre professionnel: La Chambre Arbitrale des Cafés et Poivres du Havre, 1990 *Rev. Arb.* 245

Lepp, Arbitration Appeals: A Comparison of Certain English and American Trade Associations, 39 *Arbitration* 125 (1972)

————, Arbitration Appeals: A Comparison of Certain English and American Trade Associations, 28 *Rassegna dell'Arb.* 57 (1988)

Liew, Commercial Arbitration in Korea with Special Reference to the UNCITRAL Rules, 5 *Korean J. Comp. L.* 69 (1977)

————, Commercial Arbitration in Korea with Special Reference to the UNCITRAL Rules, in *Business Laws in Korea* 905 (Kim Chan-Jin ed. 2nd ed. 1988)

Lodigiani, La Camera Arbitrale Cotoni sodi dell'Associazione Cotoniera Italiana, 19 *Rassegna dell'Arb.* 89 (1978)

Lux, MAC in Moscow, 19 *Int'l Bus. Law.* 212 (1991)

McCormack, A Lawyer's View of Arbitration Proceedings and Composition of the Arbitration Panel, 1984 *Y.B. Mar. L.* 55

Mackie, Integration of Arbitration Systems as Regards the Commodity Trades, 44 *Arbitration* 89 (1978)

————, GAFTA Arbitration Procedures, 56 *Arbitration* 150 (1990)

————, The Grain and Feed Trade Association and Immunity of Arbitrators, in *The Immunity of Arbitrators* 111 (J.D.M. Lew ed. 1990)

Makowski, Disputes Concerning Lay Days (A Practical Point of View of the Maritime Arbitration Commission), 1 *Y.B. Mar. L.* 135 (1984)

Maslov, Awards of the Maritime Arbitration Commission, 6 *Ga. J. Int'l & Comp. L.* 529 (1976)

————, Settlement of Shipping Disputes by the Maritime Arbitration Commission at the USSR Chamber of Commerce and Industry, in *IBA, Soviet Foreign Trade Reforms & East/West Arbitration* 271 (1988)

Melis, Austria as a Neutral Site for International Commercial Arbitration, 44 *Arb. J.* 31 (No. 4, 1989)

————, Austria: The Arbitral Centre of the Federal Economic Chamber, in *Handbook of Institutional Arbitration in International Trade* 33 (E. Cohn, M. Domke & F. Eisemann eds. 1977)

————, Das Schiedsgericht der Bundeskammer der Gewerblichen Wirtschaft, Wien, 2 *Jahrbuch Schiedsgerichtsbarkeit* 174 (1988)

————, Die Schiedsgerichtsbarkeit der österreichischen Handelskammer seit 1946, in *Festschrift für Ignaz Seidl-Hohenveldern* 367 (K.H. Böckstiegel, H.E. Folz, J.M. Mössner & K. Zemanek eds. 1988)

Melis, W., *A Guide to Commercial Arbitration in Austria* (Vienna 1983)

Miller, Consolidated Arbitrations in New York Maritime Disputes, 14 *Int'l Bus. Law.* 58 (1986)

Min Byoung Kook, Practical Observations on Transnational Commercial Arbitration in Korea, 14 *Korean J. Comp. L.* 1 (1986); reprinted in *Business Laws in Korea* 925 (Kim Chan-Jin ed., 2nd ed. 1988)

Moitry, Right to a Fair Trial and the European Convention on Human Rights, 6 *J. Int'l Arb.* 115 (No. 2, 1989)

Möller, Die neue Schiedsgerichtsordnung des Deutschen Ausschusses für Schiedsgerichtswesen, 34 *RIW* 605 (1988)

Montealegre Escobar, Los arbitros en el derecho colombiano y en El Centro de Arbitraje y Conciliación Mercantiles de la Cámara de Comercio de Bogotá, in *El Arbitraje en el Derecho Latinoamericano y Español* 249 (L. Perret & U. Montoya Alberti eds. 1989)

Morgan & Redmont, Arbitration in the Channel Islands, *Int'l Bus. Law.* 275 (1985)

Nanowski, International Commercial Arbitration Practices in Poland, in *ICCA, Third Int'l Arb. Congress: Proceedings* 511 (1969)

Nanowski, Z., *Z problematyki miedzynarodowego arbitrazu handlowego v Polsce* (Warsaw 1982?)

Nerz, Saudi Arabian qadi-Gerichtsbarkeit und The Commission for the Settlement of Commercial Disputes, 30 *RIW* 33 (1984)

Nestor & Capatina, Rumania: The Foreign Trade Arbitration Commission, in *Handbook of Institutional Arbitration in International Trade* 165 (E. Cohn, M. Domke & F. Eisemann eds. 1977)

Neuteufel, K., *Die Geschichte der Schiedsgerichte der Wiener Börse* (1876-1975), (Vienna 1976)

Newton, Alternative Dispute Resolution in Australia (Australian Commercial Disputes Centre Limited), in *A Handbook of Dispute Resolution* 231 (K. Mackie ed. 1991)

Norwegian Group of the International Bar Association, *International Commercial Arbitration in Action: Papers from a Conference in Oslo in 1982* (Oslo 1983)

Note, A Comment on the Rules of the Society of Maritime Arbitrators, Inc., 20 *J. Mar. L. & Com.* 199 (1989)

Orlov, Arbitration Procedure in East-West Trade, 55 *Nordic J. Int'l L.* 310 (1986)

Parker School of Foreign and Comparative Law, *The 1989 Guide to International Arbitration and Arbitrators* (Dobbs Ferry 1989)

Pechota, Arbitral Centre of the Federal Economic Chamber, Vienna, in 4 *W.A.R.* 3931 (H. Smit & V. Pechota eds. 1989)

———, Arbitrators' Institute of Canada, in 4 *W.A.R.* 4181 (H. Smit & V. Pechota eds. 1989)

———, Australian Centre for International Commercial Arbitration, in 4 *W.A.R.* 3867 (H. Smit & V. Pechota eds. 1989)

———, Australian Commercial Disputes Centre Limited, in 4 *W.A.R.* 3873 (H. Smit & V. Pechota eds. 1989)

———, Canadian Arbitration, Conciliation and Amicable Composition Centre, Inc., in 4 *W.A.R.* 4203 (H. Smit & V. Pechota eds. 1989)

———, Chamber of National and International Arbitration of Milan, in 4 *W.A.R.* 4839 (H. Smit & V. Pechota eds. 1989)

———, Court of Arbitration of the Vienna Commodity Exchange, in 4 *W.A.R.* 3945 (H. Smit & V. Pechota eds. 1989)

———, Foreign Economic and Trade Arbitration Commission of the China Council for the Promotion of International Trade, in 4 *W.A.R.* 4315 (H. Smit & V. Pechota eds. 1989)

———, Hamburg Friendly Arbitration, in 4 W.A.R. 4483 (H. Smit & V. Pechota eds. 1989)

———, International Economic Arbitration in the USSR and Eastern Europe, 8 *N.Y. L. Sch. J. Int'l & Comp. L.* 377 (1987)

———, The German Arbitration Committee, in 4 *W.A.R.* 4451 (H. Smit & V. Pechota eds. 1989)

————, The Indian Council of Arbitration, in 4 *W.A.R.* 4719 (H. Smit & V. Pechota eds. 1989)

————, The Institute of Arbitrators Australia, in 4 *W.A.R.* 3851 (H. Smit & V. Pechota eds. 1989)

————, The Maritime Arbitration Commission at the USSR Chamber of Commerce and Industry, in 4A *W.A.R.* 5485 (H. Smit & V. Pechota eds. 1989)

————, comp., The British Columbia International Commercial Arbitration Centre, in 4 *W.A.R.* 4211 (H. Smit & V. Pechota eds. 1989)

Pedersen, International Arbitration in Denmark, 14 *Case W. Res. J. Int'l L.* 357 (1982)

Perry, Dispute Resolution in the Asia/Pacific Region: The Australian Perspective, 42 *Arb. J.* 32 (No. 2, 1987)

Pestalozzi, Die Schiedsgerichtsbarkeit der Zürcher Handelskammer, in *Die Internationale Schiedsgerichtsbarkeit in der Schweiz* 183 (K.-H. Böckstiegel ed. 1989)

Petit, Le Règlement de la Chambre arbitrale de Paris et le décret du 14 mai 1980 relatif a l'arbitrage, 1981 *Rev. Arb.* 251

Pew, Jarvis & Sidel, The Maritime Arbitration Commission of the People's Republic of China: Options and Strategies, 18 *J. Mar. L. & Com.* 351 (1987)

Pohunek, Principles of Proceedings Before the Arbitration Court of the Chamber of Commerce of Czechoslovakia in Prague, in *ICCA, Fifth Int'l Arb. Congress: Proceedings* C It 1-7 (1975)

Popov, K., *Praktika na Arbitrazhniia sud pri Bulgarskata Turgovsko-promishlena palata, 1981-1985g.* (Sofia 1987)

Power, A Comparison of Soviet and American Maritime Arbitration, 21 *Vand. J. Transnat'l L.* 127 (1988)

Pozdnyakov, Commercial Arbitration in CMEA Member Countries, 4 *Int'l Tax & Bus. Law.* 272 (1986)

Przetacznik, The Arbitration Commission of the Chamber of Commerce and Industry of the Socialist Republic of Romania, in 4A *W.A.R.* 5195 (H. Smit & V. Pechota eds. 1989)

————, The Arbitration Court at the Bulgarian Chamber of Commerce and Industry, in 4 *W.A.R.* 4099 (H. Smit & V. Pechota eds. 1989)

————, The Court of Arbitration Attached to the Hungarian Chamber of Commerce, in 4 *W.A.R.* 4641 (H. Smit & V. Pechota eds. 1989)

————, The Court of Arbitration Attached to the Polish Chamber of Foreign Trade, in 4A *W.A.R.* 5081 (H. Smit & V. Pechota eds. 1989)

————, The Court of Arbitration at the Gdynia Wool Federation, in 4A *W.A.R.* 5123 (H. Smit & V. Pechota eds. 1989)

————, The Foreign Trade Court of Arbitration Attached to the Yugoslav Chamber of Economy, in 4A *W.A.R.* 5797 (H. Smit & V. Pechota eds. 1989)

Ramzaitsev, D.F., *Arbitrazh v torgovom moreplavanii* (Moscow 1960)

Ren Jianxin, Mediation, Conciliation, Arbitration and Litigation in the People's Republic of China, 15 *Int'l Bus. Law.* 395 (1987)

————, The Establishment and Development of Foreign Trade, Economic and Maritime Arbitration in China, 1983 *Y.B. Swed. & Int'l Arb.* 53

Révai, Quelques caractéristiques de l'organisation de la Cour d'Arbitrage auprès de la Chambre de Commerce de Hongrie et ses relations avec les Cours d'Arbitrage à l'étranger, in *ICCA, Third Int'l Arb. Congress: Proceedings* 541 (1969)

Ringdal, Special Features of International Arbitration in Norway, 49 *Arbitration* 91 (Aug. 1983)

Robert, Un centre national: L'Association Française d'Arbitrage (A.F.A.), 1990 *Rev. Arb.* 233

Rodriguez Sanguinetti, Uruguay: un arbitrio imprescindible: la dilucidación arbitral de controversias entre partes, 1 *Rev. Corte Esp. Arb.* 274 (1984)

Sage, Un centre régional: Le C.A.R.A. — Centre d'Arbitrage Rhône-Alps, 1990 *Rev. Arb.* 325

Sajko, Die jugoslawische Aussenhandelsschiedsgerichtsbarkeit, 29 *RIW* 916 (1983)

Schönke, A., *Das Schiedsgerichtsverfahren nach dem heutigen deutschen Recht* (Berlin 1954)

Schütze, Die Schiedsgerichtsbarkeit der Bundeskammer der gewerblichen Wirtschaft Wien, 1987 *Wertpapiermitteilungen* 609

Schütze, R., D. Tscherning & W. Wais, *Handbuch des Schiedsverfahrens. Praxis der deutschen und internationalen Schiedsgerichtsbarkeit* (2nd ed. Berlin 1990)

Sedlacek, V., *Arbitration in Czechoslovak Foreign Trade* (Prague 1982)

Semple, New Scottish Arbitration Rules, 57 *Arbitration* 79 (1991)

Shifman, Belgian Centre for the Study and the Practice of National and International Arbitration, in 4 *W.A.R.* 4029 (H. Smit & V. Pechota eds. 1989)

————, French Arbitration Association, in 4 *W.A.R.* 4545 (H. Smit & V. Pechota eds. 1989)

————, Maritime Arbitration Chamber of Paris, in 4 *W.A.R.* 4575 (H. Smit & V. Pechota eds. 1989)

————, Paris Arbitral Chamber, in 4 *W.A.R.* 4557 (H. Smit & V. Pechota eds. 1989)

————, The Copenhagen Court of International Arbitration, in 4 *W.A.R.* 4387 (H. Smit & V. Pechota eds. 1989)

Shiu Fan Chan, Settlement of Foreign Trade Disputes in the People's Republic of China, 49 *Arbitration* 282 (1984)

Singhania & Co., *International Commercial Arbitration Law, Procedures and Facilities in India* (New Delhi 1985)

Sitaru, Aspects nouveaux concernant la compétence de l'arbitrage commercial international dans le domaine des contrats conclus avec l'extérieur, 1981 *Analele Universitatii Bururesti: Drept* 51

Slade, The Arbitration Rules (1988) of the Chartered Institute of Arbitration, 54 *Arbitration* 265 (1988)

Song Sang-Hyun, Commercial Arbitration Procedures in the Republic of Korea, in *Selected Problems in Contemporary Comparative Law: Festschrift for Professor Chin Kim's Sixtieth Birthday* 262 (Seoul 1987)

Sono, The Japanese Experience, in *UNCITRAL Arbitration Model in Canada* 25 (R. Paterson & B. Thompson eds. 1987)

Stastny, La Cour d'Arbitrage près de la Chambre de Commerce de Tchéchoslovaquie à Prague et ses décisions, 13 *Rassegna dell'Arb.* 111 (1973)

Storme, M. & B. Demeulenaere, *International Commercial Arbitration in Belgium: A Handbook* (Deventer 1989)

Straatmann, Bemerkungen zur Hamburger Freundschaftlichen Arbitrage, in *Festschrift für Reimers* 199 (1979)

―――, Federal Republic of Germany: Hamburg Friendly Arbitration, in *Handbook of Institutional Arbitration* 45 (E. Cohn, M. Domke & F. Eisemann eds. 1977)

Strohbach, German Democratic Republic: The Arbitration Court Attached to the Chamber of Foreign Trade, in *Handbook of Institutional Arbitration in International Trade* 59 (E. Cohn, M. Domke & F. Eisemann eds. 1977)

―――, International Commercial Arbitration in the GDR, *Law and Legislation in the German Democratic Republic* 26 (Nos. 1-2/1984)

―――, Schiedsgerichtsbarkeit in Ostdeutschland heute, 46 *BB* (Beilage 8) (1991)

Summerskill, Maritime Arbitrations, in *Handbook of Arbitration Practice* 265 (R. Bernstein ed. 1987)

Swoboda & Möller, Der Deutsche Ausschuss für Schiedsgerichtswesen und seine Verfahrensordnung, 1 *Jahrbuch Schiedsgerichtsbarkeit* 117 (1987)

Szurski, Basic Information on Polish Law and Practice Concerning International Commercial Arbitration, in *Arbitration in Settlement of International Commercial Disputes Involving the Far East and Arbitration in Combined Transportation* 149 (P. Sanders ed. 1989)

―――, Schiedsordnung des Schiedsrichterkollegiums der Polnischen Kammer für Aussenhandel, Warschau, 2 *Jahrbuch Schiedsgerichtsbarkeit* 213 (1988)

Tajiri, Possibility of Arbitration in International Combined Transport, in *Arbitration and Settlement of International Commercial Disputes Involving the Far East and Arbitration in Combined Transportation* 377 (P. Sanders ed. 1989)

Tang An & Chen Xing-Yuan, Arbitration under Chinese Law, 6 *J. Int'l Arb.* 58 (No. 1, 1989)

Tang Houzhi & Tung Shih-chung, Legal Aspects of International Commercial Arbitration in the People's Republic of China, in *UNCITRAL Arbitration Model in Canada* 51 (R. Paterson & B. Thompson eds. 1987)

Taniguchi, Commercial Arbitration in Japan, in *Arbitration in Settlement of International Commercial Disputes Involving the Far East and Arbitration in Combined Transportation* 29 (P. Sanders ed. 1989)

Tanimoto, Arbitration by the Tokyo Maritime Arbitration Commission, 16 *Bull. Japan Shipping Exch.* 1 (Dec. 1987)

———, How to Make Use of Tokyo Maritime Arbitration, 13 *Bull. Japan Shipping Exch.* 1 (1986)

Thomas, Right to Remuneration under the Arbitration Rules of 1988 of the Chartered Institute of Arbitrators, 55 *Arbitrator* 179 (1989)

Thompson, 'Building an Arbitration and Mediation Centre: From International Foundations to Domestic Rooftops' — The Establishment of the British Columbia International Commercial Arbitration Centre, in *Arbitration in Settlement of International Commercial Disputes Involving the Far East and Arbitration in Combined Transportation* 189 (P. Sanders ed. 1989)

———, A British Columbia Perspective on International Commercial Arbitration, 13 *Can. Bus. L.J.* 70 (1987)

———, Building an Arbitration and Mediation Centre from International Foundations to Domestic Rooftops: A Case Study of the British Columbia International Commercial Arbitration Centre, in *A Handbook of Dispute Resolution* 201 (K. Mackie ed. 1991)

———, Commercial Arbitration — A New Look at a New Era, 45 *Advocate* 185 (1987)

———, The Marriage of the UNCITRAL Model Arbitration Law and the UNCITRAL Arbitration Rules, in *UNCITRAL Arbitration Model in Canada* 143 (R. Paterson & B. Thompson eds. 1987)

Timmermans, The USSR Maritime Arbitration Commission, 1987 *Lloyd's Mar. & Com. L.Q.* 350 and 468

Timmermans, W. A., *Carriage of Goods by Sea in the Practice of the USSR Maritime Arbitration Commision* (Dordrecht 1990)

Tisdall, The Hong Kong International Arbitration Centre, in *UNCITRAL Arbitration Model in Canada* 31 (R. Paterson & B. Thompson eds. 1987)

Trappe, Maritime Arbitration in Hamburg, 14 *Int'l Bus. Law.* 12 (February 1986)

————, Progress and Future Improvements in Arbitration, 42 *Arbitration* 98 (1975)

————, The Law and Institutions of Arbitration in the Federal Republic of Germany and their Relevance for English-German Business Relations, in *Handelsschiedsgerichtsbarkeit in England und in der Bundesrepublik Deutschland* 77 (K.-H. Böckstiegel ed. 1987)

Triebel & Xu Guojian, International Economic, Trade and Maritime Arbitration in the People's Republic of China: New Developments, 6 *J. Int'l Arb.* 13 (No. 2, 1989)

Tsien Hsin, Foreign Trade and Maritime Arbitration in China, *Indian Arb. Q.* 3 (No. 4, 1977)

Uwanno & Sathirathai, Introduction to the Thai Legal System. [Section C - International Commercial Arbitration], 4 *Chulalongkorn L. Rev.* 39, 105 (1985-1986)

van Delden, English Commodity Arbitrations: A Foreigner Looking Around in London, in *The Art of Arbitration* 95 (J. Schultsz & A. van den Berg eds. 1982)

Varady, Règlement de la Cour d'arbitrage du commerce extérieur auprès de la Chambre Economique de Yugoslavie, texte et commentaire, 1984 *Rev. Arb.* 151

Vigrass, Arbitration Services in the United Kingdom Relevant to Anglo-German Business Relations, in *Handelsschiedsgerichtsbarkeit in England und in der Bundesrepublik Deutschland* 143 (K.-H. Böckstiegel ed. 1987)

————, Arbitration in London, 45 *Arbitration* 104 (1979)

————, The Role of Institutions in Arbitration, in *Handbook of Arbitration Practice* 367 (R. Bernstein ed. 1987)

Wackenhuth, Die (unterbliebene) Einrede der Unzuständigkeit des Schiedsgerichts nach ausgewählten Schiedsgerichtsordnungen, 32 *RIW* 11 (1986)

Willis, Institute of Arbitrators Australia — Maritime Arbitration, 9 *Int'l Bus. Law.* 401 (1981)

Wisniewski, Awards of the Court of Arbitration at the Polish Chamber of Foreign Trade in Warsaw, 10 *Polish Y.B. Int'l L.* 269 (1980)

————, Awards of the Court of Arbitration at the Polish Chamber of Foreign Trade, 15 *Polish Y.B. Int'l L.* 301 (1986)

————, Awards of the Court of Arbitration at the Polish Chamber of Foreign Trade, 16 *Polish Y.B. Int'l L.* 191 (1987)

————, Awards of the Court of Arbitration at the Polish Chamber of Foreign Trade in Warsaw, 17 *Polish Y.B. Int'l L.* 251 (1988)

————, The Practice of the Court of Arbitration at the Polish Chamber of Foreign Trade: Major Trends and Problems as Illustrated by Chosen Awards, 1989 *Int'l Bus. L.J.* 1011

Zourek, New Rules of Arbitration Proceedings in Czechoslovakia, 1963 *Bull. Czechoslovak L.* 233

4.11 COOPERATION OF NATIONAL INSTITUTIONS

Akroyd, The Role of Arbitration in Japanese Foreign Trade, 44 *Arbitration* 136 (1978)

Bratus, Co-operation Amongst Arbitration Organizations of Eastern European Socialist Countries, in *ICCA, Third Int'l Arb. Congress: Proceedings* 219 (1969)

Gambardella & Carbone, Développement de l'arbitrage commercial en Italie: le rôle des Chambres de Commerce et la coopération entre organismes d'arbitrage au niveau national, in *ICCA, Third Int'l Arb. Congress: Proceedings* 431 (1969)

Glossner, The Need for Cooperation Between Arbitration Institutions, 47 *Arbitration* 109 (1981)

Hanak, The Experience of Socialist Lawyers in Arbitration Held in Non-Socialist Countries on Litigations Between Businessmen from East and West, 10 *Int'l Bus. Law.* 145 (1982)

Hanotiau, L'arbitrage commercial dans les relations belgo-soviétiques, 1983 *JT* 462

Hoare, Co-operation Between Specialist and Non-specialist Arbitration Bodies, in *ICCA, Third Int'l Arb. Congress: Proceedings* 463 (1969)

ICCA, Coopération entre organismes d'arbitrage/Co-operation among Arbitration Organizations. *Third Int'l Arb. Congress: Proceedings* (1969); also published in *Rev. Arb.* (No. 4, 1969)

Jakubowski, Promotion of Co-operation in the Domain of International Commercial Arbitration Practice, in *ICCA, Third Int'l Arb. Congress: Proceedings* 339 (1969)

Kopelmanas, Coopération entre organismes d'arbitrage de pays ayant des systèmes économiques ou un degré de developpement différents, in *ICCA, Third Int'l Arb. Congress: Proceedings* 229 (1969)

Krishnamurthi, Co-operation on a Regional Scale. The Bangkok Experiment, in *ICCA, Third Int'l Arb. Congress: Proceedings* 239 (1969)

Lebedev, S., *Mezdunarodnoe sotrudnichestvo v oblasti kommercheskogo arbitrazha* (Moscow 1980)

Melis, Austria as a Neutral Site for International Commercial Arbitration, 44 *Arb. J.* 31 (No. 4, 1989)

Nestor & Capatina, Règlements bilateraux de conciliation conclus par les chambres de commerce ou des associations professionnelles, in *The Art of Arbitration* 261 (J. Schultsz & A. van den Berg eds. 1982)

Straus, A Network of Arbitration Associations, in *A.I.A., Essays in Memoriam Eugenio Minoli* 487 (Turin 1974)

―――――, Co-operation amongst Arbitration Organizations of the Americas, in *ICCA, Third Int'l Arb. Congress: Proceedings* 199 (1969)

Strohbach, Arbitration Between Foreign Trade Organizations of Socialist Countries and Parties from the Capitalist Economic Sphere, 4 *Pace L. Rev.* 607 (1984)

Vigrass, The Role of Institutions in Arbitration, in *Handbook of Arbitration Practice* 367 (R. Bernstein ed. 1987)

5. THE NATURE OF ARBITRAL ADJUDICATION

5.01 THE CONTRACTUAL OR CONSENSUAL BASIS OF ARBITRATION

Aravena Arredondo, L., *Naturaleza jurídica del arbitraje* (Santiago de Chile 1969)

Aylwin Azocar, P., *El juicio arbitral* (Santiago de Chile 1958)

Barrios de Angelis, Naturaleza juridica del arbitraje privado. Su proyección en la practica, 1 *Rev. Corte Esp. Arb.* 53 (1984)

Bernini, Cultural Neutrality: A Prerequisite to Arbitral Justice, 10 *Mich. J. Int'l L.* 39 (1989)

Bunni & Myers, Let Us Not Judicialise the Arbitration Process, 53 *Arbitration* 3 (1987)

Carbonneau, Arbitral Adjudication: A Comparative Assessment of its Remedial and Substantive Status in Transnational Commerce, 19 *Tex. Int'l L.J.* 33 (1984)

Carbonneau & Firestone, Transnational Law-Making: Assessing the Impact of the Vienna Convention and the Viability of Arbitral Adjudication, 1 *Emory J. Int'l Disp. Res.* 51 (1986)

Chillón Medina, J. M. & J. F. Merino Merchán, *Tratado de arbitraje privado interno e internacional* (Madrid 1978)

Cremades, El proceso arbitral en los negocios internacionales, in *Alternativas a la justicia institucional: arbitraje, conciliación* 91 (Bogota 1988)

David, Juridictions arbitrales ou juridictions interétatiques? in *A.I.A., Essays in Memoriam Eugenio Minoli* 109 (Turin 1974)

David, R., *Arbitration in International Trade* (Deventer 1985)

DeVries, International Commercial Arbitration: A Substitute for National Courts, 57 *Tulane L. Rev.* 42 (1982)

Eisemann, Le phenomène de l'arbitrage, son utilité, ses avantages and son rôle, 53 *Rev. Droit Int'l & Droit Comp.* 106 (1976)

Ettinger, The Public Relations Value of Arbitration, 2 *Arb. J.* 304 (1947)

Fouchard, L'autonomie de l'arbitraje commercial international, 1965 *Rev. Arb.* 99 (1965)

————, Spécificité de l'arbitrage international, 1981 *Rev. Arb.* 449

Gentinetta, Befreiung der internationalen Handelsschiedsgerichtsbarkeit von der Umklammerung, 15 *AWD* 46 (1969)

Gonzales Soria, El arbitraje visto por un jurista y hombre de negocios, in *Alternativas a la justicia institucional: arbitraje, conciliación* 147 (Bogota 1988)

Heuman, Transplanting Arbitral Processes into Civil Procedure — A Swedish Perspective, 7 *Civil Just. Q.* 156 (1988)

Hoellering, Alternative Dispute Resolution and International Trade, 14 *N.Y.U. Rev. L. & Social Change* 785 (1986); also in *AAA, Arbitration & the Law,* 1986 109 (1987)

————, Emerging Techniques of Private Dispute Resolution in Long-Term Contracts: Mediation, Mini-Trial, Med-Arb, and Others, in *Arbitration & the Law: AAA General Counsel's Annual Report 1986* 15 (1987)

Jarrosson, C., *La notion d'arbitrage* (Paris 1987)

Jones, International Arbitration, 8 *Hastings Int'l & Comp. L. Rev.* 213 (1985)

Kassis, A., *Problèmes de base de l'arbitrage en droit comparé et en droit international. Vol. 1: Arbitrage juridictionnel et arbitrage contractuel* (Paris 1987)

Kitagawa, Contractual Autonomy in International Commercial Arbitration Including a Japanese Perspective, in *Liber Amicorum for Martin Domke* 133 (P. Sanders ed. 1967)

Kotzorel, A., *Private Gerichte als Alternative zur staatlichen Zivilgerichtsbarkeit: eine ökonomische Analyse* (Tübingen 1987)

Lalive, Problèmes relatifs à l'arbitrage international commercial, 120 *Recueil des Cours* 569 (1967-II)

Lazatin, Mechanics and Procedural Aspects of Commercial Arbitration, in *Commercial Arbitration* 14 (J. Ricalde ed. 1983)

Lew, The Structure and Role of Arbitration in Eastern Europe, 44 *Arbitration* 210 (July 1978)

McPherson, Arbitration, Valuation and Certainty of Terms, 60 *Austl. L.J.* 8 (1986)

Mann, Internationale Schiedsgerichte und nationale Rechtsordnung, 13 *Zeitschrift für das gesamte Handelsrecht und Wirtschaftsrecht* 97 (1968)

Meyerowitz, The Arbitration Alternative, 71 *A.B.A. J.* 78 (Feb. 1985)

Minoli, Il problema teorico fundamentale dell'arbitrato commerciale internazionale, in *Studi in memoria Carlo Furno* 627 (1973)

Munzberg, R., *Die Schranken der Parteivereinbarung in der privaten internationalen Schiedsgerichtsbarkeit* (Berlin 1970)

Mustill, Transnational Arbitration in English Law, 37 *Current Legal Problems* 133 (1984)

Nicklisch, Alternative Formen der Streitbeilegung und internationale Handelsschiedsgerichtsbarkeit, in *Festschrift für Karl Heinz Schwab* 381 (P. Gottwald & H. Prütting eds. 1990)

Oppetit, Arbitrage juridictionnel et arbitrage contractuel: à propos d'une jurisprudence récente, 1977 *Rev. Arb.* 317

Pisar, S., *Coexistence & Commerce,* Chapters 20 - 24 (New York 1970)

Ramos Mendez, Arbitraje internacional: confirmación de la doctrine jurisprudencial, 84 *Justicia* 375 (No. II, 1984)

Ricci, Sul contradditorio nell'arbitrato irrituale, 27 *Rassegna dell'Arb.* 13 (1987)

Rubino-Sammartano, Is Arbitration to Be Just a Luxury Clinic? 7 *J. Int'l Arb.* 25 (No. 3, 1990)

Rubino-Sammartano, M., *International Arbitration Law* (Deventer 1990)

Russell, F., *Russell on the Law of Arbitration* (20th ed. by A. Walton & M. Vitoria 1982)

Saario, The Principle of Party Autonomy in Arbitration of International Commercial Disputes, 1985 *Tidskrift, utgiven av Juridiska Foreningen i Finland* 500

Salter, International Commercial Arbitration: The Why, How and Where, 88 *Com. L.J.* 381 (1983)

Samuel, A., *Jurisdictional Problems in International Commercial Arbitration: A Study of Belgian, Dutch, English, French, Swedish, Swiss, U.S. and West German Law* (Zurich 1989)

Schizzerotto, G., *Dell'arbitrato* (Milan 3rd ed. 1988)

Schlosser, P., *Das Recht der internationalen privaten Schiedsgerichtsbarkeit* (2nd rev. ed. Tübingen 1989)

Schmitthoff, C., *Schmitthoff's Export Trade. The Law and Practice of International Trade* (8th ed. 1986)

Schütze, R., D. Tscherning & W. Wais, *Handbuch des Schiedsverfahrens. Praxis der deutschen und internationalen Schiedsgerichtsbarkeit* (2nd ed. Berlin 1990)

Schwab, The Legal Foundations and Limitations of Arbitration Procedure in the U.S. and Germany, in *International Arbitration: Liber Amicorum for Martin Domke* 301 (P. Sanders ed. 1967)

Schwebel, Arbitration and the Exhaustion of Local Remedies Revisited, 23 *Int'l Law.* 951 (1989)

Sillevis Smitt, Arbitrage, bemiddeling en conciliatie, in Iustitia et Amicitia. *Geschillenbeslechting in en Buiten Rechte* 93 (Arnheim 1985)

Sornarajah, Arbitration Versus Litigation, [1991] 2 *Malayan L.J.* vii

Stumpf, Vor- und Nachteile des Verfahrens vor Schiedsgerichten gegenüber dem Verfahren vor ordentlichen Gerichten, in *Festschrift für Arthur Bülow* 217 (K.-H. Böckstiegel & O. Glossner eds. 1981)

Stuyt, Misconceptions about International (Commercial) Arbitration, 5 *Neth. Y.B. Int'l L.* 35 (1974)

Summers, Private Versus State Arbitration in Latin America, 4 *Cal. W. Int'l L.J.* 121 (1973)

Tallon, The Law Applied by Arbitration Tribunals, in *The Sources of the Law of International Trade* 154 (C. Schmitthoff ed. 1984)

ter Kuile, Internationale arbitrage en Gemeenschapsrecht, in *Iustitia et Amicitia. Geschillenbeslechting in en Buiten Rechte* 33 (Arnheim 1985)

5.02 *AD HOC* ARBITRATION

Arkin, International Ad Hoc Arbitration: A Practical Alternative, 15 *Int'l Bus. Law.* 5 (1987); also 53 *Arbitration* 260 (1987)

Ball, Structuring the Arbitration in Advance — the Arbitration Clause in an International Development Agreement, in *Contemporary Problems in International Arbitration* 297 (J.D.M. Lew ed. 1986)

Barclay, Unadministered Arbitration and the UNCITRAL Draft Rules Pertaining to It, in *ICCA, Fifth Int'l Arb. Congress: Proceedings* C Ih 1-9 (1975)

Capatina, Admissibilité de l'arbitrage occasionnel de commerce exterieur en droit roumain, *Revue roumain d'études internationales* 411 (No. 4, 1981)

Cremades, Should Arbitrators Maintain Their Independence or Would It Be Desirable for Them to Have Closer Links with the Courts in Their Respective Countries? 44 *Arbitration* 83 (1978)

Gavalda, L'arbitrage ad hoc, in *First Int'l Commercial Arbitration Conference: Proceedings* 43 (N. Antaki & A. Prujiner eds. 1986)

Goldstajn, Choice of International Arbitrators, Arbitral Tribunals and Centres: Legal and Sociological Aspects, in *Essays on International Commercial Arbitration* 27 (P. Sarcevic ed. 1989)

————, Permanent and Ad Hoc Arbitration Tribunals, in *International and Economic Trade Law* 183 (C. Schmitthoff & K. Simmonds eds. Leyden 1976)

Hanak, The Experience of Socialist Lawyers in Arbitration Held in Non-Socialist Countries on Litigations Between Businessmen from East and West, 10 *Int'l Bus. Law.* 145 (1982)

Hascher, Actualité de l'arbitrage international en U.R.S.S., 1988 *Rev. Arb.* 237

Jarvin, Settling International Business Disputes: Recent Developments, *Int'l Fin. L. Rev.* 16 (No. 2, Feb. 1984)

Katona, Ad hoc Arbitration Rules: Similarities and Differences. *A Comparative Review., 3 Questions of Int'l Law: Hungarian Perspectives* 93 (H. Bokor-Szegö ed. 1986)

Lew, Arbitration Agreements: Form and Character, in *Essays on International Commercial Arbitration* 51 (P. Sarcevic ed. 1989)

Littman, Choice of Form and Place of Arbitration, 47 *Arbitration* 79 (1981)

Paulsson, International Commercial Arbitrations, in *Handbook of Arbitration Practice* 333 (R. Bernstein ed. 1987)

Pfaff, Schiedsgerichte im Ost-West-Handel, 23 *ZRV* 81 (1982)

Redfern, A. & M. Hunter, *Law and Practice of International Commercial Arbitration* (London 1986)

Schütze, R., D. Tscherning & W. Wais, *Handbuch des Schiedsverfahrens. Praxis der deutschen und internationalen Schiedsgerichtsbarkeit* (2nd ed. Berlin 1990)

Sedlacek, V., *Arbitration in Czechoslovak Foreign Trade* (Prague 1982)

Ulmer, Drafting the International Arbitration Clause, 20 *Int'l Law.* 1335 (1986)

Westermann, Gesellschaftsrechtliche Schiedsgerichte — Übersicht und Erfahrungsbericht, in *Festschrift für Robert Fischer* 853 (M. Lutter, W. Stimpel & H. Wiedermann eds. 1979)

Wiget, Fragen der Verfahrensgestaltung vor Gelegenheitsschiedsgerichten, in *Festschrift für Max Guldener* 367 (Zurich 1973)

5.03 INSTITUTIONAL AND ADMINISTERED ARBITRATION

Arkin, New Opportunities for Arbitration in East/West Trade, 3 *Transnat'l Law.* 495 (1990)

Auchter, L'arbitrage maritime dans la pratique japonaise, 25 *Droit Mar. Français* 181 (1973)

Ball, Structuring the Arbitration in Advance — the Arbitration Clause in an International Development Agreement, in *Contemporary Problems in International Arbitration* 297 (J.D.M. Lew ed. 1986)

Bond, I.C.C. Arbitration in Theory and Practice, 26 *Rassegna dell'Arb.* 141 (1986)

Cremades, Should Arbitrators Maintain Their Independence or Would It Be Desirable for Them to Have Closer Links with the Courts in Their Respective Countries? 44 *Arbitration* 83 (1978)

de Boisséson, La constitution de tribunal arbitral dans l'arbitrage institutionnel, 1990 *Rev. Arb.* 337

Fouchard, Les institutions permanentes d'arbitrage devant le juge étatique (à propos d'une jurisprudence récente), 1987 *Rev. Arb.* 225

Goldstajn, Choice of International Arbitrators, Arbitral Tribunals and Centres: Legal and Sociological Aspects, in *Essays on International Commercial Arbitration* 27 (P. Sarcevic ed. 1989)

————, Permanent and Ad Hoc Arbitration Tribunals, in *International and Economic Trade Law* 183 (C. Schmitthoff & K. Simmonds eds. Leyden 1976)

Habscheid, Statutarische Schiedsgerichte und Schiedskonkordat: Einige grundsätzliche Fragen, 57 *Schweizerische Aktiengesellschaft/La société anonyme suisse* 157 (1985)

Jarvin, Settling International Business Disputes: Recent Developments, *Int'l Fin. L. Rev.* 16 (No. 2, Feb. 1984)

Littman, Choice of Form and Place of Arbitration, 47 *Arbitration* 79 (1981)

Mezger, Das französische Dekret vom 14. Mai 1980 und die organisierte Schiedsgerichtsbarkeit, in *Festschrift für Arthur Bülow* 141 (K.-H. Böckstiegel & O. Glossner eds. 1981)

Nanowski, Authority Being Competent to Nominate Arbitrators Substitutionally, in *ICCA, Fifth Int'l Arb. Congress: Proceedings* C Io 1-11 (1975)

Paclot, La réforme du droit de l'arbitrage: l'arbitrage institutionnel, 1980 *Rev. Arb.* 598

Paulsson, International Commercial Arbitrations, in *Handbook of Arbitration Practice* 333 (R. Bernstein ed. 1987)

Pfaff, 'In einem anderen Land...' Erfahrungen westlicher Schiedsrichter in östlichen institutionellen Schiedsgerichten. Zugl. ein Beitrag zum Thema 'Schnelligkeit un Kostengünstigkeit von Schiedsverfahren, in *Festschrift für Walther J. Habscheid* 233 (W. Lindacher, D. Pfaff et al. 1989)

————, Schiedsgerichte im Ost-West-Handel, 23 *ZRV* 81 (1982)

Pisar, S., *Coexistence & Commerce*, Chapters 20 - 24 (New York 1970)

Ramzaitsev, The Law Applied by Arbitral Tribunals, in *The Sources of the Law of International Trade* 138 (C. Schmitthoff ed. 1964)

Reczei, East-West Arbitration as Administered by Institutions, 10 *Int'l Bus. L.* 141 (1982)

Redfern, A. & M. Hunter, *Law and Practice of International Commercial Arbitration* (London 1986)

Schütze, R., D. Tscherning & W. Wais, *Handbuch des Schiedsverfahrens. Praxis der deutschen und internationalen Schiedsgerichtsbarkeit* (2nd ed. Berlin 1990)

Smit, The Future of International Commercial Arbitration: A Single Transnational Institution? 25 *Colum. J. Transnat'l L.* 9 (1986)

Toller, Rechtsschutz durch ständige Schiedsgerichte. Eine Nachlese zum Schweizerischen Juristentag 1988, 85 *SJZ* 312 (1989)

Ulmer, Drafting the International Arbitration Clause, 20 *Int'l Law.* 1335 (1986)

Varady, On Appointing Authorities in International Commercial Arbitration, 2 *Emory J. Int'l Disp. Res.* 311 (1988)

Vigrass, The Role of Institutions in Arbitration, in *Handbook of Arbitration Practice* 367 (R. Bernstein ed. 1987)

5.04 AMIABLE COMPOSITION

Antaki, L'amiable composition, *In First International Commercial Arbitration Conference: Proceedings* 151 (N. Antaki & A. Prujiner eds. 1986)

Bischoff, Amiables Compositeurs in English Arbitration Law, 44 *Arbitration* 60 (1978)

Braun, A., ed., *L'arbitrage/Het scheidsgerecht* (Brussels 1983)

Horsmans, Actualité et évolution du droit belge de l'arbitrage, 1990 *Rev. Arb.* 797

Level, La reforme du droit de l'arbitrage: l'amiable composition, 1980 *Rev. Arb.* 651

Loquin, E., *L'amiable composition en droit comparé et international. Contribution à l'étude du non-droit dans l'arbitrage commercial* (Paris 1980)

Mezger, La distinction entre l'arbitre dispensé d'observer la règle de la loi et l'arbitre statuant sans appel, in *Liber Amicorum for Martin Domke* 184 (P. Sanders ed. 1967)

Nestor, L'amiable compositeur et l'arbitrage selon les règles de droit, in *A.I.A., Essays in Memoriam Eugenio Minoli* 341 (Turin 1974)

Poznanski, The Nature and Extent of an Arbitrator's Powers in International Commercial Arbitration, 4 *J. Int'l Arb.* 71 (No. 3, 1987)

Riedberg, P., *Der amiable Compositeur im internationalen privaten Schiedsgerichtsverfahren* (Frankfurt 1962)

Rubino-Sammartano, M., *International Arbitration Law* (Deventer 1990)

Schmitthoff, Extrajudicial Dispute Settlement, *Forum Internationale*, No. 6, May 1985

5.05 CONCILIATION

Blanc, La conciliation comme mode de règlement des différends dans les contrats internationaux, 40 *Revue Trimestrielle de Droit Commercial et de Droit Economique* 173 (1987)

Dore, I.I., *Arbitration and Conciliation under the UNCITRAL Rules: A Textual Analysis* (Dordrecht 1986)

Dress, International Commercial Mediation and Conciliation, 10 *Loy. L.A. Int'l & Comp. L.J.* 569 (1988)

Eisemann, Conciliation As a Means of Settlement of International Business Disputes: The UNCITRAL Rules As Compared with the ICC System, in *The Art of Arbitration* 121 (J. Schultsz & A. van den Berg eds. 1982)

Fischer-Zernin & Junker, Arbitration and Mediation: Synthesis or Antithesis? 5 *J. Int'l Arb.* 22 (No. 1, 1988)

Glossner, Zur Vollstreckbarkeit von Schlichtungsergebnissen im internationalen Bereich, in *Festschrift für Arthur Bülow* 69 (K.-H. Böckstiegel & O. Glossner eds. 1981)

Hoellering, Alternative Dispute Resolution and International Trade, 14 *N.Y.U. Rev. L. & Social Change* 785 (1986); also in *AAA, Arbitration & the Law, 1986* 109 (1987)

Jarvin, The Role of Conciliation, Contract Modification and Expert Appraisal in Settling International Commercial Disputes, 4 *Int'l Tax & Bus. Law.* 238 (1986)

Lionnet, Arbitration and Mediation — Alternatives or Opposites? 4 *J. Int'l Arb.* 69 (No. 1, 1987)

————, Schiedsgerichtsbarkeit und 'Mediation — Alternativen oder Gegensatze? in *Der Komplexe Langzeitvertrag/The Complex Long-Term Contract* 543 (F. Nicklisch ed. 1987)

López Roca, La conciliación mercantile, in *Alternativas a la justicia institucional: arbitraje, conciliación* 193 (Bogota 1988)

Nicklisch, Gutachter-, Schieds- und Schlichtungsstellen - rechtliche Einordnung und erforderliche Verfahrensgarantien, in *Festschrift für Arthur Bülow* 159 (K.-H. Böckstiegel & O. Glossner eds. 1981)

Rauh, K., *Die Schieds- und Schlichtungsordnungen der UNCITRAL* (Cologne 1983)

Reif, Conciliation as a Mechanism for the Resolution of International Economic and Business Disputes, 14 *Fordham Int'l L.J.* 578 (1990-1991)

Sillevis Smitt, Arbitrage, bemiddeling en conciliatie, in *Iustitia et Amicitia. Geschillenbeslechting in en Buiten Rechte* 93 (Arnheim 1985)

Stevens & Takahashi, The East Asian Preference for Conciliation: An Example in a Kabuki Play, in *Arbitration in Settlement of International Commercial Disputes Involving the Far East and Arbitration in Combined Transportation* 69 (P. Sanders ed. 1989). Reproduced in 5 *Arb. Int'l* 43 (1989)

Walter, Dogmatik der unterschiedlichen Verfahren zur Streitbeilegung, 103 *ZZP* 141 (1990)

5.06 SPECIALIZED ARBITRATION

Addamo, I cinquant'anni della Camera Arbitrale Italiana delle Pelli, 26 *Rassegna dell'Arb.* 128 (1986)

Billings, International Standards for Automotive Arbitration, 28 *German Y.B. Int'l L.* 425 (1985)

Chapman, FOSFA International Arbitration, 2 *Arb. Int'l* 323 (1986)

Cohen, El arbitraje marítimo. La experiencia norteamericana, in *El Arbitraje Comercial Internacional* 501 (Mexico 1983)

Cohen, M.M., ed., *Index and Digest of the Award Service of the Society of Maritime Arbitrators,* Volumes 3A & 3B (New York 1986)

Coulson, Construction Arbitration Around the World, 48 *Arbitration* 162 (1982)

Frignani, Il franchising e l'arbitrato: prime esperienze e problemi, 30 *Rassegna dell'Arb.* 162 (1990)

Goyeneche & Caivano, El arbitraje en el comercio de granos, 1985-II *Jurisprudencia Argentina* 807

Habscheid, L'expertise-arbitrage. Etude de droit comparé, in *Liber Amicorum for Martin Domke* 103 (P. Sanders ed. 1967)

Jarvis, The Soviet Maritime Arbitration Commission: A Practitioner's Perspective, 21 *Tex. Int'l L.J.* 341 (1986)

Johnson, Commodity Trade Arbitration, in *Handbook of Arbitration Practice* 189 (R. Bernstein ed. 1987)

Johnson, D., *International Commodity Arbitration* (London 1991)

Lebedev, Commentary on the Statute of the Maritime Arbitration Commission at the USSR Chamber of Commerce and Industry, 7 *Y.B. Com. Arb.* 249 (1982)

————, La Commission d'arbitrage maritime près de la Chambre de commerce de l'URSS, 1971 *Rev. Arb.* 137

Lisowski, Establishing a New Permanent Court of Arbitration in International Wool Commerce at Gdynia Wool Federation, 10 *Rassegna dell'Arb.* 31 (1970)

Liu Shujian, The New Rules Governing Maritime Arbitration in China, 21 *J. Mar. L. & Com.* 129 (1990)

McCormack, A Lawyer's View of Arbitration Proceedings and Composition of the Arbitration Panel, 1984 *Y.B. Mar. Law* 55

Mackie, Integration of Arbitration Systems as Regards the Commodity Trades, 44 *Arbitration* 89 (1978)

——, GAFTA Arbitration Procedures, 56 *Arbitration* 150 (1990)

——, Thesis on Commercial Arbitration in Commodity Trades, 57 *Arbitration* 156 (1991)

Pew, Jarvis & Sidel, The Maritime Arbitration Commission of the People's Republic of China: Options and Strategies, 18 *J. Mar. L. & Com.* 351 (1987)

Schottelius, Das Schiedsverfahren im Rahmen des DIN Deutsches Institut für Normung e.V., in *Festschrift für Arthur Bülow* 199 (K.-H. Böckstiegel & O. Glossner eds. 1981)

Shilston, Milestone in the Evolution of Modern Commercial Arbitration, 53 *Arbitration* 26 (1987)

Szurski, Basic Information on Polish Law and Practice Concerning International Commercial Arbitration, in *Arbitration in Settlement of International Commercial Disputes Involving the Far East and Arbitration in Combined Transportation* 149 (P. Sanders ed. 1989)

Timmermans, The USSR Maritime Arbitration Commission, 1987 *Lloyd's Mar. & Com. L.Q.* 350 and 468

Voûte, Een partij-arbiter in Hong Kong, 1988 *Tijdschrift voor Arbitrage* 184

5.07 PUBLIC POLICY FAVORING ARBITRATION

Akroyd, The Role of Arbitration in Japanese Foreign Trade, 44 *Arbitration* 136 (1978)

Aksen, International Arbitration Received Favorably in U.S., *N.Y.U. L.J.* *1 (1976)*

Allison, Arbitration of Private Antitrust Claims in International Trade: A Study in the Subordination of National Interests to the Demands of a World Market, 18 *N.Y.U. J. Int'l L. & Pol.* 361 (1986)

Angell, Spain's Attitude to Arbitration, *Int'l Fin. L. Rev.* 23 (June 1984)

Bartos, H., *Internationale Handelsschiedsgerichtsbarkeit:Verfahrens- prinzipien* (Frankfurt 1984)

Becker & Kleyn, Public Policy and Arbitration — The 'Unruly Horse' and the Arbitrability of Claims in America, 17 *Int'l Bus Law.* 422 (1989)

Carbonneau, Mitsubishi: The Folly of Quixotic Internationalism, 2 *Arb. Int'l* 116 (1986)

Delvolvé, Arbitration and Public Policy in Developing Countries, in *Arbitration and the Licensing Process* 6-103 (R. Goldscheider & M. de Haas eds. 1984-)

Domke, Towards an 'International' Public Policy in Commercial Arbitra- tion, in *Festschrift für Arthur Bülow* 49 (K.-H. Böckstiegel & O. Glossner eds. 1981)

Kanowitz, Alternative Dispute Resolution and the Public Interest: The Arbitration Experience, 38 *Hastings L.J.* 239 (1987)

Kerr, International Arbitration v. Litigation, 1980 *J. Bus. L.* 164 (1980)

Leacock, American Public Policy and International Arbitration, 1988 *J. Bus. L.* 518

McDermott, Significant Developments in the United States Law Governing International Commercial Arbitration, 1 *Conn. J. Int'l L.* 111 (1985-86)

Mann, Private Arbitration and Public Policy, 10 *Holdsworth L. Rev.* 11 (1985)

————, Private Arbitration and Public Policy, 4 *Civil Just. Q.* 257 (1985)

Mezghani, L'arbitrage commercial international et les imperatifs du développement, in *Centre d'Etudes, Les Entreprises Tunisiennes et l'Arbitrage Commercial International* 59 (1983)

Osakwe, The Soviet Position on International Commercial Arbitration as a Method of Resolving Transnational Disputes, in *Resolving Transnational Disputes Through International Arbitration* 184 (T. Carbonneau ed. 1984)

Siegert, Universal, Regional and National Measures to Further International Commercial Arbitration, in *Int'l Trade Arbitration* 213 (M. Domke ed. 1958)

Wilner, Acceptance of Arbitration by Developing Countries, in *Resolving Transnational Disputes Through International Arbitration* 283 (Th. Carbonneau ed. 1984)

6. DISPUTES

6.01 CATEGORIES OF DISPUTES

Holtzmann, Long Term Multinational Disputes: A Challenge to Arbitrators, in *A.A.A., New Strategies for Peaceful Resolution of International Business Disputes* 116(1971)

Sanders, Trends in the Field of International Commercial Arbitration, 145 *Recueil des Cours* 205 (1975-II)

Schlosser, Schiedsgerichtsbarkeit und öffentlich-rechtlich beeinflusste Streitgegenstände, in *Festschrift für Arthur Bülow* 189 (K.-H. Böckstiegel & O. Glossner eds. 1981)

6.02 COMMERCIAL DISPUTES

Aksen, Dispute Resolution in Commercial Contracts and Joint Ventures, in *The Moscow Conference on Law and Bilateral Economic Relations* 235 (Washington 1991)

Almond, Settlement of International Commercial Disputes, 4 *N.C. J. Int'l L. & Com. Reg.* 107 (1979)

Bauer, Some Suggested Changes to the U.S. Arbitration Act, in 1 *Fifth Int'l Congress of Maritime Arbitrators* (New York 1981)

Briseño Sierra, Arbitration and Technical Checking of Due Performance of Contracts, in *ICCA, Fourth Int'l Arb. Congress: Proceedings* 98 (1972)

Brower, Dispute Resolution in Commercial Contracts and Joint Ventures, in *The Moscow Conference on Law and Bilateral Economic Relations* 233 (Washington 1991)

Cardenas, Métodos de solución de controversias comerciales internacionales, 8 *Derecho de la Integración* 79 (No. 20, 1975)

Chew & LaFitte, The Resolution of Transnational Commercial Disputes in the People's Republic of China: A Guide for U.S. Practitioners, 8 *Yale J. World Pub. Ord.* 236 (1982)

Cremades, Arbitration and Business, in *ICCA, Sixth Int'l Arb. Congress: Proceedings* 77 (1978)

Davis, Resolving Disputes Arising from Investment and Trade in the Soviet Union, in *The Moscow Conference on Law and Bilateral Economic Relations* 237 (Washington 1991)

Devow, Commercial Dispute Resolution Between the United States and the People's Republic of China: Problems and Prospects, 7 *Suff. Transnat'l L.J.* 329 (1983)

El-Hakim, Should the Key Terms Award, Commercial and Binding Be Defined in the New York Convention? 6 *J. Int'l Arb.* 161 (No. 1, 1989)

Goldring J., *Commercial Arbitration in Japan-Australia Trade Disputes* (Sydney 1973)

Hinman, China, Modernization, and Sino-United States Trade: Will China Submit to Arbitration? 10 *Cal. W. Int'l L.J.* 53 (1980)

Kawakami & Henderson, Arbitration in U.S./Japanese Sales Disputes, 42 *Wash. L. Rev.* 541 (1967)

Kos-Rabcewicz-Zubkowski, Arbitration Agreements and Adjudication of East-West Economic Disputes, in *ICCA, Fifth Int'l Arb. Congress: Proceedings* C Ie 1-25 (1975)

Layton, Arbitration in International Commercial Agreements: The Noose Draws Tighter, 9 *Int'l Law.* 741 (1975)

Lebedev, Arbitration in Soviet-American Trade Relations, 5 *Den. J. Int'l L. & Pol'y* 337 (1975)

Lee, E., *Commercial Disputes Settlement in China* (London 1985)

Lunts, Arbitrazh po sporam sovetskich khozaistvennykh organizatsii s kapitalisticheskimi predpriatiami, 1979 *S.G.P.* 50 (No. 2)

Norberg, The Settlement of International Economic Disputes, 4 *Int'l Trade L.J.* 103 (1979)

Oppetit, L'arbitrage et les contrats commerciaux à long terme, 1976 *Rev. Arb.* 91

Park, Arbitration of International Contract Disputes, 39 *Bus. Law.* 1783 (1984)

Pfaff, D., *Die Aussenhandelsschiedsgerichtsbarkeit der sozialistischen Länder im Handel mit der Bundesrepublik Deutschland* (Heidelberg 1973)

Polonsky, Arbitration of International Contracts, 1971 *J. Bus. L.* 1

Quattrin, Arbitration in International Commerce and Prime/Subcontractors' Relationship, in *ICCA, Fourth Int'l Arb. Congress: Proceedings* 770 (1972)

Rose, F.D., ed., *International Commercial and Maritime Arbitration* (London 1988)

Sanders, Trade Arbitration between East and West, 15 *Int'l & Comp. L.Q.* 742 (1966)

Thomas, Arbitration: The Basis and Validity of a Restricted Reasons Agreement, 1986 *Lloyd's Mar. & Com. L.Q.* 235 (1986)

van den Hoven, Commercial Disputes and Their Settlement, a Factor in Business Planning, in *ICC, 60 Years of ICC Arbitration* 35 (1984)

Woychuk, Commercial Dispute Settlement in China-United States Trade, 6 *Fordham Int'l L.J.* 171 (1982)

Yamane, Resolving Disputes in U.S.-Japan Trade: The Japanese Perspective, 39 *Arb. J.* 3 (No. 4, 1984)

6.03 COMMODITY CONTRACTS

Brown & Melick, The Arbitration Alternative for Various Coal, Oil, and Gas Non-labor Dispute, in *Eastern Mineral Law Foundation, Fifth Annual Institute: Proceedings* 1 (1984)

Chapman, FOSFA International Arbitration, 2 *Arb. Int'l* 323 (1986)

de Bruin, De 'affaire C', 1989 *Tijdschrift voor Arbitrage* 1

Dudisson, Arbitration for Subcontracts in International Projects, 1 *J. Int'l Arb.* 197 (1984)

Hudson, General Average Adjustment and Arbitration in the People's Republic of China, 1976 *Lloyd's Mar. & Com. L.Q.* 135

Johnson, Commodity Trade Arbitration, in *Handbook of Arbitration Practice* 189 (R. Bernstein ed. 1987)

Johnson, D., *International Commodity Arbitration* (London 1991)

Kopelmanas, L'arbitrage et verification technique de la bonne exécution de contrats internationaux dans le domain de l'industrie, in *ICCA, Fourth Int'l Arb. Congress: Proceedings* 366 (1972)

Lisowski, Specialist Arbitration Courts in Poland and Their Role in the International Cotton and Wool Trade, in *ICCA, Fourth Int'l Arb. Congress: Proceedings* 738 (1972)

Mackie, Integration of Arbitration Systems as Regards the Commodity Trades, 44 *Arbitration* 89 (1978)

————, Thesis on Commercial Arbitration in Commodity Trades, 57 *Arbitration* 156 (1991)

Markert, T., *Rohstoffkonzessionen in der internationalen Schiedsgerichtsbarkeit* (Baden-Baden 1989)

Note, Predispute Arrangements to Arbitrate Claims Arising under the Commodity Exchange Act, 42 *Wash. & Lee L. Rev.* 939 (1985)

Schütze, Zur Wirksamkeit von internationalen Schiedsvereinbarungen und zur Wirkungserstreckung ausländischer Schiedssprüche über Ansprüche aus Börsentermingeschäften, 1 *Jahrbuch Schiedsgerichtsbarkeit* 94 (1987)

Slabotzky, A., *Grain Contracts and Arbitration for Shipments from the United States and Canada* (London 1984)

Thompson, International Chamber of Commerce — Arbitration Disputes Arising under International Construction Contracts, 5 *Int'l Bus. Law.* 225 (1977)

Timagenis, Arbitration in Piraeus — a Growing Trend, 1977 *Lloyd's Mar. & Com. L.Q.* 319

van Delden, English Commodity Arbitrations: A Foreigner Looking Around in London, in *The Art of Arbitration* 95 (J. Schultsz & A. van den Berg eds. 1982)

6.04 COMPETITION AND ANTITRUST

Allison, Arbitration Agreements and Antitrust Claims: The Need for Enhanced Accommodation of Conflicting Public Policies, 64 *N.C. L. Rev.* 219 (1986)

———, Arbitration of Private Antitrust Claims in International Trade: A Study in the Subordination of National Interests to the Demands of a World Market, 18 *N.Y.U. J. Int'l L. & Pol.* 361 (1986)

Altenmüller, R., *Die schiedsrichterliche Entscheidung kartellrechtlicher Streitigkeiten* (Tübingen 1973)

Becker, Antitrust and International Arbitration — The New American Synthesis, 13 *Int'l Bus. Law.* 445 (1985)

Bernardini, Stati Uniti: arbitrabilità di controversie in materia de legislazione antitrust, 25 *Rassegna dell'Arb.* 109 (1985)

Brown & Houck, Arbitrating International Antitrust Disputes, 13 *World Competition* 19 (No. 4, 1990)

———, Arbitrating International Antitrust Disputes, 7 *J. Int'l Arb.* 77 (No. 1, 1990)

Campbell & Vollmer, U.S. Supreme Court's Mitsubishi Decision Boosts International Arbitrations, 82 *L. Soc'y Gazette* 2830 (1985)

Carbonneau, Mitsubishi: The Folly of Quixotic Internationalism, 2 *Arb. Int'l* 116 (1986)

Cloud, Mitsubishi and the Arbitrability of Antitrust Claims: Did the Supreme Court Throw the Baby Out with the Bathwater? 18 *L. & Pol. Int'l Bus.* 341 (1986)

Comment, Arbitration and Antitrust: A Leg Up for International Arbitration [Mitsubishi Motors Corp. v. Soler Chrysler-Plymouth, Inc., 105 S. Ct. 3346 (1985)], 25 *Washburn L.J.* 536 (1986)

———, Transnational Contractual Disputes: Antitrust Joins Securities Law Claims as Arbitrable Subject Matter, 12 *Brooklyn J. Int'l L.* 731 (1986)

de Mello, Arbitrage et ordre public national découlant des règles de concurrence, 1979 *Rev. Arb.* 101

————, Arbitration and Domestic Public Policy Resulting from Regulations on Competition, in *Arbitration and the Licensing Process* 6-109 (R. Goldscheider & M. de Haas eds. 1984-)

Derains, Arbitrage et droit de concurrence, *Revue Suisse du Droit Int'l de la Concurrence* 39 (No. 14, Feb. 1982)

Donaldson, Mitsubishi and Antitrust Arbitration — It's All the Japanese You Need to Know, 1986 *B. Y. U. L. Rev.* 219 (1986)

Fox, Mitsubishi v. Soler and Its Impact on International Commercial Arbitration, 19 *J. World Trade L.* 579 (1985)

Grossen, Arbitrage et droit de la concurrence, in *Recueil de Travaux Suisses* 35 (C. Reymond & E. Bucher eds. 1984)

Jarvin, Arbitrability of Anti-Trust Disputes: the Mitsubishi v. Soler Case, 2 *J. Int'l Arb.* 69 (1985)

————, Arbitrability of Antitrust Disputes: The Mitsubishi v. Soler Case, 25 *Swiss Rev. Int'l Competition L.* 53 (Oct. 1985)

————, Skiljeforfarande och konkurrenslagstiftning; nagra anmarkningar till Mitsubishimalet [Arbitration and antitrust law: some remarks on the Mitsubishi case], 1986 *Tidskrift utgiven av Juridiska Foreningen i Finland* 219

Johnson, International Antitrust Litigation and Arbitration Clauses, 3 *J.L. & Com.* 91 (1983)

Kanowitz, Alternative Dispute Resolution and the Public Interest: The Arbitration Experience, 38 *Hastings L.J.* 239 (1987)

Kaplan, L'arbitrabilité des litiges commerciaux en matière de droit de la concurrence, 14 *Droit et Pratique du Com. Int'l* 403 (1988)

Kornblum, Nachprufbarkeit kartellrechtlicher Schiedssprüche durch die ordentliche Gerichte, 22 *NJW* 1793 (1969)

Kovar, Droit communautaire de la concurrence et arbitrage, in *Etudes offerts à Berthold Goldman* 109 (Paris 1983)

Kühn, Arbitrability of Antitrust Disputes in the Federal Republic of Germany, 3 *Arb. Int'l* 226 (1987)

————, Kartellrecht und Schiedsgerichtsbarkeit in der Bundesrepublik Deutschland, 1987 *BB* 621

Laman, Industrial Contract: Important Considerations in Preparation for International Commercial Arbitration, in *Commercial Arbitration* 57 (J. Ricalde, ed. 1983)

Lange & Wiessner, Die Schiedsfähigkeit internationaler Antitrust-Streitigkeiten: zur Mitsubishi-Entscheidung des U.S. Supreme Court, 31 *RIW* 757 (1985)

Lee, Antitrust and Commercial Arbitration: An Economic Analysis, 62 *St. John's L. Rev.* 1 (1987)

Lipner, International Antitrust Law: To Arbitrate or Not to Arbitrate, 19 *Geo. Wash. J. Int'l L. & Econ.* 395 (1985)

Loevinger, Antitrust Issues as Subjects of Arbitration, 44 *N.Y.U. L. Rev.* 1085 (1969)

Lowenfeld, The Mitsubishi Case: Another View, 2 *Arb. Int'l* 178 (1986)

McGrath, Son of Mitsubishi — Arbitration of Domestic Antitrust Disputes, 12 *Brooklyn J. Int'l L.* 693 (1986)

Moitry, Arbitrage international et droit de la concurrence: vers un ordre public de la *lex mercatoria*? 1989 *Rev. Arb.* 3

Newton, Arbitration and Antitrust: A Leg Up for International Arbitration, 25 *Washburn L.J.* 536 (1986)

Nilsson, Arbitration and Anti-trust — Enforcing Treble Damages from a Swedish Point of View, 1987 *J. Bus. L.* 227

Nissen, Antitrust and Arbitration in International Commerce, 17 *Harv. Int'l L.J.* 110 (1976)

Nobel, Privates Schiedsgerichtswesen und staatlicher Richter im 'Wettbewerb,' in *Freiheit und Verantwortung im Recht, Festschrift Arthur Meier-Hayoz* 247 (Berne 1982)

Note, Application of the Convention on the Recognition and Enforcement of Foreign Arbitral Awards: Mitsubishi Motor Corp. v. Soler Chrysler-Plymouth, Inc., 8 *Fordham Int'l L.J.* 194 (1984)

————, Arbitration: Public Policy Exception to Arbitration of Anti-trust Issues: Mitsubishi Motors Corp. v. Soler Chrysler-Plymouth, Inc. 723 F.2d 155 (1st Cir. 1983), 25 *Harv. Int'l L.J.* 427 (1984)

————, Transnational Antitrust Claims are Nonarbitrable under the Federal Arbitration Act and Art. II(1) of the Convention on the Recognition and Enforcement of Foreign Arbitral Awards: Mitsubishi v. Soler Chrysler-Plymouth, 17 *Vand. J. Transnat'l L.* 741 (1984)

Ovington, Arbitration and U.S. Antitrust Law: A Conflict of Policies, 2 *J. Int'l Arb.* 53 (No. 2, 1985)

Parnass, International Arbitration and the Comity of Error: Mitsubishi Motors Corp. v. Soler Chrysler-Plymouth, Inc., 19 *Conn. L. Rev.* 435 (1987)

Pitofsky, Arbitration and Antitrust Enforcement, 44 *N.Y.U. L. Rev.* 1072 (1969)

Renold, Arbitrage international et droit antitrust: l'arrêt Mitsubishi v. Soler de la Cour suprême des Etats-Unis, 105(127) *ZSR* 545 (1986)

Robert, Une date dans l'extension de l'arbitrage international: l'arrêt Mitsubishi c/ Soler, 1986 *Rev. Arb.* 173

Smit, Mitsubishi: It Is Not What It Seems to Be, 4 *J. Int'l Arb.* 7 (No. 3, 1987)

Smith, Determining the Arbitrability of International Antitrust Disputes, 8 *J. Comp. Bus. & Cap. Market L.* 197 (1986)

Sopata, Mitsubishi Motors Corp. v. Soler Chrysler-Plymouth, Inc.: International Arbitration and Antitrust Claims, 7 *Nw. J. Int'l L. & Bus.* 595 (1986)

Steindorf, Kartellrecht und Schiedsgerichtsbarkeit, 34 *Wirtschaft und Wettbewerb* 189 (1984)

van Hecke, Arbitrage et règles de concurrence, 1979 *Rev. Arb.* 191

Victor & Bialos, The Arbitration of Public Law Disputes: The Availability and Efficacy of This Alternative Dispute Resolution Mechanism, in *Private Investors Abroad — Problems and Solutions in International Business in 1987* 15.1 (J. Ross ed. 1987)

von Mehren, From Vynior's Case to Mitsubishi: The Future of Arbitration and Public Law, 12 *Brooklyn J. Int'l L.* 583 (1986)

von Zumbusch, Arbitrability of Antitrust Claims Under U.S., German, and EEC Law: The 'International Transaction' Criterion and Public Policy, 22 *Tex. Int'l L.J.* 291 (1987)

————, Die Schiedsfähigkeit privatrechtlicher Kartellrechtsstreitigkeiten nach US-, deutschem und EG-Recht, 1988 *GRUR Int'l* 541

Vorhees, International Commercial Arbitration and the Arbitrability of Anti-trust Claims: Mitsubishi Motors Corp. v. Soler Chrysler Plymouth, 14 *N. Ky. L. Rev.* 65(1987)

Weitbrecht, U.S. -Antitrustrecht vor internationalen Handelsschiedsgerichten (zu Mitsubishi Motors Corp. v. Soler Chrysler-Plymouth, Inc., U.S. Supreme Court, Entscheidung von 2. Juli 1985, -U.S.-, 105 S. Ct. 3346), 6 *IPRax* 313 (1986)

Werner, A Swiss Comment on Mitsubishi, 3 *J. Int'l Arb.* 81 (No. 4, 1986)

Wilkinson, Judicial Review of Foreign Arbitral Awards on Antitrust Matters After Mitsubishi Motors, 26 *Colum. J. Transnat'l L.* 407 (1988)

Zimmer, D., *Zulässigkeit und Grenzen schiedsgerichtlicher Entscheidung von Kartellrechtsstreitigkeiten* (Baden-Baden 1991)

6.05 CONSTRUCTION

Alexander, Construction Industry Arbitrations, in *Handbook of Arbitration Practice* 237 (R. Bernstein ed. 1987)

Alvarez, The Role of Arbitration in Canada — New Perspectives, 21 *U. B.C. L. Rev.* 247 (1987)

Coulson, Construction Arbitration Around the World, 48 *Arbitration* 162 (1982)

de Grandcourt, Les interférences du contentieux arbitral et des contentieux adjacents, in *First Euro-Arab Arb. Conference: Proceedings* 224 (F. Kemicha ed. 1987)

Debevoise, The Arbitrability of Gaps in Long-Term Scientific, Technical and Industrial Development Contracts, 17 *Harv. Int'l L.J.* 122 (1976)

Duncan Wallace, Deficiencies in Current International Arbitration Practice in Construction Cases, 7 *Arb. Int'l* 149 (1991)

Goudsmit, Arbitration in Construction Contracts in the Netherlands, 2 *Int'l Constr. L. Rev.* 185 (1985)

Hautot & Flécheux, La clause de règlement des différends dans les conditions F.I.D.I.C. génie civil de 1987, 1989 *Rev. Arb.* 609

Heiermann, Schiedsgerichtsvereinbarung im nationalen und internationalen Bauvertrag, 1 *Jahrbuch Schiedsgerichtsbarkeit* 23 (1987)

———, Der Schiedsvertrag im Bauwesen und Anlagenbau, 2 *Jahrbuch Schiedsgerichtsbarkeit* 66 (1988)

Hoellering, Emerging Techniques of Private Dispute Resolution in Long-Term Contracts, in *Der komplexe Langzeitvertrag/The Complex Long-Term Contract* 523 (F. Nicklisch ed. 1987)

———, The Qualification of Arbitrators for Construction Disputes, 45 *Arb. J.* 34 (No. 4, 1990)

Hunter, UNCITRAL and Construction Industry Arbitration, 2 *Int'l Constr. L. Rev.* 165 (1985)

Jarvin, Construction Disputes Under the International Chamber of Commerce (ICC) Court of Arbitration Rules, 2 *Int'l Constr. L. Rev.* 139 (1985)

Jones, Latent Conditions Disputes — Arbitration v. Litigation, 2 *Int'l Constr. L. Rev.* 99 (1985)

Kopelmanas, La procédure arbitrale dans les contrats internationaux de travaux publics, in *A.I.A., Essays in Memoriam Eugenio Minoli* 273 (Turin 1974)

Level, Caractères particuliers de l'arbitrage dans les contracts industriels et de grands travaux, in *First Euro-Arab Arb. Conference: Proceedings* 193 (F. Kemicha ed. 1987)

Mehandry, Settlement of Engineering and Building Disputes by Arbitration, 7 *I. C. A. Arb. Q.* 3 (No. 1, June 1973)

Melis, Praktische und prozedurale Probleme mit Mehrparteienschiedsgerichten bei komplexen Langzeitvertragen, in *Der komplexe Langzeitvertrag/The Complex Long-Term Contract* 569 (F. Nicklisch ed. 1987)

Myers, Could Arbitration Be Made a More Effective Method of Resolution of Construction Disputes? 19 *Int'l Bus. Law.* 313 (1991)

———, Why Conventional Arbitration Is Not Effective in Complex Long-Term Contracts, in *Der komplexe Langzeitvertrag/The Complex Long-Term Contract* 503 (F. Nicklisch ed. 1987)

Nicklisch, Der Ingenieur als Schiedsgutachter und Quasi-Schiedsrichter bei internationalen Bau- und Anlagenprojekten, in *Festschrift für Walther J. Habscheid* 217 (W. Lindacher, D. Pfaff et al. eds. 1989)

———, Privatautonomie und Schiedsgerichtsbarkeit bei internationalen Bauverträgen, 37 *RIW* 89 (1991)

Nicklisch, F., ed., *Der komplexe Langzeitvertrag. Strukturen und Internationale Schiedsgerichtsbarkeit/The Complex Long-Term Contract. Structures and International Arbitration* (Heidelberg 1987)

Niggemann, Arbitration in Construction Contracts, *Int'l Arb. Gazette* (Association Internationale des Jeunes Avocats) 211 (No. 5, July 1985)

Norris, What Has Gone Wrong with Construction Disputes: An Engineer's View, 6 *Arb. Int'l* 158 (1990)

Oehmke, T., *Construction Arbitration* (Rochester 1989)

Pearson, Role of Arbitrators and Consulting Engineers with Regard to Contracts on Civil Construction Works, in *ICCA, Fourth Int'l Arb. Congress: Proceedings* 285 (1972)

Piccinini, Arbitration in Construction and Civil Engineering Contracts, in *ICCA, Sixth Int'l Arb. Congress: Proceedings* 393 (1978)

Rao, Role of Arbitrators and Consulting Engineers in Connection with Contracts on Civil Engineering and Building Construction Works in Developing Countries, in *ICCA, Fourth Int'l Arb. Congress: Proceedings* 776 (1972)

Redfern, England as a Forum for the Arbitration of International Construction Disputes, 2 *Int'l Constr. L. Rev.* 258 (1985)

Richards, Enforceability of Arbitration Provisions in Construction Contracts, 34 *Federation of Insurance Counsel Q.* 95 (1983)

Rucareanu, Arbitration and Contracts Concerning Projects of Industrial Installations, Supply and Mountings, in *ICCA, Fourth Int'l Arb. Congress: Proceedings* 219 (1972)

Sefrioui, Interférences de l'arbitrage et des mécanismes d'organisation des travaux, in *First Euro-Arab Arb. Conference: Proceedings* 208 (F. Kemicha ed. 1987)

Seppala, La procédure pré-arbitral de règlement des litiges selon les Conditions du contrat-type de génie civil de la FIDIC, 1987 *Int'l Bus. L.J.* 579

————, The Pre-Arbitral Procedure for the Settlement of Disputes in the F.I.D.I.C. (Civil Engineering) Conditions of Contract, 3 *Int'l Constr. L.J.* 315 (1986)

————, Les décisions pré-arbitrales afférentes aux litiges en matière de construction: les décisions prises par l'ingénieur, 1991 *Int'l Bus. L.J.* 331

Singhania, Arbitration in the Construction Industry in India, 7 *J. Int'l Arb.* 49 (No. 2, 1990)

Soper, Arbitration, the Courts and the Resolution of Engineering Disputes, 42 *Arbitration* 48 (1975)

Stern, Arbitrating Disputes in Major Construction Projects, in *ICCA, Fourth Int'l Arb. Congress: Proceedings* 235 (1972)

Tackaberry, Elementary Economics and the Construction Dispute. An Outsider's Look at Swiss Law Remedies Available to the Unpaid Contractor, 7 *J. Int'l Arb.* 73 (No. 3, 1990)

von Hoffmann, International Construction Arbitration, in *Essays on International Commercial Arbitration* 223 (P. Sarcevic ed. 1989)

Yahiel & Cranston, Arbitration and Dispute Resolution in the International Construction Industry, 2 *Int'l Constr. L. Rev.* 231 (1985)

6.06 INSURANCE DISPUTES

Claasens, L'arbitrage en matière d'assurances, 1978 *Rev. Arb.* 215

Cunningham, Arbitration of Marine Insurance Disputes, 38 *Federation of Insurance & Corporate Counsel Q.* 209 (1988)

Farrug & McHugh, What's New in Arbitration? 34 *Federation of Insurance Counsel Q.* 347 (1984)

Gumbel, Thoughts on Arbitration Under Reinsurance Contracts and on an Attempt to Draft a Standard Clause, in *Festschrift für Reimer Schmidt* 883 (Karlsruhe 1976)

————, Thoughts on Arbitration under Reinsurance Contracts and on an Attempt to Draft a Standard Clause, 45 *Arbitration* 257 (1979)

Jannot, Überlegungen zu Bedeutung und Ausgestaltung von Schiedsgerichtsvereinbarungen in der Rückversicherung, in *Festschrift für Ernst C. Stiefel* 359 (M. Lutter, W. Oppenhoff, O. Sandrock & H. Winkhaus eds. 1987)

McCrindell, Arbitration in the Insurance Industry in the United Kingdom, in *ICCA, Sixth Int'l Arb. Congress: Proceedings* 149 (1978)

————, Arbitration in the English Insurance Industry, 45 *Arbitration* 229 (1979)

Nonna & Strassberg, Reinsurance Arbitration: Boon or Bust? 22 *Tort & Ins. L.J.* 586 (1987)

Piccinini, L'arbitrage en matière d'assurance et financement des crédits à l'exportation, in *ICCA, Fourth Int'l Arb. Congress: Proceedings* 492 (1972)

Sieg, Bindung des Haftpflichtversicherers an Schiedssprüche und Schiedsgutachten im Haftpflichtverhältniss, 35 *VersR* 501 (1984)

6.07 INVESTMENT DISPUTES

Agyemang, African Courts, the Settlement of Investment Disputes and the Enforcement of Awards, 33 *J. Afr. L.* 31 (1989)

Aksen, G. & R. von Mehren, eds., *International Arbitration Between Private Parties and Governments* (New York 1982)

Amerasinghe, Model Clauses for Settlement of Foreign Investment Disputes, 28 *Arb. J.* 232 (1973)

Bannerman, Digging for Gold in Ghana, 6 *Int'l Fin. L. Rev.* 29 (No. 7, 1987)

Bernardini, Considérations pratiques sur le règlement des différends relatifs aux investissements: le point de vue des utilisateurs, 21 *Rassegna dell'Arb.* 7 (1981)

————, Les arbitrages pétroliers et le droit appliqué par les arbitres, in *First Euro-Arab Arbitration Conference: Proceedings* 282 (F. Kemicha ed. 1987)

Broches, Bilateral Investment Protection Treaties and Arbitration of Investment Disputes, in *The Art of Arbitration* 63 (J. Schultsz & A. van den Berg eds. 1982)

————, Settlement of Disputes Arising out of Investment in Developing Countries, 11 *Int'l Bus. Law.* 206 (1984)

Buffenstein, Foreign Investment Arbitration and Joint Ventures, 5 *N.C.J. Int'l L. & Com. Reg.* 191 (1980)

Catranis, Probleme der Nationalisierung ausländischer Unternehmen vor internationalen Schiedsgerichten: die Libyschen Schiedsfälle, 28 *RIW* 19 (1982)

Cherian, A New Response to the Question of Law in Transnational Investment Arbitration, in *ICCA, Fifth Int'l Arb. Congress: Proceedings* C Ib 1-5 (1975)

Derman, Nationalization and the Protective Arbitration Clause, 5 *J. Int'l Arb.* 131 (No. 4, 1988)

Dimilitsa, Arbitration Agreements and Foreign Investments: The Greek State between Contractual Commitment and Sovereign Intervention, 5 *J. Int'l Arb.* 17 (No. 4, 1988)

El-Hakim, Litiges commerciaux multilatéraux dans le cadre des projets en Moyen-Orient, 1981 *Rev. Arb.* 86

El-Kosheri & Riad, The Changing Roles in the Arbitration Process (with Regard to the Applicable Law Governing the New Generation of the Petroleum Agreements), 1 *Arab Law Q.* 475 (1986); also in *First Euro-Arab Arbitration Conference: Proceedings* 253 (F. Kemicha ed. 1987)

————, The Law Governing a New Generation of Petroleum Agreements: Changes in the Arbitration Process, 1 *ICSID Rev. - Foreign Investment L.J.* 257 (1986)

Eze, Legal Structures for the Resolution of International Problems in the Domain of Private Foreign Investments: A Third World Perspective Now and in the Future, 9 *Ga. J. Int'l & Comp. L.* 535 (1979)

Feldman, Soviet Joint Ventures: Providing for Appropriate Dispute Resolution, 23 *Cornell Int'l L.J.* 107 (1990)

Fischer, Die schiedsgerichtliche Beilegung von privaten Investitionsstreitigkeiten im Lichte der Weltbankkonvention vom 18. März 1965, 1 *Verfassung und Recht in Übersee* 262 (1968)

Fishburne, Random Observations about Arbitration and East-West Investment, 10 *Int'l Law.* 119 (1976)

Forrestal, Examples of and Reasons for Increased Use of International Arbitration, in *International Arbitration Between Private Parties and Governments* 15 (G. Aksen & R. von Mehren eds. 1982)

Gallins, Bilateral Investment Protection Treaties, 2 *J. Energy & Nat. Resources L.* 77 (1984)

Gann, The U.S. Bilateral Investment Treaty Program, 21 *Stan. J. Int'l L.* 373 (1985)

Gilbert, Enforceability of Settlements of Foreign Investment Disputes, 17 *Va. J. Int'l L.* 361 (1977)

Goldman, B., *Investissement étrangers et arbitrage entre Etats et personnes privées* (Paris 1969)

Golsong, Dispute Settlement in Recently Negotiated Bilateral Investment Treaties — The Reference to the ICSID Additional Facility, in *Realism in Law-Making: Essays on International Law in Honour of Willem Riphagen* 35 (A. Bos & H. Siblezs eds. 1986)

242

Gomez Lara, Arbitraje e inversiones extranjeras, in *El Arbitraje Comercial Internacional* 363 (Mexico 1983)

Holtzmann, Settlement of Investment Disputes in East-West Trade, 10 *Int'l Law*. 123 (1976)

Irani, Settlement of International Disputes through Arbitration, in *Private Investments and International Transactions in Asian and South Pacific Countries* (New York 1975)

Joy, Arbitration of Economic Development Agreements: The Impact of Revere v. OPIC, 20 *Va. J. Int'l L.* 861 (1980)

Klitgaard, People's Republic of China Joint Venture Dispute Resolution Procedures, 1 *UCLA Pac. Basin L.J.* 1 (1982)

Mann, British Treaties for the Promotion and Protection of Investments, 52 *Brit. Y.B. Int'l L.* 241 (1981)

Mazanza, L'arbitrage dans les codes des investissements de l'Afrique noire francophone, 29 *Revue juridique et politique, indépendence et coopération* 111 (1975)

Meyer, Le nouveau code des investisssements au Burkina: changement ou continuité? 9 *Revue Burkinabe de Droit* 35 (1986)

————, Le régime juridique des investissements en Haute-Volta, 1982 *Revue Voltaique de Droit* 7

Migliorino, La surroga dello stato all'investitore privato indennizzato negli accordi bilaterali sugli investimenti, 22 *Riv. Dir. Int'le Priv. & Proc.* 275 (1986)

Nicklisch, F., ed., *Der komplexe Langzeitvertrag. Strukturen und Internationale Schiedsgerichtsbarkeit/The Complex Long-Term Contract. Structures and International Arbitration* (Heidelberg 1987)

Paulsson, Les obligations des partenaires dans un accord de développement économique: la sentence arbitrale Cameroun c/ Klöckner, 1984 *Rev. Arb.* 19

————, The ICSID Klöckner v. Cameroon Award: The Duties of Partners in North-South Economic Development Agreements, 1 *J. Int'l Arb.* 145 (1984)

————, Third World Participation in International Investment Arbitration, 2 *ICSID Rev. - Foreign Investment L.J.* 19 (1987)

Peter, Arbitration and Renegotiation Clauses, 3 *J. Int'l Arb.* 29 (No. 2, 1986)

————, International Investment Agreements - Types, Arbitration and Renegotiation, in *Der komplexe Langzeitvertrag/The Complex Long-Term Contract* 119 (F. Nicklisch ed. 1987)

————, Settlement of Investment Disputes, 5 *J. Int'l Arb.* 131 (No. 1, 1988)

Peter, W., *Arbitration and Renegotiation of International Investment Agreements: A Study with Particular Reference to Means of Conflict Avoidance Under Natural Resources Investment Agreements* (Dordrecht 1986)

Picozzi, The Settlement of International Investment Disputes, 4 *Trent L.J.* 37 (1980)

Pierros, International Commercial Arbitration: Prospects and Choices, 38-39 *Rev. Hellénique Droit Int'l* 165 (1985-86)

Pogany, Bilateral Investment Treaties: Some Recent Examples, 2 *ICSID Rev. - Foreign Investment L.J.* 457 (1987)

Rigaux, La detérmination de l'ordre juridique auquel se rattachent les arbitrages petroliers, in *First Euro-Arab Arbitration Conference: Proceedings* 298 (F. Kemicha ed. 1987)

Rubin, S.J. & R.W. Nelson, eds., *International Investment Disputes: Avoidance and Settlement* (St. Paul, MN 1985)

Rycx, L'accord sur le règlement des litiges entre Etats hôtes d'investissements arabes et ressortissants des autres Etats arabes et ses perspectives, 1981 *Rev. Arb.* 259

Shihata, The Role of ICSID and the Projected Multilateral Investment Guarantee Agency (MIGA), 41 *Aussenwirtschaft* 105 (1986)

————, The Settlement of Disputes Regarding Foreign Investment: The Role of the World Bank, with Particular Reference to ICSID and MIGA, 1 *Am. U.J. Int'l L. & Pol'y* 97 (1986); also 1 *Arab Law Q.* 265 (1986)

Sornarajah, M., *International Commercial Arbitration: The Problem of State Contracts* (Singapore 1990)

Subramanian, Arbitration in Investment and Technical Collaboration Disputes, in *ICCA, Fourth Int'l Arb. Congress: Proceedings* 820 (1972)

Taliadoros, Comment deux sentences arbitrales rendues dans le cadre de la législation hellénique relative à la protection des investissements étrangers et portant toutes deux sur un objet identique, .., 1984 *Droit et Pratique du Com. Int'l* 603

United Nations Centre on Transnational Corporations, *Bilateral Investment Treaties* (New York 1988) [United Nations Publication Sales No. E.88.II.A.1]

Varma, Petroleum Concessions in International Arbitration: Texaco Overseas Petroleum Company v. Libyan Arab Republic, 18 *Colum. J. Transnat'l L.* 259 (1979)

Vuylstehe, Foreign Investment Protection and ICSID Arbitration, 4 *Ga. J. Int'l & Comp. L.* 343 (1974)

Wegen, Dispute Settlement and Arbitration, in *International Investment Disputes: Avoidance and Settlement* 59 (S. Rubin & R. Nelson eds. 1985)

White, Expropriation of the Libyan Oil Concessions: Two Conflicting International Arbitrations, 30 *Int'l & Comp. L.Q.* 1 (1981)

Zorn & Mayerson, Cuba's Joint Venture Law: New Rules for Foreign Investment, 21 *Colum. J. Transn'l L.* 273 (1983)

6.08 MARITIME DISPUTES

Alcántara Gonzales, Enforcement of Awards, in 2 *Fifth Int'l Congress of Maritime Arbitrators* (New York 1981)

Auchter, L'arbitrage maritime dans la pratique japonaise, 25 *Droit Mar. Français* 181 (1973)

Barclay, Practical Experience in Maritime Arbitration, 49 *Arbitration* 23 and 106 (1983)

Barinova, I.I., *Kommentarii sudebnoi i arbitrazhnoi praktiki po morskim delam* (Moscow 1988)

Bauer, Maritime Arbitration in New York, 8 *Int'l Bus. Law.* 306 (1980)

Berg, Maritime RICO as Seen by an Arbitrator, 12 *Tul. Mar. L.J.* 85 (1987)

Berlingieri, International Maritime Arbitration, 10 *J. Mar. L. & Com.* 199 (1979)

Bhasin, Arbitration in International Combined Transport — A Definite Possibility, in *Arbitration in Settlement of International Commercial Disputes Involving the Far East and Arbitration in Combined Transportation* 369 (P. Sanders ed. 1989)

Broedermann, China and Admiralty — An Introduction to Chinese Maritime Law and U.S.-Chinese Shipping Relations, 15 *J. Mar. L. & Com.* 539, 562 (1984)

Bulow, Consequential Damages and the Duty to *Mitigate in New York Maritime Arbitrations, 1984* Lloyd's Mar. & Com. L.Q. 622

Butler, Soviet Maritime Arbitration, in *International Commercial and Maritime Arbitration* 37 (F.D. Rose ed. 1988)

Butler, W., ed., *Soviet Commercial and Maritime Arbitration* (Dobbs Ferry, NY 1980)

Byrne, The Effect of RICO on Maritime Arbitration, 12 *Tul. Mar. L.J.* 77 (1987)

Carbone & Luzzatto, Arbitration Clauses, Carriage by Sea and Uniform Law, in *Studies on the Revision of the Brussels Convention on Bills of Lading* 353 (Genoa 1974); also in 76 *Dir. Mar.* 253 (1974)

China Maritime Arbitration Commission, *Selection of Awards and Conciliation Statements* (1984—1988), (Beijing 1989)

Cleveland, How to Save Maritime Arbitration in New York (A Modest Proposal), in 2 *Fifth Int'l Congress of Maritime Arbitrators* (New York 1981)

Cohen, A New Yorker Looks at London Maritime Arbitration, 1986 *Lloyd's Mar. & Com. L.Q.* 57 (No. 1)

————, A Venue Problem with the Arbitration Clauses Found in Printed Form Charters, 7 *J. Mar. L. & Com.* 541 (1976)

————, Miscelaneous Problems with Arbitration Clauses in Printed Form Charters, 78 Il *Dir. Mar.* 141 (1976)

Cohen, M.M., ed., *Index and Digest of the Award Service of the Society of Maritime Arbitrators,* Volumes 3A & 3B (New York 1986)

Costabel, Non-Domestic Arbitration Clauses, Stay of Proceedings and Recognition of Foreign Awards in Italy, 2 *Fifth Int'l Congress of Maritime Arbitrators* (New York 1981)

Darling, Salvage Arbitration, in *International Commercial and Maritime Arbitration* 95 (F.D. Rose ed. 1988)

Davies, Some Powers of the Arbitrator Under English Law, in 1 *Fifth Int'l Congress of Maritime Arbitrators* (New York 1981)

————, A View of London Maritime Arbitration, 52 *Arbitration* 150 (1986)

Freear, Practice and Procedure under the ICC-CMI International Maritime Arbitration Rules, 1 *Fifth Int'l Congress of Maritime Arbitrators* (New York 1981)

Heifets, Jurisdictions of Permanent USSR Arbitration Courts Distinguished, in *ICCA, Fifth Int'l Arb. Congress: Proceedings* C Izb 1-4 (1975)

Istomin, Maritime Arbitration and Sources of International Legal Adjustment of Merchant Marine Fleet Commercial Operation Issues, in *ICCA, Fourth Int'l Arb. Congress: Proceedings* 725 (1972)

Ivanov, Provision on Arbitration at Carriage of Cargoes Under Bills of Lading, in *ICCA, Fifth Int'l Arb. Congress: Proceedings* C Iza 1-4 (1975)

Iwasaki, Survey of Maritime Arbitration in New York, 15 *J. Mar. L. & Com.* 69 (1984)

Jackson, The Hague-Visby Rules and Forum, Arbitration and Choice of Law Clauses, 1980 *Lloyd's Mar. & Com. L.Q.* 159 (1980)

Jambu-Merlin, The New French Arbitration Act, in 1 *Fifth Int'l Congress of Maritime Arbitrators* (New York 1981)

Japikse, Combined Transport and Arbitration, in *Arbitration in Settlement of International Commercial Disputes Involving the Far East and Arbitration in Combined Transportation* 357 (P. Sanders ed. 1989)

Jarvis, An Annotated Bibliography of English-Language Materials on Maritime Arbitration, 14 *Tul. Mar. L.J.* 49 (1989)

————, Problems with and Solutions for New York Maritime Arbitration, 1986 *Lloyd's Mar. & Com. L.Q.* 535

Jarvis & Mellman, A Comment of the Rules of the Maritime Arbitration Board of Miami, 19 *J. Mar. L. & Com.* 463 (1988)

Kalpin, A. G., *Spory, svyazannye s torgovym moreplavaniem. Nauchno-prakticheskii komentarii arbitrazhnoi praktiki* (Moscow 1971)

Keane, Waiver of Maritime Arbitration, 8 *J. Mar. L. & Com.* 195 (1977)

Kheifets, O pravilakh proizvodstva del v Morskoi arbitrazhnoi komissii, 1988 *Khozaistvo i Pravo* 60 (No. 3)

————, Recognition and Enforcement of Foreign Court Judgements and Arbitral Awards in Maritime Disputes, 1985 *Soviet Y.B. Mar. L.* 87

Kimball, Vacating Maritime Arbitration Awards: Is It Really Possible? 13 *J. Mar. L. & Com.* 71 (1981)

Kühl, S. G., *Schiedsgerichtsbarkeit im Seehandel* (Kehl am Rhein 1990)

Lebedev, 'Combined Transport' Disputes in Soviet Arbitration Practice, in *Arbitration in Settlement of International Commercial Disputes Involving the Far East and Arbitration in Combined Transportation* 347 (P. Sanders ed. 1989)

————, Application of Law by the Maritime Arbitration Commission in Settling Disputes, 6 *Ga. J. Int'l & Comp.L.* 519 (1976)

————, Commentary on the Statute of the Maritime Arbitration Commission at the USSR Chamber of Commerce and Industry, 7 *Y.B. Com. Arb.* 249 (1982)

————, La Commission d'arbitrage maritime près de la Chambre de commerce de l'URSS, 1971 *Rev. Arb.* 137

Lux, MAC in Moscow, 19 *Int'l Bus. Law.* 212 (1991)

McCormack, A Lawyer's View of Arbitration Proceedings and Composition of the Arbitration Panel, 1984 *Y.B. Mar. Law* 55

————, Arbitration in Combined Transportation — A Rare Bird, in *Arbitration in Settlement of International Commercial Disputes Involving the Far East and Arbitration in Combined Transportation* 325 (P. Sanders ed. 1989)

McIntosh, The Practice of Maritime Arbitration in London: Recent Developments in the Law, 1983 *Lloyd's Mar. & Com. Q.* 235

McMahon, The Hague Rules and Incorporation of Charter Party Arbitration Clauses into Bills of Lading, 2 *J. Mar. L. & Com.* 1 (1970)

Makowski, Disputes Concerning Lay Days (A Practical Point of View of the Maritime Arbitration Commission), 1 *Y.B. Mar. L.* 135 (1984)

Malpica de Lamadrid, El arbitraje internacional y el derecho marítimo, in *El Arbitraje Comercial Internacional* 413 (Mexico 1983)

Mankabady, Arbitration in Shipping Disputes Under English Law, 14 *N. Ky. L. Rev.* 13 (1987)

Mello Ruiz, Los contratos en el transporte marítimo y la solución arbitral, in *El Arbitraje Comercial Internacional* 447 (Mexico 1983)

Meyer, Arbitrators: Qualification, Challenge and Withdrawal, in 1 *Fifth Int'l Congress of Maritime Arbitrators* (New York 1981)

Migeal, ICC-CMI Arbitration Rules, in 1 *Fifth Int'l Congress of Maritime Arbitrators* (New York 1981)

Miller, Consolidated Arbitrations in New York Maritime Disputes, 14 *Int'l Bus. Law.* 58 (1986)

Mooney, Interim Awards — Their Usage and Enforceability in the United States, in 2 *Fifth Int'l Congress of Maritime Arbitrators* (New York 1981)

Mordiglia, Enforcement of Foreign Arbitration Awards in Italy, in 2 *Fifth Int'l Congress of Maritime Arbitrators* (New York 1981)

Nariman, Arbitration in Combined Transportation, in *Arbitration in Settlement of International Commercial Disputes Involving the Far East and Arbitration in Combined Transportation* 373 (P. Sanders ed. 1989)

Norwegian Group of the International Bar Association, *International Commercial Arbitration in Action: Papers from a Conference in Oslo in 1982* (Oslo 1983)

O'Brien, Arbitration, Charter Parties and Changes in the Law, in 2 *Fifth Int'l Congress of Maritime Arbitrators* (New York 1981)

O'Hare, Cargo Dispute Resolution and the Hamburg Rules, 29 *Int'l & Comp. L.Q.* 219 (1980)

Ohashi, M., *Maritime Arbitration in Tokyo: Its Legal Aspects* (Tokyo 1979)

Orsini, Sole Arbitrator or a Three Person Board, and When, in 1 *Fifth Int'l Congress of Maritime Arbitrators* (New York 1981)

Pineus, ICC/CMI Arbitration Rules, 14 *Europ. Transport L.* 839 (1979)

Power, A Comparison of Soviet and American Maritime Arbitration, 21 *Vand. J. Transnat'l L.* 127 (1988)

Ramos Mendez, The Relationship between Civil and Criminal Actions and Arbitration Agreements in Maritime Disaster Cases under Spanish Law, 2 *Y.B. Mar. L.* 125 (1985—1986)

Ramzaitsev, D.F., *Arbitrazh v torgovom moreplavanii* (Moscow 1960)

Raymos, Punitive Damage Awards in Maritime Arbitration: A Legitimate Part of the Arbitrator's Arsenal? 10 *Mar. Law.* 251 (1985)

Rose, F.D., ed., *International Commercial and Maritime Arbitration* (London 1988)

Sommer, Maritime Arbitration — Some of the Legal Aspects, 49 *Tul. L. Rev.* 1035 (1975)

Stansfield, Letters of Indemnity in Arbitration, 1 *Emory J. Int'l Disp. Res.* 275 (1987)

Stoedter, The International Maritime Arbitration Rules (ICC-CMI), 8 *Int'l Bus. Law.* 302 (1980)

Strohbach, Legal Aspects of Arbitration under the International Court of Arbitration for Marine and Inland Navigation [Gdynia Arbitration Court], in *A.I.A, Essays in Memoriam Eugenio Minoli* 495 (Turin 1974)

Summerskill, Maritime Arbitrations, in *Handbook of Arbitration Practice* 265 (R. Bernstein ed. 1987)

Tajiri, Possibility of Arbitration in International Combined Transport, in *Arbitration and Settlement of International Commercial Disputes Involving the Far East and Arbitration in Combined Transportation* 377 (P. Sanders ed. 1989)

Thomas, Admiralty Security and the Arbitral Process, 1983 *Lloyd's Mar. & Com. L.Q.* 493

Timmermans, The USSR Maritime Arbitration Commission, 1987 *Lloyd's Mar. & Com. L.Q.* 350 and 468

Timmermans, W. A., *Carriage of Goods by Sea in the Practice of the USSR Maritime Arbitration Commision* (Dordrecht 1990)

Trappe, L'arbitrage en matière d'assistance maritime, 18 *Europ. Transport L.* 719 (1983)

———, Legal Issues in Maritime Arbitration, 48 *Arbitration* 202 (1983)

Villareal, Fotopulos & Overly, International Maritime Arbitration, 12 *Stetson L. Rev.* 342 (1983)

Waehler, J.P., *Die Aussenhandels- und Seeschiedsgerichtsbarkeit in der UdSSR* (Berlin 1974)

Walker, Arbitration: History and Practice from a Maritime Perspective, in *Commercial and Labor Arbitration in Central America* 173 (A. Garro ed. 1991)

Willis, Institute of Arbitrators Australia — Maritime Arbitration, 9 *Int'l Bus. Law.* 401 (1981)

Wills, Is Court Enforced Discovery Proper in Aid of an Arbitration Governed by the U.S. Arbitration Act? in 1 *Fifth Int'l Congress of Maritime Arbitrators* (New York 1981)

Wodehouse, New York Arbitration As Seen by a Londoner, 1986 *Lloyd's Mar. & Com. L.Q.* 43

Zubrod, Delay in Maritime Arbitrations — Post-Hearing and Otherwise, an Arbitrator's View, 10 *Md. J. Int'l L. & Trade* 175 (1986)

————, Maritime Arbitration in New York, 39 *Arb. J.* 16 (No. 4, 1984)

6.09 PATENTS, TRADEMARKS, COPYRIGHT, TRANSFER OF TECHNOLOGY

Aghina & Crimaldi, Arbitrage en matière de contrats de licence de brevet et know-how, in *ICCA, Fourth Int'l Arb. Congress: Proceedings* 483 (1972)

Alvarez Soberanis, El arbitraje en los contratos de asistencia de tecnologia, in *El Arbitraje Comercial Internacional* 341 (Mexico 1983)

Anand, Arbitration in the Context of Technology Transfer Agreements: The Case of India, 7 *J. Int'l Arb.* 87 (No. 2, 1990)

Boguslavskii, Examination of disputes arising out of contracts in the field of scientific and technological co-operation, in *ICCA, Fourth Int'l Arb. Congress: Proceedings* 472 (1972)

Carmicheal, The Arbitration of Patent Disputes, in *Arbitration and the Licensing Process* 5-28.11 (R. Goldscheider & M. de Haas eds. 1984); reprinted from 38 *Arb. J.* (No. 1, March 1938)

Chillón Medina & Merino Merchán, International Arbitration of Transfer of Technology Contracts in Spanish Law, in *ICCA, Sixth Int'l Arb. Congress: Proceedings* 339 (1978)

Cremades, L'arbitrage dans les contrats internationaux de transfert de technologie passés par les entreprises espagnoles, 1972 *Rev. Arb.* 72

Comment, Arbitration and Intellectual Property: A Survey of Arbitration in Patent, Trademark and Copyright Cases, 48 *Alb. L. Rev.* 797 (1984)

Davis, Resolving Patent Disputes by Arbitration and Minitrial, 65 *J. Pat. Off. Soc'y* 275 (1984); reprinted in *Arbitration and the Licensing Process* 8-17 (R. Goldscheider & M. de Haas eds. 1984-)

de Berti, Arbitration and Technology: The Italian Experience, in *ICCA, Sixth Int'l Arb. Congress: Proceedings* 347 (1978)

Delvolvé, Le rôle de l'arbitrage en matière de transfer de technologie, in *ICCA, Sixth Int'l Arb. Congress: Proceedings* 357 (1978)

Derains, Arbitrage et brevets d'invention, 1975 *Droit et Pratique Com. Int'l* 91

————, L'expérience de la Cour d'arbitrage de la Chambre de commerce internationale en matière de propriété industrielle, 1977 *Rev. Arb.* 40

Devitt & Donahey, International Arbitration in Patent Disputes, 65 *J. Pat. Off. Soc'y* 621 (No. 11, Nov. 1983)

Dobkin, Arbitration of Patent Disputes under the U.S. Arbitration Act, 23 *Arb. J.* 1 (1968)

Domke, Arbitration of Know-How and Franchise Disputes, in *ICCA, Fourth Int'l Arb. Congress: Proceedings* 689 (1972)

Dresser, Agreements to Arbitrate Patent Disputes, 67 *J. Patent & Trademark Office Soc'y* 551 (1985)

Dunshee de Abranches, Arbitration and Contracts Concerned with Scientific, Technical and Research Work, Including Agreements on the Use of Inventions, Know-How, Etc., in *ICCA, Fourth Int'l Arb. Congress: Proceedings* 443 (1972)

Eckstrom, L., *Licensing in Foreign and Domestic Operations.* Volume I, Chapter 7: Arbitration (by Steven Z. Szczepanski), (New York 1972, updated 1987)

Farley, The Role of Arbitration in the Resolution of Patent Disputes, 3 *Touro L. Rev.* 47 (1986)

Fiammenghi, Brevetti ed arbitrato: una penalizzazione che andrebbe eliminata, 30 *Rassegna dell'Arb.* 150 (1990)

————, Motivi che impendiscono la definizione arbitrale delle controversie in materia di brevetti di invenzioni, 25 *Rassegna dell'Arb.* 123 (1985)

Field, Patent Arbitration — Past, Present and Future, 24 *J. Law and Technology* 233 (Fall 1983)

Gilbert & Devolvé, Lack of Exploitation of the Technique by the Acquirer and Arbitration, in *Arbitration and the Licensing Process* 6-63 (R. Goldscheider and M. de Haas eds. 1984-)

Goldman, Arbitration and Transfer of Technology in Latin America, in *Arbitration and the Licensing Process* 5-29 (R. Goldscheider & M. de Haas eds. 1984-)

Goldscheider, R. & M. de Haas, eds., *Arbitration and the Licensing Process* (New York 1984-)

Goldsmith, Patent, Trademark and Copyright Arbitration Guide, 53 *J. Pat. Off. Soc'y* 224 (1971)

Gray, Arbitration Under Section 294 and Patent Licensing, in 2 *The Law and Business of Licensing: Licensing in the 1980s* 2C-213 (R. Goldscheider & T. Arnold eds. 1987)

Guyet, La proprieté industrielle et l'arbitrage en Suisse, in *Recueil de Travaux Suisses* 45 (C. Reymond & E. Bucher eds. 1984)

Hoellering, Arbitration of Patent Disputes, in *Arbitration & the Law: AAA General Counsel's Annual Report 1987-88* 163 (1988)

―――, New Opportunities for Patent Arbitration in the United States, in *Arbitration and the Licensing Process* 5-28.1 (R. Goldscheider & M. de Haas eds. 1984); reprinted from *N.Y.L.J.*, Dec. 16, 1982

Holtzmann, Arbitration and Contracts Concerned with Scientific, Research and Technical Work, in *ICCA, Fourth Int'l Arb. Congress: Proceedings* 479 (1972)

―――, New Uses for Arbitration in Soviet-American Contracts for Industrial, Scientific, and Technical Development, 5 *Den. J. Int'l L. & Pol'y*, Spec. Issue 357 (1975)

Jakubowski, Les problémes de loi applicable et de l'arbitrage dans la coopération industrielle entre l'Est et l'Ouest, in *ICC, Hommage à Frederic Eisemann* 103 (1978)

Janicke & Borovoy, Resolving Patent Disputes by Arbitration: An Alternative to Litigation, 62 *J. Pat. Off. Soc'y* 337 (1980)

Jarvin, Arbitrating International Disputes, in 3 *The Law and Business of Licensing: Licensing in the 1980s* 2G-217 (R. Goldscheider & T. Arnold eds. 1987)

―――, Arbitrating International Disputes, 23 *Les Nouvelles (J. Licencing Exec. Soc'y)* 15 (1988)

Kamenov, Problèmes de procédure dans l'arbitrage portant sur les litiges nés des contrats de coopération industrielles, scientifique et technique, in *ICCA, Fourth Int'l Arb. Congress: Proceedings* 500 (1972)

Kaplan, Arbitration and Intellectual Property: A Survey of Arbitration in Patent, Trademark and Copyright Cases, 48 *Alb. L. Rev.* 797 (1984); reprinted in 18 *Intellectual Property L. Rev.* 439 (1986)

Keutgen, Arbitrage et proprieté intellectuelle, 1978 *Rev. Arb.* 175

255

Lécuyer-Thieffry, Un nouveau domaine pour l'arbitrage aux Etats-Unis: la validité et la contrefaçon des brevets, 1985 *Rev. Arb.* 405

Lefkowitz, The Trademark Forum: A Place for Arbitration in Proceedings Before the Trademark Trial and Appeal Board, 72 *Trademark Rep.* 275 (1982); reprinted in *Arbitration and the Licensing Process* 5-28.33 (R. Goldscheider & M. de Haas eds. 1984-)

Loyer, Nonobservation of Secrecy and Arbitration in the Transfer of Technology, in *Arbitration and the Licensing Process* 6-49 (R. Goldscheider & M. de Haas eds. 1984-)

Madson, Arbitration Provisions in Franchise Agreements, in *Arbitration and the Licensing Process* 1-35 (R. Goldscheider & M. de Haas eds. 1984-)

Manbeck, Voluntary Arbitration of Patent Disputes — Background to 35 U.S.C. 294, in *Arbitration and the Licensing Process* 5-28.25 (R. Goldscheider & M. de Haas eds. 1984-)

Mattei, Arbitration and Contracts of International Industrial Cooperation, in *A.I.A., Essays in memoriam Eugenio Minoli* 301 (Turin 1974)

Minoli, Arbitrage et coopération internationale en vue du développement industriel, scientifique et technique, in *ICCA, Fourth Int'l Arb. Congress:Proceedings* 54 (1972)

Moreau, Know-How, Non observation of Secrecy, and Arbitration, in *Arbitration and the Licensing Process* 6 (R. Goldscheider & M. de Haas eds. 1984-)

Naryshkina, Arbitration and Technology Transfer Serve the Cause of International Industrial Cooperation, in *ICCA, Sixth Int'l Arb. Congress: Proceedings* 319 (1978)

Nelson, Planning for Resolution of Disputes in International Technology Transactions, 7 *B. C. Int'l & Comp. L. Rev.* 269 (1984)

Nicklisch, Projekte über neue Technologien und internationale Schiedsgerichtsbarkeit, 1 *Jahrbuch Schiedsgerichtsbarkeit* 63 (1987)

Oppetit, Arbitration in the Fields of Patents After the Law of July 13, 1978, in *Arbitration and the Licensing Process* 6-91 (R. Goldscheider & M. de Haas eds. 1984-)

Padis, De la validité en droit français de le clause compromissoire inserée dans un contrat national ou international d'ingénieries (know-how), in *ICCA, Fourth Int'l Arb. Congress: Proceedings* 466 (1972)

Pedrazzini, Arbitration and Technology: Some Remarks on Swiss Law, in *ICCA, Sixth Int'l Arb. Congress: Proceedings* 385 (1978)

Pfaff, Grenzbewegungen der Schiedsfähigkeit — Patentnichtigkeit im Schiedsverfahren, in *Beiträge zum internationalen Verfahrensrecht und zur Schiedsgerichtsbarkeit. Festschrift für Heinrich Nagel* 278 (W. Habscheid & K. Schwab eds. 1987)

Piergrossi, Problems of Arbitrability of Patent and Licensing Controversies in Italian and United States Law, in *ICCA, Fourth Int'l Arb. Congress: Proceedings* 752 (1972); 6 *N.Y.U. J. Int'l L. & Pol.* 85 (1973)

Rangel Medina, El arbitraje en los contratos sobre usos de marcas y explotación de patentes, in *El Arbitraje Comercial Internacional* 323 (Mexico 1983)

Recchia, Nouvelles questions constitutionnelles sur les droits de propriété industrielle et l'arbitrage en Italie, 1977 *Rev. Arb.* 93

Robert, Arbitrage et coopération internationale en vue du développement industriel, scientifique et technique, in *ICCA, Fourth Int'l Arb. Congress: Proceedings* 620 (1972)

Savarese, Arbitration and Contracts for the Transfer of Technology in the Experience of Some Italian State-owned Companies, in *ICCA, Sixth Int'l Arb. Congress: Proceedings* 405 (1978)

Schlicher, The Patent Arbitration Law: A New Procedure for Resolving Patent Infringement Disputes, 40 *Arb. J.* 7 (No. 4, 1985)

Schweyer, A., *Patentnichtigkeit und Patentverletzung und deren Beurteilung durch private Schiedsgerichte nach dem Recht der Schweiz, Deutschlands, Italiens und Frankreich* (St. Gallen 1981)

Sebestyen, Arbitrage et coopération industrielle internationale, 1977 *Rev. Arb.* 33

Simpson, Licensing Disputes in England and Scotland — Arbitration or Litigation? in *Arbitration and the Licensing Process* 5-97 (R. Goldscheider & M. de Haas eds. 1984-)

257

Stork, The Use of Arbitration in Copyright Disputes: IBM v. Fujitsu, 3 *High Technology L.J.* 241 (1988)

Strohbach, Arbitral Jurisdiction and Contracts on Scientific-Technical and Research Work Including Licensing and Know-How Agreements, in *ICCA, Fourth Int'l Arb. Congress: Proceedings* 409 (1972)

Stumpf, Arbitration and Contracts Concerned with Scientific, Technical and Research Work, Including Agreements on the Use of Inventions, Know-how, etc., in *ICCA, Fourth Int'l Arb. Congress: Proceedings* 428 (1972)

————, Arbitration and Technology, in *ICCA, Sixth Int'l Arb. Congress: Proceedings* 411 (1978)

Timberg, Antitrust Aspects of Patent Litigation Arbitration and Settlement, 59 *J. Pat. Off. Soc'y* 244 (1977); reprinted in *Arbitration and the Licensing Process* 3-39 (R. Goldscheider & M. de Haas eds. 1984-)

Trumpy, Limiting Arbitration Clauses, 19 *Nouvelles - J. Licensing Executives Society* 213 (1984)

Tupman, Arbitration of Intellectual Property Disputes under U.S. Law, 42 *Arb. J.* 3 (No. 4, 1987)

6.10 SECURITIES TRANSACTIONS

Applebaum, Predispute Arbitration Agreements Between Brokers and Investors: The Extension of Wilko to Section 10(b) Claims, 46 *Md. L. Rev.* 339 (1987)

Bedell, Harrison & Harvey, The McMahon Mandate: Compulsory Arbitration of Securities and RICO Claims, 19 *Loy. U. Chi. L.J.* 1 (1987)

Chapman, Comment, The Case for Domestic Arbitration of Federal Securities Claims: Is the Wilko Doctrine Still Valid? 16 *Sw. U.L. Rev.* 619 (1986)

Coulson, Arbitration as a Means of Resolving Conflicts Arising out of International Securities Transactions, 4 *B.U. Int'l L.J.* 99 (1986)

Dellet, Arbitration, Forum Selection, and Choice of Law in International Securities Transactions, 42 *Wash. and Lee L. Rev.* 1069 (1985)

Escudero, The Enforceability of Predispute Arbitration Agreements under 10(b) and 10b-5 Claims, 43 *Wash. & Lee L. Rev.* 923 (1986)

Fletcher, Privatizing Securities Disputes through the Enforcement of Arbitration Agreements, 71 *Minn. L. Rev.* 393 (1987)

Fletcher C.E., *Arbitrating Securities Disputes* (New York 1990)

Friedman, Arbitrating Your Case under the Securities Arbitration Rules of the American Arbitration Association, in *Arbitration & the Law 1987-88: AAA General Counsel's Annual Report* 92 (1988); also in 43 *Arb. J.* 23 (No. 2, 1988)

Hoblin, P., *Securities Arbitration: Procedures, Strategies, Cases* (New York 1988)

Hoellering, Shearson/American Express v. McMahon: Broadened Domain of Arbitration in U.S.A., 4 *J. Int'l Arb.* 153 (No. 3, 1987)

Ishizumi, International Commercial Arbitration and Federal Securities Regulations: Reconciling Two Conflicting Policies, 6 *J. Comp. Bus. & Cap. Market L.* 81 (1984)

Jarvis, The Use of Civil RICO in International Arbitration: Some Thoughts after Shearson/American Express v. McMahon, 1 *Transnat'l Law.* 1 (1988)

Katsoris, The Arbitration of a Public Securities Dispute, 53 *Fordham L. Rev.* 279 (1984)

Lindsay, 'Public' Rights and Private Forums: Predispute Arbitration Agreements and Securities Litigation, 20 *Loy. L.A. L. Rev.* 643 (1987)

Lipton, Discovery Procedures and the Selection and Training of Arbitrators: A Study of Securities Industry Practices, 26 *Am. Bus. L.J.* 435 (1988)

Malcolm & Segall, The Arbitrability of Claims Arising under Section 10(b) of the Securities Exchange Act: Should Wilko Be Extended? 50 *Alb. L. Rev.* 725 (1986)

Nelson, The Arbitrability of Securities Disputes between Brokers and Customers — Phillips v. Merrill Lynch, Pierce, Fenner & Smith, Inc., 20 *Creighton L. Rev.* 1009 (1987)

Note, Arbitrability of Implied Rights of Action under Section 10(b) of the Securities Exchange Act, 61 *N.Y.U. L. Rev.* 506 (1986)

————, Arbitrability of Claims Arising under the Securities Exchange Act of 1934, 1986 *Duke L.J.* 548

————, Arbitration, Forum Selection, and Choice of Law Agreements in International Security Transactions, 42 *Wash. & Lee L. Rev.* 1069 (1985)

Olson, International Arbitration and Securities Laws, 1976 *Sec. L. Rev.* 747 (1976)

Patkin, Arbitration of Extraterritorial Discovery Disputes Between the Securities and Exchange Commission and a Foreign Broker-Dealer: A New Approach to the Restatement Balancing Test, 5 *B.U. Int'l L.J.* 413 (1987)

Peterson, The Arbitrability of Claims Under the Federal Securities Laws, 12 *J. Corp. L.* 535 (1987)

Poser, Arbitrability of International Securities Disputes, 12 *Brooklyn J. Int'l L.* 675 (1986)

Practising Law Institute, *Resolving Securities Disputes: Arbitration and Litigation,* (New York 1986)

Rabbino, International Commercial Arbitration — The Relationship between Arbitration and the Federal Securities Laws. Alberto-Culver Co. v. Scherk, 7 *N.Y.U. J. Int'l L. & Pol.* 383 (1974)

Reder, Securities Law and Arbitration: The Enforceability of Predispute Arbitration Clauses in Broker-Customer Agreements, 1990 *Colum. Bus. L. Rev.* 91

Rotunda, Cautionary Lessons from American Securities Arbitration: Litigation v. Arbitration, 5 *Arb. Int'l* 199 (1989)

Sanchez, Should Claims Involving Public Customers Arising Under the Securities Exchange Act of 1934 Be Subject to Compulsory Arbitration? 10 *Harv. J. L. & Pub. Pol'y* 173 (1987)

Taylor, The Arbitrability of Federal Securities Claims: Wilko's Swan Song, 42 *U. Miami L. Rev.* 203 (1987)

Vaca, Arbitrating Civil RICO and Implied Causes of Action Arising under Section 10(b) of the Securities Exchange Act of 1934, 36 *Cath. U.L. Rev.* 455 (1987)

Victor & Bialos, The Arbitration of Public Law Disputes: The Availability and Efficacy of This Alternative Dispute Resolution Mechanism, in *Private Investors Abroad— Problems and Solutions in International Business in 1987* 15.1 (J. Ross ed. 1987)

6.11 OTHER

Bartels, M., *Contractual Adaptation and Conflict Resolution* (Frankfurt 1985)

Bedell, Harrison & Harvey, The McMahon Mandate: Compulsory Arbitration of Securities and RICO Claims, 19 *Loy. U. Chi. L.J.* 1 (1987)

Behre, Arbitration: A Permissible or Desirable Method of Resolving Disputes Involving Federal Acquisition and Assistance Contracts? 16 *Pub. Cont. L.J.* 66 (1986)

Chambreuil, Arbitrage international et garanties bancaires, 1991 *Rev. Arb.* 33

Daughtrey, Enforcement of Arbitration Clauses Against Deceived Franchisees, 21 *U. Rich. L. Rev.* 391 (1987)

Dohm, Bankgarenties und Schiedsgerichtsbarkeit, 5 *Bull. Swiss. Arb. A.* 92 (1987)

El-Alem, Arbitration in Disputes Relating to Libyan Administrative Contracts, 3 *Int'l Constr. L. Rev.* 21 (1985)

————, L'arbitrage dans les litiges relatifs aux contrats administratifs libyens, 1983 *Rev. Arb.* 295

Ellison & Ellison, Arbitration in Pensions, 46 *Arbitration* 234 (1980)

Fogarasi, Gordon & Venuti, Use of International Arbitration to Resolve Double Taxation Cases, 18 *Management Int'l J.* 319 (1989)

Foussard, L'arbitrage en droit administrative, 1990 *Rev. Arb.* 3

Frignani, Il franchising e l'arbitrato: prime esperienze e problemi, 30 *Rassegna dell'Arb.* 162 (1990)

Hennington, Computer Arbitration: Taking the Byte Out of Data Processing Disputes, 19 *Cumb. L. Rev.* 279 (1989)

Horsmans, Actualité et évolution du droit belge de l'arbitrage, 1990 *Rev. Arb.* 797

Jacot-Guillarmod, L'arbitrage privé face à l'article 6, para. 1 de la Convention européenne des Droit de l'Homme, in *Protecting Human Rights: The European Dimension. Studies in Honour of Gérard J. Wiarda* 281 (F. Matscher & H. Petzold eds. 1988)

Jarrosson, L'arbitrage et la Convention européenne des droit de l'Homme, 1989 *Rev. Arb.* 573

Kwatra, Arbitration in International Tax Disputes: A New Approach, 5 *J. Int'l Arb.* 151 (No. 4, 1988)

———, Resolving International Tax Disputes, [1988](1) *Comp. L.J.* 54

Lindencrona & Mattsson, Arbitration in Taxation, in 1982 *Y.B. Swed. Int'l Arb.* 50

Lindencrona, G. & N. Mattsson, *Arbitration in Taxation* (Deventer 1981)

Maktouf, Resolving International Tax Disputes through Arbitration, 4 *Arb. Int'l* 32 (1988)

Montoya Alberti, Arbitration, Foreign Law and Jurisdiction in International Loan Agreements in Some Countries of Latin America, in *Arbitration in Settlement of International Commercial Disputes Involving the Far East and Arbitration in Combined Transportation* 99 (P. Sanders ed. 1989)

———, El arbitraje en los contratos de prestamo internacionales, in *El Arbitraje en el Derecho Latinoamericano y Español* 481 (L. Perret & U. Montoya Alberti eds. 1989)

Mutz, Schiedsgerichtsbarkeit im internationalen Eisenbahnfrachtrecht, 1988 *Zeitschrift für d. intern. Eisenbahnverkehr* 73 (Nos. 7/8)

Nerz, Die Schiedsfähigkeit von Rechtsstreitigkeiten zwischen einem Agenten und seinem Prinzipal in Saudi-Arabien, 31 *RIW* 465 (1985)

Nutley, Rent Review and Property Valuation Arbitrations, in *Handbook of Arbitration Practice* 311 (R. Bernstein ed. 1987)

Note, Resolving the Conflict between Arbitration Clauses and Claims under Unfair and Deceptive Practices Acts, 64 *B.U. L. Rev.* 377 (1984)

———, The Effectiveness of Arbitration for the Resolution of Consumer Disputes, 6 *N.Y.U. Rev. L. & Soc. Change* 175 (1977)

263

Punzi, Le clausole arbitrali nell'ordinamento sportivo, 26 *Rassegna dell'Arb.* 165 (1986)

Rucellai, Nuclear Supply Contracts, Liability for Damages and Arbitration, in *ICCA, Sixth Int'l Arb. Congress: Proceedings* 399 (1978)

Ruiz del Rio, Arbitration Clauses in International Loans, 4 *J. Int'l Arb.* 45 (No. 3, 1987)

Rutherford, Documents Only Arbitrations in Consumer Disputes, in *Handbook of Arbitration Practice* 217 (R. Bernstein ed. 1987)

Samuel & Gearhart, Sporting Arbitration and the International Olympic Committee's Court of Arbitration for Sport, 6 *J. Int'l Arb.* 39 (No. 4, 1989)

Sandrock, Are Disputes Over the Application of Article VIII, Section 2(b) of the IMF Treaty Arbitrable? 23 *Int'l Law.* 933 (1989)

Scott, Settlement of Disputes Within the IEA Emergency Sharing System, 19 *St. Mary's L.J.* 897 (1988)

Simma, The Court of Arbitration for Sport, in *Festschrift für Ignaz Seidl-Hohenveldern* 573 (K.-H. Böckstiegel, H.E. Folz, J.M. Mössner & K. Zemanek eds. 1988)

Tarte, Clergy Arbitrator Liability: A Potential Pitfall of Alternative Dispute Resolution in the Church, 32 *Catholic Law.* 310 (1988)

Taylor, The Arbitrability of Federal Securities Claims: Wilko's Swan Song, 42 *U. Miami L. Rev.* 203 (1987)

Victor & Bialos, The Arbitration of Public Law Disputes: The Availability and Efficacy of This Alternative Dispute Resolution Mechanism, in *Private Investors Abroad— Problems and Solutions in International Business in 1987* 15.1 (J. Ross ed. 1987)

Westermann, Gesellschaftsrechtliche Schiedsgerichte — Übersicht und Erfahrungsbericht, in *Festschrift für Robert Fischer* 853 (M. Lutter, W. Stimpel & H. Wiedermann eds. 1979)

Zepeda, Fideicomiso y arbitraje, in *El Arbitraje Comercial Internacional* 373 (Mexico 1983)

6.12 ARBITRABILITY

Allison, Arbitration of Private Antitrust Claims in International Trade: A Study in the Subordination of National Interests to the Demands of a World Market, 18 *N.Y.U. J. Int'l L. & Pol.* 361 (1986)

————, Arbitration Agreements and Antitrust Claims: The Need for Enhanced Accommodation of Conflicting Public Policies, 64 *N.C. L. Rev.* 219 (1986)

Ball, Structuring the Arbitration in Advance — the Arbitration Clause in an International Development Agreement, in *Contemporary Problems in International Arbitration* 297 (J.D.M. Lew ed. 1986)

Becker, Antitrust and International Arbitration — The New American Synthesis, 13 *Int'l Bus. Law.* 445 (1985)

Becker & Kleyn, Public Policy and Arbitration — The 'Unruly Horse' and the Arbitrability of Claims in America, 17 *Int'l Bus Law.* 422 (1989)

Bedell, Harrison & Grant, Arbitrability: Current Developments in the Interpretation and Enforceability of Arbitration Agreements, 13 *J. Contemp. L.* 1 (1987)

Bedell, Harrison & Harvey, The McMahon Mandate: Compulsory Arbitration of Securities and RICO Claims, 19 *Loy. U. Chi. L.J.* 1 (1987)

Bernardini, Stati Uniti: arbitrabilità di controversie in materia de legislazione antitrust, 25 *Rassegna dell'Arb.* 109 (1985)

Böckstiegel, Public Policy and Arbitrability, in *Comparative Arbitration Practice and Public Policy in Arbitration* 177 (P. Sanders ed. 1987)

Booysen, The Municipal Enforcement of Arbitration Awards against States in Terms of Arbitration Conventions, with Special Reference to the New York Convention — Does International Law Provide for a Municipal Law Concept of an Arbitrable Act of State? 12 *South Afr. Y.B. Int'l L.* 73 (1986-1987)

Bork, Der Begriff der objektiven Schiedsfähigkeit (Par. 1025 Abs. 1 ZPO), 100 *ZZP* 249 (1987)

Campbell & Vollmer, U.S. Supreme Court's Mitsubishi Decision Boosts International Arbitrations, 82 *L. Soc'y Gazette* 2830 (1985)

Carbonneau, Mitsubishi: The Folly of Quixotic Internationalism, 2 *Arb. Int'l* 116 (1986)

————, The Exuberant Pathway to Quixotic Internationalism: Assessing the Folly of Mitsubishi, 19 *Vand. J. Transnat'l L.* 265 (1986)

Cloud, Mitsubishi and the Arbitrability of Antitrust Claims: Did the Supreme Court Throw the Baby Out with the Bathwater? 18 *L. & Pol. Int'l Bus.* 341 (1986)

Czimpiel & Kurth, Schiedsvereinbarung und Wechselforderung im deutschen und internationalen Privatrecht, 40 *NJW* 2118 (1987)

Comment, Arbitration and Antitrust: A Leg Up for International Arbitration [Mitsubishi Motors Corp. v. Soler Chrysler-Plymouth, Inc., 105 S. Ct. 3346 (1985)], 25 *Washburn L.J.* 536 (1986)

————, Enforcing International Commercial Arbitration Agreements — Post-Mitsubishi Motors Corp. v. Soler Chrysler-Plymouth, Inc., 36 *Am. U.L. Rev.* 57 (1986)

————, International Commercial Arbitration: The Non-arbitrable Subject Matter Defense, 9 *Den. J. Int'l L. & Pol.* 119 (1980)

————, Transnational Contractual Disputes: Antitrust Joins Securities Law Claims as Arbitrable Subject Matter, 12 *Brooklyn J. Int'l L.* 731 (1986)

Debevoise, The Arbitrability of Gaps in Long-Term Scientific, Technical and Industrial Development Contracts, 17 *Harv. Int'l L.J.* 122 (1976)

de Mello, Arbitrage et ordre public national découlant des règles de concurrence, 1979 *Rev. Arb.* 101

Derains, Arbitrage et droit de concurrence, *Revue Suisse du Droit Int'l de la Concurrence* 39 (No. 14, Feb. 1982)

Dilger, Schiedsgerichtsbarkeit und Volstreckung ausländischer Entscheidungen in den Golfstaaten, in *Vetragspraxis und Streiterledigung im Wirschaftverkehr mit arabischen Staaten* 101 (K.-H. Böckstiegel ed. 1981)

Donaldson, Mitsubishi and Antitrust Arbitration — It's All the Japanese You Need to Know, 1986 *B.Y.U. L. Rev.* 219 (1986)

Foster, C.A., *The Law and Practice of Commercial Arbitration in North Carolina* (Durham 1986)

266

Foustoucos, Conditions Required for the Validity of an Arbitration Agreement, 5 *J. Int'l Arb.* 113 (No. 4, 1988)

Fox, Mitsubishi v. Soler and Its Impact on International Commercial Arbitration, 19 *J. World Trade L.* 579 (1985)

Gaillard, Le point de vue d'un utilisateur étranger, 1989 *Int'l Bus. L.J.* 793

Geisinger & Renold, Arbitrage international, ordre public et reconnaissance en Suisse de sentences arbitrales étrangères, in *Le Juriste Suisse Face au Droit et aux Jugements Etrangers: Ouverture ou Repli?* 89 (F. Knoepfler ed. 1988)

Goldman, International Arbitration in Europe, in *IBA, Soviet Foreign Trade Reforms & East/West Arbitration* 217 (1988)

————, The Applicable Law: General Principles of Law—the Lex Mercatoria, in *Contemporary Problems in Int'l Arbitration* 113 (J.D.M. Lew ed. 1986)

Goodman, Arbitrability and Antitrust: Mitsubishi Motors Corp. v. Soler Chrysler-Plymouth, 23 *Colum. J. Transnat'l L.* 655 (1986)

Graham, The Internationalization of Commercial Arbitration in Canada: A Preliminary Reaction, 13 *Can. Bus. L.J.* 1 (1987)

Gregory, International Commercial Arbitration: Comments on Professor Graham's Paper, 13 *Can. Bus. L.J.* 42 (1987)

Groos, Schiedsgerichtsbarkeit im deutsch-französischen Wirtschaftsverkehr, 33 *RIW* 343 (1987)

Grossen, Arbitrage et droit de la concurrence, in *Recueil de Travaux Suisses* 35 (C. Reymond & E. Bucher eds. 1984)

Hanotiau, L'arbitrage international en Belgique, in *L'arbitrage* 143 (L. Matray & G. de Leval eds. 1989)

Hoellering, Arbitrability in the Wake of Byrd and Mitsubishi, in *Arbitration & the Law: AAA General Counsel's Annual Report 1986* 59 (1987)

————, Arbitrability of Disputes, 41 *Bus. Law.* 125 (1985)

————, Shearson/American Express v. McMahon: Broadened Domain of Arbitration in U.S.A., 4 *J. Int'l Arb.* 153 (No. 3, 1987)

Horsmans, Actualité et évolution du droit belge de l'arbitrage, 1990 *Rev. Arb.* 797

Jarvin, Arbitrability of Anti-Trust Disputes: the Mitsubishi v. Soler Case, 2 *J. Int'lArb.* 69 (1985)

―――, Arbitrability of Antitrust Disputes: The Mitsubishi v. Soler Case, 25 *Swiss Rev. Int'l Competition L.* 53 (Oct. 1985)

―――, Skiljeforfarande och konkurrenslagstiftning; nagra anmarkningar till Mitsubishimalet [Arbitration and antitrust law: some remarks on the Mitsubishi case], 1986 *Tidskrift utgiven av Juridiska Foreningen i Finland* 219

Johnson, International Antitrust Litigation and Arbitration Clauses, 3 *J.L. & Com.* 91 (1983)

Kaplan, L'arbitrabilité des litiges commerciaux en matière de droit de la concurrence, 14 *Droit et Pratique du Com. Int'l* 403 (1988)

Kovar, Droit communautaire de la concurrence et arbitrage, in *Etudes offerts à Berthold Goldman* 109 (Paris 1983)

Kühn, Arbitrability of Antitrust Disputes in the Federal Republic of Germany, 3 *Arb. Int'l* 226 (1987)

Lalive, The New Swiss Law on International Arbitration, 4 *Arb. Int'l* 2 (1988)

Lange & Wiessner, Die Schiedsfähigkeit internationaler Antitrust-Streitigkeiten: zur Mitsubishi-Entscheidung des U.S. Supreme Court, 31 *RIW* 757 (1985)

Lew, *Determination of Arbitrators' Jurisdiction and the Public Policy Limitations on that Jurisdiction, in Contemporary Problems in Int'l Arbitration* 73 (J.D.M. Lew ed. 1986)

―――, EEC Restrictions on Arbitration, 47 *Arbitration* 117 (1981)

Lipner, International Antitrust Law: To Arbitrate or Not to Arbitrate, 19 *Geo. Wash. J. Int'l L. & Econ.* 395 (1985)

Lowenfeld, The Mitsubishi Case: Another View, 2 *Arb. Int'l* 178 (1986)

McClendon, Subject-Matter Arbitrability in International Cases: Mitsubishi Motors Closes the Circle, 11 *N.C. J. Int'l L. & Com. Reg.* 81 (1986)

―――, Arbitrability of Statutory Claims, in *AAA, Arbitration & the Law 1986* 63 (1987)

Malcolm & Segall, The Arbitrability of Claims Arising under Section 10(b) of the Securities Exchange Act: Should Wilko Be Extended? 50 *Alb. L. Rev.* 725 (1986)

Merino Merchán, La exepción de sumisión de la cuestión litigiosa a arbitraje, 5 *Rev. Corte Esp. Arb.* 235 (1988—1989)

Morgan, Contract Theory and the Sources of Rights: An Approach to the Arbitrability Question, 60 *S. Cal. L. Rev.* 1059 (1987)

Munzberg, R., *Die Schranken der Parteivereinbarung in der privaten internationalen Schiedsgerichtsbarkeit* (Berlin 1970)

Mustill, Sir Michael J. & S. C. Boyd, *The Law and Practice of Commercial Arbitration in England* (2nd ed. 1989)

Nariman, Problems of Public Policy — the Indian Perspective, in *Comparative Arbitration Practice and Public Policy in Arbitration* 336 (P. Sanders ed. 1987)

Nelson, The Arbitrability of Securities Disputes between Brokers and Customers — Phillips v. Merrill Lynch, Pierce, Fenner & Smith, Inc., 20 *Creighton L. Rev.* 1009 (1987)

Newton, Arbitration and Antitrust: A Leg Up for International Arbitration, 25 *Washburn L.J.* 536 (1986)

Nicklisch, F., ed., *Der komplexe Langzeitvertrag. Strukturen und Internationale Schiedsgerichtsbarkeit/The Complex Long-Term Contract. Structures and International Arbitration* (Heidelberg 1987)

Nolting, Mangelnde Feststellung des für Formwirksamkeit der Schiedsklausel und Schiedsfähigkeit massgeblichen Rechts, 7 *IPRax* 349 (1987)

Nuber, J., *Die objektive Schiedsfähigkeit im Zusammenhang mit der Gültigkeit der Schiedsvereinbarung (anwendbares Recht) und mit der Vollstreckung* (ordre public), (Zurich 1986)

Note, Application of the Convention on the Recognition and Enforcement of Foreign Arbitral Awards: Mitsubishi Motor Corp. v. Soler Chrysler-Plymouth, Inc., 8 *Fordham Int'l L.J.* 194 (1984)

———, Arbitrability of Implied Rights of Action under Section 10(b) of the Securities Exchange Act, 61 *N.Y.U. L. Rev.* 506 (1986)

———, Arbitrability of Claims Arising under the Securities Exchange Act of 1934, 1986 *Duke L.J.* 548

————, Transnational Antitrust Claims are Nonarbitrable under the Federal Arbitration Act and Art. II(1) of the Convention on the Recognition and Enforcement of Foreign Arbitral Awards: Mitsubishi v. Soler Chrysler-Plymouth, 17 *Vand. J. Transnat'l L.* 741 (1984)

O'Neill, Recent Developments in International Commercial Arbitration: an American Perspective, 4 *J. Int'l Arb.* 7 (No. 1, 1987); also in 53 *Arbitration* 177 (1987)

Oehmke, T., *International Arbitration* (Rochester 1990)

Olson, International Arbitration and Securities Laws, 1976 *Sec. L. Rev.* 747 (1976)

Overby, Arbitrability of Disputes under the Federal Arbitration Act, 71 *Iowa L. Rev.* 1137 (1986)

Ovington, Arbitration and U.S. Antitrust Law: A Conflict of Policies, 2 *J. Int'l Arb.* 53 (No. 2, 1985)

Park, Private Adjudicators and the Public Interest: The Expanding Scope of International Arbitration, 12 *Brooklyn J. Int'l L.* 629 (1986)

Parnass, International Arbitration and the Comity of Error: Mitsubishi Motors Corp. v. Soler Chrysler-Plymouth, Inc., 19 *Conn. L. Rev.* 435 (1987)

Peterson, The Arbitrability of Claims Under the Federal Securities Laws, 12 *J. Corp. L.* 535 (1987)

Pfaff, Grenzbewegungen der Schiedsfähigkeit — Patentnichtigkeit im Schiedsverfahren, in *Beiträge zum internationalen Verfahrensrecht und zur Schiedsgerichtsbarkeit. Festschrift für Heinrich Nagel* 278 (W. Habscheid & K. Schwab eds. 1987)

Piergrossi, Problems of Arbitrability of Patent and Licensing Controversies in Italian and United States Law, in *ICCA, Fourth Int'l Arb. Congress: Proceedings* 752 (1972); 6 *N.Y.U. J. Int'l L. & Pol.* 85 (1973)

Poser, Arbitrability of International Securities Disputes, 12 *Brooklyn J. Int'l L.* 675 (1986)

Renold, Arbitrage international et droit antitrust: l'arrêt Mitsubishi v. Soler de la Cour suprême des Etats-Unis, 105(127) *ZSR* 545 (1986)

Robert, Une date dans l'extension de l'arbitrage international: l'arrêt Mitsubishi c/ Soler, 1986 *Rev. Arb.* 173

Rokison, The Sources and Limits of the Arbitrator's Powers in England, in *Contemporary Problems of International Arbitration* 86 (J.D.M. Lew ed. 1986); also 52 *Arbitration* 219 (1986)

Rubino-Sammartano, M., *International Arbitration Law* (Deventer 1990)

Rucellai, Joint Venture, Arbitral Audit, and Arbitration, in *A.I.A., Essays in Memoriam Eugenio Minoli* 449 (Turin 1974)

Ruiz del Rio, Arbitration Clauses in International Loans, 4 *J. Int'l Arb.* 45 (No. 3, 1987)

Russell, F., *Russell on the Law of Arbitration* (20th ed. by A. Walton & M. Vitoria 1982)

Saleh, The Settlement of Disputes in the Arab World: Arbitration and Other Methods, 1 *Arab Law Q.* 198 (1986); reprinted in 4 *Int'l Tax & Bus. Law.* 280 (1986)

Samuel, A., *Jurisdictional Problems in International Commercial Arbitration: A Study of Belgian, Dutch, English, French, Swedish, Swiss, U.S. and West German Law* (Zurich 1989)

Sandrock, Arbitration between U.S. and West German Companies: An Example of Effective Dispute Resolution in International Business Transactions, 9 *U. Pa. J. Int'l Bus. L.* 27 (1987)

————, Are Disputes Over the Application of Article VIII, Section 2(b) of the IMF Treaty Arbitrable? 23 *Int'l Law.* 933 (1989)

————, Gerichtsstands- oder Schiedsklauseln in Verträgen zwischen U.S.-amerikanischen und deutschen Unternehmen: was ist zu empfehlen? in *Festschrift für Ernst C. Stiefel* 625 (M. Lutter, W. Oppenhoff, O. Sandrock & H. Winkhaus eds. 1987)

Saravalle, Arbitrato internazionale e leggi antitrust: il caso Mitsubishi, 22 *Riv. Dir. Int'le Priv. & Proc.* 597 (1986)

Schmidt, Präklusion und Einlassung auf die schiedsgerichtliche Verhandlung zur Hauptsache — Vertragsdenken und Prozessdenken in der jüngeren Praxis, in *Beiträge zum internationalen Verfahrensrecht und zur Schiedsgerichtsbarkeit. Festschrift für Heinrich Nagel* 373 (W. Habscheid & K. Schwab eds. 1987)

Schmitthoff, C., *Schmitthoff's Export Trade. The Law and Practice of International Trade* (8th ed. 1986)

Smit, Mitsubishi: It Is Not What It Seems to Be, 4 *J. Int'l Arb.* 7 (No. 3, 1987)

Smith, Determining the Arbitrability of International Antitrust Disputes, 8 *J. Comp. Bus. & Cap. Market L.* 197 (1986)

Sopata, Mitsubishi Motors Corp. v. Soler Chrysler-Plymouth, Inc.: International Arbitration and Antitrust Claims, 7 *Nw. J. Int'l L. & Bus.* 595 (1986)

Sornarajah, The Enforcement of Foreign Arbitral Awards in Singapore, 1988 *Malayan L.J.* lxxxvi

Stalev, Arbitrazh za poplvane na praznini v dlgosrochni vnshnotrgovski dogovori, 1983 *Vaprosy na mezhdunarodnoto chastno pravo* (Sofia) 93

Strohbach, International Arbitration and Public Policy. Comment on the Legal Practice in the German Democratic Republic, in *Comparative Arbitration Practice and Public Policy in Arbitration* 358 (P. Sanders ed. 1987)

Taylor, The Arbitrability of Federal Securities Claims: Wilko's Swan Song, 42 *U. Miami L. Rev.* 203 (1987)

ter Kuile, Internationale arbitrage en Gemeenschapsrecht, in *Iustitia et Amicitia. Geschillenbeslechting in en Buiten Rechte* 33 (Arnheim 1985)

Tschanz, Le droit américain et la Convention de New York, in *First International Commercial Arbitration Conference: Proceedings* 249 (N. Antaki & A. Prujiner eds. 1986)

van den Berg, A. J., *The New York Arbitration Convention of 1958* (Deventer 1981)

van Hecke, Arbitrage et règles de concurrence, 1979 *Rev. Arb.* 191

van Houtte, L'arbitrage: son territoire et ses frontières, 53 *Rev. Droit Int'l & Droit Comp.* 140 (1976)

Ventura, Convençao de arbitragem, 46 *Revista da Ordem dos Advogados* 289 (1986)

Victor & Bialos, The Arbitration of International Antitrust Claims: A Bold Supreme Court Experiment in Alternative Dispute Resolution, in *Fordham Corporate Law Institute: Annual Proceedings: Antitrust & Trade Policy in the U.S. and the European Community* 184 (New York 1986)

————, The Arbitration of Public Law Disputes: The Availability and Efficacy of This Alternative Dispute Resolution Mechanism, in *Private Investors Abroad - Problems and Solutions in International Business in 1987* 15.1 (J. Ross ed. 1987)

von Mehren, From Vynior's Case to Mitsubishi: The Future of Arbitration and Public Law, 12 *Brooklyn J. Int'l L.* 583 (1986)

von Zumbusch, Arbitrability of Antitrust Claims Under U.S., German, and EEC Law: The 'International Transaction' Criterion and Public Policy, 22 *Tex. Int'l L.J.* 291 (1987)

————, Die Schiedsfähigkeit privatrechtlicher Kartellrechtsstreitigkeiten nach U.S.-, deutschem und EG-Recht, 1988 *GRUR Int'l* 541

Vorhees, International Commercial Arbitration and the Arbitrability of Anti-trust Claims: Mitsubishi Motors Corp. v. Soler Chrysler Plymouth, 14 *N. Ky. L. Rev.* 65 (1987)

Walder Bohner, Die neuen Zürcher Bestimmungen über die Schieds-gerichtsbarkeit im Lichte des Konkordats, 72 *SJZ* 249 (1976)

Walsh, Arbitration in International Commercial Transactions: Mitsubishi Motors Corp. v. Soler Chrysler-Plymouth, Inc. and Its Aftermath, 13 *Syracuse J. Int'l L. & Com.* 200 (1986)

Weitbrecht, U.S.-Antitrustrecht vor internationalen Handelsschieds-gerichten (zu Mitsubishi Motors Corp. v. Soler Chrysler-Plymouth, Inc., U.S. Supreme Court, Entscheidung von 2. Juli 1985, -U.S.-, 105 S. Ct. 3346), 6 *IPRax* 313 (1986)

Werner, A Swiss Comment on Mitsubishi, 3 *J. Int'l Arb.* 81 (No. 4, 1986)

Wilkinson, Judicial Review of Foreign Arbitral Awards on Antitrust Matters After Mitsubishi Motors, 26 *Colum. J. Transnat'l L.* 407 (1988)

Zall, International Commercial Arbitration: The Nonarbitrable Subject Matter Defense, 9 *Den. J. Int'l L. & Pol'y* 119 (1980)

7. PARTIES

7.01 CAPACITY OF PARTIES

Audit, L'arbitrage transnational et les contrats d'Etat: Bilan et perspectives/ Transnational Arbitration and State Contracts, in *L'arbitrage transnational et les contrats d'Etat/Transnational Arbitration and State Contracts 23,* 77 (Dordrecht 1988)

Batiffol, Arbitration Clauses Concluded Between French Government-Owned Enterprises and Foreign Private Parties, 7 *Colum. J. Transnat'l L.* 32 (1968)

Cafani Panico, Clausola compromissoria e capacità delle persone giuridiche, 24 *Diritto Comunitario e degli Scambi Internazionali* 480 (1985)

Gaillard, Le point de vue d'un utilisateur étranger, 1989 *Int'l Bus. L.J.* 793

Mádl, Competence of Arbitral Tribunals in International Commercial Arbitration, in *Essays on International Commercial Arbitration* 92 (P. Sarcevic ed. 1989)

Renggli, P., *Die Grenzen der Parteifreiheit im internationalen privatrechtlichen Schiedsverfahren, unter besonderer Berücksichtigung des Genferprotokolls von 1923* (Bern 1955)

Roth, Schiedsklauseln in Gesellschaftsverträgen, in *Beiträge zum internationalen Verfahrensrecht und zur Schiedsgerichtsbarkeit. Festschrift für Heinrich Nagel* 318 (W. Habscheid & K. Schwab eds. 1987)

Ventura, Convençao de arbitragem, 46 *Revista da Ordem dos Advogados* 289 (1986)

7.02 EQUALITY OF PARTIES

Coleman, A Preliminary Investigation of Possible Areas of Discrimination Against Foreign Litigants in Japanese Courts on Arbitration Practice, in *Business Transactions with China, Japan and South Korea* 9-1 (P. Saney & H. Smit eds. 1983)

Geisinger & Renold, Arbitrage international, ordre public et reconnaissance en Suisse de sentences arbitrales étrangères, in *Le Juriste Suisse Face au Droit et aux Jugements Etrangers: Ouverture ou Repli?* 89 (F. Knoepfler ed. 1988)

Holtzmann, H. & J. Neuhaus, *A Guide to the UNCITRAL Model Law on International Commercial Arbitration: Legislative History and Commentary* (Deventer 1989)

7.03 NATIONALITY

Ebb, Developing Views on What Constitutes a 'Foreign Arbitration Agreement' and a 'Foreign Award' under the New York Convention, 1 *Am. Rev. Int'l Arb.* 364 (1990)

Leurent, Problèmes soulevés par les demandes des double nationaux devant le Tribunal des différends irano-americains, 74 *Rev. Crit. Droit Int'l Privé* 273 & 477 (1985)

Matray, La loi belge du 27 mars 1985 et ses repércussions sur l'arbitrage commercial international, 64 *Rev. Droit Int'l & Droit Comp.* 243 (1987)

Rubino-Sammartano, International and Foreign Arbitration, 5 *J. Int'l Arb.* 85 (No. 3, 1988)

Stern, Les questions de nationalité des personnes physiques et de nationalité et de contrôle des personnes morales devant le Tribunal des différends irano-américains, 30 *Ann. Français Droit Int'l* 425 (1984)

Straus, Arbitration of Disputes Between Multinational Corporations, in *A.A.A., New Strategies* 109 (1971)

Vagts, The Multinational Enterprise and Dispute-Settlement Machinery, in *A.A.A., New Strategies* 97 (1971)

van den Berg, When Is an Arbitral Award Non-Domestic Under the New York Convention of 1958? 6 *Pace L. Rev.* 25 (1985)

7.04 SOVEREIGN PARTIES; SOVEREIGN IMMUNITY

Aksen, Arbitration under International Commercial Contracts. Current Issues and Practical Problems: Enforcement of Awards against Governments - The Libyan Awards, in *Essays on International Law* 104 (New Delhi 1981)

——, El arbitraje comercial internacional entre gobiernos, in *El Arbitraje Comercial Internacional* 511 (Mexico 1983)

Asken, G. & R. von Mehren, eds., *International Arbitration Between Private Parties and Governments* (New York 1982)

Amerasinghe, Dispute Settlement Machinery in Relations Between States and Multinational Enterprises — with Particular Reference to the ICSID, 11 *Int'l Law.* 45 (1977)

Arbitration Institute of the Stockholm Chamber of Commerce, *Arbitration in Sweden* (2nd rev. ed. 1984)

Atkeson & Ramsey, Proposed Amendment of the Foreign Sovereign Immunities Act, 79 *Am. J. Int'l L.* 770 (1985)

Audit, L'arbitrage transnational et les contrats d'Etat: Bilan et perspectives/ Transnational Arbitration and State Contracts, in *L'arbitrage transnational et les contrats d'Etat/Transnational Arbitration and State Contracts 23*, 77 (Dordrecht 1988)

Batiffol, Arbitration Clauses Concluded Between French Government-Owned Enterprises and Foreign Private Parties, 7 *Colum. J. Transnat'l L.* 32 (1968)

Berger, Internationale Schiedsgerichtsbarkeit und Staatsimmunität: Die Revision des U.S. Foreign Sovereign Immunities Act, 35 *RIW* 956 (1989)

Bernini & van den Berg, The Enforcement of Arbitral Award Against a State: The Problem of Immunity from Execution, in *Contemporary Problems in Int'l Arbitration* 359 (J.D.M. Lew ed. 1986)

Blessing & Burckhardt, Sovereign Immunity — A Pitfall in State Arbitration? in *Recueil de Travaux Suisses* 107 (C. Reymond & E. Bucher eds. 1984)

Böckstiegel, Arbitration of Disputes Between States and Private Enterprises in the International Chamber of Commerce, 59 *Am. J. Int'l L.* 579 (1965)

————, Arbitration on Contracts Between States and Foreign Private Enterprises, in *ICCA, Fourth Int'l Arb. Congress: Proceedings* 670 (1972)

————, Specific Problems of International Arbitration Between States and Private Enterprises, in *ICCA, Fifth Int'l Arb. Congress: Proceedings* C IIIe 1-12 (1975)

————, States in the International Arbitral Process, 2 *Arb. Int'l* 22 (No. 1, Jan. 1986)

————, States in the International Arbitral Process, in *Contemporary Problems in Int'l Arbitration* 40 (J.D.M. Lew ed. 1986)

————, The Legal Rules Applicable in International Commercial Arbitration Involving States or State-controlled Enterprises, in *ICC, 60 Years of ICC Arbitration* 117 (1984)

Booysen, The Municipal Enforcement of Arbitration Awards against States in Terms of Arbitration Conventions, with Special Reference to the New York Convention — Does International Law Provide for a Municipal, Law Concept of an Arbitrable Act of State? 12 *South Afr. Y.B. Int'l L.* 73 (1986-1987)

Booysen, H., *The Application of the New York Convention to Arbitration to which a State is a Party* (Saarbrücken 1987)

Bourel, Arbitrage international et immunités des Etats étrangères (A propos d'une jurisprudence récente), 1982 *Rev. Arb.* 119

Boutin, De la teoria de la doble personalidad del Estado y el arbitraje internacional en el nuevo Código Judicial Panameño, in *El Arbitraje en el Derecho Latinoamericano y Español* 459 (L. Perret & U. Montoya Alberti eds. 1989)

Cahier, The Strengths and Weaknesses of International Arbitration Involving a State as a Party, in *Contemporary Problems in Int'l Arbitration* 241 (J.D.M. Lew ed. 1986)

Capelli & Percibaldi, The Application of the New York Convention to Disputes between States and between State Entities and Private Individuals: The Problem of Sovereign Immunity, 12 *Int'l Law.* 197 (1978)

Carabiber, L'immunité de juridiction et d'exécution des Etats collectivités et établissements publics au regard de l'obligation assumée par une clause compromissoire inserée dans les contrats internationaux de droit privé, in *Liber Amicorum for Martin Domke* 23 (P. Sanders ed. 1967)

————, L'arbitrage international entre gouvernements et particuliers, 76 *Recueil des Cours* 217 (1950-I)

Carver, The Strengths and Weaknesses of International Arbitration Involving a State As a Party: Practical Implications, 1 *Arb. Int'l* 179 (1985); reprinted in *Contemporary Problems in Int'l Arbitration* 264 (J.D.M. Lew ed. 1986)

Chafic, Quelques réfléxions sur la philosophie de l'arbitrage commercial, in *Euro-Arab Arbitration II* 17 (F. Kemicha ed. 1989)

Chapelle, L'arbitrage et les tiers: le droit des personnes morales (groupes de sociétés; interventions d'Etat), 1988 *Rev. Arb.* 475

Chukwumerije, ICSID Arbitration and Sovereign Immunity, 19 *Anglo-Am. L. Rev.* 166 (1990)

Crawford & Johnson, Arbitrating with Foreign States and their Instrumentalities, 5 *Int'l Fin. L. Rev.* 11 (No. 4, 1986)

Delaume, Contractual Waivers of Sovereign Immunity: Some Practical Considerations, 5 *ICSID Rev. - Foreign Investment L.J.* 232 (1990)

————, Foreign Sovereign Immunity: Impact on Arbitration, 38 *Arb. J.* 34 (No. 2, 1983)

————, Judicial Decisions Related to Sovereign Immunity and Transnational Arbitration, 2 *ICSID Rev. - Foreign Investment L.J.* 403 (1987)

————, Le CIRDI et l'immunité des Etats, 1983 *Rev. Arb.* 143

————, SEEE v. Yugoslavia: Epitaph or Interlude? 4 *J. Int'l Arb.* 25 (No. 3, 1987)

————, Sovereign Immunity and International Arbitration, 3 *Arb. Int'l* 28 (No. 1, 1987)

————, Sovereign Immunity and Transnational Arbitration, in *Contemporary Problems in Int'l Arbitration* 313 (J.D.M. Lew ed. 1986)

————, State Contracts and Transnational Arbitration, 75 *Am. J. Int'l L.* 784 (1981)

————, The Finality of Arbitration Involving States: Recent Developments, 5 *Arb. Int'l* 21 (1989)

Delaume, G., *Law and Practice of Transnational Contracts* (Dobbs Ferry, NY 1988)

de Magalhaes, Do Estado na arbitragem privada, 22 *Revista de Informaçao Legislativa* 125 (April-June 1985)

de Magalhaes, J. & L.O. Batista, *Arbitragem comercial* (Rio de Janeiro 1986)

Dimilitsa, Arbitration Agreements and Foreign Investments: The Greek State between Contractual Commitment and Sovereign Intervention, 5 *J. Int'l Arb.* 17 (No. 4, 1988)

Domke, Arbitration Between Governmental Bodies and Foreign Private Firms, 17 *Arb. J.* 129 (1962)

————, Government Immunity in Foreign Trade Arbitration: A Comparative Survey of Recent Practice, in *ICC, Hommage à Fréderic Eisemann* 45 (1978)

Eisemann, Report on the Present Situation of International Commercial Arbitration Between States or State Entities and Foreign Private Parties, in *ICCA, Fifth Int'l Arb. Congress: Proceedings* C IIIa 1-14 (1975)

Feldman, Enforcement of Foreign Arbitral Awards in the U.S. Courts, 3 *Int'l Arb. Rep.* 15 (No. 11, 1988)

————, Waiver of Foreign Sovereign Immunity by Agreement to Arbitrate: Legislation Proposed by the American Bar Association, 40 *Arb. J.* 24 (No. 1, 1985)

Flamme, L'arbitrage dans les rapports entre personnes de droit public et personnes de droit privé, 1966 *Rev. Arb.* 86

Forrestal, Examples of and Reasons for Increased Use of International Arbitration, in *International Arbitration Between Private Parties and Governments* 15 (G. Aksen & R. von Mehren eds. 1982)

Fox, Sovereign Immunity and Arbitration, in *Contemporary Problems in Int'l Arbitration* 323 (J.D.M. Lew ed. 1986)

————, States and the Undertaking to Arbitrate, 37 *Int'l & Comp. L.Q.* 1 (1988)

Gaillard, Le point de vue d'un utilisateur étranger, 1989 *Int'l Bus. L.J.* 793

Goldman, B., *Investissement étrangers et arbitrage entre Etats et personnes privées* (Paris 1969)

Greenwood, State Contracts in International Law: The Lybian Oil Arbitrations, 53 *Brit. Y.B. Int'l L.* 27 (1982)

Grigera Naón, El estado y el arbitraje, in *El Arbitraje en el Derecho Latinoamericano y Español* 73 (L. Perret & U. Montoya Alberti eds. 1989)

Guyomar, L'arbitrage concernant les rapports entre Etats et particuliers, 5 *Ann. Français Droit Int'l* 333 (1959)

Hermann, Disputes Between States and Foreign Companies, in *Contemporary Problems in Int'l Arbitration* 250 (J.D.M. Lew ed. 1986)

Jimenez de Aréchaga, L'arbitrage entre les Etats et les sociétés privées, in *Mélanges en l'honneur de Gilbert Gidel* 367 (Paris 1961)

Kahale, Arbitration and Choice of Law Clauses as Waivers of Jurisdictional Immunity, 14 *N.Y.U. J. Int'l L. & Pol.* 29 (1981)

———, New Legislation in the United States Facilitates Enforcement of Arbitral Agreements and Awards Against Foreign States, 6 *J. Int'l Arb.* 57 (No. 2, 1989)

Kahn, Souveraineté de l'Etat et règlement du litige. Régime juridique du contrat d'Etat, 1985 *Rev. Arb.* 641

Kawagishi, The Function of the Arbitration Clauses in State Contracts, 82 *KGZ* 1 (No. 3, 1983)

Lalive, Arbitration with Foreign States or State-Controlled Entities, in *Private Investors Abroad— Problems and Solutions in International Business in 1988* 9.1 (J. Moss ed. 1989)

———, Arbitration with Foreign States or State-Controlled Entities: Some Practical Questions, in *Contemporary Problems in Int'l Arbitration* 289 (J.D.M. Lew ed. 1986)

———, Contracts Between a State or a State Agency and a Foreign Company: Theory and Practice: Choice of Law in a New Arbitration Case, 13 *Int'l Comp. L.Q.* 987 (1964)

———, Quelques observations sur l'imunité d'exécution des Etats et l'arbitrage international, in *International Law at a Time of Perplexity. Essays in Honour of Shabtai Rosenne* 369 (Y. Dinstein ed. 1989)

———, Some Threats to International Investment Arbitration, 1 *ICSID Rev. - Foreign Investment L.J.* 26 (1986)

————, Transnational (or Truly International) Public Policy and International Arbitration, in *Comparative Arbitration Practice and Public Policy in Arbitration* 256 (P. Sanders ed. 1987)

Langkeit, J., *Staatenimmunität und Schiedsgerichtsbarkeit. Verzichtet ein Staat durch Unterzeichnung einer Schiedsgerichtsvereinbarung auf seine Immunität?* (Heidelberg 1989)

Larschan & Mirfendereski, The Status of Counterclaims under International Law, with Particular Reference to International Arbitration Involving a Private Party and a Foreign State, 15 *Den. J. Int'l L. & Pol'y* 11 (1986)

Leboulanger, Groupes d'Etat(s) et l'arbitrage, 1989 *Rev. Arb.* 415

Lelewer, International Commercial Arbitration as a Model for Resolving Treaty Disputes, 21 *N.Y.U. J. Int'l L. & Pol.* 379 (1989)

Lipstein, International Arbitration Between Individuals and Governments and the Conflict of Laws, in *Contemporary Problems of International Law: Essays in Honour of Georg Schwarzenberger* 177 (B. Cheng & E.D. Brown eds. 1988)

Lliteras, El arbitraje internacional entre estados y particulares, 20 *Comparative Juridical Review* 111 (1983)

Loftis, Securing Arbitral Awards: Waiving Immunity Under the Foreign Sovereign Immunities Act and Ensuring Equitable Remedy by Pre-Award Attachment Under the New York Convention, 9 *Suff. Transnat'l L.J.* 235 (1985)

McGovan, Arbitration Clauses as Waivers of Immunity from Jurisdiction and Execution under the Foreign Sovereign Immunity Act of 1976, 5 *N.Y. L. Sch. J. Int'l & Comp. L.* 409 (1984)

Mádl, Competence of Arbitral Tribunals in International Commercial Arbitration, in *Essays on International Commercial Arbitration* 92 (P. Sarcevic ed. 1989)

Mann, State Contracts and International Arbitration, 42 *Brit. Y.B. Int'l L.* 13 (1967)

Mezghani, Souverenaité de l'Etat et participation a l'arbitrage, 1985 *Rev. Arb.* 543

Montoya Alberti, Arbitration, Foreign Law and Jurisdiction in International Loan Agreements in Some Countries of Latin America, in *Arbitration in Settlement of International Commercial Disputes Involving the Far East and Arbitration in Combined Transportation* 99 (P. Sanders ed. 1989)

Mustill, Sir Michael J. & S. C. Boyd, *The Law and Practice of Commercial Arbitration in England* (2nd ed. 1989)

Nilsson, Problems of Sovereign Immunity under the Swedish Law of Arbitration, 1982 *Y.B. Swed. & Int'l Arb.* 41

Note, The Validity of the Foreign Sovereign Immunity Defense in Suits Under the Convention on the Recognition and Enforcement of Foreign Arbitral Awards, 7 *Fordham Int'l L. J.* 321 (1983-84)

O'Neill, American Legal Developments in Commercial Arbitration Involving Foreign States and State Enterprises, 6 *J. Int'l Arb.* 117 (No. 1, 1989)

Oparil, Waiver of Sovereign Immunity in the United States and Great Britain by an Arbitration Agreement, 3 *J. Int'l Arb.* 61 (No. 4, 1986)

Oppetit, Arbitrage et contrats d'Etats: l'arbitrage Framatone et autres c/ Atomic Energy Organization of Iran, 111 *J. Droit Int'l (Clunet)* 37 (1984)

————, Les Etats et l'arbitrage international: esquisse de systématisation, 1985 *Rev. Arb.* 493

Osakwe, A Soviet Perspective on Foreign Sovereign Immunity: Law and Practice, 23 *Va. J. Int'l L.* 13 (1982)

Paasivirta, E., *Participation of States in International Contracts and Arbitral Settlement of Disputes* (Helsinki 1990)

Paulsson, May a State Invoke Its Internal Law to Repudiate Consent to International Commercial Arbitration? Reflections on the Benteler v. Belgium Preliminary Award, 2 *Arb. Int'l* 90 (1986)

Pavlis, International Arbitration and the Inapplicability of the Act of State Doctrine, 14 *N.Y.U. J. Int'l L. & Pol.* 65 (1981)

Przetacznik, The Sovereign Immunity of Foreign States and International Commercial Arbitration, 57 *Rev. Droit Int'l Sci. Dipl. & Pol.* 188 and 291 (1979)

Regli, J.-P., *Contrats d'Etat et arbitrage entre Etats et personnes privées* (Geneva 1983)

Reymond, Souveraineté de l'Etat et participation a l'arbitrage, 1985 *Rev. Arb.* 517

Richard, Enforcement of Foreign Arbitral Awards under the United Nations Convention of 1958: A Survey of Recent Federal Case Law, 11 *Md. J. Int'l L. & Trade* 13 (1987)

Rothstein, Recognizing and Enforcing Arbitral Agreements and Awards Against Foreign States: The Mathias Amendments to the Foreign Sovereign Immunities Act and Title 9, 1 *Emory J. Int'l Disp. Res.* 101 (1986)

Schreuer, Ch. H., *State Immunity: Some Recent Developments.* Chapter 4: Arbitration (Cambridge 1988)

Schwebel, Some Aspects of International Law in Arbitration between States and Aliens, in *Private Investors Abroad - Problems and Solutions in International Business in 1986* 12-1 (J. Moss ed. 1986)

Schwebel, S.M., *International Arbitration: Three Salient Problems* (Cambridge 1987)

Seppala, International Commercial Arbitration and States and State-Controlled Enterprises: Some Comments on a Recent ICC Conference, 1 *Int'l Constr. L. Rev.* 159 (1984)

Shattuck, Claims Against the Sovereign and Its Instrumentalities: The Arbitration Agreement, 41 *Arb. J.* 7 (No. 2, 1986)

Shifman, Maritime International Nominees Establishment v. Republic of Guinea: Effect on U.S. Jurisdiction of an Agreement by a Foreign Sovereign to Arbitrate before the ICSID, 16 *J. Int'l L. & Econ.* 451 (1982)

Shihata, The Institute of International Law's Resolution on Arbitration between States and Foreign Enterprises — A Comment, 5 *ICSID Rev. - Foreign Investment L.J.* 65 (1990)

Sillevis Smitt, Arbitration Clause and Sovereign Immunity, in *ICCA, Fifth Int'l Arb. Congress: Proceedings* C IIIf 1-4 (1975)

Simmonds, International Arbitration between States and Corporate Entities: A Cautionary Note, in *Contemporary Problems in Int'l Arbitration* 273 (J.D.M. Lew ed. 1986)

Singhania, Arbitrating State Contracts, 2 *Lex et Juris - The Law Magazine* 43 (No. 6, 1987)

Sornarajah, M., *International Commercial Arbitration: The Problem of State Contracts* (Singapore 1990)

Ssekandi, Contracts between a State and a Foreign Private Company. Reflections on the Effectiveness of the Arbitration Process, 2 *East Afr. L.J.* 281 (1966)

Sujan, M.A., *The Law Relating to Government Arbitration* (New Delhi 1985)

Sullivan, Implicit Waiver of Sovereign Immunity by Consent to Arbitration: Territorial Scope and Procedural Limits. Comment, 18 *Tex. Int'l L.J.* 329 (1983)

Tankoano, La place du droit public de l'Etat dans l'arbitrage international avec une personne privée, 42 *Revue Juridique et Politique, Indépendence et Coopération* 938 (1988); also 1 *Afr. J. Int'l & Comp. L.* 69 (1989)

Tesón, State Contracts and Oil Expropriations: The Aminoil-Kuwait Arbitration, 24 *Va. J. Int'l L.* 323 (1984)

Toop, S., *Mixed International Arbitration: Studies in Arbitration Between States and Private Persons* (Cambridge 1990)

Tschanz, Contrats d'Etat et mesures unilatérales de l'Etat devant l'arbitre international, 74 *Rev. Crit. Droit Int'l Privé* 47 (1985)

van Marwijk Kooy, Arbitration and Sovereign Immunity, in *ICCA, Fourth Int'l Arb. Congress: Proceedings* 140 (1972)

Vedel, Le problème de l'arbitrage entre gouvernements ou personnes de droit public et personnes de droit privé, 1961 *Rev. Arb.* 116

Ventura, Convençao de arbitragem, 46 *Revista da Ordem dos Advogados* 289 (1986)

Verhoeven, Arbitrage entre Etats et entreprises étrangères: des règles spécifiques? 1985 *Rev. Arb.* 609

von Mehren, Arbitration between States and Foreign Enterprises: The Significance of the Institute of International Law's Santiago de Compostella Resolution, 5 *ICSID Rev. - Foreign Investment L.J.* 54 (1990)

von Mehren & Kourides, International Arbitration between States and Foreign Private Parties: The Libyan Nationalization Case, 75 *Am. J. Int'l L.* 476 (1981)

————, The Libyan Nationalizations: TOPCO/CALASIATIC v. Libyan Arbitration, 12 *Natural Resources Law.* 419 (1979)

Voyame, L'Etat et l'arbitrage commercial international, in *Recueil de Travaux Suisses* 15 (C. Reymond & E. Bucher eds. 1984)

Wengler, Nouveaux aspects de la problématique des contrats entre Etats et personnes privées, 1978-79 *Revue Belge Droit Int'l* 415

Westberg, The Applicable Law Issue in International Business Transactions with Government Parties: Ruling of the Iran-United States Claims Tribunal, 2 *ICSID Rev. - Foreign Investment L.J.* 473 (1987)

Westberg, J., *International Business Transactions Involving Government Parties — Awards of the Iran-United States Claims Tribunal* (Washington 1991)

Wetter, Pleas of Sovereign Immunity and Act of Sovereignty before International Arbitral Tribunals, 2 *J. Int'l Arb.* 7 (1985)

Wortley, Quelques devéloppements modernes qui touchent les controverses entre les particuliers et les Etats et les entités étatiques, in *Liber Amicorum for Martin Domke* 348 (P. Sanders ed. 1967)

7.05 PUBLIC ORGANIZATIONS AND ENTERPRISES

Audit, L'arbitrage transnational et les contrats d'Etat: Bilan et perspectives/ Transnational Arbitration and State Contracts, in *L'arbitrage transnational et les contrats d'Etat/Transnational Arbitration and State Contracts 23*, 77 (Dordrecht 1988)

Behre, Arbitration: A Permissible or Desirable Method of Resolving Disputes Involving Federal Acquisition and Assistance Contracts? 16 *Pub. Cont. L.J.* 66 (1986)

Böckstiegel, The Legal Rules Applicable in International Commercial Arbitration Involving States or State-controlled Enterprises, in *ICC, 60 Years of ICC Arbitration* 117 (1984)

Böckstiegel, K.-H., *Arbitration and State Enterprises. Survey on the National and International State of Law and Practice* (Deventer 1984)

Bouony, Les personnes morales de droit public et l'arbitrage, in *Centre d'Etudes, Les Entreprises Tunisiennes et l'Arbitrage Commercial International* 247 (1983)

Flamme, L'arbitrage dans les rapports entre personnes de droit public et personnes de droit privé, 1966 *Rev Arb.* 86

Horsmans, Actualité et évolution du droit belge de l'arbitrage, 1990 *Rev. Arb.* 797

Lalive, Contracts between a State or a State Agency and a Foreign Company: Theory and Practice: Choice of Law in a New Arbitration Case, 13 *Int'l Comp. L.Q.* 987 (1964)

———, Arbitration with Foreign States or State-Controlled Entities, in *Private Investors Abroad— Problems and Solutions in International Business in 1988* 9.1 (J. Moss ed. 1989)

———, Arbitration with Foreign States or State-Controlled Entities: Some Practical Questions, in *Contemporary Problems in Int'l Arbitration* 289 (J.D.M. Lew ed. 1986)

Leboulanger, Groupes d'Etat(s) et l'arbitrage, 1989 *Rev. Arb.* 415

———, Etats, politique et arbitrage. L'affaire du Plateau des Pyramides, 1986 *Rev. Arb.* 3

Malouche, Les entreprises public et l'arbitrage en droit tunisien, 1989 *Rev. Arb.* 374

Mestre, Les établissements publics industriels et commerciaux et le recours a l'arbitrage, 1976 *Rev. Arb.* 4

O'Neill, American Legal Developments in Commercial Arbitration Involving Foreign States and State Enterprises, 6 *J. Int'l Arb.* 117 (No. 1, 1989)

Pozdnyakov, Commercial Arbitration in Relations of Soviet FTOs with Firms of Capitalist Countries, in *USSR Contract Law* (V. Pozdnyakov ed. 1982)

————, The Foreign Trade Corporation as a Side in an Arbitration Dispute, in *ICCA, Fourth Int'l Arb. Congress: Proceedings* 129 (1974)

Révai, Arbitrages entre les sujets de droit des pays de l'Est et de l'Ouest, 24 *Acta Juridica (Budapest)* 207 (1982)

Savarese, Arbitration and Contracts for the Transfer of Technology in the Experience of Some Italian State-owned Companies, in *ICCA, Sixth Int'l Arb. Congress: Proceedings* 405 (1978)

Seppala, International Commercial Arbitration and States and State-Controlled Enterprises: Some Comments on a Recent ICC Conference, 1 *Int'l Constr. L. Rev.* 159 (1984)

Storme, Arbitrage entre personnes de droit public et de droit privé, 1978 *Rev. Arb.* 113; 1979 *Tijdschrift voor Privaatrecht* 179

Strohbach, Arbitration between Foreign Trade Organizations of Socialist Countries and Parties from the Capitalist Economic Sphere, 4 *Pace L. Rev.* 607 (1984)

Szasz, Public Corporations as Parties to Arbitration. Procedural Aspects, in *ICC, 60 Years of ICC Arbitration* 213 (1984)

Terki, L'arbitrage et l'entreprise publique en Afrique du Nord, 66 *Rev. Droit Int'l & Droit Comp.* 124 (1989)

Westberg, J., *International Business Transactions Involving Government Parties - Awards of the Iran-United States Claims Tribunal* (Washington 1991)

Zourek, Some Comments on the Difficulties Encountered in the Juridical Settlement of Disputes Arising from Trade between Countries with Different Economic and Social Structure, 86 *J. Droit Int'l (Clunet)* 639 (1959)

7.06 DEATH, DISSOLUTION, MERGER, SUCCESSION AND SUBSTITUTION OF PARTIES

Heuman, L., *Current Issues in Swedish Arbitration* (Deventer and Stockholm 1990)

Hobér, Party Substitution under Swedish Arbitration Law, 1983 *Y.B. Swed. & Int'l Arb.* 43

Mustill, Sir Michael J. & S. C. Boyd, *The Law and Practice of Commercial Arbitration in England* (2nd ed. 1989)

Roth, Schiedsklauseln in Gesellschaftsverträgen, in *Beiträge zum Internationalen Verfahrensrecht und zur Schiedsgerichtsbarkeit. Festschrift für Heinrich Nagel* 318 (W. Habscheid & K. Schwab eds. 1987)

Samuel, A., *Jurisdictional Problems in International Commercial Arbitration: A Study of Belgian, Dutch, English, French, Swedish, Swiss, U.S. and West German Law* (Zurich 1989)

7.07 BANKRUPTCY OF A PARTY

Aksen, The Application of the New York Convention by the United States, 4 *Y.B. Com. Arb.* 341 (1979)

Ancel, Arbitrage et procédures collectives après la loi du 26 janvier 1985, 1987 *Rev. Arb.* 128

Cárdenas, Arbitration and Bankruptcy Procedures — The Agentina Reply: 'La Nación v. La Razón,' 19 *Int'l Bus. Law* 527 (1991)

Crozier, The Status of International Arbitration Awards Under Canadian Insolvency Law, 18 *Can. Bus. L.J.* 294 (1991)

Deitrick, The Conflicting Policies between Arbitration and Bankruptcy, 40 *Bus. Law.* 33 (1984)

Jestaedt, T., *Schiedsverfahren und Konkurs* (Berlin 1985)

Massoff, Authority of United States Bankruptcy Courts to Stay International Arbitral Proceedings, 11 *Fordham Int'l L.J.* 148 (1987)

Mustill, Sir Michael J. & S. C. Boyd, *The Law and Practice of Commercial Arbitration in England* (2nd ed. 1989)

Note, Authority of United States Bankruptcy Courts to Stay International Arbitral Proceedings, 11 *Fordham Int'l L.J.* 148 (1987)

Oehmke, T., *International Arbitration* (Rochester 1990)

Schlosser, Quelles nouvelles de l'arbitrage Outre-Rhin? 1987 *Rev. Arb.* 293

Schwebel & Lahne, Public Policy and Arbitral Procedure, in *Comparative Arbitration Practice and Public Policy in Arbitration* 205 (P. Sanders ed. 1987)

Victor & Bialos, The Arbitration of Public Law Disputes: The Availability and Efficacy of This Alternative Dispute Resolution Mechanism, in *Private Investors Abroad - Problems and Solutions in International Business in 1987* 15.1 (J. Ross ed. 1987)

Westbrook, The Coming Encounter: International Arbitration and Bankruptcy, 67 *Minn. L. Rev.* 595 (1983)

7.08 RESPONSIBILITY OF PARTIES

Carver, Legal and Moral Obligations of the Counsel and of the Parties, in *Euro-Arab Arbitration II* 53 (F. Kemicha ed. 1989)

Gaillard, Les manoevres dilatoires des parties et des arbitres dans l'arbitrage commercial international, 1990 *Rev. Arb.* 759

Jarvin, L'obligation de coopérer de bonne fois: examples d'application au plan de l'arbitrage international, in *ICC, L'apport de la jurisprudence arbitrale* 157 (1986)

8. AGREEMENT TO ARBITRATE

8.01 EXISTENCE OF AN AGREEMENT TO ARBITRATE

Arbitration Institute of the Stockholm Chamber of Commerce, *Arbitration in Sweden* (2nd rev. ed. 1984)

Armenta Deu, Perspectivas de futuro de la cláusula compromisoria arbitral, 2 *Revista Juridica de Cataluña* 49 (1984)

Aylwin Azocar, P., *El juicio arbitral* (Santiago de Chile 1958)

Backhausen, G., *Schiedsgerichtsbarkeit unter besonderer Berücksichtigung des Schiedsvertragsrechts* (Vienna 1990)

Bakshi, Arbitration Agreement: A Very Important Judgment, 1985(1) *Company L.J.* 195

Basedow, Vertragsstatut und Arbitrage nach neuem IPR, 1 *Jahrbuch Schiedsgerichtsbarkeit* 3 (1987)

Bernini, Arbitration During the Progress of Long-term Contracts, 43 *Arbitration* 51 (Summer 1976)

————, Demostración de las técnicas para la solución de problemas en la celebración y cumplimiento de contratos a largo plazo, in *El Arbitraje Comercial Internacional* 151 (Mexico 1983)

Bin, Il compromesso e la clausola compromissoria in arbitrato irrituale, 45 *Riv. Trim. Dir. & Proc. Civ.* 373 (1991)

Bohm, Zur Rechtsnatur des Schiedsvertrages unter nationalen Gesichtspunkten, 9 *ZRV* 262 (1968)

Bourdin, La convention d'arbitrage international en droit français depuis le Décret du 12 mai 1981, in *Droit et pratique de l'arbitrage international en France* 11 (Y. Derains ed. 1984)

Brierley, La Convention d'arbitrage en droit québécois interne, 1987 *C.P. du N.* 507,

————, La validité de la clause compromissoire demeure-t-elle incertaine en droit québécois? 1975 *Rev. Arb.* 154

————, Quebec's New (1986) Arbitration Law, 13 *Can. Bus. L.J.* 58 (1987)

Bucher, A., *Die neue internationale Schiedsgerichtsbarkeit in der Schweiz* (Basel 1989)

————, *Le nouvel arbitrage international en Suisse. Théorie et pratique de droit* (Basel 1988)

Bucher, A. & P.-Y. Tschanz, *International Arbitration in Switzerland* (Basel 1989)

Chillón Medina, J. M. & J. F. Merino Merchán, *Tratado de arbitraje privado interno e internacional* (Madrid 1978)

Chowdhuri, S.K.R. & H.K. Saharay, *Arbitration Law*. 2nd ed. (Calcutta 1986)

Colas, Clause compromissoire, compromis et arbitrage en droit nouveau, 28 *Rev. du Barreau* 129 (1968)

Cremades, Les effets de la clause d'arbitrage dans la jurisprudence espagnole récente, in *The Art of Arbitration* 83 (J. Schultsz & A. van den Berg, eds. 1982)

Cremades, B. M., *Panorámica Española del Arbitraje Comercial Internacional* (Madrid 1975)

D'Aloisio, International Arbitration: Arbitration (Foreign Awards and Agreements) Act, 1974 (CTH), 5 *Austl. Bus. L. Rev.* 295 (1977)

David, R., *Arbitration in International Trade* (Deventer 1985)

de Bruin, De 'affaire C,' 1989 *Tijdschrift voor Arbitrage* 1

Delaume, L'arbitrage transnational et les tribunaux nationaux, 111 *J. Droit Int'l (Clunet)* 521 (1984)

de Magalhaes J. & L.O. Batista, *Arbitragem comercial* (Rio de Janeiro 1986)

Derains, International Commercial Arbitration in Civil Law Countries, in *Arbitration in Settlement of International Commercial Disputes Involving the Far East and Arbitration in Combined Transportation* 229 (P. Sanders ed. 1989)

Derains & Schaf, Clauses d'arbitrage et groupes de sociétés, 1985 *Int'l Bus. L.J.* 231

Derains, Y., ed., *Droit et pratique de l'arbitrage international en France* (Paris 1984)

Deshpande, Practice Versus the Law in Arbitration, 6 *J. Int'l Arb.* 55 (No. 4, 1989)

————, The Applicable Law in International Commercial Arbitration, 31 *J. Ind. L. Inst.* 127 (1989)

Dietrich, Internationale Schiedsvereinbarungen vor amerikanischen Gerichten, 40 *Rabels Z.* 1 (1976)

Dobratz, Schiedsklausel und Vollstreckung im Aussenhandel, 8 *AWD* 188 (1962)

Duintjer Tebbens, A Facelift for Dutch Arbitration Law, 34 *Neth. Int'l L. Rev.* 141 (1987)

Dunshee de Abranches, C.A., ed., *El arbitraje comercial en Iberoamérica* (Madrid 1982)

Ebenroth & Parche, Schiedsgerichtsklauseln als alternative Streiterledigungsmechanismen in internationalen Konsortialkreditverträgen und Umschuldungsabkommen, 36 *RIW* 341 (1990)

————, Arbitration Clauses as Alternative Mechanisms for the Settlement of Conflicts Involving International Syndicate Loan Agreements and Restructuring Agreements, 38 *Neth. Int'l L. Rev.* 1 (1991)

Ehlers, Le consentement à une convention d'arbitrage en droit danois, 1978 *Rev. Arb.* 571

Eisemann, Arbitrage et garanties contractuelles (garanties de soumission, de bonne exécution et de remboursement), in *ICCA, Fourth Int'l Arb. Congress: Proceedings* 151 (1972)

Eyzaguirre Echeverria, R., *El arbitraje comercial en la legislación chilena y su regulación international* (Santiago de Chile 1981)

Foustoucos, Conditions Required for the Validity of an Arbitration Agreement, 5 *J. Int'l Arb.* 113 (No. 4, 1988)

García Rubio, El Convenio arbitral en la Ley de Arbitraje de 5 de diciembre de 1988, 5 *Rev. Corte Esp. Arb.* 71 (1988-89)

Gildeggen, R., *Internationale Schieds- und Schiedsverfahrensvereinbarungen in algemeinen Geschäftsbedingungen vor deutschen Gerichten* (Frankfurt 1991)

Ginsburgs, Recognition of Arbitration Agreements in Post-war Soviet Bilateral Treaty Practice, 11 *Rev. Soc. L.* 13 (1985)

Glossner, International Commercial Arbitration — Some Practical Aspects, in *Liber Amicorum for Martin Domke* 95 (P. Sanders ed. 1967)

―――, The Conduct of ICC Arbitration Proceedings, in *Contemporary Problems in International Arbitration* 210 (J.D.M. Lew ed. 1986)

Glossner, O., *Commercial Arbitration in the Federal Republic of Germany* (Deventer 1984)

González Campos, Sobre el convenio de arbitraje en el derecho internacional privado español, 2 *Anuario Der. Int'l* 13 (1975)

Goutal, L'arbitrage et les tiers: le droit des contrats, 1988 *Rev. Arb.* 439

Graham, The Internationalization of Commercial Arbitration in Canada: A Preliminary Reaction, 13 *Can. Bus. L.J.* 1 (1987)

Grigera Naón, Mandatory Provisions of Law Regarding Arbitration Agreements in Latin America, in *Arbitration in Settlement of International Commercial Disputes Involving the Far East and Arbitration in Combined Transportation* 121 (P. Sanders ed. 1989)

Heiermann, Schiedsgerichtsvereinbarung im nationalen und internationalen Bauvertrag, 1 *Jahrbuch Schiedsgerichtsbarkeit* 23 (1987)

―――, Der Schiedsvertrag im Bauwesen und Anlagenbau, 2 *Jahrbuch Schiedsgerichtsbarkeit* 66 (1988)

Henn, G., *Schiedsverfahrensrecht: ein Handbuch* (Heidelberg 1986)

Hoellering, Provisions of U.S. Law on Arbitration Agreements, in *Arbitration & the Law: AAA General Counsel's Annual Report 1987-88* 170 (1988)

Horsmans, La sentence arbitrale, la convention d'arbitrage et l'ordre public interne belge, 16 *Tijdschrift voor Privaatrecht* 231 (1979)

Hunter, Achievement of the Intention of the Parties: Arbitration Agreements and the First Procedural Steps in International Arbitrations, 47 *Arbitration* 213 (1982)

Keilin, A.D., *Sudoustroistvo i grazhdanskii protsess kapitalisticheskikh gosudarstv. III - Arbitrazh* (Moscow 1961)

Kessler J., *Die Bindung des Schiedsgerichts an das materielle Recht* (Cologne 1964)

————, *Schiedsgerichtsvertrag und Schiedsverfahren* (Munich 1970)

Klingmüller, Zu den Grundlagen von Schiedsgeichtsvereinbarungen in Saudisch-Arabien, in *Vertragspraxis und Streiterledigung im Wirtschaftverkehr mit arabischen Staaten* 5 (K.-H. Böckstiegel ed. 1981)

Kos-Rabcewicz-Zubkowski, L., *East European Rules on the Validity of International Arbitration Agreements* (Manchester and Dobbs Ferry, NY 1970)

Krüger, Probleme des saudi-arabischen internationalen Vertrags- und Schiedsrecht, in *Vertragspraxis und Streiterledigung im Wirtschaftsverkehr mit arabischen Staaten* 61 (K.-H. Böckstiegel ed. 1981)

Lalive, L'influence des clauses arbitrales, 11 *Revue belge de droit int'l* 570 (1975)

————, Problèmes relatifs à l'arbitrage international commercial, 120 *Recueil des Cours* 569 (1967-II)

————, The New Swiss Law on International Arbitration, 4 *Arb. Int'l* 2 (1988)

Laschet, Rechtsmittel gegen Prozess-, Vorab- oder Zwischenentscheidungen eines Schiedsgerichtes oder einer Schiedsgerichtsorganisation, in *Beiträge zum internationalen Verfahrensrechts und zur Schiedsgerichtbarkeit. Festschrift für Heinrich Nagel* 167 (W. Habscheid & K. Schwab eds. 1987)

Lécuyer-Thieffry, C. & P. Thieffry, *Le règlement des litiges civils et commerciaux avec les Etats-Unis* (Paris 1986)

Lebedev, S., *Mezhdunarodnyi kommercheskii arbitrazh: kompetentsia arbitrov i soglashenie stran* (Moscow 1988)

Lee, E., *Encyclopedia of International Commercial Arbitration* (London 1986)

Lew, Arbitration Agreements: Form and Character, in *Essays on International Commercial Arbitration* 51 (P. Sarcevic ed. 1989)

Lombard, Arbitration Has Worked at Exxon, 42 *Arb. J.* 3 (No. 1, 1987)

Lucke, Arbitration Clauses in South Australia, 5 *Adel. L. Rev.* 244 (1975)

Moreau, B. & T. Bernard, *Droit interne et droit international de l'arbitrage* (2nd ed. 1985)

Mustill, Sir Michael J. & S. C. Boyd, *The Law and Practice of Commercial Arbitration in England* (2nd ed. 1989)

Nerz, Abfassen von Schiedsklauseln in Verträgen mit saudiarabischen Parteien, 33 *RIW* 23 (1987)

————, The Structuring of an Arbitration Clause in a Contract with a Saudi Party, 1 *Arab L. Q.* 380 (1986)

Nolting, Mangelnde Feststellung des für Formwirksamkeit der Schiedsklausel und Schiedsfähigkeit massgeblichen Rechts, 7 *IPRax* 349 (1987)

Oehmke, T., *International Arbitration* (Rochester 1990)

Pire, La convention d'arbitrage, in *L'Arbitrage* 31 (L. Matray & G. de Leval eds. 1989)

Poudret, La clause arbitrale par référence selon la Convention de New York et l'art. 6 du Concordat sur l'arbitrage, in *Mélanges Guy Flattet* 523 (Lausanne 1985)

Pryles, M. & K. Iwasaki, *Dispute Resolution in Australia-Japan Transactions* (Sydney 1983)

Raeschke-Kessler, Neuere Entwicklungen im Bereich der Internationalen Schiedsgerichtsbarkeit, 41 *NJW* 3041 (1988)

Ramos Mendez, Les clauses d'arbitrage international et leur validité selon le droit espagnol, 1982 *Rev. Arb.* 147

————, The Relationship between Civil and Criminal Actions and Arbitration Agreements in Maritime Disaster Cases under Spanish Law, 2 *Y.B. Mar. L.* 125 (1985-1986)

Redfern, International Commercial Arbitration. Jurisdiction Denied: the Pyramid Collapses, 1986 *J. Bus. L.* 15

Redfern, A. & M. Hunter, *Law and Practice of International Commercial Arbitration* (2nd ed. 1991)

Reiter & Carleton, Arbitration Clauses and Submissions, 3 *Int'l Constr. L. Rev.* 181 (1986)

Rendon Graniel & Zivy, Jurisprudence méxicaine: la validité de la clause arbitrale internationale, 1987 *Int'l Bus. L.J.* 629

Revoredo de Debakey, La selección de las leyes aplicables a la validez del acuerdo arbitral y al fondo de la controversia en el arbitraje comercial internacional, 7 *Anuario Hispano-Luso-Americano de Derecho Internacional* 329 (1984)

Robert, J. & B. Morceau, *L'arbitrage — droit interne, droit international privé* (5th ed. Paris 1983)

Rokison, The Sources and Limits of the Arbitrator's Powers in England, in *Contemporary Problems of International Arbitration* 86 (J.D.M. Lew ed. 1986); also 52 *Arbitration* 219 (1986)

Rubino-Sammartano, M., *International Arbitration Law* (Deventer 1990)

Russell, F., *Russell on the Law of Arbitration* (20th ed. by A. Walton & M. Vitoria 1982)

Samtleben, Schiedsklauseln in Peru and Venezuela, 33 *RIW* 20 (1987)

Samuel, A., *Jurisdictional Problems in International Commercial Arbitration: A Study of Belgian, Dutch, English, French, Swedish, Swiss, U.S. and West German Law* (Zurich 1989)

Sareika, La clause compromissoire et l'article 68 du Code de procédure civile du Québec, 1977 *Rev. Arb.* 250

Sareika, W., *Die Gültigkeit von Schiedsgerichtsvereinbarungen nach kanadischem und deutschem Recht* (Frankfurt 1978)

Schizzerotto, G., *Dell'arbitrato* (Milan 3rd ed. 1988)

Schlosser, P., *Das Recht der internationalen privaten Schiedsgerichtsbarkeit* (2nd rev. ed. Tübingen 1989)

Schmidt, Präklusion und Einlassung auf die schiedsgerichtliche Verhandlung zur Hauptsache — Vertragsdenken und Prozessdenken in der jüngeren Praxis, in *Beiträge zum internationalen Verfahrensrecht und zur Schiedsgerichtsbarkeit. Festschrift für Heinrich Nagel* 373 (W. Habscheid & K. Schwab eds. 1987)

————, Statutarische Schiedsklauseln zwischen prozessualer und verbandsrechtlicher Legitimation: Ein Beitrag zum Anwendungsbereich des Par. 1048 *ZPO*, 44 *JZ* 1077 (1989)

Schönke, A., *Das Schiedsgerichtsverfahren nach dem heutigen deutschen Recht* (Berlin 1954)

Schütze, R., D. Tscherning & W. Wais, *Handbuch des Schiedsverfahrens. Praxis der deutschen und internationalen Schiedsgerichtsbarkeit* (2nd ed. Berlin 1990)

Sharkey, J. & J. Dorter, *Commercial Arbitration* (Sydney 1986)

Smit, A-National Arbitration, 63 *Tul. L. Rev.* 629 (1989)

Strieder, J., *Rechtliche Einordnung und Behandlung des Schiedsrichtervertrages* (Cologne 1984)

Suarez, La clausula compromisoria y el compromiso como motivos de excepción previa, 2 *Revista de la Universidad Externado de Colombia* 79 (1983)

Taha, Arbitration Clauses in Iraqi Contracts, 13 *Middle E. Exec. Rep.* 15 (No. 6, 1990)

ter Kuile, Internationale arbitrage en Gemeenschapsrecht, in *Iustitia et Amicitia. Geschillenbeslechting in en Buiten Rechte* 33 (Arnheim 1985)

Tschanz, La convention d'arbitrage, 1989 *Int'l Bus. L.J.* 749

Ulmer, Drafting the International Arbitration Clause, 20 *Int'l Law.* 1335 (1986)

van Houtte & Hudson, Les conventions d'arbitrage conclues entre partenaires commerciaux arabes et européens, 1990 *Int'l Bus. L.J.* 65

van den Berg, A. J., *The New York Arbitration Convention of 1958* (Deventer 1981)

Ventura, Convençao de arbitragem, 46 *Revista da Ordem dos Advogados* 289 (1986)

————, Convençao de arbitragem e clausulas contratuais gerais, 46 *Revista da Ordem dos Advogados* 5 (1986)

von Hülsen, H.-V., *Die Gültigkeit von internationalen Schiedsvereinbarungen* (Berlin 1973)

Weinreb, Arbitration Clauses in Multilateral International Agreements, 1975 *J. Bus. L.* 287

Wetter, Salient Features of Swedish Arbitration Clauses, 1983 *Y.B. Swed. & Int'l Arb.* 33

Zaccheo, Contratto e clausola compromissoria, 41 *Riv. Trim. Dir. & Proc. Civ.* 423 (1987)

8.02 REQUIREMENT OF WRITTEN FORM

Böckstiegel, Abschluss von Schiedsvertragen durch konkludentes Handeln oder Stillschweigen, in *Festschrift für Arthur Bülow* 1 (K.-H. Böckstiegel & O. Glossner eds. 1981)

Brierley, La validité de la clause compromissoire demeure-t-elle incertaine en droit québécois? 1975 *Rev. Arb.* 154

Bucher, A., *Die neue internationale Schiedsgerichtsbarkeit in der Schweiz* (Basel 1989)

————, *Le nouvel arbitrage international en Suisse. Théorie et pratique de droit* (Basel 1988)

Bucher, A. & P.-Y. Tschanz, *International Arbitration in Switzerland* (Basel 1989)

Cohen, De la validité formelle des clauses compromissoires conclues par télex, 75 *SJZ* 259 (1979)

de Bruin, De 'affaire C', 1989 *Tijdschrift voor Arbitrage* 1

Fasching, Die Form der Schiedsvereinbarung, 44 *ÖJZ* 289 (1989)

Holtzmann, H. & J. Neuhaus, *A Guide to the UNCITRAL Model Law on International Commercial Arbitration: Legislative History and Commentary* (Deventer 1989)

Kos-Rabcewicz-Zubkowski, Central and East European Rules on the Form of International Arbitration Agreement, 3 *La Revue Juridique Themis* 415 (1969)

Lew, Arbitration Agreements: Form and Character, in *Essays on International Commercial Arbitration* 51 (P. Sarcevic ed. 1989)

Mádl, Competence of Arbitral Tribunals in International Commercial Arbitration, in *Essays on International Commercial Arbitration* 92 (P. Sarcevic ed. 1989)

Mann, An 'Agreement in Writing' to Arbitrate, 3 *Arb. Int'l* 171 (1987)

Morviducci, La forma de la clausola compromissoria secondo la Convenzione di New York del 1958, 56 *Riv. Dir. Int'le* 732 (1973)

Picardi, La forme de la convention d'arbitrage, 26 *Rassegna dell'Arb.* 157 (1986)

Samuel, A., *Jurisdictional Problems in International Commercial Arbitration: A Study of Belgian, Dutch, English, French, Swedish, Swiss, U.S. and West German Law* (Zurich 1989)

Sandrock, Arbitration between U.S. and West German Companies: An Example of Effective Dispute Resolution in International Business Transactions, 9 *U. Pa. J. Int'l Bus. L.* 27 (1987)

Schwartz, La forme écrite de l'art. II, al. 2 de la Convention de New York pour la reconnaissance et l'exécution des sentences arbitrales étrangères du 10 juin 1958, 64 *SJZ* 49 (1968)

van den Berg, A. J., *The New York Arbitration Convention of 1958* (Deventer 1981)

Ventura, Convençao de arbitragem e clausulas contratuais gerais, 46 *Revista da Ordem dos Advogados* 5 (1986)

Wackenhuth, Die Schriftform für Schiedsvereinbarungen nach dem UN-Übereinkommen und Allgemeine Geschäftsbedingungen, 99 *ZZP* 445 (1986)

8.03 STANDARD AND MODEL ARBITRATION CLAUSES

Amerasinghe, How to Use the International Centre for Settlement of Investment Disputes by Reference to its Model Clauses, 13 *Indian J. Int'l L.* 530 (1973)

————, Model Clauses for Settlement of Foreign Investment Disputes, 28 *Arb. J.* 232 (1973)

Beyly, The Manager and Arbitration, 3 *J. Int'l Arb.* 7 (No. 1, 1986)

Bond, How to Draft an Arbitration Clause, 6 *J. Int'l Arb.* 65 (No. 2, 1989)

Branson & Tupman, Selecting an Arbitral Forum: A Guide to Cost-Effective International Arbitration, 24 *Va. J. Int'l L.* 917 (1984)

Brenner, International Arbitration: There Is No Standard Clause, 49 *Arbitration* 20 (August 1983)

Coulson, Soviet-American Contract Arbitration, 1983 *Y.B. Swed. & Int'l Arb.* 20

de Bruin, De 'affaire C,' 1989 *Tijdschrift voor Arbitrage* 1

Derman, Nationalization and the Protective Arbitration Clause, 5 *J. Int'l Arb.* 131 (No. 4, 1988)

Gaillard, Some Notes on the Drafting of ICSID Arbitration Clauses, 3 *ICSID Rev. - Foreign Investment L.J.* 136 (1988)

Gumbel, Thoughts on Arbitration under Reinsurance Contracts and on an Attempt to Draft a Standard Clause, in *Festschrift für Reimer Schmidt* 883 (Karlsruhe 1976); reprinted in 45 *Arbitration* 257 (1979)

Lebedev, The 1977 Optional Clause for Soviet-American Contracts, 27 *Am. J. Comp. L.* 469 (1979)

Lee, E., *Encyclopedia of International Commercial Arbitration* (London 1986)

Lew, Arbitration Agreements: Form and Character, in *Essays on International Commercial Arbitration* 51 (P. Sarcevic ed. 1989)

Pestalozzi, The Validity of Arbitration Clauses under N.Y. UCC 2-207 (The Battle of Forms), in *Dr. Lee Jaechul, In Celebration of His 60th Birthday, 2 Studies on Modern Civil & Commercial Law* 615 (1984)

Redfern, A. & M. Hunter, *Law and Practice of International Commercial Arbitration* (London 1986)

Rhodes & Sloan, The Pitfalls of International Commercial Arbitration, 17 *Vand. J. Transnat'l L.* 19 (1984)

Sanders, Arbitration Clause for Optional Use in USA-USSR Trade, 3 *Y.B. Com. Arb.* 299 (1978)

Tetley, Arbitration Clauses in Ocean Bills of Lading, 2 *Y.B. Mar. L.* 51 (1985—1986)

Ulmer, Drafting the International Arbitration Clause, 20 *Int'l Law.* 1335 (1986)

8.04 SEPARABILITY

Bedell, Harrison & Grant, Arbitrability: Current Developments in the Interpretation and Enforceability of Arbitration Agreements, 13 *J. Contemp. L.* 1 (1987)

Budin, Nature et cessibilité d'une convention d'arbitrage en droit suisse, 1979 *Rev. Arb.* 435

Doi, The Effect of an Arbitration Clause in a Voidable Contract: Separability Doctrine Adopted by the Supreme Court of Japan, in *Law in East and West/ Recht in Ost und West* 609 (Tokyo 1988)

Furnish, Commercial Arbitration Agreements and the Uniform Commercial Code, 67 *Calif. L. Rev.* 317 (1979)

Gardner, The Doctrine of Separability in Soviet Arbitration Law: An Analysis of Sojuzneftexport v. JOC Oil Co., 28 *Colum. J. Transnat'l L.* 301 (1990)

Goldman, International Arbitration in Europe, in *IBA, Soviet Foreign Trade Reforms & East/West Arbitration* 217 (1988)

Grigera Naón, La autonomia del acuerdo arbitral, *La Ley*, Sept. 5, 1989

————, The Scope of the Separability of the Arbitration Agreement under Argentine Law, 1 *Am. Rev. Int'l Arb.* 261 (1990)

Groos, Schiedsgerichtsbarkeit im deutsch-französischen Wirtschaftsverkehr, 33 *RIW* 343 (1987)

Hobér, Arbitration in Moscow, 3 *Arb. Int'l* 119 (1987)

————, The Doctrine of Separability under Swedish Arbitration Law, Including Comments on the Position of American and Soviet Law, 68 *Svensk Juristtidning* 257 (1983)

Klein, Du caractère autonome de la clause compromissoire, notamment en matière d'arbitrage international, 50 *Rev. Crit. Droit Int'l Privé* 499 (1961)

Lebedev, S., *Mezhdunarodnyi kommercheskii arbitrazh: kompetentsia arbitrov i soglashenie stran* (Moscow 1988)

Lessing, Sauer-Getriebe K.G. v. White Hydraulics, Inc.— Applicability of the Federal Arbitration Act to International Commercial Arbitration, 2 *Int'l Tax & Bus. Law.* 331 (1984)

Lew, Arbitration Agreements: Form and Character, in *Essays on International Commercial Arbitration* 51 (P. Sarcevic ed. 1989)

Mádl, Competence of Arbitral Tribunals in International Commercial Arbitration, in *Essays on International Commercial Arbitration* 92 (P. Sarcevic ed. 1989)

Paulsson, The Contribution of English and American Legislation, in *Euro-Arab Arbitration III* 104 (F. Kemicha ed. 1991)

Redfern, The Jurisdiction of an International Commercial Arbitrator, 3 *J. Int'l Arb.* 19 (1986); also 52 *Arbitrator* 254 (1986)

Saario, The Doctrine of the Autonomy of the Arbitration Clause, 1987 *Tidskrift, utgiven av Juridiska Forenningen i Finland* 358

Sajko, The New York Arbitration Convention of 1958 from the Yugoslav Point of View: Selected Issues, in *Essays on International Commercial Arbitration* 199 (P. Sarcevic ed. 1989)

Samuel, Developments in English Arbitration Law since the 1984 Antaios Decision, 5 *J. Int'l Arb.* 9 (No. 3, 1988)

————, Separability in English Law — Should an Arbitration Clause Be Regarded as an Agreement Separate and Collateral to a Contract in Which It Is Contained? 3 *J. Int'l Arb.* 95 (No. 3, 1986)

Samuel, A., *Jurisdictional Problems in International Commercial Arbitration: A Study of Belgian, Dutch, English, French, Swedish, Swiss, U.S. and West German Law* (Zurich 1989)

Sanders, L'autonomie de la clause compromissoire, in *ICC, Hommage à Fréderic Eisemann* 31 (1978)

Sandrock, Arbitration between U.S. and West German Companies: An Example of Effective Dispute Resolution in International Business Transactions, 9 *U. Pa. J. Int'l Bus. L.* 27 (1987)

Sanoff, SNE v. JOC Oil Ltd.: A Recent Development in the Theory of the Separability of the Arbitration Clause, 1 *Am. Rev. Int'l Arb.* 157 (1990)

Schlosser, P., *Das Recht der internationalen privaten Schiedsgerichtsbarkeit* (2nd rev. ed. Tübingen 1989)

Schwab, Die Entscheidung des Schiedsgerichts über seine eigene Zuständigkeit: Eine Stellungsnahme zum Verhältnis von Hauptvertrag und Schiedsvertrag und zur sog. Kompetenz-Kompetenz des Schiedsgerichts, 22 *KTS* 17 (1961)

Schwebel, S.M., *International Arbitration: Three Salient Problems* (Cambridge 1987)

Strenger, Do juizo arbitral, 607 *Rev. Trib.* 24 (May 1986)

Tschanz, La convention d'arbitrage, 1989 *Int'l Bus. L.J.* 749

van den Berg, A.J., *The New York Arbitration Convention of 1958* (Deventer 1981)

Ventura, Convençao de arbitragem, 46 *Revista da Ordem dos Advogados* 289 (1986)

Wetter, The Importance of Having a Connection, 3 *Arb. Int'l* 329 (1987)

Zaccheo, Contratto e clausola compromissoria, 41 *Riv. Trim. Dir. & Proc. Civ.* 423 (1987)

8.05 LAW APPLICABLE TO ARBITRATION AGREEMENT

Bogdan, Some Arbitration-related Problems of Swedish Private International Law, 1990 *Y.B. Swed. & Int'l Arb.* 70

Nuber, J., *Die objektive Schiedsfähigkeit im Zusammenhang mit der Gültigkeit der Schiedsvereinbarung (anwendbares Recht) und mit der Vollstreckung (ordre public),* (Zurich 1986)

Tschanz, La convention d'arbitrage, 1989 *Int'l Bus. L.J.* 749

van Niekerk, Aspects of Proper Law, Curial Law and International Commercial Arbitration, 2 *S.A. Mercantile L.J.* 117 (1990)

von Hülsen, H.-V., *Die Gültigkeit von internationalen Schiedsvereinbarungen* (Berlin 1973)

8.06 OPERATION AND EFFECT

Bentil, Judicial Intervention and International Commercial Arbitration, 130 *Solicitors' J.* 191 (1986)

Berger, The Modern Trend Towards Exclusion of Recourse Against Transnational Arbitral Awards: A European Perspective, 12 *Fordham Int'l L. J.* 605 (1989)

Bucher, Les voies de recours, 1989 *Int'l Bus. L.J.* 771

Delaume, The Finality of Arbitration Involving States: Recent Developments, 5 *Arb. Int'l* 21 (1989)

Doi, International Commercial Arbitration in Japan, in *Liber Amicorum for Martin Domke* 65 (P. Sanders ed. 1967)

Eisemann, Arbitrage et garanties contractuelles (garanties de soumission, de bonne exécution et de remboursement), in *ICCA, Fourth Int'l Arb. Congress: Proceedings* 151 (1972)

Garro, Enforcement of Arbitration Agreements and Jurisdiction of Arbitral Tribunals in Latin America, 1 *J. Int'l Arb.* 293 (No. 4, 1984)

Goldman, International Arbitration in Europe, in *IBA, Soviet Foreign Trade Reforms & East/West Arbitration* 217 (1988)

Heuman, L., *Current Issues in Swedish Arbitration* (Deventer and Stockholm 1990)

Hobér, Arbitration in Moscow, 3 *Arb. Int'l* 119 (1987)

Kos-Rabcewicz-Zubkowski, Absolute Lack of Jurisdiction of Courts When an Undertaking to Arbitrate is Stipulated in a Contract, 24 *Inter-American Bar Association Conference: Proceedings* 143 (Panama, Feb. 4-10, 1984)

Lalive, The New Swiss Law on International Arbitration, 4 *Arb. Int'l* 2 (1988)

Lew, Arbitration Agreements: Form and Character, in *Essays on International Commercial Arbitration* 51 (P. Sarcevic ed. 1989)

Malik, Arbitration Clause in an International Contract: Whether a Bar to Local Civil Jurisdiction, 8 *Indian J. Leg. Studies* 160 (1988)

Mustill, Sir Michael J. & S. C. Boyd, *The Law and Practice of Commercial Arbitration in England* (2nd ed. 1989)

Poudret, Challenge and Enforcement of Arbitral Awards in Switzerland, 4 *Arb. Int'l* 278 (1988)

Pryles, Comparative Aspects of Prorogation and Arbitration Agreements, 25 *Int'l & Comp. L.Q.* 543 (1976)

Redfern, International Commercial Arbitration: Winning the Battle, in *Private Investors Abroad— Problems and Solutions in International Business in 1989* 11-1 (C. Holgren ed. 1989)

Rhodes, Judicial Review of Commercial Arbitration, 14 *Hong Kong L.J.* 159 (1984)

Schmidt, Präklusion und Einlassung auf die schiedsgerichtliche Verhandlung zur Hauptsache — Vertragsdenken und Prozessdenken in der jüngeren Praxis, in *Beiträge zum internationalen Verfahrensrecht und zur Schiedsgerichtsbarkeit. Festschrift für Heinrich Nagel* 373 (W. Habscheid & K. Schwab eds. 1987)

Schmitthoff, C., *Schmitthoff's Export Trade. The Law and Practice of International Trade* (8th ed. 1986)

Thomas, Restraining Concurrent Foreign Legal Proceedings, 1983 *Lloyd's Mar. & Com. L.Q.* 692

Ventura, Convençao de arbitragem, 46 *Revista da Ordem dos Advogados* 289 (1986)

8.07 DEFECTS AND INVALIDITY

Brierley, La validité de la clause compromissoire demeure-t-elle incertaine en droit québécois? 1975 *Rev. Arb.* 154

de Nova, Nullità del contratto e arbitrato irrituale, 45 *Riv. Trim. Dir. & Proc. Civ.* 401 (1991)

Eisemann, La clause d'arbitrage pathologique, in *A.I.A., Essays in Memoriam Eugenio Minoli* 129 (Turin 1974)

Foussard, Le juge administratif et l'arbitrage (Remarques à propos de l'arrêt A.R.E.A. du Conseil d'Etat du 3 mars 1989), 1989 *Rev. Arb.* 167

Laschet, Rechtsmittel gegen Prozess-, Vorab- oder Zwischenentscheidungen eines Schiedsgerichtes oder einer Schiedsgerichtsorganisation, in *Beiträge zum internationalen Verfahrensrechts und zur Schiedsgerichtbarkeit. Festschrift für Heinrich Nagel* 167 (W. Habscheid & K. Schwab eds. 1987)

Mustill, Sir Michael J. & S. C. Boyd, *The Law and Practice of Commercial Arbitration in England* (2nd ed. 1989)

Park & Paulsson, Arbitrage commercial et contrats internationaux, 45 *Rev. Barreau* 215 (1985)

Scalbert & Marville, Les clauses compromissoires pathologiques, 1988 *Rev. Arb.* 117

Schmitthoff, Defective Arbitration Clauses, 1975 *J. Bus. L.* 9

van den Berg, A.J., *The New York Arbitration Convention of 1958* (Deventer 1981)

Ventura, Convençao de arbitragem, 46 *Revista da Ordem dos Advogados* 289 (1986)

Warren, The Concept of 'Null and Void' in International Commercial Arbitration, 45 *Arb. J.* 57 (No. 4, 1990)

8.08 TERMINATION

Deshpande, Court, Contract and Arbitration, 26 *J. Ind. L. Inst.* 378 (1984)

Hobér, Schiedsort Stockholm: Verjährung und das anzuwendende Recht, 2 *Jahrbuch Schiedsgerichtsbarkeit* 80 (1988)

Keane, Waiver of Maritime Arbitration, 8 *J. Mar. L. & Com.* 195 (1977)

Paulsson, May a State Invoke Its Internal Law to Repudiate Consent to International Commercial Arbitration? Reflections on the Benteler v. Belgium Preliminary Award, 2 *Arb. Int'l* 90 (1986)

Philippe, Pacta sunt servanda et rebus sic stantibus, in *ICC, L'apport de la jurisprudence arbitrale* 181 (1986)

Poznanski, The Nature and Extent of an Arbitrator's Power in International Commercial Arbitration, 4 *J. Int'l Arb.* 71 (No. 3, 1987)

Raeschke-Kessler & Bühler, Aufsicht über den Schiedsrichter durch den ICC-Schiedsgerichtshof (Paris) und rechtliches Gehör der Parteien, 8 *ZIP* 1157 (1987)

Ventura, Convençao de arbitragem, 46 *Revista da Ordem dos Advogados* 289 (1986)

8.09 ENFORCEABILITY OF ARBITRATION AGREEMENTS

Ebb, Developing Views on What Constitutes a 'Foreign Arbitration Agreement' and a 'Foreign Award' under the New York Convention, 1 *Am. Rev. Int'l Arb.* 364 (1990)

Ginsburgs, G., *The Soviet Union and International Cooperation in Legal Matters. Part I: Recognition of Arbitral Agreements and Execution of Foreign Commercial Arbitral Awards* (Dordrecht 1988)

Kahale, New Legislation in the United States Facilitates Enforcement of Arbitral Agreements and Awards Against Foreign States, 6 *J. Int'l Arb.* 57 (No. 2, 1989)

McDermott, Enforcement of Arbitration Agreements in the United States and in the Asia-Pacific Region, 10 *Loy. L.A. Int'l & Comp. L.J.* 615 (1988)

Pisar, S., *Coexistence & Commerce*, Chapters 20-24 (New York 1970)

Pryles, Legal Issues Concerning International Arbitrations, 64 *Austl. L.J.* 470 (1990)

Reder, Securities Law and Arbitration: The Enforceability of Predispute Arbitration Clauses in Broker-Customer Agreements, 1990 *Colum. Bus. L. Rev.* 91

Schütze, Zur Wirksamkeit von internationalen Schiedsvereinbarungen und zur Wirkungserstreckung ausländischer Schiedssprüche über Ansprüche aus Börsentermingeschäften, 1 *Jahrbuch Schiedsgerichtsbarkeit* 94 (1987)

Sutti, Giurisdizione italiana ed arbitrato estero: problemi di connessione, 26 *Riv. Dir. Int'le Priv. & Proc.* 631 (1990)

Young, Arbitration and the European Communities' Judgments Convention, in *International Commercial and Maritime Arbitration* 77 (F.D. Rose ed. 1988)

9. ARBITRATION AND THIRD PARTIES

9.01 THIRD PARTIES IN ARBITRAL PROCEEDINGS

Chapelle, L'arbitrage et les tiers: le droit des personnes morales (groupes de sociétés; interventions d'Etat), 1988 *Rev. Arb.* 475

Delvolvé, L'arbitrage et les tiers: le droit de l'arbitrage: les solutions contractuelles: la clause d'arbitrage multipartite, 1988 *Rev. Arb.* 501

Goutal, L'arbitrage et les tiers: le droit des contrats, 1988 *Rev. Arb.* 439

Matray, Quelques problèmes de l'arbitrage commercial international (doctrine et jurisprudence), in *L'Arbitrage* 289 (L. Matray & G. de Leval eds. 1989)

Mustill, Sir Michael J. & S. C. Boyd, *The Law and Practice of Commercial Arbitration in England* (2nd ed. 1989)

Oppetit, L'arbitrage et les tiers: présentation générale, 1988 *Rev. Arb.* 433

Rubellin-Devichi, L'arbitrage et les tiers: le droit de l'arbitrage: les solutions juridictionnelles, 1988 *Rev. Arb.* 515

Tan, Multiple Parties and Causes of Action in Arbitration Proceedings, 1988 *Malayan L.J.* li

10. MULTI-PARTY ARBITRATION

10.01 MULTIPLE PARTIES IN ARBITRATION

Aksen, Les arbitrages multiparties aux Etats-Unis, 1981 *Rev. Arb.* 98

―――, Multi-party Arbitrations in the United States, in *Arbitration and the Licensing Process* 5-3 (R. Goldscheider & M. de Haas eds. 1984-)

Alvarez, The Role of Arbitration in Canada — New Perspectives, 21 *U. B.C. L. Rev.* 247 (1987)

Arbitration Institute of the Stockholm Chamber of Commerce, *Arbitration in Sweden* (2nd rev. ed. 1984)

Austmann, Commercial Multi-Party Arbitration: A Case-by-Case Approach, 1 *Am. Rev. Int'l Arb.* 341 (1990)

Bartels, Multiparty Arbitration Clauses, 2 *J. Int'l Arb.* 61 (No. 2, 1985)

Bernini, L'arbitrato nelle controversie commerciali che interessano più di due parti, 20 *Rassegna dell'Arb.* 127 (1980)

Braggion, Validity of Multi-Party Arbitration Clauses under Italian Law, 18 *Int'l Bus. Law.* 412 (1990)

―――, La validité en droit italien des clauses d'arbitrage multipartite et ses conséquences aux effets de l'exécution des sentences arbitrales sur la base de la Convention de New York de 1958, 1991 *Int'l Bus. L.J.* 847

Braun, A., ed., *L'arbitrage/Het scheidsgerecht* (Brussels 1983)

Colman, A.D., *The Practice and Procedure of the Commercial Court* (2nd ed. London 1986)

Cremades, El grupo de empresas y su tratamiento en el arbitraje comercial internacional, in *El Arbitraje en el Derecho Latinoamericano y Español* 295 (L. Perret & U. Montoya Alberti eds. 1989)

Delvolvé, L'arbitrage et les tiers: le droit de l'arbitrage: les solutions contractuelles: la clause d'arbitrage multipartite, 1988 *Rev. Arb.* 501

Derains & Schaf, Clauses d'arbitrage et groupes de sociétés, 1985 *Int'l Bus. L.J.* 231

Devitt, Multiparty Controversies in International Construction Arbitrations, 17 *Int'l Law.* 669 (1983)

Dika, The Problem of Multiparty Arbitration from the Standpoint of Yugoslav Law, in 5 *Hague-Zagreb Essays* 125 (C. Voskuil & J. Wade eds. 1985)

Dore, I., *Theory and Practice of Multiparty Commercial Arbitration, With Special Reference to the UNCITRAL Framework* (London 1990)

Duintjer Tebbens, A Facelift for Dutch Arbitration Law, 34 *Neth. Int'l L. Rev.* 141 (1987)

Eisemann, Multiparty International Business Disputes — Minimizing the Risks of Conflicting Decisions, 1 *Int'l Contr.* 43 (1980)

El-Hakim, Multilaterale Streitigkeiten im Rahmen von Schiedsverfahren bei Wirtschaftprojekten im Nahen Osten, in *Vertragspraxis und Streiterledigung im Wirtschaftverkehr mit arabischen Staaten* 83 (K.-H. Böckstiegel ed. 1981)

Franks, A Further Approach to Multilateral Arbitration, in *ICCA, Sixth Int'l Arb. Congress: Proceedings* 127 (1978)

Fraser, International Arbitration of Multi-Party Contract Disputes: The Need for Change, 6 *Loy. L.A. Int'l & Comp. L.J.* 427 (1983)

Gaillard, L'affaire SOFIDIF ou les difficultés de l'arbitrage multipartite (à propos de l'arrêt rendu par la Cour d'Appel de Paris le 19 décembre 1986), 1987 *Rev. Arb.* 275

Habscheid, Zum Problem der Mehrparteienschiedsgerichtsbarkeit, in *Recueil de Travaux Suisses* 173 (C. Reymond & E. Bucher eds. 1984)

International Chamber of Commerce, *Guide on Multi-party Arbitration — According to the Rules of the ICC Court of Arbitration* (Paris 1982)

————, *Multi-party Arbitration* (Paris 1991)

Jakubowski, L'arbitrage international dans les litiges commerciaux multilatéraux, 1981 *Rev. Arb.* 66; also 49 *Droit polonais contemporain* 27 (1981)

Jarvin, Choosing the Place of Arbitration: Where Do We Stand? 16 *Int'l Bus. Law.* 417 (1988)

————, Multi-Party Arbitration: Identifying the Issues, 8 *N.Y.L. Sch. J. Int'l & Comp. L.* 317 (1987)

————, Settling International Business Disputes: Recent Developments, *Int'l Fin. L. Rev.* 16 (No. 2, Feb. 1984)

Kassis, L'arbitrage multipartite et les clauses de consolidation, 14 *Droit et Pratique du Com. Int'l* 221 (1988)

Laschet, Die Mehrparteienschiedsgerichtsbarkeit, in *Festschrift für Arthur Bülow* 85 (K.-H. Böckstiegel & O. Glossner eds. 1981)

Leboulanger, Groupes d'Etat(s) et l'arbitrage, 1989 *Rev. Arb.* 415

Luther, Das Drei-Mann-Schiedsgericht bei der Entscheidung von Streitigkeiten zwischen drei oder mehr Vertragspartnern, in *Festschrift für Ernst von Caemmerer* 571 (Tübingen 1978)

McCormack, Arbitration in Combined Transportation — A Rare Bird, in *Arbitration in Settlement of International Commercial Disputes Involving the Far East and Arbitration in Combined Transportation* 325 (P. Sanders ed. 1989)

Medalie, The Libyan Producers' Agreement Arbitration: Developing Innovative Procedures in a Complex Multiparty Arbitration, 7 *J. Int'l Arb.* 7 (No. 2, 1990)

Melis, Praktische und prozedurale Probleme mit Mehrparteienschiedsgerichten bei komplexen Langzeitvertragen, in *Der komplexe Langzeitvertrag/ The Complex Long-Term Contract* 569 (F. Nicklisch ed. 1987)

Mustill, Sir Michael J. & S. C. Boyd, *The Law and Practice of Commercial Arbitration in England* (2nd ed. 1989)

Polish Chamber of Foreign Trade, *International Arbitration in Multi-Party Commercial Disputes; Materials of an International Symposium, Warsaw, June 29th - July 2nd, 1980* (Warsaw 1982)

Reymond, Des connaissances personnelles de l'arbitre à son information privilégiée, 1991 *Rev. Arb.* 3

Rubino-Sammartano, Multi-Party Arbitration, 9 *Int'l Bus. Law.* 436 (1981)

Schlosser, Party-Appointed Arbitrators and Multiple Defendants Having Conflicting Interests, in *Law in East and West/Recht in Ost und West* 739 (Tokyo 1988)

Schwab, Mehrparteien-schiedsgerichtsbarkeit und Streitgenossenschaft, in *Festschrift für Walther J. Habscheid* 285 (W. Lindacher, D. Pfaff et al. eds. 1989)

Schwartz, Multiparty Disputes and Consolidated Arbitrations: An Oxymoron or the Solution to a Continuing Dilemma? 22 *Case W. Res. J. Int'l L.* 341 (1990)

Seppala & Gogek, Multi-Party Arbitration under ICC Rules, 9 *Int'l Fin. L. Rev.* 32 (No. 11, 1989)

Stipanowich, Arbitration and the Multiparty Dispute: The Search for Workable Solutions., 72 *Iowa L. Rev.* 473 (1987)

Tan, Multiple Parties and Causes of Action in Arbitration Proceedings, 1988 *Malayan L.J.* li

Tandeau de Marsac, Multi-Party Arbitration: Problems and Remedies, 2 *Int'l Contr.* 31 (1981)

van Compernolle, L'arbitrage dans les relations commerciales internationales: questions de procédure, 66 *Rev. Droit Int'l & Droit Comp.* 101 (1989)

————, L'arbitrage multipartite, in *L'Arbitrage* 81 (L. Matray & G. de Leval eds. 1989)

van den Berg, A. J., *The New York Arbitration Convention of 1958* (Deventer 1981)

van Marwijk Kooy, Multi-Party Arbitration, in 5 *Hague-Zagreb Essays* 139 (C. Voskuil & J. Wade eds. 1985)

Veeder, Multi-Party Disputes: Consolidation under English Law, 2 *Arb. Int'l* 310 (1986)

Ventura, Convençao de arbitragem, 46 *Revista da Ordem dos Advogados* 289 (1986)

von Hoffmann, International Construction Arbitration, in *Essays on International Commercial Arbitration* 223 (P. Sarcevic ed. 1989)

————, Mehrparteienschiedsgerichtsbarkeit und Internationale Handelskammer, in *Beiträge zum internationalen Verfahrensrecht und zur Schiedsgerichtsbarkeit. Festschrift für Heinrich Nagel* 112 (W. Habscheid & K. Schwab eds. 1987)

Weinreb, Arbitration Clauses in Multilateral International Agreements, 1975 *J. Bus. L.* 287

Wetter, A Multi-Party Arbitration Scheme for International Joint Ventures, 3 *Arb. Int'l* 2 (No. 1, 1987)

11. ARBITRATORS AND ARBITRAL TRIBUNALS

11.01 IN GENERAL

Arbitration Institute of the Stockholm Chamber of Commerce, *Arbitration in Sweden* (2nd rev. ed. 1984)

Aylwin Azocar, P., *El juicio arbitral* (Santiago de Chile 1958)

Bartos, H., *Internationale Handelsschiedsgerichtsbarkeit: Verfahrensprinzipien* (Frankfurt 1984)

Blessing, The Major Western and Soviet Arbitration Rules: A Comparison of the Rules of UNCITRAL, UNCITRAL Model Law, LCIA, ICC, AAA and the Rules of the USSR Chamber of Commerce and Industry, 6 *J. Int'l Arb.* 7 (No. 3,1989)

Bond, The International Arbitrator: From the Perspective of the ICC International Court of Arbitration, 12 *Nw. J. Int'l L. & Bus.* 1 (1991)

Chillón Medina, J. M. & J. F. Merino Merchán, *Tratado de arbitraje privado interno e internacional* (Madrid 1978)

David, L'obligation pour les arbitres de statuer en droit dans les arbitrages de commerce international, in *Problèmes de droit contempotain: mélanges Louis Baudouin* 305 (1974)

David, R., *Arbitration in International Trade* (Deventer 1985)

Delaume, L'arbitrage transnational et les tribunaux nationaux, 111 *J. Droit Int'l (Clunet)* 521 (1984)

Derains, Y., ed., *Droit et pratique de l'arbitrage international en France* (Paris 1984)

Dunshee de Abranches, C.A., ed., *El arbitraje comercial en Iberoamérica* (Madrid 1982)

Eyzaguirre Echeverria, R., *El arbitraje comercial en la legislación chileña y su regulación international* (Santiago de Chile 1981)

Feuerle, International Arbitration and Choice of Law Under Art. 42 of the Convention on the Settlement of Investment Disputes, 4 *Yale Stud. World Pub. Ord.* 89 (1977)

Goldstajn, Choice of International Arbitrators, Arbitral Tribunals and Centres: Legal and Sociological Aspects, in *Essays on International Commercial Arbitration* 27 (P. Sarcevic ed. 1989)

Goodman-Everard, Cultural Diversity in International Arbitration — A Challenge for Decision-Makers and Decision-Making, 7 *Arb. Int'l* 155 (1991)

Henn, G., *Schiedsverfahrensrecht: ein Handbuch* (Heidelberg 1986)

Jagenburg, Schiedsgerichtsbarkeit zwischen Wunsch und Wirklichkeit, in *Festschrift für Walter Oppenhoff zum 80. Geburtstag* 147 (W. Jagenburg, G. Maier-Reimer & T. Verhoeven eds. 1985)

Keilin, A.D., *Sudoustroistvo i grazhdanskii protsess kapitalisticheskikh gosudarstv. III - Arbitrazh* (Moscow 1961)

Kessler, J., *Schiedsgerichtsvertrag und Schiedsverfahren* (Munich 1970)

Lee, E., *Encyclopedia of International Commercial Arbitration* (London 1986)

Loussouarn, Les arbitres, in *Droit et pratique de l'arbitrage international en France* 37 (Y. Derains ed. Paris 1984)

Montealegre Escobar, Los arbitros en el derecho colombiano y en El Centro de Arbitraje y Conciliación Mercantiles de la Cámara de Comercio de Bogotá, in *El Arbitraje en el Derecho Latinoamericano y Español* 249 (L. Perret & U. Montoya Alberti eds. 1989)

Moreau, B. & T. Bernard, *Droit interne et droit international de l'arbitrage* (2nd ed. 1985)

Mustill, Sir Michael J. & S.C. Boyd, *The Law and Practice of Commercial Arbitration in England* (2nd ed. 1989)

Nordenson, The Arbitral Tribunal, 1990 *Y.B. Swed. & Int'l Arb.* 19

Redfern, A. & M. Hunter, *Law and Practice of International Commercial Arbitration* (2nd ed. 1991)

Reiner, Die internationale Schiedsgerichtsbarkeit nach österreichischem und französischem Recht. Ein Vergleich zweier Reformen jüngeren Datums, 27 *ZRV* 162 (1986)

Robert, J. & B. Morceau, *L'arbitrage — droit interne, droit international privé* (5th ed. Paris 1983)

Rubino-Sammartano, M., *International Arbitration Law* (Deventer 1990)

Russell, F., *Russell on the Law of Arbitration* (20th ed. by A. Walton & M. Vitoria 1982)

Schizzerotto, G., *Dell'arbitrato* (Milan 3rd ed. 1988)

Schmitthoff, C., *Schmitthoff's Export Trade. The Law and Practice of International Trade* (8th ed. 1986)

Schönke, A., *Das Schiedsgerichtsverfahren nach dem heutigen deutschen Recht* (Berlin 1954)

Schütze, R., D. Tscherning & W. Wais, *Handbuch des Schiedsverfahrens. Praxis der deutschen und internationalen Schiedsgerichtsbarkeit* (2nd ed. Berlin 1990)

Sharkey, J. & J. Dorter, *Commercial Arbitration* (Sydney 1986)

Strenger, Do juizo arbitral, 607 *Rev. Trib.* 24 (May 1986)

Vassogne, L'arbitre, le juge et l'ordre public économique (remarques adventices), 1987 *Rev. Arb.* 87

11.02 COMPOSITION OF ARBITRAL TRIBUNAL

Ball, Structuring the Arbitration in Advance — the Arbitration Clause in an International Development Agreement, in *Contemporary Problems in International Arbitration* 297 (J.D.M. Lew ed. 1986)

Blessing, International Arbitration Procedures, 17 *Int'l Bus. Law.* 408 and 451(1989)

de Leval, La designation et la mission des arbitres. Notes succinctes sur le droit positif applicable en Belgique, 53 *Rev. Droit Int'l & Droit Comp.* 170 (1976)

Glossner, The Conduct of ICC Arbitration Proceedings, in *Contemporary Problems in International Arbitration* 210 (J.D.M. Lew ed. 1986)

Goldstajn, Choice of International Arbitrators, Arbitral Tribunals and Centres: Legal and Sociological Aspects, in *Essays on International Commercial Arbitration* 27 (P. Sarcevic ed. 1989)

Helal, International Commercial Arbitration, 53 *Arbitration* 258 (1987)

Herrmann, The UNCITRAL Model Law on International Commercial Arbitration — Its Salient Features and Prospects, in *First Int'l Commercial Arbitration Conference: Proceedings* 351 (N. Antaki & A. Prujiner eds. 1986)

Hintz, Recht und Praxis der Streiterledigung im Ost-West-Handel am Beispiel des Handels zwischen der UdSSR und der Bundesrepublik Deutschland, 32 *RIW* 506 (1986)

Holtzmann & Bernini, Hypothetical Case for Use in a Comparative Study of Arbitration Practice in Various Legal Systems, in *Comparative Arbitration Practice and Public Policy in Arbitration* 19 (P. Sanders ed. 1987)

Holtzmann H. & J. Neuhaus, *A Guide to the UNCITRAL Model Law on International Commercial Arbitration: Legislative History and Commentary* (Deventer 1989)

Littman, Composition of Arbitral Tribunal and Making the Award, 24 *Rassegna dell'Arb.* 37 (1984)

McCormack, A Lawyer's View of Arbitration Proceedings and Composition of the Arbitration Panel, 1984 *Y.B. Mar. Law* 55

Nordenson, The Arbitral Tribunal, 1990 *Y.B. Swed. & Int'l Arb.* 19

Orsini, Sole Arbitrator or a Three Person Board, and When, in 1 *Fifth Int'l Congress of Maritime Arbitrators* (New York 1981)

Prujiner, La gestion des arbitrages commerciaux internationaux: l'exemple de la Cour d'arbitrage de la CCI, 115 *J. Droit Int'l (Clunet)* 662 (1988)

Subramanian, Composition of Arbitral Tribunals, in *ICCA, Third Int'l Arb. Congress: Proceedings* 553 (1969)

Voskuil & Freedberg-Swartzburg, Composition of the Arbitral Tribunal, in *Essays on International Commercial Arbitration* 64 (P. Sarcevic ed. 1989)

Voûte, Een partij-arbiter in Hong Kong, 1988 *Tijdschrift voor Arbitrage* 184

11.03 DESIGNATION OF ARBITRATORS

Bond, How to Draft an Arbitration Clause, 6 *J. Int'l Arb.* 65 (No. 2, 1989)

Branson & Tupman, Selecting an Arbitral Forum: A Guide to Cost-Effective International Arbitration, 24 *Va. J. Int'l L.* 917 (1984)

Bucher, A., *Die neue internationale Schiedsgerichtsbarkeit in der Schweiz* (Basel 1989)

————, *Le nouvel arbitrage international en Suisse. Théorie et pratique de droit* (Basel 1988)

Bucher, A. & P.-Y. Tschanz, *International Arbitration in Switzerland* (Basel 1989)

Chowdhuri, S.K.R. & H.K. Saharay, *Arbitration Law.* 2nd ed. (Calcutta 1986)

Cox, The Selection Process and the Appointment of Arbitrators, 46 *Arb. J.* 28 (No. 2, 1991); also in *Commercial Arbitration for the 1990s* (R. Medalie ed. 1991)

Cremades, B.M., *Panorámica Española del Arbitraje Comercial Internacional* (Madrid 1975)

Dallal, Appointment of an Arbitrator under ICC Rules in Jordan, 2 *Int'l Constr. L. Rev.* 177 (1985)

de Leval, La designation et la mission des arbitres. Notes succinctes sur le droit positif applicable en Belgique, 53 *Rev. Droit Int'l & Droit Comp.* 170 (1976)

Derains, Mesures dilatoires en matière d'arbitrage et moyens de s'y opposer, in *Festschrift für Arthur Bülow* 31 (K.-H. Böckstiegel & O. Glossner eds. 1981)

Duintjer Tebbens, A Facelift for Dutch Arbitration Law, 34 *Neth. Int'l L. Rev.* 141 (1987)

Glossner, International Commercial Arbitration — Some Practical Aspects, in *Liber Amicorum for Martin Domke* 95 (P. Sanders ed. 1967)

Goldman, International Arbitration in Europe, in *IBA, Soviet Foreign Trade Reforms & East/West Arbitration* 217 (1988)

Hintz, Recht und Praxis der Streiterledigung im Ost-West-Handel am Beispiel des Handels zwischen der UdSSR und der Bundesrepublik Deutschland, 32 *RIW* 506 (1986)

Hobér, Arbitration in Moscow, 3 *Arb. Int'l* 119 (1987)

Holtzmann, H. & J. Neuhaus, *A Guide to the UNCITRAL Model Law on International Commercial Arbitration: Legislative History and Commentary* (Deventer 1989)

Indian Council of Arbitration, *International Seminar on Commercial Arbitration* (18-19 March 1968), (New Delhi 1968)

International Chamber of Commerce, *The Arbitral Process and the Independence of Arbitrators/La procédure arbitrale et l'indépendence des arbitres* (Paris 1991)

Karrer, Les rapports entre le tribunal arbitral, les tribunaux étatiques et l'institution arbitrale, 1989 *Int'l Bus. L.J.* 761

Klein, Zur Ernennung von Schiedsrichtern durch im voraus bezeichnete Dritte, 6 *IPRax* 53 (1986)

Kopelmanas, La rédaction des clauses d'arbitrage et le choix des arbitres, in *ICC, Hommage à Fréderic Eisemann* 23 (1978)

Lalive, The New Swiss Law on International Arbitration, 4 *Arb. Int'l* 2 (1988)

Mádl, Competence of Arbitral Tribunals in International Commercial Arbitration, in *Essays on International Commercial Arbitration* 92 (P. Sarcevic ed. 1989)

Matray, Rédaction d'une clause d'arbitrage et choix d'arbitres compétents en matière internationale, 56 *Rev. Droit Int'l & Droit Comp.* 51 (1979)

Mirabelli, Contratti nell'arbitrato (con l'arbitro; con l'istituzione arbitrale), 30 *Rassegna dell'Arb.* 3 (1990)

Mustill, Sir Michael J. & S. C. Boyd, *The Law and Practice of Commercial Arbitration in England* (2nd ed. 1989)

Nagel, Gedanken über die Beschleunigung des Schiedsverfahren, in *Festschrift für Karl Firsching* 191 (Munich 1985)

Nanowski, Authority Being Competent to Nominate Arbitrators Substitutionally, in *ICCA, Fifth Int'l Arb. Congress: Proceedings* C Io 1-11 (1975)

Paterson, International Commercial Arbitration Act: An Overview, in *UNCITRAL Arbitration Model in Canada* 113 (R. Paterson & B. Thompson eds. 1987)

Paulsson, The Contribution of English and American Legislation, in *Euro-Arab Arbitration III* 104 (F. Kemicha ed. 1991)

Pedrazzini, Essentialia e accidentialia della clausola compromissoria, in *Recueil de Travaux Suisses* 71 (C. Reymond & E. Bucher eds. 1984)

Pisar, S., *Coexistence & Commerce*, Chapters 20-24 (New York 1970)

Prujiner, La gestion des arbitrages commerciaux internationaux: l'exemple de la Cour d'arbitrage de la CCI, 115 *J. Droit Int'l (Clunet)* 662 (1988)

Real, G.K.L., *Der Schiedsrichtervertrag* (Cologne 1983)

Redfern, International Commercial Arbitration: Winning the Battle, in *Private Investors Abroad— Problems and Solutions in International Business in 1989* 11-1 (C. Holgren ed. 1989)

Reymond, Des connaissances personnelles de l'arbitre à son information privilégiée, 1991 *Rev. Arb.* 3

Rhodes & Sloan, The Pitfalls of International Commercial Arbitration, 17 *Vand. J. Transnat'l L.* 19 (1984)

Robine, Le choix des arbitres, 1990 *Rev. Arb.* 315

Schwab, Schiedsrichterernennung und Schiedsrichtervertrag, in *Festschrift für Gerhard Schiedermair* 499 (Munich 1976)

Schwebel & Lahne, Public Policy and Arbitral Procedure, in *Comparative Arbitration Practice and Public Policy in Arbitration* 205 (P. Sanders ed. 1987)

Smit, The Future of International Commercial Arbitration, 2 *West's Int'l L. Bull.* 5 (Issue 4, Fall 1984)

———, The Future of International Commercial Arbitration: A Single Transnational Institution? 25 *Colum. J. Transnat'l L.* 9 (1986)

Stumpf, Ost-West-Schiedsgerichtsbarkeit: Schiedsgerichte mit Sitz in dritten Ländern, 33 *RIW* 821 (1987)

Sujan, M.A., *The Law Relating to Government Arbitration* (New Delhi 1985)

Sweeney, Judicial Review of Arbitral Proceedings, in 2 *Fifth Int'l Congress of Maritime Arbitrators* (New York 1981)

Trammer, Choice of Arbitrators, 6 *I.C.A. Arb. Q.* 8 (No. 1, June 1971)

Voskuil & Freedberg-Swartzburg, Composition of the Arbitral Tribunal, in *Essays on International Commercial Arbitration* 64 (P. Sarcevic ed. 1989)

11.04 SELECTION BY ARBITRAL INSTITUTION

Briner, The Appointment of Arbitrators by the Organization Responsible for the Arbitration Court, in *Recueil de Travaux Suisses* 147 (C. Reymond & E. Bucher 1984)

Cox, The Selection Process and the Appointment of Arbitrators, 46 *Arb. J.* 28 (No. 2, 1991); also in *Commercial Arbitration for the 1990s* (R. Medalie ed. 1991)

de Boisséson, La constitution de tribunal arbitral dans l'arbitrage institutionnel, 1990 *Rev. Arb.* 337

Mann, Zur Ernennung von Schiedsrichtern durch vertraglich bezeichnete Dritte, in *Liber Amicorum Adolf F. Schnitzer* 325 (Geneva 1979)

Nanowski, Authority Being Competent to Nominate Arbitrators Substitutionally, in *ICCA, Fifth Int'l Arb. Congress: Proceedings* C Io 1-11 (1975)

Parker School of Foreign and Comparative Law, *The 1989 Guide to International Arbitration and Arbitrators* (Dobbs Ferry 1989)

Varady, On Appointing Authorities in International Commercial Arbitration, 2 *Emory J. Int'l Disp. Res.* 311 (1988)

Vigrass, The Role of Institutions in Arbitration, in *Handbook of Arbitration Practice* 367 (R. Bernstein ed. 1987)

11.05 SOLE ARBITRATOR

Goldstajn, The Relationship between International Commercial Arbitration and National Adjudication, in 4 *Hague-Zagreb Essays* 297 (C. Voskuil & J. Wade eds. 1981)

Klein, Zur Ernennung von Schiedsrichtern durch im voraus bezeichnete Dritte, 6 *IPRax* 53 (1986)

Lalive, De la désignation par un tiers de l'arbitre international, in *Mélanges en l'honneur de Wilhelm Schoenenberger* 373 (1968)

McCormack, A Lawyer's View of Arbitration Proceedings and Composition of the Arbitration Panel, 1984 *Y.B. Mar. Law* 55

Mann, Zur Ernennung von Schiedsrichtern durch vertraglich bezeichnete Dritte, in *Liber Amicorum Adolf F. Schnitzer* 325 (Geneva 1979)

Mustill, Sir Michael J. & S. C. Boyd, *The Law and Practice of Commercial Arbitration in England* (2nd ed. 1989)

Nanowski, Authority Being Competent to Nominate Arbitrators Substitutionally, in *ICCA, Fifth Int'l Arb. Congress: Proceedings* C Io 1-11 (1975)

Prujiner, La gestion des arbitrages commerciaux internationaux: l'exemple de la Cour d'arbitrage de la CCI, 115 *J. Droit Int'l (Clunet)* 662 (1988)

Wenner, Swiss Judges as Arbitrators or as Nominators for Arbitrators, 35 *Arb. J.* 22 (No. 4, 1980)

11.06 TRIBUNAL OF TWO ARBITRATORS

Mustill, Sir Michael J. & S. C. Boyd, *The Law and Practice of Commercial Arbitration in England* (2nd ed. 1989)

Samuel, Tribunal of Two, 53 *Arbitration* 141 (1987)

11.07 TRIBUNAL OF THREE ARBITRATORS

Beyly, The Manager and Arbitration, 3 *J. Int'l Arb.* 7 (No. 1, 1986)

Eisemann, L''arbitre-parties,' in *Liber Amicorum for Martin Domke* 78 (P. Sanders ed. 1967)

————, The Partisan Arbitrator, 4 *I. C. A. Arb. Q.* 3 (No. 2, July-Sept. 1969)

Goldstajn, The Relationship between International Commercial Arbitration and National Adjudication, in 4 *Hague-Zagreb Essays* 297 (C. Voskuil & J. Wade eds. 1981)

Holtzmann, H. & J. Neuhaus, *A Guide to the UNCITRAL Model Law on International Commercial Arbitration: Legislative History and Commentary* (Deventer 1989)

Lalive, Problèmes relatifs à l'arbitrage international commercial, 120 *Recueil des Cours* 569 (1967-II)

Luther, Das Drei-Mann-Schiedsgericht bei der Entscheidung von Streitigkeiten zwischen drei oder mehr Vertragspartnern, in *Festschrift für Ernst von Caemmerer* 571 (Tübingen 1978)

Mann, Zur Ernennung von Schiedsrichtern durch vertraglich bezeichnete Dritte, in *Liber Amicorum Adolf F. Schnitzer* 325 (Geneva 1979)

Mosk, The Role of Party-Appointed Arbitrators in International Arbitration: The Experience of the Iran-United States Claims Tribunal, 1 *Transnat'l Law.* 253 (1988)

Mustill, Sir Michael J. & S. C. Boyd, The Law and Practice of Commercial Arbitration in England (2nd ed. 1989)

Nanowski, Authority Being Competent to Nominate Arbitrators Substitutionally, in *ICCA, Fifth Int'l Arb. Congress: Proceedings* C Io 1-11 (1975)

Prujiner, La gestion des arbitrages commerciaux internationaux: l'exemple de la Cour d'arbitrage de la CCI, 115 *J. Droit Int'l (Clunet)* 662 (1988)

Raeschke-Kessler & Bühler, Aufsicht über den Schiedsrichter durch den ICC-Schiedsgerichtshof (Paris) und rechtliches Gehör der Parteien, 8 *ZIP* 1157 (1987)

Schlosser, Party-Appointed Arbitrators and Multiple Defendants Having Conflicting Interests, in *Law in East and West/Recht in Ost und West* 739 (Tokyo 1988)

11.08 CAPACITY AND QUALIFICATIONS OF ARBITRATORS

Baden Hellard, Management Functions and the Arbitrator, in *ICCA, Fourth Int'l Arb. Congress: Proceedings* 659 (1972)

Briner, The Appointment of Arbitrators by the Organization Responsible for the Arbitration Court, in *Recueil de Travaux Suisses* 147 (C. Reymond & E. Bucher 1984)

Bucher, A., *Die neue internationale Schiedsgerichtsbarkeit in der Schweiz* (Basel 1989)

————, *Le nouvel arbitrage international en Suisse. Théorie et pratique de droit* (Basel 1988)

Bucher, A. & P.-Y. Tschanz, *International Arbitration in Switzerland* (Basel 1989)

Bülow, The Professional Qualifications of the Arbitrator, 6 *I.C.A. Arb. Q.* 3 (No. 3, Oct.-Dec. 1971)

Cherian, A Proposal to Amend Article 14(1) (Qualifications of Arbitrators) of the World Bank Convention on the Settlement of Investment Disputes Between States and Nationals of Other States, in *ICCA, Fifth Int'l Arb. Congress: Proceedings* C Ig 1-4 (1975)

de Leval, La designation et la mission des arbitres. Notes succinctes sur le droit positif applicable en Belgique, 53 *Rev. Droit Int'l & Droit Comp.* 170 (1976)

Fitch, Professionalism and Ethics of the Arbitrator, 2 *Arbitrator* 97 (1983)

Glossner, International Commercial Arbitration — Some Practical Aspects, in *Liber Amicorum for Martin Domke* 95 (P. Sanders ed. 1967)

Graham, The Internationalization of Commercial Arbitration in Canada: A Preliminary Reaction, 13 *Can. Bus. L.J.* 1 (1987)

Helal, International Commercial Arbitration, 53 *Arbitration* 258 (1987)

Hoellering, The Qualification of Arbitrators for Construction Disputes, 45 *Arb. J.* 34 (No. 4, 1990)

Holtzmann & Bernini, Hypothetical Case for Use in a Comparative Study of Arbitration Practice in Various Legal Systems, in *Comparative Arbitration Practice and Public Policy in Arbitration* 19 (P. Sanders ed. 1987)

Matray, Rédaction d'une clause d'arbitrage et choix d'arbitres compétents en matière internationale, 56 *Rev. Droit Int'l & Droit Comp.* 51 (1979)

Meason & Smith, Non-Lawyers in International Commercial Arbitration: Gathering Splinters on the Bench, 12 *Nw. J. Int'l L. & Bus.* 24 (1991)

Meyer, Arbitrators: Qualification, Challenge and Withdrawal, in 1 *Fifth Int'l Congress of Maritime Arbitrators* (New York 1981)

Mustill, Sir Michael J. & S. C. Boyd, *The Law and Practice of Commercial Arbitration in England* (2nd ed. 1989)

Nordenson, The Arbitral Tribunal, 1990 *Y.B. Swed. & Int'l Arb.* 19

Real, G.K.L., *Der Schiedsrichtervertrag* (Cologne 1983)

Schlosser, Quelles nouvelles de l'arbitrage Outre-Rhin? 1987 *Rev. Arb.* 293

Shelton, The Expertise of the Arbitrator, 3 *Arbitrator* 5 (1984)

Shilston, Milestone in the Evolution of Modern Commercial Arbitration, 53 *Arbitration* 26 (1987)

———, The Evolution of Modern Commercial Arbitration, 4 *J. Int'l Arb.* 45 (No. 2, 1987)

Smit, The Future of International Commercial Arbitration, 2 *West's Int'l L. Bull.* 5 (Issue 4, Fall 1984)

Swoboda, M., *Fachleute als Richter — Schiedsgerichtsbarkeit in der Bundesrepublik Deutschland* (Schriftreihe des Deutschen Industrie- und Handelstag), (1984)

Tupman, Challenge and Disqualification of Arbitrators in International Commercial Arbitration, 38 *Int'l & Comp. L.Q.* 26 (1989)

Uff, Arbitral Procedure: Use of Legal and Technical Expertise, 53 *Arbitration* 23 (1987)

Vigrass, Arbitrators — Selection and Training, 47 *Arbitrator* 112 (1981)

Voskuil & Freedberg-Swartzburg, Composition of the Arbitral Tribunal, in *Essays on International Commercial Arbitration* 64 (P. Sarcevic ed. 1989)

11.09 NATIONALITY OF ARBITRATORS

Garro, The Colombian Supreme Court Holds Unconstitutional the Use of Foreign Arbitrators Under New Arbitration Law, 1 *Am. Rev. Int'l Arb.* 594 (1990)

Goldstajn, Choice of International Arbitrators, Arbitral Tribunals and Centres: Legal and Sociological Aspects, in *Essays on International Commercial Arbitration* 27 (P. Sarcevic ed. 1989)

Hobér, Arbitration in Moscow, 3 *Arb. Int'l* 119 (1987)

Holtzmann & Bernini, Hypothetical Case for Use in a Comparative Study of Arbitration Practice in Various Legal Systems, in *Comparative Arbitration Practice and Public Policy in Arbitration* 19 (P. Sanders ed. 1987)

Melis, East-West Arbitration, 47 *Arbitration* 84 (1981)

Nobili, I costi fiscali dell'arbitrato in Italia: sviluppi recenti, 26 *Rassegna dell'Arb.* 13 (1986)

Pearson, The Arbitrator's Nationality and Other Ties, 6 *I.C.A. Arb. Q.* 3 (No. 1, June 1971)

Shihata, Obstacles Facing International Arbitration, 4 *Int'l Tax & Bus. Law.* 209 (1986)

Tupman, Challenge and Disqualification of Arbitrators in International Commercial Arbitration, 38 *Int'l & Comp. L.Q.* 26 (1989)

Voskuil & Freedberg-Swartzburg, Composition of the Arbitral Tribunal, in *Essays on International Commercial Arbitration* 64 (P. Sarcevic ed. 1989)

11.10 INDEPENDENCE AND IMPARTIALITY

Adlerstein, Zur Unabhängigkeit des Schiedsrichters, in *Studien zum Recht der internationalen Schiedsgerichtsbarkeit* 9 (K.-H. Böckstiegel ed. 1979)

Bakshi, The Arbitrator and His Norms of Conduct, 3 *The Lawyers* 41 (No. 5, 1988)

Bartos ,H., *Internationale Handelsschiedsgerichtsbarkeit:Verfahrensprinzipien* (Frankfurt 1984)

Baur, F., *Neuere Probleme der privaten Schiedsgerichtsbarkeit* (Berlin 1980)

Bedjaoui, Obligations légales et morales de l'arbitre, in *Euro-Arab Arbitration II* 41 (F. Kemicha ed. 1989)

————, The Arbitrator: One Man — Three Roles, 5 *J. Int'l Arb.* 7 (No. 1, 1988)

Bernini, Cultural Neutrality: A Prerequisite to Arbitral Justice, 10 *Mich. J. Int'l L.* 39 (1989)

————, The Ethical Implications of the Arbitral Functions: Standards of Behaviour of Arbitrators, 23 *Revue de Droit Comparé/Comparative Law Review* (Tokyo)(No. 3, 1989)

Bond, I.C.C. Arbitration in Theory and Practice, 26 *Rassegna dell'Arb.* 141 (1986)

————, The Selection of ICC Arbitrators and the Requirement of Independence, 4 *Arb. Int'l* 300 (1988)

Branson, Ethics for International Arbitrators, 3 *Arb. Int'l* 72 (No. 1, 1987)

————, IBA Rules of Ethics for International Arbitrators, 15 *Int'l Bus. Law.* 335 (1987)

Bucher, Zur Unabhängigkeit des parteibennanten Schiedsrichters, in *Recht und Wirtschaft heute. Festgabe für Max Kummer* 599 (Berne 1980)

Cardenas & de Vanosci, Arbitraje comercial internacional: la actuación de los arbitros; su perfil ético, 18 *Revista del Derecho Comercial* (ARG) 595 (1985)

Carter, International Bar Association: Guidelines for International Arbitrators (1986). Introductory Note, 26 *I.L.M.* 583 (1987)

Coulson, An American Critique of the IBA's Ethics for International Arbitrators, 4 *J. Int'l Arb.* 103 (No. 2, 1987)

de Mello, Refléxions sur les règles deontologiques élaborées par L'International Bar Association pour les arbitres internationaux, 1988 *Rev. Arb.* 339

Domke, The Arbitrator's Duty to Disclose, *J. Bus. L.* 162 (1969)

Duintjer Tebbens, A Facelift for Dutch Arbitration Law, 34 *Neth. Int'l L. Rev.* 141 (1987)

Eisemann, L''arbitre-parties', in *Liber Amicorum for Martin Domke* 78 (P. Sanders ed. 1967)

————, The Arbitrator's Independence, 6 *I. C. A. Arb. Q.* 5 (No. 1, June 1971)

————, The Partisan Arbitrator, 4 *I. C. A. Arb. Q.* 3 (No. 2, July-Sept. 1969)

Fitch, Professionalism and Ethics of the Arbitrator, 2 *Arbitrator* 97 (1983)

Geisinger & Renold, Arbitrage international, ordre public et reconnaissance en Suisse de sentences arbitrales étrangères, in *Le Juriste Suisse Face au Droit et aux Jugements Etrangers: Ouverture ou Repli?* 89 (F. Knoepfler ed. 1988)

Glick, Bias, Fraud, Misconduct and Partiality of the Arbitrator, 22 *Arb. J.* 161 (1967)

Goldstajn, Choice of International Arbitrators, Arbitral Tribunals and Centres: Legal and Sociological Aspects, in *Essays on International Commercial Arbitration* 27 (P. Sarcevic ed. 1989)

Holtzmann, Code of Ethics for Arbitrators in Commercial Disputes: Introductory Note to the American Code of Ethics for Arbitrators in Commercial Disputes, 10 *Y.B. Com. Arb.* 131 (1985)

————, The First Code of Ethics for Arbitrators in Commercial Disputes, 33 *Bus. Law.* 309 (1977)

Holtzmann & Bernini, Hypothetical Case for Use in a Comparative Study of Arbitration Practice in Various Legal Systems, in *Comparative Arbitration Practice and Public Policy in Arbitration* 19 (P. Sanders ed. 1987)

Hunter, Ethics of the International Arbitrator, 53 *Arbitration* 219 (1987)

Hunter & Paulsson, A Code of Ethics for Arbitrators in International Commercial Arbitrations? *Int'l Bus. Law.* 153 (April 1985)

International Chamber of Commerce, T*he Arbitral Process and the Independence of Arbitrators/La procédure arbitrale et l'indépendence des arbitres* (Paris 1991)

Kellor, F., *American Arbitration* (New York 1948)

Kornblum, Das 'Gebot überparteilicher Rechtspflege' und der deutsche schiedsrechtliche ordre public, 40 *NJW* 1105 (1987)

Kornblum, U., *Probleme der schiedsrichterlichen Unabhängigkeit* (Munich 1968)

Lalive, On the Neutrality of the Arbitrator and the Place of Arbitration, in *Recueil de Travaux Suisses* 23 (C. Reymond & E. Bucher eds. 1984)

Matray, L'arbitre-partie en matière internationale, 53 *Rev. Droit Int'l & Droit Comp.* 152 (1976)

————, Quelques problèmes de l'arbitrage commercial international (doctrine et jurisprudence), in *L'Arbitrage* 289 (L. Matray & G. de Leval eds. 1989)

Minoli, Relations between the Parties and the Arbitrator, 5 *I. C. A. Arb. Q.* 3 (No. 4, Jan.-March 1971)

Mosk, The Role of Party-Appointed Arbitrators in International Arbitration: The Experience of the Iran-United States Claims Tribunal, 1 *Transnat'l Law.* 253 (1988)

Mustill, Sir Michael J. & S. C. Boyd, *The Law and Practice of Commercial Arbitration in England* (2nd ed. 1989)

Nariman, Standards of Behaviour of Arbitrators, 4 *Arb. Int'l* 311 (1988)

Parker School of Foreign and Comparative Law, *The 1989 Guide to International Arbitration and Arbitrators* (Dobbs Ferry 1989)

Petersen & Rezler, The Impact of Opinion 11 on the Publication of Arbitration Awards, 1986 *Mo. J. Disp. Res.* 73

Richard, Enforcement of Foreign Arbitral Awards under the United Nations Convention of 1958: A Survey of Recent Federal Case Law, 11 *Md. J. Int'l L. & Trade* 13 (1987)

Robert, La règle morale dans l'arbitrage commercial international, in *A.I.A., Essays in Memoriam Eugenio Minoli* 439 (Turin 1974)

Schlosser, Die Unparteilichkeit des Schiedsrichteramtes, 93 *ZZP* 121 (1980)

Shenton, Arbitral Impartiality: The Attitude of the English Courts, 8 *Int'l Bus. Law.* 76 (1980)

Shilston, Milestone in the Evolution of Modern Commercial Arbitration, 53 *Arbitration* 26 (1987)

————, The Evolution of Modern Commercial Arbitration, 4 *J. Int'l Arb.* 45 (No. 2, 1987)

Smit, The Future of International Commercial Arbitration, 2 *West's Int'l L. Bull.* 5 (Issue 4, Fall 1984)

Smith, Impartiality of the Party-Appointed Arbitrator, 6 *Arb. Int'l* 320 (1990)

Sweeney, Judicial Review of Arbitral Proceedings, in 2 *Fifth Int'l Congress of Maritime Arbitrators* (New York 1981)

Szasz, Public Corporations as Parties to Arbitration. Procedural Aspects, in *ICC, 60 Years of ICC Arbitration* 213 (1984)

Tupman, Challenge and Disqualification of Arbitrators in International Commercial Arbitration, 38 *Int'l & Comp. L.Q.* 26 (1989)

Voskuil & Freedberg-Swartzburg, Composition of the Arbitral Tribunal, in *Essays on International Commercial Arbitration* 64 (P. Sarcevic ed. 1989)

11.11 CHALLENGE OF ARBITRATORS

Bakshi, Misconduct by Arbitrators, 1988(1) *Company L.J.* 40

———, Misconduct by the Arbitrator, 1989(2) *Company* L.J. 49

Bucher, A., *Die neue internationale Schiedsgerichtsbarkeit in der Schweiz* (Basel 1989)

———, *Le nouvel arbitrage international en Suisse. Théorie et pratique de droit* (Basel 1988)

Bucher, A. & P.-Y. Tschanz, *International Arbitration in Switzerland* (Basel 1989)

Cardenas & de Vanosci, Arbitraje comercial internacional: la actuación de los arbitros; su perfil ético, 18 *Revista del Derecho Comercial* (ARG) 595 (1985)

Chowdhuri, S.K.R. & H.K. Saharay, *Arbitration Law.* 2nd ed. (Calcutta 1986)

Duintjer Tebbens, A Facelift for Dutch Arbitration Law, 34 *Neth. Int'l L. Rev.* 141 (1987)

Hobér, Arbitration in Moscow, 3 *Arb. Int'l* 119 (1987)

Holtzmann, H. & J. Neuhaus, *A Guide to the UNCITRAL Model Law on International Commercial Arbitration: Legislative History and Commentary* (Deventer 1989)

International Chamber of Commerce, *The Arbitral Process and the Independence of Arbitrators/La procédure arbitrale et l'indépendence des arbitres* (Paris 1991)

Karrer, Les rapports entre le tribunal arbitral, les tribunaux étatiques et l'institution arbitrale, 1989 *Int'l Bus. L.J.* 761

Laschet, Rechtsmittel gegen Prozess-, Vorab- oder Zwischenentscheidungen eines Schiedsgerichtes oder einer Schiedsgerichtsorganisation, in *Beiträge zum internationalen Verfahrensrechts und zur Schiedsgerichtbarkeit. Festschrift für Heinrich Nagel* 167 (W. Habscheid & K. Schwab eds. 1987)

Marti & Kohler, La récusation des arbitres en droit suisse, in *Mélanges offerts à Raymond Vander Elst* 595 (Brussels 1986

Meyer, Arbitrators: Qualification, Challenge and Withdrawal, in 1 *Fifth Int'l Congress of Maritime Arbitrators* (New York 1981)

Nordenson, The Arbitral Tribunal, 1990 *Y.B. Swed. & Int'l Arb.* 19

Note, Challenge of Arbitrators: Is an Institutional Decision Final? 2 *Arb. Int'l* 261 (1986)

Parlade, Remedies after Arbitration Award, in *Commercial Arbitration* 75 (J. Ricalde ed. 1983)

Paterson, International Commercial Arbitration Act: An Overview, in *UNCITRAL Arbitration Model in Canada* 113 (R. Paterson & B. Thompson eds. 1987)

Paulsson, Vicarious Hypochondria and Institutional Arbitration, 6 *Arb. Int'l* 226 (1990)

————, Vicarious Hypochondria and Institutional Arbitration, 1990 *Y.B. Swed. & Int'l Arb.* 96

Prujiner, La gestion des arbitrages commerciaux internationaux: l'exemple de la Cour d'arbitrage de la CCI, 115 *J. Droit Int'l (Clunet)* 662 (1988)

Sharkey, J. & J. Dorter, *Commercial Arbitration* (Sydney 1986)

Smit, A-National Arbitration, 63 *Tul. L. Rev.* 629 (1989)

Sweeney, Judicial Review of Arbitral Proceedings, in 2 *Fifth Int'l Congress of Maritime Arbitrators* (New York 1981)

Tupman, Challenge and Disqualification of Arbitrators in International Commercial Arbitration, 38 *Int'l & Comp. L.Q.* 26 (1989)

Voskuil & Freedberg-Swartzburg, Composition of the Arbitral Tribunal, in *Essays on International Commercial Arbitration* 64 (P. Sarcevic ed. 1989)

Wenger, Zur Ablehnung von Schiedsrichtern im schweizerischen Schiedsverfahrensrecht, 8 *IPRax* 116 (1988)

11.12 REMOVAL AND RESIGNATION OF ARBITRATORS

Briguglio, Die Schiedsrichterablehnung im italianischen Recht und nach den Regeln der ICC-Schiedsordnung, 2 *Jahrbuch Schiedsgerichtsbarkeit* 23 (1988)

Bucher, A., *Die neue internationale Schiedsgerichtsbarkeit in der Schweiz* (Basel 1989)

————, *Le nouvel arbitrage international en Suisse. Théorie et pratique de droit* (Basel 1988)

Bucher, A. & P.-Y. Tschanz, *International Arbitration in Switzerland* (Basel 1989)

Gelinas, L'exécution des sentences arbitrales internationales au Québec: commentaire, in *First International Commmercial Arbitration Conference: Proceedings* 305 (N. Antaki & A. Prujiner eds. 1986)

Laschet, Erneut zur Frage der Ablehnung von Schiedsrichtern in Frankreich — Beschluss der Cour d'Appel de Paris vom 15.1.1985, 1985 *KTS* 627

Marti & Kohler, La récusation des arbitres en droit suisse, in *Mélanges offerts à Raymond Vander Elst* 595 (Brussels 1986)

Meyer, Arbitrators: Qualification, Challenge and Withdrawal, in 1 *Fifth Int'l Congress of Maritime Arbitrators* (New York 1981)

Prujiner, La gestion des arbitrages commerciaux internationaux: l'exemple de la Cour d'arbitrage de la CCI, 115 *J. Droit Int'l (Clunet)* 662 (1988)

Real, G.K.L., *Der Schiedsrichtervertrag* (Cologne 1983)

Sharkey, J. & J. Dorter, *Commercial Arbitration* (Sydney 1986)

Thomas, Removal of Arbitrators by the Court, 48 *Arbitration* 136 (1982)

11.13 RESPONSIBILITY OF ARBITRATORS

Carlston, Psychological and Sociological Aspects of the Judicial and Arbitration Processes, in *Liber Amicorum for Martin Domke* 44 (P. Sanders ed. 1967)

Cremades, Should Arbitrators Be Immune from Liability? 10 *Int'l Fin. L. Rev.* 32 (No. 3, 1991)

Domke, Die Haftpflicht des Schiedsrichters in rechtsvergleichender Sicht, in *Festschrift für Martin Luther* (Munich 1976)

Eisemann, Deontologie de l'arbitre commercial international, in *ICCA, Third Int'l Arb. Congress: Proceedings* 261 (1969)

Gaillard, Les manoevres dilatoires des parties et des arbitres dans l'arbitrage commercial international, 1990 *Rev. Arb.* 759

Goldman, The Complementary Roles of Judges and Arbitrators in Ensuring that International Commercial Arbitration Is Effective, in *ICC, 60 Years of ICC Arbitration* 257 (1984)

Hausmaninger, Civil Liability of Arbitrators — Comparative Analysis and Proposals for Reform, 7 *J. Int'l Arb.* 7 (No. 4, 1990)

Kemicha, F., ed., *Euro-Arab Arbitration II/Arbitrage Euro-Arabe II* (London 1989)

Kühn, The Liability of Arbitrators in West Germany, 8 *Int'l Bus. Law.* 345 (1980)

Lew, J., ed., *The Immunity of Arbitrators* (London 1990)

McLaughlin, Arbitral Immunity, in *International Commercial and Maritime Arbitration* 55 (F.D. Rose ed. 1988)

Melis, Taak en verantwoordelijkheid van arbitrage-instituten, 1988 *Tijdschrift voor Arbitrage*

Mirabelli, Contratti nell'arbitrato (con l'arbitro; con l'istituzione arbitrale), 30 *Rassegna dell'Arb.* 3 (1990)

Mustill, Sir Michael J. & S. C. Boyd, *The Law and Practice of Commercial Arbitration in England* (2nd ed. 1989)

Nordenson, The Arbitral Tribunal, 1990 *Y.B. Swed. & Int'l Arb.* 19

Prütting, Zur Rechtsstellung des Schiedsrichters - dargestellt am richterlichen Beratungsgeheimnis, in *Festschrift für Karl Heinz Schwab* 409 (P. Gottwald & H. Prütting eds. 1990)

Reymond, Des connaissances personnelles de l'arbitre à son information privilégiée, 1991 *Rev. Arb.* 3

Robine, The Liability of Arbitrators and Arbitral Institutions in International Arbitrations under French Law, 5 *Arb. Int'l* 323 (1989)

Shenton, The Liability of Arbitrators, England, 8 *Int'l Bus. Law.* 335 (1980)

Teed, Liability of Arbitrators for Negligence, 10 *Can. Arb. J.* 14 (No. 1, 1985)

Traverso, The Liability of Arbitrators in Italy, 8 *Int'l Bus. Law.* 339 (1980)

11.14 IMMUNITY OF ARBITRATORS

Branson & Wallace, Immunity of Arbitrators under United States Law, in *The Immunity of Arbitrators* 85 (J.D.M. Lew ed. 1990)

Coulson, American Arbitration Association and Immunity of Arbitrators, in *The Immunity of Arbitrators* 97 (J.D.M. Lew ed. 1990)

Cremades, Immunity of Arbitrators under Spanish Law, in *The Immunity of Arbitrators* 71 (J.D.M. Lew ed. 1990)

————, Should Arbitrators Be Immune from Liability? 10 *Int'l Fin. L. Rev.* 32 (No. 3, 1991)

Davies, Immunity of the Arbitrator, 43 *Arbitration* 3 (Summer 1976)

Delvolvé, Immunity of Arbitrators under French Law, in *The Immunity of Arbitrators* 29 (J.D.M. Lew ed. 1990)

Grigera Naón, Immunity of Arbitrators under Argentine Law, in *The Immunity of Arbitrators* 5 (J.D.M. Lew ed. 1990)

Haug, Immunity of Arbitrators under Norwegian Law, in *The Immunity of Arbitrators* 65 (J.D.M. Lew ed. 1990)

Hausmaninger, Civil Liability of Arbitrators — Comparative Analysis and Proposals for Reform, 7 *J. Int'l Arb.* 7 (No. 4, 1990)

Hjerner, The Immunity of Arbitrators under Swedish Law, in *The Immunity of Arbitrators* 81 (J.D.M. Lew ed. 1990)

Iwasaki, Immunity of Arbitrators under Japanese Law, in *The Immunity of Arbitrators* 53 (J.D.M. Lew ed. 1990)

Lalive, Immunity of Arbitrators under Swiss Law, in *The Immunity of Arbitrators* 117 (J.D.M. Lew ed. 1990)

Lew, J., ed., *The Immunity of Arbitrators* (London 1990)

Mackie, The Grain and Feed Trade Association and Immunity of Arbitrators, in *The Immunity of Arbitrators* 111 (J.D.M. Lew ed. 1990)

McLaughlin, Arbitral Immunity, in *International Commercial and Maritime Arbitration* 55 (F.D. Rose ed. 1988)

Melis, Immunity of Arbitrators under Austrian Law, in *The Immunity of Arbitrators* 15 (J.D.M. Lew ed. 1990)

Parra, The International Centre for the Settlement of Investment Disputes and Immunity of Arbitrators, in *The Immunity of Arbitrators* 105 (J.D.M. Lew ed. 1990)

Pryles, Immunity of Arbitrators under Australian Law, in *The Immunity of Arbitrators* 13 (J.D.M. Lew ed. 1990)

Triebel & Hyden, Immunity of Arbitrators under German Law, in *The Immunity of Arbitrators* 39 (J.D.M. Lew 1990)

van den Berg, Immunity of Arbitrators under Netherlands Law, in *The Immunity of Arbitrators* 59 (J.D.M. Lew ed. 1990)

11.15 COMPENSATION OF ARBITRATORS

Cox, The Selection Process and the Appointment of Arbitrators, 46 *Arb. J.* 28 (No. 2, 1991); also in *Commercial Arbitration for the 1990s* (R. Medalie ed. 1991)

Delalande, Les honoraires dans l'arbitrage institutionnel, 1990 *Rev. Arb.* 367

Mustill, Sir Michael J. & S. C. Boyd, *The Law and Practice of Commercial Arbitration in England* (2nd ed. 1989)

Nordenson, The Arbitral Tribunal, 1990 *Y.B. Swed. & Int'l Arb.* 19

Real, G.K.L., *Der Schiedsrichtervertrag* (Cologne 1983)

Thomas, Right to Remuneration under the Arbitration Rules of 1988 of the Chartered Institute of Arbitrators, 55 *Arbitrator* 179 (1989)

Werner, Remuneration of Arbitrators by the International Chamber of Commerce, 5 *J. Int'l Arb.* 135 (No. 3, 1988)

11.16 TRAINING OF ARBITRATORS

Barclay, Preparación y especialización de arbitros, in *El Arbitraje Comercial Internacional* 195 (Mexico 1983)

Derains, The International Chamber of Commerce Continuing Education of Lawyers and Arbitrators, 5 *Y.B. Com. Arb.* 301 (1980)

Goode, The Proposed London School of International Arbitration, 47 *Arbitration* 279 (1982)

Harris, The Recruitment and Training of Maritime Arbitrators, 7 *J. Int'l Arb.* 43 (No. 2, 1990)

Hoellering, Training and Development of Commercial Arbitrators (U.S.A.), 10 *Y.B. Com. Arb.* 551 (1985)

James, The Training of Future Arbitrators, Technical Assessors and Expert Witnesses, in *ICCA, Fourth Int'l Arb. Congress: Proceedings* 695 (1972)

Krishnamurthi, Training Facilities at the Indian Council of Arbitration, 5 *Y.B. Com. Arb.* 305 (1980)

Lew, The School of International Arbitration, London, 5 *J. Int'l Arb.* 127 (No. 3, 1988)

Lipton, Discovery Procedures and the Selection and Training of Arbitrators: A Study of Securities Industry Practices, 26 *Am. Bus. L.J.* 435 (1988)

Vigrass, Arbitrators — Selection and Training, 47 *Arbitrator* 112 (1981)

————, The Role of Institutions in Arbitration, in *Handbook of Arbitration Practice* 367 (R. Bernstein ed. 1987)

12. AUTHORITY OF THE ARBITRAL TRIBUNAL

12.01 DECISION MAKING IN GENERAL

Blessing, International Arbitration Procedures, 17 *Int'l Bus. Law.* 408 and 451 (1989)

Coulson, Do We Know How Arbitration Panels Decide? 6 *J. Int'l Arb.* 7 (No. 2, 1989)

Deshpande, International Commercial Arbitration: Uniformity of Jurisdiction, 5 *J. Int'l Arb.* 115 (No. 2, 1988)

Garro, Enforcement of Arbitration Agreements and Jurisdiction of Arbitral Tribunals in Latin America, 1 *J. Int'l Arb.* 293 (No. 4, 1984)

Kassis, The Questionable Validity of Arbitration and Awards under the Rules of the International Chambre of Commerce, 6 *J. Int'l Arb.* 79 (No. 2, 1989)

Knoepfler & Schweizer, Making of Awards and Termination of Proceedings, in *Essays on International Commercial Arbitration* 160 (P. Sarcevic ed. 1989)

Laschet, Rechtsmittel gegen Prozess-, Vorab- oder Zwischenentscheidungen eines Schiedsgerichtes oder einer Schiedsgerichtsorganisation, in *Beiträge zum internationalen Verfahrensrechts und zur Schiedsgerichtbarkeit. Festschrift für Heinrich Nagel* 167 (W. Habscheid & K. Schwab eds. 1987)

Poznanski, The Nature and Extent of an Arbitrator's Powers in International Commercial Arbitration, 4 *J. Int'l Arb.* 71 (No. 3, 1987)

Ventura, Convençao de arbitragem, 46 *Revista da Ordem dos Advogados* 289 (1986)

353

12.02 RIGHT TO DECIDE ON JURISDICTION

Baker & Davis, Arbitral Proceedings under the UNCITRAL Rules: The Experience of the Iran-United States Claims Tribunal, 23 *Geo. Wash. J. Int'l L. & Econ.* 267 (1989)

Blessing, International Arbitration Procedures, 17 *Int'l Bus. Law.* 408 and 451 (1989)

Böckstiegel, Applying the UNCITRAL Rules: The Experience of the Iran-United States Claims Tribunal, 4 *Int'l Tax & Bus. Law.* 266 (1986)

Bucher, A., *Die neue internationale Schiedsgerichtsbarkeit in der Schweiz* (Basel 1989)

————, *Le nouvel arbitrage international en Suisse. Théorie et pratique de droit* (Basel 1988)

Bucher, A. & P.-Y.Tschanz, *International Arbitration in Switzerland* (Basel 1989)

Forni, Il potere dell'arbitro di statuire sulla propia competenza e l'arbitrabilità del litigio, in *Recueil de Travaux Suisses* 191 (C. Reymond & E. Bucher eds. 1984)

Gaillard, L'affaire SOFIDIF ou les difficultés de l'arbitrage multipartite (à propos de l'arrêt rendu par la Cour d'Appel de Paris le 19 décembre 1986), 1987 *Rev. Arb.* 275

————, Les manoevres dilatoires des parties et des arbitres dans l'arbitrage commercial international, 1990 *Rev. Arb.* 759

Glossner, The Conduct of ICC Arbitration Proceedings, in *Contemporary Problems in International Arbitration* 210 (J.D.M. Lew ed. 1986)

Goldman, The Complementary Roles of Judges and Arbitrators in Ensuring that International Commercial Arbitration Is Effective, in *ICC, 60 Years of ICC Arbitration* 257 (1984)

Grigera Naón, Mandatory Provisions of Law Regarding Arbitration Agreements in Latin America, in *Arbitration in Settlement of International Commercial Disputes Involving the Far East and Arbitration in Combined Transportation* 121 (P. Sanders ed. 1989)

Habscheid, Das Problem der Kompetenz-Kompetenz des Schiedsgerichts, 78 *SJZ* 321 (1982)

Herrmann, The UNCITRAL Model Law on International Commercial Arbitration — Its Salient Features and Prospects, in *First Int'l Commercial Arbitration Conference: Proceedings* 351 (N. Antaki & A. Prujiner eds. 1986)

Holtzmann, H. & J. Neuhaus, *A Guide to the UNCITRAL Model Law on International Commercial Arbitration: Legislative History and Commentary* (Deventer 1989)

Jarvin, The Sources and Limits of the Arbitrator's Powers, 2 *Arb. Int'l* 140 (1986)

Laschet, Rechtsmittel gegen Prozess-, Vorab- oder Zwischenentscheidungen eines Schiedsgerichtes oder einer Schiedsgerichtsorganisation, in *Beiträge zum internationalen Verfahrensrechts und zur Schiedsgerichtbarkeit. Festschrift für Heinrich Nagel* 167 (W. Habscheid & K. Schwab eds. 1987)

Lebedev S., *Mezhdunarodnyi kommercheskii arbitrazh: kompetentsia arbitrov i soglashenie stran* (Moscow 1988)

Mádl, Competence of Arbitral Tribunals in International Commercial Arbitration, in *Essays on International Commercial Arbitration* 92 (P. Sarcevic ed. 1989)

Mayer, L'autonomie de l'arbitre international dans l'appréciation de sa propre compétence, 217 *Recueil des Cours* 319 (1989)

Mezger, Compétence-compétence des arbitres et indépendence de la Convention arbitrale dans la Convention dite Européenne sur l'Arbitrage Commercial International de 1961, in *A.I.A., Essays in Memoriam Eugenio Minoli* 315 (Turin 1974)

————, Neueste Entwicklung von Gesetzgebung und Rechtssprechung (bis Anfang 1988) zur Zwischenentscheidung der Schiedsrichter über ihre eigene Zuständigkeit, in *Festschrift für Walther J. Habscheid* 177 (W. Lindacher, D. Pfaff et al. eds. 1989)

Mustill, Sir Michael J. & S. C. Boyd, *The Law and Practice of Commercial Arbitration in England* (2nd ed. 1989)

Paulsson, The Contribution of English and American Legislation, in *Euro-Arab Arbitration III* 104 (F. Kemicha ed. 1991)

Poncet, Challenges to the Jurisdiction of International Arbitrators: An Important Decision of the Swiss Supreme Court, 50 *Arbitration* 156 (1984)

Poznanski, The Nature and Extent of an Arbitrator's Power in International Commercial Arbitration, 4 *J. Int'l Arb.* 71 (No. 3, 1987)

Redfern, The Jurisdiction of an International Commercial Arbitrator, 3 *J. Int'l Arb.* 19 (1986); also 52 *Arbitrator* 254 (1986)

Rokison, The Sources and Limits of the Arbitrator's Powers in England, in *Contemporary Problems of International Arbitration* 86 (J.D.M. Lew ed. 1986); also 52 *Arbitration* 219 (1986)

Samuel, A., *Jurisdictional Problems in International Commercial Arbitration: A Study of Belgian, Dutch, English, French, Swedish, Swiss, U.S. and West German Law* (Zurich 1989)

Sandrock, Arbitration between U.S. and West German Companies: An Example of Effective Dispute Resolution in International Business Transactions, 9 *U. Pa. J. Int'l Bus. L.* 27 (1987)

Schlosser, P., *Das Recht der internationalen privaten Schiedsgerichtsbarkeit* (2nd rev. ed. Tübingen 1989)

Schmitthoff, The Jurisdiction of the Arbitrator, in *The Art of Arbitration* 285 (J. Schultsz & A. van den Berg eds. 1982)

Schwab, Die Entscheidung des Schiedsgerichts über seine eigene Zuständigkeit: Eine Stellungsnahme zum Verhältnis von Hauptvertrag und Schiedsvertrag und zur sog. Kompetenz-Kompetenz des Schiedsgerichts, 22 *KTS* 17 (1961)

Schweizer & Guillod, L'exception de litispendance et l'arbitrage international: quelques refléxions sur le pour et le contre, in *Le Juriste Suisse Face au Droit et aux Jugements Etrangers: Ouverture ou Repli?* 71 (F. Knoepfler ed. 1988)

Soper, Authority and the English Arbitrator, 46 *Arbitration* 195 (1980)

Tschanz, International Arbitration in the United States: The Need for a New Act, 3 *Arb. Int'l* 309 (1987)

Wetter, The Importance of Having a Connection, 3 *Arb. Int'l* 329 (1987)

12.03 RIGHT TO DETERMINE THE VALIDITY OF THE ARBITRATION AGREEMENT

Cremades, Arbitration Agreement and Jurisdiction of Arbitral Tribunal, 24 *Rassegna dell'Arb.* 27 (1984)

Lalive, Problèmes relatifs à l'arbitrage international commercial, 120 *Recueil des Cours* 569 (1967-II)

Mezger, Compétence-compétence des arbitres et indépendence de la Convention arbitrale dans la Convention dite Européenne sur l'Arbitrage Commercial International de 1961, in *A.I.A., Essays in Memoriam Eugenio Minoli* 315 (Turin 1974)

Redfern, The Jurisdiction of an International Commercial Arbitrator, 3 *J. Int'l Arb.* 19 (1986); also 52 *Arbitrator* 254 (1986)

Ventura, Convençao de arbitragem, 46 *Revista da Ordem dos Advogados* 289 (1986)

12.04 RIGHT TO DETERMINE APPLICABLE LAW

Blessing, International Arbitration Procedures, 17 Int'l Bus. Law. 408 and 451 (1989)

Crook, Applicable Law in International Arbitration: The Iran-U.S. Claims Tribunal Experience, 83 Am. J. Int'l L. 278 (1989)

Derains, Determination de la lex contractus, in ICC, L'apport de la jurisprudence arbitrale 7 (1986)

Gaillard, The Use of Comparative Law in International Commercial Arbitration, in Arbitration in Settlement of International Commercial Disputes Involving the Far East and Arbitration in Combined Transportation 283 (P. Sanders ed. 1989); reprinted in 55 Arbitration 263 (1989)

Lando, The Law Applicable to the Merits of the Dispute, 2 Arb. Int'l 104 (1986)

————, The Law Applicable to the Merits of the Dispute, in Essays on International Commercial Arbitration 129 (P. Sarcevic ed. 1989)

————, The Law Applicable to the Merits of the Dispute, in Contemporary Problems in International Arbitration 101 (J.D.M. Lew ed. 1986)

Mezger, The Arbitrator and Private International Law, in International Trade Arbitration 229 (M. Domke ed. 1958)

Poznanski, The Nature and Extent of an Arbitrator's Powers in International Commercial Arbitration, 4 J. Int'l Arb. 71 (No. 3, 1987)

Sajko, The New York Arbitration Convention of 1958 from the Yugoslav Point of View: Selected Issues, in Essays on International Commercial Arbitration 199 (P. Sarcevic ed. 1989)

Schiffer, Sonderanknüpfung ausländischen 'öffentlichen' Rechts durch Richterrecht in der Internationalen Handelsschiedsgerichtsbarkeit, 11 IPRax 84 (1991)

van Houtte, Conduct of Arbitral Proceedings, in Essays on International Commercial Arbitration 113 (P. Sarcevic ed. 1989)

12.05 RIGHT TO DECIDE *EX AEQUO ET BONO*; POWERS OF THE *AMIABLE COMPOSITEUR*

Bischoff, Amiables Compositeurs in English Arbitration Law, 44 *Arbitration* 60 (1978)

Blessing, International Arbitration Procedures, 17 *Int'l Bus. Law.* 408 and 451 (1989)

Bucher, A., *Die neue internationale Schiedsgerichtsbarkeit in der Schweiz* (Basel 1989)

————, *Le nouvel arbitrage international en Suisse. Théorie et pratique de droit* (Basel 1988)

Bucher, A. & P.-Y.Tschanz, *International Arbitration in Switzerland* (Basel 1989)

Galgano, L'equità degli arbitri, 45 *Riv. Trim. Dir. & Proc. Civ.* 409 (1991)

Harrison, Equity Clauses and Arbitration, 85 *L. Soc'y Gazette* 35 (No. 43, 1988)

Jolidon, La sentence en equité dans le Concordat suisse sur l'arbitrage, in *Recueil de Travaux Suisses* 259 (C. Reymond & E. Bucher eds. 1984)

Mezger, La distinction entre l'arbitre dispense d'observer la règle de la loi et l'arbitre statuant sans appel, in *Liber Amicorum for Martin Domke* 184 (P. Sanders ed. 1967)

Nestor, L'amiable compositeur et l'arbitrage selon les règles de droit, in *A.I.A., Essays in Memoriam Eugenio Minoli* 341 (Turin 1974)

Poznanski, The Nature and Extent of an Arbitrator's Powers in International Commercial Arbitration, 4 *J. Int'l Arb.* 71 (No. 3, 1987)

Riedberg, P., *Der amiable Compositeur im internationalen privaten Schiedsgerichtsverfahren* (Frankfurt 1962)

12.06 RIGHTS PERTAINING TO THE CONDUCT
OF PROCEEDINGS

de Leval, Les mesures provisoires et conservatoires en matière d'arbitrage, in *L'Arbitrage* 111 (L. Matray & G. de Leval eds. 1989)

Dermine, L'arbitre et les mesures d'instruction, in *L'Arbitrage* 73 (L. Matray & G. de Leval eds. 1989)

Habscheid, Einstweiliger Rechtsschutz durch Schiedsgericht nach dem schweizerischen Gesetz über das Internationale Privatrecht (IPRG), 9 *IPRax* 134 (1989)

Hjerner, On Partial Awards, Orders and Other Decisions in Arbitral Proceedings, in Particular with Respect to Arbitration in Sweden, 1984 *Y.B. Swed. & Int'l Arb.* 31

Holtzmann H. & J. Neuhaus, *A Guide to the UNCITRAL Model Law on International Commercial Arbitration: Legislative History and Commentary* (Deventer 1989)

Jarvin, The Sources and Limits of the Arbitrator's Powers, 2 *Arb. Int'l* 140 (1986)

Kassis, The Questionable Validity of Arbitration and Awards under the Rules of the International Chambre of Commerce, 6 *J. Int'l Arb.* 79 (No. 2, 1989)

Kohl B., *Vorläufiger Rechtsschutz in international en Handels-schiedsverfahren* (Berne 1990)

Laschet, Rechtsmittel gegen Prozess-, Vorab- oder Zwischenentscheidungen eines Schiedsgerichtes oder einer Schiedsgerichtsorganisation, in *Beiträge zum internationalen Verfahrensrechts und zur Schiedsgerichtbarkeit. Festschrift für Heinrich Nagel* 167 (W. Habscheid & K. Schwab eds. 1987)

Oehmke, T., *International Arbitration* (Rochester 1990)

Poznanski, The Nature and Extent of an Arbitrator's Power in International Commercial Arbitration, 4 *J. Int'l Arb.* 71 (No. 3, 1987)

Sandrock & Nöcker, Einstweilige Massnahmen internationaler Schieds-gerichte: Blosse Papiertiger? 1 *Jahrbuch Schiedsgerichtsbarkeit* 74 (1987)

Soper, Authority and the English Arbitrator, 46 *Arbitration* 195 (1980)

Tan, Multiple Parties and Causes of Action in Arbitration Proceedings, 1988 *Malayan L.J.* li

12.07 TERMINATION OF AUTHORITY

Böckstiegel, Applying the UNCITRAL Rules: The Experience of the Iran-United States Claims Tribunal, 4 *Int'l Tax & Bus. Law.* 266 (1986)

de Leval, La designation et la mission des arbitres. Notes succinctes sur le droit positif applicable en Belgique, 53 *Rev. Droit Int'l & Droit Comp.* 170 (1976)

Mádl, Competence of Arbitral Tribunals in International Commercial Arbitration, in *Essays on International Commercial Arbitration* 92 (P. Sarcevic ed. 1989)

Mustill, Sir Michael J. & S. C. Boyd, *The Law and Practice of Commercial Arbitration in England* (2nd ed. 1989)

Poznanski, The Nature and Extent of an Arbitrator's Power in International Commercial Arbitration, 4 *J. Int'l Arb.* 71 (No. 3, 1987)

Raeschke-Kessler & Bühler, Aufsicht über den Schiedsrichter durch den ICC-Schiedsgerichtshof (Paris) und rechtliches Gehör der Parteien, 8 *ZIP* 1157 (1987)

Real, G.K.L., *Der Schiedsrichtervertrag* (Cologne 1983)

Voskuil & Freedberg-Swartzburg, Composition of the Arbitral Tribunal, in *Essays on International Commercial Arbitration* 64 (P. Sarcevic ed. 1989)

Wenger, Zur Ablehnung von Schiedsrichtern im schweizerischen Schiedsverfahrensrecht, 8 *IPRax* 116 (1988)

13. APPLICABLE LAW

13.01 IN GENERAL

Alvarez Gonzalez, Arbitraje y derecho aplicable (Anotaciones al Título X de la Ley 36/1988 de Arbitraje), 5 *Rev. Corte Esp. Arb.* 171 (1988—1989)

Arbitration Institute of the Stockholm Chamber of Commerce, *Arbitration in Sweden* (2nd rev. ed. 1984)

Ball, Structuring the Arbitration in Advance — the Arbitration Clause in an International Development Agreement, in *Contemporary Problems in International Arbitration* 297 (J.D.M. Lew ed. 1986)

Böckstiegel, Die Bestimmung des anwendbaren Rechts in der Praxis internationaler Schiedsgerichtsverfahren, in *Festschrift für Günther Beitzke zum 70. Geburtstag* 443 (Berlin 1979)

Bond, How to Draft an Arbitration Clause, 6 *J. Int'l Arb.* 65 (No. 2, 1989)

Boyd, 'Arbitrator not to bound by the Law' Clauses, 6 *Arb. Int'l* 122 (1990)

Broches, The Convention on the Settlement of Investment Disputes between States and Nationals of Other States: Applicable Law and Default Procedure, in *Liber Amicorum for Martin Domke* 12 (P. Sanders ed. 1967)

Collins, The Law Governing the Agreement and Procedure in International Commercial Arbitration in England, in *Contemporary Problems in International Arbitration* 126 (J.D.M. Lew ed. 1986)

Delaume, L'arbitrage transnational et les tribunaux nationaux, 111 *J. Droit Int'l (Clunet)* 521 (1984)

Delaume, G., *Transnational Contracts, Applicable Law and Settlement of Disputes: A Study in Conflict Avoidance* (Dobbs Ferry, NY 1975)

Dellet, Arbitration, Forum Selection, and Choice of Law in International Securities Transactions, 42 *Wash. and Lee L. Rev.* 1069 (1985)

Derains, Public Policy and the Law Applicable to the Dispute in International Arbitration, in *Comparative Arbitration Practice and Public Policy in Arbitration* 227 (P. Sanders ed. 1987)

363

Deshpande, International Commercial Arbitration: Uniformity of Jurisdiction, 5 *J. Int'l Arb.* 115 (No. 2, 1988)

Dilger, Schiedsgerichtsbarkeit und Volstreckung ausländischer Entscheidungen in den Golfstaaten, in *Vetragspraxis und Streiterledigung im Wirschaftverkehr mit arabischen Staaten* 101 (K.-H. Böckstiegel ed. 1981)

Ebenroth & Parche, Schiedsgerichtsklauseln als alternative Streiterledigungsmechanismen in internationalen Konsortialkreditverträgen und Umschuldungsabkommen, 36 *RIW* 341 (1990)

————, Arbitration Clauses as Alternative Mechanisms for the Settlement of Conflicts Involving International Syndicate Loan Agreements and Restructuring Agreements, 38 *Neth. Int'l L. Rev.* 1 (1991)

Eisemann, Zur Rechtswahl in der Schiedsgerichtsbarkeit bei Kaufvertragen, in *Festschrift für Arthur Bülow* 59 (K.-H. Böckstiegel & O. Glossner eds. 1981)

Foustoucos, Conditions Required for the Validity of an Arbitration Agreement, 5 *J. Int'l Arb.* 113 (No. 4, 1988)

Gaillard, Le point de vue d'un utilisateur étranger, 1989 *Int'l Bus. L.J.* 793

Gamboa Serrano, Ley aplicable en el arbitraje internacional, in *Alternativas a la justicia institucional: arbitraje, conciliación* 123 (Bogota 1988)

Gentinetta, Was ist Lex fori privater internationaler Schiedsgerichte? 84 *ZSR* 139 (1965)

Gentinetta, J., *Die lex fori internationaler Handelsschiedsgerichte* (Bern 1973)

Gergtz, The Selection of Choice of Law Provisions in International Commercial Arbitration: A Case for Contractual Depeçage, 12 *Nw. J. Int'l L. & Bus.* 163 (1991)

Goldman, La lex mercatoria dans les contrats et l'arbitrage internationaux; realités et perspectives, 106 *J. Droit Int'l (Clunet)* 475 (1979)

Haardt, Choice of Law Clauses in Arbitration Agreements, in 1 *Hague-Zagreb Essays* 215 (C. Voskuil & N. Katitic eds. 1974)

Hjerner, Choice of Law Problems in International Arbitration with Particular Reference to Arbitration in Sweden, 1982 *Y.B. Swed. & Int'l Arb.* 18

Hobér, Das anzuwendende Recht beim internationalen Schiedsverfahren in Schweden, 32 *RIW* 685 (1986)

International Chamber of Commerce, *L'apport de la jurisprudence arbitrale. Seminaire des 7 et 8 avril 1986* (Paris 1986)

Iwasaki, Drafting Arbitration Clauses Designating Tokyo As Arbitration Site, 11 *Bull. Japan Shipping Exch.* 1 (1985)

Jakubowski, Choice of Law Clauses in Arbitration Agreements, in 1 *Hague-Zagreb Essays* 225 (C. Voskuil & N. Katicic eds. 1974)

Kahale, Arbitration and Choice of Law Clauses as Waivers of Jurisdictional Immunity, 14 *N.Y.U. J. Int'l L. & Pol.* 29 (1981)

Kessler, J., *Die Bindung des Schiedsgerichts an das materielle Recht* (Cologne 1964)

Kitagawa, Applicable Law of the UNCITRAL Rules, in *ICCA, Fifth Int'l Arb. Congress: Proceedings* C Ik 1-6 (1975)

Lalive, Problèmes relatifs à l'arbitrage international commercial, 120 *Recueil des Cours* 569 (1967-II)

Lando, The Law Applicable to the Merits of the Dispute, in *Essays on International Commercial Arbitration* 129 (P. Sarcevic ed. 1989)

Lebedev, Application of Law by the Maritime Arbitration Commission in Settling Disputes, 44 *Arbitration* 18 (1977)

Lee, E., *Encyclopedia of International Commercial Arbitration* (London 1986)

Lew, Applicable Law in Commercial Arbitration, 47 *Arbitration* 92 (1981)

Lew, J., *Applicable Law in International Commercial Arbitration. A Study in Commercial Arbitration Awards* (Dobbs Ferry 1978)

——, *Contemporary Problems in International Arbitration* (London 1986)

Mann, Lex Facit Arbitrum, in *Liber Amicorum for Martin Domke* 157 (P. Sanders ed. 1967)

Marin Lopez, La Ley aplicable al convenio arbitral, 5 *Rev. Corte Esp. Arb.* 191(1988—1989)

Marriott, Arbitrating International Commercial Disputes in the United Kingdom, 44 *Arb. J.* 3 (No. 3, 1989)

Masood, Law Applicable in Arbitration of Investment Disputes under the World Bank Convention, 15 *J. Ind. L. Inst.* 311 (1973)

Mezger, Du consentement en matière "d'electio juris" et de clause compromissoire, 50 *Rev. Crit. Droit Int'l Privé* 37 (1971)

Minakov, K voprosu ob opredelenii prava, primenimogo k soglasheniu ob arbitrazhe (arbitrazhnoi ogovorke), 1976 *Soviet Y.B. Int'l L.* 136

Moreau, B. & T. Bernard, *Droit interne et droit international de l'arbitrage* (2nd ed. 1985)

Mostafa, The Applicable Law in Commerce Arbitration between American and Egyptian Parties, 32 *Rev. Egyptienne Droit Int'l* 179 (1976)

Mustill, Sir Michael J. & S. C. Boyd, *The Law and Practice of Commercial Arbitration in England* (2nd ed. 1989)

Note, Arbitration, Forum Selection, and Choice of Law Agreements in International Security Transactions, 42 *Wash. & Lee L. Rev.* 1069 (1985)

Ochoa Bunsow, A., *El derecho applicable en el arbitraje comercial international* (Mexico 1980)

Park & Paulsson, Arbitrage commercial et contrats internationaux, 45 *Rev. Barreau* 215 (1985)

Pedrazzini, Essentialia e accidentialia della clausola compromissoria, in *Recueil de Travaux Suisses* 71 (C. Reymond & E. Bucher eds. 1984)

Praendl, Measure of Damages in International Commercial Arbitration, 23 *Stan. J. Int'l L.* 263 (1987)

Pryles, Comparative Aspects of Prorogation and Arbitration Agreements, 25 *Int'l & Comp. L.Q.* 543 (1976)

Redfern, The Arbitration between the Government of Kuwait and Aminoil, 55 *Brit. Y.B. Int'l L.* 65 (1984)

Redfern, A. & M. Hunter, *Law and Practice of International Commercial Arbitration* (2nd ed. 1991)

Robert, De la place de la loi dans l'arbitrage, in *Liber Amicorum for Martin Domke* 226 (P. Sanders ed. 1967)

Robert, J. & B. Morceau, *L'arbitrage — droit interne, droit international privé* (5th ed. Paris 1983)

Sajko, The New York Arbitration Convention of 1958 from the Yugoslav Point of View: Selected Issues, in *Essays on International Commercial Arbitration* 199 (P. Sarcevic ed. 1989)

Sanders, Trends in the Field of International Commercial Arbitration, 145 *Recueil des Cours* 205 (1975-II)

Sandrock, Arbitration between U.S. and West German Companies: An Example of Effective Dispute Resolution in International Business Transactions, 9 *U. Pa. J. Int'l Bus. L.* 27 (1987)

————, Choice of Law and Choice of Forum in Civil Law Jurisdictions, in *Drafting and Enforcing Contracts in Civil and Common Law Jurisdictions* 145 (K. Yelpaala, M. Rubino-Sammartano & D. Campbell eds. 1986)

————, Zügigkeit und Leichtigkeit versus Grundlichkeit: Internationale Schiedsverfahren in der Bundesrepublik Deutschland, 41 *JZ* 370 (1986)

Smit, A-National Arbitration, 63 *Tul. L. Rev.* 629 (1989)

Stumpf, Ost-West-Schiedsgerichtsbarkeit: Schiedsgerichte mit Sitz in dritten Ländern, 33 *RIW* 821 (1987)

Subramanian, Trade Terms and International Contracts, in *ICCA, Sixth Int'l Arb. Congress: Proceedings* 459 (1978)

ter Kuile, Internationale arbitrage en Gemeenschapsrecht, in *Iustitia et Amicitia. Geschillenbeslechting in en Buiten Rechte* 33 (Arnheim 1985)

Thomas, Arbitration Agreements as a Signpost of the Proper Law, 1984 *Lloyd's Mar. & Com. L.Q* 141

————, Proper Law of Arbitration Agreements, 1984 *Lloyd's Mar. & Com. L. Q.* 304

Timmermans, The USSR Maritime Arbitration Commission, 1987 L*loyd's Mar. & Com. L.Q.* 350 and 468

Ulmer, Drafting the International Arbitration Clause, 20 *Int'l Law.* 1335 (1986)

van Houtte, Le droit applicable a l'arbitrage commercial international, 57 *Rev. Droit Int'l & Droit Comp.* 285 (1980)

van Niekerk, Aspects of Proper Law, Curial Law and International Commercial Arbitration, 2 *SA Mercantile L.J.* 117 (1990)

von Hoffmann, B., *Internationale Handelsschiedsgerichtsbarkeit. Die Bestimmung des massgeblichen Rechts* (Frankfurt 1970)

Wetter, Choice of Law in International Arbitration Proceedings in Sweden, 1984 *Y.B. Swed. & Int'l Arb.* 16

13.02 LAW APPLICABLE TO PROCEDURE

Audit, L'arbitrage transnational et les contrats d'Etat: Bilan et perspectives/ Transnational Arbitration and State Contracts, in *L'arbitrage transnational et les contrats d'Etat/Transnational Arbitration and State Contracts* 23, 77 (Dordrecht 1988)

Becker, Choice of Law and the Federal Arbitration Act: The Shock of Volt, 45 *Arb. J.* 32 (No. 2, 1990)

Böckstiegel, The Relevance of National Arbitration Law for Arbitration under the UNCITRAL Rules, 1 *J. Int'l Arb.* 223 (No. 3, 1984)

Cohen, La soumission de l'arbitrage international à la loi française (Commentaire de l'article 1495 NCPC), 1991 *Rev. Arb.* 155

Coing, Materielles Recht und Verfahrensrecht in der internationalen Schiedsgerichtsbarkeit, in *Law and International Trade* 19 (Frankfurt 1973)

Collins, The Law Governing the Agreement and Procedure in International Commercial Arbitration in England, in *Contemporary Problems in International Arbitration* 126 (J.D.M. Lew ed. 1986)

Danilowicz, The Choice of Applicable Law in International Arbitration, 9 *Hastings Int'l & Comp. L. Rev.* 235 (1986)

De Ly, The Place of Arbitration in the Conflict of Laws of International Commercial Arbitration: An Exercise in Arbitration Planning, 12 *Nw. J. Int'l L. & Bus.* 48 (1991)

Goldman, L'arbitre, les conflits des lois et la lex mercatoria, in *First Int'l Commercial Arbitrational Conference: Proceedings* 104 (N. Antaki & A. Prujiner eds. 1986)

Herrmann, The UNCITRAL Model Law on International Commercial Arbitration — Its Salient Features and Prospects, in *First Int'l Commercial Arbitration Conference: Proceedings* 351 (N. Antaki & A. Prujiner eds. 1986)

Hirsch, The Place of Arbitration and the Lex Arbitri, 34 *Arb. J.* 43 (No. 3, 1979)

Hobér, Arbitration in Moscow, 3 *Arb. Int'l* 119 (1987)

Holtzmann, H. & J. Neuhaus, *A Guide to the UNCITRAL Model Law on International Commercial Arbitration: Legislative History and Commentary* (Deventer 1989)

Mann, English Procedural Law and Foreign Arbitrations, 19 *Int'l & Comp. L.Q.* 693 (1970)

————, Schiedsrichter und Recht, in *Festschrift für Werner Flume* 593 (Cologne 1978)

Matray, Quelques problèmes de l'arbitrage commercial international (doctrine et jurisprudence), in *L'Arbitrage* 289 (L. Matray & G. de Leval eds. 1989)

Nolting, Mangelnde Feststellung des für Formwirksamkeit der Schiedsklausel und Schiedsfähigkeit massgeblichen Rechts, 7 *IPRax* 349 (1987)

Note, The UNCITRAL Model Law—Lex Facit Arbitrum, 2 *Arb. Int'l* 241 (1986)

Pacific Rim Advisory Council, *Pacific Rim: Commercial Arbitration Procedures* (San Diego, CA 1985)

Park, The Lex Loci Arbitri and International Commercial Arbitration, 32 *Int'l & Comp. L.Q.* 21 (1983)

Park & Paulsson, The Binding Force of International Arbitral Awards, 23 *Va. J. Int'l L.* 253 (1983)

Poudret, Challenge and Enforcement of Arbitral Awards in Switzerland, 4 *Arb. Int'l* 278 (1988)

Rao, Proper Law of Contract with Arbitration Clauses, 29 *J. Ind. L. Inst.* 60 (1987)

Reiner, Die internationale Schiedsgerichtsbarkeit nach österreichischem und französischem Recht. Ein Vergleich zweier Reformen jüngeren Datums, 27 *ZRV* 162 (1986)

Rubino-Sammartano, Nationality of Awards and Applicable Substantive and Procedural Law, 48 *Arbitration* 47 (1982)

Rubino-Sammartano, M., *International Arbitration Law* (Deventer 1990)

Sanders, Trends in the Field of International Commercial Arbitration, 145 *Recueil des Cours* 205 (1975-II)

Schlosser, Die Fortbildung des Prozessrechts durch die Internationale Schiedsgerichtsbarkeit, in *Rechtsfortsbildung durch internationale Schiedsgerichtsbarkeit* 5 (K.-H. Böckstiegel ed. 1989)

Trappe, Links between Arbitrators and the Courts, 44 *Arbitration* 69 (1978)

van Compernolle, L'arbitrage dans les relations commerciales internationales: questions de procédure, 66 *Rev. Droit Int'l & Droit Comp.* 101 (1989)

van Niekerk, Aspects of Proper Law, Curial Law and International Commercial Arbitration, 2 *SA Mercantile L.J.* 117 (1990)

Wilner, Determining the Law Governing Performance in International Commercial Arbitration, 19 *Rutgers L. Rev.* 646 (1965)

13.03 LAW APPLICABLE TO THE MERITS

Ancel, The Tronc Commun Doctrine: Logics and Experience in International Arbitration, 7 *J. Int'l Arb.* 65 (No. 3, 1990)

Bernardini, Les arbitrages pétroliers et le droit appliqué par les arbitres, in *First Euro-Arab Arbitration Conference: Proceedings* 282 (F. Kemicha ed. 1987)

Blom, Conflict of Laws Aspects of the International Commercial Arbitration Act, in *UNCITRAL Arbitration Model in Canada* 127 (R. Paterson & B. Thompson eds. 1987)

Bogdan, Some Arbitration-Related Problems of Swedish Private International Law, 1990 *Y.B. Swed. & Int'l Arb.* 70

Branson & Wallace, Choosing the Substantive Law to Apply in International Commercial Arbitration, 27 *Va. J. Int'l L.* 39 (1986)

Cherian, A New Response to the Question of Law in Transnational Investment Arbitration, in *ICCA, Fifth Int'l Arb. Congress: Proceedings* C Ib 1-5 (1975)

Coing, Materielles Recht und Verfahrensrecht in der internationalen Schiedsgerichtsbarkeit, in *Law and International Trade* 19 (Frankfurt 1973)

Crane, Arbitral Freedom from Substantive Law, 14 *Arb. J.* 163 (1959)

Crook, Applicable Law in International Arbitration: The Iran-U.S. Claims Tribunal Experience, 83 *Am. J. Int'l L.* 278 (1989)

Danilowicz, The Choice of Applicable Law in International Arbitration, 9 *Hastings Int'l & Comp. L. Rev.* 235 (1986)

Derains, L'ordre public et le droit applicable au fond du litige dans l'arbitrage international, 1986 *Rev. Arb.* 375

————, Public Policy and the Law Applicable to the Dispute in International Arbitration, in *Comparative Arbitration Practice and Public Policy in Arbitration* 227 (P. Sanders ed. 1987)

Dimitrakou-Deliyanni, Arbitrage commercial international et contrats internationaux en matière de représentation commerciale, 38-39 *Rev. Hellénique Droit Int'l* 147 (1985-86)

Drobnig, Internationale Schiedsgerichtsbarkeit und wirtschaftsrechtliche Eingriffsnormen, in *Festschrift für Gerhard Kegel* 97 (Musielak & Schurig eds. 1987)

Duintjer Tebbens, A Facelift for Dutch Arbitration Law, 34 *Neth. Int'l L. Rev.* 141 (1987)

Eisemann, Zur Rechtswahl in der Schiedsgerichtsbarkeit bei Kaufvertragen, in *Festschrift für Arthur Bülow* 59 (K.-H. Böckstiegel & O. Glossner eds. 1981)

El-Kosheri & Riad, The Changing Roles in the Arbitration Process (with Regard to the Applicable Law Governing the New Generation of the Petroleum Agreements), 1 *Arab L. Q.* 475 (1986); also in *First Euro-Arab Arbitration Conference: Proceedings* 253 (F. Kemicha ed. 1987)

Erecinski, Zagadnienia prawa wlasciwego i postepowania dowodowego w miedzynarodowym arbitrazu handlowym, 42 *Panstwo i Prawo* 49 (No. 9, 1987)

Fumagalli, La legge applicabile al merito della controversia nell'arbitrato commerciale internazionale, 21 *Riv. Dir. Int'le Priv. & Proc.* 465 (1985)

Gaillard, The Use of Comparative Law in International Commercial Arbitration, in *Arbitration in Settlement of International Commercial Disputes Involving the Far East and Arbitration in Combined Transportation* 283 (P. Sanders ed. 1989); reprinted in 55 *Arbitration* 263 (1989)

Goldman, International Arbitration in Europe, in *IBA, Soviet Foreign Trade Reforms & East/West Arbitration* 217 (1988)

————, L'arbitre, les conflits des lois et la lex mercatoria, in *First Int'l Com. Arb. Conference: Proceedings* 104 (N. Antaki & A. Prujiner eds. 1986)

————, Le droit applicable selon la Convention de la B.I.R.D., du 18 mars 1965, pour le règlement des différends relatifs aux investissements entre Etats et ressortissants d'autre Etats, in *Investissements étrangers et arbitrage entre Etats et personnes privées* 133 (Paris 1969)

Hertzfeld, Applicable Law and Dispute Settlement in Soviet Joint Ventures, 3 *ICSID Rev. - Foreign Investment L.J.* 249 (1988)

Hintz, Recht und Praxis der Streiterledigung im Ost-West-Handel am Beispiel des Handels zwischen der UdSSR und der Bundesrepublik Deutschland, 32 *RIW* 506 (1986)

Hobér, Arbitration in Moscow, 3 *Arb. Int'l* 119 (1987)

Horsmans, L'interprétation des contrats internationaux, in *ICC, L'apport de la jurisprudence arbitrale* 123 (1986)

Jakubowski, Les problèmes de loi applicable et de l'arbitrage dans la coopération industrielle entre l'Est et l'Ouest, in *ICC, Hommage à Fréderic Eisemann* 103 (1978)

Klein, The Law to Be Applied by the Arbitrators to the Substance of the Dispute, in *The Art of Arbitration* 189 (J. Schultsz & A. van den Berg eds. 1982)

Koslow, The Arbitrator's Power to Award Punitive Damages in International Contract Actions, 19 *N.Y.U. J. Int'l L. & Pol.* 203 (1986)

Lalive, Contracts between a State or a State Agency and a Foreign Company: Theory and Practice: Choice of Law in a New Arbitration Case, 13 *Int'l Comp. L.Q.* 987 (1964)

———, Le droit applicable au fond du litige en matière d'arbitrage, 17 *Rassegna dell'Arb.* 1 (1977)

———, Possible Conflict of Laws Rules and the Rules Applicable to the Substance of the Dispute, 24 *Rassegna dell'Arb.* 49 (1984)

Lando, The Law Applicable to the Merits of the Dispute, 2 *Arb. Int'l* 104 (1986)

———, The Law Applicable to the Merits of the Dispute, in *Essays on International Commercial Arbitration* 129 (P. Sarcevic ed. 1989)

———, The Law Applicable to the Merits of the Dispute, in *Contemporary Problems in International Arbitration* 101 (J.D.M. Lew ed. 1986)

Lebedev, Application of Law by the Maritime Arbitration Commission in Settling Disputes, 6 *Ga. J. Int'l & Comp. L.* 519 (1976)

Lowenfeld, The Two-Way Mirror: International Arbitration as Comparative Procedure, 7 *Mich. Y.B. Int'l Legal Stud.* 163 (1985)

Matray, Quelques problèmes de l'arbitrage commercial international (doctrine et jurisprudence), in *L'Arbitrage* 289 (L. Matray & G. de Leval eds. 1989)

Mayer, L'interference des lois de police, in *ICC, L'apport de la jurisprudence arbitrale* 31 (1986)

Moitry, L'arbitre international et l'obligation de boycottage imposée par un Etat, 118 *J. Droit Int'l (Clunet)* 349 (1991)

Monaco, Le droit applicable au fond du litige dans la convention sur l'arbitrage commercial international, 9 *Nederlands Tijtschrift voor Int'l Ret* 331 (1962)

Park, El arbitraje comercial internacional y la lex loci arbitri: perspectiva de la Ley de Arbitraje inglesa, 2 *Rev. Corte Esp. Arb.* 57 (1957)

Perez Bevia, Sobre la ley aplicable por el árbitro al fondo de la controversia en el derecho internacional privado español, 5 *Rev. Corte Esp. Arb.* 213 (1988—1989)

Ramzaitsev, The Law Applied by Arbitral Tribunals, in *The Sources of the Law of International Trade* 138 (C. Schmitthoff ed. 1964)

Revoredo de Debakey, La selección de las leyes aplicables a la validez del acuerdo arbitral y al fondo de la controversia en el arbitraje comercial international, 7 *Anuario Hispano-Luso-Americano de Derecho Internacional* 329 (1984)

Rigaux, La detérmination de l'ordre juridique auquel se rattachent les arbitrages petroliers, in *First Euro-Arab Arbitration Conference: Proceedings* 298 (F. Kemicha ed. 1987)

Rubino-Sammartano, Le tronc commun des lois nationales en présence (refléxions sur le droit applicable par l'arbitrage international), 1987 *Rev. Arb.* 133

————, Nationality of Awards and Applicable Substantive and Procedural Law, 48 *Arbitration* 47 (1982)

Rubino-Sammartano, M., *International Arbitration Law* (Deventer 1990)

Sandrock, Die Fortbildung des materiellen Rechts durch die internationale Schiedsgerichtsbarkeit, in *Rechtsfortbildung durch internationale Schiedsgerichtsbarkeit* 21 (K.-H. Böckstiegel ed. 1989)

Schiffer, Sonderanknüpfung ausländischen 'öffentlichen' Rechts durch Richterrecht in der Internationalen Handelsschiedsgerichtsbarkeit, 11 *IPRax* 84 (1991)

Schlosser, P., *Das Recht der internationalen privaten Schiedsgerichtsbarkeit* (2nd rev. ed. Tübingen 1989)

Schmidt, L'interprétation des contrats internationaux par la Commission Arbitrale du Commerce Extérieur de l'URSS, 1985 *Int'l Bus. L.J.* 239

Smit, The Future of International Commercial Arbitration: A Single Transnational Institution? 25 *Colum. J. Transnat'l L.* 9 (1986)

Spiro, England Rejects Delocalized Contracts and Arbitration, 33 *Int'l & Comp. L.Q.* 193 (1984)

Stewart, The Iran-United States Claims Tribunal: A Review of Developments 1983-84, 16 *L. & Pol. Int'l Bus.* 677 (1984)

Strenger, The Application by the Arbitrator of Public Policy Rules to the Substance of the Dispute, in *Comparative Arbitration Practice and Public Policy in Arbitration* 353 (P. Sanders ed. 1987)

Tallon, The Law Applied by Arbitration Tribunals, in *The Sources of the Law of International Trade* 154 (C. Schmitthoff ed. 1984)

Tesón, State Contracts and Oil Expropriations: The Aminoil-Kuwait Arbitration, 24 *Va. J. Int'l L.* 323 (1984)

van Houtte, Arbitrage en toepasselijk recht, 19 *Tijdschrift voor Privaatrecht* 703 (1982)

van Niekerk, Aspects of Proper Law, Curial Law and International Commercial Arbitration, 2 *SA Mercantile L.J.* 117 (1990)

Westberg, The Applicable Law Issue in International Business Transactions with Government Parties: Ruling of the Iran-United States Claims Tribunal, 2 *ICSID Rev. - Foreign Investment L.J.* 473 (1987)

13.04 APPLICABLE CONFLICT-OF-LAWS SYSTEMS

Blom, Conflict of Laws Aspects of the International Commercial Arbitration Act, in *UNCITRAL Arbitration Model in Canada* 127 (R. Paterson & B. Thompson eds. 1987)

Bucher, A., *Die neue internationale Schiedsgerichtsbarkeit in der Schweiz* (Basel 1989)

————, *Le nouvel arbitrage international en Suisse. Théorie et pratique de droit* (Basel 1988)

Bucher, A. & P.-Y. Tschanz, *International Arbitration in Switzerland* (Basel 1989)

Croff, The Applicable Law in an International Commercial Arbitration: Is It Still a Conflict of Laws Problem? 16 *Int'l Law.* 613 (1982)

Crook, Applicable Law in International Arbitration: The Iran-U.S. Claims Tribunal Experience, 83 *Am. J. Int'l L.* 278 (1989)

Danilowicz, The Choice of Applicable Law in International Arbitration, 9 *Hastings Int'l & Comp. L. Rev.* 235 (1986)

De Ly, The Place of Arbitration in the Conflict of Laws of International Commercial Arbitration: An Exercise in Arbitration Planning, 12 *Nw. J. Int'l L. & Bus.* 48 (1991)

Derains, L'application cumulative par l'arbitre des systèmes de conflit de lois intéressés au litige, 1972 *Rev. Arb.* 00

Goldman, L'arbitre, les conflits des lois et la lex mercatoria, in *First Int'l Commercial Arbitration Conference: Proceedings* 104 (N. Antaki & A. Prujiner eds. 1986)

————, Les conflits de lois dans l'arbitrage international de droit privé, 109 *Recueil de Cours* 347 (1963-II)

Hobér, Arbitration in Moscow, 3 *Arb. Int'l* 119 (1987)

Kassis, L'arbitre, les conflits de lois et la lex mercatoria, in *First Int'l Commercial Arbitration Conference: Proceedings* 133 (N. Antaki & A. Prujiner eds. 1986)

Lalive, Les règles de conflit de lois appliqués au fond du litige par l'arbitrage international siégeant en Suisse, 1976 *Rev. Arb.* 135

―――, Possible Conflict of Laws Rules and the Rules Applicable to the Substance of the Dispute, 24 *Rassegna dell'Arb.* 49 (1984)

Lando, Conflict-of-Law Rules for Arbitrators, in *Festschrift für Konrad Zweigert* 157 (Tübingen 1981)

―――, The Law Applicable to the Merits of the Dispute, in *Contemporary Problems in International Arbitration* 101 (J.D.M. Lew ed. 1986)

―――, The Law Applicable to the Merits of the Dispute, in *Essays on International Commercial Arbitration* 129 (P. Sarcevic ed. 1989)

Lew, Applicable Law in Commercial Arbitration, 47 *Arbitration* 92 (1981)

Lipstein, International Arbitration between Individuals and Governments and the Conflict of Laws, in *Contemporary Problems of International Law: Essays in Honour of Georg Schwarzenberger* 177 (B. Cheng & E.D. Brown eds. 1988)

Lowenfeld, The Two-Way Mirror: International Arbitration as Comparative Procedure, 7 *Mich. Y.B. Int'l Legal Stud.* 163 (1985)

Lynch, Conflict of Laws in Arbitration Agreements between Developed and Developing Countries, 11 *Ga. J. Int'l & Comp. L.* 669 (1981)

McClelland, Toward a More Mature System of International Commercial Arbitration: The Establishment of Uniform Rules of Procedure and the Elimination of the Conflict of Laws Questions, 5 *N.C.J. Int'l L. & Com. Reg.* 169 (1980)

Majoros, Das Kollisionsrecht der Konventionskonflikte etabliert sich: Die Regel der maximalen Wirksamkeit in der Doctrine des schweizerischen Bundesgerichts (Entscheidung Denysiana v. 14. März 1984), in *Festschrift für Karl H. Neumayer* 431 (W. Barfuss, B. Dutois, H. Forkel, U. Immenga & F. Majoros eds. 1985)

Perez Bevia, Sobre la ley aplicable por el árbitro al fondo de la controversia en el derecho internacional privado español, 5 *Rev. Corte Esp. Arb.* 213 (1988—1989)

Robert, De la règle de conflit à la règle materielle en matière d'arbitrage international (spécialement en droit international privé français), in *The Art of Arbitration* 273 (J. Schultsz & A. van den Berg eds. 1982)

Samuel, Developments in English Arbitration Law since the 1984 Antaios Decision, 5 *J. Int'l Arb.* 9 (No. 3, 1988)

Schwab, Kollisionsrechtliche Fragen des deutschen internationalen Schiedsverfahrensrechts, in *Festschrift für Martin Luther* 163 (Munich 1976)

Toop, S., *Mixed International Arbitration: Studies in Arbitration between States and Private Persons* (Cambridge 1990)

Wetter, Choice of Law in International Arbitration Proceedings in Sweden, 2 *Arb. Int'l* 294 (1986)

13.05 INTERNATIONAL AND TRANSNATIONAL LAW

Bebr, Arbitration Tribunals and Article 177 of the EEC Treaty, 22 *Common Mkt. L. Rev.* 489 (1985)

Bucher, A., *Die neue internationale Schiedsgerichtsbarkeit in der Schweiz* (Basel 1989)

————, *Le nouvel arbitrage international en Suisse. Théorie et pratique de droit* (Basel 1988)

Bucher, A. & P.-Y. Tschanz, *International Arbitration in Switzerland* (Basel 1989)

Cassoni, Lo jus gentium come metodo per la disciplina del contratto internazionale e dell'arbitrato commerciale internazionale, 25 *Diritto Comunitario e degli Scambi Internazionali* 289 (1986)

Crook, Applicable Law in International Arbitration: The Iran-U.S. Claims Tribunal Experience, 83 *Am. J. Int'l L.* 278 (1989)

Danilowicz, The Choice of Applicable Law in International Arbitration, 9 *Hastings Int'l & Comp. L. Rev.* 235 (1986)

Derains, Les normes d'application immédiate dans la jurisprudence arbitrale internationale, in *Le droit des relations économiques internationales. Etudes offertes à Berthold Goldman* 29 (Paris 1983)

Enderlein, Uniform Law and Its Application by Judges and Arbitrators, in *International Uniform Law in Practice* 329 (Rome and Dobbs Ferry, NY 1988)

Lalive, Transnational (or Truly International) Public Policy and International Arbitration, in *Comparative Arbitration Practice and Public Policy in Arbitration* 256 (P. Sanders ed. 1987)

Lando, The Law Applicable to the Merits of the Dispute, in *Essays on International Commercial Arbitration* 129 (P. Sarcevic ed. 1989)

Lipstein, International Arbitration between Individuals and Governments and the Conflict of Laws, in *Contemporary Problems of International Law: Essays in Honour of Georg Schwarzenberger* 177 (B. Cheng & E.D. Brown eds. 1988)

Loquin, L'application de règles anationales dans l'arbitrage commercial international, in *ICC, L'apport de la jurisprudence arbitrale* 67 (1986)

Majoros, Das Kollisionsrecht der Konventionskonflikte etabliert sich: Die Regel der maximalen Wirksamkeit in der Doctrine des schweizerischen Bundesgerichts (Entscheidung Denysiana v. 14 März 1984), in *Festschrift für Karl H. Neumayer* 431 (W. Barfuss, B. Dutois, H. Forkel, U. Immenga & F. Majoros eds. 1985)

Schmidt, L'interprétation des contrats internationaux par la Commission Arbitrale du Commerce Extérieur de l'URSS, 1985 *Int'l Bus. L.J.* 239

Schmitthoff, Arbitration and EEC Law, 24 *Common Mkt. L. Rev.* 143 (1987)

Thieffry, Arbitration and the New Rules Applicable to International Sales Contracts under the United Nations Convention, 4 *Arb. Int'l* 52 (1988)

Toop, S., *Mixed International Arbitration: Studies in Arbitration between States and Private Persons* (Cambridge 1990)

van Niekerk, Aspects of Proper Law, Curial Law and International Commercial Arbitration, 2 *SA Mercantile L.J.* 117 (1990)

van den Berg, Should an International Arbitrator Apply the New York Arbitration Convention of 1958? in *The Art of Arbitration* 39 (J. Schultsz & A. van den Berg eds. 1982)

von Mehren, To What Extent is International Commercial Arbitration Autonomous? in *Le droit des relations économiques internationales: Etudes offertes à Berthold Goldman* 217 (Paris 1983)

13.06 *LEX MERCATORIA*

Carbonneau, T., ed., *Lex Mercatoria and Arbitration: A Discussion of the New Law Merchant* (Ardsley-on-Hudson, NY 1990)

Cassoni, Lo jus gentium come metodo per la disciplina del contratto internazionale e dell'arbitrato commerciale internazionale, 25 *Diritto Comunitario e degli Scambi Internazionali* 289 (1986)

Cremades & Plehn, The New Lex Mercatoria and the Harmonization of the Laws of International Commercial Transactions, 2 *B.U. Int'l L. J.* 317 (1984)

Crook, Applicable Law in International Arbitration: The Iran-U.S. Claims Tribunal Experience, 83 *Am. J. Int'l L.* 278 (1989)

Danilowicz, The Choice of Applicable Law in International Arbitration, 9 *Hastings Int'l & Comp. L. Rev.* 235 (1986)

Dasser, F., *Internationale Schiedsgerichte und lex mercatoria* (Zurich 1989)

De Ly, F., *De lex mercatoria, inleiding op de studien van het transnationaal handelsrecht* (Antwerp and Apeldorn 1989)

Delaume, The Proper Law of State Contracts and the Lex Mercatoria: A Reappraisal, 3 *ICSID Rev. - Foreign Investment L.J.* 79 (1988)

Delaume, G., *Law and Practice of Transnational Contracts* (Dobbs Ferry, NY 1988)

Derains, L'obligation de minimiser le dommage dans la jurisprudence arbitrale, 1987 *Int'l Bus. L.J.* 375

————, Le statut des usages du commerce international devant les juridictions arbitrales, 1973 *Rev. Arb.* 122

Durovic, Uloga arbitraze u stvaranju medunarodnog privrednog prava, 1986 *Jugoslovenska Revija za Medunarodno Pravo* 204 (summary in French at 216)

Fouchard, Les usages, l'arbitre et le juge, in *Le droit des relations économiques internationales: Etudes offertes à Berthold Goldman* 67 (Paris 1983)

Gaillard, The Use of Comparative Law in International Commercial Arbitration, in *Arbitration in Settlement of International Commercial Disputes Involving the Far East and Arbitration in Combined Transportation* 283 (P. Sanders ed. 1989); reprinted in 55 *Arbitration* 263 (1989)

Giardina, Arbitrato transnazionale e lex mercatoria di fronte alla Corte di Cassazione, 18 *Riv. Dir. Int'le Priv. & Proc.* 754 (1982)

Goldman, L'arbitre, les conflits des lois et la lex mercatoria, in *First Int'l Com. Arb. Conference: Proceedings* 104 (N. Antaki & A. Prujiner eds. 1986)

————, La lex mercatoria dans les contrats et l'arbitrage internationaux; realités et perspectives, 106 *J. Droit Int'l (Clunet)* 475 (1979)

————, The Applicable Law: General Principles of Law — the Lex Mercatoria, in *Contemporary Problems in Int'l Arbitration* 113 (J.D.M. Lew ed. 1986)

Highet, The Enigma of the Lex Mercatoria, 63 *Tul. L. Rev.* 613 (1989)

Indian Council of Arbitration, *International Seminar on Commercial Arbitration* (18-19 March, 1968), (New Delhi 1968)

Jarvin, The Sources and Limits of the Arbitrator's Powers, 2 *Arb. Int'l* 140 (1986)

Kahn, Les principes généraux du droit devant les arbitres du commerce international, 116 *J. Droit Int'l (Clunet)* 305 (1989)

Kassis, L'arbitre, les conflits de lois et la lex mercatoria, in *First Int'l Commercial Arbitration Conference: Proceedings* 133 (N. Antaki & A. Prujiner eds. 1986)

Kassis, A., *Théorie générale des usages du commerce* [Chapters VIII and IX deal with arbitration] (Paris 1984)

Lalive, Transnational (or Truly International) Public Policy and International Arbitration, in *Comparative Arbitration Practice and Public Policy in Arbitration* 256 (P. Sanders ed. 1987)

Lando, The Law Applicable to the Merits of the Dispute, 2 *Arb. Int'l* 104 (1986)

————, The Law Applicable to the Merits of the Dispute, in *Contemporary Problems in International Arbitration* 101 (J.D.M. Lew ed. 1986)

————, The Law Applicable to the Merits of the Dispute, in *Essays on International Commercial Arbitration* 129 (P. Sarcevic ed. 1989)

————, The Lex Mercatoria in International Commercial Arbitration, 34 *Int'l & Comp. L.Q.* 747 (1985)

Lew, Applicable Law in Commercial Arbitration, 47 *Arbitration* 92 (1981)

————, Bona Fides in International Commercial Arbitration, in 3 *Hague-Zagreb Essays* 244 (C. Voskuil & J. Wade eds. 1980)

Lowenfeld, Lex Mercatoria: An Arbitrator's View, 6 *Arb. Int'l* 133 (1990)

————, Lex Mercatoria: An Arbitrator's View, in *Lex Mercatoria and Arbitration* 37 (Th. Carbonneau ed. 1990)

————, The Two-Way Mirror: International Arbitration as Comparative Procedure, 7 *Mich. Y.B. Int'l Legal Stud.* 163 (1985)

Matray, Quelques problèmes de l'arbitrage commercial international (doctrine et jurisprudence), in *L'Arbitrage* 289 (L. Matray & G. de Leval eds. 1989)

Moitry, Arbitrage international et droit de la concurrence: vers un ordre public de la lex mercatoria? 1989 *Rev. Arb.* 3

Mustill, The New Lex Mercatoria: The First Twenty-five Years, in *Liber Amicorum for The Rt. Hon. Lord Wilberforce* 149 (M. Bos & I. Brownlie eds. 1987)

————, The New Lex Mercatoria: The First Twenty-five Years, 4 *Arb. Int'l* 86 (1988)

Note, General Principles of Law in International Commercial Arbitration, 101 *Harv. L. Rev.* 1816 (1988)

Park, Judicial Controls in the Arbitral Process, 5 *Arb. Int'l* 230 (1989)

Paulsson, La Lex mercatoria dans l'arbitrage C.C.I., 1990 *Rev. Arb.* 55

Ramzaitsev, International Trade Traditions in Arbitration Practice, in *ICCA, Fourth Int'l Arb. Congress: Proceedings* 793 (1972)

————, Primenenie mezhdunarodnykh obychaev v kommercheskom arbitrazhe v SSSR (The Application of International Custom in Commercial Arbitration in the Soviet Union), 1961 *Soviet Y.B. Int'l L.* 387

————, The Law Applied by Arbitral Tribunals, in *The Sources of the Law of International Trade* 138 (C. Schmitthoff ed. 1964)

Schlesinger & Gundisch, Allgemeine Rechtsgrundsätze als Sachnormen im Schiedsgerichtsverfahren, 28 *Rabels Zeitschrift* 41 (1964)

Smit, Proper Choice of Law and the Lex Mercatoria Arbitralis, in *Lex Mercatoria and Arbitration* 59 (Th. Carbonneau ed. 1990)

Stern, Lex mercatoria et arbitrage international: à propos des Mélanges Goldman, 1983 *Rev. Arb.* 447

Stoecker, The Lex Mercatoria: To What Extent Does It Exist? 7 *J. Int'l Arb.* 101 (No. 1, 1990)

Subramanian, Trade Terms and International Contracts, in *ICCA, Sixth Int'l Arb. Congress: Proceedings* 459 (1978)

Toop, S., *Mixed International Arbitration: Studies in Arbitration between States and Private Persons* (Cambridge 1990)

Triebel & Petzold, Grenzen der lex mercatoria in der internationalen Schiedsgerichtsbarkeit, 34 *RIW* 245 (1988)

Weise, P.-F., *Lex mercatoria: Materielles Recht vor der internationalen Handelsschiedsgerichtsbarkeit* (Berne 1990)

von Hoffmann, Lex mercatoria vor internationalen Schiedsgerichten, 1984 *IPRax* 106 (No. 4, 1984)

————, Grundsätzliches zur Anwendung der 'lex mercatoria' durch internationale Schiedsgerichte, in *Festschrift für Gerhard Kegel* 215 (H.-J. Musielak & K. Schurig eds. 1987)

13.07 INTERNATIONAL PUBLIC ORDER

Courteault & Flécheux, La notion de l'ordre public international dans la jurisprudence de la Cour de Cassation française, in *ICCA, Sixth Int'l Arb. Congress: Proceedings* 257 (1978)

Holquín Holquín, El concepto de orden público en la Convención de Nueva York y otros comentarios, in *Alternativas a la justicia institucional: arbitraje, conciliación* 131 (Bogota 1988)

Kornblum, 'Ordre public transnational,' 'ordre public international' und 'ordre public intern' im Recht der privaten Schiedsgerichtsbarkeit, in *Beiträge zum internationalen Verfahrensrecht und zur Schiedsgerichtsbarkeit. Festschrift für Heinrich Nagel* 140 (W. Habscheid & K. Schwab eds. 1987)

Lalive, Ordre public transnational (ou réellement international) et arbitrage international, 1986 *Rev. Arb.* 329

———, Transnational (or Truly International) Public Policy and International Arbitration, in *Comparative Arbitration Practice and Public Policy in Arbitration* 256 (P. Sanders ed. 1987)

Matray, Arbitrage et ordre public international, in *The Art of Arbitration* 241 (J. Schultsz & A. van den Berg eds. 1982)

———, Quelques problèmes de l'arbitrage commercial international (doctrine et jurisprudence), in *L'Arbitrage* 289 (L. Matray & G. de Leval eds. 1989)

14. THE ARBITRAL PROCESS

14.01 COMMENCEMENT OF ARBITRAL PROCEEDINGS

Blessing, International Arbitration Procedures, 17 *Int'l Bus. Law.* 408 and 451 (1989)

Carpi, Il procedimento nell'arbitrato irrituale, 45 *Riv. Trim. Dir. & Proc. Civ.* 389 (1991)

Holtzmann, H. & J. Neuhaus, *A Guide to the UNCITRAL Model Law on International Commercial Arbitration: Legislative History and Commentary* (Deventer 1989)

Karrer, Starting International Arbitration — Pitfalls in the Runway, in *Recueil de Travaux Suisses* 139 (C. Reymond & E. Bucher eds. 1984)

Kreindler, A Defendant's Initial 'Rights and Duties' in an ICC Arbitration, 10 *Int'l Fin. L. Rev.* 29 (No. 8, 1991); also in 6 *Int'l Arb. Rep.* 32 (No. 9, 1991)

McCormack, A Lawyer's View of Arbitration Proceedings and Composition of the Arbitration Panel, 1984 *Y.B. Mar. L.* 55

Mustill, Sir Michael J. & S. C. Boyd, *The Law and Practice of Commercial Arbitration in England* (2nd ed. 1989)

van Houtte, Conduct of Arbitral Proceedings, in *Essays on International Commercial Arbitration* 113 (P. Sarcevic ed. 1989)

14.02 REPRESENTATION AND LEGAL ASSISTANCE

American Bar Association (Section of International Law & Practice), Recommendation and Report, 4 *Int'l Arb. Rep.* D-1 (No. 8, 1989)

Bartlett, Taking Legal Advice in Relation to an Arbitration: Arbitrator's Direct Access to the Bar, 55 *Arbitration* 165 (1989)

Bernini, Cultural Neutrality: A Prerequisite to Arbitral Justice, 10 *Mich. J. Int'l L.* 39 (1989)

Carver, Legal and Moral Obligations of the Counsel and of the Parties, in *Euro-Arab Arbitration* II 53 (F. Kemicha ed. 1989)

Heyn, Parteivertretung durch Anwälte im Schiedsgerichtsverfahren, 11 *NJW* 1667 (1958)

Holtzmann & Bernini, Hypothetical Case for Use in a Comparative Study of Arbitration Practice in Various Legal Systems, in *Comparative Arbitration Practice and Public Policy in Arbitration* 19 (P. Sanders ed. 1987)

Jones, Re-thinking the Role of the Lawyer in the Arbitration Process, 53 *Arbitration* 229 (1987)

Katzenbach, Business Executives and Lawyers in International Trade, in *ICC, 60 Years of ICC Arbitration* 67 (1984)

Lowenfeld, Singapore and the Local Bar: Aberration or Ill Omen? 5 *J. Int'l Arb.* 71 (No. 3, 1988)

Mooney, Representation in Arbitrations in Malaysia and Singapore, 1989 *Malayan L.J.* cvii

Polkinghorne, The Right of Representation in a Foreign Venue, 4 *Arb. Int'l* 333 (1988)

Redfern, International Commercial Arbitration: Winning the Battle, in *Private Investors Abroad— Problems and Solutions in International Business in 1989* 11-1 (C. Holgren ed. 1989)

Rivkin, Keeping Lawyers Out of International Arbitrations, 9 *Int'l Fin. L. Rev.* 11 (No. 2, 1990)

Thomas, Disqualifying Lawyers in Arbitrations: Do the Arbitrators Play Any Proper Role? 1 *Am. Rev. Int'l Arb.* 562 (1990)

14.03 CHOICE OF FORUM; PLACE OF PROCEEDINGS

American Arbitration Association, *Survey of International Arbitration Sites* (New York 1984)

Baker & Davis, Arbitral Proceedings Under the UNCITRAL Rules: The Experience of the Iran-United States Claims Tribunal, 23 *Geo. Wash. J. Int'l L. & Econ.* 267 (1989)

Ball, Structuring the Arbitration in Advance - the Arbitration Clause in an International Development Agreement, in *Contemporary Problems in International Arbitration* 297 (J.D.M. Lew ed. 1986)

Böckstiegel, Zu den Thesen von einer 'delokalisierten' internationalen Schiedsgerichtsbarkeit, *Festschrift für Walter Oppenhoff* 1 (Munich 1985)

Bond, How to Draft an Arbitration Clause, 6 *J. Int'l Arb.* 65 (No. 2, 1989)

Branson & Tupman, Selecting an Arbitral Forum: A Guide to Cost-Effective International Arbitration, 24 *Va. J. Int'l L.* 917 (1984)

Bucher, Die Schweiz als traditioneller Sitzort internationaler Schiedsgerichte, in *Die Internationale Schiedsgerichtsbarkeit in der Schweiz* 119 (K.-H. Böckstiegel ed. 1989)

Cohen, A Venue Problem with the Arbitration Clauses Found in Printed Form Charters, 7 *J. Mar. L. & Com.* 541 (1976)

Craig, The Uses and Abuses of Appeal from International Arbitration Awards, in *Private Investors Abroad— Problems and Solutions in International Business in 1987* 14.1 (J. Moss ed. 1987)

————, Uses and Abuses of Appeal from Awards, 4 *Arb. Int'l* 174 (1988)

Crawford & Feldman, American Perceptions of London as a Situs for International Commercial Arbitration, 2 *Arb. Int'l* 232 (1986)

De Ly, The Place of Arbitration in the Conflict of Laws of International Commercial Arbitration: An Exercise in Arbitration Planning, 12 *Nw. J. Int'l L. & Bus.* 48 (1991)

Dellet, Arbitration, Forum Selection, and Choice of Law in International Securities Transactions, 42 *Wash. & Lee L. Rev.* 1069 (1985)

Derains, France as a Place for International Arbitration, in *The Art of Arbitration* 111 (J. Schultsz & A. van den Berg eds. 1982)

—————, International Commercial Arbitration in Civil Law Countries, in *Arbitration in Settlement of International Commercial Disputes Involving the Far East and Arbitration in Combined Transportation* 229 (P. Sanders ed. 1989)

—————, Le choix du lieu de l'arbitrage, 1986 *Revue de Droit des Affaires Int'les/Int'l Bus. L.J.* 109

Deshpande, International Commercial Arbitration: Uniformity of Jurisdiction, 5 *J. Int'l Arb.* 115 (No. 2, 1988)

Everard Goodman, Choosing a Place for International Arbitration: The New York Option, 2 *J. Int'l Arb.* 39 (No. 2, 1985)

Flower; Killian; Northrup & Range, A Survey of Arbitral Forums: Their Significance and Procedure, 5 *N.C.J. Int'l L. & Com. Reg.* 219 (1980)

Glossner, International Commercial Arbitration — Some Practical Aspects, in *Liber Amicorum for Martin Domke* 95 (P. Sanders ed. 1967)

Goldstajn, Choice of International Arbitrators, Arbitral Tribunals and Centres: Legal and Sociological Aspects, in *Essays on International Commercial Arbitration* 27 (P. Sarcevic ed. 1989)

Hintz, Recht und Praxis der Streiterledigung im Ost-West-Handel am Beispiel des Handels zwischen der UdSSR und der Bundesrepublik Deutschland, 32 *RIW* 506 (1986)

Hirsch, The Place of Arbitration and the Lex Arbitri, 34 *Arb. J.* 43 (No. 3, 1979)

Hoellering, Arbitration in the United States, 76 *Am. Soc. Int'l L. Proc.* 175 (1982)

Holtzmann, The Desirability of Including More Specific Provisions Concerning Place of Arbitration in the Model Clause in the UNCITRAL Rules, in *ICCA, Fifth Int'l Arb. Congress: Proceedings* C Iv 1-3 (1975)

—————, The Importance of Choosing the Right Place to Arbitrate an International Case, in *Private Investors Abroad: Problems and Solutions in International Business* 183 (New York 1977)

Holtzmann H. & J. Neuhaus, *A Guide to the UNCITRAL Model Law on International Commercial Arbitration: Legislative History and Commentary* (Deventer 1989)

Indian Council of Arbitration, *International Seminar on Commercial Arbitration* (18-19 March, 1968), (New Delhi 1968)

Iwasaki, Drafting Arbitration Clauses Designating Tokyo As Arbitration Site, 11 *Bull. Japan Shipping Exch.* 1 (1985)

————, Selection of Situs: Criteria and Priorities, 2 *Arb. Int'l* 57 (No. 1, Jan. 1986)

Jarvin, Choosing the Place of Arbitration: Where Do We Stand? 16 *Int'l Bus. Law.* 417 (1988)

————, London As a Place for International Arbitration: Some Observations in Light of the Arbitration Act 1979 and the Bank Mellat v. Helleniki Techniki Case, 1 *J. Int'l Arb.* 59 (1984)

————, The Place of Arbitration, 1990 *Y.B. Swed. & Int'l Arb.* 85

Kuster, Zurich, siège d'arbitrage international, 1982 *Rev. Arb.* 3

Lalive, On the Neutrality of the Arbitrator and the Place of Arbitration, in *Recueil de Travaux Suisses* 23 (C. Reymond & E. Bucher eds. 1984)

Lee, E., *Encyclopedia of International Commercial Arbitration* (London 1986)

Lefkowitz, The Trademark Forum: A Place for Arbitration in Proceedings Before the Trademark Trial and Appeal Board, 72 *Trademark Rep.* 275 (1982); reprinted in *Arbitration and the Licensing Process* 5-28.33 (R. Goldscheider & M. de Haas eds. 1984-)

Littman, Choice of Form and Place of Arbitration, 47 *Arbitration* 79 (1981)

McClendon, The World Arbitration Institute: Attracting International Arbitration to the United States, in *Private Investors Abroad— Problems and Solutions in International Business* 145 (New York 1985)

McClendon, J.S. & R.E. Everard Goodman, *International Commercial Arbitration in New York* (Ardsley-on-Hudson, NY 1986)

Mann, England Rejects Delocalised Contracts and Arbitration, 33 *Int'l & Comp. L.Q.* 193 (1984)

Matray, Quelques problèmes de l'arbitrage commercial international (doctrine et jurisprudence), in *L'Arbitrage* 289 (L. Matray & G. de Leval eds. 1989)

Mendes, Canada: A New Forum to Develop the Cultural Psychology of International Commercial Arbitration, 3 *J. Int'l Arb.* 71 (No. 3, 1986)

Note, Arbitration, Forum Selection, and Choice of Law Agreements in International Security Transactions, 42 *Wash. & Lee L. Rev.* 1069 (1985)

———, Changed Circumstances and the Iranian Claims Arbitration: Applications to Forum Selection Clauses and Frustration of Contract, 16 *Geo. Wash. J. Int'l L. & Econ.* 335 (1982)

O'Connell, Arbitration and Forum Selection Clauses in International Business: The Supreme Court Takes on Internationalist View, 43 *Fordham L. Rev.* 424 (1974)

O'Neill, Has Switzerland Solved Its Problems as a Site for Arbitration? 45 *Arb. J.* 16 (No. 4, 1990)

———, Recent Developments in International Commercial Arbitration: an American Perspective, 4 *J. Int'l Arb.* 7 (No. 1, 1987); also in 53 *Arbitration* 177 (1987)

Panchaud, Le siège de l'arbitrage international de droit privé, 61 *SJZ* 369 (1965); also in 1966 *Rev. Arb.* 2

Park, Judicial Controls in the Arbitral Process, 5 *Arb. Int'l* 230 (1989)

Park & Paulsson, Arbitrage commercial et contrats internationaux, 45 *Rev. Barreau* 215 (1985)

Paulsson, Delocalization of International Commercial Arbitration: When and Why it Matters, 32 *Int'l & Comp. L.Q.* 53 (1983)

———, International Commercial Arbitrations, in *Handbook of Arbitration Practice* 333 (R. Bernstein ed. 1987)

Pedrazzini, Essentialia e accidentialia della clausola compromissoria, in *Recueil de Travaux Suisses* 71 (C. Reymond & E. Bucher eds. 1984)

Pfaff, Schiedsgerichte im Ost-West-Handel, 23 *ZRV* 81 (1982)

Philip, The Significance of the Place of Arbitration in International Arbitration, 1985 *Y.B. Swed. & Int'l Arb.* 37 (1985)

Prujiner, La gestion des arbitrages commerciaux internationaux: l'exemple de la Cour d'arbitrage de la CCI, 115 *J. Droit Int'l (Clunet)* 662 (1988)

Redfern, International Commercial Arbitration: Winning the Battle, in *Private Investors Abroad— Problems and Solutions in International Business in 1989* 11-1 (C. Holgren ed. 1989)

————, The Importance of the Forum in International Commercial Arbitration, 1 *Int'l Contr.* 317 (1980)

Rogers, Forum Non Conveniens in Arbitration, 4 *Arb. Int'l* 240 (1988)

Sandrock, Arbitration between U.S. and West German Companies: An Example of Effective Dispute Resolution in International Business Transactions, 9 *U. Pa. J. Int'l Bus. L.* 27 (1987)

————, Choice of Law and Choice of Forum in Civil Law Jurisdictions, in *Drafting and Enforcing Contracts in Civil and Common Law Jurisdictions* 145 (K. Yelpaala, M. Rubino-Sammartano & D. Campbell eds. 1986)

————, Die Entscheidung von Streitigkeiten durch Schiedsgerichte, in *Französisches Vertragsrecht für deutsche Exporteure* 54 (C. Witz & T.M. Bopp eds. 1989)

Shenton & Toland, London as a Venue for International Arbitration: The Arbitration Act, 1979, 12 *L. & Pol'y Int'l Bus.* 643 (1980)

Strohbach, On the Venue of Arbitration, in *ICCA, Fifth Int'l Arb. Congress: Proceedings* C Il 1-7 (1975)

Sutton, Choosing a Forum for International Commercial Arbitration in London, 76 *Am. Soc. Int'l L. Proc.* 178 (1982)

Taylor, National Iranian Oil Co. v. Ashland Oil, Inc.: All Dressed Up and Nowhere to Arbitrate, 63 *N.Y.U. L. Rev.* 1142 (1988)

Triebel & Viertel, Die Bundesrepublik Deutschland wird als Schiedsgerichtsort im internationalen Schiedsverfahren gemieden: Zur Reformbedürftigkeit des par. 1039 ZPO, 41 *BB* 1168 (1986)

Tupman, Selecting an Arbitral Forum: A Guide to Cost-Effective International Arbitration, 24 *Va. J. Int'l L.* 917 (1984)

Ulmer, Drafting the International Arbitration Clause, 20 *Int'l Law.* 1335 (1986)

van den Berg, When Is an Arbitral Award Non-Domestic Under the New York Convention of 1958? 6 *Pace L. Rev.* 25 (1985)

Vanderelst, Increasing the Appeal of Belgium as an International Arbitration Forum? The Belgian Law of March 27, 1985 Concerning the Annulment of Arbitral Awards, 3 *J. Int'l Arb.* 77 (No. 2, 1986)

van Houtte, Conduct of Arbitral Proceedings, in *Essays on International Commercial Arbitration* 113 (P. Sarcevic ed. 1989)

Vartian, Choice of Confirmation Forum in International Commercial Arbitration, 21 *Tex. Int'l L.J.* 67 (1986)

Wetter, Sweden as the Location of International Arbitration Proceedings, in *Private Investors Abroad: Problems and Solutions in International Business* 223 (New York 1977)

Zubrod, Maritime Arbitration in New York, 39 *Arb. J.* 16 (No. 4, 1984)

14.04 LANGUAGES

Baker & Davis, Arbitral Proceedings Under the UNCITRAL Rules: The Experience of the Iran-United States Claims Tribunal, 23 *Geo. Wash. J. Int'l L. & Econ.* 267 (1989)

Ball, Structuring the Arbitration in Advance — the Arbitration Clause in an International Development Agreement, in *Contemporary Problems in International Arbitration* 297 (J.D.M. Lew ed. 1986)

Bond, How to Draft an Arbitration Clause, 6 *J. Int'l Arb.* 65 (No. 2, 1989)

Holtzmann, H. & J. Neuhaus, *A Guide to the UNCITRAL Model Law on International Commercial Arbitration: Legislative History and Commentary* (Deventer 1989)

Matray, Quelques problèmes de l'arbitrage commercial international (doctrine et jurisprudence), in *L'Arbitrage* 289 (L. Matray & G. de Leval eds. 1989)

Miller, Consolidation in Hong Kong — the Shui On Case, 3 *Arb. Int'l* 87 (No. 1, 1987)

Mustill, Sir Michael J. & S. C. Boyd, *The Law and Practice of Commercial Arbitration in England* (2nd ed. 1989)

van Houtte, Conduct of Arbitral Proceedings, in *Essays on International Commercial Arbitration* 113 (P. Sarcevic ed. 1989)

14.05 TIME LIMITS: CALCULATION OF PERIODS OF TIME

Blessing, International Arbitration Procedures, 17 *Int'l Bus. Law.* 408 and 451 (1989)

Bredow & Bühler, Zur Änderung der Schiedsgerichtsordnung der Internationalen Handelskammer, 8 *IPRax* 69 (1988)

Bühler, Staatsgerichtliche Aufhebungskontrolle am Schiedsort? Zur Reform Belgiens, 7 *IPRax* 253 (1987)

Junker, Verjährungsunterbrechung beim Übergang vom Zivilprozess zum Schiedsverfahren, 48 *KTS* 37 (1987)

Mustill, Sir Michael J. & S.C. Boyd, *The Law and Practice of Commercial Arbitration in England* (2nd ed. 1989)

Prujiner, La gestion des arbitrages commerciaux internationaux: l'exemple de la Cour d'arbitrage de la CCI, 115 *J. Droit Int'l (Clunet)* 662 (1988)

Raeschke-Kessler & Bühler, Aufsicht über den Schiedsrichter durch den ICC-Schiedsgerichtshof (Paris) und rechtliches Gehör der Parteien, 8 *ZIP* 1157 (1987)

Schwebel & Lahne, Public Policy and Arbitral Procedure, in *Comparative Arbitration Practice and Public Policy in Arbitration* 205 (P. Sanders ed. 1987)

Steyn, Delays and Delaying Tactics in International Arbitration, 49 *Arbitration* 9 (August 1983)

Thomas, Power of the Court to Extend Time for Commencing Arbitration Proceedings, 1981 *Lloyd's Mar. Com. L.Q.* 529

————, The Legal Remedies for Dilatoriness in the Pre-hearing Arbitral Procedure, 1983 *Lloyd's Mar. Com. L.Q.* 315

14.06 WAIVERS

Baker & Davis, Arbitral Proceedings under the UNCITRAL Rules: The Experience of the Iran-United States Claims Tribunal, 23 *Geo. Wash. J. Int'l L. & Econ.* 267 (1989)

Deshpande, Court, Contract and Arbitration, 26 *J. Ind. L. Inst.* 378 (1984)

Kahale, Arbitration and Choice of Law Clauses as Waivers of Jurisdictional Immunity, 14 *N.Y.U. J. Int'l L. & Pol.* 29 (1981)

Keane, Waiver of Maritime Arbitration, 8 *J. Mar. L. & Com.* 195 (1977)

McGovan, Arbitration Clauses as Waivers of Immunity from Jurisdiction and Execution under the Foreign Sovereign Immunity Act of 1976, 5 *N.Y. L. Sch. J. Int'l & Comp.L.* 409 (1984)

Mustill, Sir Michael J. & S. C. Boyd, *The Law and Practice of Commercial Arbitration in England* (2nd ed. 1989)

Poznanski, The Nature and Extent of an Arbitrator's Power in International Commercial Arbitration, 4 *J. Int'l Arb.* 71 (No. 3, 1987)

Wiget, Fragen der Verfahrensgestaltung vor Gelegenheitsschiedsgerichten, in *Festschrift für Max Guldener* 367 (Zurich 1973)

14.07 FAILURE TO ARBITRATE; DEFAULT

Baker & Davis, Arbitral Proceedings under the UNCITRAL Rules: The Experience of the Iran-United States Claims Tribunal, 23 *Geo. Wash. J. Int'l L. & Econ.* 267 (1989)

Bingham, The Problem of Delay in Arbitration, 5 *Arb. Int'l* 333 (1989); also in 56 *Arbitration* 164 (1990)

Blessing, International Arbitration Procedures, 17 *Int'l Bus. Law.* 408 and 451 (1989)

Broches, The Convention on the Settlement of Investment Disputes between States and Nationals of Other States: Applicable Law and Default Procedure, in *Liber Amicorum for Martin Domke* 12 (P. Sanders ed. 1967)

Davenport, Stale Arbitrations — Again, 104 *L.Q. Rev.* 493 (1988)

Hanotiau, Default Procedure (dans l'arbitrage commercial international), [1986] 7 *Int'l Arb. Gazette* 300

Holtzmann, H. & J. Neuhaus, *A Guide to the UNCITRAL Model Law on International Commercial Arbitration: Legislative History and Commentary* (Deventer 1989)

Mustill, Sir Michael J. & S. C. Boyd, *The Law and Practice of Commercial Arbitration in England* (2nd ed. 1989)

Rokison, The Sources and Limits of the Arbitrator's Powers in England, in *Contemporary Problems of International Arbitration* 86 (J.D.M. Lew ed. 1986); also 52 *Arbitration* 219 (1986)

Sethu, Abandonment in Contract, 1987 *Malayan L.J.* xli

Tan, Unmeritorious Claims and Defences in Arbitration Proceedings, 1987 *Malayan L.J.* cxvii

van Houtte, Conduct of Arbitral Proceedings, in *Essays on International Commercial Arbitration* 113 (P. Sarcevic ed. 1989)

Vis, Want of Prosecution in English Commercial Arbitration, in *The Art of Arbitration* 311 (J. Schultsz & A. van den Berg eds. 1982)

Wenger, Säumnis und Säumnisfolgen im internationalen Schiedsverfahren, in *Recueil de Travaux Suisses* 245 (C. Reymond & E. Bucher eds. 1984)

Wiget, Fragen der Verfahrensgestaltung vor Gelegenheitsschiedsgerichten, in *Festschrift für Max Guldener* 367 (Zurich 1973)

15. ARBITRATION PROCEDURE

15.01 MODE AND COURSE OF PROCEEDINGS IN GENERAL

Arbitration Institute of the Stockholm Chamber of Commerce, *Arbitration in Sweden* (2nd rev. ed. 1984)

Aylwin Azocar, P., *El juicio arbitral* (Santiago de Chile 1958)

Bartos, H., *Internationale Handelsschiedsgerichtsbarkeit: Verfahrensprinzipien* (Frankfurt 1984)

Bernstein, Reducing Delays in Arbitration, 49 *Arbitration* 277 (May 1984)

Blessing, The Major Western and Soviet Arbitration Rules: A Comparison of the Rules of UNCITRAL, UNCITRAL Model Law, LCIA, ICC, AAA and the Rules of the USSR Chamber of Commerce and Industry, 6 *J. Int'l Arb.* 7 (No. 3, 1989)

Chillón Medina, J. M. & J. F. Merino Merchán, *Tratado de arbitraje privado interno e internacional* (Madrid 1978)

Chowdhuri, S.K.R. & H.K. Saharay, *Arbitration Law* (2nd ed. Calcutta 1986)

Cremades, B. M., *Panorámica Española del Arbitraje Comercial Internacional* (Madrid 1975)

David, R., *Arbitration in International Trade* (Deventer 1985)

Derains, International Commercial Arbitration in Civil Law Countries, in *Arbitration in Settlement of International Commercial Disputes Involving the Far East and Arbitration in Combined Transportation* 229 (P. Sanders ed. 1989)

————, Mesures dilatoires en matière d'arbitrage et moyens de s'y opposer, in *Festschrift für Arthur Bülow* 31 (K.-H. Böckstiegel & O. Glossner eds. 1981)

Derains, Y., ed., *Droit et pratique de l'arbitrage international en France* (Paris 1984)

Dunshee de Abranches, C.A., ed., *El arbitraje comercial en Iberoamérica* (Madrid 1982)

401

Erecinski, Zagadnienia prawa wlasciwego i postepowania dowodowego w miedzynarodowym arbitrazu handlowym, 42 *Panstwo i Prawo* 49 (No. 9, 1987)

Eyzaguirre Echeverria, R., *El arbitraje comercial en la legislación chileña y su regulación international* (Santiago de Chile 1981)

Fletcher, Unrealised Expectations — the Root of Procedural Confusion in International Arbitration, 2 *J. Int'l Arb.* 7 (No. 3, 1985); also 54 *Arbitration* 40 (1988)

Foster, C.A., *The Law and Practice of Commercial Arbitration in North Carolina* (Durham 1986)

Gaillard, Les manoevres dilatoires des parties et des arbitres dans l'arbitrage commercial international, 1990 *Rev. Arb.* 759

Gill, W.H., *Evidence and Procedure in Arbitration* (London 1965)

Goekjian, The Conduct of International Arbitration, 11 *Law. Am.* 409 (1979)

Goldman, The Applicable Law: General Principles of Law — the Lex Mercatoria, in *Contemporary Problems in Int'l Arbitration* 113 (J.D.M. Lew ed. 1986)

Golsong, A Guide to Procedural Issues in International Arbitration, 18 *Int'l Law.* 633 (1984)

Groos, Schiedsgerichtsbarkeit im deutsch-französischen Wirtschaftsverkehr, 33 *RIW* 343 (1987)

Habscheid & Schlosser, Improvement of Civil Litigation by Lessons Derived from Arbitration, in *Justice and Efficiency* 149 (W. Wedekind ed. 1989)

Hagberg, Salient Features of the Swedish Arbitral Procedure, 1990 *Y.B. Swed. & Int'l Arb.* 34

Harris, Saving Time in Arbitration, 53 *Arbitration* 147 (1987)

Henn, G., *Schiedsverfahrensrecht: ein Handbuch* (Heidelberg 1986)

Herrmann, The UNCITRAL Model Law on International Commercial Arbitration — Its Salient Features and Prospects, in *First Int'l Commercial Arbitration Conference: Proceedings* 351 (N. Antaki & A. Prujiner eds. 1986)

Hintz, Recht und Praxis der Streiterledigung im Ost-West-Handel am Beispiel des Handels zwischen der UdSSR und der Bundesrepublik Deutschland, 32 *RIW* 506 (1986)

Holtzmann, Delays in International Arbitration — Role of the Arbitrator, 14 *Int'l Bus. Law.* 120 (1986)

————, What an Arbitrator Can Do to Overcome Delays in International Arbitration, 52 *Arbitration* 167 (1986)

Jarrosson, Le rôle respectif de l'institution, de l'arbitre et des parties dans l'instance arbitrale, 1990 *Rev. Arb.* 381

Kessler, J., *Schiedsgerichtsvertrag und Schiedsverfahren* (Munich 1970)

Kimbrough, Viabilité générale de l'arbitrage à Singapour: l'accession a la Convention de New York comble la dernière lacune, 1986 *Int'l Bus. L.J.* 783

Lécuyer-Thieffry, C. & P. Thieffry, *Le règlement des litiges civils et commerciaux avec les Etats-Unis* (Paris 1986)

Lebedev, Conduct of Arbitral Proceedings, 24 *Rassegna dell'Arb.* 41 (1984)

Lee, E., *Encyclopedia of International Commercial Arbitration* (London 1986)

Level, *La procédure arbitrale, in Droit et pratique de l'arbitrage international en France* 51 (Y. Derains ed., Paris 1984)

Lew, J., ed., *Contemporary Problems in International Arbitration* (London 1986)

Lloyd, How to Manage Complex International Arbitration, 45 *Arb. J.* 30 (No. 3, 1990)

McCormack, A Lawyer's View of Arbitration Proceedings and Composition of the Arbitration Panel, 1984 *Y.B. Mar. Law* 55

Marchais, Setting up the Initial Procedural Framework in ICSID Arbitration, 5 *News from ICSID* 5 (No. 1, Winter 1988)

Moreau, B. & T. Bernard, *Droit interne et droit international de l'arbitrage* (2nd ed. 1985)

Mustill, Sir Michael J. & S. C. Boyd, *The Law and Practice of Commercial Arbitration in England* (2nd ed. 1989)

Nagel, Gedanken über die Beschleunigung des Schiedsverfahren, in *Festschrift für Karl Firsching* 191 (Munich 1985)

Nordenson, The Arbitral Proceedings in International Arbitration in Sweden, 1984 *Y.B. Swed. & Int'l Arb.* 6

Oehmke, T., *International Arbitration* (Rochester 1990)

Pacific Rim Advisory Council, *Pacific Rim: Commercial Arbitration Procedures* (San Diego, CA 1985)

Park, National Law and Commercial Justice: Safeguarding Procedural Integrity in International Arbitration, 63 *Tul. L. Rev.* 674 (1989)

Paterson, International Commercial Arbitration Act: An Overview, in *UNCITRAL Arbitration Model in Canada* 113 (R. Paterson & B. Thompson eds. 1987)

Poppleton, The Arbitrator's Role in Expediting the Large and Complex Commercial Cases, 36 *Arb. J.* (No. 4, 1981); reprinted in *Arbitration and the Licensing Process* 7-3 (R. Goldscheider & M. de Haas eds. 1984-)

Redfern, A. & M. Hunter, *Law and Practice of International Commercial Arbitration* (2nd. ed. 1991)

Robert, J. & B. Morceau, *L'arbitrage — droit interne, droit international privé* (5th ed. Paris 1983)

Russell, F., *Russell on the Law of Arbitration* (20th ed. by A. Walton & M. Vitoria 1982)

Sarikas, Procedural Problems of International Arbitration, in *ICCA, Fourth Int'l Arb. Congress: Proceedings* 807 (1972)

Schizzerotto, G., *Dell'arbitrato* (Milan 3rd ed. 1988)

Schlosser, P., *Das Recht der internationalen privaten Schiedsgerichtsbarkeit* (2nd rev. ed. Tübingen 1989)

Schönke, A., *Das Schiedsgerichtsverfahren nach dem heutigen deutschen Recht* (Berlin 1954)

Schütze, R., D. Tscherning & W. Wais, *Handbuch des Schiedsverfahrens. Praxis der deutschen und internationalen Schiedsgerichtsbarkeit* (2nd ed. Berlin 1990)

Sharkey, J. & J. Dorter, *Commercial Arbitration* (Sydney 1986)

Shilston, Milestone in the Evolution of Modern Commercial Arbitration, 53 *Arbitration* 26 (1987)

Steyn, Remedies Against the Reluctant Respondent: The Position Under English Law, 5 *Arb. Int'l* 294 (1989)

Tackaberry, The Conduct of Arbitration Proceedings Under English Law, in *Contemporary Problems in International Arbitration* 216 (J.D.M. Lew ed. 1986); also 52 *Arbitration* 227 (1986)

Thomas, The Legal Remedies for Dilatoriness in the Pre-hearing Arbitral Procedure, 1983 *Lloyd's Mar. Com. L.Q.* 315

van Houtte, Conduct of Arbitral Proceedings, in *Essays on International Commercial Arbitration* 113 (P. Sarcevic ed. 1989)

Wetter, The Conduct of the Arbitration, 2 *J. Int'l Arb.* 7 (No. 2, 1985)

Wight, Developments in Commercial Arbitration, in *A Handbook of Dispute Resolution* 55 (K. Mackie ed. 1991)

Zubrod, Delay in Maritime Arbitrations — Post-Hearing and Otherwise, an Arbitrator's View, 10 *Md. J. Int'l L. & Trade* 175 (1986)

15.02 TERMS OF REFERENCE

Bond, I.C.C. Arbitration in Theory and Practice, 26 *Rassegna dell'Arb.* 141 (1986)

————, ICC Terms of Reference Rule Saves Time and Money While Promoting Common Understanding, 6 *Int'l Arb. Rep.* 33 (No. 8, 1991)

de Bournonville, Au sujet des demandes incidents en matière d'arbitrage, in *L'arbitrage* 55 (L. Matray & G. de Leval eds. 1989)

Derains, Mesures dilatoires en matière d'arbitrage et moyens de s'y opposer, in *Festschrift für Arthur Bülow* 31 (K.-H. Böckstiegel & O. Glossner eds. 1981)

Glossner, The Conduct of ICC Arbitration Proceedings, in *Contemporary Problems in International Arbitration* 210 (J.D.M. Lew ed., 1986)

Goldman, International Arbitration in Europe, in *IBA, Soviet Foreign Trade Reforms & East/West Arbitration* 217 (1988)

Goldsmith, How to Draft Terms of Reference, 3 *Arb. Int'l* 298 (1987)

Hafter, Gespräche zwischen Schiedsgericht und Parteien — Ein Beitrag zur Technik der Fuhrung von Schiedsgerichten, in *Recueil de Travaux Suisses* 203 (C. Reymond & E. Bucher eds. 1984)

Holtzmann & Bernini, Hypothetical Case for Use in a Comparative Study of Arbitration Practice in Various Legal Systems, in *Comparative Arbitration Practice and Public Policy in Arbitration* 19 (P. Sanders ed. 1987)

Jarvin, The Sources and Limits of the Arbitrator's Powers, 2 *Arb. Int'l* 140 (1986)

Karrer, Starting International Arbitration — Pitfalls in the Runway, in *Recueil de Travaux Suisses* 139 (C. Reymond & E. Bucher eds. 1984)

Nicklisch, Terms of Reference: Sinn und Zweck der Terms of Reference, Technik der Abfassung, 34 *RIW* 763 (1988)

Prujiner, La gestion des arbitrages commerciaux internationaux: l'exemple de la Cour d'arbitrage de la CCI, 115 *J. Droit Int'l (Clunet)* 662 (1988)

Rhodes & Sloan, The Pitfalls of International Commercial Arbitration, 17 *Vand. J. Transnat'l L.* 19 (1984)

Sandrock, Die Terms of Reference und die Grenzen ihrer Präklusionswirkungen. Ein Rechtsinstitut der Verfahrensordnung des Schiedsgerichtshofes der Internationalen Handelskammer in Paris und seine Geheimnisse, 33 *RIW* 649 (1987)

15.03 PRELIMINARY QUESTIONS; REFEREE PROCEDURE

Arnaldez & Schäfer, Le règlement de référé pré-arbitrale de la Chambre de commerce internationale, 1990 *Rev. Arb.* 835

Holtzmann & Bernini, Hypothetical Case for Use in a Comparative Study of Arbitration Practice in Various Legal Systems, in *Comparative Arbitration Practice and Public Policy in Arbitration* 19 (P. Sanders ed. 1987)

Karrer, Starting International Arbitration — Pitfalls in the Runway, in *Recueil de Travaux Suisses* 139 (C. Reymond & E. Bucher eds. 1984)

Lécuyer-Thieffry, Examination of ICC's New Pre-Arbitral Referee Procedure, 1 *World Arb. & Med. Rep.* 13 (No. 1, 1990)

Paulsson, A Better Mousetrap: 1990 ICC Rules for a Pre-arbitral Referee Procedure, 18 *Int'l Bus. Law.* 214 (1990)

Seppala, Les décisions pré-arbitrales afférentes aux litiges en matière de construction: les décisions prises par l'ingénieur, 1991 *Int'l Bus. L.J.* 331

Sharkey, J. & J. Dorter, *Commercial Arbitration* (Sydney 1986)

Smit, Provisional Relief in International Arbitration: The ICC and Other Proposed Rules, 1 *Am. Rev. Int'l Arb.* 388 (1990)

Soper, The Importance of the Preliminary Proceedings, 41 *Arbitration* 17 (1974)

Tackaberry, The Conduct of Arbitration Proceedings under English Law, in *Contemporary Problems in International Arbitration* 216 (J.D.M. Lew ed. 1986); also 52 *Arbitration* 227 (1986)

15.04 WRITTEN PROCEEDINGS

Harris, Documents-only Arbitrations, 49 *Arbitration* 221 (Feb. 1984)

Nutley, Rent Review and Property Valuation Arbitrations, in *Handbook of Arbitration Practice* 311 (R. Bernstein ed. 1987)

Rutherford, Documents Only Arbitrations in Consumer Disputes, in *Handbook of Arbitration Practice* 217 (R. Bernstein ed. 1987)

van Houtte, Conduct of Arbitral Proceedings, in *Essays on International Commercial Arbitration* 113 (P. Sarcevic ed. 1989)

15.05 PRE-HEARING CONFERENCES

Holtzmann, Delays in International Arbitration — Role of the Arbitrator, 14 *Int'l Bus. Law.* 120 (1986)

Holtzmann & Bernini, Hypothetical Case for Use in a Comparative Study of Arbitration Practice in Various Legal Systems, in *Comparative Arbitration Practice and Public Policy in Arbitration* 19 (P. Sanders ed. 1987)

Mustill, Sir Michael J. & S.C. Boyd, *The Law and Practice of Commercial Arbitration in England* (2nd ed. 1989)

Pellerin, Les droits des parties dans l'instance arbitrale, 1990 *Rev. Arb.* 395

Shilston, The Evolution of Modern Commercial Arbitration, 4 *J. Int'l Arb.* 45 (No. 2, 1987)

Soper, Authority and the English Arbitrator, 46 *Arbitration* 195 (1980)

van Houtte, Conduct of Arbitral Proceedings, in *Essays on International Commercial Arbitration* 113 (P. Sarcevic ed. 1989)

15.06 CONSOLIDATION OF PROCEEDINGS

Aksen, Multi-Party Arbitrations in the United States, in *Arbitration and the Licensing Process* 5-3 (R. Goldscheider & M. de Haas eds. 1984-)

Austmann, Commercial Multi-Party Arbitration: A Case-by-Case Approach, 1 *Am. Rev. Int'l Arb.* 341 (1990)

Chiu, Consolidation of Arbitral Proceedings and International Commercial Arbitration, 7 *J. Int'l Arb.* 53 (No. 2, 1990)

Dika, The Problem of Multiparty Arbitration from the Standpoint of Yugoslav Law, in 5 *Hague-Zagreb Essays* 125 (C. Voskuil & J. Wade eds. 1985)

Dore, I., *Theory and Practice of Multiparty Commercial Arbitration, With Special Reference to the UNCITRAL Framework* (London 1990)

Foster, C.A., *The Law and Practice of Commercial Arbitration in North Carolina* (Durham 1986)

Hascher, Consolidation of Arbitration by American Courts: Fostering or Hampering International Commercial Arbitration? 1 *J. Int'l Arb.* 127 (No. 2, 1984)

International Chamber of Commerce, *Multi-party Arbitration* (Paris 1991)

Kassis, L'arbitrage multipartite et les clauses de consolidation, 14 *Droit et Pratique du Com. Int'l* 221 (1988)

Laschet, Anordnung gemeinsamer Verhandlung zweier getrennter Schiedsverfahren durch ein Schiedsgericht in England — Aufhebung durch den High Court, 6 *IPRax* 182 (1986)

McCormack, Arbitration in Combined Transportation — A Rare Bird, in *Arbitration in Settlement of International Commercial Disputes Involving the Far East and Arbitration in Combined Transportation* 325 (P. Sanders ed. 1989)

Miller, Consolidated Arbitrations in New York Maritime Disputes, 14 *Int'l Bus. Law.* 58 (1986)

Paterson, International Commercial Arbitration Act: An Overview, in *UNCITRAL Arbitration Model in Canada* 113 (R. Paterson & B. Thompson eds. 1987)

Schwartz, Multiparty Disputes and Consolidated Arbitrations: An Oxymoron or the Solution to a Continuing Dilemma? 22 *Case W. Res. J. Int'l L.* 341 (1990)

Tan, Multiple Parties and Causes of Action in Arbitration Proceedings, 1988 *Malayan L.J.* li

Thompson, The Same Tribunal for Different Arbitrations, 4 *J. Int'l Arb.* 111 (No. 2, 1987)

van den Berg, Consolidated Arbitrations and the 1958 New York Arbitration Convention, 2 *Arb. Int'l* 367 (1986)

Veeder, Multi-Party Disputes: Consolidation under English Law, 2 *Arb. Int'l* 310 (1986)

von Hoffmann, International Construction Arbitration, in *Essays on International Commercial Arbitration* 223 (P. Sarcevic ed. 1989)

15.07 STATEMENT OF CLAIM AND DEFENSE; COUNTERCLAIMS; SET-OFFS

Baker & Davis, Arbitral Proceedings under the UNCITRAL Rules: The Experience of the Iran-United States Claims Tribunal, 23 *Geo. Wash. J. Int'l L. & Econ.* 267 (1989)

Holtzmann & Bernini, Hypothetical Case for Use in a Comparative Study of Arbitration Practice in Various Legal Systems, in *Comparative Arbitration Practice and Public Policy in Arbitration* 19 (P. Sanders ed. 1987)

Holtzmann, H. & J. Neuhaus, *A Guide to the UNCITRAL Model Law on International Commercial Arbitration: Legislative History and Commentary* (Deventer 1989)

Larschan & Mirfendereski, The Status of Counterclaims under International Law, with Particular Reference to International Arbitration Involving a Private Party and a Foreign State, 15 *Den. J. Int'l L. & Pol'y* 11 (1986)

Lazatin, Mechanics and Procedural Aspects of Commercial Arbitration, in *Commercial Arbitration* 14 (J. Ricalde ed. 1983)

Renteln, Encoutering Counterclaims, 15 *Den. J. Int'l L. & Pol'y* 379 (1987)

Stewart, The Iran-United States Claims Tribunal: A Review of Developments 1983-84, 16 *L. & Pol. Int'l Bus.* 677 (1984)

Tackaberry, The Conduct of Arbitration Proceedings under English Law, in *Contemporary Problems in International Arbitration* 216 (J.D.M. Lew ed. 1986); also 52 *Arbitration* 227 (1986)

Tan, Unmeritorious Claims and Defences in Arbitration Proceedings, 1987 *Malayan L.J.* cxvii

van Houtte, Conduct of Arbitral Proceedings, in *Essays on International Commercial Arbitration* 113 (P. Sarcevic ed. 1989)

15.08 HEARING

Baker & Davis, Arbitral Proceedings under the UNCITRAL Rules: The Experience of the Iran-United States Claims Tribunal, 23 *Geo. Wash. J. Int'l L. & Econ.* 267 (1989)

Blessing, International Arbitration Procedures, 17 *Int'l Bus. Law.* 408 and 451 (1989)

Gaillard, Le principe de confidentialité de l'arbitrage commercial international, 1987 *Recueil Dalloz Sirey No. 22,* at 153

Glass, The Function of the Hearing in International Commercial Arbitration, in *ICCA, Fifth Int'l Arb. Congress: Proceedings* C Iq 1-4 (1975)

Hermanns, Zur Frage der Verletzung des rechtlichen Gehörs im schiedsgerichtlichen Verfahren, 1987 *IPRax* 353

Holtzmann & Bernini, Hypothetical Case for Use in a Comparative Study of Arbitration Practice in Various Legal Systems, in *Comparative Arbitration Practice and Public Policy in Arbitration* 19 (P. Sanders ed. 1987)

Lowenfeld, The Two-Way Mirror: International Arbitration as Comparative Procedure, 7 *Mich. Y.B. Int'l Legal Stud.* 163 (1985)

Mustill, Sir Michael J. & S. C. Boyd, *The Law and Practice of Commercial Arbitration in England* (2nd ed. 1989)

Paulsson, International Commercial Arbitrations, in *Handbook of Arbitration Practice* 333 (R. Bernstein ed. 1987)

————, The Rules of Evidence in the Arbitral Procedure: Comparative Study, in *Euro-Arab Arbitration II* 90 (F. Kemicha ed. 1989)

Poznanski, The Nature and Extent of an Arbitrator's Power in International Commercial Arbitration, 4 *J. Int'l Arb.* 71 (No. 3, 1987)

Sharkey, J. & J. Dorter, *Commercial Arbitration* (Sydney 1986)

Wackenhuth, Nochmals: Verletzung des rechtlichen Gehörs im schiedsgerichtlichen Verfahren, 7 *IPRax* 355 (1987)

15.09 EVIDENCE

Alley, Pre-Hearing Obtaining of Evidence in Arbitrations, in *Pre-Trial and Pre-Hearing Procedures Worldwide* 417 (Ch. Platto ed. 1990)

Baker & Davis, Arbitral Proceedings under the UNCITRAL Rules: The Experience of the Iran-United States Claims Tribunal, 23 *Geo. Wash. J. Int'l L. & Econ.* 267 (1989)

Bakshi, Arbitration Law and Evidentiary Aspects, 1987(2) *Company L.J.* 63

Barclay, Harmonization of Evidence, in *ICCA, Fifth Int'l Arb. Congress: Proceedings* C IIb 1-4 (1975)

Bernini, Cultural Neutrality: A Prerequisite to Arbitral Justice, 10 *Mich. J. Int'l L.* 39 (1989)

Blessing, International Arbitration Procedures, 17 *Int'l Bus. Law.* 408 and 451 (1989)

Branson, Continuous Ownership of a Claim: A Hard Case at the Iran-United States Claims Tribunal Makes Bad Law, 3 *Arb. Int'l* 164 (1987)

Brower, Discovery and Production of Evidence in the U.S.: Theory and Practice, in *ICC, Taking of Evidence in International Arbitral Proceedings* 7 (1990)

Bucher, A., *Die neue internationale Schiedsgerichtsbarkeit in der Schweiz* (Basel 1989)

————, *Le nouvel arbitrage international en Suisse. Théorie et pratique de droit* (Basel 1988)

Bucher, A. & P.-Y. Tschanz, *International Arbitration in Switzerland* (Basel 1989)

Callender, The Expert, the Arbitrator and the Rules of Evidence, 47 *Arbitration* 197 (1982)

Capatina, Asistenta juridica internationala in litigiile arbitrale de comert exterior, 40 *Revista Romana de Drept* 10 (No. 4, 1984)

Croal, Misconception about Discovery in English Arbitration, 51 *Arbitration* 532 (Nov. 1985) de Boisséson, Introduction comparative aux systèmes d'administration des preuves dans les pays de common law et des pays de tradition romaniste/Comparative Introduction to the System of Producing Evidence in Common Law Countries and Countries of Roman Law Tradition, in *ICC, Taking of Evidence in International Arbitral Proceedings* 85 (1990)

Delvolvé, Practices for Presenting Evidence in International Commercial Arbitration, in *ICCA, 5th Int'l Arb. Congress: Proceedings* C IIc 1-10 (1975)

de Mello, International Bar Association: Règles complémentaires de preuve a usage de l'arbitrage international: commentaire, 1986 *Rev. Arb.* 660

Dieryck, Procédure et moyens de preuve (dans l'arbitrage commercial international), [1986] 7 *Int'l Arb. Gazette* 277

———, Procédure et moyens de preuve dans l'arbitrage commercial international, 1988 *Rev. Arb.* 267

Erecinski, Evidence in Polish International Commercial Arbitration, 1987 *Y.B. Socialist Legal Systems* 331

———, Problems in the Administration of Evidence Arising from the Rules of the International Commercial Arbitration, 17 *Polish Y.B. Int'l L.* 41 (1988)

Fischer-Zernin & Junker, Between Scylla and Charybdis: Fact Gathering in German Arbitration, 4 *J. Int'l Arb.* 9 (No. 2, 1987)

Foster, C.A., *The Law and Practice of Commercial Arbitration in North Carolina* (Durham 1986)

Gill, W.H., *Evidence and Procedure in Arbitration* (London 1965)

Goldman, International Arbitration in Europe, in *IBA, Soviet Foreign Trade Reforms & East/West Arbitration* 217 (1988)

Gothberg, Coercive Measures for Obtaining Production of Documentary Evidence in Arbitration Proceedings, 8 *Int'l Arb. Gazette* 361 (1986)

Hagberg, Evidence in Swedish Arbitral Procedure, 1982 *Y.B. Swed. & Int'l Arb.* 29

Heuman, L., *Current Issues in Swedish Arbitration* (Deventer and Stockholm 1990)

Hill, M. & A. Sinicropi, *Evidence in Arbitration* (2nd ed. Washington, DC 1987)

Hobér, Arbitration in Moscow, 3 *Arb. Int'l* 119 (1987)

Hoellering, Remedies in Arbitration, 20 *The Forum* 516 (1984-85)

Holland & Hantke, Beschränkung auf den Urkunden-Beweis im Schiedsverfahren, in *Festschrift für Arthur Bülow* 75 (K.-H. Böckstiegel & O. Glossner eds. 1981)

Holtzmann & Bernini, Hypothetical Case for Use in a Comparative Study of Arbitration Practice in Various Legal Systems, in *Comparative Arbitration Practice and Public Policy in Arbitration* 19 (P. Sanders ed. 1987)

International Chamber of Commerce, *Taking of Evidence in International Arbitral Proceedings/L'administration de la preuve dans les procédures arbitrales internationales* (Paris 1990)

Jakubowski, Proposals for Promoting the Development of Practices Which Might Be Commonly Acceptable for Presenting Evidence in International Commercial Arbitration, in *ICCA, Fifth Int'l Arb. Congress: Proceedings* C IIa 1-7 (1975)

————, The Continental Case in Eastern Europe, 41 *Arbitration* 106 (1974)

Jarvin, Choosing the Place of Arbitration: Where Do We Stand? 16 *Int'l Bus. Law.* 417 (1988)

Junker, Discovery in deutsch-amerikanischen Rechtsverkehr— Entwicklungslinien und Perspektiven, 33 *RIW* 1 (1987)

Kemicha, F., ed., *Euro-Arab Arbitration II/Arbitrage Euro-Arabe II* (London 1989)

Langeveld, Iets over getuigen in internationale arbitrages, 1988 *Tijdschrift voor Arbitrage* 156

Lipton, Discovery Procedures and the Selection and Training of Arbitrators: A Study of Securities Industry Practices, 26 *Am. Bus. L.J.* 435 (1988)

Lowenfeld, The Two-Way Mirror: International Arbitration as Comparative Procedure, 7 *Mich. Y.B. Int'l Legal Stud.* 163 (1985)

McCabe, Arbitral Discovery and the Iran-United States Claims Tribunal Experience, 20 *Int'l Law.* 499 (1986)

Marriott, Evidence in International Arbitration, 5 *Arb. Int'l* 280 (1989)

Matray, Les traits caractéristiques de l'administration de la preuve dans certaines procédures de type romaniste, in *ICC, Taking of Evidence in International Arbitral Proceedings* 113 (1990)

Medalie, The Libyan Producers' Agreement Arbitration: Developing Innovative Procedures in a Complex Multiparty Arbitration, 7 *J. Int'l Arb.* 7 (No. 2, 1990)

Misra, Suggestions Regarding Unification of Guidelines for Presentation of Evidence in International Arbitration, in *ICCA, Fifth Int'l Arb. Congress: Proceedings* C IIh 1-2 (1975)

Morgan, Discovery in Arbitration, 3 *J. Int'l Arb.* 9 (No. 3, 1986)

Mustill, Sir Michael J. & S. C. Boyd, *The Law and Practice of Commercial Arbitration in England* (2nd ed. 1989)

Niblett, The Challenge of Presenting Technical Evidence, 16 *Int'l Bus. Law.* 236 (1988)

Park, Discovery, 51 *Arbitration* 352 (1985)

Patkin, Arbitration of Extraterritorial Discovery Disputes between the Securities and Exchange Commission and a Foreign Broker-Dealer: A New Approach to the Restatement Balancing Test, 5 *B.U. Int'l L.J.* 413 (1987)

Paulsson, International Commercial Arbitrations, in *Handbook of Arbitration Practice* 333 (R. Bernstein ed. 1987)

————, The Rules of Evidence in the Arbitral Procedure: Comparative Study, in *Euro-Arab Arbitration II* 90 (F. Kemicha ed. 1989)

Perrot, The Civil Law Approach to Evidence, 41 *Arbitration* 75 (1974)

Poznanski, The Nature and Extent of an Arbitrator's Power in International Commercial Arbitration, 4 *J. Int'l Arb.* 71 (No. 3, 1987)

Rhodes & Sloan, The Pitfalls of International Commercial Arbitration, 17 *Vand. J. Transnat'l L.* 19 (1984)

Robert, Administration of Evidence in International Commercial Arbitration, 1 *Y.B. Com. Arb.* 221 (1976)

Rokison, The Sources and Limits of the Arbitrator's Powers in England, in *Contemporary Problems of International Arbitration* 86 (J.D.M. Lew ed. 1986); also 52 *Arbitration* 219 (1986)

418

Rubino-Sammartano, A Civil Law Approach to the UNCITRAL Model Law and to Arbitral Rules of Evidence, 51 *Arbitration* 278 (1985)

———, La legge uniforme arbitrale delle Nazioni Unite, in embrione, e le rules of evidence arbitrali, 39 *Foro Padano* 97 (1984)

———, La prova nell'arbitrato internazionale. Necessità di una disciplina e di armonizzazione, 26 *Rassegna dell'Arb.* 37 (1986)

———, Rules of Evidence in International Arbitration: A Need for Discipline and Harmonization, 3 *J. Int'l Arb.* 87 (No. 2, 1986); also in *53 Arbitration* 85 (1987)

———, The Civil Law Approach to Evidence, 48 *Arbitration* 331 (1983)

Rubino-Sammartano, M., *International Arbitration Law* (Deventer 1990)

Russell, F., *Russell on the Law of Arbitration* (20th ed. by A. Walton & M. Vitoria 1982)

Schwebel & Lahne, Public Policy and Arbitral Procedure, in *Comparative Arbitration Practice and Public Policy in Arbitration* 205 (P. Sanders ed. 1987)

Sebestyen, Arbitration Procedure for Evidence, in *ICCA, Fifth Int'l Arb. Congress: Proceedings* C IId 1-2 (1975)

Sharkey, J. & J. Dorter, *Commercial Arbitration* (Sydney 1986)

Shenton, An Introduction to the IBA Rules of Evidence, 1 *Arb. Int'l* 118 (1985); also in 51 *Arbitration* 553 (Nov. 1985)

———, Supplementary Rules Governing the Presentation and Reception of Evidence in International Commercial Arbitration, 10 *Y.B. Com. Arb.* 145 (1985); reprinted in *Contemporary Problems in Int'l Arbitration* 188 (J.D.M. Lew ed. 1986)

Stalev, The Continental Case of Eastern Europe, 41 *Arbitration* 95 (1974)

Stein, Pre-Hearing Discovery in International Arbitrations in the U.S., 2 *Forum New York* (No. 1, 1985)

Straus, The Practice of the Iran-U.S. Claims Tribunal in Receiving Evidence from Parties and from Experts, 3 *J. Int'l Arb.* 57 (No. 3, 1986)

Sutton, Discovery and Production of Evidence in Arbitral Proceedings: the U.S. and England Distinguished, in *ICC, Taking of Evidence in International Proceedings* 57 (1990)

Tackaberry, Evidence at Hearings and in Documents-Only Arbitrations, in *Handbook of Arbitration Practice* 159 (R. Bernstein ed. 1987)

————, The Conduct of Arbitration Proceedings Under English Law, in *Contemporary Problems in International Arbitration* 216 (J.D.M. Lew ed. 1986); also 52 *Arbitration* 227 (1986)

Tibrewal, Presenting Evidence in International Commercial Arbitration, in *ICCA, Fifth Int'l Arb. Congress: Proceedings* C IIf 1-5 (1975)

Triebel, An Outline of the Swiss/German Rules of Civil Procedure and Practice Relating to Evidence, 47 *Arbitration* 221 (1982)

————, Rules of Procedure and Practice Relating to Evidence in Arbitration Proceedings in Continental Europe, 16 *Indian Council of Arbitration Q.* 3 (No. 4, Jan. -March 1982)

Tupman, Discovery and Evidence in U.S. Arbitration: The Prevailing Views, 44 *Arb. J.* 27 (No. 1, 1989)

Uff, Arbitral Procedure: Use of Legal and Technical Expertise, 53 *Arbitration* 23 (1987)

van Houtte, Conduct of Arbitral Proceedings, in *Essays on International Commercial Arbitration* 113 (P. Sarcevic ed. 1989)

Volk, Discovery in Arbitration in the United States, in *Second Bermuda Int'l Arb. Conference: Collection of Papers* (Hamilton, Bermuda, April 19-22, 1983)

Walder-Bohner, Zeugen vor Schiedsgericht, in *Recueil de Travaux Suisses* 213 (C. Reymond & E. Bucher eds. 1984)

Willens & Beaverman, Case Study on Use of Procedural Flexibility in Arbitration, 1 *Int'l Arb. Rep.* 296 (1986)

15.10 EXPERTS

Baker & Davis, Arbitral Proceedings under the UNCITRAL Rules: The Experience of the Iran-United States Claims Tribunal, 23 *Geo. Wash. J. Int'l L. & Econ.* 267 (1989)

Bühler, Technical Expertise: An Additional Means for Preventing or Settling Commercial Disputes, 6 *J. Int'l Arb.* 135 (No. 1, 1989)

Callender, The Expert, the Arbitrator and the Rules of Evidence, 47 *Arbitration* 197 (1982)

de Hauteclocque, French Judicial Expertise Procedure and International Arbitration, 4 *J. Int'l Arb.* 77 (No. 2, 1987)

Demont & Vermeille, L'arbitrage, son tribunal, sa procédure vus par l'expert, in *Recueil de Travaux Suisses* 235 (C. Reymond & E. Bucher eds. 1984)

Holtzmann, Use of Impartial Technical Experts to Resolve Engineering and Other Technological Disputes Before Arbitration, in *A.I.A., Essays in Memoriam Eugenio Minoli* 233 (Turin 1974)

Holtzmann & Bernini, Hypothetical Case for Use in a Comparative Study of Arbitration Practice in Various Legal Systems, in *Comparative Arbitration Practice and Public Policy in Arbitration* 19 (P. Sanders ed. 1987)

Holtzmann, H. & J. Neuhaus, *A Guide to the UNCITRAL Model Law on International Commercial Arbitration: Legislative History and Commentary* (Deventer 1989)

Horsmans, Actualité et évolution du droit belge de l'arbitrage, 1990 *Rev. Arb.* 797

James, The Training of Future Arbitrators, Technical Assessors and Expert Witnesses, in *ICCA, Fourth Int'l Arb. Congress: Proceedings* 695 (1972)

Kamenov, Problèmes de procédure dans l'arbitrage portant sur les litiges nés des contrats de coopération industrielles, scientifique et technique, in *ICCA, Fourth Int'l Arb. Congress: Proceedings* 500 (1972)

Kopelmanas, Le rôle de l'expertise dans l'arbitrage commercial international, 1979 *Rev. Arb.* 205

Miller, The Expert Witness, 47 *Arbitration* 287 (1982)

Mustill, Sir Michael J. & S. C. Boyd, *The Law and Practice of Commercial Arbitration in England* (2nd ed. 1989)

Paulsson, International Commercial Arbitrations, in *Handbook of Arbitration Practice* 333 (R. Bernstein ed. 1987)

————, The Rules of Evidence in the Arbitral Procedure: Comparative Study, in *Euro-Arab Arbitration II* 90 (F. Kemicha ed. 1989)

Poznanski, The Nature and Extent of an Arbitrator's Powers in International Commercial Arbitration, 4 *J. Int'l Arb.* 71 (No. 3, 1987)

Stewart, The Iran-United States Claims Tribunal: A Review of Developments 1983-84, 16 *L. & Pol'y Int'l Bus.* 677 (1984)

Straus, The Practice of the Iran-U.S. Claims Tribunal in Receiving Evidence from Parties and from Experts, 3 *J. Int'l Arb.* 57 (No. 3, 1986)

Tackaberry, The Conduct of Arbitration Proceedings Under English Law, in *Contemporary Problems in International Arbitration* 216 (J.D.M. Lew ed. 1986); also 52 *Arbitration* 227 (1986)

Uff, Arbitral Procedure: Use of Legal and Technical Expertise, 53 *Arbitration* 23 (1987)

van Houtte, Conduct of Arbitral Proceedings, in *Essays on International Commercial Arbitration* 113 (P. Sarcevic ed. 1989)

Warner, The Engineer in Court and International Arbitration, 52 *Arbitration* 107 (1986)

16. INTERIM MEASURES OF PROTECTION

16.01 IN GENERAL

Aden, Der einstweilige Rechtsschutz im Schiedsgerichtsverfahren, 40 *BB* 2277 (1985)

Baker & Davis, Arbitral Proceedings Under the UNCITRAL Rules: The Experience of the Iran-United States Claims Tribunal, 23 *Geo. Wash. J. Int'l L. & Econ.* 267 (1989)

Blessing, International Arbitration Procedures, 17 *Int'l Bus. Law.* 408 and 451 (1989)

Böckstiegel, Applying the UNCITRAL Rules: The Experience of the Iran-United States Claims Tribunal, 4 *Int'l Tax & Bus. Law.* 266 (1986)

Bösch, A., *Einstweiliger Rechtsschutz in der internationalen Handelsschiedsgerichtsbarkeit* (Berne 1989)

Branson & Tupman, Selecting an Arbitral Forum: A Guide to Cost-Effective International Arbitration, 24 *Va. J. Int'l L.* 917 (1984)

Brinkmann, G., *Schiedsgerichtsbarkeit und Massnahmen des einstweiligen Rechtsschutzes* (Berlin 1977)

Brower & Tupman, Court-Ordered Provisional Measures under the New York Convention, 80 *Am. J. Int'l L.* 24 (1986)

Bucher, A., *Die neue internationale Schiedsgerichtsbarkeit in der Schweiz* (Basel 1989)

————., *Le nouvel arbitrage international en Suisse. Théorie et pratique de droit* (Basel 1988)

Bucher, A. & P.-Y. Tschanz, *International Arbitration in Switzerland* (Basel 1989)

Caron, Interim Measures of Protection: Theory and Practice in Light of the Iran-United States Claims Tribunal, 46 *Zeitschrift für ausländisches öffentliches Recht und Völkerrecht* 465 (1986)

Cremades, Is Exclusion of Concurrent Courts' Jurisdiction over Conservatory Measures to Be Introduced through a Revision of the Convention? 6 *J. Int'l Arb.* 105 (No. 3, 1989)

Delaume, ICSID Tribunals and Provisional Measures — A Review of the Cases, 1 *ICSID Rev. - Foreign Investment L.J.* 392 (1986)

de Leval, Les mesures provisoires et conservatoires en matière d'arbitrage, in *L'Arbitrage* 111 (L. Matray & G. de Leval eds. 1989)

Friedland, Provisional Measures in ICSID Arbitration, 2 *Arb. Int'l* 335 (1986)

Gaillard, Le point de vue d'un utilisateur étranger, 1989 *Int'l Bus. L.J.* 793

Habscheid, Einstweiliger Rechtsschutz durch Schiedsgericht nach dem schweizerischen Gesetz über das Internationale Privatrecht (IPRG), 9 *IPRax* 134 (1989)

Hausmaninger, Ch., *Die einstweilige Verfügung im schiedsgerichtlichen Verfahren* (Vienna 1989)

Hoellering, Interim Measures and Arbitration: The Situation in the United States, 46 *Arb. J.* 22 (No. 2, 1991)

————, Interim Relief in International Arbitration, in *Arbitration and the Licensing Process* 3-55 (R. Goldscheider & M. de Haas eds. 1984-); reprinted from 1984 *Wis. Int'l L.J.* 3

Knoepfler & Schweizer, Les mesures provisoires et l'arbitrage, in *Recueil de Travaux Suisses* 221 (C. Reymond & E. Bucher eds. 1984)

Kohl B., *Vorläufiger Rechtsschutz in internationalen Handelsschiedsverfahren* (Berne 1990)

Kühn, Preliminary Remedies in Arbitration Matters, 12 *Int'l Bus. Law.* 111 (March 1984)

Kühn, Vorläufiger Rechtsschutz und Schiedsgerichtsbarkeit, 1 *Jahrbuch Schiedsgerichtsbarkeit* 47 (1987)

Laschet, Schiedsgerichtsbarkeit und einstweiliger Rechtsschutz, 99 *ZZP* 271 (1986)

Lessing, Schiedsgerichtsbarkeit und Massnahmen des provisorischen Rechtsschutzes: Jüngste Entwicklungen in den Vereinigten Staaten, 25 *ZRV* 26 (1984)

McDonell, The Availability of Provisional Relief in International Commercial Arbitration, 22 *Colum. J. Transnat'l L.* 273 (1984)

Manheim, Arbitrator's Power to Grant Injunction and Temporary Attachment (in Hebrew), 36 *Hapraklit (Israel)* 233 (1985)

Marchais, Mesure provisoires et autonomie du système d'arbitrage CIRDI, 14 *Droit et Pratique du Com. Int'l* 275 (1988)

Masood, Provisional Measures of Protection in Arbitration under the World Bank Convention, 1 *Delhi L. Rev.* 138 (1972)

Mustill, Sir Michael J. & S. C. Boyd, *The Law and Practice of Commercial Arbitration in England* (2nd ed. 1989)

Ouakrat, L'arbitrage et les mesures provisoires, 14 *Droit et Pratique du Com. Int'l* 239 (1988)

Paterson, International Commercial Arbitration Act: An Overview, in *UNCITRAL Arbitration Model in Canada* 113 (R. Paterson & B. Thompson eds. 1987)

Ramos Mendez, Arbitrage international et mesures conservatoires, 1985 *Rev. Arb.* 51

————, Arbitraje internacional y medidas cautelares, 84 *Justicia* 843 (1984)

Reichert, Provisional Remedies in the Context of International Commercial Arbitration, 3 *Int'l Tax & Bus. Law.* 368 (1986)

Rubino-Sammartano, M., *International Arbitration Law* (Deventer 1990)

Sandrock & Nöcker, Einstweilige Massnahmen internationaler Schiedsgerichte: Blosse Papiertiger? 1 *Jahrbuch Schiedsgerichtsbarkeit* 74 (1987)

Schlosser, Einstweiliger Rechtsschutz durch staatliche Gerichte im Dienste der Schiedsgerichtsbarkeit, 99 *ZZP* 241 (1986)

Shilston, Milestone in the Evolution of Modern Commercial Arbitration, 53 *Arbitration* 26 (1987)

Smit, Provisional Relief in International Arbitration: The ICC and Other Proposed Rules, 1 *Am. Rev. Int'l Arb.* 388 (1990)

————, Substance and Procedure in International Arbitration, 65 *Tul. L. Rev.* 1309 (1991)

Stewart, The Iran-United States Claims Tribunal: A Review of Developments 1983 -84, 16 *L. & Pol'y Int'l Bus.* 677 (1984)

von Hoffmann, International Construction Arbitration, in *Essays on International Commercial Arbitration* 223 (P. Sarcevic ed. 1989)

16.02 INTERIM MEASURES RELATING TO PROPERTY

Baker & Davis, Arbitral Proceedings under the UNCITRAL Rules: The Experience of the Iran-United States Claims Tribunal, 23 *Geo. Wash. J. Int'l L. & Econ.* 267 (1989)

Brody, An Argument for Pre-Award Attachment in International Arbitration under the New York Convention, 18 *Cornell Int'l L.J.* 99 (1985)

Hausmaninger, Ch., *Die einstweilige Verfügung im schiedsgerichtlichen Verfahren* (Vienna 1989)

Holmes, Pre-Award Attachment under the UN Convention on the Recognition and Enforcement of Foreign Arbitral Awards, 21 *Va. J. Int'l L.* 785 (1981)

Lécuyer-Thieffry, Examination of ICC's New Pre-Arbitral Referee Procedure, 1 *World Arb. & Med. Rep.* 13 (No. 1, 1990)

Mustill, Sir Michael J. & S. C. Boyd, *The Law and Practice of Commercial Arbitration in England* (2nd ed. 1989)

Newman & Burrows, New York Law Revision Changes Attachment Picture, 1 *Int'l Arb. Rep.* 301 (1986)

Note, Pre-Arbitration Attachment: Is It Available in International Disputes? 1 *Rev. Litigation* 211 (1981)

Rhodes & Sloan, The Pitfalls of International Commercial Arbitration, 17 *Vand. J. Transnat'l L.* 19 (1984)

van den Berg, Some Recent Problems in the Practice of Enforcement under the New York and ICSID Conventions, in *Arbitration and the Courts: Fifth ICSID/ AAA/ICC Colloquium* (Washington 1987)

16.03 INTERIM MEASURES RELATING
TO EVIDENCE

Gothberg, Coercive Measures for Obtaining Production of Documentary Evidence in Arbitration Proceedings, 8 *Int'l Arb. Gazette* 361 (1986)

Hausmaninger, Ch., *Die einstweilige Verfügung im schiedsgerichtlichen Verfahren* (Vienna 1989)

Kühn, Vorläufiger Rechtsschutz und Schiedsgerichtsbarkeit, 1 *Jahrbuch Schiedsgerichtsbarkeit* 47 (1987)

Leahy & Pierce, Sanctions to Control Party Misbehavior in International Arbitration, 26 *Va. J. Int'l L.* 291 (1986)

Mustill, Sir Michael J. & S. C. Boyd, *The Law and Practice of Commercial Arbitration in England* (2nd ed. 1989)

16.04 ORDERS FOR SECURITY

Baker & Davis, Arbitral Proceedings under the UNCITRAL Rules: The Experience of the Iran-United States Claims Tribunal, 23 *Geo. Wash. J. Int'l L. & Econ.* 267 (1989)

Hobér, Arbitration in Moscow, 3 *Arb. Int'l* 119 (1987)

Leahy & Pierce, Sanctions to Control Party Misbehavior in International Arbitration, 26 *Va. J. Int'l L.* 291 (1986)

Lee, Security for Costs in International Arbitration, 5 *Bus. L. Rev.* 286 (1984)

Mustill, Sir Michael J. & S. C. Boyd, *The Law and Practice of Commercial Arbitration in England* (2nd ed. 1989)

Samuel, Developments in English Arbitration Law since the 1984 Antaios Decision, 5 *J. Int'l Arb.* 9 (No. 3, 1988)

Thomas, Admiralty Security and the Arbitral Process, 1983 *Lloyd's Mar. & Com. L.Q.* 493

————, The Availability of a Security Obtained in Rem to the Arbitral Process under English Law, in 2 *Fifth Int'l Congress of Maritime Arbitrators* (New York 1981)

17. AWARDS

17.01 IN GENERAL

Alvarez Rodriguez, Formación, contenido y efectos del laudo arbitral en la Ley española de Arbitraje, 5 *Rev. Corte Esp. Arb.* 95 (1988-89)

Arbitration Institute of the Stockholm Chamber of Commerce, *Arbitration in Sweden* (2nd rev. ed. 1984)

Aylwin Azocar, P., *El juicio arbitral* (Santiago de Chile 1958)

Barclay, The Arbitration Award, 45 *Arbitration* 118 (1979)

Bartos, H., *Internationale Handelsschiedsgerichtsbarkeit: Verfahrensprinzipien* (Frankfurt 1984)

Blessing, International Arbitration Procedures, 17 I*nt'l Bus. Law.* 408 and 451 (1989)

————, The Major Western and Soviet Arbitration Rules: A Comparison of the Rules of UNCITRAL, UNCITRAL Model Law, LCIA, ICC, AAA and the Rules of the USSR Chamber of Commerce and Industry, 6 *J. Int'l Arb.* 7 (No. 3, 1989)

Böckstiegel, Applying the UNCITRAL Rules: The Experience of the Iran-United States Claims Tribunal, 4 *Int'l Tax & Bus. Law.* 266 (1986)

Bond, I.C.C. Arbitration in Theory and Practice, 26 *Rassegna dell'Arb.* 141 (1986)

Buzaid, Do juizo arbitral, 217 *Rev. Trib.* 7 (1960)

Capatina, Nouvelles tendances dans la réglementation des effets des sentences arbitrales étrangères, [1977] 1 *Revue Roumaine des Sciences Sociales, Série de Sciences Juridiques* 63

Carbonneau, Arbitral Adjudication: A Comparative Assessment of Its Remedial and Substantive Status in Transnational Commerce, 19 *Tex. Int'l L. J.* 33 (1984)

Chillón Medina, J. M. & J. F. Merino Merchán, *Tratado de arbitraje privado interno e internacional* (Madrid 1978)

David, R., *Arbitration in International Trade* (Deventer 1985)

Derains, Y., ed., *Droit et pratique de l'arbitrage international en France* (Paris 1984)

Diez-Canseco, El juicio arbitral, 34 *Revista juridica del Perú* 289 (1983)

El-Hakim, Should the Key Terms Award, Commercial and Binding Be Defined in the New York Convention? 6 *J. Int'l Arb.* 161 (No. 1, 1989)

Ester Ledesma, Eficacia del laudo arbitral, in *El Arbitraje en el Derecho Latinoamericano y Español* 99 (L. Perret & U. Montoya Alberti eds. 1989)

Eyzaguirre Echeverria, R., *El arbitraje comercial en la legislación chileña y su regulación international* (Santiago de Chile 1981)

Foster, C.A., *The Law and Practice of Commercial Arbitration in North Carolina* (Durham 1986)

Goldman, International Arbitration in Europe, in *IBA, Soviet Foreign Trade Reforms & East/West Arbitration* 217 (1988)

Hagberg, Salient Features of the Swedish Arbitral Procedure, 1990 *Y.B. Swed. & Int'l Arb.* 34

Henn, G., *Schiedsverfahrensrecht: ein Handbuch* (Heidelberg 1986)

Hintz, Recht und Praxis der Streiterledigung im Ost-West-Handel am Beispiel des Handels zwischen der UdSSR und der Bundesrepublik Deutschland, 32 *RIW* 506 (1986)

Holtzmann, H. & J. Neuhaus, *A Guide to the UNCITRAL Model Law on International Commercial Arbitration: Legislative History and Commentary* (Deventer 1989)

Horsmans, La sentence arbitrale, la convention d'arbitrage et l'ordre public interne belge, 16 *Tijdschrift voor Privaatrecht* 231 (1979)

Jolidon, La sentence en equité dans le Concordat suisse sur l'arbitrage, in *Recueil de Travaux Suisses* 259 (C. Reymond & E. Bucher eds. 1984)

Keilin, A.D., *Sudoustroistvo i grazhdanskii protsess kapitalisticheskikh gosudartstv. III: - Arbitrazh* (Moscow 1961)

Kessler, J., *Schiedsgerichtsvertrag und Schiedsverfahren* (Munich 1970)

Knoepfler & Schweizer, Making of Awards and Termination of Proceedings, in *Essays on International Commercial Arbitration* 160 (P. Sarcevic ed. 1989)

Lee, E., *Encyclopedia of International Commercial Arbitration* (London 1986)

Lew, J., *Applicable Law in International Commercial Arbitration. A Study in Commercial Arbitration Awards* (Dobbs Ferry 1978)

Littman, Composition of Arbitral Tribunal and Making the Award, 24 *Rassegna dell'Arb.* 37 (1984)

Moreau, B. & T. Bernard, *Droit interne et droit international de l'arbitrage* (2nd ed. 1985)

Mustill, Sir Michael J. & S. C. Boyd, *The Law and Practice of Commercial Arbitration in England* (2nd ed. 1989)

Pacific Rim Advisory Council, *Pacific Rim: Commercial Arbitration Procedures* (San Diego, CA 1985)

Paterson, International Commercial Arbitration Act: An Overview, in *UNCITRAL Arbitration Model in Canada* 113 (R. Paterson & B. Thompson eds. 1987)

Perrot, L'arbitrage international en droit français, 27 *Rassegna dell'Arb.* 1 (1987)

Recchia, Nuove prospettive dell'arbitrato commerciale in Italia, 23 *Rassegna dell'Arb.* 41 (1983)

Redfern, A. & M. Hunter, *Law and Practice of International Commercial Arbitration* (2nd ed. 1991)

Rhodes & Sloan, The Pitfalls of International Commercial Arbitration, 17 *Vand. J. Transnat'l L.* 19 (1984)

Robert, J. & B. Morceau, *L'arbitrage — droit interne, droit international privé* (5th ed. Paris 1983)

Rubino-Sammartano, M., *International Arbitration Law* (Deventer 1990)

Russell, F., *Russell on the Law of Arbitration* (20th ed. by A. Walton & M. Vitoria 1982)

Schizzerotto, G., *Dell'arbitrato* (3rd ed. Milan 1988)

Schlosser, Conflits entre jugements judiciares et arbitrage, 1981 *Rev. Arb.* 371

Schönke, A., *Das Schiedsgerichtsverfahren nach dem heutigen deutschen Recht* (Berlin 1954)

Schütze, R., D. Tscherning & W. Wais, *Handbuch des Schiedsverfahrens. Praxis der deutschen und internationalen Schiedsgerichtsbarkeit* (2nd ed. Berlin 1990)

Sharkey, J. & J. Dorter, *Commercial Arbitration* (Sydney 1986)

Shilston, The Evolution of Modern Commercial Arbitration, 4 *J. Int'l Arb.* 45 (No. 2, 1987)

Strenger, Do juizo arbitral, 607 *Rev. Trib.* 24 (May 1986)

Taliadoros, Comment deux sentences arbitrales rendues dans le cadre de la législation hellénique relative à la protection des investissements étrangers et portant toutes deux sur un objet identique, ..., 1984 *Droit et Pratique du Com. Int'l* 603

Turner, C., *Yorston, Fortescue & Turner Australian Mercantile Law.* 17th ed. Chapter 25: Commercial Arbitration and Awards (Sydney 1985)

van den Berg, A. J., *The New York Arbitration Convention of 1958* (Deventer 1981)

Vulliemin, J.-M., *Jugement et sentence arbitrale: étude de droit international privé et de droit comparé* (2nd ed., Lausanne 1990)

17.02 TIME LIMIT FOR RENDERING AWARD

Bakshi, Time Limits in Arbitration: Reform Needed, 1987 (1) *Company L .J.* 13

Blessing, International Arbitration Procedures, 17 *Int'l Bus. Law.* 408 and 451 (1989)

Bredow & Bühler, Zur Änderung der Schiedsgerichtsordnung der Internationalen Handelskammer, 8 *IPRax* 69 (1988)

Derains, International Commercial Arbitration in Civil Law Countries, in *Arbitration in Settlement of International Commercial Disputes Involving the Far East and Arbitration in Combined Transportation* 229 (P. Sanders ed. 1989)

Jarvis, The Problem of Post-Hearing Delay in Maritime Arbitrations: When Did You Say We Would Receive the Arbitral Award? 9 *Md. J. Int'l L. & Trade* 19 (1985)

Less, Late Arbitration Awards Enforceable Where Party Fails to Make Timely Objection, 21 *Suff. U.L. Rev.* 447 (1987)

Nordenson, The Arbitral Proceedings in International Arbitration in Sweden, 1984 *Y.B. Swed. & Int'l Arb.* 6

Parlade, Remedies after Arbitration Award, in *Commercial Arbitration* 75 (J. Ricalde ed. 1983)

Prujiner, La gestion des arbitrages commerciaux internationaux: l'exemple de la Cour d'arbitrage de la CCI, 115 *J. Droit Int'l (Clunet)* 662 (1988)

Raeschke-Kessler & Bühler, Aufsicht über den Schiedsrichter durch den ICC-Schiedsgerichtshof (Paris) und rechtliches Gehör der Parteien, 8 *ZIP* 1157 (1987)

Samuel, A., *Jurisdictional Problems in International Commercial Arbitration: A Study of Belgian, Dutch, English, French, Swedish, Swiss, U.S. and West German Law* (Zurich 1989)

17.03 FORMAL REQUIREMENTS

Bernini, Il riconoscimento all'estero del lodo arbitrale irrituale, 45 *Riv. Trim. Dir. & Proc. Civ.* 357 (1991)

Bin, Il compromesso e la clausola compromissoria in arbitrato irrituale, 45 *Riv. Trim. Dir. & Proc. Civ.* 373 (1991)

Blessing, International Arbitration Procedures, 17 *Int'l Bus. Law.* 408 and 451 (1989)

Bucher, A., *Die neue internationale Schiedsgerichtsbarkeit in der Schweiz* (Basel 1989)

————., *Le nouvel arbitrage international en Suisse. Théorie et pratique de droit* (Basel 1988)

Bucher, A. & P.-Y.Tschanz, *International Arbitration in Switzerland* (Basel 1989)

Carpi, Il procedimento nell'arbitrato irrituale, 45 *Riv. Trim. Dir. & Proc. Civ.* 389(1991)

de Nova, Nullità del contratto e arbitrato irrituale, 45 *Riv. Trim. Dir. & Proc. Civ.* 401(1991)

Derains, International Commercial Arbitration in Civil Law Countries, in *Arbitration in Settlement of International Commercial Disputes Involving the Far East and Arbitration in Combined Transportation* 229 (P. Sanders ed. 1989)

Ferrante, Profili pratici della formazione del lodo, 26 *Rassegna dell'Arb.* 1 (1986)

Fulton, The Art of Writing Arbitral Decisions, 10 *Can. Arb. J.* 25 (No. 1, 1985)

Gaillard, Les manoevres dilatoires des parties et des arbitres dans l'arbitrage commercial international, 1990 *Rev. Arb.* 759

Galgano, L'equità degli arbitri, 45 *Riv. Trim. Dir. & Proc. Civ.* 409 (1991)

Knoepfler & Schweizer, Making of Awards and Termination of Proceedings, in *Essays on International Commercial Arbitration* 160 (P. Sarcevic ed. 1989)

Lorcher, Kein Schiedsspruch ohne Unterschrift des Vorsitzenden? 43 *BB* 78 (1988)

Lucchesi, Zur Frage der Anerkennung und Vollstreckung des "lodo irrituale" (=formfreien Schiedsspruches) ausserhalb Italiens, 24 *ZRV* 1 (1983)

Montesano, Aspetti problematici dell'arbitrato irrituale dopo la riforma del 1983, 45 *Riv. Trim. Dir. & Proc. Civ.* 214 (1991)

Mustill, Sir Michael J. & S. C. Boyd, *The Law and Practice of Commercial Arbitration in England* (2nd ed. 1989)

Sandrock, Das Gesetz zur Neuregelung des Internationalen Privatrechts und die internationale Schiedsgerichtsbarkeit, 33 *RIW Beilage 2 zu Heft* 5/1987 (1987)

Schwebel & Lahne, Public Policy and Arbitral Procedure, in *Comparative Arbitration Practice and Public Policy in Arbitration* 205 (P. Sanders ed. 1987)

Shilston, Milestone in the Evolution of Modern Commercial Arbitration, 53 *Arbitration* 26 (1987)

Tarzia, Nullità e annullamento del lodo arbitrale irrituale, 45 *Riv. Trim. Dir. & Proc. Civ.* 451 (1991)

Triebel & Viertel, Die Bundesrepublik Deutschland wird als Schiedsgerichtsort im internationalen Schiedsverfahren gemieden: Zur Reformbedürftigkeit des par. 1039 ZPO, 41 *BB* 1168 (1986)

Wenger, Zur Anwendbarkeit des New Yorker Übereinkommen über die Anerkennung und Vollstreckung ausländischer Schiedssprüche auf einem "freien" Schiedsspruch (lodo irrituale) des italienischen Rechts, 2 *IPRax* 135 (1982)

17.04 SUBSTANTIVE REQUIREMENTS

Bentil, Judicial Intervention and International Commercial Arbitration, 130 *Solicitors' J.* 191 (1986)

Bond, The New Swiss Law on International Arbitration and the Arbitral Institutions, 1989 *Int'l Bus. L.J.* 785

Broches, Awards Rendered Pursuant to the ICSID Convention: Binding Force, Finality, Recognition, Enforcement, Execution, 2 *ICSID Rev. - Foreign Investment L.J.* 287 (1987)

Delaume, The Finality of Arbitration Involving States: Recent Developments, 5 *Arb. Int'l* 21 (1989)

El-Hakim, Conditions de validité dans le droit et la pratique des pays arabes, in *Euro-Arab Arbitration II* 131 (F. Kemicha ed. 1989)

———, Should the Key Terms Award, Commercial and Binding Be Defined in the New York Convention? 6 *J. Int'l Arb.* 161 (No. 1, 1989)

Feldman, The Annulment Proceedings and the Finality of ICSID Arbitral Awards, 2 *ICSID Rev.- Foreign Investment L.J.* 85 (1987)

Ferrante, Sull'indivisibilità del lodo arbitrale, 30 *Rassegna dell'Arb.* 155 (1930)

Firth, The Finality of a Foreign Arbitral Award, 25 *Arb. J.* 1 (1970); also in *A.A.A., New Strategies* 121 (1971)

Fouchard, Conditions de validité en droit conventionnel et droit comparé, in *Euro-Arab Arbitration II* 121 (F. Kemicha ed. 1989)

Jaffe, The Judicial Trend toward Finality of Commercial Arbitral Awards in England, 24 *Tex. Int'l L.J.* 67 (1989)

Kemicha, F., ed., *Euro-Arab Arbitration II/Arbitrage Euro-Arabe II* (London 1989)

Lalive, Enforcing Awards, in *ICC, 60 Years of ICC Arbitration* 317 (1984)

Mustill, Sir Michael J. & S. C. Boyd, *The Law and Practice of Commercial Arbitration in England* (2nd ed. 1989)

Schmitthoff, Finality of Arbitral Awards and Judicial Review, in *Contemporary Problems in International Arbitration* 230 (J.D.M. Lew ed. 1986)

Thieffry, The Finality of Awards in International Arbitration, 2 *J. Int'l Arb.* 27 (1985)

17.05 REASONS

Beresford-Hartwell, The Reasoned Award, 54 *Arbitration* 36 (1988)

Bingham, Reasons and Reasons for Reasons: Differences between a Court Judgment and an Arbitration Award, 4 *Arb. Int'l* 141 (1988)

Carbonneau, Etude historique et comparée de l'arbitrage: vers un droit matériel de l'arbitrage commercial international fondé sur la motivation des sentences, 36 *Rev. Int'l Droit Comp.* 727 (1984)

———, Rendering Arbitral Awards with Reasons: The Elaboration of a Common Law of International Transactions, 23 *Colum. J. Transnat'l L.* 579 (1985)

Conrick, Where the Kings Writ Does Not Run: The Origins and Effect of the Arbitration Act 1979, 1 *Queensl. Inst. Tech. L.J.* 1 (1985)

Delvolvé, Essai sur la motivation des sentences arbitrales, 1989 *Rev. Arb.* 149

Domke, Arbitral Awards without Written Opinions: Comparative Aspects of International Commercial Arbitration, in *Legal Essays in Honour of H.E. Yntema* 249 (The Hague 1961)

Geisinger & Renold, Arbitrage international, ordre public et reconnaissance en Suisse de sentences arbitrales étrangères, in *Le Juriste Suisse Face au Droit et aux Jugements Etrangers: Ouverture ou Repli?* 89 (F. Knoepfler ed. 1988)

Glossner, The Conduct of ICC Arbitration Proceedings, in *Contemporary Problems in International Arbitration* 210 (J.D.M. Lew ed. 1986)

Hardenberg, De motivering van arbitrale vonnissen, 1990 *Tijdschrift voor Arbitrage* 48

Harmer, Structure and Content of a Reasoned Award, 54 *Arbitration* 163 (1988)

Knoepfler & Schweizer, Making of Awards and Termination of Proceedings, in *Essays on International Commercial Arbitration* 160 (P. Sarcevic ed. 1989)

Motulsky, L'exequatur des sentences étrangères non motivée, 1967 *Rev. Arb.* 103

Mustill, Sir Michael J. & S. C. Boyd, *The Law and Practice of Commercial Arbitration in England* (2nd ed. 1989)

Rhidian, Arbitration: The Basis and Validity of a Restricted Reasons Agreement, [1986] *Lloyd's Mar. & Com. L.Q.* 235

Rhodes, Judicial Review of Commercial Arbitration, 14 *Hong Kong L.J.* 159 (1984)

Samuel, Developments in English Arbitration Law since the 1984 Antaios Decision, 5 *J. Int'l Arb.* 9 (No. 3, 1988)

Santhanam, Arbitration Award without Reasons: Validity, 1989(2) *Company L.J.* 8

Schmitthoff, Extrajudicial Dispute Settlement, *Forum Internationale*, (No.6, May 1985)

Schmitthoff, C., *Schmitthoff's Export Trade. The Law and Practice of International Trade* (8th ed. 1986)

Schwebel & Lahne, Public Policy and Arbitral Procedure, in *Comparative Arbitration Practice and Public Policy in Arbitration* 205 (P. Sanders ed. 1987)

Sims, Trust Your Arbitrator? 137 *New L.J.* 855 (1987)

Steyn, Reasoned Awards under the Arbitration Act 1979, 47 *Arbitration* 264 (1982)

Sweeney, Judicial Review of Arbitral Proceedings, in 2 *Fifth Int'l Congress of Maritime Arbitrators* (New York 1981)

Thomas, Arbitration: The Basis and Validity of a Restricted Reasons Agreement, 1986 *Lloyd's Mar. & Com. L.Q.* 235 (1986)

van den Berg, A. J., *The New York Arbitration Convention of 1958* (Deventer 1981)

17.06 CONFIRMATION OR AUTHENTICATION

Jarvin, An International Chamber of Commerce Perspective, in *UNCITRAL Arbitration Model in Canada* 55 (R. Paterson & B. Thompson eds. 1987)

————, The Enforcement of ICC Arbitral Award, 1988 *Int'l Bus. L.J.* 241

Loquin, L'examen du projet de sentence par l'institution et la sentence au deuxième degré, 1990 *Rev. Arb.* 427

Paulsson, Vicarious Hypochondria and Institutional Arbitration, 1990 *Y.B. Swed. & Int'l Arb.* 96; also in 6 *Arb. Int'l* 226 (1990)

Prujiner, La gestion des arbitrages commerciaux internationaux: l'exemple de la Cour d'arbitrage de la CCI, 115 *J. Droit Int'l (Clunet)* 662 (1988)

Smit, The Future of International Commercial Arbitration: A Single Transnational Institution? 25 *Colum. J. Transnat'l L.* 9 (1986)

Sujan, M.A., *The Law Relating to Government Arbitration* (New Delhi 1985)

Tanimoto, Necessity of Establishing of Custom and of Arbitration Award Based on the Custom, in *ICCA, Fourth Int'l Arb. Congress: Proceedings* 826 (1972)

17.07 TYPES OF AWARDS

Bucher, A., *Die neue internationale Schiedsgerichtsbarkeit in der Schweiz* (Basel 1989)

————., *Le nouvel arbitrage international en Suisse. Théorie et pratique de droit* (Basel 1988)

Bucher, A. & P.-Y.Tschanz, *International Arbitration in Switzerland* (Basel 1989)

Caron, Interim Measures of Protection: Theory and Practice in Light of the Iran-United States Claims Tribunal, 46 *Zeitschrift für ausländisches öffentliches Recht und Völkerrecht* 465 (1986)

Comment, Enforcement of Interim Awards, 3 *Forum New York* 4 (No. 2, 1986)

Derains, International Commercial Arbitration in Civil Law Countries, in *Arbitration in Settlement of International Commercial Disputes Involving the Far East and Arbitration in Combined Transportation* 229 (P. Sanders ed. 1989)

Duintjer Tebbens, A Facelift for Dutch Arbitration Law, 34 *Neth. Int'l L. Rev.* 141 (1987)

Habscheid, Teil-, Zwischen- und Vorabschiedsprüche im schweizerischen und deutschen Recht, ihre Anfechtbarkeit und die Rechtsfolgen ihrer Aufhebung durch das Staatsgericht (unter besonderer Berücksichtigung der Streitgenossenschaft), 106 *ZSR* 669 (1987)

Hjerner, On Partial Awards, Orders and Other Decisions in Arbitral Proceedings, in Particular with Respect to Arbitration in Sweden, 1984 *Y.B. Swed. & Int'l Arb.* 31

Knoepfler & Schweizer, Making of Awards and Termination of Proceedings, in *Essays on International Commercial Arbitration* 160 (P. Sarcevic ed. 1989)

Laschet, Zur Anerkennung ausländischer Zwischenschiedssprüche, 4 *IPRax* 72 (1984)

McDonell, The Availability of Provisional Relief in International Commercial Arbitration, 22 *Colum. J. Transnat'l L.* 273 (1984)

Mirimanoff, Objection to Arbitrators Following the Annulment of a Partial Award: A Potential Jeopardy of Arbitration in Switzerland? 3 *J. Int'l Arb.* 101 (No. 2, 1986)

Monteleone, Il nuovo regime giuridico dei lodi arbitrali rituali, 40 *Riv. Dir. Proc.* 552 (1985)

Mooney, Interim Awards — Their Usage and Enforceability in the United States, in 2 *Fifth Int'l Congress of Maritime Arbitrators* (New York 1981)

Panchaud, La sentence arbitrale partielle, in *A.I.A., Essays in Memoriam Eugenio Minoli* 385 (Turin 1974)

Paulsson, May a State Invoke Its Internal Law to Repudiate Consent to International Commercial Arbitration? Reflections on the Benteler v. Belgium Preliminary Award, 2 *Arb. Int'l* 90 (1986)

Penna, Partial Final Awards, in *AAA, Arbitration & the Law, 1986* 67 (1987)

Perrot, Arbitrage interne et arbitrage international. Les recours devant la Cour d'appel empêchent-ils l'arbitre de poursuivre sa mission? 1987 *Rev. Arb.* 107

Rokison, The Sources and Limits of the Arbitrator's Powers in England, in *Contemporary Problems of International Arbitration* 86 (J.D.M. Lew ed. 1986); also 52 *Arbitration* 219 (1986)

Schmitthoff, Extrajudicial Dispute Settlement, *Forum Internationale*, (No .6, May 1985)

Tan, Unmeritorious Claims and Defences in Arbitration Proceedings, 1987 *Malayan L.J.* cxvii

Zubrod, Interim Decisions and Partial Final Awards in United States Arbitrations, in *Second Bermuda Int'l Arb. Conference: A Collection of Papers* (Hamilton, Bermuda, April 19-22, 1983)

17.08 NATIONALITY OF AWARDS

Bajons, Zur Nationalität internationaler Schiedssachen: der Fall 'Norsolor' vor den österreichischen Gerichten, in *Festschrift für Winfried Kralik* 3 (Vienna 1986)

Berger, The Modern Trend Towards Exclusion of Recourse against Transnational Arbitral Awards: A European Perspective, 12 *Fordham Int'l L. J.* 605 (1989)

Booysen, The Municipal Enforcement of Arbitration Awards against States in Terms of Arbitration Conventions, with Special Reference to the New York Convention — Does International Law Provide for a Municipal Law Concept of an Arbitrable Act of State? 12 *South Afr. Y.B. Int'l L.* 73 (1986-1987)

Bühler, Staatsgerichtliche Aufhebungskontrolle am Schiedsort? Zur Reform Belgiens, 7 *IPRax* 253 (1987)

Delaume, Arbitration with Governments: Domestic and International, 17 *Int'l Law.* 687 (1983)

————, SEEE v. Yugoslavia: Epitaph or Interlude? 4 *J. Int'l Arb.* 25 (No. 3, 1987)

Deshpande, Jurisdiction over 'Foreign' and 'Domestic' Awards in the New York Convention 1958, 7 *Arb. Int'l* 123 (1991)

Ebb, Developing Views on What Constitutes a 'Foreign Arbitration Agreement' and a 'Foreign Award' under the New York Convention, 1 *Am. Rev. Int'l Arb.* 364 (1990)

Feldman, An Award Made in New York Can Be a Foreign Arbitration Award, 39 *Arb. J.* 14 (March 1984)

Ferrante, About the Nature (National or A-National, Contractual or Jurisdictional) of ICC Awards under the New York Convention, in *The Art of Arbitration* 129 (J. Schultsz & A. van den Berg eds. 1982)

————, Profili pratici della formazione del lodo, 26 *Rassegna dell'Arb.* 1 (1986)

Gelinas, L'exécution des sentences arbitrales internationales au Québec: commentaire, in *First International Commmercial Arbitration Conference: Proceedings* 305 (N. Antaki & A. Prujiner eds. 1986)

Gomez, International Arbitration: A Case for Delocalization, 3 *Sri Lanka J. Int'l L.* 61 (1991)

Groos, Schiedsgerichtsbarkeit im deutsch-französischen Wirtschaftsverkehr, 33 *RIW* 343 (1987)

Hardenberg, The Awards of the Iran-U.S. Claims Tribunal Seen in Connection with the Law of the Netherlands, 12 *Int'l Bus. Law.* 337 (1984)

Herrmann, The UNCITRAL Model Law on International Commercial Arbitration — Its Salient Features and Prospects, in *First Int'l Commercial Arbitration Conference: Proceedings* 351 (N. Antaki & A. Prujiner eds. 1986)

Hunter, Achievement of the Intention of the Parties: Arbitration Agreements and the First Procedural Steps in International Arbitrations, 47 *Arbitration* 213 (1982)

Lake & Dana, Judicial Review of Awards of the Iran-United States Claims Tribunal: Are the Tribunal's Awards Dutch? 16 *L. & Pol'y Int'l Bus.* 755 (1984)

Lew, Nationality of International Commercial Arbitration, 5 *Bus. L. Rev.* 318 (1984)

Mann, Where Is an Award 'Made'? 1 *Arb. Int'l* 107 (1985)

———, Zur Nationalität des Schiedsspruchs, in *Festschrift für Walter Oppenhoff* 215 (Munich 1985)

Minoli, Il problema teorico fundamentale dell'arbitrato commerciale internazionale, in *Studi in memoria Carlo Furno* 627 (1973)

Mok Young-Joon, The Principle of Reciprocity in the United Nations Convention on the Recognition and Enforcement of Foreign Arbitral Awards of 1958, 21 *Case W. Res. J. Int'l L.* 123 (1989)

Park, Judicial Controls in the Arbitral Process, 5 *Arb. Int'l* 230 (1989)

———, Private Adjudicators and the Public Interest: The Expanding Scope of International Arbitration, 12 *Brooklyn J. Int'l L.* 629 (1986)

Paulsson, Arbitration Unbound: Award Detached from the Law of its Country of Origin, 30 *Int'l & Comp. L.Q.* 358 (1981)

———, Arbitre et juge en Suède: exposé générale et réflexions sur la délocalisation des sentences arbitrales, 1980 *Rev. Arb.* 441

————, Delocalization of International Commercial Arbitration: When and Why It Matters, 32 *Int'l & Comp. L.Q.* 53 (1983)

Pisar, The United Nations Convention on Foreign Arbitral Awards, 1959 *J. Bus. L.* 219; reprinted in 33 *S. Cal. L. Rev.* 14 (1959)

Poznanski, The Nature and Extent of an Arbitrator's Powers in International Commercial Arbitration, 4 *J. Int'l Arb.* 71 (No. 3, 1987)

Rigaux, La detérmination de l'ordre juridique auquel se rattachent les arbitrages petroliers, in *First Euro-Arab Arbitration Conference: Proceedings* 298 (F. Kemicha ed. 1987)

Rubino-Sammartano, International and Foreign Arbitration, 5 *J. Int'l Arb.* 85 (No. 3, 1988)

————, Nazionalità degli arbitrati e regolamento della Camera di Commercio Internazionale, 20 *Rassegna dell'Arb.* 179 (1980)

————, Nationality of Awards and Applicable Substantive and Procedural Law, 48 *Arbitration* 47 (1982)

Samuel, A., *Jurisdictional Problems in International Commercial Arbitration: A Study of Belgian, Dutch, English, French, Swedish, Swiss, U.S. and West German Law* (Zurich 1989)

Sanders, Trends in the Field of International Commercial Arbitration, 145 *Recueil des Cours* 205 (1975-II)

Sarcevic, The Setting Aside and Enforcement of Arbitral Awards under the UNCITRAL Model law, in *Essays on International Commercial Arbitration* 177 (P. Sarcevic ed. 1989)

Schlosser, Das internationale an der internationalen privaten Schiedsgerichtsbarkeit, 28 *RIW* 857 (1982)

————, Quelles nouvelles de l'arbitrage Outre-Rhin? 1987 Rev. Arb. 293

————, What Is International in the Legal Basis of International Arbitration? 1985 *Comp. L. Rev.* 113 (No. 1, 1985) and 85 (No. 2, 1985)

Schultsz, The Bill on Applicability of Dutch Law to Awards Rendered by the Iran-United States Claims Tribunal, in *Legislation in the Netherlands and International Arbitration* 32 (1986)

Smit, A-National Arbitration, 63 *Tul. L. Rev.* 629 (1989)

————, The Future of International Commercial Arbitration: A Single Transnational Institution? 25 *Colum. J. Transnat'l L.* 9 (1986)

Strohbach, Towards an International Arbitral Award, in *The Art of Arbitration* 305 (J. Schultsz & A. van den Berg eds. 1982)

Thompson, 'Detachment' from the National Law in International Commercial Arbitration, 48 *Arbitration* 105 (1982)

Toop, S., *Mixed International Arbitration: Studies in Arbitration between States and Private Persons* (Cambridge 1990)

Triebel & Petzold, Grenzen der lex mercatoria in der internationalen Schiedsgerichtsbarkeit, 34 *RIW* 245 (1988)

van den Berg, Non-Domestic Arbitral Awards under the 1958 New York Convention, 2 *Arb. Int'l* 191 (1986)

————, Recent Enforcement Problems under the New York and ICSID Conventions, 5 *Arb. Int'l* 2 (1989)

————, Some Recent Problems in the Practice of Enforcement under the New York and ICSID Conventions, in *Arbitration and the Courts: Fifth ICSID/AAA/ICC Colloquium* (Washington 1987)

————, When Is an Arbitral Award Non-Domestic under the New York Convention of 1958? 6 *Pace L. Rev.* 25 (1985)

van den Berg, A. J., *The New York Arbitration Convention of 1958* (Deventer 1981)

Watté, Le sort des sentences arbitrales en droit belge depuis la loi du 27 mars 1985, 21 *Revue belge de droit international* 496 (1988)

17.09 RELIEF AND REMEDIES

Bedell, Punitive Damages in Arbitration, 21 *J. Marshall L. Rev.* 21 (1987)

Berg, Punitive Damages: Are They Properly Awarded in Arbitration? 1 *Int'l Arb. Rep.* 248 (1986)

Boyd, Interest for the Late Payment of Money, 1 *Arb. Int'l* 153 (1985)

Branson & Wallace, Awarding Interest in International Commercial Arbitration: Establishing a Uniform Approach, 28 *Va. J. Int'l L.* 919 (1988)

Carper, Punitive Damages in Commercial Arbitration, 53 *Arbitration* 276 (1987)

Farnsworth, Punitive Damages in Arbitration, 7 *Arb. Int'l* 3 (1991)

Heuman, L., *Current Issues in Swedish Arbitration* (Deventer and Stockholm 1990)

Hjerner, Awarding Interest in Swedish Arbitration, 1985 *Y.B. Swed. & Int'l Arb.* 29

Hoellering, Remedies in Arbitration, 20 *The Forum* 516 (1984-85)

Hunter & Triebel, Awarding Interest in International Arbitration, 6 *J. Int'l Arb.* 7 (No. 1, 1989)

Jones, Punitive Damages as an Arbitration Remedy, 4 *J. Int'l Arb.* 35 (No. 2, 1987)

————, Punitive Damages in Arbitration in the USA, 14 *Int'l Bus. Law.* 188 (1986)

————, Win Punitive Damages in Arbitration, 1987 *ABA J.* 86

Koslow, The Arbitrator's Power to Award Punitive Damages in International Contract Actions, 19 *N.Y.U. J. Int'l L. & Pol.* 203 (1986)

Maskell, Arbitration — Interest and Costs, 54 *Arbitration* 258 (1988)

Mustill, Sir Michael J. & S. C. Boyd, *The Law and Practice of Commercial Arbitration in England* (2nd ed. 1989)

Nilsson, Arbitration and Anti-Trust — Enforcing Treble Damages from a Swedish Point of View, 1987 *J. Bus. L.* 227

Note, Arbitration: The Award of Punitive Damages as a Public Policy Question, 43 *Brooklyn L. Rev.* 546 (1976)

————, Punitive Damages in Arbitration: The Search for a Workable Rule, 63 *Cornell L. Rev.* 272 (1978)

Praendl, Measure of Damages in International Commercial Arbitration, 23 *Stan. J. Int'l L.* 263 (1987)

Raymos, Punitive Damage Awards in Maritime Arbitration: A Legitimate Part of the Arbitrator's Arsenal? 10 *Mar. Law.* 251 (1985)

Richmond, Interest, 54 *Arbitration* 167 (1988)

Rokison, The Sources and Limits of the Arbitrator's Powers in England, in *Contemporary Problems of International Arbitration* 86 (J.D.M. Lew ed. 1986); also 52 *Arbitration* 219 (1986)

Ruga, An Argument Against the Availability of Punitive Damages in Commercial Arbitration, 62 *St. John's L. Rev.* 270 (1988)

Samuel, Pre-Award Interest: England and Scotland, 5 *Arb. Int'l* 310 (1989)

Schwytz, Kosten und Kostenentscheidung im schiedsgerichtlichen Verfahren, 1974 *BB* 673

Seidl-Hohenveldern, L'évaluations des dommages dans les arbitrages transnationaux, 33 *Ann. Français Droit Int'l* 7 (1987)

Shell, The Power to Punish: Authority of Arbitrators to Award Multiple Damages and Attorney's Fees, 72 *Mass. L. Rev.* 26 (1987)

Stipanowich, Punitive Damages in Arbitration: Garrity v. Lyle Stuart, Inc. Reconsidered, 66 *B.U. L. Rev.* 953 (1986)

Thomas, Commercial Arbitration: The Vexed Issue of Interest Awards, 1982 *Lloyd's Mar. & Com. L.Q.* 667

Tolson, Conflicts Presented by Arbitral Awards of Punitive Damages, 4 *Arb. Int'l* 255 (1988)

———, Punitive Damage Awards in International Arbitration: Does the Safety Valve of Public Policy Render Them Unenforceable in Foreign States? 20 *Loy. L.A. L. Rev.* 455 (1987)

Wetter, Interest as an Element of Damages in the Arbitral Process, 5 *Int'l Fin. L. Rev.* 20 (No. 12, 1986)

17.10 DISSENTING AND SEPARATE OPINIONS

Blessing, International Arbitration Procedures, 17 *Int'l Bus. Law.* 408 and 451 (1989)

Holtzmann & Bernini, Hypothetical Case for Use in a Comparative Study of Arbitration Practice in Various Legal Systems, in *Comparative Arbitration Practice and Public Policy in Arbitration* 19 (P. Sanders ed. 1987)

Levy, Dissenting Opinions in International Arbitration in Switzerland, 5 *Arb. Int'l* 35 (1989)

Niggemann, The ICSID Klockner v. Cameroon Award: The Dissenting Opinion, 1 *J. Int'l Arb.* 331 (1984)

————, Die dritte Annulierung eines ICSID-Schiedsspruches — Die Entscheidung in Sachen Mine v. Guinea, 11 *IPRax* 77 (1991)

17.11 AMENDMENTS AND RECTIFICATION

Duintjer Tebbens, A Facelift for Dutch Arbitration Law, 34 *Neth. Int'l L. Rev.* 141 (1987)

Knoepfler & Schweizer, Making of Awards and Termination of Proceedings, in *Essays on International Commercial Arbitration* 160 (P. Sarcevic ed. 1989)

Poznanski, The Nature and Extent of an Arbitrator's Powers in International Commercial Arbitration, 4 *J. Int'l Arb.* 71 (No. 3, 1987)

Samuel, Developments in English Arbitration Law since the 1984 Antaios Decision, 5 *J. Int'l Arb.* 9 (No. 3, 1988)

Thomas, The Power of Arbitrators to Cure Accidental Errors, 1985 *Lloyd's Mar. & Com. L. Q.* 263

17.12 INTERPRETATION OF THE AWARD

Bernardini, Questioni sull'interpretazione e l'esecuzione del lodo, in *Arbitrato nazionale e internazionale: interpretazione ed esecuzione del lodo* 27 (G. Carli ed. 1989)

Blessing, International Arbitration Procedures, 17 *Int'l Bus. Law.* 408 and 451 (1989)

Dermine, L'interprétation des sentences arbitrales, 53 *Rev. Droit Int'l & Droit Comp.* 206 (1976)

Di Cagno, Sull'interpretazione della nuova disciplina dell'arbitrato, in *Arbitrato nazionale e internazionale: interpretazione ed esecuzione del lodo* 41 (G. Carli ed. 1989)

Irti, L'interpretazione del lodo arbitrale, in *Arbitrato nazionale e internazionale: interpretazione ed esecuzione del lodo* 3 (G. Carli ed. 1989)

Knoepfler & Schweizer, Making of Awards and Termination of Proceedings, in *Essays on International Commercial Arbitration* 160 (P. Sarcevic ed. 1989)

Lalive, Arbitrato commerciale internazionale e ordinamenti interni, in *Arbitrato nazionale e internazionale: interpretazione ed esecuzione del lodo* 49 (G. Carlo ed. 1989)

Mirabelli, Riflessioni sull'interpretazione del lodo, in *Arbitrato nazionale e internazionale: interpretazione ed esecuzione del lodo* 53 (G. Carli ed. 1989)

Perror, L'interpretation des sentences arbitrales, 1969 *Rev. Arb.* 7

Poudret, L'interprétation des sentences arbitrales (étude de droit suisse et de droit comparé), in *Recueil de Travaux Suisses* 269 (C. Reymond & E. Bucher eds. 1984)

17.13 DELIVERY TO THE PARTIES

Dalla Verita, Note sull'impugnazione del lodo arbitrale, 42 *Riv. Trim. Dir. & Proc. Civ.* 614 (1988)

Ferrante, Profili pratici della formazione del lodo, 26 *Rassegna dell'Arb.* 1 (1986)

Knoepfler & Schweizer, Making of Awards and Termination of Proceedings, in *Essays on International Commercial Arbitration* 160 (P. Sarcevic ed. 1989)

Sandrock, Das Gesetz zur Neuregelung des Internationalen Privatrechts und die internationale Schiedsgerichtsbarkeit, 33 *RIW Beilage 2 zu Heft* 5/1987 (1987)

17.14 DEPOSIT OF AWARD

Dalla Verita, Note sull'impugnazione del lodo arbitrale, 42 *Riv. Trim. Dir. & Proc. Civ.* 614 (1988)

Gelinas, L'exécution des sentences arbitrales internationales au Québec: commentaire, in *First International Commmercial Arbitration Conference: Proceedings* 305 (N. Antaki & A. Prujiner eds. 1986)

Kagel, An International Registry for Arbitration Awards, in *Int'l Trade Arbitration* 209 (M. Domke ed. 1958)

Knoepfler & Schweizer, Making of Awards and Termination of Proceedings, in *Essays on International Commercial Arbitration* 160 (P. Sarcevic ed. 1989)

Lalive, Arbitrato commerciale internazionale e ordinamenti interni, in *Arbitrato nazionale e internazionale: interpretazione ed esecuzione del lodo* 49 (G. Carlo ed. 1989)

Lau, Probleme der Niederlegung von Schiedssprüchen und von Schiedsvergleichen, 40 *MDR* 545 (1986)

Levoni, A., *L'arbitrato dopo la riforma* (Milano 1985)

Lotti, Sull'impugnabilità del lodo rituale non reso esecutivo, 43 *Riv. Dir. Proc.* 646 (1988)

Malagu, Natura giuridica del lodo arbitrale non depositato ed imposta di registro, 38 *Riv. Trim. Dir. & Proc. Civ.* 259 (1984)

Punzi, L'arbitrato di fronte alla riforma generale ed alle riforme parziali del processo civile, 26 *Rassegna dell'Arb.* 23 (1986)

———, Sull'inammissibilità dell'impugnazione immediata con le azioni c.d. negoziali del lodo arbitrale non dichiarato esecutivo, 26 *Rassegna dell'Arb.* 183 (1986)

———, Sulla legittimazione ad effettuare il deposito del lodo arbitrale, 24 *Rassegna dell'Arb.* 231 (1984)

Sandrock, Das Gesetz zur Neuregelung des Internationalen Privatrechts und die internationale Schiedsgerichtsbarkeit, 33 *RIW Beilage 2 zu Heft* 5/1987 (1987)

Walter, Der nicht niedergelegte Schiedsspruch (zu Par. 1039 Abs. 3 *ZPO* n.F.), 34 *RIW* 945 (1988)

17.15 CONFIDENTIALITY AND PUBLICATION

Gaillard, Le principe de confidentialité de l'arbitrage commercial international, 1987 *Recueil Dalloz Sirey No. 22,* at 153

Glossner, The Conduct of ICC Arbitration Proceedings, in *Contemporary Problems in International Arbitration* 210 (J.D.M. Lew ed. 1986)

Hardenberg, Het openbaar maken van arbitrale vonnissen, 1989 *Tijdschrift voor Arbitrage* 65

Harris, Arbitration and Confidentiality, 85 *L. Soc'y Gazette* 25 (No. 43, 1988)

Hunter, Publication of Arbitral Awards, 1987 *Lloyd's Mar. & Com. L.Q.* 139; also in 54 *Arbitration* 55 (1988)

Knoepfler & Schweizer, Making of Awards and Termination of Proceedings, in *Essays on International Commercial Arbitration* 160 (P. Sarcevic ed. 1989)

Lalive, Problèmes relatifs à l'arbitrage international commercial, 120 *Recueil des Cours* 569 (1967-II)

Lew, The Case for the Publication of Arbitration Awards, in *The Art of Arbitration* 223 (J. Schultsz & A. van den Berg eds. 1982)

Loyer, Non-observation of Secrecy and Arbitration in the Transfer of Technology, in *Arbitration and the Licensing Process* 6-49 (R. Goldscheider & M. de Haas eds. 1984-)

Mustill, Sir Michael J. & S. C. Boyd, *The Law and Practice of Commercial Arbitration in England* (2nd ed. 1989)

Note, Confidentiality in ICSID Arbitration After AMCO ASIA CORP. v. INDONESIA: Watchword or White Elephant? 10 *Fordham Int'l L. J.* 93 (1986)

Petersen & Rezler, The Impact of Opinion 11 on the Publication of Arbitration Awards, 1986 *Mo. J. Disp. Res.* 73

Pfaff, Zum Problem der Veröffentlichung von Schiedssprüchen der internationalen Handels-Schiedsgerichtsbarkeit, in *Um Recht und Freiheit, Festschrift für von der Heydte* 1127 (1977)

Sanders, Aspects de l'arbitrage international, 53 *Rev. Droit Int'l & Droit Comp.* 129 (1976)

Shilston, Cultural Diversity in Commercial Arbitration Practice, 55 *Arbitration* 260 (1989)

Smit, The Future of International Commercial Arbitration, 2 *West's Int'l L. Bull.* 5 (Issue 4, Fall 1984)

van Delden, English Commodity Arbitrations: A Foreigner Looking Around in London, in *The Art of Arbitration* 95 (J. Schultsz & A. van den Berg eds. 1982)

Westerling, Publishing of Arbitral Awards, 1983 *Y.B. Swed. & Int'l Arb.* 59

Yates, Arbitration or Court Litigation for Private International Dispute Resolution: The Lesser of Two Evils, in *Resolving Transnational Disputes Through International Arbitration* 224 (Th. Carbonneau ed. 1984)

17.16 EFFECTS

Broches, Awards Rendered Pursuant to the ICSID Convention: Binding Force, Finality, Recognition, Enforcement, Execution, 2 *ICSID Rev. - Foreign Investment L.J.* 287 (1987)

Bucher, A., *Die neue internationale Schiedsgerichtsbarkeit in der Schweiz* (Basel 1989)

—————, *Le nouvel arbitrage international en Suisse. Théorie et pratique de droit* (Basel 1988)

Bucher, A. & P.-Y. Tschanz, *International Arbitration in Switzerland* (Basel 1989)

Carlisle, Getting a Full Bite of the Apple: When Should the Doctrine of Issue Preclusion Make an Administrative or Arbitral Determination Binding in a Court of Law? 55 *Fordham L. Rev.* 63 (1986)

Chillón Medina, J. M. & J. F. Merino Merchán, *Tratado de arbitraje privado interno e internacional* (Madrid 1978)

Chowdhuri, S.K.R. & H.K. Saharay, *Arbitration Law* (2nd ed. Calcutta 1986)

Ferrante, About the Nature (National or A-National, Contractual or Jurisdictional) of ICC Awards under the New York Convention, in *The Art of Arbitration* 129 (J. Schultsz & A. van den Berg eds. 1982)

Garbagnati, Sull'efficacia di cosa giudicata del lodo arbitrale rituale, 40 *Riv. Dir. Proc.* 425 (1985)

Hulbert, Arbitral Procedure and the Preclusive Effect in International Commercial Arbitration, 7 *Int'l Tax & Bus. Law.* 155 (1989)

Kessler, J., *Die Bindung des Schiedsgerichts an das materielle Recht* (Cologne 1964)

Knoepfler & Schweizer, Making of Awards and Termination of Proceedings, in *Essays on International Commercial Arbitration* 160 (P. Sarcevic ed. 1989)

Levoni, A., *L'arbitrato dopo la riforma* (Milano 1985)

Lew, Bona Fides in International Commercial Arbitration, in 3 *Hague-Zagreb Essays* 244 (C. Voskuil & J. Wade eds. 1980)

Monégier du Sorbier, L'exécution de la sentence, 1990 *Rev. Arb.* 465

Mustill, Sir Michael J. & S. C. Boyd, *The Law and Practice of Commercial Arbitration in England* (2nd ed. 1989)

Page, Res Judicata, Collateral Estoppel, Arbitration Awards, in *Arbitration & the Law 1987-88: AAA General Counsel's Annual Report* 39 (1988)

Park & Paulsson, The Binding Force of International Arbitral Awards, 23 *Va. J. Int'l L.* 253 (1983)

Poudret, Challenge and Enforcement of Arbitral Awards in Switzerland, 4 *Arb. Int'l* 278 (1988)

Punzi, L'efficacia del lodo arbitrale nelle convenzioni internazionali e nell'ordinamento interno, 25 *Rassegna dell'Arb.* 305 (1985)

Russell, F., *Russell on the Law of Arbitration* (20th ed. by A. Walton & M. Vitoria 1982)

Selvaggi, Legge 9 febbraio 1983 n.28 e l'efficacia del lodo arbitrale, 23 *Rassegna dell'Arb.* 69 (1983)

Tarzia, Efficacia del lodo e impugnazione nell'arbitrato rituale e irrituale, 42 *Riv. Dir. Proc.* 14 (1987)

———, Efficacia ed impugnabilità del lodo nell'arbitrato rituale, 25 *Rassegna dell'Arb.* 1 (1985)

Walter, Die Vollstreckbarerklärung als Voraussetzung bestimmter Wirkungen des Schiedsspruch, in *Festschrift für Karl Heinz Schwab* 539 (P. Gottwald & H. Prütting eds. 1990)

17.17 APPEALS TO ARBITRAL TRIBUNAL

Craig, The Appeal of Arbitral Awards: Ideas for the Future, 2 *Int'l Arb. Rep.* 776 (1987)

————, The Uses and Abuses of Appeal from International Arbitration Awards, in *Private Investors Abroad - Problems and Solutions in International Business in 1987* 14.1 (J. Moss ed. 1987)

————, Uses and Abuses of Appeal from Awards, 4 *Arb. Int'l* 174 (1988)

de Berranger, L'article 52 de la Convention de Washington du 18 mars 1965 et les premiers enseignements de sa pratique, 1988 *Rev. Arb.* 95

Feldman, The Annulment Proceedings and the Finality of ICSID Arbitral Awards, 2 *ICSID Rev.- Foreign Investment L.J.* 85 (1987)

Golsong, Schwächung des Schiedsdispositifs bei Investitionsstreitigkeiten. Das ICSID-Annulierungsverfahren und seine mögliche Fortentwicklung, in *Festschrift für Walther J. Habscheid* 113 (W. Lindacher, D. Pfaff et al. eds. 1989)

Lattanzi, Convenzione de Washington sulle controversie relative ad investimenti e invalidità delle sentenze arbitrali, 70 *Riv. Dir. Int'le* 521 (1987)

Lepp, Arbitration Appeals: A Comparison of Certain English and American Trade Associations, 39 *Arbitration* 125 (1972)

————, Arbitration Appeals: A Comparison of Certain English and American Trade Associations, 28 *Rassegna dell'Arb.* 57 (1988)

Pirrwitz, Annulment of Arbitral Awards under Article 52 of the Washington Convention on the Settlement of Investment Disputes Between States and Nationals of Other States, 23 *Tex. Int'l L.J.* 73 (1988)

Poznanski, The Nature and Extent of an Arbitrator's Powers in International Commercial Arbitration, 4 *J. Int'l Arb.* 71 (No. 3, 1987)

Rambaud, L'annulation des sentences Klöckner et Amco, 32 *Ann. Français Droit Int'l* 259 (1986)

Redfern, ICSID — Losing Its Appeal? 3 *Arb. Int'l* 98 (1987)

Rubino-Sammartano, An International Arbitral Court of Appeal as an Alternative to Long Attacks and Recognition Proceedings, 6 *J. Int'l Arb.* 180 (No. 1, 1989)

————, Third Generation Arbitration. Appeals to a New Panel Within Arbitration Proceedings? 4 *J. Int'l Arb.* 75 (No. 1, 1987); also in 54 *Arbitration* 59 (1988)

Schatz, The Effect of the Annulment Decisions in AMCO v. Indonesia and Klockner v. Cameroon on the Future of the International Centre for the Settlement of Investment Disputes, 3 *Am. U. J. Int'l L. & Pol'y* 481 (1988)

Schlechtriem, Zur Überprufbarkeit von ICSID-Schiedssprüchen: Die Aufhebungsentscheidung im Falle Klöckner/Kamerun, 6 *IPRax* 69 (1986)

Schlosser, Right and Remedy in Common Law Arbitration and in German Arbitration Law, 4 *J. Int'l Arb.* 27 (No. 1, 1987)

17.18 SETTLEMENT

Baur, F., *Der Schiedsrichterliche Vergleich* (Munich 1971)

Blessing, International Arbitration Procedures, 17 *Int'l Bus. Law.* 408 and 451 (1989)

Glossner, The Conduct of ICC Arbitration Proceedings, in *Contemporary Problems in International Arbitration* 210 (J.D.M. Lew ed. 1986)

Holtzmann & Bernini, Hypothetical Case for Use in a Comparative Study of Arbitration Practice in Various Legal Systems, in *Comparative Arbitration Practice and Public Policy in Arbitration* 19 (P. Sanders ed. 1987)

Jagenburg, Schiedsgerichtsbarkeit zwischen Wunsch and Wirklichkeit, in *Festschrift für Walter Oppenhoff* zum 80. *Geburtstag* 147 (W. Jagenburg, G. Maier-Reimer & T. Verhoeven eds. 1985)

Knoepfler & Schweizer, Making of Awards and Termination of Proceedings, in *Essays on International Commercial Arbitration* 160 (P. Sarcevic ed. 1989)

Pierce, Termination of Arbitration by Mediation: Domestic and Foreign-Related Mediation Agreements, 18 *Hong Kong L.J.* 467 (1988)

Redfern, Enforcement of International Arbitral Awards and Settlement Agreements, 54 *Arbitration* 124 (1988)

Schütze, R., D. Tscherning & W. Wais, *Handbuch des Schiedsverfahrens. Praxis der deutschen und internationalen Schiedsgerichtsbarkeit* (2nd ed. Berlin 1990)

18. COSTS

18.01 IN GENERAL

Baumgartner, P., *Die Kosten des Schiedsgerichtsprozesses* (Zurich 1982)

Blessing, International Arbitration Procedures, 17 *Int'l Bus. Law.* 408 and 451 (1989)

Branson & Tupman, Selecting an Arbitral Forum: A Guide to Cost-Effective International Arbitration, 24 *Va. J. Int'l L.* 917 (1984)

Bühler, Grundsätze und Praxis des Kostenrechts im ICC-Schiedsverfahren, 87 *ZVR* 431 (1988)

Gill, W.H., *Evidence and Procedure in Arbitration* (London 1965)

Hall, Taxation of Costs in Arbitration, 48 *Arbitration* 327 (1983)

Henn, G., *Schiedsverfahrensrecht: ein Handbuch* (Heidelberg 1986)

Karrer, Arbitration Saves! Costs: Poker and Hide-and Seek, 3 *J. Int'l Arb.* 35 (No. 1, 1986)

Kritzer & Anderson, The Arbitration Alternative: A Comparative Analysis of Case Processing Time, Disposition Mode, and Cost in the American Arbitration Association and the Courts, 8 *Just. Sys. J.* 6 (1983)

Mustill, Sir Michael J. & S. C. Boyd, *The Law and Practice of Commercial Arbitration in England* (2nd ed. 1989)

Nobili, I costi fiscali dell'arbitrato in Italia: sviluppi recenti, 26 *Rassegna dell'Arb.* 13 (1986)

Nordenson, The Arbitral Proceedings in International Arbitration in Sweden, 1984 *Y.B. Swed. & Int'l Arb.* 6

Oehmke, T., *International Arbitration* (Rochester 1990)

Prujiner, La gestion des arbitrages commerciaux internationaux: l'exemple de la Cour d'arbitrage de la CCI, 115 *J. Droit Int'l (Clunet)* 662 (1988)

Rhodes & Sloan, The Pitfalls of International Commercial Arbitration, 17 *Vand. J. Transnat'l L.* 19 (1984)

Russell, F., *Russell on the Law of Arbitration* (20th ed. by A. Walton & M. Vitoria 1982)

Sandrock, Die Entscheidung von Streitigkeiten durch Schiedsgerichte, in *Französisches Vertragsrecht für deutsche Exporteure* 54 (C. Witz & T.M. Bopp eds. 1989)

Schwab, K.H. & G. Walter, *Schiedsgerichtsbarkeit: Systematischer Kommentar zu den Vorschriften der Zivilprozessordnung, des Arbeitsgerichtsgesetzes, der Staatsverträge und der Kostengesetze über das privatrechtliche Schiedsgerichtsvefahren* (4th ed. Munich 1990)

Schwytz, Kosten und Kostenentscheidung im schiedsgerichtlichen Verfahren, 1974 *BB* 673

Sharkey, J. & J. Dorter, *Commercial Arbitration* (Sydney 1986)

Shilston, The Evolution of Modern Commercial Arbitration, 4 *J. Int'l Arb.* 45 (No. 2, 1987)

Smit, The Future of International Commercial Arbitration, 2 *West's Int'l L. Bull.* 5 (Issue 4, Fall 1984)

Thomas, Costs, Discretion and Issues of Technical Misconduct, 1982 *Lloyd's Mar. & Com. L.Q.* 288

Uff, Cost Effectiveness in Construction Arbitration, 47 *Arbitration* 174 (1982)

Wetter, Methods of Settling International Commercial Disputes, 3 *Int'l Arb. Rep.* 21 (No. 5, 1988)

Wilson, Saving Costs in International Arbitration, 6 *Arb. Int'l* 151 (1990)

18.02 ARBITRATION FEES

Barclay, Is the Arbitrator Worth His Salt? in 2 *Fifth Int'l Congress of Maritime Arbitrators* (New York 1981)

Bond, The 1986 Reform of ICC's Practice Relating to Costs and Payments, 2 *Arb. Int'l* 358 (1986)

————, Neuregelung der Kostenfestsetzung und Zahlungsweise in ICC-Schiedsverfahren, 7 *IPRax* 58 (1987)

Branson & Tupman, Selecting an Arbitral Forum: A Guide to Cost-Effective International Arbitration, 24 *Va. J. Int'l L.* 917 (1984)

Hall, Arbitrations and the New Supreme Court Costs Rules, 52 *Arbitration* 174 (1986)

Lazatin, Mechanics and Procedural Aspects of Commercial Arbitration, in *Commercial Arbitration* 14 (J. Ricalde ed. 1983)

Mustill, Sir Michael J. & S. C. Boyd, *The Law and Practice of Commercial Arbitration in England* (2nd ed. 1989)

Prujiner, La gestion des arbitrages commerciaux internationaux: l'exemple de la Cour d'arbitrage de la CCI, 115 *J. Droit Int'l (Clunet)* 662 (1988)

18.03 EXPENSES OF PARTIES

Bühler, Grundsätze und Praxis des Kostenrechts im ICC-Schiedsverfahren, 87 *ZVR* 431 (1988)

Fasching, Die Kostenersatzanspruch des Beklagten bei Unzuständigkeitsanspruch des Schiedsgerichtes, in *Festschrift für Walther J. Habscheid* 93 (W. Lindacher, D. Pfaff et al. eds. 1989)

18.04 DEPOSIT OF COSTS

Baker & Davis, Arbitral Proceedings Under the UNCITRAL Rules: The Experience of the Iran-United States Claims Tribunal, 23 *Geo. Wash. J. Int'l L. & Econ.* 267 (1989)

Bentil, Judicial Intervention and International Commercial Arbitration, 130 *Solicitors' J.* 191 (1986)

Lee, Security for Costs in International Arbitration, 5 *Bus. L. Rev.* 286 (1984)

Mustill, Sir Michael J. & S. C. Boyd, *The Law and Practice of Commercial Arbitration in England* (2nd ed. 1989)

Prujiner, La gestion des arbitrages commerciaux internationaux: l'exemple de la Cour d'arbitrage de la CCI, 115 *J. Droit Int'l (Clunet)* 662 (1988)

Samuel, Developments in English Arbitration Law since the 1984 Antaios Decision, 5 *J. Int'l Arb.* 9 (No. 3, 1988)

Thomas, Security for Costs in Arbitration, 1982 *Lloyd's Mar. & Com. L.Q.* 463 (1982)

18.05 APPORTIONING OF COSTS

Boyd, Interest for the Late Payment of Money, 1 *Arb. Int'l* 153 (1985)

Branson & Wallace, Awarding Interest in International Commercial Arbitration: Establishing a Uniform Approach, 28 *Va. J. Int'l L.* 919 (1988)

Deak, Repartizarea intre parti a taxei arbitrale in litigiile solutionate de Comisia de Arbitraj de pe linga Camera de Comert si Industrie, 40 *Revista Romana de Drept* 20 (No. 3, 1984)

Heuman, L., *Current Issues in Swedish Arbitration* (Deventer and Stockholm 1990)

Hjerner, Awarding Interest in Swedish Arbitration, 1985 *Y.B. Swed. & Int'l Arb.* 29

Hoellering, Remedies in Arbitration, 20 *The Forum* 516 (1984-85)

Hunter & Triebel, Awarding Interest in International Arbitration, 6 *J. Int'l Arb.* 7 (No. 1, 1989)

Maskell, Arbitration — Interest and Costs, 54 *Arbitration* 258 (1988)

Mustill, Sir Michael J. & S. C. Boyd, *The Law and Practice of Commercial Arbitration in England* (2nd ed. 1989)

Praendl, Measure of Damages in International Commercial Arbitration, 23 *Stan. J. Int'l L.* 263 (1987)

Richmond, Interest, 54 *Arbitration* 167 (1988)

Samuel, Pre-Award Interest: England and Scotland, 5 *Arb. Int'l* 310 (1989)

Schwytz, Kosten und Kostenentscheidung im schiedsgerichtlichen Verfahren, 1974 *BB* 673

Thomas, Commercial Arbitration: The Vexed Issue of Interest Awards, 1982 *Lloyd's Mar. & Com. L.Q.* 667

Ulmer, Drafting the International Arbitration Clause, 20 *Int'l Law.* 1335 (1986)

Wetter, Interest as an Element of Damages in the Arbitral Process, 5 *Int'l Fin. L. Rev.* 20 (No. 12, 1986)

19. ARBITRATION AND THE COURTS

19.01 JURISDICTION AND POWERS OF THE COURTS IN MATTERS OF ARBITRATION GENERALLY

Abromson, The English Arbitration Act of 1979: A Symbiotic Relationship Between the Courts and Arbitration Tribunals, 5 *Suff. Transnat'l L.J.* 7 (1980)

Agbosu, Arbitration under the Customary Law, 15 *Rev. Ghana L.* 204 (1983-86)

Aliaga Grez, Alvaro, *Los recursos procesales en el juicio arbitral* (Santiago de Chile 1985)

Bates, Commercial Arbitration and the Courts in Australia: Signs and Change, 1987 *J. Bus. L.* 527; also in 54 *Arbitration* 160 (1988)

Baum, Arbitration and Court Intervention: Recent Swiss, U.S. Examples, 1 *Int'l Arb. Rep.* 449 (1986)

Bellet, The Evolution of French Judicial Views on International Arbitration, 34 *Arb. J.* 28 (No. 1, 1979)

Bentil, Making England a More Attractive Venue for International Commercial Arbitration by Less Judicial Oversight, 5 *J. Int'l Arb.* 49 (No. 1, 1988)

Bernini, Links Between Arbitrators and the Courts, 44 *Arbitration* 77 (1978)

Böckstiegel, Arbitration and Courts— Recent Developments — Conclusions for Contracts and Arbitration Practice, in *ICCA, Sixth Int'l Arb. Congress: Proceedings* 239 (1978)

————, Schiedsgerichte und staatliche Gerichte, 25 *RIW* 161 (1979)

Boyd, The Role of National Law and the National Courts in England, In *Contemporary Problems in International Arbitration* 149 (J.D.M. Lew ed. 1986)

Bühler, Staatsgerichtliche Aufhebungskontrolle am Schiedsort? Zur Reform Belgiens, 7 *IPRax* 253 (1987)

Bucher, A., *Die neue internationale Schiedsgerichtsbarkeit in der Schweiz* (Basel 1989)

————, *Le nouvel arbitrage international en Suisse. Théorie et pratique de droit* (Basel 1988)

Bucher, A. & P.-Y. Tschanz, *International Arbitration in Switzerland* (Basel 1989)

Bull, S., *The Arbitral Process and the Courts* (Wellington 1983)

Carbonneau, The Elaboration of a French Court Doctrine on International Commercial Arbitration: A Study in Liberal Civilian Judicial Creativity, 55 *Tul. L. Rev.* 1 (1980)

Craig, The Uses and Abuses of Appeal from International Arbitration Awards, in *Private Investors Abroad - Problems and Solutions in International Business in 1987* 14.1 (J. Moss ed. 1987)

————, Uses and Abuses of Appeal from Awards, 4 *Arb. Int'l* 174 (1988)

Cremades, Is Exclusion of Concurrent Courts' Jurisdiction over Conservatory Measures to Be Introduced through a Revision of the Convention? 6 *J. Int'l Arb.* 105 (No. 3, 1989)

————, Should Arbitrators Maintain Their Independence or Would It Be Desirable for Them to Have Closer Links with the Courts in Their Respective Countries? 44 *Arbitration* 83 (1978)

Cremades, B. M. & E. G. Cabiedes, *Litigating in Spain. Considerations for Foreign Practitioners, Including International Judicial Assistance, Enforcement of Foreign Judgments, Bankruptcy, Arbitration and Other Civil Proceedings in Spain* (Deventer 1989)

David, R., *Arbitration in International Trade* (Deventer 1985)

Delaume, Court Intervention in Arbitral Proceedings, in *Resolving Transnational Disputes through International Arbitration* 195 (T. Carbonneau ed. 1984)

————, ICSID Arbitration and the Courts, 77 *Am. J. Int'l L.* 784 (1983)

————, L'arbitrage transnational et les tribunaux nationaux, 111 *J. Droit Int'l (Clunet)* 521 (1984)

Delvolvé, La reforme du droit de l'arbitrage: l'intervention du juge, 1980 *Rev. Arb.* 607

Derains, International Commercial Arbitration in Civil Law Countries, in *Arbitration in Settlement of International Commercial Disputes Involving the Far East and Arbitration in Combined Transportation* 229 (P. Sanders ed. 1989)

Derains, Y., ed., *Droit et pratique de l'arbitrage international en France* (Paris 1984)

Deshpande, How International Arbitration Can Always Prevail over Litigation, 4 *J. Int'l Arb.* 9 (No. 4, 1987)

――――, International Commercial Arbitration and Domestic Courts in India, 2 *J. Int'l Arb.* 45 (No. 1, 1985)

――――, International Commercial Arbitration: Uniformity of Jurisdiction, 5 *J. Int'l Arb.* 115 (No. 2, 1988)

――――, Judicial Interpretation of Commercial Arbitration, 16 *I.C.A. Arb. Q.* 3 (No. 1, April-March 1981)

Doi, International Commercial Arbitration in Japan, in *Liber Amicorum for Martin Domke* 65 (P. Sanders ed. 1967)

Donaldson, Relationship Between the Courts and Arbitration Under the European Common Law Systems, 47 *Arbitration* 72 (1981)

Dorter, J. & G. Widmer, *Arbitration (Commercial) in Australia— Law and Practice* (Sydney 1979)

Drouillat, L'intervention du juge dans la procédure arbitrale (de la clause compromissoire à la sentence), 1980 *Rev. Arb.* 253

Eisemann, L'arbitrage commercial international et le juge américain, 1 *Droit et Pratique du Com. Int'l* 653 (1975)

Esplugues, 'National Intervention' in International Commercial Arbitration, 19 *Revue Générale de Droit* 81 (1988)

Eyzaguirre Echeverria, R., *El arbitraje comercial en la legislación chilena y su regulación international* (Santiago de Chile 1981)

Fouchard, La coopération du Président du Tribunal de Grande Instance à l'arbitrage, 1985 *Rev. Arb.* 5

――――, Les institutions permanentes d'arbitrage devant le juge étatique (à propos d'une jurisprudence récente), 1987 *Rev. Arb.* 225

Gildeggen, R., *Internationale Schieds- und Schiedsverfahrensvereinbarungen in algemeinen Geschäftsbedingungen vor deutschen Gerichten* (Frankfurt 1991)

Glossner, Eine zentrale Gerichtsinstanz für internationale Schiedsverfahren in der Bundesrepublik Deutschland? 32 *RIW* 214 (1986)

Goldman, The Complementary Roles of Judges and Arbitrators in Ensuring that International Commercial Arbitration Is Effective, in *ICC, 60 Years of ICC Arbitration* 257 (1984)

Gottwald, Die sachliche Kontrolle internationaler Schiedssprüche durch staatliche Gerichte, in *Beiträge zum internationalen Verfahrensrecht und zur Schiedsgerichtsbakeit. Festschrift für Heinrich Nagel* 54 (W. Habscheid & K. Schwab eds. 1987)

Habscheid, Les jurisdictions et l'arbitrage, in *ICCA, Sixth Int'l Arb. Congress: Proceedings* 261 (1978)

Hanak, Arbitration and the Courts, 24 *Rassegna dell'Arb.* 33 (1984)

Hanotiau, Devéloppements récents en matière d'arbitrage commercial international en Belgique, 1988 *Int'l Bus. L.J.* 839

Henn, G., *Schiedsverfahrensrecht: ein Handbuch* (Heidelberg 1986)

Herrmann, The Role of the Courts under the UNCITRAL Model Law Script, in *Contemporary Problems in Int'l Arbitration* 164 (J.D.M. Lew ed. 1986)

Hjerner, Recourse to Law Courts in International Arbitration in Sweden, in *ICC, Hommage à Fréderic Eisemann* 61 (1978)

Holtzmann, Arbitration and the Courts: Partners in a System of International Jurisdiction, in *ICCA, Sixth Int'l Arb. Congress: Proceedings* 193 (1978); also *Rev. Arb.* 253 (1978)

————, El arbitraje y los tribunales: socios de un sistema de derecho internacional, in *El Arbitraje Comercial Internacional* 91 (Mexico 1983)

————, L'arbitrage et les tribunaux: des associés dans un système de justice internationale, 1978 *Rev. Arb.* 253

Holtzmann, H. & J. Neuhaus, *A Guide to the UNCITRAL Model Law on International Commercial Arbitration: Legislative History and Commentary* (Deventer 1989)

Iwasaki, Drafting Arbitration Clauses Designating Tokyo as Arbitration Site, 11 *Bull. Japan Shipping Exch.* 1 (1985)

Jaffe, Judicial Supervision of Commercial Arbitration in England, 55 *Arbitration* 184 (1989)

————, The Judicial Trend Toward Finality of Commercial Arbitral Awards in England, 24 *Tex. Int'l L.J.* 67 (1989)

Jarvin, Choosing the Place of Arbitration: Where Do We Stand? 16 *Int'l Bus. Law.* 417 (1988)

Karrer, Les rapports entre le tribunal arbitral, les tribunaux étatiques et l'institution arbitrale, 1989 *Int'l Bus. L.J.* 761

Kerr, Arbitration and the Courts: the UNCITRAL Model Law, 34 *Int'l & Comp. L.Q.* 1 (1985)

Kessler, J., *Schiedsgerichtsvertrag und Schiedsverfahren* (Munich 1970)

Lalive, The New Swiss Law on International Arbitration, 4 *Arb. Int'l* 2 (1988)

Leahy & Pierce, Sanctions to Control Party Misbehavior in International Arbitration, 26 *Va. J. Int'l L.* 291 (1986)

Lebedev, Sudebnyi kontrol za pravoprimenitelnoi deyatelnostiu arbitrov (Angliiskii zakon 1979 goda), 29 *Pravovedenie* 88 (January-February 1985)

Lew, J., ed., *Contemporary Problems in International Arbitration* (London 1986)

Lloyd, Arbitration and the Commercial Court, 49 *Arbitration* 13 (1983)

Longo, Arbitration and the Courts: Hypothesis for a Bridging Over, in *ICCA, Sixth Int'l Arb. Congress: Proceedings* 267 (1978)

Loumiet, United States: Florida International Arbitration Act. Introductory Note, 26 *I.L.M.* 949 (1987)

Lutz, International Arbitration and Judicial Intervention, 10 *Loy. L.A. Int'l & Comp. L.J.* 621 (1988)

Marchais, Judicial Attitudes Towards Decisions Taken by Arbitral Institutions — Current Trends — the Experience of ICSID, in *Arbitration and the Courts: Fifth ICSID/AAA/ICC Colloquium* (Washington 1987)

475

Mayer, L'insértion de la sentence dans l'ordre juridique français, in *Droit et pratique de l'arbitrage international en France* 81 (Y. Derains ed. Paris 1984)

Melis, Arbitration and the Courts, 51 *Arbitration* 453 (1985)

———, Arbitration and the Courts in Austria — International Aspects, in *The Art of Arbitration* 253 (J. Schultsz & A. van den Berg eds. 1982)

Mirabelli, Recchia & Galli Fonseca, Les juges italiens et l'arbitrage commercial international, in *ICCA, Sixth Int'l Arb. Congress: Proceedings* 273 (1978)

Moussali, Arbitrage international: Syrie, 1991 *Int'l Bus. L.J.* 401

Mustill, Distinctive Features of English Commercial Arbitration, 14 *Arkiv for Sjorett* 321 (1976-77)

———, Sir Michael J. & S. C.Boyd, *The Law and Practice of Commercial Arbitration in England* (2nd ed. 1989)

Nathan, Arbitrate or Litigate — Powers of the Court, 55 *Arbitration* 285(1989)

Neumann, Limiting Judicial Review in International Commercial Arbitration: The New Swiss and Belgian Laws Offer Less Than They Promise, 1 *Am. Rev. Int'l Arb.* 435 (1990)

Nobel, Privates Schiedsgerichtswesen und staatlicher Richter im 'Wettbewerb,' in *Freiheit und Verantwortung im Recht, Festschrift Arthur Meier-Hayoz* 247 (Berne 1982)

Park, Judicial Supervision of Transnational Commercial Arbitration: The English Arbitration Act of 1979, 21 *Harv. Int'l L.J.* 87 (1980)

Park & Paulsson, Arbitrage commercial et contrats internationaux, 45 *Rev. Barreau* 215 (1985)

Parker School of Foreign and Comparative Law, *International Commercial Arbitration and the Courts* (Dobbs Ferry 1990)

Paulsson, Arbitre et juge en Suède: exposé générale et réflexions sur la délocalisation des sentences arbitrales, 1980 *Rev. Arb.* 441

———, The Role of Swedish Court in Transnational Commercial Arbitration, 21 *Va. J. Int'l L.* 211 (1981)

Perrot, Arbitrage interne et arbitrage international. Les recours devant la Cour d'appel empêchent-ils l'arbitre de poursuivre sa mission? 1987 *Rev. Arb.* 107

Polebaum & Conlan, U.S. Rules on Proper Venue in Which to Petition to Vacate a Foreign Arbitration Award, 19 *Int'l Bus. Law.* 219 (1991)

Poudret, Le recours au Tribunal fédéral en matière d'arbitrage interne et international, 6 *ASA Bulletin* 33 (1988)

Redfern, The Jurisdiction of an International Commercial Arbitrator, 3 *J. Int'l Arb.* 19 (1986); also 52 *Arbitrator* 254 (1986)

Rhodes, Judicial Review of Commercial Arbitration, 14 *Hong Kong L.J.* 159 (1984)

Robert, J. & B. Morceau, *L'arbitrage — droit interne, droit international privé* (5th ed. Paris 1983)

Rubellin-Devichi, L'arbitrage et les tiers: le droit de l'arbitrage: les solutions juridictionnelles, 1988 *Rev. Arb.* 515

Rubino-Sammartano, M., *International Arbitration Law* (Deventer 1990)

Russell, F., *Russell on the Law of Arbitration* (20th ed. by A. Walton & M. Vitoria 1982)

Sacks, Arbitration in Connecticut: Issues in Judicial Intervention Under the Connecticut Arbitration Statutes, 17 *Conn. L. Rev.* 387 (1985)

Samuel, A., *Jurisdictional Problems in International Commercial Arbitration: A Study of Belgian, Dutch, English, French, Swedish, Swiss, U.S. and West German Law* (Zurich 1989)

Sanders, L'intervention du juge dans la procédure arbitral (de la clause compromissoire a la sentence), 1980 *Rev. Arb.* 238

Sarcevic, The Setting Aside and Enforcement of Arbitral Awards under the UNCITRAL Model law, in *Essays on International Commercial Arbitration* 177 (P. Sarcevic ed. 1989)

Schlosser, Conflits entre jugements judiciares et arbitrage, 1981 *Rev. Arb.* 371

———, Coordinated Transnational Interaction in Civil Litigation and Arbitration, 12 *Mich. J. Int'l L.* 150 (1990)

Schmitthoff, The Supervisory Jurisdiction of the English Courts, in *Liber Amicorum for Martin Domke* 289 (P. Sanders ed. 1967)

Schönke, A., *Das Schiedsgerichtsverfahren nach dem heutigen deutschen Recht* (Berlin 1954)

Schweizer & Guillod, L'exception de litispendance et l'arbitrage international: quelques refléxions sur le pour et le contre, in *Le Juriste Suisse Face au Droit et aux Jugements Etrangers: Ouverture ou Repli?* 71 (F. Knoepfler ed. 1988)

Shilston, Milestone in the Evolution of Modern Commercial Arbitration, 53 *Arbitration* 26 (1987)

Sprott, A., *Judicial Control of Arbitration* (Auckland 1988)

Tiewul & Tsegah, Arbitration and the Settlement of Commercial Disputes: A Selective Survey of African Practice, 24 *Int'l & Comp. L.Q.* 393 (1975)

Travers, Commercial Arbitration in New South Wales: Too Much Judicial Interference? 4 *J. Int'l Arb.* 121 (No. 2, 1987)

van Houtte, International Arbitration and National Adjudication, in 4 *Hague-Zagreb Essays on the Law of International Trade* 321 (C. Voskuil & J. Wade eds. 1981)

Vassogne, L'arbitre, le juge et l'ordre public économique (remarques adventices), 1987 *Rev. Arb.* 87

von Mehren, International Commercial Arbitration: The Contribution of the French Jurisprudence, 46 *La. L. Rev.* 1045 (1986)

Wallace, Control by the Courts: A Plea for More, Not Less, 6 *Arb. Int'l* 253 (1990)

19.02 PROCEEDINGS TO DETERMINE OR MODIFY ARBITRATION AGREEMENT

Becker, The Supervisory and Adjunctive Jurisdiction of American Courts in Arbitration Cases, in *Contemporary Problems in International Arbitration* 207 (J.D.M. Lew ed. 1986)

Böckstiegel, Public Policy and Arbitrability, in *Comparative Arbitration Practice and Public Policy in Arbitration* 177 (P. Sanders ed. 1987)

Dietrich, Internationale Schiedsvereinbarungen vor amerikanischen Gerichten, 40 *Rabels Z.* 1 (1976)

Mustill, Sir Michael J. & S. C. Boyd, *The Law and Practice of Commercial Arbitration in England* (2nd ed. 1989)

Nicklisch, Agreement to Arbitrate to Fill Contractual Gaps, 5 *J. Int'l Arb.* 35 (No. 3, 1988)

Rendon Graniel & Zivy, Jurisprudence méxicaine: la validité de la clause arbitrale internationale, 1987 *Int'l Bus. L.J.* 629

Samuel, Developments in English Arbitration Law since the 1984 Antaios Decision, 5 *J. Int'l Arb.* 9 (No. 3, 1988)

Schmitthoff, The Supervisory Jurisdiction of the English Courts, in *Liber Amicorum for Martin Domke* 289 (P. Sanders ed. 1967)

19.03 PROCEEDINGS TO COMPEL ARBITRATION

Aksen, The Application of the New York Convention by the United States, 4 *Y.B. Com. Arb.* 341 (1979)

Becker, The Supervisory and Adjunctive Jurisdiction of American Courts in Arbitration Cases, in *Contemporary Problems in International Arbitration* 207 (J.D.M. Lew ed. 1986)

Bedell, Harrison & Grant, Arbitrability: Current Developments in the Interpretation and Enforceability of Arbitration Agreements, 13 *J. Contemp. L.* 1 (1987)

Comment, Enforcing International Commercial Arbitration Agreements — Post-Mitsubishi Motors Corp. v. Soler Chrysler-Plymouth, Inc., 36 *Am. U.L. Rev.* 57 (1986)

Daughtrey, Enforcement of Arbitration Clauses Against Deceived Franchisees, 21 *U. Rich. L. Rev.* 391 (1987)

Escudero, The Enforceability of Predispute Arbitration Agreements under 10(b) and 10b-5 Claims, 43 *Wash. & Lee L. Rev.* 923 (1986)

Fletcher, Privatizing Securities Disputes through the Enforcement of Arbitration Agreements, 71 *Minn. L. Rev.* 393 (1987)

Garro, Enforcement of Arbitration Agreements and Jurisdiction of Arbitral Tribunals in Latin America, 1 *J. Int'l Arb.* 293 (No. 4, 1984)

Herrmann, The Role of the Courts under the UNCITRAL Model Law Script, in *Contemporary Problems in Int'l Arbitration* 164 (J.D.M. Lew ed. 1986)

Hunter, Judicial Assistance for the Arbitrator, in *Contemporary Problems in International Arbitration* 195 (J.D.M. Lew ed. 1986)

Kochery, The Enforcement of Arbitration Agreements in the Federal Courts: Erie v. Tompkins, 39 *Cornell L. Q.* 74 (1953)

McClendon, Subject-Matter Arbitrability in International Cases: Mitsubishi Motors Closes the Circle, 11 *N.C. J. Int'l L. & Com. Reg.* 81 (1986)

Merchant & Merchant, The Law Relating to Recognition and Enforcement of Foreign Arbitral Agreements and Awards in the United States of America and India, in *ICCA, Fifth Int'l Arb. Congress: Proceedings* C Im 1-10 (1975)

Note, Arbitration: Public Policy Exception to Arbitration of Anti-trust Issues: Mitsubishi Motors Corp. v. Soler Chrysler Plymouth, Inc. 723 F.2d 155 (1st Cir. 1983), 25 *Harv. Int'l L.J.* 427 (1984)

Pacific Rim Advisory Council, *Pacific Rim: Commercial Arbitration Procedures* (San Diego, CA 1985)

Parker School of Foreign and Comparative Law, *International Commercial Arbitration and the Courts* (Dobbs Ferry 1990)

Poznanski, The Nature and Extent of an Arbitrator's Power in International Commercial Arbitration, 4 *J. Int'l Arb.* 71 (No. 3, 1987)

Recchia, G., *Enforcement of Foreign Arbitration Agreements and Awards in Italy and the United States: A Comparative Study* (Naples 1970)

Rothstein, Recognizing and Enforcing Arbitral Agreements and Awards Against Foreign States: The Mathias Amendments to the Foreign Sovereign Immunities Act and Title 9, 1 *Emory J. Int'l Disp. Res.* 101 (1986)

Samuel, Developments in English Arbitration Law since the 1984 Antaios Decision, 5 *J. Int'l Arb.* 9 (No. 3, 1988)

Sandrock, Arbitration between U.S. and West German Companies: An Example of Effective Dispute Resolution in International Business Transactions, 9 *U. Pa. J. Int'l Bus. L.* 27 (1987)

Sterk, Enforceability of Agreements to Arbitrate: An Examination of the Public Policy Defense, 2 *Cardozo L. Rev.* 481 (1981)

Swan, Compelling Arbitration and Judicial Review of Arbitral Awards, 11 *Law. Am.* 475 (1979)

Tiewul, The Enforcement of Arbitration Agreements and Awards, 11 *Univ. Ghana L.J.* 143 (1974)

van den Berg, A. J., *The New York Arbitration Convention of 1958* (Deventer 1981)

19.04 STAY OF COURT PROCEEDINGS PENDING ARBITRATION

Blom, Conflict of Laws Aspects of the International Commercial Arbitration Act, in *UNCITRAL Arbitration Model in Canada* 127 (R. Paterson & B. Thompson eds. 1987)

Costabel, Non-Domestic Arbitration Clauses, Stay of Proceedings and Recognition of Foreign Awards in Italy, 2 *Fifth Int'l Congress of Maritime Arbitrators* (New York 1981)

Hitters, Posibilidad de prorrogar la jurisdicción en favor de tribunales o arbitros extrajeros. Limitaciones, 1984-III *Jurisprudencia Argentina* 763

Mustill, Sir Michael J. & S. C. Boyd, *The Law and Practice of Commercial Arbitration in England* (2nd ed. 1989)

Parker School of Foreign and Comparative Law, *International Commercial Arbitration and the Courts* (Dobbs Ferry 1990)

Paterson, International Commercial Arbitration Act: An Overview, in *UNCITRAL Arbitration Model in Canada* 113 (R. Paterson & B. Thompson eds. 1987)

Sharkey, J. & J. Dorter, *Commercial Arbitration* (Sydney 1986)

van den Berg, A. J., *The New York Arbitration Convention of 1958* (Deventer 1981)

19.05 JUDICIAL CONSOLIDATION OF ARBITRAL PROCEEDINGS

Austmann, Commercial Multi-Party Arbitration: A Case-by-Case Approach, 1 *Am. Rev. Int'l Arb.* 341 (1990)

Barron, Court-Ordered Consolidation of Arbitration Proceedings in the United States, 4 *J. Int'l Arb.* 81 (No. 1, 1987)

Branson & Wallace, Court-Ordered Consolidated Arbitrations in the United States: Recent Authority Assures Parties the Choice, 5 *J. Int'l Arb.* 89 (No. 1, 1988)

Chiu, Consolidation of Arbitral Proceedings and International Commercial Arbitration, 7 *J. Int'l Arb.* 53 (No. 2, 1990)

Duintjer Tebbens, A Facelift for Dutch Arbitration Law, 34 *Neth. Int'l L. Rev.* 141 (1987)

Kassis, L'arbitrage multipartite et les clauses de consolidation, 14 *Droit et Pratique du Com. Int'l* 221 (1988)

McCormack, Arbitration in Combined Transportation — A Rare Bird, in *Arbitration in Settlement of International Commercial Disputes Involving the Far East and Arbitration in Combined Transportation* 325 (P. Sanders ed. 1989)

McKellar, To Consolidate or Not to Consolidate: A Study of Federal Court Decisions, 44 *Arb. J.* 15 (No. 4, 1989)

Miller, Consolidation in Hong Kong — the Shui On Case, 3 *Arb. Int'l* 87 (No. 1, 1987)

Parker School of Foreign and Comparative Law, *International Commercial Arbitration and the Courts* (Dobbs Ferry 1990)

Rubellin-Devichi, L'arbitrage et les tiers: le droit de l'arbitrage: les solutions juridictionnelles, 1988 *Rev. Arb.* 515

Samuel, A., *Jurisdictional Problems in International Commercial Arbitration: A Study of Belgian, Dutch, English, French, Swedish, Swiss, U.S. and West German Law* (Zurich 1989)

Schwartz, Multiparty Disputes and Consolidated Arbitrations: An Oxymoron or the Solution to a Continuing Dilemma? 22 *Case W. Res. J. Int'l L.* 341 (1990)

Tan, Multiple Parties and Causes of Action in Arbitration Proceedings, 1988 *Malayan L.J.* li

Veeder, Multi-Party Disputes: Consolidation under English Law, 2 *Arb. Int'l* 310 (1986)

19.06 JUDICIAL APPOINTMENT OF ARBITRATORS

Aksen, The Application of the New York Convention by the United States, 4 *Y.B. Com. Arb.* 341 (1979)

Deshpande, Court, Contract and Arbitration, 26 *J. Ind. L. Inst.* 378 (1984)

Dwor, Some Consequences of a Badly Drafted Arbitration Agreement, 54 *Arbitration* 252 (1988)

Goldstajn, The Relationship between International Commercial Arbitration and National Adjudication, in 4 *Hague-Zagreb Essays* 297 (C. Voskuil & J. Wade eds. 1981)

Hobér, Arbitration and the Swedish Courts, 1990 *Y.B. Swed. & Int'l Arb.* 53

Hunter, Judicial Assistance for the Arbitrator, in *Contemporary Problems in International Arbitration* 195 (J.D.M. Lew ed. 1986)

Parker School of Foreign and Comparative Law, *International Commercial Arbitration and the Courts* (Dobbs Ferry 1990)

Robert, Le rôle du juge pour la constitution du tribunal arbitral et pendant le deroulement de la procédure selon la récente législation française sur l'arbitrage, in *Festschrift für Arthur Bülow* 179 (K.-H. Böckstiegel & O. Glossner eds. 1981)

Trappe, Links Between Arbitrators and the Courts, 44 *Arbitration* 69 (1978)

Varady, On Appointing Authorities in International Commercial Arbitration, 2 *Emory J. Int'l Disp. Res.* 311 (1988)

Voskuil & Freedberg-Swartzburg, Composition of the Arbitral Tribunal, in *Essays on International Commercial Arbitration* 64 (P. Sarcevic ed. 1989)

Wenner, Swiss Judges as Arbitrators or as Nominators for Arbitrators, 35 *Arb. J.* 22 (No. 4, 1980)

19.07 JUDICIAL ASSISTANCE IN PROCEDURAL MATTERS

Capatina, L'accès des tribunaux arbitraux a l'entraide judiciaire internationale, 111 *J. Droit Int'l (Clunet)* 549 (1984)

———, L'entraide judiciare internationale et l'arbitrage de commerce extérieur, *Revue roumain d'études internationales* (No. 5, 1983)

Duintjer Tebbens, A Facelift for Dutch Arbitration Law, 34 *Neth. Int'l L. Rev.* 141 (1987)

Fischer-Zernin & Junker, Between Scylla and Charybdis: Fact Gathering in German Arbitration, 4 *J. Int'l Arb.* 9 (No. 2, 1987)

Gothberg, Coercive Measures for Obtaining Production of Documentary Evidence in Arbitration Proceedings, 8 *Int'l Arb. Gazette* 361 (1986)

Heuman, L., *Current Issues in Swedish Arbitration* (Deventer and Stockholm 1990)

Hobér, Arbitration and the Swedish Courts, 1990 *Y.B. Swed. & Int'l Arb.* 53

Holtzmann, H. & J. Neuhaus, *A Guide to the UNCITRAL Model Law on International Commercial Arbitration: Legislative History and Commentary* (Deventer 1989)

Hunter, Judicial Assistance for the Arbitrator, in *Contemporary Problems in International Arbitration* 195 (J.D.M. Lew ed. 1986)

Hurlburt, Setting Aside Private Non-labour Arbitration Awards for Errors of Law — Some Recent Decisions, 26 *Alta. L. Rev.* 345 (1988)

Karrer, Les rapports entre le tribunal arbitral, les tribunaux étatiques et l'institution arbitrale, 1989 *Int'l Bus. L.J.* 761

Lutz, International Arbitration and Judicial Intervention, 10 *Loy. L.A. Int'l & Comp. L.J.* 621 (1988)

Moreau, The Intervention of the Judge During the Arbitration in Both French and Comparative Law, in *ICCA, Sixth Int'l Arb. Congress: Proceedings* 287 (1978)

Parker School of Foreign and Comparative Law, *International Commercial Arbitration and the Courts* (Dobbs Ferry, NY 1990)

Patkin, Arbitration of Extraterritorial Discovery Disputes Between the Securities and Exchange Commission and a Foreign Broker-Dealer: A New Approach to the Restatement Balancing Test, 5 *B.U. Int'l L.J.* 413 (1987)

Robert, Le rôle du juge pour la constitution du tribunal arbitral et pendant le deroulement de la procédure selon la récente législation française sur l'arbitrage, in *Festschrift für Arthur Büllow* 179 (K.-H. Böckstiegel & O. Glossner eds. 1981)

van Houtte, Conduct of Arbitral Proceedings, in *Essays on International Commercial Arbitration* 113 (P. Sarcevic ed. 1989)

Wills, Is Court Enforced Discovery Proper in Aid of an Arbitration Governed by the U.S. Arbitration Act? in 1 *Fifth Int'l Congress of Maritime Arbitrators* (New York 1981)

19.08 JUDICIAL GRANTING OF INTERIM RELIEF

Allison & Nevin, Attachments and Other Similar Remedies in Arbitration Matters: The Quebec Perspective, in *Interim Court Remedies in Support of Arbitration* 179 (D. Shenton & W. Kühn eds. 1987)

Bagner, Attachments and Other Interim Court Remedies in Support of Arbitration in Sweden, 1985 *Y.B. Swed. & Int'l Arb.* 24

———, Attachments and Other Interim Court Remedies in Support of Arbitration: Sweden, in *Interim Court Remedies in Support of Arbitration* 143 (D. Shenton & W. Kühn eds. 1987)

Baker & Davis, Arbitral Proceedings Under the UNCITRAL Rules: The Experience of the Iran-United States Claims Tribunal, 23 *Geo. Wash. J. Int'l L. & Econ.* 267 (1989)

Becker, Attachments and International Arbitration — An Addendum, 2 *Arb. Int'l* 365 (1986)

———, Attachments in Aid of International Arbitration — The American Position, 1 *Arb. Int'l* 40 (1985)

———, The Supervisory and Adjunctive Jurisdiction of American Courts in Arbitration Cases, in *Contemporary Problems in International Arbitration* 207 (J.D.M. Lew ed. 1986)

Bombau, Attachments and Other Interim Court Remedies in Support of Arbitration: The Argentine Perspective, in *Interim Court Remedies in Support of Arbitration* 111 (D. Shenton & W. Kühn eds. 1987)

Bösch, A., *Einstweiliger Rechtsschutz in der internationalen Handelsschiedsgerichtsbarkeit* (Berne 1989)

Buhart, Attachments and Other Interim Court Remedies in Support of Arbitration: French Law, in *Interim Court Remedies in Support of Arbitration* 163 (D. Shenton & W. Kühn eds. 1987)

———, Interim Court Remedies in Support of Arbitration, 12 *Int'l Bus. Law.* 107 (1984)

Cosman, Attachments and Other Interim Court Remedies in Support of Arbitration, 10 *Can. Arb. J.* 2 (No. 1, 1985)

————, Attachments and Other Interim Court Remedies in Support of Arbitration: The Canadian Perspective, in *Interim Court Remedies in Support of Arbitration* 191 (D. Shenton & W. Kühn eds. 1987)

Cremades, Attachments and Other Interim Court Remedies in Support of Arbitration: The Spanish Courts, in *Interim Court Remedies in Support of Arbitration* 215 (D. Shenton & W. Kühn eds. 1987)

————, Is Exclusion of Concurrent Courts' Jurisdiction over Conservatory Measures to Be Introduced through a Revision of the Convention? 6 *J. Int'l Arb.* 105 (No. 3, 1989)

de Leval, Les mesures provisoires et conservatoires en matière d'arbitrage, in *L'Arbitrage* 111 (L. Matray & G. de Leval eds. 1989)

Duintjer Tebbens, A Facelift for Dutch Arbitration Law, 34 *Neth. Int'l L. Rev.* 141 (1987)

Ebb, Flight of Assets from the Jurisdiction 'In the Twinkling of a Telex': Pre- and Post-Award Conservatory Relief in International Commercial Arbitration, 7 *J. Int'l Arb.* 9 (No. 1, 1990)

Fiotto, The United States Arbitration Act and Preliminary Injunctions: A New Interpretation of an Old Statute, 66 *B. U. L. Rev.* 1041 (1986)

Freimüller, Attachments in Switzerland and Their Validation in International Commercial Arbitration, 2 *Bull. Swiss Arb. A.* 72 (1984)

————, Interim Court Remedies in Support of Arbitration, 12 *Int'l Bus. Law.* 119 (March 1984)

————, Attachments and Other Interim Court Remedies in Support of Arbitration: Switzerland, in *Interim Court Remedies in Support of Arbitration* 245 (D. Shenton & W. Kühn eds. 1987)

Friedland, ICSID and Court-Ordered Provisional Remedies: An Update, 4 *Arb. Int'l* 161 (1988)

————, Provisional Measures in ICSID Arbitration, 2 *Arb. Int'l* 335 (1986)

Gaillard, Le point de vue d'un utilisateur étranger, 1989 *Int'l Bus. L.J.* 793

Hanamizu, Attachments and Other Interim Court Remedies in Support of Arbitration: Japan, in *Interim Court Remedies in Support of Arbitration* 127 (D. Shenton & W. Kühn eds. 1987)

489

Hausmaninger, Ch., *Die einstweilige Verfügung im schiedsgerichtlichen Verfahren* (Vienna 1989)

Hobér, Arbitration and the Swedish Courts, 1990 *Y.B. Swed. & Int'l Arb.* 53

Hoellering, Interim Measures and Arbitration: The Situation in the United States, 46 *Arb. J.* 22 (No. 2, 1991)

————, Interim Relief in Aid of International Commercial Arbitration, 1984 *Wis. Int'l L.J.* 1 (Symposium)

————, Interim Relief in International Arbitration, in *Arbitration and the Licensing Process* 3-55 (R. Goldscheider & M. de Haas eds. 1984-); reprinted from 1984 *Wis. Int'l L.J.* 3

Holmes, Pre-Award Attachment under the U.N. Convention on the Recognition and Enforcement of Foreign Arbitral Awards, 21 *Va. J. Int'l L.* 785 (1981)

Holtzmann, H. & J. Neuhaus, *A Guide to the UNCITRAL Model Law on International Commercial Arbitration: Legislative History and Commentary* (Deventer 1989)

Hunter, Judicial Assistance for the Arbitrator, in *Contemporary Problems in International Arbitration* 195 (J.D.M. Lew ed. 1986)

Jarvin, Is Exclusion of Concurrent Courts' Jurisdiction over Conservatory Measures to Be Introduced by a Revision of the Convention? 6 *J. Int'l Arb.* 171 (No. 1, 1989)

Karrer, Les rapports entre le tribunal arbitral, les tribunaux étatiques et l'institution arbitrale, 1989 *Int'l Bus. L.J.* 761

Kennedy-Grant, Attachments and Other Interim Court Remedies in Support of Arbitration — The New Zealand Position, in *Interim Court Remedies in Support of Arbitration* 261 (D. Shenton & W. Kühn eds. 1987)

Knoepfler & Schweizer, Les mesures provisoires et l'arbitrage, in *Recueil de Travaux Suisses* 221 (C. Reymond & E. Bucher eds. 1984)

Kühn, Interim Court Remedies in Support of Arbitration: Germany, in *Interim Court Remedies in Support of Arbitration* 5 (D. Shenton & W. Kühn eds. 1987)

————, Vorläufiger Rechtsschutz und Schiedsgerichtsbarkeit, 1 *Jahrbuch Schiedsgerichtsbarkeit* 47 (1987)

Lessing, Sauer-Getriebe K.G. v. White Hydraulics, Inc.— Applicability of the Federal Arbitration Act to International Commercial Arbitration, 2 *Int'l Tax & Bus. Law.* 331 (1984)

————, Schiedsgerichtsbarkeit und Massnahmen des provisorischen Rechtsschutzes: Jüngste Entwicklungen in den Vereinigten Staaten, 25 *ZRV* 26 (1984)

Loftis, Securing Arbitral Awards: Waiving Immunity under the Foreign Sovereign Immunities Act and Ensuring Equitable Remedy by Pre-Award Attachment under the New York Convention, 9 *Suff. Transnat'l L.J.* 235 (1985)

McLachlan, Transnational Applications of Mareva Injunctions and Anton Piller Orders, 36 *Int'l & Comp. L.Q.* 669 (1987)

Matsuura, Schiedsgerichtsbarkeit und erstweiliger Rechtsschutz, in *Festschrift für Karl Heinz Schwab* 321 (P. Gottwald & H. Prütting eds. 1990)

Meier, Provisional Judicial Remedies in Arbitration: The United States Position, in *Interim Court Remedies in Support of Arbitration* 31 (D. Shenton & W. Kühn eds. 1987)

Mills, State International Arbitration Statutes and the U.S. Arbitration Act: Unifying the Availability of Interim Relief, 13 *Fordham Int'l L.J.* 604 (1989 - 1990)

Ng, Singapore, in *Interim Court Remedies in Support of Arbitration* 89 (D. Shenton & W. Kühn eds. 1987)

Note, An Argument for Pre-Award Attachment in International Arbitration under the New York Convention, 18 *Cornell Int'l L.J.* 99 (1985)

————, Attachment under the United Nations Convention on the Recognition and Enforcement of Foreign Arbitral Awards, 36 *Wash. & Lee L. Rev.* 1135 (1979)

————, Pre-Arbitration Attachment: Is It Available in International Disputes? 1 *Rev. Litigation* 211 (1981)

————, Pre-Award Attachment under the U.N. Convention of the Recognition and Enforcement of Foreign Arbitral Awards, 21 *Va. J. Int'l L.* 788 (1981)

————, The Use of Pre-Judgment Attachments and Temporary Injunctions in International Commercial Arbitration Proceedings: A Comparative Analysis of the British and American Approaches, 50 *U. Pitt. L. Rev.* 667 (1989)

O'Neill, American Legal Developments in Commercial Arbitration Involving Foreign States and State Enterprises, 6 *J. Int'l Arb.* 117 (No. 1, 1989)

Parker School of Foreign and Comparative Law, *International Commercial Arbitration and the Courts* (Dobbs Ferry 1990)

Perry, Attachments and Other Interim Court Remedies in Support of Arbitration — The Australian Position, in *Interim Court Remedies in Support of Arbitration* 68 (D. Shenton & W. Kühn eds. 1987)

Pew & Jarvis, Pre-Award Attachment in International Arbitration: The Law in New York, 7 *J. Int'l Arb.* 31 (No. 3, 1990)

Reichert, Provisional Remedies in the Context of International Commercial Arbitration, 3 *Int'l Tax & Bus. Law.* 368 (1986)

Sandrock & Nöcker, Einstweilige Massnahmen internationaler Schieds-gerichte: Blosse Papiertiger? 1 *Jahrbuch Schiedsgerichtsbarkeit* 74 (1987)

Shenton, Attachments and Interim Court Remedies in Support of Arbitra-tion: The English Courts, in *Interim Court Remedies in Support of Arbitration* 53 (D. Shenton & W. Kühn eds. 1987)

————, Interim Court Remedies in Support of Arbitration, 12 *Int'l Bus. Law.* 101 (1984)

Shenton, D. & W. Kühn, *Interim Court Remedies in Support of Arbitration: A Country-by-Country Analysis* (London 1987)

Singhania, Attachments and Other Court Remedies in Support of Arbitration Available in India, in *Interim Court Remedies in Support of Arbitration* 153 (D. Shenton & W. Kühn eds. 1987)

Tschanz, International Arbitration in the United States: The Need for a New Act, 3 *Arb. Int'l* 309 (1987)

Tupman & Brower, Court-Ordered Provisional Measures under the New York Convention, 80 *Am. J. Int'l L.* 24 (1986)

Ughi, Attachments and Other Interim Court Remedies in Support of Arbitration: Italy, in *Interim Court Remedies in Support of Arbitration* 99 (D. Shenton & W. Kühn eds. 1987)

————, Interim Court Remedies in Support of Arbitration, 12 *Int'l Bus. Law.* 115 (1984)

van den Berg, Recent Enforcement Problems under the New York and ICSID Conventions, 5 *Arb. Int'l* 2 (1989)

van den Berg, A. J., *The New York Arbitration Convention of 1958* (Deventer 1981)

von Mehren, The Enforcement of Arbitral Awards under Conventions and United States Law, 9 *Yale J. World Pub. Ord.* 343 (1983)

Williams, Attachments and Other Interim Court Remedies in Support of Arbitration: South Africa, in *Interim Court Remedies in Support of Arbitration* 281 (D. Shenton & W. Kühn eds. 1987)

19.09 STAY OR TERMINATION OF ARBITRATION BY JUDICIAL ORDER

Budin, La suspension dans l'arbitrage international, 1986 *Rev. Arb.* 415

Cremades, Le caractère prejudiciel de la procédure pénal et la procédure d'arbitrage, in *Festschrift für Arthur Bülow* 25 (K.-H. Böckstiegel & O. Glossner eds. 1981)

Massoff, Authority of United States Bankruptcy Courts to Stay International Arbitral Proceedings, 11 *Fordham Int'l L.J.* 148 (1987)

Mustill, Sir Michael J. & S. C.Boyd, *The Law and Practice of Commercial Arbitration in England* (2nd ed. 1989)

Note, Appealability of District Court Orders Granting or Denying Stays of Arbitration under 28 U.S.C. 1291(a)(1), 36 *Case W. Res. L. Rev.* 1 (1985-86)

————, Authority of United States Bankruptcy Courts to Stay International Arbitral Proceedings, 11 *Fordham Int'l L.J.* 148 (1987)

Parker School of Foreign and Comparative Law, *International Commercial Arbitration and the Courts* (Dobbs Ferry 1990)

Schmitthoff, C., *Schmitthoff's Export Trade. The Law and Practice of International Trade* (8th ed. 1986)

19.10 JUDICIAL CONFIRMATION OF AWARD

Lew, Arbitration Agreements: Form and Character, in *Essays on International Commercial Arbitration* 51 (P. Sarcevic ed. 1989)

Parker School of Foreign and Comparative Law, *International Commercial Arbitration and the Courts* (Dobbs Ferry, NY 1990)

Parlade, Remedies after Arbitration Award, in *Commercial Arbitration* 75 (J. Ricalde ed. 1983)

Solveni, Dichiarazione di efficacia in Italia di lodi arbitrali inglesi convertiti in sentenze della High Court of Justice ai sensi della Sez. 26 dell'Arbitration Act, 1950, 88 *Dir. Mar.* 451 (1986)

19.11 RECOURSE AGAINST AWARD GENERALLY

Barker, Judicial Review of English Arbitration in the Wake of the Nema and Evia, 23 *Va. J. Int'l L.* 432 (1983)

Barona Vilar, El recurso de anulación del laudo arbitral, 5 *Rev. Corte Esp. Arb.* 111 (1988-89)

Béguin, La logique du régime des voies de recours en matière d'arbitrage commercial international, in *Houin Collection. Etudes offertes à Roger Houin* 241 (Paris 1985)

Berger, Die Regelung der gerichtlichen Anfechtbarkeit internationaler Schiedssprüche in europäischen Schiedsgerichtsgesetzen, 35 *RIW* 850 (1989)

Bernini, Appeal against the Award and Enforcement of the Award, 24 *Rassegna dell'Arb.* 55 (1984)

Bucher, Les voies de recours, 1989 *Int'l Bus. L.J.* 771

Budin, La suspension dans l'arbitrage international, 1986 *Rev. Arb.* 415

Conrick, Where the Kings Writ Does Not Run: The Origins and Effect of the Arbitration Act 1979, 1 *Queensl. Inst. Tech. L.J.* 1 (1985)

Craig, The Uses and Abuses of Appeal from International Arbitration Awards, in *Private Investors Abroad - Problems and Solutions in International Business in 1987* 14.1 (J. Moss ed. 1987)

————, Uses and Abuses of Appeal from Awards, 4 *Arb. Int'l* 174 (1988)

El-Hakim, Conditions de validité dans le droit et la pratique des pays arabes, in *Euro-Arab Arbitration II* 131 (F. Kemicha ed. 1989)

Fouchard, Conditions de validité en droit conventionnel et droit comparé, in *Euro-Arab Arbitration II* 121 (F. Kemicha ed. 1989)

Gaillard, Le point de vue d'un utilisateur étranger, 1989 *Int'l Bus. L.J.* 793

Habscheid, Teil-, Zwischen- und Vorabschiedsprüche im schweizerischen und deutschen Recht, ihre Anfechtbarkeit und die Rechtsfolgen ihrer Aufhebung durch das Staatsgericht (unter besonderer Berücksichtigung, der Streitgenossenschaft), 106 *ZSR* 669 (1987)

Hobér, Judicial Review in International Arbitration: The Swedish Supreme Court Decision in the Uganda Case, 1 *Am. Rev. Int'l Arb.* 596 (1990)

Jaffe, The Judicial Trend Toward Finality of Commercial Arbitral Awards in England, 24 *Tex. Int'l L.J.* 67 (1989)

Kaufmann-Kohler, Specificity of International Arbitration — Its Increasing Role in Case Law Illustrated by Geneva Court Practice on Application for Stays Imposed on Arbitral Awards, in *Recueil de Travaux Suisses* 297 (C. Reymond & E. Bucher eds. 1984)

Klaric, Judicial Intervention and International Commercial Arbitration: The Australian Perspective, 16 *Austl. Bus. L. Rev.* 440 (1988)

Knoepfler & Schweizer, L'arbitrage international et des voies de recours: à propos du projet de Loi fédérale sur le DIP, in *Mélanges Guy Flattet* 491 (Lausanne 1985)

Kolkey, Attacking Arbitral Awards: Rights of Appeal and Review in International Arbitrations, 22 *Int'l Law.* 693 (1988)

Lalive, Enforcing Awards, in *ICC, 60 Years of ICC Arbitration* 317 (1984)

Lamm, Arbitration Awards: Post Award Review and Enforcement Proceedings, 5 *Int'l Litigation Q.* 169 (No. 3, 1989)

Laschet, Erneut zur Frage der Ablehnung von Schiedsrichtern in Frankreich — Beschluss der Cour d'Appel de Paris vom 15.1.1985, 1985 *KTS* 627

Lewis, Leave of Appeal under the Arbitration Act 1979, 1982 *Lloyd's Mar. & Com. L.Q.* 271

Loussouarn, La réforme du droit de l'arbitrage: les voies de recours, 1980 *Rev. Arb.* 671

Moreau, B. & T. Bernard, *Droit interne et droit international de l'arbitrage* (2nd ed. 1985)

Mustill, Sir Michael J. & S. C. Boyd, *The Law and Practice of Commercial Arbitration in England* (2nd ed. 1989)

Park, Judicial Controls in the Arbitral Process, 5 *Arb. Int'l* 230 (1989)

Paterson, International Commercial Arbitration Act: An Overview, in *UNCITRAL Arbitration Model in Canada* 113 (R. Paterson & B. Thompson eds. 1987)

Paulsson, Arbitrage international et voies de recours: La Cour suprême de Suède dans le sillage des solutions belge et helvétique, 117 *J. Droit Int'l (Clunet)* 588 (1990)

——, Means of Recourse Against Arbitral Awards Under U.S. Law, 6 *J. Int'l Arb.* 101 (No. 2, 1989)

——, Rights of Recourse in Sweden, 5 *Arb. Int'l* 291 (1989)

——, The Contribution of English and American Legislation, in *Euro-Arab Arbitration III* 104 (F. Kemicha ed. 1991)

Perrot, Les voies de recours en matière d'arbitrage, 1980 *Rev. Arb.* 268

Poudret, Les voies de recours en matière d'arbitrage international en Suisse selon le Concordat et la nouvelle loi fédérale, 1988 *Rev. Arb.* 595

——, Refléxions à propos de la recevabilité du recours en réforme ou en nulité au Tribunal fédérale en matière d'arbitrage, 106 *ZSR* 765 (1987)

Redfern, A. & M. Hunter, *Law and Practice of International Commercial Arbitration* (2nd ed. 1991)

Rhodes, Judicial Review of Commercial Arbitration, 14 *Hong Kong L.J.* 159 (1984)

Rubino-Sammartano, M., *International Arbitration Law* (Deventer 1990)

Samuel, Developments in English Arbitration Law since the 1984 Antaios Decision, 5 *J. Int'l Arb.* 9 (No. 3, 1988)

Sarcevic, The Setting Aside and Enforcement of Arbitral Awards under the UNCITRAL Model Law, in *Essays on International Commercial Arbitration* 177 (P. Sarcevic ed. 1989)

Schizzerotto, G., *Dell'arbitrato* (3rd ed. Milan 1988)

Schlosser, L'arbitrage et les voies de recours, 1980 *Rev. Arb.* 286

——, La procédure des voies de recours en matière d'arbitrage. Etude de droit comparé, in *ICCA, Sixth Int'l Arb. Congress: Proceedings* 301 (1978); also in 1978 *Rev. Arb.* 345

Schmitthoff, C., *Schmitthoff's Export Trade. The Law and Practice of International Trade* (8th ed. 1986)

Sharkey, J. & J. Dorter, *Commercial Arbitration* (Sydney 1986)

Stanton, The Court of Appeal of Paris and Lack of Arbitral Jurisdiction, 2 *Arb. Int'l* 220 (1986)

Tarzia, Nullità e annullamento del lodo arbitrale irrituale, 45 *Riv. Trim. Dir. & Proc. Civ.* 451 (1991)

Toral Moreno, Procede el amparo contra laudos de arbitros nombrados por particulares? 1-3 *Revista de Derecho Procesal* 5 (1975)

Tschanz, International Arbitration in the United States: The Need for a New Act, 3 *Arb. Int'l* 309 (1987)

Walder-Bohner, Frage der Anfechtung von Schiedsgerichtsentscheiden durch Rechtsmittel (Ein Gegenvorschlag zum Entwurf des Bundesrates über das Internationale Privatrecht), 79 *SJZ* 356 (1983)

Wallace, Control by the Courts: A Plea for More, Not Less, 6 *Arb. Int'l* 253 (1990)

Westerling, Void and Challengeable Awards in Swedish Arbitral Procedure, 1984 *Y.B. Swed. & Int'l Arb.* 45

Zubrod, A History of Appeal of Arbitration Awards in the United States, in 2 *Fifth Int'l Congress of Maritime Arbitrators* (New York 1981)

19.12 PROCEDURE AND GROUNDS FOR SETTING ASIDE

Aksen, The Application of the New York Convention by the United States, 4 *Y.B. Com. Arb.* 341 (1979)

Alvarez, Judicial Intervention and Review under the International Commercial Arbitration Act, in *UNCITRAL Arbitration Model in Canada* 137 (R. Paterson & B. Thompson eds. 1987)

Baur, F., *Neuere Probleme der privaten Schiedsgerichtsbarkeit* (Berlin 1980)

Blom, Conflict of Laws Aspects of the International Commercial Arbitration Act, in *UNCITRAL Arbitration Model in Canada* 127 (R. Paterson & B. Thompson eds. 1987)

Böckstiegel, Public Policy and Arbitrability, in *Comparative Arbitration Practice and Public Policy in Arbitration* 177 (P. Sanders ed. 1987)

Briner, Die Anfechtung und Vollstreckung des Schiedsentscheides, in *Die Internationale Schiedsgerichtsbarkeit in der Schweiz* 99 (K.-H. Böckstiegel ed. 1989)

Bucher, Les voies de recours, 1989 *Int'l Bus. L.J.* 771

————, Unabdingbarkeit der Nichtigkeitsbeschwerde nach schweizerischem Konkordat über die Schiedsgerichtsbarkeit, 6 *IPRax* 187 (1986)

Bucher, A., *Die neue internationale Schiedsgerichtsbarkeit in der Schweiz* (Basel 1989)

————, *Le nouvel arbitrage international en Suisse. Théorie et pratique de droit* (Basel 1988)

Bucher, A. & P.-Y. Tschanz, *International Arbitration in Switzerland* (Basel 1989)

Carabiber, L'arbitrage international et la réserve de l'ordre public, 1956 *Rev. Arb.* 118

Courteault & Flécheux, La notion de l'ordre public international dans la jurisprudence de la Cour de Cassation française, in *ICCA, Sixth Int'l Arb. Congress: Proceedings* 257 (1978)

Dalla Verita, Note sull'impugnazione del lodo arbitrale, 42 *Riv. Trim. Dir. & Proc. Civ.* 614 (1988)

David, R., *Arbitration in International Trade* (Deventer 1985)

Duintjer Tebbens, A Facelift for Dutch Arbitration Law, 34 *Neth. Int'l L. Rev.* 141 (1987)

Garbagnati, Ancora in tema d'impugnazione per nullità del lodo arbitrale rituale, 45 *Riv. Dir. Proc.* 1 (1990)

Gonzales Soria, J., *La intervención judicial en el arbitraje. Recursos jurisdiccionales y ejecución judicial del laudo arbitral* (Madrid 1988)

Gottwald, Die sachliche Kontrolle internationaler Schiedssprüche durch staatliche Gerichte, in *Beiträge zum internationalen Verfahrensrecht und zur Schiedsgerichtsbakeit. Festschrift für Heinrich Nagel* 54 (W. Habscheid & K. Schwab eds. 1987)

Grade, The Annulment of Arbitral Awards in Belgium, 5 *Int'l Fin. L. Rev.* 35 (No. 11, 1986)

Grigera Naón, Public Policy and International Commercial Arbitration: The Argentine Perspective, 3 *J. Int'l Arb.* 5 (No. 2, 1986)

Groos, Schiedsgerichtsbarkeit im deutsch-französischen Wirtschaftsverkehr, 33 *RIW* 343 (1987)

Heini, Der materiellrechtliche Ordre public im neuen schweizerischen Recht der internationalen Schiedsgerichtsbarkeit, in *Festschrift für Walther J. Habscheid* 153 (W. Lindacher, D. Pfaff et al. eds. 1989)

Herrmann, The Role of the Courts under the UNCITRAL Model Law Script, in *Contemporary Problems in Int'l Arbitration* 164 (J.D.M. Lew ed. 1986)

Hobér, Arbitration and the Swedish Courts, 1990 *Y.B. Swed. & Int'l Arb.* 53

——, Arbitration in Moscow, 3 *Arb. Int'l* 119 (1987)

Holtzmann, H. & J. Neuhaus, *A Guide to the UNCITRAL Model Law on International Commercial Arbitration: Legislative History and Commentary* (Deventer 1989)

Horsmans, L'arbitrage et l'ordre public interne belge, 1978 *Rev. Arb.* 79

————, La sentence arbitrale, la convention d'arbitrage et l'ordre public interne belge, 16 *Tijdschrift voor Privaatrecht* 231 (1979)

Jaffe, The Judicial Trend toward Finality of Commercial Arbitral Awards in England, 24 *Tex. Int'l L.J.* 67 (1989)

Kimball, Vacating Maritime Arbitration Awards: Is It Really Possible? 13 *J. Mar. L. & Com.* 71 (1981)

Kolkey, Attacking Arbitral Awards: Rights of Appeal and Review in International Arbitrations, 22 *Int'l Law.* 693 (1988)

Kornblum, Das 'Gebot überparteilicher Rechtspflege' und der deutsche schiedsrechtliche ordre public, 40 *NJW* 1105 (1987)

Lalive, The New Swiss Law on International Arbitration, 4 *Arb. Int'l* 2 (1988)

Lebedev, S., ed., *Handbook on Foreign Trade Arbitration in the CMEA Member Countries* (Moscow 1983)

Lee Tae Hee, Arbitration of International Commercial Disputes in Korea, 3 *Arb. Int'l* 14 (No. 1, 1987)

Lepp & Migeal, Powers of the Arbitrators, in 1 *Fifth International Congress of Maritime Arbitrators* (New York 1981)

Linsmeau, L'annulation des sentences arbitrales en droit belge, in *L'Arbitrage* 91 (L. Matray & G. de Leval eds. 1989)

Martens & Matray, Arbitrage et ordre public interne, 1978 *Rev. Arb.* 95

Matray, Arbitrage et ordre public international, in *The Art of Arbitration* 241 (J. Schultsz & A. van den Berg eds. 1982)

————, La loi belge du 27 mars 1985 et ses repércussions sur l'arbitrage commercial international, 64 *Rev. Droit Int'l & Droit Comp.* 243 (1987)

Meisel, The Changing Role of the High Court in Relation to Supervision of Commercial Arbitrations, 25 *Les Cahiers de Droit* 653 (1984)

Mirimanoff, Objection to Arbitrators Following the Annulment of a Partial Award: A Potential Jeopardy of Arbitration in Switzerland? 3 *J. Int'l Arb.* 101 (No. 2, 1986)

Mustill, Sir Michael J. & S. C. Boyd, *The Law and Practice of Commercial Arbitration in England* (2nd ed. 1989)

Park, Judicial Controls in the Arbitral Process, 5 *Arb. Int'l* 230 (1989)

Parker School of Foreign and Comparative Law, *International Commercial Arbitration and the Courts* (Dobbs Ferry 1990)

Parlade, Remedies after Arbitration Award, in *Commercial Arbitration* 75 (J. Ricalde ed. 1983)

Poudret, Challenge and Enforcement of Arbitral Awards in Switzerland, 4 *Arb. Int'l* 278 (1988)

————, Refléxions à propos de la recevabilité du recours en réforme ou en nulité au Tribunal fédérale en matière d'arbitrage, 106 *ZSR* 765 (1987)

Poznanski, The Nature and Extent of an Arbitrator's Powers in International Commercial Arbitration, 4 *J. Int'l Arb.* 71 (No. 3, 1987)

Punzi, Sull'inammissibilità dell'impugnazione immediata con le azioni c.d. negoziali del lodo arbitrale non dichiarato esecutivo, 26 *Rassegna dell'Arb.* 183 (1986)

Raeschke-Kessler, Neuere Entwicklungen im Bereich der Internationalen Schiedsgerichtsbarkeit, 41 *NJW* 3041 (1988)

Redfern, A. & M. Hunter, *Law and Practice of International Commercial Arbitration* (2nd ed. 1991)

Samuel, A., *Jurisdictional Problems in International Commercial Arbitration: A Study of Belgian, Dutch, English, French, Swedish, Swiss, U.S. and West German Law* (Zurich 1989)

Sanders, Trends in the Field of International Commercial Arbitration, 145 *Recueil des Cours* 205 (1975-II)

Sarcevic, The Setting Aside and Enforcement of Arbitral Awards under the UNCITRAL Model Law, in *Essays on International Commercial Arbitration* 177 (P. Sarcevic ed. 1989)

Schmitthoff, Finality of Arbitral Awards and Judicial Review, in *Contemporary Problems in International Arbitration* 230 (J.D.M. Lew ed. 1986)

Schütze, R., D. Tscherning & W. Wais, *Handbuch des Schiedsverfahrens. Praxis der deutschen und internationalen Schiedsgerichtsbarkeit* (2nd ed. Berlin 1990)

Schulthess, H.K., *Der verfahrensrechtliche Ordre public in der internationalen Schiedsgerichtsbarkeit in der Schweiz* (Zurich 1981)

Stanton, The Court of Appeal of Paris and Lack of Arbitral Jurisdiction, 2 *Arb. Int'l* 220 (1986)

Storme, M. & B. Demeulenaere, *International Commercial Arbitration in Belgium: A Handbook* (Deventer 1989)

Strenger, Aplicaçao de normas de ordem publica nos laudos arbitrais, 606 *Rev. Trib.* 9 (April 1986)

Strohbach, On the Setting Aside of Arbitration Awards, in *ICC, Hommage à Fréderic Eisemann* 77 (1978)

Sujan, M.A., *The Law Relating to Government Arbitration* (New Delhi 1985)

Sweeney, Judicial Review of Arbitral Proceedings, in 2 *Fifth Int'l Congress of Maritime Arbitrators* (New York 1981)

Thomas, Costs, Discretion and Issues of Technical Misconduct, 1982 *Lloyd's Mar. & Com. L.Q.* 288

Timmermans, The USSR Maritime Arbitration Commission, 1987 *Lloyd's Mar. & Com. L.Q.* 350 and 468

Tschanz, International Arbitration in the United States: The Need for a New Act, 3 *Arb. Int'l* 309 (1987)

Vigoriti, Corte d'Appello Firenze e l'impugnazione del lodo arbitrale (1987—1989), 30 *Rassegna dell'Arb.* 33 (1990)

von Winterfeld, Noch einmal: Der deutsche ordre public in der internationalen Schiedsgerichtsbarkeit, 1987 *NJW* 3059

Warren, The Concept of 'Null and Void' in International Commercial Arbitration, 45 *Arb. J.* 57 (No. 4, 1990)

Westerling, Void and Challengeable Awards in Swedish Arbitral Procedure, 1984 *Y.B. Swed. & Int'l Arb.* 45

19.13 REVIEW ON THE MERITS

Briner, La révision des sentences arbitrales dans les cantons faisant partie du Concordat intercantonal sur l'arbitrage, in *Recueil de Travaux Suisses* 285 (C. Reymond & E. Bucher 1984)

Craig, The Uses and Abuses of Appeal from International Arbitration Awards, in *Private Investors Abroad - Problems and Solutions in International Business in 1987* 14.1 (J. Moss ed. 1987)

Craig, Uses and Abuses of Appeal from Awards, 4 *Arb. Int'l* 174 (1988)

Deshpande, Court, Contract and Arbitration, 26 *J. Ind. L. Inst.* 378 (1984)

Jaffe, The Judicial Trend Toward Finality of Commercial Arbitral Awards in England, 24 *Tex. Int'l L.J.* 67 (1989)

Kornblum, Nachprufbarkeit kartellrechtlicher Schiedssprüche durch die ordentliche Gerichte, 22 *NJW* 1793 (1969)

Lake & Dana, Judicial Review of Awards of the Iran-United States Claims Tribunal: Are the Tribunal's Awards Dutch? 16 *L. & Pol'y Int'l Bus.* 755 (1984)

Marriott, Arbitrating International Commercial Disputes in the United Kingdom, 44 *Arb. J.* 3 (No. 3, 1989)

Mustill, Sir Michael J. & S. C. Boyd, *The Law and Practice of Commercial Arbitration in England* (2nd ed. 1989)

Parker School of Foreign and Comparative Law, *International Commercial Arbitration and the Courts* (Dobbs Ferry 1990)

Parlade, Remedies after Arbitration Award, in *Commercial Arbitration* 75 (J. Ricalde ed. 1983)

Samuel, The 1979 Arbitration Act — Judicial Review of Arbitration Awards on the Merits in England, 2 *J. Int. Arb.* 53 (No. 4, 1985)

Schmitthoff, Finality of Arbitral Awards and Judicial Review, in *Contemporary Problems in International Arbitration* 230 (J.D.M. Lew ed. 1986)

Schmitthoff, C., *Schmitthoff's Export Trade. The Law and Practice of International Trade* (8th ed. 1986)

Swan, Compelling Arbitration and Judicial Review of Arbitral Awards, 11 *Law. Am.* 475 (1979)

Thomas, The Antaios: The Nema Guidelines Reconsidered, 1985 *J. Bus. L.* 200

van den Berg, A. J., *The New York Arbitration Convention of 1958* (Deventer 1981)

19.14 REMISSION

Briner, La révision des sentences arbitrales dans les cantons faisant partie du Concordat intercantonal sur l'arbitrage, in *Recueil de Travaux Suisses* 285 (C. Reymond & E. Bucher 1984)

Jaffe, The Judicial Trend Toward Finality of Commercial Arbitral Awards in England, 24 *Tex. Int'l L.J.* 67 (1989)

Knoepfler & Schweizer, Making of Awards and Termination of Proceedings, in *Essays on International Commercial Arbitration* 160 (P. Sarcevic ed. 1989)

Mustill, Sir Michael J. & S. C. Boyd, *The Law and Practice of Commercial Arbitration in England* (2nd ed. 1989)

Parker School of Foreign and Comparative Law, *International Commercial Arbitration and the Courts* (Dobbs Ferry 1990)

20. RECOGNITION AND ENFORCEMENT OF ARBITRAL AWARDS

20.01 IN GENERAL

Alcala Zamora, La ejecución de sentencias arbitrales en México, 11 *Boletin del Instituto de Derecho Comparado de México* 45 (1958)

Aliaga Grez, Alvaro, *Los recursos procesales en el juicio arbitral* (Santiago de Chile 1985)

Arbitration Institute of the Stockholm Chamber of Commerce, *Arbitration in Sweden*, (2nd rev. ed. 1984)

Bernini, Appeal against the Award and Enforcement of the Award, 24 *Rassegna dell'Arb.* 55 (1984)

Bertin, Le rôle du juge dans l'exécution de la sentence arbitrale, 1983 *Rev. Arb.* 281

Billioud de Nuzillet, Enforcement of Arbitral Awards, in *Arbitration and the Licensing Process* 3-3 (R. Goldscheider & M. de Haas eds. 1984-)

Branson & Tupman, Selecting an Arbitral Forum: A Guide to Cost-Effective International Arbitration, 24 *Va. J. Int'l L.* 917 (1984)

Bull, S., *The Arbitral Process and the Courts* (Wellington 1983)

Chillón Medina, J. M. & J. F. Merino Merchán, *Tratado de arbitraje privado interno e internacional* (Madrid 1978)

Comment, Enforcement of Interim Awards, 3 *Forum New York* 4 (No. 2, 1986)

David, R., *Arbitration in International Trade* (Deventer 1985)

Delaume, L'arbitrage transnational et les tribunaux nationaux, 111 *J. Droit Int'l (Clunet)* 521 (1984)

Doi, Recognition and Enforcement of Foreign Judgments and Arbitral Awards in *Japan, Quarterly of the Japan Commercial Arbitration Association* 1 (Nos. 13/14, 1963)

Dorter, J. & G. Widmer, *Arbitration (Commercial) in Australia— Law and Practice* (Sydney 1979)

El-Hakim, L'exécution des sentences arbitrales, in *Etudes Dediées à Alex Weill, Paris* 227 (1983)

Eyzaguirre Echeverria, R., *El arbitraje comercial en la legislación chilena y su regulación international* (Santiago de Chile 1981)

Fouchard, L'arbitrage commercial international, in 2 *Bibliothèque de droit international privé* (Paris 1965)

Giardina, The Question of General Recognition and Enforcement of Arbitral Awards, 22 *Rassegna dell'Arb.* 289 (1982)

Glossner, Eine zentrale Gerichtsinstanz für internationale Schiedsverfahren in der Bundesrepublik Deutschland? 32 *RIW* 214 (1986)

Glossner, O., *Commercial Arbitration in the Federal Republic of Germany* (Deventer 1984)

Henn, G., *Schiedsverfahrensrecht: ein Handbuch* (Heidelberg 1986)

Hjerner, Recourse to Law Courts in International Arbitration in Sweden, in *ICC, Hommage à Fréderic Eisemann* 61 (1978)

Hunter, Judicial Assistance for the Arbitrator, in *Contemporary Problems in International Arbitration* 195 (J.D.M. Lew ed. 1986)

Kimbrough, Viabilité générale de l'arbitrage à Singapour: l'accession a la Convention de New York comble la dernière lacune, 1986 *Int'l Bus. L.J.* 783

Lalive, Enforcing Awards, in *ICC, 60 Years of ICC Arbitration* 317 (1984)

Leahy & Pierce, Sanctions to Control Party Misbehavior in International Arbitration, 26 *Va. J. Int'l L.* 291 (1986)

Lew, The Recognition and Enforcement of Arbitration Agreements and Awards in the Middle East, 1 *Arb. Int'l* 161 (1985)

———, The Recognition and Enforcement of Arbitration Awards in England, 10 *Int'l Law.* 425 (1976)

Lew, J., ed., *Contemporary Problems in International Arbitration* (London 1986)

Loumiet, United States: Florida International Arbitration Act. Introductory Note, 26 *I.L.M.* 949 (1987)

Mayer, L'insértion de la sentence dans l'ordre juridique français, in *Droit et pratique de l'arbitrage international en France* 81 (Y. Derains ed. Paris 1984)

Moreau, B. & T. Bernard, *Droit interne et droit international de l'arbitrage* (2nd ed. 1985)

Mustill, Distinctive Features of English Commercial Arbitration, 14 *Arkiv for Sjorett* 321 (1976-77)

Mustill, Sır Michael J. & S. C. Boyd, *The Law and Practice of Commercial Arbitration in England* (2nd ed. 1989)

Parker School of Foreign and Comparative Law, *International Commercial Arbitration and the Courts* (Dobbs Ferry 1990)

Recchia, G., *Enforcement of Foreign Arbitration Agreements and Awards in Italy and the United States: A Comparative Study* (Naples 1970)

Redfern, A. & M. Hunter, *Law and Practice of International Commercial Arbitration* (2nd ed. 1991)

Robert, J. & B. Morceau, *L'arbitrage — droit interne, droit international privé* (5th ed. Paris 1983)

Sharkey, J. & J. Dorter, *Commercial Arbitration* (Sydney 1986)

Tiewul, The Enforcement of Arbitration Agreements and Awards, 11 *U. Ghana L.J.* 143 (1974)

Tiewul & Tsegah, Arbitration and the Settlement of Commercial Disputes: A Selective Survey of African Practice, 24 *Int'l & Comp. L.Q.* 393 (1975)

van den Berg, A. J., *The New York Arbitration Convention of 1958* (Deventer 1981)

20.02 ENFORCEABILITY

Aden, M., *Internationale Handelsschiedsgerichtsbarkeit. Kommentar zu den Verfahrensordnungen* (Heidelberg 1988)

Agyemang, African Courts, the Settlement of Investment Disputes and the Enforcement of Awards, 33 *J. Afr. L.* 31 (1989)

Aksen, Arbitration under International Commercial Contracts. Current Issues and Practical Problems: Enforcement of Awards against Governments — The Libyan Awards, in *Essays on International Law* 104 (New Delhi 1981)

Alangoya, Die Vollstreckung ausländischer Schiedsprüche nach türkischem Recht, in *Festschrift für Karl Heinz Schwab* 1 (P. Gottwald & H. Prütting eds. 1990)

Alcántara Gonzales, Enforcement of Awards, in 2 *Fifth Int'l Congress of Maritime Arbitrators* (New York 1981)

Anton, Arbitration: International Aspects, 1986 *The Scots Law Times* 45 and 53

Arnold, Die Vollstreckung ausländischer Urteile und Schiedssprüche in Aethiopien, 1968 *AWD* 309 (1968)

Arroyo, Recognition and Enforcement of Foreign Arbitral Awards in Spanish Law, 6 *Bus. L.J.* 763 (1985)

Ayiter, Vollstreckbarkeit ausländischer Schiedssprüche in der Türkei, in *Konflikt und Ordnung, Festschrift für Murad Ferid* 15 (Munich 1978)

Bakshi, Arbitration Law: Foreign Awards, 3 *The Lawyers* 33 (No. 4, 1988)

Bakshi, Foreign Forum for Enforcing Awards, 1987(1) *Company L.J.* 16

Baptista & Latorre, Oservaçoes praticas sobre a homologaçao de sentencas e de laudos arbitrais estrangeiros no Brasil, 276 *Revista Forense* 311 (1981)

Barbosa Moreira, Improving the Procedures for the Enforcement and Recognition of Foreign Judgments and Arbitral Awards, in *Justice and Efficiency* 191 (W. Wedekind ed. 1989)

Bentil, Judicial Intervention and International Commercial Arbitration, 130 *Solicitors' J.* 191 (1986)

Bernardini, Questioni sull'interpretazione e l'esecuzione del lodo, in *Arbitrato nazionale e internazionale: interpretazione ed esecuzione del lodo* 27 (G. Carli ed. 1989)

Bernini, Esecuzione del lodo arbitrale, in *Arbitrato nazionale e internazionale: interpretazione ed esecuzione del lodo* 13 (G. Carli ed. 1989)

————, Il riconoscimento all'estero del lodo arbitrale irrituale, 45 *Riv. Trim. Dir. & Proc. Civ.* 357 (1991)

————, Observations Regarding Recognition and Enforcement of Foreign Arbitral Awards in Italy, in *A.I.A., Essays in Memoriam Eugenio Minoli* 39 (Turin 1974)

————, The Enforcement of Arbitration Awards, 47 *Arbitration* 99 (1981)

————, The Enforcement of Foreign Arbitral Awards by National Judiciaries: A Trial of the New York Convention's Ambit and Workability, in *The Art of Arbitration* 51 (J. Schultsz & A. van den Berg eds. 1982)

Bernini & van den Berg, The Enforcement of Arbitral Award against a State: The Problem of Immunity from Execution, in *Contemporary Problems in Int'l Arbitration* 359 (J.D.M. Lew ed. 1986)

Bertram-Nothnagel, Enforcement of Foreign Judgments and Arbitral Awards in West Germany, 17 *Va. J. Int'l L.* 385 (1977)

Bongco, The Enforcement of Foreign Arbitration Agreements and Awards in the Philippines, 21 *Arb. J.* 34 (1966)

Brierley, Quebec's New (1986) Arbitration Law, 13 *Can. Bus. L.J.* 58 (1987)

Briner, Die Anfechtung und Vollstreckung des Schiedsentscheides, in *Die Internationale Schiedsgerichtsbarkeit in der Schweiz* 99 (K.-H. Böckstiegel ed. 1989)

Broches, Awards Rendered Pursuant to the ICSID Convention: Binding Force, Finality, Recognition, Enforcement, Execution, 2 *ICSID Rev. - Foreign Investment L.J.* 287 (1987)

Brücher, Vollstreckung und Sicherung der Vollstreckung ausländischer Schiedssprüche, 13 *ADW* 337 (1967)

Bucher, A., *Die neue internationale Schiedsgerichtsbarkeit in der Schweiz* (Basel 1989)

————, *Le nouvel arbitrage international en Suisse. Théorie et pratique de droit* (Basel 1988)

Bucher, A. & P.-Y. Tschanz, *International Arbitration in Switzerland* (Basel 1989)

Butler, W., *Arbitration in the Soviet Union* (Dobbs Ferry 1989)

Capatina, Limites du droit de contrôle exercé par l'instance roumaine d'exéquatur en matière de regularité internationale des sentences arbitrales étrangères, 1973 *Revue Roumaine d'Etudes Internationales* 250 (No. 4)

Capatina & Zilberstein, La reconnaissance et l'exécution des décisions judiciares civiles et des sentences arbitrales étrangères dans le droit de la République Socialiste de Roumanie, 16 *Revue Roumaine des Sciences Sociales, Série de Sciences Juridiques* 285 (1972)

Carbonneau, Arbitral Adjudication: A Comparative Assessment of its Remedial and Substantive Status in Transnational Commerce, 19 *Tex. Int'l L.J.* 33 (1984)

Carli, G., ed., *Arbitrato nazionale e internazionale: interpretazione ed esecuzione del lodo* (Milan 1989)

Castel, Canada and International Arbitration, 36 *Arb. J.* 5 (1981)

Cheung, Enforcement of Foreign Arbitral Awards in the People's Republic of China, 34 *Am. J. Comp. L.* 295 (1985)

Chowdhuri, S.K.R. & H.K. Saharay, *Arbitration Law.* (2nd ed., Calcutta 1986)

Chrocziel & Westin, Die Vollstreckbarkeit ausländischer Urteile und Schiedsprüche, 87 *ZVR* 145 (1988)

Cohen, La reconnaissance et l'exécution au Canada des sentences arbitrales étrangères, 47 *Rev. Barreau* 435 (1987)

Costabel, Non-Domestic Arbitration Clauses, Stay of Proceedings and Recognition of Foreign Awards in Italy, 2 *Fifth Int'l Congress of Maritime Arbitrators* (New York 1981)

Craig, The Uses and Abuses of Appeal from International Arbitration Awards, in *Private Investors Abroad - Problems and Solutions in International Business in 1987* 14.1 (J. Moss ed. 1987)

————, Uses and Abuses of Appeal from Awards, 4 *Arb. Int'l* 174 (1988)

Cremades, Evolution récente du droit espagnol en matière d'arbitrage, 1988 *Rev. Arb.* 223

Cremades, B.M., *Panorámica Española del arbitraje comercial internacional* (Madrid 1975)

Cremades, B. M. & E. G. Cabiedes, *Litigating in Spain. Considerations for Foreign Practitioners, Including International Judicial Assistance, Enforcement of Foreign Judgments, Bankruptcy, Arbitration and Other Civil Proceedings in Spain* (Deventer 1989)

Crespi-Reghizzi & Hascher, La reconnaissance et l'exécution des jugements étrangers et des sentences arbitrales étrangères. Le nouveau droit soviétique de l'Ordonnance du 21 juin 1988, 118 *J. Droit Int'l (Clunet)* 90 (1991)

Damjanov, C., *Isplnyaemost na chuzhdestranni sdebni ta arbitrazhni reshenia* (Sofia 1977)

de Magalhaes, Execuçao de laudo arbitral, 599 *Rev. Trib.* 9 (Sept. 1985)

de Magalhaes, J. & L.O. Batista, *Arbitragem comercial* (Rio de Janeiro 1986)

Deshpande, Enforcement of Foreign Awards in India, U.K. and U.S.A., 4 *J. Int'l Arb.* 41 (No. 1, 1987)

Dilger, Schiedsgerichtsbarkeit und Volstreckung ausländischer Entscheidungen in den Golfstaaten, in *Vetragspraxis und Streiterledigung im Wirschaftverkehr mit arabischen Staaten* 101 (K.-H. Böckstiegel ed. 1981)

Dobratz, Schiedsklausel und Vollstreckung im Aussenhandel, 8 *AWD* 188 (1962)

Doi, International Commercial Arbitration in Japan, in *Liber Amicorum for Martin Domke* 65 (P. Sanders ed. 1967)

Domke, On the Enforcement Abroad of American Arbitration Awards, 17 *L. & Contemp. Probs.* 547 (1952)

Donnini, Su alcuni aspetti della riforma dell'arbitrato: in particolare la riconoscibilità del lodo all'estero, 25 *Rassegna dell'Arb.* 283 (1985)

Duintjer Tebbens, A Facelift for Dutch Arbitration Law, 34 *Neth. Int'l L. Rev.* 141 (1987)

Dunshee de Abranches, C.A., ed., *El arbitraje comercial en Iberoamérica* (Madrid 1982)

Ebb, Developing Views on What Constitutes a 'Foreign Arbitration Agreement' and a 'Foreign Award' under the New York Convention, 1 *Am. Rev. Int'l Arb.* 364 (1990)

Ebke & Parker, Foreign-Country Money Judgments and Arbitral Awards and the Restatement (Third) of the Foreign Relations Law of the United States: A Conventional Approach, 24 *Int'l Law.* 21 (1990)

El-Hakim, L'exécution des sentences arbitrales en Syrie, 1987 *Droit des Aff. Int'les/Int'l Bus. L.J.* 233

Esplugues Mota, Reflexiones en torno a una frustración: El Título IX de la nueva Ley española de Arbitraje relativo a la ejecución en España de los laudos arbitrales extranjeros, 5 *Rev. Corte Esp. Arb.* 143 (1988-89)

Eyzaguirre Echeverria & Siqueiros, Arbitration in Latin America, in *Arbitration in Settlement of International Commercial Disputes Involving the Far East and Arbitration in Combined Transportation* 81 (P. Sanders ed. 1989)

Ezejiofor, Enforcement of Arbitration Awards in Nigeria, 1981 *J. Bus. L.* 319 (1981)

Ferrante, About the Nature (National or A-National, Contractual or Jurisdictional) of ICC Awards Under the New York Convention, in *The Art of Arbitration* 129 (J. Schultsz & A. van den Berg eds. 1982)

Filip & Capatina, Les effets des sentences arbitrales étrangères en matière de rapports de commerce extérieur, conformément au droit de la République socialiste de Roumanie, 1967 *Revue Roumaine d'Etudes Internationales* 105

Forsyth, Enforcement of Arbitral Awards, Choice of Law in Contract, Characterization and a New Attitude to Private International Law, 104 *South Afr. L.J.* 4 (1987)

Foustoucos, La reconnaissance et l'exécution en Grèce des sentences arbitrales étrangères après la récente réforme du droit de l'arbitrage, 1974 *Rev. Arb.* 265

―――, Sentences arbitrales nationals et étrangères: exécution et voies de recours en Grèce, 1991 *Int'l Bus. L.J.* 285

Fragistas, L'exécution en Grèce des sentences arbitrales étrangères, 1957 *Rev. Arb.* 74

Gaja, Sul coordinamento fra le norme relative al riconoscimento delle sentenze arbitrali straniere, 7 *Rassegna dell'Arb.* 147 (1967)

Gelinas, L'exécution des sentences arbitrales internationales au Québec: commentaire, in *First International Commmercial Arbitration Conference: Proceedings* 305 (N. Antaki & A. Prujiner eds. 1986)

Ghanem, The Enforcement of Arbitral Awards and Foreign Judgments in the Yemen Arab Republic, 3 *Arab. L.Q.* 81 (1988)

Giardina, L'esecuzione delle sentenze CIRDI, 22 *Rassegna dell'Arb.* 69 (1982)

———, L'exécution des sentences du Centre international pour le règlement des différends relatifs aux investissements, 71 *Rev. Crit. Droit Int'l Privé* 273 (1982)

———, The International Center for Settlement of Investment Disputes between States and Nationals of Other States (ICSID), in *Essays on International Commercial Arbitration* 214 (P. Sarcevic ed. 1989)

Gilbert, Enforceability of Settlements of Foreign Investment Disputes, 17 *Va. J. Int'l L.* 361 (1977)

Gingerich, Indonesia to Enforce Foreign Arbitral Awards, 12 *East Asian Exec. Rep.* 9 (No. 6, 1990)

Ginsburgs, Execution of Foreign Arbitration Awards: The Heritage of Domestic Legislation, Bilateral Treaties, and Intra-COMECON Ententes, in *The Impact of Perestroika on Soviet Law* 457 (A.J. Schmidt ed. 1990)

———, Execution of Foreign Commercial Awards in Post-War Soviet Bilateral Treaty Practice, 9 *Can. Y.B. Int'l L.* 59 (1971)

———, Soviet International Trade Contracts and the Execution of Foreign Commercial Arbitral Awards, in *Contemporary Soviet Law. Essays in Honor of John N. Hazard* 195 (D. Barry, W. Butler & G. Ginsburgs eds. 1974)

Ginsburgs, G., *The Soviet Union and International Cooperation in Legal Matters. Part I: Recognition of Arbitral Agreements and Execution of Foreign Commercial Arbitral Awards* (Dordrecht 1988)

Glossner, International Commercial Arbitration — Some Practical Aspects, in *Liber Amicorum for Martin Domke* 95 (P. Sanders ed. 1967)

Goni, La nouvelle politique d'exécution des sentences arbitrales étrangères en Espagne, 35 *Droit Mar. Français* 55 (1983)

517

Gonzales Soria, J., *La intervención judicial en el arbitraje. Recursos jurisdiccionales y ejecución judicial del laudo arbitral* (Madrid 1988)

Graham, The Internationalization of Commercial Arbitration in Canada: A Preliminary Reaction, 13 *Can. Bus. L.J.* 1 (1987)

Hahn, Die Anerkennung und Vollstreckung von ICSID-Schiedssprüchen in Frankreich, 37 *RIW* 459 (1991)

Hariani, Enforcement of Foreign Arbitration Agreements and Awards in India, 7 *Indian J. Int'l L.* 31 (1967)

Harnik, Recognition and Enforcement of Foreign Arbitral Awards, 31 *Am. J. Comp. L.* 703 (1983)

Hascher, Actualité de l'arbitrage international en U.R.S.S., 1988 *Rev. Arb.* 237

Herrmann, The Role of the Courts under the UNCITRAL Model Law Script, in *Contemporary Problems in Int'l Arbitration* 164 (J.D.M. Lew ed. 1986)

Heuman, L., *Current Issues in Swedish Arbitration* (Deventer and Stockholm 1990)

Hintz, Recht und Praxis der Streiterledigung im Ost-West-Handel am Beispiel des Handels zwischen der UdSSR und der Bundesrepublik Deutschland, 32 *RIW* 506 (1986)

Hobér, Arbitration and the Swedish Courts, 1990 *Y.B. Swed. & Int'l Arb.* 53

————, Arbitration in Moscow, 3 *Arb. Int'l* 119 (1987)

Hornick, The Recognition and Enforcement of Foreign Judgments in Indonesia, 18 *Harv. Int'l L.J.* 97 (1977)

Horomides, The Enforcement of Foreign Arbitral Awards in Greece, 3 *Arb. Int'l* 240 (1987)

Hosoi, Matters of Comity and Enforcement of Foreign Judgments and Awards in Japan, 15 *Bull. Japan Shipping Exch.* 34 (1987)

————, The Role of Japanese and American Lawyers in Maritime Dispute Settlement: Foreign Judgments and Awards in Japan, 3 *Y.B. Mar. L.* 105 (1986-1987)

Huet, Les procédures de reconnaissance et d'exécution des jugements étrangers et de sentences arbitrales, en droit international privé français, 115 *J. Droit Int'l (Clunet)* 5 (1988)

Ibrahim, Enforcement of Foreign Arbitral Awards, 1981 *Rev. Egyptienne Droit Int'l* 1 (1981)

Illueca, La ejecución de las sentencias arbitrales extranjeras en Panamá, 11 *Anuario de Derecho* (Panama) 77 (1981)

Iwasaki, Drafting Arbitration Clauses Designating Tokyo As Arbitration Site, 11 *Bull. Japan Shipping Exch.* 1 (1985)

Jakubowski, The Recognition and Enforcement of Foreign Arbitral Awards in Poland, *Polish Y.B. Int'l L.* 65 (1975)

Jambholkar, Enforcement of Foreign Awards in India: A Critique of Judicial Practice, 12 *Indian J. Int'l L.* 109 (1972)

Jarvin, Enforcement of an Arbitration Award in Oman, 2 *J. Int. Arb.* 81 (No. 4, 1985)

———, The Enforcement of ICC Arbitral Award, 1988 *Int'l Bus. L.J.* 241

Jeantet, L'accueil des sentences étrangères or internationales dans l'ordre juridique français, 1981 *Rev. Arb.* 503

Jessel & Holst, Anerkennung und Vollstreckung ausländischer Entscheidungen sowie Rechtshilfe in Zivilsachen nach dem bulgarischen Recht, 24 *WGO, Monatshefte für Osteuropäisches Recht* 255 (1982)

Jillani, Recognition and Enforcement of Foreign Arbitral Awards in Pakistan, 37 *Int'l & Comp. L.Q.* 926 (1988)

Kakinuki, Dispute Resolution in Japan: Choosing the Right Alternative, 9 *East Asian Exec. Rep.* 7 (No. 11, 1987)

Kang Seok Jeon, Non-Judicial Dispute Resolution Procedures in the Republic of Korea with an Emphasis on Arbitration, 14 *Korean J. Comp. L.* 31 (1986)

Kerameus, Arbitrage international et ordre juridique hellénique, 1987 *Rev. Arb.* 35

————, Improving the Procedures for the Recognition and Enforcement of Foreign Judgments and Arbitral Awards, in *Justice and Efficiency* 226 (W. Wedekind ed. 1989)

Kerr, The Enforcement of a Taiwanese Arbitration Award, 6 *Arb. Int'l* 167 (1990)

Kheifets, Recognition and Enforcement of Foreign Court Judgements and Arbitral Awards in Maritime Disputes, 1985 *Soviet Y.B. Mar. L.* 87

Klein, A propos de l'exécution en Suisse des sentences arbitrales étrangères, in *Festgabe zum Schweizerischen Juristentag* 157 (Basel 1985)

Kono & Trunk, Anerkennung und Vollstreckung ausländischer Urteile in Japan, 102 *ZZP* 319 (1989)

Koral, L'action en exécution dans l'arbitrage international et nouveau projet de loi turc sur le droit international de procédure civile, 28 *Annales de la Faculté de Droit d'Istanbul* 3 (1981)

————, L'exécution des sentences arbitrales étrangères en Turquie. A propos des progrès jurisprudentiels récents, 1989 *Rev. Arb.* 467

Krings, L'exécution des sentences arbitrales, 53 *Rev. Droit Int'l & Droit Comp.* 181 (1976)

Krüger, Neues internationales Privatrecht in der Turkei, 23 *ZRV* 169 (1982)

————, Probleme des saudi-arabischen internationalen Vertrags- und Schiedsrecht, in *Vertragspraxis und Streiterledigung im Wirtschaftsverkehr mit arabischen Staaten* 61 (K.-H. Böckstiegel ed. 1981)

Kühn, Arbitrability of Antitrust Disputes in the Federal Republic of Germany, 3 *Arb. Int'l* 226 (1987)

————, Die Anfechtung und Vollstreckung des Schiedsentscheides. Eine kritische Würdigung der neuen schweizerischen Regelung unter Berücksichtigung ihrer Auswirkungen im deutschen Vollstreckbarerklärungsverfahren, in *Die Internationale Schiedsgerichtsbarkeit in der Schweiz* 163 (K.-H. Böckstiegel ed. 1989)

Lake & Dana, Judicial Review of Awards of the Iran-United States Claims Tribunal: Are the Tribunal's Awards Dutch?, 16 *L. & Pol'y Int'l Bus.* 755 (1984)

Lane & Morton, Enforcement of a Foreign Award in Oman, 2 *Arb. Int'l* 75 (No. 1, Jan 1986); 1 *Int'l Arb. Report* 28 (1986)

Larsen, Enforcement of Foreign Judgments in Latin America: Trends and Individual Differences, 17 *Tex. Int'l L.J.* 213 (1982)

Laschet, Zur Anerkennung ausländischer Zwischenschiedssprüche, 4 *IPRax* 72 (1984)

Lécuyer-Thieffry, C. & P. Thieffry, *Le règlement des litiges civils et commerciaux avec les Etats-Unis* (Paris 1986)

Lebedev, S., ed., *Handbook on Foreign Trade Arbitration in the CMEA Member Countries* (Moscow 1983)

León Gomez, Ejecución de la sentencia arbitral en Honduras, in *El Arbitraje en el Derecho Latinoamericano y Español* 349 (L. Perrot & U. Montoya Alberti eds. 1989)

Lewis, What Goes Around Comes Around: Can Iran Enforce Awards of the Iran-U.S. Claims Tribunal in the United States? 26 *Colum. J. Transnat'l L.* 515 (1988)

Lorenzen, Commercial Arbitration — Enforcement of Foreign Awards, 45 *Yale L.J.* 39 (1935)

Lucchesi, Zur Frage der Anerkennung und Vollstreckung des 'lodo irrituale' (=formfreien Schiedsspruches) ausserhalb Italiens, 24 *ZRV* 1 (1983)

McClendon, Enforcement of Foreign Arbitral Awards in the United States, 4 *Nw. J. Int'l L. & Bus.* 58 (1982)

McDermott, A Survey of Methods for the Enforcement of Foreign Judgments and Foreign Arbitral Awards in the Asia-Pacific Region, 12 *Loy. L.A. Int'l & Comp. L.J.* 114 (1989)

Majoros, Exécution de décisions étrangères et procédure d'exéquatur en Europe de l'Est: Tour d'horizon avec des références de droit comparé, in *Le Juriste Suisse Face au Droit et aux Jugements Etrangers: Ouverture ou Repli?* 135 (F. Knoepfler ed. 1988)

Melis, East-West Arbitration, in *ICC, Hommage à Fréderic Eisemann* 97 (1978)

———, Enforcement of Arbitral Awards in Eastern Europe, in *Contemporary Problems in International Arbitration* 332 (J.D.M. Lew ed. 1986)

———, Enforcement of Foreign Awards in European Member-Countries of the Council for Mutual Economic Assistance, 2 *Arbitration Int'l* 33 (No. 1, Jan. 1986)

Merchant & Merchant, The Law Relating to Recognition and Enforcement of Foreign Arbitral Agreements and Awards in the United States of America and India, in *ICCA, Fifth Int'l Arb. Congress: Proceedings* C Im 1-10 (1975)

Mezger, Beschränkung des Geltungbereich von Par. 1044 ZPO durch internationale Übereinkommen, 17 *AWD* 322 (1971)

———, Die Anerkennung jugoslawischer und anderer osteuropäischer Schiedssprüche in der Bundesrepublik, 15 *NJW* 278 (1962)

———, Vollstreckung ausländischer Schiedssprüche, 16 *AWD* 258 (1970)

Minoli, L'esecuzione delle sentenze arbitrali straniere in Italia, 12 *Rassegna dell'Arb.* 66 (1972)

Montoya Alberti, El arbitraje en los contratos de prestamo internacionales, in *El Arbitraje en el Derecho Latinoamericano y Español* 481 (L. Perret & U. Montoya Alberti eds. 1989)

Mooney, Interim Awards — Their Usage and Enforceability in the United States, in 2 *Fifth Int'l Congress of Maritime Arbitrators* (New York 1981)

Mordiglia, Enforcement of Foreign Arbitration Awards in Italy, in 2 *Fifth Int'l Congress of Maritime Arbitrators* (New York 1981)

Mosk, Enforcement of International Arbitral Awards, 2 *Calif. Int'l Practitioner* 9 (1990-91)

Motulsky, L'exequatur des sentences étrangères non motivée, 1967 *Rev. Arb.* 103

Mustill, Sir Michael J. & S. C. Boyd, *The Law and Practice of Commercial Arbitration in England* (2nd ed. 1989)

Nariman, Foreign Arbitral Awards in India: Problems, Pitfalls, and Progress, 6 *J. Int'l Arb.* 25 (No. 1, 1989)

———, Problems of Public Policy — the Indian Perspective, in *Comparative Arbitration Practice and Public Policy in Arbitration* 336 (P. Sanders ed. 1987)

Nattier, International Commercial Arbitration in Latin America: Enforcement of Arbitral Agreements and Awards, 21 *Tex. Int'l L. J.* 397 (1986)

Nerz, Vollstreckbarkeit ausländischer Schiedssprüche im Königreich Saudi-Arabien, 29 *RIW* 811 (1983)

Nestor & Capatina, Applicabilité des réglementations du droit commun roumain pour l'autorisation de l'exécution des sentences arbitrales provenant d'un autre pays socialiste membre du CAEM, [1973] 4 *Revue Roumaine d'Etudes Internationales* 246

Nobili, I costi fiscali dell'arbitrato in Italia: sviluppi recenti, 26 *Rassegna dell'Arb.* 13 (1986)

Nomura, Some Aspects of the Use of Commercial Arbitration by Japanese Corporations, 33 *Osaka Univ. L. Rev.* 47 (March 1986); also in *East and West: Legal Philosophies in Japan* 50 (M. Yasaki ed. 1987)

Nuber, J., *Die objektive Schiedsfähigkeit im Zusammenhang mit der Gültigkeit der Schiedsvereinbarung (anwendbares Recht) und mit der Vollstreckung* (ordre public), (Zurich 1986)

Note, Enforcing Foreign Judgments and Arbitration Awards, 5 *Int'l Fin. L. Rev.* 26 (No. 7, 1986)

————, Enforcing International Commercial Arbitration Agreements and Awards Not Subject to the New York Convention, 23 *Va. J. Int'l L.* 75 (1982)

Orban, The Challenge to the Enforcement of Socialist Arbitral Awards, 17 *Va. J. Int'l L.* 375 (1977)

Ozbakan, La reconnaissance et l'exécution des jugements étrangers en Turquie, 70 *SJZ* 353 (1983)

Pacific Rim Advisory Council, *Pacific Rim: Commercial Arbitration Procedures* (San Diego, CA 1985)

Park & Paulsson, Arbitrage commercial et contrats internationaux, 45 *Rev. Barreau* 215 (1985)

Parker School of Foreign and Comparative Law, *International Commercial Arbitration and the Courts* (Dobbs Ferry 1990)

Patchett, K.W., *Recognition of Commercial Judgments and Awards in the Commonwealth* (London 1984)

Paterson, International Commercial Arbitration Act: An Overview, in *UNCITRAL Arbitration Model in Canada* 113 (R. Paterson & B. Thompson eds. 1987)

Paulsson, The Extent of Independence of International Arbitration from the Law of the Situs, in *Contemporary Problems in Int'l Arbitration* 141 (J.D.M. Lew ed. 1986)

Pessoa Vaz & Alvaro Dias, La reconnaissance et l'exécution des jugements étrangers judiciaires et arbitraux en matière civile et commerciale au Portugal, 33-34 *Documentaçao e Direito Comparado* 513 (1988)

Peyre, Le juge de l'exéquatur: fantôme ou réalité? 1985 *Rev. Arb.* 231

Pisar, S., *Coexistence & Commerce*, Chapters 20-24 (New York 1970)

Poudret, Challenge and Enforcement of Arbitral Awards in Switzerland, 4 *Arb. Int'l* 278 (1988)

Prujiner, L'exécution des sentences arbitrales internationales au Québec, in *First International Commercial Arbitration Conference: Proceedings* 289 (N. Antaki & A. Prujiner eds. 1986)

Pryles, International Dispute Resolution and Litigation in Australia, 16 *Int'l Bus. Law.* 454 (1988)

————, Legal Issues Concerning International Arbitrations, 64 *Austl. L.J.* 470 (1990)

Pryles, M. & K. Iwasaki, *Dispute Resolution in Australia-Japan Transactions* (Sydney 1983)

Punzi, L'arbitrato di fronte alla riforma generale ed alle riforme parziali del processo civile, 26 *Rassegna dell'Arb.* 23 (1986)

Quilling, The Recognition and Enforcement of Foreign Country Judgments and Arbitral Awards: A North-South Perspective, 11 *Ga. J. Int'l & Comp. L.* 635 (1981)

Raeschke-Kessler, Neuere Entwicklungen im Bereich der Internationalen Schiedsgerichtsbarkeit, 41 *NJW* 3041 (1988)

Ranouil, Exécution: mérites comparés de la sentence arbitrale et de la décision de justice, 14 *Droit et Pratique du Com. Int'l* 427 (1988)

Razumov, Public Policy as a Condition for Recognition and Enforcement of Foreign Court Judgments and Arbitral Awards in the USSR, in *Comparative Arbitration Practice and Public Policy in Arbitration* 348 (P. Sanders ed. 1987)

Recchia, Enforcement of American Arbitration Awards in Italy, 2 *N.Y.U.J. Int'l L. & Pol.* 219 (1969)

Recchia, G., *Enforcement of Foreign Arbitration Agreements and Awards in Italy and the United States: A Comparative Study* (Naples 1970)

Rechsteiner, Die neuere brasilianische Rechtssprechung zur Anerkennung ausländischer Schiedsprüche, 26 *ZRV* 100 (1985)

Redfern, Enforcement of International Arbitral Awards and Settlement Agreements, 54 *Arbitration* 124 (1988)

Remiro Brotons, La reconnaissance et l'exécution des sentences arbitrales étrangères, 184 *Recueil des Cours* 169 (1984-I)

Remiro Brotons, A., *Ejecución de sentencias arbitrales extranjeras. Los convenios internacionales y su aplicación en España* (Madrid 1980)

Ricci, Problemi sulla recezione all'estero dei lodi rituali italiani, 41 *Riv. Dir. Proc.* 117 (1986)

Richard, Enforcement of Foreign Arbitral Awards under the United Nations Convention of 1958: A Survey of Recent Federal Case Law, 11 *Md. J. Int'l L. & Trade* 13 (1987)

Rosenn, Enforcement of Foreign Arbitral Awards in Brazil, 28 *Am. J. Comp. L.* 498 (1980)

Rothstein, Recognizing and Enforcing Arbitral Agreements and Awards Against Foreign States: The Mathias Amendments to the Foreign Sovereign Immunities Act and Title 9, 1 *Emory J. Int'l Disp. Res.* 101 (1986)

Rubino-Sammartano, The Keban Arbitration (a report on the judgment of the Supreme Court of Turkey), 46 *Arbitration* 241 (1980)

Rubino-Sammartano, M., *International Arbitration Law* (Deventer 1990)

Sajko, The New York Arbitration Convention of 1958 from the Yugoslav Point of View: Selected Issues, in *Essays on International Commercial Arbitration* 199 (P. Sarcevic ed. 1989)

Saleh, The Recognition and Enforcement of Foreign Arbitral Awards in the States of the Arab Middle East, in *Contemporary Problems in International Arbitration* 340 (J.D.M. Lew ed. 1986)

Samtleben, Arbitragem comercial no direito internacional privado Brazileiro, in *Estudos em Homenagem ao Prof. Doutor A. Ferrer-Correia* 691 (Coimbra 1986)

Samuel, The Recognition and Enforcement of Foreign Judgments and Arbitral Awards in England with a Comparative Look at the United States of America, in *Le Juriste Suisse Face au Droit et aux Jugements Etrangers: Ouverture ou Repli?* 105 (F. Knoepfler ed. 1988)

Sanders, Arbitration (Including Recognition and Enforcement of Awards), 27 *Neth. Int'l L. Rev.* 392 (1980)

Sandrock, Arbitration between U.S. and West German Companies: An Example of Effective Dispute Resolution in International Business Transactions, 9 *U. Pa. J. Int'l Bus. L.* 27 (1987)

Sandrock & Hentzen, Enforcing Foreign Arbitral Awards in the Federal Republic of Germany: The Example of a United States Award, 2 *Transnat'l Law.* 49 (1989)

Sarcevic, The Setting Aside and Enforcement of Arbitral Awards under the UNCITRAL Model law, in *Essays on International Commercial Arbitration* 177 (P. Sarcevic ed. 1989)

Sareika, The Enforcement of Commercial Arbitral Awards under Canadian Law, 8 *Int'l Bus. Law.* 173 (1980)

Schaafsma, Recognition and Enforcement of Foreign Country Judgments and Arbitral Awards in the Netherlands, in *Enforcement of Foreign Country Judgments* (Commercial Law & Practice Course Handbook Series, No.104) 151 (New York: Practicing Law Institute 1974)

Schlesinger, L'esecuzione del lodo arbitrale rituale, 43 *Riv. Dir. Proc.* 751 (1988); also in *Arbitrato nazionale e internazionale: interpretazione ed esecuzione del lodo* 55 (G. Carli ed. 1989)

Schlosser, Die Durchsetzung von Schiedssprüchen und ausländischen Urteilen im Urkundenprozess und mittels eines inländischen Arrests, in *Festschrift für Karl Heinz Schwab* 435 (P. Gottwald & H. Prütting eds. 1990)

————, Verfahrensintegrität und Anerkennung von Schiedsprüchen im deutsch-amerikanischen Verhältnis, 31 *NJW* 455 (1978)

Schmitthoff, Arbitration and EEC Law, 24 *Common Mkt. L. Rev.* 143 (1987)

Schrameyer, Die Anerkennung ausländischer Entscheidungen in Mexico, 1966 *AWD* 253

Schütze, Anerkennung und Vollstreckbarerklärung von Zivilurteilen und Schiedssprüchen im deutsch-saudiarabischen Verhältnis, 30 *RIW* 261 (1984)

———, Die Anerkennung und Vollstreckbarerklärung ausländischer Schiedssprüche in der Volksrepublik China, 8 *IPRax* 311 (1988)

———, Die Anerkennung und Vollstreckbarerklärung ausländischer Zivilurteile und Schiedssprüche in Bhutan, *Juristische Rundschau* 498 (1981)

———, Die Anerkennung und Vollstreckbarerklärung ausländischer Zivilurteile und Schiedssprüche in Liberia, 33 *RIW* 598 (1987)

———, Die Anerkennung und Vollstreckbarerklärung von Zivilurteilen und Schiedssprüchen im deutsch-chinesischen Rechtsverkehr, 32 *RIW* 269 (1986)

Schütze, R., D. Tscherning & W. Wais, *Handbuch des Schiedsverfahrens. Praxis der deutschen und internationalen Schiedsgerichtsbarkeit* (2nd ed. Berlin 1990)

Schurmann, Plan eines zentralen Gerichtshofs für die Anerkennung von Schiedssprüchen, 33 *RIW* 415 (1987)

Sedlacek, V., *Arbitration in Czechoslovak Foreign Trade* (Prague 1982)

Seidl-Hohenveldern, Austrian Public Policy and the Enforcement of Foreign Arbitral Awards, 4 *Arb. Int'l* 322 (1988)

Sharkey, J. & J. Dorter, *Commercial Arbitration* (Sydney 1986)

Shenton, The Enforcement of International Commercial Arbitral Awards in English Courts, 8 *Int'l Bus. Law.* 35 (1980)

Shroff, Enforcement in India of Foreign Commercial Awards, 21 *J. Ind. L. Inst.* 31 (1979)

Siqueiros, Reconocimiento y ejecución de laudos extranjeros en la República Mexicana, in *El Arbitraje Comercial Internacional* 285 (Mexico 1983)

———, Resolution of Commercial Disputes: Enforcement of Foreign Arbitral Awards in Mexico, in *Doing Business in Mexico* 18-1 (S. Lefler ed. 1980)

Solveni, Dichiarazione di efficacia in Italia di lodi arbitrali inglesi convertiti in sentenze della High Court of Justice ai sensi della Sez. 26 dell'Arbitration Act, 1950, 88 *Dir. Mar.* 451 (1986)

Sornarajah, The Enforcement of Foreign Arbitral Awards in Singapore, 1988 *Malayan L.J.* lxxxvi

Stevens, Spunti in tema di esecuzione e impugnazione del lodo, in *Arbitrato nazionale e internazionale: interpretazione ed esecuzione del lodo* 45 (G. Carli ed. 1989)

Stojkovic, Anerkennung und Vollstreckung ausländischer Schiedssprüche in Jugoslawien, 30 *Rabels Z.* 685 (1966)

Storme, M. & B. Demeulenaere, *International Commercial Arbitration in Belgium: A Handbook* (Deventer 1989)

Strohbach, H., *Die Anerkennung und Vollstreckung schiedsgerichtlicher Entscheidungen in der Deutschen Demokratischen Republik* (Berlin 1977)

Stumpf, Ost-West-Schiedsgerichtsbarkeit: Schiedsgerichte mit Sitz in dritten Ländern, 33 *RIW* 821 (1987)

Suwit Suwan, International Commercial Arbitration and Enforcement of Foreign Judgements, 8 *Law J. of Marut Bunnag Int'l L.* Office 7 (No. 2, 1981)

Tanaka, Enforcement of American Awards in Japan, 10 *Arb. J.* 88 (1955)

Thieffry, L'exécution des sentences arbitrales, 1983 *Rev. Arb.* 423

Thieffry, P. & C. Lecuyer-Thieffry, *Le règlement des litiges civils et commerciaux avec les Etats-Unis* (Paris 1986)

Timagenis, Admissibility and Enforcement of Foreign Court Decisions and Arbitration Awards in Greece, 1984 *Lloyd's Mar. & Com. L.Q.* 488

Timmermans, The USSR Maritime Arbitration Commission, 1987 *Lloyd's Mar. & Com. L.Q.* 350 and 468

Troller, Arbitration and Enforcement of Arbitration Awards in Arab Countries, 2 *Int'l Contr.* 397 (1981)

Tueller, Problems of Arbitration of International Contract Disputes and Recognition and Enforcement of Foreign Judgments in the Federal Republic of Germany: A Recent Decision of the Bundesgerichtshof, 17 *Stan. J. Int'l L.* 207 (1981)

Ungar, The Enforcement of Arbitral Awards Under UNCITRAL's Model Law on International Commercial Arbitration, 25 *Colum. J. Transnat'l L.* 717 (1987)

Ünal, The New York Convention and the Recognition and Enforcement of Foreign Arbitral Awards in Turkish Law, 7 *J. Int'l Arb.* 55 (No. 4, 1990)

van den Berg, A. J., *The New York Arbitration Convention of 1958* (Deventer 1981)

van Houtte, International Arbitration and National Adjudication, in 4 *Hague-Zagreb Essays on the Law of International Trade* 321 (C. Voskuil & J. Wade eds. 1981)

Varady, Les développements nouveaux concernant la reconnaissance et l'exécution des sentences arbitrales étrangères en Yougoslavie, 1983 *Rev. Arb.* 163

Vasquez Martinez, La ejecución de sentencias y laudos extranjeros en el derecho guatelmalteco, 2 *Boletín de la Asociación de Abogados de Guatemala* 3 (March - April 1960)

Velinov, Priznavane i izpulnenie na chuzdestrannite resheniia spored dogovorite za pravna pomosht skliucheni ot NRB, 32 *Sotsialistichesko Pravo* 26 (August 1983)

Vigoriti, Recent Developments in the Recognition and Execution of Foreign Judgments and Arbitral Awards in Italy, 6 *Civil Just. Q.* 248 (1987)

Villela, Reconhecimento de decisoes arbitrais estrangeiras, 19 *Revista de Informaçao Legislativa* 53 (No. 75, July-Sept. 1982)

von Mehren, The Enforcement of Arbitral Awards under Conventions and United States Law, 9 *Yale J. World Pub. Ord.* 343 (1983)

von Rhein, Zur Anerkennung und Vollstreckung von schweizerischen Gerichtsentscheidungen, Schiedssprüchen und Vergleichen in der Bundesrepublik Deutschland, 82 *SJZ* 141 (1986)

Walder-Bohner, H. U., *Die Einführung in das internationale Zivilprozessrecht der Schweiz: Anerkennung und Vollstreckung ausländischer Entscheidungen, Zuständigkeit der schweizerischen Gerichte, Schiedsgerichtsbarkeit und weitere Fragen nach IPRG und Staatsverträgen* (Zurich 1989)

Weeraratna, The Enforcement of Arbitral Awards in Sri Lanka, [1988] 2 *Bar Association Law Journal* 4

Westin, Enforcing Foreign Commercial Judgments and Arbitral Awards in the United States, West Germany, and England, 19 *L. & Pol'y Int'l Bus.* 325 (1987)

Wysocka, B., *Uznawanie i wykonywanie zagranicznych orzeczen arbitrazowych w Polsce* (Warsaw 1987)

Zdravkovic, Certains cas de la jurisprudence yougoslave et étrangère sur l'exécution des sentences arbitrales étrangères, in *ICCA, Fifth Int'l Arb. Congress: Proceedings* C Izi 1-16 (1975)

Zheng, Private International Law in the People's Republic of China: Principles and Procedures, 22 *Tex. Int'l L.J.* 231 (1987)

Zilberstein, Die Zwangsvollstreckung von ausländischen gerichtlichen und schiedsgerichtlichen Entscheidungen in Rumänien, 40 *Rabels Z.* 56 (1976)

20.03 APPLICABLE LAW

Aksen, American Arbitration Accession Arrives in the Age of Aquarius: United States Implements United Nations Convention on the Recognition and Enforcement of Foreign Arbitral Awards, 3 *Sw. U. L. Rev.* 1 (1971); also in *A.A.A., New Strategies for Peaceful Resolution of Int'l Business Disputes* 37 (1971)

————, The Application of the New York Convention by the United States, 4 *Y.B. Com. Arb.* 341 (1979)

Aksen & Dorman, Application of the New York Convention by United States Courts: A Twenty Year Review, 2 *Am. Rev. Int'l Arb.* 65 (1991)

Bakshi, Foreign Forum for Enforcing Awards, 1987(1) *Company L.J.* 16

Barclay, Enforcement of Arbitration Awards, 41 *Arbitration* 194 (1974)

Baxi, Goodbye to Unification? The Indian Supreme Court and the United Nations Arbitration Convention, 15 *J. Ind. L. Inst.* 353 (1973)

Berglin, The Application in United States Courts of the Public Policy Provisions of the Convention on the Recognition and Enforcement of Foreign Arbitral Awards, 4 *Dick. J. Int'l L.* 167 (1986)

Bernini, The Enforcement of Arbitration Awards, 47 *Arbitration* 99 (1981)

————, The Enforcement of Foreign Arbitral Awards by National Judiciaries: A Trial of the New York Convention's Ambit and Workability, in *The Art of Arbitration* 51 (J. Schultsz & A. van den Berg eds. 1982)

Block, Le droit belge de l'arbitrage et la Convention de New York du 10 juin 1958, in *L'Arbitrage* 129 (L. Matray & G. de Leval eds. 1989)

Bombau & Zivy, Influence of the 1958 New York Convention on Recognition and Enforcement of Foreign Arbitral Awards in Argentina, 1990 *Int'l Bus. L.J.* 815

Booysen, H., *The Application of the New York Convention to Arbitration to which a State Is a Party* (Saarbrücken 1987)

Brown, Enforcement of Foreign Arbitral Awards — the United Nations Convention on the Recognition and Enforcement of Foreign Arbitral Awards, 14 *Ga. J. Int'l & Comp. L.* 217 (1984)

Bucher, A., *Die neue internationale Schiedsgerichtsbarkeit in der Schweiz* (Basel 1989)

————, *Le nouvel arbitrage international en Suisse. Théorie et pratique de droit* (Basel 1988)

Bucher, A. & P.-Y. Tschanz, *International Arbitration in Switzerland* (Basel 1989)

Bülow, La convention des parties relative à la procedure d'arbitrage visée a l'Art. V, par.1, litt. d) de la Convention de New York, in *A.I.A., Essays in Memoriam Eugenio Minoli* 81 (Turin 1974)

Carpi, L'esecutorietà della sentenza arbitrale secondo la Convenzione di New York, 43 *Riv. Dir. Proc.* 386 (1988); also in *Arbitrato nazionale e internazionale: interpretazione es esecuzione del lodo* 31 (G. Carli ed. 1989)

Cole, Public Policy Exception to the New York Convention on the Recognition and Enforcement of Arbitral Awards, 1 *Ohio St. J. Disp. Res.* 365 (1986)

Cremades, La reconnaissance en Espagne des décisions judiciaires et des actes authentiques français, 1975 *Rev. Crit. Droit Int'l Privé* 355 and 595

————, The Enforcement of British Arbitral Awards in Spain, 45 *Arbitration* 30 and 97 (1979)

de Bruin, De 'affaire C,' 1989 *Tijdschrift voor Arbitrage* 1

Deshpande, Jurisdiction over 'Foreign' and 'Domestic' Awards in the New York Convention 1958, 7 *Arb. Int'l* 123 (1991)

Domke, The United States Implementation of the United Nations Arbitral Convention, 19 *Am. J. Comp. L.* 575 (1971)

Ebb, At the End of a Long Trail: How the Bombay High Court Strengthened International Arbitration in India, 44 *Arb. J.* 28 (No. 2, 1989)

Evans & Ellis, International Commercial Arbitration: A Comparison of Legal Regimes, 8 *Tex. Int'l L.J.* 17 (1973)

Fois, Primi orientamenti giurisprudenziali in Italia circa l'interpretazione della Convenzione di New York sull'Arbitrato, 12 *Riv. Dir. Int'le Priv. & Proc.* 299 (1976)

Gaja, G., ed., *The New York Convention* (Dobbs Ferry, NY 1979)

Giardina, Court Decisions in Italy Interpreting and Implementing the New York Convention, 7 *J. Int'l Arb.* 77 (No. 2, 1990)

————, L'applicazione in Italia della Convenzione di New York sull'Arbitrato, 7 *Riv. Dir. Int'le Priv. & Proc.* 268 (1971)

Glossner, Das Übereinkommen von New York über die Anerkennung und Vollstreckung ausländischer Schiedsprüche von 1958 - ein Fazit, in *Recht über See. Festschrift für Wilhelm Stödter* 47 (H. Ipsen ed. 1979)

Gonzalez Campos, El Convenio entre España y Francia de 28 de mayo de 1969 sobre reconocimiento y ejecución de decisiones extranjeras, in 2 *Estudios de Derecho internacional público y privado. Homenaje al Profesor Sela* 993 (1970)

Heller, Zur Vollstreckung eines jugoslawischen Schiedsspruches in Österreich, 9 *IPRax* 315 (1989)

Hornick, Indonesia — Foreign Arbitral Awards Not Enforceable, 7 *East Asian Exec. Rep.* 11 (No. 11, 1985)

Horomides, The Enforcement of Foreign Arbitral Awards in Greece, 3 *Arb. Int'l* 240 (1987)

Hosoi, Practical Aspects of the Recognition and Enforcement in Japan of Foreign Arbitration Awards Under the 1958 New York Convention, 10 *Bull. Japan Shipping Exch.* 31 (No. 10, March 1984)

Huet, Les procédures de reconnaissance et d'exécution des jugements étrangers et de sentences arbitrales, en droit international privé français, 115 *J. Droit Int'l (Clunet)* 5 (1988)

Iwasaki, Application of New York Convention by Japanese Courts, 10 *Bull. Japan Shipping Exch.* 1 (1984)

Kennedy, Enforcing International Commercial Agreements and Awards Not Subject to the New York Convention, 23 *Va. J. Int'l L.* 75 (1982)

Krings, L'exécution des sentences arbitrales, 53 *Rev. Droit Int'l & Droit Comp.* 181 (1976)

Leahy & Orentlicher, Enforcement of Arbitral Awards Issued by the Additional Facility of the International Centre for Settlement of Investment Disputes (ICSID), 2 *J. Int'l Arb.* 15 (No. 3, 1985)

533

Love, Arbitration: the Convention on the Recognition and Enforcement of Foreign Arbitral Awards, as Implemented by U.S. Law, Applies to Arbitration Awards Involving Wholly Foreign Interests and Rendered in the United States, 15 *J.Mar. L. & Com.* 134 (1984)

Lucchesi, Zur Frage der Anerkennung und Vollstreckung des 'lodo irrituale' (=formfreien Schiedsspruches) ausserhalb Italiens, 24 *ZRV* 1 (1983)

Lüer, German Court Decisions Interpreting and Implementing the New York Convention, 7 *J. Int'l Arb.* 127 (No. 1, 1990)

McClendon, Enforcement of Foreign Arbitral Awards in the United States, 4 *Nw. J. Int'l L. & Bus.* 58 (1982)

McLaughlin & Genevro, Enforcement of Arbitral Awards Under the New York Convention — Practice in U.S.Courts, 3 *Int'l Tax & Bus. Law.* 249 (1986)

McMahon, Implementation of U.N. Convention on Foreign Arbitral Awards in the U.S., in *A.A.A., New Strategies for Peaceful Resolution of Int'l Business Disputes* 75 (1971); also in 2 *J. Mar. L. & Com.* 735 (1971)

Martinez, Recognition and Enforcement on International Arbitral Awards under the United Nations Convention of 1958: The 'Refusal' Provisions, 24 *Int'l Law.* 487 (1990)

Melis, Enforcement of Arbitral Awards in Eastern Europe, in *Contemporary Problems in International Arbitration* 332 (J.D.M. Lew ed. 1986)

Mendes & Binavince, Canada and the New York Convention on Foreign Arbitral Awards, 1984 *Can. Arb. J.* 2 (Spring 1984)

Mendes, Canada: A New Forum to Develop the Cultural Psychology of International Commercial Arbitration, 3 *J. Int'l Arb.* 71 (No. 3, 1986)

Mezger, Beschränkung des Geltungbereich von Par. 1044 ZPO durch internationale Übereinkommen, 17 *AWD* 322 (1971)

Mirabelli, The Application of the New York Convention by the Italian Courts, 4 *Y.B. Com. Arb.* 362 (1979)

Moussali, Arbitrage International: Syrie, 1991 *Int'l Bus. L.J.* 401

Nariman, Foreign Arbitral Awards in India: Problems, Pitfalls, and Progress, 6 *J. Int'l Arb.* 25 (No. 1, 1989)

Nicotina, Oggetto e limiti dell'accertamento giudiciale nel giudicio do delibazione di lodo estero secondo la Convenzione di New York, 25 *Rassegna dell'Arb.* 129 (1985)

Note, Application of the Convention on the Recognition and Enforcement of Foreign Arbitral Awards: Mitsubishi Motor Corp. v. Soler Chrysler-Plymouth, Inc., 8 *Fordham Int'l L.J.* 194 (1984)

————, Enforcement of Foreign Arbitral Awards under the United Nations Convention of 1958: A Survey of Recent Federal Case Law. Notes and Comments, 11 *Md. J. Int'l L. & Trade* 13 (1987)

————, Enforcing International Commercial Arbitration Agreements and Awards Not Subject to the New York Convention, 23 *Va. J. Int'l L.* 75 (1982)

————, International Commercial Arbitration: Domestic Recognition and Enforcement of the Inter-American Convention on International Commercial Arbitration, 10 *Syracuse J. Int'l L. & Com.* 169 (1983)

————, The Validity of the Foreign Sovereign Immunity Defense in Suits Under the Convention on the Recognition and Enforcement of Foreign Arbitral Awards, 7 *Fordham Int'l L. J.* 321 (1983-84)

Oppetit, Le refus d'exécution d'une sentence arbitrale étrangère dans le cadre de la Convention de New York, 1971 *Rev. Arb.* 97

Palmer, Mitsubishi: the Erosion of the New York Convention and International Arbitration, 1984 *Wis. Int'l L.J.* 151 (Symposium)

Parker School of Foreign and Comparative Law, *International Commercial Arbitration and the Courts* (Dobbs Ferry 1990)

Patchett, K.W., *Recognition of Commercial Judgments and Awards in the Commonwealth* (London 1984)

Paulsson, The Contribution of English and American Legislation, in *Euro-Arab Arbitration* III 104 (F. Kemicha ed. 1991)

Poudret, Challenge and Enforcement of Arbitral Awards in Switzerland, 4 *Arb. Int'l* 278 (1988)

Quigley, Convention on Foreign Arbitral Awards, 58 *A.B.A. J.* 821 (1972)

Rached, S., *At-Takhim fi Al-llakat Ad-Dawliyat Al-Khassat* [Arbitration in Private International Law Relations], Vol. 1 [Arbitration Convention], (Cairo 1984)

Raeschke-Kessler & Bühler, *Aufsicht über den Schiedsrichter durch den ICC-Schiedsgerichtshof (Paris) und rechtliches Gehör der Parteien*, 8 *ZIP* 1157 (1987)

Ramos Mendez, *First Applications by the Spanish Supreme Court of the New York Convention of June 10, 1958 to the Exequatur of Foreign Arbitral Awards*, 10 *Int'l Trade L. & Prac.* 95 (1984)

Recchia, *Nuove prospettive dell'arbitrato commerciale in Italia*, 23 *Rassegna dell'Arb.* 41 (1983)

Recchia, G., *Enforcement of Foreign Arbitration Agreements and Awards in Italy and the United States: A Comparative Study* (Naples 1970)

Remiro Brotons, A., *Ejecución de sentencias arbitrales extranjeras. Los convenios internacionales y su aplicación en España* (Madrid 1980)

Ricci, *Problemi sulla recezione all'estero dei lodi rituali italiani*, 41 *Riv. Dir. Proc.* 117 (1986)

Riccomagno, *Recognition and Enforcement of Foreign Arbitral Awards in Italy under the New York Convention of 1958*, 1 *Y.B. Mar. L.* 119 (1984)

Richard, *Enforcement of Foreign Arbitral Awards under the United Nations Convention of 1958: A Survey of Recent Federal Case Law*, 11 *Md. J. Int'l L. & Trade* 13 (1987)

Ruiloba Santana, *El Convenio hispano-francés de 28 de mayo de 1969 sobre reconocimiento y ejecución de sentencias extranjeras y actas autenticas en materia civil y mercantil*, 23 *Rev. Esp. Der. Int'l* 42 (1970)

Report, *Canada and the United Nations Convention on Arbitral Awards*, 9 *Can. Arb. J.* 2 (No. 1, 1984)

Sanders, *A Twenty Year's Review of the Convention on the Recognition and Enforcement of Foreign Arbitral Awards*, 13 *Int'l Law.* 269 (1979); reprinted in *Arbitration and the Licensing Process* 3 (R. Goldscheider & M. de Haas eds. 1984)

———, *Trends in the Field of International Commercial Arbitration*, 145 *Recueil des Cours* 205 (1975-II)

Sandrock & Hentzen, *Enforcing Foreign Arbitral Awards in the Federal Republic of Germany: The Example of a United States Award*, 2 *Transnat'l Law.* 49 (1989)

Schultsz, Recognition and Enforcement of Foreign Arbitral Awards without a Convention Being Applicable, in *The Art of Arbitration* 295 (J. Schultsz & A. van den Berg eds. 1982)

Sidel & Mao Tong, China: Recognition and Enforcement of Foreign Arbitral Awards under the N.Y. Convention, 10 *East Asian Exec. Rep.* 14 (No. 5, 1988)

Smit, A-National Arbitration, 63 *Tul. L. Rev.* 629 (1989)

Sornarajah, The Enforcement of Foreign Arbitral Awards in Singapore, 1988 *Malayan L.J.* lxxxvi

Sornarajah, M., *International Commercial Arbitration: The Problem of State Contracts* (Singapore 1990)

Trooboff & Goldstein, Foreign Arbitral Awards and the 1958 New York Convention: Experience to Date in the United States Courts, 17 *Va. J. Int'l L.* 469 (1977)

Tupman, Staying Enforcement of Arbitral Awards under the New York Convention, 3 *Arb. Int'l* 223 (1987)

Ünal, The New York Convention and the Recognition and Enforcement of Foreign Arbitral Awards in Turkish Law, 7 *J. Int'l Arb.* 55 (No. 4, 1990)

United Nations, Study on the Application and Interpretation of the Convention on the Recognition and Enforcement of Foreign Arbitral Awards: Report of the Secretary-General, UN Doc. A/CN.9/168 (1979); reprinted in 10 *UNCITRAL Y.B.* 100 (1979)

van den Berg, Does the New York Arbitration Convention of 1958 Apply Retroactively? 1 *Arb. Int'l* 103 (1985)

———, Non-Domestic Arbitral Awards under the 1958 New York Convention, 2 *Arb. Int'l* 191 (1986)

———, Recent Enforcement Problems under the New York and ICSID Conventions, 5 *Arb. Int'l* 2 (1989)

———, Some Recent Problems in the Practice of Enforcement under the New York and ICSID Conventions, in *Arbitration and the Courts: Fifth ICSID/AAA/ICC Colloquium* (Washington 1987)

———, Some Recent Problems in the Practice of Enforcement under the New York and ICSID Conventions, 2 *ICSID Rev. - Foreign Investment L.J.* 439 (1987)

————, When Is an Arbitral Award Non-Domestic Under the New York Convention of 1958? 6 *Pace L. Rev.* 25 (1985)

van den Berg, A. J., *The New York Arbitration Convention of 1958* (Deventer 1981)

Vigoriti, Recent Developments in the Recognition and Execution of Foreign Judgments and Arbitral Awards in Italy, 6 *Civil Just. Q.* 248 (1987)

von Mehren, The Enforcement of Arbitral Awards under Conventions and United States Law, 9 *Yale J. World Pub. Ord.* 343 (1983)

von Preuschen, Die Vollstreckung ausländischer Schiedssprüche in Japan nach dem Inkrafttreten des UN-Übereinkommens, 10 *AWD* 112 (1964)

Walter, Das Schiedsverfahren im deutsch-italienischen Rechtsverkehr, 28 *RIW* 693 (1982)

Wenger, Zur Anwendbarkeit des New Yorker Übereinkommen über die Anerkennung und Vollstreckung ausländischer Schiedssprüche auf einem 'freien' Schiedsspruch (lodo irrituale) des italienischen Rechts, 2 *IPRax* 135 (1982)

Wysocka, B., *Uznawanie i wykonywanie zagranicznych orzeczen arbitrazowych w Polsce* (Warsaw 1987)

Young, Arbitration and the European Communities' Judgments Convention, in *International Commercial and Maritime Arbitration* 77 (F.D. Rose ed. 1988)

Zdravkovic, Certains cas de la jurisprudence yougoslave et étrangère sur l'exécution des sentences arbitrales étrangères, in *ICCA, Fifth Int'l Arb. Congress: Proceedings* C Izi 1-16 (1975)

20.04 FORMAL REQUIREMENTS

Herrmann, The UNCITRAL Model Law on International Commercial Arbitration — Its Salient Features and Prospects, in *First Int'l Commercial Arbitration Conference: Proceedings* 351 (N. Antaki & A. Prujiner eds. 1986)

Mordiglia, Enforcement of Foreign Arbitration Awards in Italy, in 2 *Fifth Int'l Congress of Maritime Arbitrators* (New York 1981)

Samuel, The Recognition and Enforcement of Foreign Judgments and Arbitral Awards in England with a Comparative Look at the United States of America, in *Le Juriste Suisse Face au Droit et aux Jugements Etrangers: Ouverture ou Repli?* 105 (F. Knoepfler ed. 1988)

van den Berg, A. J., *The New York Arbitration Convention of 1958* (Deventer 1981)

20.05 PROCEDURE FOR ENFORCEMENT

Anderegg, Zum 'Doppelexequatur' ausländischer Schiedssprüche, 53 *Rabels Z.* 171 (1989)

Barbosa Moreira, Improving the Procedures for the Enforcement and Recognition of Foreign Judgments and Arbitral Awards, in *Justice and Efficiency* 191 (W. Wedekind ed. 1989)

Bimpong-Buta, The Legal Effect of Executive Confirmation of Findings or Awards by Quasi-Judicial Bodies in Ghana, 32 *J. Afr. L.* 95 (1988)

Dalla Verita, Note sull'impugnazione del lodo arbitrale, 42 *Riv. Trim. Dir. & Proc. Civ.* 614 (1988)

Dolinger, Brazilian Confirmation of Foreign Judgments, 19 *Int'l Law.* 853 (1985); reprinted in *Modern Legal Systems Cyclopedia, Supplement One* 360.1 (K.R. Redden ed. 1987)

Giardina, Court Decisions in Italy Interpreting and Implementing the New York Convention, 7 *J. Int'l Arb.* 77 (No. 2, 1990)

Horomides, The Enforcement of Foreign Arbitral Awards in Greece, 3 *Arb. Int'l* 240 (1987)

Kerameus, Improving the Procedures for the Recognition and Enforcement of Foreign Judgments and Arbitral Awards, in *Justice and Efficiency* 226 (W. Wedekind ed. 1989)

Lamm, Arbitration Awards: Post Award Review and Enforcement Proceedings, 5 *Int'l Litigation Q.* 169 (No. 3, 1989)

Lotti, Sull'impugnabilità del lodo rituale non reso esecutivo, 43 *Riv. Dir. Proc.* 646 (1988)

Majoros, Exécution de décisions étrangères et procédure d'exéquatur en Europe de l'Est: Tour d'horizon avec des références de droit comparé, in *Le Juriste Suisse Face au Droit et aux Jugements Etrangers: Ouverture ou Repli?* 135 (F. Knoepfler ed. 1988)

Mordiglia, Enforcement of Foreign Arbitration Awards in Italy, in 2 *Fifth Int'l Congress of Maritime Arbitrators* (New York 1981)

Nicotina, G., *La dichiarazione di esecutività del lodo arbitrale* (aggiornato con le innovazione legislative del 9-2-1983 n.28), (Padova 1983)

Parker School of Foreign and Comparative Law, *International Commercial Arbitration and the Courts* (Dobbs Ferry 1990)

Rechsteiner, Die neuere brasilianische Rechtssprechung zur Anerkennung ausländischer Schiedsprüche, 26 *ZRV* 100 (1985)

Rosenn, Enforcement of Foreign Arbitral Awards in Brazil, 28 *Am. J. Comp. L.* 498 (1980)

Schlosser, Die Durchsetzung von Schiedssprüchen und ausländischen Urteilen im Urkundenprozess und mittels eines inländischen Arrests, in *Festschrift für Karl Heinz Schwab* 435 (P. Gottwald & H. Prütting eds. 1990)

Schurmann, Plan eines zentralen Gerichtshofs für die Anerkennung von Schiedssprüchen, 33 *RIW* 415 (1987)

Tarzia, Dichiarazione di esecutività e attuazione del lodo, 27 *Rassegna dell'Arb.* 195 (1987); also in *Arbitrato nazionale e internazionale: interpretazione ed esecuzione del lodo* 59 (G. Carli ed. 1989)

van den Berg, A. J., *The New York Arbitration Convention of 1958* (Deventer 1981)

Wysocka, B., *Uznawanie i wykonywanie zagranicznych orzeczen arbitrazowych w Polsce* (Warsaw 1987)

20.06 GROUNDS FOR REFUSAL TO ENFORCE

Aksen, Arbitration Under International Commercial Contracts. Current Issues and Practical Problems: Enforcement of Awards against Governments — The Libyan Awards, in *Essays on International Law* 104 (New Delhi 1981)

Baur, F., *Neuere Probleme der privaten Schiedsgerichtsbarkeit* (Berlin 1980)

Béguin, Le droit français de l'arbitrage international et la Convention de New York du 10 juin 1958, in *First International Commercial Arbitration Conference: Proceedings* 218 (N. Antaki & A. Prujiner eds. 1986)

Berglin, The Application in United States Courts of the Public Policy Provisions of the Convention on the Recognition and Enforcement of Foreign Arbitral Awards, 4 *Dick. J. Int'l L.* 167 (1986)

Bernini, The Enforcement of Arbitration Awards, 47 *Arbitration* 99 (1981)

Bernini & van den Berg, The Enforcement of Arbitral Award Against a State: The Problem of Immunity from Execution, in *Contemporary Problems in Int'l Arbitration* 359 (J.D.M. Lew ed. 1986)

Böckstiegel, Public Policy and Arbitrability, in *Comparative Arbitration Practice and Public Policy in Arbitration* 177 (P. Sanders ed. 1987)

Booysen, The Municipal Enforcement of Arbitration Awards against States in Terms of Arbitration Conventions, with Special Reference to the New York Convention — Does International Law Provide for a Municipal Law Concept of an Arbitrable Act of State? 12 *South Afr. Y.B. Int'l L.* 73 (1986-1987)

Bourel, Arbitrage international et immunités des Etats étrangères (A propos d'une jurisprudence récente), *Rev. Arb.* 119 (1982)

Brierley, Quebec's New (1986) Arbitration Law, 13 *Can. Bus. L.J.* 58 (1987)

Bucher, A., *Die neue internationale Schiedsgerichtsbarkeit in der Schweiz* (Basel 1989)

————, *Le nouvel arbitrage international en Suisse. Théorie et pratique de droit* (Basel 1988)

Bucher, A. & P.-Y. Tschanz, *International Arbitration in Switzerland* (Basel 1989)

542

Budin, L'exécution des sentences arbitrales étrangères en Suisse et les limites de l'ordre public, 1977 *Rev. Arb.* 107

Bülow, La convention des parties relative à la procedure d'arbitrage visée a l'Art. V, par.1, litt. d) de la Convention de New York, in *A.I.A., Essays in Memoriam Eugenio Minoli* 81 (Turin 1974)

Capelli & Percibaldi, The Application of the New York Convention to Disputes between States and between State Entities and Private Individuals: The Problem of Sovereign Immunity, 12 *Int'l Law.* 197 (1978)

Carabiber, L'immunité de juridiction et d'exécution des Etats collectivités et établissements publics au regard de l'obligation assumée par une clause compromissoire inserée dans les contrats internationaux de droit privé, in *Liber Amicorum for Martin Domke* 23 (P. Sanders ed. 1967)

————, L'arbitrage international et la réserve de l'ordre public, 1956 *Rev. Arb.* 118

Cole, Public Policy Exception to the New York Convention on the Recognition and Enforcement of Arbitral Awards, 1 *Ohio St. J. Disp. Res.* 365 (1986)

Coll, United States Enforcement of Arbitral Awards Against Sovereign States: Implications of the ICSID Convention, 17 *Harv. J. Int'l L.* 401 (1976)

Crawford, Les Etats et l'exécution des sentences arbitrales dans les droits américain et anglais, 1985 *Rev. Arb.* 689

Comment, International Commercial Arbitration: The Non-Arbitrable Subject Matter Defense, 9 *Den. J. Int'l L. & Pol'y* 119 (1980)

de Bruin, De 'affaire C,' 1989 *Tijdschrift voor Arbitrage* 1

Delaume, Judicial Decisions Related to Sovereign Immunity and Transnational Arbitration, 2 *ICSID Rev. - Foreign Investment L.J.* 403 (1987)

————, SEEE v. Yugoslavia: Epitaph or Interlude? 4 *J. Int'l Arb.* 25 (No. 3, 1987)

————, Sovereign Immunity and Transnational Arbitration, in *Contemporary Problems in Int'l Arbitration* 313 (J.D.M. Lew ed. 1986)

Ebb, At the End of a Long Trail: How the Bombay High Court Strengthened International Arbitration in India, 44 *Arb. J.* 28 (No. 2, 1989)

Evans, The Nonarbitrability of Subject Matter Defense to Enforcement of Foreign Arbitral Awards in United States Federal Courts, 21 *N.Y.U. J. Int'l L. & Pol.* 329 (1989)

Feldman, Enforcement of Foreign Arbitral Awards in the U.S. Courts, 3 *Int'l Arb. Rep.* 15 (No. 11, 1988)

Ferrante, About the Nature (National or A-National, Contractual or Jurisdictional) of ICC Awards Under the New York Convention, in *The Art of Arbitration* 129 (J. Schultsz & A. van den Berg eds. 1982)

————, Enforcement of Foreign Arbitral Awards in Italy and Public Policy, in *ICC, Hommage à Frederic Eisemann* 83 (1978)

Flécheux, Les difficultés d'exécution en France des sentences rendues contre les Etats ou leur émanations, 1985 *Rev. Arb.* 675

Fox, Sovereign Immunity and Arbitration, in *Contemporary Problems in Int'l Arbitration* 323 (J.D.M. Lew ed. 1986)

García de Enterría, The Role of Public Policy in International Commercial Arbitration, 21 *L. & Pol'y Int'l Bus.* 389 (1990)

Geisinger & Renold, Arbitrage international, ordre public et reconnaissance en Suisse de sentences arbitrales étrangères, in *Le Juriste Suisse Face au Droit et aux Jugements Etrangers: Ouverture ou Repli?* 89 (F. Knoepfler ed. 1988)

Giardina, The International Center for Settlement of Investment Disputes between States and Nationals of Other States (ICSID), in *Essays on International Commercial Arbitration* 214 (P. Sarcevic ed. 1989)

Gonzales Soria, J., *La intervención judicial en el arbitraje. Recursos jurisdiccionales y ejecución judicial del laudo arbitral* (Madrid 1988)

Grigera Naón, Public Policy and International Commercial Arbitration: The Argentine Perspective, 3 *J. Int'l Arb.* 5 (No. 2, 1986)

Groos, Schiedsgerichtsbarkeit im deutsch-französischen Wirtschaftsverkehr, 33 *RIW* 343 (1987)

Herrmann, The Role of the Courts under the UNCITRAL Model Law Script, in *Contemporary Problems in Int'l Arbitration* 164 (J.D.M. Lew ed. 1986)

Hobér, Defenses to Recognition and Enforcement of Foreign Arbitral Awards in the United States, 48 *Nordisk Tidskrift for International Ret* 38 (1978)

Holtzmann, H. & Neuhaus, J., *A Guide to the UNCITRAL Model Law on International Commercial Arbitration: Legislative History and Commentary* (Deventer 1989)

Horomides, The Enforcement of Foreign Arbitral Awards in Greece, 3 *Arb. Int'l* 240 (1987)

Horsmans, L'arbitrage et l'ordre public interne belge, 1978 *Rev. Arb.* 79

――――, La sentence arbitrale, la convention d'arbitrage et l'ordre public interne belge, 16 *Tijdschrift voor Privaatrecht* 231 (1979)

Junker, The Public Policy Defense to Recognition and Enforcement of Foreign Arbitral Awards, 7 *Calif. W. Int'l L.J.* 228 (1977)

Kahale, New Legislation in the United States Facilitates Enforcement of Arbitral Agreements and Awards Against Foreign States, 6 *J. Int'l Arb.* 57 (No. 2, 1989)

Kornblum, 'Ordre public transnational,' 'ordre public international' und 'ordre public interne' im Recht der privaten Schiedsgerichtsbarkeit, in *Beiträge zum internationalen Verfahrensrecht und zur Schiedsgerichtsbarkeit. Festschrift für Heinrich Nagel* 140 (W. Habscheid & K. Schwab eds. 1987)

――――, Das 'Gebot überparteilicher Rechtspflege' und der deutsche schiedsrechtliche ordre public, 40 *NJW* 1105 (1987)

Kuner, The Public Policy Exception to the Enforcement of Foreign Arbitral Awards in the United States and West Germany under the New York Convention, 7 *J. Int'l Arb.* 71 (No. 4, 1990)

Lalive, Quelques observations sur l'imunité d'exécution des Etats et l'arbitrage international, in *International Law at a Time of Perplexity. Essays in Honour of Shabtai Rosenne* 369 (Y. Dinstein ed. 1989)

――――, *Arbitrage international et ordre public suisse, Revue de Droit Suisse* 529 (1978)

Le Pera, Where to Vacate and How to Resist Enforcement of Foreign Arbitral Awards: I.S.E.C. v. Bridas, 2 *Am. Rev. Int'l Arb.* 48 (1991)

Lee Tae Hee, Arbitration of International Commercial Disputes in Korea, 3 *Arb. Int'l* 14 (No. 1, 1987)

Lorenzen, Commercial Arbitration — Enforcement of Foreign Awards, 45 *Yale L.J.* 39 (1935)

McLaughlin & Genevro, Enforcement of Arbitral Awards Under the New York Convention — Practice in U.S.Courts, 3 *Int'l Tax & Bus. Law.* 249 (1986)

Martens & Matray, Arbitrage et ordre public interne, 1978 *Rev. Arb.* 95

Martinez, Recognition and Enforcement on International Arbitral Awards under the United Nations Convention of 1958: The 'Refusal' Provisions, 24 *Int'l Law.* 487 (1990)

Matray, Arbitrage et ordre public international, in *The Art of Arbitration* 241 (J. Schultsz & A. van den Berg eds. 1982)

Mezger, Verstoss gegen die öffentliche Ordnung bei Beurteilung ausländischer Schiedssprüche, 23 *NJW* 368 (1970)

Moitry, Right to a Fair Trial and the European Convention on Human Rights, 6 *J. Int'l Arb.* 115 (No. 2, 1989)

Montoya Alberti, El arbitraje en los contratos de prestamo internacionales, in *El Arbitraje en el Derecho Latinoamericano y Español* 481 (L. Perret & U. Montoya Alberti eds. 1989)

Moussali, Arbitrage International: Syrie, 1991 *Int'l Bus. L.J.* 401

Nariman, Foreign Arbitral Awards in India: Problems, Pitfalls, and Progress, 6 *J. Int'l Arb.* 25 (No. 1, 1989)

Nilsson, Problems of Sovereign Immunity under the Swedish Law of Arbitration, 1982 *Y.B. Swed. & Int'l Arb.* 41

Note, The Recognition and Enforcement of Foreign Arbitral Awards: Defenses to Arbitrability, 37 *S.C. L. Rev.* 719 (1986)

Olmstead, Enforcement of a Foreign Arbitral Award against a Government — A Catch, in *1981 Private Investors Abroad: Problems and Solutions in International Business* 213 (New York 1981)

Oppetit, Le refus d'exécution d'une sentence arbitrale étrangère dans le cadre de la Convention de New York, 1971 *Rev. Arb.* 97

Park, Private Adjudicators and the Public Interest: The Expanding Scope of International Arbitration, 12 *Brooklyn J. Int'l L.* 629 (1986)

Parker School of Foreign and Comparative Law, *International Commercial Arbitration and the Courts* (Dobbs Ferry 1990)

Raeschke-Kessler & Bühler, Aufsicht über den Schiedsrichter durch den ICC-Schiedsgerichtshof (Paris) und rechtliches Gehör der Parteien, 8 *ZIP* 1157 (1987)

Rechsteiner, Die neuere brasilianische Rechtssprechung zur Anerkennung ausländischer Schiedsprüche, 26 *ZRV* 100 (1985)

Redfern, International Commercial Arbitration. Jurisdiction Denied: the Pyramid Collapses, 1986 *J. Bus. L.* 15

Richard, Enforcement of Foreign Arbitral Awards under the United Nations Convention of 1958: A Survey of Recent Federal Case Law, 11 *Md. J. Int'l L. & Trade* 13 (1987)

Rovine, U.S. Public Policy on Recognition, Enforcement of Foreign Awards, 1 *Int'l Arb. Rep.* 41 (1986)

Sajko, The New York Arbitration Convention of 1958 from the Yugoslav Point of View: Selected Issues, in *Essays on International Commercial Arbitration* 199 (P. Sarcevic ed. 1989)

Samuel, Developments in English Arbitration Law since the 1984 Antaios Decision, 5 *J. Int'l Arb.* 9 (No. 3, 1988)

———, The Recognition and Enforcement of Foreign Judgments and Arbitral Awards in England with a Comparative Look at the United States of America, in *Le Juriste Suisse Face au Droit et aux Jugements Etrangers: Ouverture ou Repli?* 105 (F. Knoepfler ed. 1988)

Sanders, Trends in the Field of International Commercial Arbitration, 145 *Recueil des Cours* 205 (1975-II)

Sandrock, Arbitration between U.S. and West German Companies: An Example of Effective Dispute Resolution in International Business Transactions, 9 *U. Pa. J. Int'l Bus. L.* 27 (1987)

Sandrock & Hentzen, Enforcing Foreign Arbitral Awards in the Federal Republic of Germany: The Example of a United States Award, 2 *Transnat'l Law.* 49 (1989)

Schütze, Zur Wirksamkeit von internationalen Schiedsvereinbarungen und zur Wirkungserstreckung ausländischer Schiedssprüche über Ansprüche aus Börsentermingeschäften, 1 *Jahrbuch Schiedsgerichtsbarkeit* 94 (1987)

Schulthess, H. K., *Der verfahrensrechtliche Ordre public in der internationalen Schiedsgerichtsbarkeit in der Schweiz* (Zurich 1981)

Seidl-Hohenveldern, Austrian Public Policy and the Enforcement of Foreign Arbitral Awards, 4 *Arb. Int'l* 322 (1988)

Sornarajah, The Enforcement of Foreign Arbitral Awards in Singapore, 1988 *Malayan L.J.* lxxxvi

Toop, S., *Mixed International Arbitration: Studies in Arbitration between States and Private Persons* (Cambridge 1990)

Tschanz, Le droit américain et la Convention de New York, in *First International Commercial Arbitration Conference: Proceedings* 249 (N. Antaki & A. Prujiner eds. 1986)

Tupman, Staying Enforcement of Arbitral Awards under the New York Convention, 3 *Arb. Int'l* 223 (1987)

van den Berg, Recent Enforcement Problems under the New York and ICSID Conventions, 5 *Arb. Int'l* 2 (1989)

————, Some Recent Problems in the Practice of Enforcement under the New York and ICSID Conventions, in *Arbitration and the Courts: Fifth ICSID/AAA/ICC Colloquium* (Washington 1987)

van den Berg, A. J., *The New York Arbitration Convention of 1958* (Deventer 1981)

von Mehren, The Enforcement of Arbitral Awards under Conventions and United States Law, 9 *Yale J. World Pub. Ord.* 343 (1983)

von Winterfeld, Noch einmal: Der deutsche ordre public in der internationalen Schiedsgerichtsbarkeit, 1987 *NJW* 3059

Warren, The Concept of 'Null and Void' in International Commercial Arbitration, 45 *Arb. J.* 57 (No. 4, 1990)

West, The Express Defenses of the N.Y. Convention on Foreign Arbitral Awards, 5 *N.Y. L. Sch. J. Int'l & Comp. L.* 103 (1983)Warren, The Concept of 'Null and Void' in International Commercial Arbitration, 45 *Arb. J.* 57 (No. 4, 1990)

————, The Express Defenses of the N.Y. Convention on Foreign Arbitral Awards, 5 *N.Y. L. Sch. J. Int'l & Comp. L.* 103 (1983)

20.07 PARTIAL AND PROVISIONAL ENFORCEMENT

Duintjer Tebbens, A Facelift for Dutch Arbitration Law, 34 *Neth. Int'l L. Rev.* 141 (1987)

van den Berg, A. J., *The New York Arbitration Convention of 1958* (Deventer 1981)

20.08 POSTPONEMENT OF THE DECISION ON ENFORCEMENT

Kotora, New Rules of Arbitration Proceedings and Recognition and Enforcement of Foreign Awards and Judicial Decisions in Czechoslovakia, 7 *Diritto negli Scambi Int'li* 225 (1968)

Parker School of Foreign and Comparative Law, *International Commercial Arbitration and the Courts* (Dobbs Ferry, NY 1990)

Sarevic, The Setting Aside and Enforcement of Arbitral Awards under the UNCITRAL Model law, in *Essays on International Commercial Arbitration* 177 (P. Sarcevic ed. 1989)

Tupman, Staying Enforcement of Arbitral Awards under the New York Convention, 3 *Arb. Int'l* 223 (1987)

PART TWO

COUNTRY-BY-COUNTRY
BIBLIOGRAPHY

AFRICA

Agyemang, African Courts, the Settlement of Investment Disputes and the Enforcement of Awards, 33 *J. Afr. L.* 31 (1989)

―――――, African States and ICSID Arbitration, 21 *Comp. & Int'l L.J. Southern Afr.* 177 (1988)

Atanda, Review of Arbitration Law and Practice in Sub-Saharan Africa, 1 *Am. Rev. Int'l Arb.* 123 (1990)

Brown, Commercial Arbitration and the European Economic Community, 2 *J. Int'l Arb.* 21 (1985)

Mazanza, L'arbitrage dans les codes des investissements de l'Afrique noire francophone, 29 *Revue juridique et politique, indépendence et coopération* 111 (1975)

Spedding, Interpretation of Art. 132 of the Lome II Convention. Arbitration or Court Proceeding, 12 *Int'l Bus. Law.* 382 (1984)

Tiewul & Tsegah, Arbitration and the Settlement of Commercial Disputes: A Selective Survey of African Practice, 24 *Int'l & Comp. L.Q.* 393 (1975)

ALGERIA

Derains, Clauses et procédures d'arbitrage internationales dans le pays arabes, in *First Euro-Arab Arb. Conference: Proceedings* 150 (F. Kemicha ed. 1987)

El-Ahdab, A. H., *Arbitration with the Arab Countries* (Deventer 1990)

————, *L'arbitrage dans les pays arabes* (Paris 1988)

Issad, Algeria: National Report, 4 *Y.B. Com. Arb.* 3 (1979) and 12 *Y.B. Com. Arb.* 360 (1987)

————, L'arbitrage en Algérie, 1977 *Rev. Arb.* 219

————, La pratique de l'arbitrage international en Algérie, in *First Euro-Arab Arb. Conference: Proceedings* 114 (F. Kemicha ed. 1987)

Kassis, Particularités et problèmes de l'arbitrage dans les droits des pays arabes, 63 *Rev. Droit Int'l & Droit Comp.* 7 (1986)

Krüger, Probleme des algerischen internationalen Vertrags- und Schiedsrecht, in *Vertragspraxis und Streiterledigung im Wirtschaftsverkehr mit arabischen Staaten* 17 (K.-H. Böckstiegel ed. 1981)

Mebroukine, Le Règlement d'arbitrage algéro-français du 27 mars 1983, 1986 *Rev. Arb.* 191

Mezghani, Les pays arabes du Maghreb, in *First Euro-Arab Arb. Conference: Proceedings* 39 (F. Kemicha ed. 1987)

Pechota, Algeria, in 2 *W.A.R.* 501 (H. Smit & V. Pechota eds. 1987)

Sachs, Das bilaterale französisch-algerische Schiedsabkommen vom 27. März 1983 - Ein Muster auch für andere Staaten? 6 *IPRax* 309 (1986)

Sefrioui, Pratique de l'arbitrage et tendances reformatrices nouvelles, in *Euro-Arab Arbitration III* 61 (F. Kemicha ed. 1991)

Stewart & Pechota, Franco-Algerian Agreement on the Settlement by Arbitration of Disputes Arising from Commercial Contracts, 1983, in 3 *W.A.R.* 3630 (H. Smit & V. Pechota eds. 1987)

Stumpf, Schiedsgerichtsbarkeit in arabischen Ländern, 1 *Jahrbuch Schiedsgerichtsbarkeit* 102 (1987)

Terki, L'arbitrage et l'entreprise publique en Afrique du Nord, 66 *Rev. Droit Int'l & Droit Comp.* 124 (1989)

Ziadé, Selective Bibliography on Arbitration and Arab Countries, 3 *ICSID Rev. -Foreign Investment L.J.* 423 (1988)

ANTIGUA AND BARBUDA

Pechota, Antigua and Barbuda, in 2 *W.A.R.* 563 (H. Smit & V. Pechota eds. 1987)

ARAB LEAGUE

Derains, Clauses et procédures d'arbitrage internationales dans le pays arabes, in *First Euro-Arab Arb. Conference: Proceedings* 150 (F. Kemicha ed. 1987)

El-Ahdab, A. H., *Arbitration with the Arab Countries* (Deventer 1990)

————, *L'arbitrage dans les pays arabes* (Paris 1988)

Kassis, Particularités et problèmes de l'arbitrage dans les droits des pays arabes, 63 *Rev. Droit Int'l & Droit Comp.* 7 (1986)

Mezghani, Les pays arabes du Maghreb, in *First Euro-Arab Arb. Conference: Proceedings* 39 (F. Kemicha ed. 1987)

Sefrioui, Pratique de l'arbitrage et tendances reformatrices nouvelles, in *Euro-Arab Arbitration III* 61 (F. Kemicha ed. 1991)

Stumpf, Schiedsgerichtsbarkeit in arabischen Ländern, 1 *Jahrbuch Schiedsgerichtsbarkeit* 102 (1987)

Terki, L'arbitrage et l'entreprise publique en Afrique du Nord, 66 *Rev. Droit Int'l & Droit Comp.* 124 (1989)

Ziadé, Selective Bibliography on Arbitration and Arab Countries, 3 *ICSID Rev. -Foreign Investment L.J.* 423 (1988)

ARGENTINA

Alvarado Velloso, El arbitraje: solución eficiente de conflictos de intereses, in *Der komplexe Langzeitvertrag/The Complex Long-Term Contract* 475 (F. Nicklisch ed. 1987)

Ayarragaray, C., *Naturaleza del Proceso Arbitral* (Buenos Aires 1970)

Barclay, Arbitration in Latin America, 43 *Arbitration* 105 (1977)

Bombau, Attachments and Other Interim Court Remedies in Support of Arbitration: The Argentine Perspective, in *Interim Court Remedies in Support of Arbitration* 111 (D. Shenton & W. Kühn eds. 1987)

Bombau & Zivy, Influence of the 1958 New York Convention on Recognition and Enforcement of Foreign Arbitral Awards in Argentina, 1990 *Int'l Bus. L.J.* 815

Buchanan, Public Policy and International Commercial Arbitration, 26 *Am. Bus. L.J.* 511 (1988)

Dunshee de Abranches, C.A., ed., *El arbitraje comercial en Iberoamérica* (Madrid 1982)

Ester Ledesma, Eficacia del laudo arbitral, in *El Arbitraje en el Derecho Latinoamericano y Español* 99 (L. Perret & U. Montoya Alberti eds. 1989)

Fargosi, Commercial Arbitration in Argentina, 20 *U. Miami Inter-Am. L. Rev.* 687 (1989)

————, Commercial Arbitration in Argentina, in *Commercial and Labor Arbitration in Central America* 15 (A. Garro ed. 1991)

Garro, Argentina, in 2 *W.A.R.* 629 (H. Smit & V. Pechota eds. 1987)

Goldman, Arbitration and Transfer of Technology in Latin America, in *Arbitration and the Licensing Process* 5-29 (R. Goldscheider & M. de Haas eds. 1984-)

Goyeneche & Caivano, El arbitraje en el comercio de granos, 1985-II *Jurispr. Arg.* 807

Grigera Naón, Arbitration in Latin America: Overcoming Traditional Hostility, 5 *Arb. Int'l* 137 (1989)

————, Argentina, 15 *Y.B. Com. Arb.* 295 (1990)

————, Argentina, in *Int'l Handbook Com. Arb.* (A. van den Berg, gen. ed. 1984), Suppl. 11, Jan. 1990

————, Argentinien nach der Ratifizierung des New Yorker Abkommens über die Anerkennung und Vollstreckung von ausländischen Schiedssprüchen von 1958, 2 *Jahrbuch Schiedsgerichtsbarkeit* 111 (1988)

————, El arbitraje comercial en el derecho argentino interno e internacional privado, *Revista de derecho mercantil* 115 (1982)

————, El arbitraje comercial international en la Argentina, *Pensamiento Económico Revista de la Cámara Argentina de Comercio* 79 (No. 435, 1986)

————, El estado y el arbitraje, in *El Arbitraje en el Derecho Latino-americano y Español* 73 (L. Perret & U. Montoya Alberti eds. 1989)

————, Immunity of Arbitrators under Argentine Law, in *The Immunity of Arbitrators* 5 (J.D.M. Lew ed. 1990)

————, La autonomia del acuerdo arbitral, *La Ley*, Sept. 5, 1989

————, La ley modelo de la CNUDMI sobre arbitraje comercial internacional y el derecho argentino, 1989-A *La Ley* 1021

————, Mandatory Provisions of Law Regarding Arbitration Agreements in Latin America, in *Arbitration in Settlement of International Commercial Disputes Involving the Far East and Arbitration in Combined Transportation* 121 (P. Sanders ed. 1989)

————, Public Policy and International Commercial Arbitration: An Argentine View, in *Comparative Arbitration Practice and Public Policy in Arbitration* 329 (P. Sanders ed. 1987)

————, Public Policy and International Commercial Arbitration: The Argentine Perspective, 3 *J. Int'l Arb.* 5 (No. 2, 1986)

————, Ratification by Argentina of the 1958 New York Convention on Recognition and Enforcement of Foreign Arbitral Awards, 6 *J. Int'l Arb.* 121 (No. 3, 1989)

————, The Scope of the Separability of the Arbitration Agreement Under Argentine Law, 1 *Am. Rev. Int'l Arb.* 261 (1990)

Grigera Naón & Samtleben, Schiedsgerichtsbarkeit in Argentinien, 29 *RIW* 721 (1983)

Hitters, Posibilidad de prorrogar la jurisdicción en favor de tribunales o arbitros extrajeros. Limitaciones., 1984-III *Jurispr. Arg.* 763

International Chamber of Commerce, Argentina/Argentine, in *Commercial Arbitration and the Law/L'Arbitrage commercial et la Loi* (Basel 1951)

Lucas Sosa, Nuevas perspectivas del arbitraje: un enfoque procesal desde Argentina, in *El Arbitraje en el Derecho Latinoamericano y Español* 115 (L. Perret & U. Montoya Alberti eds. 1989)

Malamud, Argentina: National Report, 3 *Y.B. Com. Arb.* 17 (1978) and 8 *Y.B. Com. Arb.* 65 (1983)

Malamud, J., *El Arbitraje Comercial y el Nuevo Código de Procedimientos* (Buenos Aires 1968)

Montoya Alberti, Arbitration, Foreign Law and Jurisdiction in International Loan Agreements in Some Countries of Latin America, in *Arbitration in Settlement of International Commercial Disputes Involving the Far East and Arbitration in Combined Transportation* 99 (P. Sanders ed. 1989)

————, El arbitraje en los contratos de prestamo internacionales, in *El Arbitraje en el Derecho Latinoamericano y Español* 481 (L. Perret & U. Montoya Alberti eds. 1989)

Nattier, International Commercial Arbitration in Latin America: Enforcement of Arbitral Agreements and Awards, 21 *Tex. Int'l L. J.* 397 (1986)

Piaggi, El arbitraje international y la realidad argentina, *La Ley,* Apr. 6, 1983, at 1

Ray, La responsibilidad de transportistas en las reglas de Hamburgo y la solución arbitral de controversias, in *El Arbitraje Comercial Internacional* 461 (Mexico 1983)

Vinals Blake, La importancia del arbitraje en el comercio nacional e internacional, *Revista del Derecho Industria* 453 (1983)

AUSTRALIA

Bates, Commercial Arbitration and the Courts in Australia: Signs and Change, 1987 *J. Bus. L.* 527; also in 54 *Arbitration* 160 (1988)

Bernini, Recent Legislations and International Unification of the Law on Arbitration, in *First International Commercial Arbitration Conference: Proceedings* 315 (N. Antaki & A. Prujiner eds. 1986)

Brazil, Resolution of Trade Disputes in the Asian Pacific Region, 10 *Adel. L. Rev.* 49 (1985)

Conrick, Arbitration, 17 *Queensl. L. Soc'y J.* 335 (1987)

Croft, Australia Adopts the UNCITRAL Model Law, 5 *Arb. Int'l* 189 (1989)

———, International Commercial Arbitration: Developments in the State of Victoria, Australia, in *UNCITRAL Arbitration Model in Canada* 35 (R. Paterson & B. Thompson eds. 1987)

D'Aloisio, International Arbitration: Arbitration (Foreign Awards and Agreements) Act, 1974 (CTH), 5 *Austl. Bus. L. Rev.* 295 (1977)

de Fina, Arbitration Law Reforms, International Facilities and Rules, Australian Development, 52 *Arbitration* 158 (1986)

———, International Commercial Arbitration in Australia, in *Arbitration in Settlement of International Commercial Disputes Involving the Far East and Arbitration in Combined Transportation* 209 (P. Sanders ed. 1989)

Dore, I., *Theory and Practice of Multiparty Commercial Arbitration, With Special Reference to the UNCITRAL Framework* (London 1990)

Dorter, J. & G. Widmer, *Arbitration (Commercial) in Australia - Law and Practice* (Sydney 1979)

Finlay, An Overview of Commercial Arbitration in Australia, 4 *J. Int'l Arb.* 103 (No. 4, 1987)

Fox, States and the Undertaking to Arbitrate, 37 *Int'l & Comp. L.Q.* 1 (1988)

Gaillard, The UNCITRAL Model Law and Recent Statutes on International Arbitration in Europe and North America, 2 *ICSID Rev. - Foreign Investment L.J.* 424 (1987)

Goldring, Australia, 2 *Y.B. Com. Arb.* 3 (1977); 9 *Y.B.* 39 (1984)(jointly with D. Skapinker); 13 *Y.B.* 381 (1988)(jointly with A.G. Christie); 14 *Y.B.* 488 (1989); 15 *Y.B.* 299 (1990)

————, Australian Law and International Commercial Arbitration, 15 *Colum. J. Transnat'l L.* 216 (1976)

————, The 1958 United Nations Convention on Recognition and Enforcement of Foreign Arbitral Awards and the Australian Constitution, 5 *Fed. L. Rev.* 203 (1972-73)

Goldring, J., *Commercial Arbitration in Japan-Australia Trade Disputes* (Sydney 1973)

Goldring & Christie, Australia, in *Int'l Handbook Com. Arb.* (A. van den Berg, gen. ed. 1984), Suppl. 8, Dec. 1987

Hanna, The Commercial Arbitration Bill 1984, 3 *The Arbitrator* 77 (1984)

Klaric, Judicial Intervention and International Commercial Arbitration: The Australian Perspective, 16 *Austl. Bus. L. Rev.* 440 (1988)

Kolkey, Attacking Arbitral Awards: Rights of Appeal and Review in International Arbitrations, 22 *Int'l Law.* 693 (1988)

Longo, Towards a 'Common Core' of Legal Rules on Commercial Arbitration, 59 *Austl. L.J.* 407 (1985)

Lucke, Arbitration Clauses in South Australia, 5 *Adel. L. Rev.* 244 (1975)

McCardell, Arbitration in Australia, 53 *Arbitration* 136 (1987)

McPherson, Arbitration, Valuation and Certainty of Terms, 60 *Austl. L.J.* 8 (1986)

Najar & Polkinghorne, Australia's Adoption of the UNCITRAL Model Law, 4 *Int'l Arb. Rep.* 21 (No. 3, 1989)

Newton, Alternative Dispute Resolution in Australia (Australian Commercial Disputes Centre Limited), in *A Handbook of Dispute Resolution* 231 (K. Mackie ed. 1991)

O'Keefe, P.J., *Arbitration in International Trade* (Sydney 1975)

Pacific Rim Advisory Council, *Pacific Rim: Commercial Arbitration Procedures* (San Diego, CA 1985)

Parker School of Foreign and Comparative Law, *International Commercial Arbitration and the Courts* (Dobbs Ferry, NY 1990)

Pechota, Australian Centre for International Commercial Arbitration, in 4 *W.A.R.* 3867 (H. Smit & V. Pechota eds. 1989)

————, Australian Commercial Disputes Centre Limited, in 4 *W.A.R.* 3873 (H. Smit & V. Pechota eds. 1989)

————, The Institute of Arbitrators Australia, in 4 *W.A.R.* 3851 (H. Smit & V. Pechota eds. 1989)

Perry, Attachments and Other Interim Court Remedies in Support of Arbitration — The Australian Position, in *Interim Court Remedies in Support of Arbitration* 68 (D. Shenton & W. Kühn eds. 1987)

————, Dispute Resolution in the Asia/Pacific Region: The Australian Perspective, 42 *Arb. J.* 32 (No. 2, 1987)

Pryles, Immunity of Arbitrators under Australian Law, in *The Immunity of Arbitrators* 13 (J.D.M. Lew ed. 1990)

————, International Arbitration in Australia, 1 *Am. Rev. Int'l Arb.* 37 (1990)

————, International Dispute Resolution and Litigation in Australia, 16 *Int'l Bus. Law.* 454 (1988)

————, Legal Issues Concerning International Arbitrations, 64 *Austl. L.J.* 470 (1990)

Pryles, M. & K. Iwasaki, *Dispute Resolution in Australia-Japan Transactions* (Sydney 1983)

Rath, Australia, 3 *Int'l Commercial Arbitration: A World Handbook* 2 (P. Sanders ed. 1965)

Rogers, International Arbitration and Australia, 1 *Com. Arbitrator* 14 (No. 3, June 1982)

————, The UNCITRAL Model Law: An Australian Perspective, 6 *Arb. Int'l* 348 (1990)

Scotford, Commercial Arbitration: New South Wales Commercial Arbitration Bill 1984, 1985 *Lloyd's Mar. & Com. L.Q.* 136

Sharkey, J. & J. Dorter, *Commercial Arbitration* (Sydney 1986)

Simmonds, K., B. Hill & S. Jarvin, eds., *Commercial Arbitration Law in Asia and the Pacific* (Paris & Dobbs Ferry, NY 1987)

Sykes, E. & M. Pryles, *Australian Private International Law*, Second ed. Chapter 4: Arbitration (Sydney 1987)

Tedeschi, Commercial Arbitration in Australia, 15 *Rassegna dell'Arb.* 117 (1975)

Travers, Commercial Arbitration in New South Wales: Too Much Judicial Interference? 4 *J. Int'l Arb.* 121 (No. 2, 1987)

Turner, C., *Yorston, Fortescue & Turner Australian Mercantile Law.* 17th ed. Chapter 25: Commercial Arbitration and Awards (Sydney 1985)

Willis, Institute of Arbitrators Australia — Maritime Arbitration, 9 *Int'l Bus. Law.* 401 (1981)

AUSTRIA

Aden, M., *Internationale Handelsschiedsgerichtsbarkeit. Kommentar zu den Verfahrensordnungen* (Heidelberg 1988)

American Arbitration Association, *New Strategies for Peaceful Resolution of International Business Disputes* (Dobbs Ferry, NY 1971)

Backhausen, G., *Schiedsgerichtsbarkeit unter besonderer Berücksichtigung des Schiedsvertragsrechts* (Vienna 1990)

Bajons, Zur Nationalität internationaler Schiedssachen: der Fall 'Norsolor' vor den österreichischen Gerichten, in *Festschrift für Winfried Kralik* 3 (Vienna 1986)

Berger, Die Regelung der gerichtlichen Anfechtbarkeit internationaler Schiedssprüche in europäischen Schiedsgerichtsgesetzen, 35 *RIW* 850 (1989)

———, The Modern Trend Towards Exclusion of Recourse Against Transnational Arbitral Awards: A European Perspective, 12 *Fordham Int'l L. J.* 605 (1989)

Bernini, Recent Legislations and International Unification of the Law on Arbitration, in *First International Commercial Arbitration Conference: Proceedings* 315 (N. Antaki & A. Prujiner eds. 1986)

Eckstrom, L. *Licensing in Foreign and Domestic Operations.* Volume I, Chapter 7: Arbitration (by Steven Z. Szczepanski), (New York 1972, updated 1987)

Ender, Austria, in 1 *Union Internationale des Avocats, Arbitrage International Commercial/International Commercial Arbitration* (P. Sanders ed. 1957)

Fasching, Die Form der Schiedsvereinbarung, 44 *ÖJZ* 289 (1989)

Fasching, H.W., *Schiedsgericht und Schiedsverfahren im österreichischen und internationalen Rechte* (Vienna 1973)

Fischer, Das Recht der internationalen Schiedsgerichtsbarkeit 'revisited,' 31 *Österreichische Zeitschrift für öffentliches Recht und Völkerrecht* 279 (1980)

Hausmaninger, Ch., *Die einstweilige Verfügung im schiedsgerichtlichen Verfahren* (Vienna 1989)

Heller, Zur Vollstreckung eines jugoslawischen Schiedsspruches in Österreich, 9 *IPRax* 315 (1989)

International Chamber of Commerce, *Arbitration Law in Europe* (Paris 1981)

————, Austria/Autriche, in *Commercial Arbitration and the Law/ L'Arbitrage commercial et la Loi* (Basel 1949)

Klein, F.-E., *Considérations sur l'arbitrage en droit international privé* (Basel 1955)

Krilyszyn & Bajons, Zur Internationalisierung des österreichischen Schiedsrecht, 1 *Jahrbuch Schiedsgerichtsbarkeit* 234 (1987)

MacLaren, Commercial Arbitration in the United States and Overseas, in *Arbitration and the Licensing Process* 5 (R. Goldscheider & M. de Haas eds. 1984-)

Melis, Arbitration and the Courts in Austria — International Aspects, in *The Art of Arbitration* 253 (J. Schultsz & A. van den Berg eds. 1982)

————, Austria, in *Int'l Handbook Com. Arb.* (A. van den Berg, gen. ed. 1984), Suppl. 10, June 1989

————, Austria as a Neutral Site for International Commercial Arbitration, 44 *Arb. J.* 31 (No. 4, 1989)

————, Austria, 4 *Y.B. Com. Arb.* 21 (1979); 9 *Y.B.* 42 (1984); 15 *Y.B.* 302 (1990)

————, Austria: The Arbitral Centre of the Federal Economic Chamber, in *Handbook of Institutional Arbitration in International Trade* 33 (E. Cohn, M. Domke & F. Eisemann eds. 1977)

————, Das Schiedsgericht der Bundeskammer der Gewerblichen Wirtschaft, Wien, 2 *Jahrbuch Schiedsgerichtsbarkeit* 174 (1988)

————, Die Schiedsgerichtsbarkeit der österreichischen Handelskammer seit 1946, in *Festschrift für Ignaz Seidl-Hohenveldern* 367 (K.H. Böckstiegel, H.E. Folz, J.M. Mössner & K. Zemanek eds. 1988)

————, Immunity of Arbitrators under Austrian Law, in *The Immunity of Arbitrators* 15 (J.D.M. Lew ed. 1990)

————, La réforme autrichienne de l'arbitrage (loi du 2 fébrier 1983), 1987 *Rev. Arb.* 451

————, Zur Neuorderung der Bestimmungen über die Schiedsgerichtsbarkeit in der österreichischen Zivilprozessordnung, in *Festschrift für Arthur Bülow* 129 (K.-H. Böckstiegel & O. Glossner eds. 1981)

Melis, W., *A Guide to Commercial Arbitration in Austria* (Vienna 1983)

Neuteufel, Art. XXIX EGEO und das New Yorker Übereinkommen über die Anerkennung und Vollstreckung ausländischer Schiedssprüche, 1984 *ÖJZ* 320

Neuteufel, K., *Die Geschichte der Schiedsgerichte der Wiener Börse* (1876-1975) (Vienna 1976)

Parker School of Foreign and Comparative Law, *International Commercial Arbitration and the Courts* (Dobbs Ferry, NY 1990)

————, *The 1989 Guide to International Arbitration and Arbitrators* (Dobbs Ferry 1989)

Pechota, Arbitral Centre of the Federal Economic Chamber, Vienna, in 4 *W.A.R.* 3931 (H. Smit & V. Pechota eds. 1989)

————, Austria, in 2 *W.A.R.* 813 (H. Smit & V. Pechota eds. 1987)

————, Court of Arbitration of the Vienna Commodity Exchange, in 4 W.A.R. 3945 (H. Smit & V. Pechota eds. 1989)

Real, G.K.L., *Der Schiedsrichtervertrag* (Cologne 1983)

Rechberger, Das Anerkennungs- und Vollstreckungsabkommen zwischen Österreich und dem Fürstentum Liechtenstein, 16 *ZRV* 122 (1975)

Reiner, Die internationale Schiedsgerichtsbarkeit nach österreichischem und französischem Recht. Ein Vergleich zweier Reformen jüngeren Datums, 27 *ZRV* 162 (1986)

Reiner, A., *Handbuch der ICC Schiedsgerichtsbarkeit. Die Verfahrensordnung des Schiedsgerichtshofes der Internationalen Handelskammer* (Vienna 1989)

Schönherr, Neuerungen im Schiedsverfahren nach österreichischem Recht, 29 *RIW* 745 (1983)

Schütze, Die Schiedsgerichtsbarkeit der Bundeskammer der gewerblichen Wirtschaft Wien, 1987 *Wertpapiermitteilungen* 609

Seidl-Hohenveldern, Austrian Public Policy and the Enforcement of Foreign Arbitral Awards, 4 *Arb. Int'l* 322 (1988)

Tupman, Staying Enforcement of Arbitral Awards under the New York Convention, 3 *Arb. Int'l* 223 (1987)

Vulliemin, J.-M., *Jugement et sentence arbitrale* (2nd ed. Zurich 1990)

Wehli, Arbitral Tribunals under Austrian Law, 1 *Int'l Y.B. Civil & Com. Arb.* 114 (1928)

Zdravkovic, Certains cas de la jurisprudence yougoslave et étrangere sur l'exécution des sentences arbitrales étrangères, in *ICCA, Fifth Int'l Arb. Congress: Proceedings* C Izi 1-16 (1975)

BAHAMAS

Sterling, The Bahamas, in 2 *W.A.R.* 881 (H. Smit & V. Pechota   eds. 1987)

BAHRAIN

Dilger, Schiedsgerichtsbarkeit und Volstreckung ausländischer Entscheidungen in den Golfstaaten, in *Vetragspraxis und Streiterledigung im Wirschaftverkehr mit arabischen Staaten* 101 (K.-H. Böckstiegel ed. 1981)

El-Ahdab, A. H., *Arbitration with the Arab Countries* (Deventer 1990)

————, *L'arbitrage dans les pays arabes* (Paris 1988)

International Bar Association, *Arab Comparative & Commercial Law: The International Approach: Proceedings of the I.B.A. First Arab Regional Conference*, Cairo 15-19 February 1987 (London 1987)

Kemicha, F., ed., *Euro-Arab Arbitration II/Arbitrage Euro-Arabe II* (London 1989)

Krüger, Zur Einrede der Schiedsgerichtsbarkeit in Bahrain, 35 *RIW* 821 (1989)

Radhi, Settlement of Disputes through Arbitration: Arbitration in Bahrain, in 1 *Arab Comparative & Commercial Law: The International Aproach: Proceedings I.B.A. Conference* 199 (1987)

Saleh, The Recognition and Enforcement of Foreign Arbitral Awards in the States of the Arab Middle East, in *Contemporary Problems in International Arbitration* 340 (J.D.M. Lew ed. 1986)

Saleh, S., *Commercial Arbitration in the Arab Middle East* (London 1984)

Troller, Arbitration and Enforcement of Arbitration Awards in Arab Countries, 2 *Int'l Contr.* 397 (1981)

Zainalabedine, Commercial Arbitration Principles and Procedures: An Applied Study on Bahrain's Experience in Arbitration and Settlement of Commercial Disputes, in *Euro-Arab Arbitration II* 167 (F. Kemicha ed. 1989)

Ziadé, Selective Bibliography on Arbitration and Arab Countries, 3 *ICSID Rev. -Foreign Investment L.J.* 423 (1988)

BANGLADESH

Islam, Mediation in Bangladesh: A Lawyer's Perspective, 8 *L. & Int'l Affairs* 29 (1985)

BELGIUM

Berger, Die Regelung der gerichtlichen Anfechtbarkeit internationaler Schiedssprüche in europäischen Schiedsgerichtsgesetzen, 35 *RIW* 850 (1989)

————, The Modern Trend Towards Exclusion of Recourse Against Transnational Arbitral Awards: A European Perspective, 12 *Fordham Int'l L. J.* 605 (1989)

Bernini, Recent Legislations and International Unification of the Law on Arbitration, in *First International Commercial Arbitration Conference: Proceedings* 315 (N. Antaki & A. Prujiner eds. 1986)

Block, Le droit belge de l'arbitrage et la Convention de New York du 10 juin 1958, in *L'Arbitrage* 129 (L. Matray & G. de Leval eds. 1989)

Braun, A., ed., *L'arbitrage/Het scheidsgerecht* (Brussels 1983)

Bühler, Staatsgerichtliche Aufhebungskontrolle am Schiedsort? Zur Reform Belgiens, 7 *IPRax* 253 (1987)

Carabiber, L'immunité de juridiction et d'exécution des Etats collectivités et établissements publics au regard de l'obligation assumée par une clause compromissoire insérée dans les contrats internationaux de droit privé, in *Liber Amicorum for Martin Domke* 23 (P. Sanders ed. 1967)

de Bournonville, Au sujet des demandes incidents en matière d'arbitrage, in *L'arbitrage* 55 (L. Matray & G. de Leval eds. 1989)

de Leval, La designation et la mission des arbitres. Notes succinctes sur le droit positif applicable en Belgique, 53 *Rev. Droit Int'l & Droit Comp.* 170 (1976)

————, Les mesures provisoires et conservatoires en matière d'arbitrage, in *L'Arbitrage* 111 (L. Matray & G. de Leval eds. 1989)

De Ly, Judicial Review of Decisions of the I.C.C. Court of International Arbitration, 7 *J. Int'l Arb.* 153 (No. 1, 1990)

Dermine, L'arbitre et les mesures d'instruction, in *L'Arbitrage* 73 (L. Matray & G. de Leval eds. 1989)

————, L'interprétation des sentences arbitrales, 53 *Rev. Droit Int'l & Droit Comp.* 206 (1976)

Dermine, L., *L'arbitrage commercial en Belgique: Commentaire de la loi du 4 juillet 1972* (Brussels 1975)

Dieryck, Procédure et moyens de preuve (dans l'arbitrage commercial international), [1986] 7 *Int'l Arb. Gazette* 277

Eckstrom, L., *Licensing in Foreign and Domestic Operations*. Volume I, Chapter 7: Arbitration (by Steven Z. Szczepanski) (New York 1972, updated 1987)

Friedland, Provisional Measures in ICSID Arbitration, 2 *Arb. Int'l* 335 (1986)

Gaillard, The UNCITRAL Model Law and Recent Statutes on International Arbitration in Europe and North America, 2 *ICSID Rev. - Foreign Investment L.J.* 424 (1987)

Gomez, International Arbitration: A Case for Delocalization, 3 *Sri Lanka J. Int'l L.* 61 (1991)

Grade, The Annulment of Arbitral Awards in Belgium, 5 *Int'l Fin. L. Rev.* 35 (No. 11, 1986)

Hanotiau, Default Procedure (dans l'arbitrage commercial international), [1986] 7 *Int'l Arb. Gazette* 300

————, International Commercial Arbitration in Belgium, 1 *Am. Rev. Int'l Arb.* 1 (1990)

————, L'arbitrage commercial dans les relations belgo-soviétiques, 1983 *JT* 462

————, L'arbitrage international en Belgique, in *L'arbitrage* 143 (L. Matray & G. de Leval eds. 1989)

————, Developpements récents en matière d'arbitrage commercial international en Belgique, 1988 *Int'l Bus. L.J.* 839

Horsmans, Actualité et évolution du droit belge de l'arbitrage, 1990 *Rev. Arb.* 797

————, L'arbitrage et l'ordre public interne belge, 1978 *Rev. Arb.* 79

————, L'importance de l'arbitrage pour le juriste belge, in *L'Arbitrage* 3 (L. Matray & G. de Leval eds. 1989)

————, La sentence arbitrale, la convention d'arbitrage et l'ordre public interne belge, 16 *Tijdschrift voor Privaatrecht* 231 (1979)

Huys, M., Centre belge pour l'Etude et la Pratique de l'Arbitrage National et International CEPANI: Schiedsordnung, 1 *Jahrbuch Schiedsgerichtsbarkeit* 176 (1987)

Huys, M. & G. Keutgen, *L'arbitrage en droit belge et international* (Brussels 1981)

International Chamber of Commerce, *Arbitration Law in Europe* (Paris 1981)

———, Belgium/Belgique, in *Commercial Arbitration and the Law/ L'Arbitrage commercial et la Loi* (Basel 1949)

Jarvin, Choosing the Place of Arbitration: Where Do We Stand? 16 *Int'l Bus. Law.* 417 (1988)

Kassis, A., *Problèmes de base de l'arbitrage en droit comparé et en droit international.* Vol. 1: *Arbitrage juridictionnel et arbitrage contractuel* (Paris 1987)

Keutgen & Huys, L'arbitrage et la Convention de New York, 91 *JT* 232 (1976)

Klein, F.-E., *Considérations sur l'arbitrage en droit international privé* (Basel 1955)

Krings, L'exécution des sentences arbitrales, 53 *Rev. Droit Int'l & Droit Comp.* 181 (1976)

———, Un magistrat de l'ordre judiciare peut-il être designé en tant qu'arbitre? 56 *Rev. Droit Int'l & Droit Comp.* 278 (1979)

Ledoux, La Convention de New York et la Convention européenne sur l'arbitrage international et les concessions de vente en Belgique, 91 *JT* 305 (1976)

Legras de Grandcourt, Evolution contemporaine des législations européennes, in *Euro-Arab Arbitration* III 119 (F. Kemicha ed. 1991)

Linsmeau, L'annulation des sentences arbitrales en droit belge, in *L'Arbitrage* 91 (L. Matray & G. de Leval eds. 1989)

Linsmeau, L'arbitrage volontaire en droit privé belge, in *Répertoire pratique de droit belge, Complément* VII (1990)

MacLaren, Commercial Arbitration in the United States and Overseas, in *Arbitration and the Licensing Process* 5 (R. Goldscheider & M. de Haas eds. 1984-)

Matray, Belgium, in *Int'l Handbook Com. Arb.* (A. van den Berg gen. ed. 1984), Suppl. 8, Dec. 1987

———, Belgium: National Report, 5 *Y.B. Com. Arb.* 1 (1980); 11 *Y.B. Com. Arb.* 57 (1986)

———, L'arbitre-partie en matière internationale, 53 *Rev. Droit Int'l & Droit Comp.* 152 (1976)

———, Le droit belge de l'arbitrage, in *L'Arbitrage* 231 (L. Matray & G. de Leval eds. 1989)

———, La loi belge du 27 mars 1985 et ses repercussions sur l'arbitrage commercial international, 64 *Rev. Droit Int'l & Droit Comp.* 243 (1987)

Matray, L. & G. de Leval, eds., *L'Arbitrage. Travaux offerts au Professeur Albert Fettweis* (Brussels 1989)

Neumann, Limiting Judicial Review in International Commercial Arbitration: The New Swiss and Belgian Laws Offer Less Than They Promise, 1 *Am. Rev. Int'l Arb.* 435 (1990)

Park, Judicial Controls in the Arbitral Process, 5 *Arb. Int'l* 230 (1989)

Parker School of Foreign and Comparative Law, *International Commercial Arbitration and the Courts* (Dobbs Ferry 1990)

Paulsson, Arbitrage international et voies de recours: La Cour suprême de Suède dans le sillage des solutions belge et helvétique, 117 *J. Droit Int'l (Clunet)* 588 (1990)

———, Arbitration Unbound in Belgium, 2 *Arb. Int'l* 68 (1986)

———, May a State Invoke Its Internal Law to Repudiate Consent to International Commercial Arbitration? Reflections on the Benteler v. Belgium Preliminary Award, 2 *Arb. Int'l* 90 (1986)

Pire, La convention d'arbitrage, in *L'Arbitrage* 31 (L. Matray & G. de Leval eds. 1989)

Real, G.K.L., *Der Schiedsrichtervertrag* (Cologne 1983)

Robert, El arbitraje en los paises de la Comunidad Europea, in *El Arbitraje Comercial Internacional* 223 (Mexico 1983)

Samuel, A., *Jurisdictional Problems in International Commercial Arbitration: A Study of Belgian, Dutch, English, French, Swedish, Swiss, U.S. and West German Law* (Zurich 1989)

Sauvepanne, Die Schiedsgerichtsbarkeit in der Benelux, 7 *Jahrbuch für internationales Recht* 86 (1956)

Shifman, Belgian Centre for the Study and the Practice of National and International Arbitration, in 4 *W.A.R.* 4029 (H. Smit & V. Pechota eds. 1989)

———, Belgium, in 2 *W.A.R.* 945 (H. Smit & V. Pechota eds. 1987)

Storme, Arbitrage entre personnes de droit public et de droit privé, 1978 *Rev. Arb.* 113; 1979 *Tijdschrift voor Privaatrecht* 179

———, Aspects importants du droit arbitral belge, 53 *Rev. Droit Int'l & Droit Comp.* 116 (1976)

———, Belgium: A Paradise for International Commercial Arbitration, 14 *Int'l Bus. Law.* 294 (1986)

———, Das Territorium im Recht: Die Stellung der Schiedsgerichtsbarkeit im belgischen Recht, in *Festschrift für Walther J. Habscheid* 317 (W. Lindacher, D. Pfaff et al. eds. 1989)

Storme, M. & B. Demeulenaere, *International Commercial Arbitration in Belgium: A Handbook* (Deventer 1989)

van Compernolle, L'arbitrage multipartite, in *L'Arbitrage* 81 (L. Matray & G. de Leval eds. 1989)

Vanderelst, Increasing the Appeal of Belgium as an International Arbitration Forum? The Belgian Law of March 27, 1985 Concerning the Annulment of Arbitral Awards, 3 *J. Int'l Arb.* 77 (No. 2, 1986)

van Houtte, Arbitrage en toepasselijk recht, 19 *Tijdschrift voor Privaatrecht* 703 (1982)

———, L'arbitrabilité de la résiliation des concessions de vente exclusive, in *Mélanges offerts à Raymond Vander Elst* 821 (Brussels 1986)

———, La loi belge du 27 mars 1985 sur l'arbitrage international, 1986 *Rev. Arb.* 29

Vulliemin, J.-M., *Jugement et sentence arbitrale* (2nd ed. Zurich 1990)

Watté, Le sort des sentences arbitrales en droit belge depuis la loi du 27 mars 1985, 21 *Revue belge de droit international* 496 (1988)

BHUTAN

Schütze, Die Anerkennung und Vollstreckbarerklärung ausländischer Zivilurteile und Schiedssprüche in Bhutan, *Juristische Rundschau* 498 (1981)

BOLIVIA

Eckstrom, L., *Licensing in Foreign and Domestic Operations*. Volume I, Chapter 7: Arbitration (by Steven Z. Szczepanski), (New York 1972, updated 1987)

Garro, Bolivia, in 2 *W.A.R.* 967 (H. Smit & V. Pechota eds. 1987)

International Chamber of Commerce, Bolivia/Bolivie, in *Commercial Arbitration and the Law/L'Arbitrage commercial et la Loi* (Basel 1951)

MacLaren, Commercial Arbitration in the United States and Overseas, in *Arbitration and the Licensing Process* 5 (R. Goldscheider & M. de Haas eds. 1984-)

Samtleben, Schiedsgerichtsbarkeit in den Andenpaktstaaten, 30 *RIW* 600 (1984)

BRAZIL

Ascarelli & Sciascia, Brazilian Law and Practice, 5 *Arb. J.* 204 (1950)

Azeredo Santos, Commercial Arbitration in Brazil, in *Sixty Years of ICC Arbitration - A Look at the Future* 51 (1984)

Baptista & Latorre, Oservaçoes praticas sobre a homologaçao de sentencas e de laudos arbitrais estrangeiros no Brasil, 276 *Revista Forense* 311 (1981)

Barclay, Arbitration in Latin America, 43 *Arbitration* 105 (1977)

Buchanan, Public Policy and International Commercial Arbitration, 26 *Am. Bus. L.J.* 511 (1988)

Buzaid, Do juizo arbitral, 217 *Rev. Trib.* 7 (1960)

Clare, Enforcement of the Arbitration Clause in Brazilian Loan Agreements, 1982 *Int'l Fin. L. Rev.* 18 (No. 3)

de Magalhaes, Arbitragem internacional privada, 279 *Revista Forense* 99 (1982)

―――, Do Estado na arbitragem privada, 22 *Revista de Informacao Legislativa* 125 (April-June 1985)

―――, Execuçao de laudo arbitral, 599 *Rev. Trib.* 9 (Sept. 1985)

de Magalhaes J. & L.O. Batista, *Arbitragem comercial* (Rio de Janeiro 1986)

de Oliveira Novaes, Difficulties in Resolving Conflicts Regarding High Technology Contracts in Brazil, 16 *Int'l Bus. Law.* 177 (1988)

Dolinger, Brazilian Confirmation of Foreign Judgments, 19 *Int'l Law.* 853 (1985); reprinted in *Modern Legal Systems Cyclopedia,* Supplement One 360.1 (K.R. Redden ed. 1987)

Dunshee de Abranches, C.A., ed., *El arbitraje comercial en Iberoamérica* (Madrid 1982)

Eckstrom, L., *Licensing in Foreign and Domestic Operations.* Volume I, Chapter 7: Arbitration (by Steven Z. Szczepanski), (New York 1972, updated 1987)

Garro, Brazil, in 2 *W.A.R.* 1017 (H. Smit & V. Pechota eds. 1987)

Goldman, Arbitration and Transfer of Technology in Latin America, in *Arbitration and the Licensing Process* 5-29 (R. Goldscheider & M. de Haas eds. 1984-)

Grigera Naón, Mandatory Provisions of Law Regarding Arbitration Agreements in Latin America, in *Arbitration in Settlement of International Commercial Disputes Involving the Far East and Arbitration in Combined Transportation* 121 (P. Sanders ed. 1989)

Huck, Deficiencias da arbitragem comercial internacional, 593 *Rev. Trib.* 26 (March 1985)

International Chamber of Commerce, Brazil/Bresil, in *Commercial Arbitration and the Law/L'Arbitrage commercial et la Loi* (Basel 1951)

Larsen, Enforcement of Foreign Judgments in Latin America: Trends and Individual Differences, 17 *Tex. Int'l L.J.* 213 (1982)

MacLaren, Commercial Arbitration in the United States and Overseas, in *Arbitration and the Licensing Process* 5 (R. Goldscheider & M. de Haas eds. 1984-)

Marotta Rangel, Brazil: National Report, 3 *Y.B. Com. Arb.* 31 (1978) and 7 *Y.B. Com. Arb.* 57 (1982)

———, Brazil, in *Int'l Handbook Com. Arb.* (A. van den Berg, gen. ed. 1984), Suppl. 9, Sept. 1988

Montoya Alberti, Arbitration, Foreign Law and Jurisdiction in International Loan Agreements in Some Countries of Latin America, in *Arbitration in Settlement of International Commercial Disputes Involving the Far East and Arbitration in Combined Transportation* 99 (P. Sanders ed. 1989)

———, El arbitraje en los contratos de prestamo internacionales, in *El Arbitraje en el Derecho Latinoamericano y Español* 481 (L. Perret & U. Montoya Alberti eds. 1989)

Nattier, International Commercial Arbitration in Latin America: Enforcement of Arbitral Agreements and Awards, 21 *Tex. Int'l L. J.* 397 (1986)

Olavo Baptista, Arbitragem e joint venture internacionais, in *El Arbitraje en el Derecho Latinoamericano y Español* 185 (L. Perret & U. Montoya Alberti eds. 1989)

581

Paes de Barros Leaes, Arbitragem comercial international, in 7 *Enciclopedia Juridica Saraiva* 359 (Sao Paulo 1978)

Paes de Barros Leaes, L.G., *Ensaio sobre arbitragens comercials* (Sao Paulo 1966)

Parker School of Foreign and Comparative Law, *International Commercial Arbitration and the Courts* (Dobbs Ferry, NY 1990)

Pestalozzi, Arbitration and Its New Prospects in Brazil, 4 *J. Int'l Arb.* 131 (No. 3, 1987)

Rechsteiner, Die neuere brasilianische Rechtssprechung zur Anerkennung ausländischer Schiedsprüche, 26 *ZRV* 100 (1985)

Rosenn, Enforcement of Foreign Arbitral Awards in Brazil, 28 *Am. J. Comp. L.* 498 (1980)

Samtleben, Aktuelle Fragen der internationalen Handelsschiedsgerichtsbarkeit in Brasilien, 35 *RIW* 769 (1989)

———, Arbitragem comercial no direito internacional privado Brazileiro, in *Estudos em Homenagem ao Prof. Doutor A. Ferrer-Correia* 691 (Coimbra 1986)

———, Arbitragem no Brazil, 77 *Revista da Faculdade de Direito, Universidade de Sao Paulo* 185 (1982)

———, Arbitration in Brazil, 18 *U. Miami Inter-Am. L. Rev.* 1 (1986)

———, Schiedsgerichtsbarkeit in Brasilien, 27 *RIW* 376 (1981)

Silva Soares, Arbitragem no comercio internacional, in 156 *Arquivos do Ministerio da Justica* 233 (Brazilia, Oct.-Dec. 1980)

Silva Soares, G., *Concessoes de exploraçao de petróleo e arbitragens internacionais* (Sao Paulo 1977)

Strenger, Do juizo arbitral, 607 *Rev. Trib.* 24 (May 1986)

———, International Arbitration: Doctrine and Practice in Brazil, 5 *J. Int'l Arb.* 41 (No. 1, 1988)

———, The Application by the Arbitrator of Public Policy Rules to the Substance of the Dispute, in *Comparative Arbitration Practice and Public Policy in Arbitration* 353 (P. Sanders ed. 1987)

————, Aplicaçao de normas de ordem publica nos laudos arbitrais, 606 *Rev. Trib.* 9 (April 1986)

Villela, Reconhecimento de decisoes arbitrais estrangeiras, 19 *Revista de Informaçao Legislativa* 53 (No. 75, July-Sept. 1982)

BULGARIA

Atanassoff, Joint ventures et arbitrage commercial international en Bulgarie, 1990 *Int'l Bus. L.J.* 579

Blessing, Proper Law and Dispute Resolution Arising out of East-West Joint Ventures, in *Eastern Bloc Joint Ventures* 107 (D. Winter ed. 1990)

Bulgarian Chamber of Commerce and Industry, *International Commercial Arbitration in Bulgaria* (Sofia 1989)

Damjanov, C., *Isplnyaemost na chuzhdestranni sdebni ta arbitrazhni reshenia* (Sofia 1977)

Georgiev, Le règlement de la Cour d'arbitrage près de la Chambre de commerce et d'industrie de Bulgarie, 1980 *Rev. Arb.* 44

Grzybowski, Arbitral Tribunals for Foreign Trade in Socialist Countries, 37 *Law & Contemp. Probs.* 592 (1972)

International Chamber of Commerce, Bulgaria/Bulgarie, in *Commercial Arbitration and the Law/L'Arbitrage commercial et la Loi* (Basel 1951)

Jessel & Holst, Anerkennung und Vollstreckung ausländischer Entscheidungen sowie Rechthilfe in Zivilsachen nach dem bulgarischen Recht, 24 *WGO, Monatshefte für Osteuropäisches Recht* 255 (1982)

Kos-Rabcewicz-Zubkowski, Central and East European Rules on the Form of International Arbitration Agreement, 3 *La Revue Juridique Themis* 415 (1969)

Kos-Rabcewicz-Zubkowski, L., *East European Rules on the Validity of International Arbitration Agreements* (Manchester and Dobbs Ferry, NY 1970)

Kudryashev & Kozhevnikov, Vneshnetorgovyi arbitrazh v stranakh-chlenakh SEV, *Vneshniaia torgovlia* 52 (No. 4, 1984)

Kuss, Neuere Entwicklungen und Perspektiven der Ost - West - Schieds-gerichts-barkeit, 33 *RIW* 584 (1987)

Lebedev, International Commercial Arbitration in the Socialist Countries Members of the CMEA, 158 *Recueil des Cours* 87 (1977-V)

Lebedev, S., ed., *Handbook on Foreign Trade Arbitration in the CMEA Member Countries* (Moscow 1983)

Majoros, Exécution de décisions étrangères et procédure d'exéquatur en Europe de l'Est: Tour d'horizon avec des références de droit comparé, in *Le Juriste Suisse Face au Droit et aux Jugements Etrangers: Ouverture ou Repli?* 135 (F. Knoepfler ed. 1988)

Melis, Enforcement of Arbitral Awards in Eastern Europe, in *Contemporary Problems in International Arbitration* 332 (J.D.M. Lew ed. 1986)

Minakov, A.I., *Arbitrazhnye soglashenia i praktika rassmotreniya vneshneekonomicheskikh sporov* (Moscow 1985)

Pechota, A New Law on International Commercial Arbitration in Bulgaria, 1 *Am. J. Int'l Arb.* 310 (1990)

————, International Economic Arbitration in the USSR and Eastern Europe, 8 *N.Y. L. Sch. J. Int'l & Comp. L.* 377 (1987)

Pisar, S., *Coexistence & Commerce*, Chapters 20-24 (New York 1970)

Popov, K., *Praktika na Arbitrazhniia sud pri Bulgarskata Turgovsko-promishlena palata*, 1981-1985g. (Sofia 1987)

Pozdnyakov, Commercial Arbitration in CMEA Member Countries, 4 *Int'l Tax & Bus. Law.* 272 (1986)

Przetacznik, The Arbitration Court at the Bulgarian Chamber of Commerce and Industry, in 4 *W.A.R.* 4099 (H. Smit & V. Pechota eds. 1989)

Sipkov, The Law of Foreign Trade in the People's Republic of Bulgaria, 37 *Law & Contemp. Probs.* 485 (1972)

Stalev, Arbitrazh za poplvane na praznini v dlgosrochni vnshnotrgovski dogovori, 1983 *Vaprosy na mezhdunarodnoto chastno pravo* (Sofia) 93

————, Bulgarian People's Republic, in *Int'l Handbook Com. Arb.* (A. van den Berg, gen. ed. 1984), Suppl. 12, January 1991

————, Bulgaria: National Report, 1 *Y.B. Com. Arb.* 18 (1976); 7 *Y.B. Com. Arb.* 60 (1982); 11 *Y.B. Com. Arb.* 61 (1986)

————, Das neue bulgarische Gesetz über die internationale Handelsschiedsgerichtsbarkeit, 2 *Jahrbuch Schiedsgerichtsbarkeit* 208 (1988)

————, The Continental Case of Eastern Europe, 41 *Arbitration* 95 (1974)

Strohbach, The CMEA Countries, in *Arbitration in Settlement of International Commercial Disputes Involving the Far East and Arbitration in Combined Transportation* 133 (P. Sanders ed. 1989)

Stumpf, Ost-West-Schiedsgerichtsbarkeit: Schiedsgerichte mit Sitz in dritten Ländern, 33 *RIW* 821 (1987)

Topalov, Problems of Foreign Trade Arbitration in the People's Republic of Bulgaria, 11 *Rassegna dell'Arb.* 1 (1971)

Velinov, Priznavane i izpulnenie na chuzdestrannite resheniia spored dogovorite za pravna pomosht skliucheni ot NRB, 32 *Sotsialistichesko Pravo* 26 (August 1983)

BURKINA FASO

Meyer, Le nouveau code des investisssements au Burkina: changement ou continuité? 9 *Revue Burkinabe de Droit* 35 (1986)

————, Le régime juridique des investissements en Haute-Volta, 1982 *Revue Voltaique de Droit* 7

CAMEROON

Dorman, Cameroon, in 2 *W.A.R.* 1081 (H. Smit & V. Pechota eds. 1987)

International Chamber of Commerce, Cameroon/Cameroun, in *Commercial Arbitration and the Law/L'Arbitrage commercial et la Loi* (Basel 1964)

CANADA

Allison & Nevin, Attachments and Other Similar Remedies in Arbitration Matters: The Quebec Perspective, in *Interim Court Remedies in Support of Arbitration* 179 (D. Shenton & W. Kühn eds. 1987)

Alvarez, Judicial Intervention and Review Under the International Commercial Arbitration Act, in *UNCITRAL Arbitration Model in Canada* 137 (R. Paterson & B. Thompson eds. 1987)

————, La nouvelle législation canadienne sur l'arbitrage commercial international, 1986 *Rev. Arb.* 529

————, The Role of Arbitration in Canada - New Perspectives, 21 *U. B.C. L. Rev.* 247 (1987)

Anderson & Rugman, The Canada-U.S. Free Trade Agreement: A Legal and Economic Analysis of the Dispute Settlement Mechanism, 6 *J. Int'l Arb.* 65 (No. 4, 1989)

Antaki, A Critical Evaluation of International Commercial Arbitration, in *Resolving International Business Disputes through Arbitration: Materials of the Conference in Toronto, Jan. 19 & 20, 1987*

Antaki, N. & A. Prujiner, eds., *Actes du 1er Colloque sur l'Arbitrage Commercial International/Proceedings of the First International Commercial Arbitration Conference* (Montreal 1986)

Apuzzo & Kerr, International Arbitration — The Dispute Settlement Procedures Chosen for the Canada-U.S. Free Trade Agreement, 5 *J. Int'l Arb.* 7 (No. 4, 1988)

Azrieli, Dispute Resolution Under Chapter 18 of the Canada-United States Free Trade Agreement, 1 *Am. Rev. Int'l Arb.* 419 (1990)

Blom, Conflict of Laws Aspects of the International Commercial Arbitration Act, in *UNCITRAL Arbitration Model in Canada* 127 (R. Paterson & B. Thompson eds. 1987)

Brierley, Aspects of the Promise to Arbitrate in the Law of Quebec, 30 *Rev. Barreau* 473 (1970)

————, International Trade Arbitration: The Canadian Viewpoint, in *Canadian Perspectives on International Law and Organization* (R. St.J. Macdonald, ed. 1974)

————, La Convention d'arbitrage en droit québécois interne, 1987 *C.P. du N.* 507

————, La validité de la clause compromissoire demeure-t-elle incertaine en droit québécois? 1975 *Rev. Arb.* 154

————, Overview of International Commercial Arbitration in Quebec and in the Canadian Common Law Provinces, in *First International Commercial Arbitration Conference: Proceedings* 273 (N. Antaki & A. Prujiner eds. 1986)

————, Quebec Arbitration Law: A New Era Begins, 40 *Arb. J.* 20 (No. 3, 1985)

————, Quebec's New (1986) Arbitration Law, 13 *Can. Bus. L.J.* 58 (1987)

————, Une loi nouvelle pour le Québec en matière d'arbitrage, 47 *Rev. Barreau* 259 (1987)

Carbonneau, American and Other National Variations on the Theme of International Commercial Arbitration, 18 *Ga. J. Int'l & Comp. L.* 143 (1988)

Castel, Canada and International Arbitration, 36 *Arb. J.* 5 (1981)

Chiasson, Canada: No Man's Land No More, 3 *J. Int'l Arb.* 67 (No. 2, 1986)

Chiasson & Lalonde, Recent Canadian Legislation on Arbitration, 2 *Arb. Int'l* 370 (1986)

Cohen, La reconnaissance et l'exécution au Canada des sentences arbitrales étrangères, 47 *Rev. Barreau* 435 (1987)

Colas, Clause compromissoire, compromis et arbitrage en droit nouveau, 28 *Rev. Barreau* 129 (1968)

Collins, Arbitration in Canada, 54 *Arbitration* 257 (1988)

Cosman, Enforcing International Arbitration Awards, in *Resolving Int'l Business Disputes through Arbitration.* Materials of the Conference held in Toronto on Jan. 19 & 20, 1987

————, Attachments and Other Interim Court Remedies in Support of Arbitration, 10 *Can. Arb. J.* 2 (No. 1, 1985)

————, Attachments and Other Interim Court Remedies in Support of Arbitration: The Canadian Perspective, in *Interim Court Remedies in Support of Arbitration* 191 (D. Shenton & W. Kühn eds. 1987)

Crozier, The Status of International Arbitration Awards Under Canadian Insolvency Law, 18 *Can. Bus. L.J.* 294 (1991)

Davidson, International Commercial Arbitration Law in Canada, 12 *Nw. J. Int'l L. & Bus.* 97 (1991)

Dorais, L'arbitrage commercial — développements législatifs, 47 *Rev. Barreau* 273 (1987)

Dorman, Canada, in 2 *W.A.R.* 1143 (H. Smit & V. Pechota eds. 1987)

Dwor, Some Consequences of a Badly Drafted Arbitration Agreement, 54 *Arbitration* 252 (1988)

Ferland, L'arbitrage sans action en justice dans la province de Québec, 31 *Rev. Barreau* 69 (1971)

Ferland, Ph., *L'arbitrage conventionnel* (Montreal 1983)

Gaillard, The UNCITRAL Model Law and Recent Statutes on International Arbitration in Europe and North America, 2 *ICSID Rev. - Foreign Investment L.J.* 424 (1987)

Gelinas, L'exécution des sentences arbitrales internationales au Québec: commentaire, in *First International Commercial Arbitration Conference: Proceedings* 305 (N. Antaki & A. Prujiner eds. 1986)

Graham, International Commercial Arbitration: The Developing Canadian Profile, in *UNCITRAL Arbitration Model in Canada* 77 (R. Paterson & B. Thompson eds. 1987)

————, Proposals for a New Alberta Arbitration Act, 16 *Can. Bus. L.J.* 185 (1990)

————, The Internationalization of Commercial Arbitration in Canada: A Preliminary Reaction, 13 *Can. Bus. L.J.* 1 (1987)

————, The New York Convention of 1958: A Canadian Perspective, in *First International Commercial Arbitration Conference: Proceedings* 185 (N. Antaki & A. Prujiner eds. 1986)

———, The Present Status of International Commercial Arbitration in Canada, in *Arbitration in Settlement of International Commercial Disputes Involving the Far East and Arbitration in Combined Transportation* 185 (P. Sanders ed. 1989); reprinted in 55 *Arbitration* 266 (1989)

Gregory, International Commercial Arbitration: Comments on Professor Graham's Paper, 13 *Can. Bus. L.J.* 42 (1987)

Guthrie, Arbitration in Commercial Disputes, 41 *Advocate* 511 (1983)

Herrmann, A Revolution in Canadian Arbitration, 2 *Int'l Arb. Rep.* 164 (1987)

———, The British Columbia Enactment of the UNCITRAL Model Law, in *UNCITRAL Arbitration Model in Canada* 65 (R. Paterson & B. Thompson eds. 1987)

Hunter, Arbitration in British Columbia, Canada, 3 *Int'l Constr. L. Rev.* 420(1986)

Jarvin, Canada's Determined Move Towards International Commercial Arbitration, 3 *J. Int'l Arb.* 111 (No. 3, 1986)

———, Choosing the Place of Arbitration: Where Do We Stand? 16 *Int'l Bus. Law.* 417 (1988)

Klein, F.-E., *Considérations sur l'arbitrage en droit international privé* (Basel 1955)

Kokonis & Kelly, Canada: Arbitration, in A1 *World Litigation Law & Practice* CAN 13-1 (R. Myrick ed. 1986)

Kos-Rabcewicz-Zubkowski, Absolute Lack of Jurisdiction of Courts When an Undertaking to Arbitrate is Stipulated in a Contract, 24 *Inter-American Bar Association Conference: Proceedings* 143 (Panama, Feb. 4-10, 1984)

———, Arbitration in the Code of Civil Procedure of Quebec, 8 *Rassegna dell'Arb.* 85 (1968); also 2 *La Revue Juridique Themis* 143 (1968)

———, Assistance accordé par les tribunaux d'Etats aux tribunaux d'arbitrage (Province de Québec, Canada), in *ICCA, Third Int'l Arb. Congress: Proceedings* 487 (1969)

———, Canada, in *Int'l Handbook Com. Arb.* (A. van den Berg gen. ed. 1984), Suppl. 10, June 1989

————, Canada: National Report, 2 *Y.B. Com. Arb.* 16 (1977); 8 *Y.B. Com. Arb.* 68 (1983); 12 *Y.B. Com. Arb.* 361 (1987); 13 *Y.B. Com. Arb.* 393 (1988) and 14 *Y.B. Com. Arb.* 493 (1989)

————, Elementos esenciales de los acuerdos de arbitraje en Canada, in *El Arbitraje Comercial Internacional* 237 (Mexico 1983)

————, International Arbitration Laws in Canada: Adaptation of UNCITRAL Model Law on International Commercial Arbitration, 5 *J. Int'l Arb.* 43 (No. 3, 1988)

————, International Arbitration Laws in Canada: Recent Legislation (Ontario and Saskatchewan), 5 *J. Int'l Arb.* 164 (No. 4, 1988)

————, International Commercial Arbitration in the Common Law Provinces of Canada, 44 *Arb. J.* 14 (No. 3, 1989)

————, L'adaptation de la loi-type de la C.N.U.D.C.I. dans les provinces de common law au Canada, 1989 *Rev. Arb.* 37

Kos-Rabcewicz-Zubkowski, L., *Commercial and Civil Law Arbitration in Canada* (Ottawa 1978)

Lalonde, The New Environment for Commercial Arbitration in Canada, 1 *Rev. Int'l Bus. L.* 31 (1987); also in 1988 *Int'l Bus. L. J.* 963

————, The New Environment for Commercial Arbitration in Canada, 29 *Rassegna dell'Arb.* 13 (1989)

Lalonde, Buchanan & Ross, Domestic and International Commercial Arbitration in Quebec, Current Status and Perspectives for the Future, 45 *Rev. Barreau* 705 (1985)

McLaren, R.H. & E.E. Palmer, *The Law and Practice of Commercial Arbitration* (Toronto 1982)

Mendes, Canada: A New Forum to Develop the Cultural Psychology of International Commercial Arbitration, 3 *J. Int'l Arb.* 71 (No. 3, 1986)

Mendes & Binavince, Canada and the New York Convention on Foreign Arbitral Awards, 1984 *Can. Arb. J.* 2 (Spring 1984)

Morris, The Problem of Uniform Arbitration Legislation in Canada, 13 *Arb. J.* 103 (1958)

Nöcker, Das neue Schiedsverfahrenrecht in Kanada, 34 *RIW* 363 (1988)

Nöcker, T., *Das Recht der Schiedsgerichtsbarkeit in Kanada* (Heidelberg 1988)

Nöcker & Hentzen (Matthias K.), The New Legislation on Arbitration in Canada, 22 *Int'l Law.* 829 (1988)

Oehmke, T., *International Arbitration* (Rochester 1990)

Pacific Rim Advisory Council, *Pacific Rim: Commercial Arbitration Procedures* (San Diego, CA 1985)

Parker School of Foreign and Comparative Law, *International Commercial Arbitration and the Courts* (Dobbs Ferry, NY 1990)

Paterson, International Commercial Arbitration Act: An Overview, in *UNCITRAL Arbitration Model in Canada* 113 (R. Paterson & B. Thompson eds. 1987)

Paterson R. & B. Thompson, eds., *UNCITRAL Arbitration Model in Canada. Canadian International Commercial Arbitration Legislation* (Toronto 1987)

Pechota, Arbitrators' Institute of Canada, in 4 *W.A.R.* 4181 (H. Smit & V. Pechota eds. 1989)

———, Canadian Arbitration, Conciliation and Amicable Composition Centre, Inc., in 4 *W.A.R.* 4203 (H. Smit & V. Pechota eds. 1989)

———, comp., The British Columbia International Commercial Arbitration Centre, in 4 *W.A.R.* 4211 (H. Smit & V. Pechota eds. 1989)

Pomerleau, L'arbitrage interprovincial et international au Canada: aspects constitutionnel et législatif, 1985 *Rev. Arb.* 373 (1985)

Proceedings of the First International Commercial Arbitration Conference, Quebec City, October 1985 (N. Antaki & A. Prujiner eds.), (Montreal 1986)

Prujiner, L'exécution des sentences arbitrales internationales au Québec, in *First International Commercial Arbitration Conference: Proceedings* 289 (N. Antaki & A. Prujiner eds. 1986)

———, Les nouvelles règles de l'arbitrage au Québec, 1987 *Rev. Arb.* 425 (1987)

Report, Canada and the United Nations Convention on Arbitral Awards, 9 *Can. Arb. J.* 2 (No. 1, 1984)

Sareika, Arbitration in Canada, 46 *Arbitration* 43 and 116 (1980)

———, La clause compromissoire et l'article 68 du Code de procédure civile du Québec, 1977 *Rev. Arb.* 250

———, Rechtsprechung zum kanadischen Recht der Schiedsgerichtsbarkeit, 22 *RIW* 261 (1976)

———, The Enforcement of Commercial Arbitral Awards under Canadian Law, 8 *Int'l Bus. Law.* 173 (1980)

Sareika, W., *Die Gültigkeit von Schiedsgerichtsvereinbarungen nach kanadischem und deutschem Recht* (Frankfurt 1978)

Thompson, 'Building an Arbitration and Mediation Centre: From International Foundations to Domestic Rooftops' — The Establishment of the British Columbia International Commercial Arbitration Centre, in *Arbitration in Settlement of International Commercial Disputes Involving the Far East and Arbitration in Combined Transportation* 189 (P. Sanders ed. 1989)

———, A British Columbia Perspective on International Commercial Arbitration, 13 *Can. Bus. L.J.* 70 (1987)

———, Building An Arbitration and Mediation Centre from International Foundations to Domestic Rooftops: A Case Study of the British Columbia International Commercial Arbitration Centre, in *A Handbook of Dispute Resolution* 201 (K. Mackie ed. 1991)

———, Commercial Arbitration — a New Look at a New Era, 45 *Advocate* 185(1987)

———, The Marriage of the UNCITRAL Model Arbitration Law and the UNCITRAL Arbitration Rules, in *UNCITRAL Arbitration Model in Canada* 143 (R. Paterson & B. Thompson eds. 1987)

Thuilleaux, La loi de 1986 sur l'arbitrage au Québec, au regard de la loi française sur l'arbitrage, 1988 *Int'l Bus. L.J.* 905

Tremblay, Domestic and International Arbitration in Quebec, 13 *Commonwealth L. Bull.* 277 (1987)

Wilkinson, The Arbitration Act of Ontario, 6 *Can. Arb. J.* 17 (No. 1, 1981)

————, Reports of Proposed Changes in Ontario Arbitration Act, 7 *Can. Arb. J.* (Annual Meeting Edition) 26 (1982)

CENTRAL AMERICA

Garro, A., ed., *Commercial and Labor Arbitration in Central America* (Ardsley-on-Hudson, NY 1991)

CHILE

Aliaga Grez, A., *Los recursos procesales en el juicio arbitral* (Santiago de Chile 1985)

Aravena Arredondo, L., *Naturaleza jurídica del arbitraje* (Santiago de Chile 1969)

Aylwin Azocar, P., *El juicio arbitral* (Santiago de Chile 1958)

Dunshee de Abranches, C.A., ed., *El arbitraje comercial en Iberoamérica* (Madrid 1982)

Eckstrom, L., *Licensing in Foreign and Domestic Operations. Volume I, Chapter 7: Arbitration* (by Steven Z. Szczepanski), (New York 1972, updated 1987)

Eyzaguirre Echeverria, Chile: National Report, 3 *Y.B. Com. Arb.* 45 (1978)

Eyzaguirre Echeverria, R., *El arbitraje comercial en la legislación chilena y su regulación international* (Santiago de Chile 1981)

Fuchs, Das Schiedsgerichtswesen in Chile, 3 *Internationales Jahrbuch für Schiedsgerichtswesen in Zivil- und Handelssachen* 63 (1931)

Goldman, Arbitration and Transfer of Technology in Latin America, in *Arbitration and the Licensing Process* 5-29 (R. Goldscheider & M. de Haas eds. 1984-)

Landeta Verdi, P., *El arbitraje comercial* (Santiago de Chile 1962)

Larsen, Enforcement of Foreign Judgments in Latin America: Trends and Individual Differences, 17 *Tex. Int'l L.J.* 213 (1982)

León, Arbitraje comercial internacional en Chile, in *El Arbitraje en el Derecho Latinoamericano y Español* 199 (L. Perrot & U. Montoya Alberti eds. 1989)

MacLaren, Commercial Arbitration in the United States and Overseas, in *Arbitration and the Licensing Process* 5 (R. Goldscheider & M. de Haas eds. 1984-)

Montoya Alberti, Arbitration, Foreign Law and Jurisdiction in International Loan Agreements in Some Countries of Latin America, in *Arbitration in Settlement of International Commercial Disputes Involving the Far East and Arbitration in Combined Transportation* 99 (P. Sanders ed. 1989)

————, El arbitraje en los contratos de prestamo internacionales, in *El Arbitraje en el Derecho Latinoamericano y Español* 481 (L. Perret & U. Montoya Alberti eds. 1989)

Pacific Rim Advisory Council, *Pacific Rim: Commercial Arbitration Procedures* (San Diego, CA 1985)

Samtleben, Schiedsgerichtsbarkeit in Chile, 29 *RIW* 167 (1983)

Stumpf, Ost-West-Schiedsgerichtsbarkeit: Schiedsgerichte mit Sitz in dritten Ländern, 33 *RIW* 821 (1987)

CHINA

Bernini, Recent Legislations and International Unification of the Law on Arbitration, in *First International Commercial Arbitration Conference: Proceedings* 315 (N. Antaki & A. Prujiner eds. 1986)

Brazil, Resolution of Trade Disputes in the Asian Pacific Region, 10 *Adel. L. Rev.* 49 (1985)

Broedermann, China and Admiralty —— An Introduction to Chinese Maritime Law and U.S.-Chinese Shipping Relations, 15 *J. Mar. L. & Com.* 539, 562(1984)

Cheung, Enforcement of Foreign Arbitral Awards in the People's Republic of China, 34 *Am. J. Comp. L.* 295 (1985)

Chew, A Procedural and Substantive Analysis of Fairness of Chinese and Soviet Foreign Trade Arbitrations, 21 *Tex. Int'l L.J.* 291 (1986)

Chew & LaFitte, The Resolution of Transnational Commercial Disputes in the People's Republic of China: A Guide for U.S. Practitioners, 8 *Yale J. World Pub. Ord.* 236 (1982)

China Maritime Arbitration Commission, *Selection of Awards and Conciliation Statements* (1984-1988) (Beijing 1989)

Coulson, *Aspects of Pacific Arbitration - The U.S.A. View, Paper presented to Int'l Conf. Growth of Arb. in the Pacific, Auckland, NZ, Sept. 1985*

Deslandres & Deschandol, Conception et pratique du règlement extrajudiciare des litiges commerciaux en Chine populaire, 15 *Droit et Pratique du Com. Int'l* 498 (1989)

Devow, Commercial Dispute Resolution Between the United States and the People's Republic of China: Problems and Prospects, 7 *Suff. Transnat'l L.J.* 329 (1983)

Dong Yougan, Arbitration Cases Concerning the Responsibilities of the Party Failing to Fulfil the Contractual Obligations, *China Patents & Trademarks* 99 (No. 3, 1985)

——, Arbitration Cases Handled by the Foreign Economic and Trade Arbitration Commission, *China Patents and Trademarks* 101 (No. 1, 1987)

Doty, An Evaluation of the People's Republic of China's Participation in International Commercial Arbitration: Pragmatic Prospectus, 12 *Cal. W. Int'l L.J.* 130 (1982)

Ellis & Shea, Foreign Commercial Dispute Settlement in the People's Republic of China, 6 *Int'l Trade L.J.* 155 (1980-81)

Fabro, Les institutions chinoises d'arbitrage commercial international, 1977 *Rev. Arb.* 377

Farina, Talking Disputes into Harmony: China Approaches International Commercial Arbitration, 4 *Am. U.J. Int'l L. & Pol'y* 137 (1989)

Foucault, L'arbitrage dans le règlement des litiges économiques et commerciaux avec la Chine, 1986 *Rev. Arb.* 131

Goossen, Chinese Contract Law and the New Civil Code, 8 *East Asian Exec. Rep.* 9 (No. 7, July 1986)

―――, Non-judicial Dispute Resolution in the People's Republic of China, 7 *Bus. L. Rev.* 331 (1986)

Grenner, The Evolution of Foreign Trade Arbitration in the People's Republic of China, 21 *N.Y.U. J. Int'l L. & Pol.* 293 (1989)

Hinman, China, Modernization, and Sino-United States Trade: Will China Submit to Arbitration? 10 *Cal. W. Int'l L.J.* 53 (1980)

Hudson, General Average Adjustment and Arbitration in the People's Republic of China, 1976 *Lloyd's Mar. & Com. L.Q.* 135

Ingreselli, International Dispute Resolution and the People's Republic of China, 12 *Int'l Bus. Law.* 376 (1984)

International Chamber of Commerce, China/Chine, in *Commercial Arbitration and the Law/L'Arbitrage commercial et la Loi* (Basel 1958)

Jen Tsien-Hsin & Liu Shao-Shan, People's Republic of China: National Report, 3 *Y.B. Com. Arb.* 153 (1978)

Klitgaard, People's Republic of China Joint Venture Dispute Resolution Procedures, 1 *UCLA Pac. Basin L.J.* 1 (1982)

Kolkey, Fora for the Resolution of International Business Disputes when Doing Business with the People's Republic of China, 12 *Loy. L.A. Int'l & Comp. L.J.* 102 (1989)

Lecat, L'arbitrage dans les contrats avec la Chine, 1986 *Cahiers Juridiques et Fiscaux* 447

Lee, How to Settle Commercial Disputes in China, 4 *Int'l Fin. L. Rev.* 33 (No. 2, 1985)

Lee, E., *Encyclopedia of International Commercial Arbitration* (London 1986)

————, *Commercial Disputes Settlement in China* (London 1985)

Liu Shujian, The New Rules Governing Maritime Arbitration in China, 21 *J. Mar. L. & Com.* 129 (1990)

Lockett, Dispute Settlement in the People's Republic of China: The Developing Role of Arbitration in Foreign Trade and Maritime Disputes, 16 *Geo. Wash. J. Int'l & Econ.* 239 (1982)

McClelland, A Survey of Pacific Rim Commercial Arbitration, 40 *Arb. J.* 3 (No. 1, 1985)

McCobb, Foreign Trade Arbitration in the People's Republic of China, 5 *N.Y.U. J. Int'l L. & Pol.* 205 (1972)

MacNeil, Contract in China: Law, Practice, and Dispute Resolution, 38 *Stan. L. Rev.* 303 (1986)

Moser, International Commercial Arbitration in the People's Republic of China: A Primer, 18 *Int'l Bus. Law.* 254 (1990)

Nafziger & Ruan Jiafang, Chinese Methods of Resolving International Trade, Investment, and Maritime Disputes, 23 *Willamette L. Rev.* 619 (1987)

Nee, O., ed., *Commercial, Business and Trade Laws: People's Republic of China.* Binder II, Booklet 8: *Arbitration* (Dobbs Ferry, NY 1987)

Note, Commercial Dispute Resolution between the United States and the People's Republic of China: Problems and Prospects, 7 *Suff. Transnat'l L.J.* 329 (1983)

————, Enforcing Foreign Judgments and Arbitration Awards, 5 *Int'l Fin. L. Rev.* 26 (No. 7, 1986)

Pechota, China, in 2 *W.A.R.* 1283 (H. Smit & V. Pechota eds. 1987)

602

————, Foreign Economic and Trade Arbitration Commission of the China Council for the Promotion of International Trade, in 4 *W.A.R.* 4315 (H. Smit & V. Pechota eds. 1989)

Pettit, Dispute Resolution in the People's Republic of China, 39 *Arb. J.* 3 (No. 1, 1984)

Pew; Jarvis & Sidel, The Maritime Arbitration Commission of the People's Republic of China: Options and Strategies, 18 *J. Mar. L. & Com.* 351 (1987)

Pierce, Termination of Arbitration by Mediation: Domestic and Foreign-Related Mediation Agreements, 18 *Hong Kong L.J.* 467 (1988)

Rafferty, Far from the Tiger's Mouth: Present Practice and Future Prospects for the Settlement of Foreign Commercial Disputes in the People's Republic of China, 3 *J. L. & Com.* 115 (1983)

Ren Jianxin, Mediation, Conciliation, Arbitration and Litigation in the People's Republic of China, 15 *Int'l Bus. Law.* 395 (1987)

————, The Establishment and Development of Foreign Trade, Economic and Maritime Arbitration in China, 1983 *Y.B. Swed. & Int'l Arb.* 53

Robinson & Doumar, It Is Better to Enter a Tiger's Mouth Than a Court of Law or Dispute Resolution Alternatives in U.S.-China Trade, 5 *Dick. J. Int'l L.* 247 (1987)

Sacks, Arbitration of Disputes Between the People's Republic of China and U.S. Corporations, in *Arbitration and the Licensing Process* 5-83 (R. Goldscheider & M. de Haas eds. 1984-)

Salbaing, Dispute Settlement in China, in *Doing Business in China* 21-1 (W. Streng & A. Wilcox gen. eds. 1990)

Schütze, Die Anerkennung und Vollstreckbarerklärung ausländischer Schiedssprüche in der Volksrepublik China, 8 *IPRax* 311 (1988)

————, Die Anerkennung und Vollstreckbarerklärung von Zivilurteilen und Schiedssprüchen im deutsch-chinesischen Rechtsverkehr, 32 *RIW* 269 (1986)

Shi Weisan, Arbitration and Conciliation: Resolving Commercial Disputes in China, 12 *Loy. L.A. Int'l & Comp. L.J.* 93 (1989)

Shiu Fan Chan, Settlement of Foreign Trade Disputes in the People's Republic of China, 49 *Arbitration* 282 (1984)

Shum, International Economic and Trade Arbitration in China, 1990 *J. Bus. L.* (1990)

―――, Maritime Arbitration in the People's Republic of China, 1990 *Lloyd's Mar. & Com. L.Q.* 114

Sidel & Mao Tong, China: Recognition and Enforcement of Foreign Arbitral Awards under the N.Y. Convention, 10 *East Asian Exec. Rep.* 14 (No. 5, 1988)

Tang An & Chen Xing-Yuan, Arbitration under Chinese Law, 6 *J. Int'l Arb.* 58 (No. 1, 1989)

Tang Houzhi, Arbitration ― A Method Used by China to Settle Foreign Trade and Economic Disputes, 4 *Pace L. Rev.* 519 (1984)

―――, Arbitration and Conciliation in China (An Outline), 52 *Arbitration* 89 (1986)

―――, International Commercial Arbitration in the Far East ― the PRC Example, in *Arbitration in Settlement of International Commercial Disputes Involving the Far East and Arbitration in Combined Transportation* 43 (P. Sanders ed. 1989); reprinted in 55 *Arbitration* 197 (1989)

―――, People's China: No Stranger to International Arbitration, 45 *Arb. J.* 27 (No. 4, 1990)

Tang Houzhi & Tung Shih-Chung, Legal Aspects of International Commercial Arbitration in the People's Republic of China, in *UNCITRAL Arbitration Model in Canada* 51 (R. Paterson & B. Thompson eds. 1987)

Trappe, Conciliation in the Far East, 5 *Arb. Int'l* 173 (1989)

Triebel & Xu Guojian, International Economic, Trade and Maritime Arbitration in the People's Republic of China: New Developments, 6 *J. Int'l Arb.* 13 (No. 2, 1989)

Tsien Hsin, Foreign Trade and Maritime Arbitration in China, *I.C.A. Arb. Q.* 3 (No. 4, 1977)

Verkhovskoy, Particularities of Arbitration in the People's Republic of China, 5 *Int'l Trade L. & Prac.* 271 (1979)

Wang Wen Lin, People's Republic of China, 3 *Int'l Commercial Arbitration: A World Handbook* 126 (P. Sanders ed. 1965)

Woychuk, Commercial Dispute Settlement in China-United States Trade, 6 *Fordham Int'l L.J.* 171 (1982)

Zheng, Private International Law in the People's Republic of China: Principles and Procedures, 22 *Tex. Int'l L.J.* 231 (1987)

Zhu Mingxing, Main Features of Chinese Court Arbitration and Maritime Litigation in China, 11 *Loy. L.A. Int'l & Comp. L.J.* 311 (1989)

COLUMBIA

Angel, La reforma de la justicia en Colombia: arbitraje y conciliación, in *Alternativas a la justicia institucional: arbitraje, conciliación* 59 (Bogota 1988)

Aramburú Menchaca, International Commercial Arbitration in the Andean Pact (Observations for a Community Regime), in *The Art of Arbitration* 27 (J. Schultsz & A. van den Berg eds. 1982)

Benetti Salgar, El arbitraje en el derecho interno colombiano, in *El Arbitraje en el Derecho Latinoamericano y Español* 205 (L. Perret & U. Montoya Alberti eds. 1989)

Cardoso Isaza, Conciliación y arbitraje: alternativas para una reforma a la administración de justicia en Colombia, in *Alternativas a la justicia institucional: arbitraje, conciliación* 69 (Bogota 1988)

————, Documentos de trabajo elaborados por Jorge Cardoso Isaza y sometidos al estudio de la Comisión de Reformas Civiles y Comerciales, creada por el Gobierno Nacional, in *Alternativas a la justicia institucional: arbitraje, conciliación* 77 (Bogota 1988)

Dias Rubio, Colombia: National Report, 3 *Y.B. Com. Arb.* 58 (1978)

Dunshee de Abranches, C.A., ed., *El arbitraje comercial en Iberoamérica* (Madrid 1982)

Duque Echeverri, Apuntes sobre el arbitramento mercantil, 3 *Revista de Derecho Mercantil* (1974)

Duque Echeverri, E., *Del arbitramento mercantil* (Medellin 1976)

Gamboa Serrano, Ley aplicable en el arbitraje internacional, in *Alternativas a la justicia institucional: arbitraje, conciliación* 123 (Bogota 1988)

Garro, Colombia, in 2 *W.A.R.* 1357 (H. Smit & V. Pechota eds. 1987)

————, The Colombian Supreme Court Holds Unconstitutional the Use of Foreign Arbitrators Under New Arbitration Law, 1 *Am. Rev. Int'l Arb.* 594 (1990)

Goldman, Arbitration and Transfer of Technology in Latin America, in *Arbitration and the Licensing Process* 5-29 (R. Goldscheider & M. de Haas eds. 1984-)

Holquín Holquín, El concepto de orden público en la Convención de Nueva York y otros comentarios, in *Alternativas a la justicia institucional: arbitraje, conciliación* 131 (Bogota 1988)

Monroy Cabra, Consideraciones sobre el arbitraje comercial en Colombia, in *Alternativas a la justicia institucional: arbitraje, conciliación* 33 (Bogota 1988)

————, El arbitraje internacional y el derecho colombiano, in *El Arbitraje en el Derecho Latinoamericano y Español* 235 (L. Perret & U. Montoya Alberti eds. 1989)

Monroy Cabra, M.G., *Arbitraje Comercial* (Bogota 1982)

Montealegre Escobar, Los arbitros en el derecho colombiano y en El Centro de Arbitraje y Conciliación Mercantiles de la Cámara de Comercio de Bogotá, in *El Arbitraje en el Derecho Latinoamericano y Español* 249 (L. Perret & U. Montoya Alberti eds. 1989)

Montoya Alberti, Arbitration, Foreign Law and Jurisdiction in International Loan Agreements in Some Countries of Latin America, in *Arbitration in Settlement of International Commercial Disputes Involving the Far East and Arbitration in Combined Transportation* 99 (P. Sanders ed. 1989)

————, El arbitraje en los contratos de prestamo internacionales, in *El Arbitraje en el Derecho Latinoamericano y Español* 481 (L. Perret & U. Montoya Alberti eds. 1989)

Morales Molina, El arbitraje nacional e internacional en Colombia, in *Alternativas a la justicia institucional: arbitraje, conciliación* 17 (Bogota 1988)

Note, Enforcing Foreign Judgments and Arbitration Awards, 5 *Int'l Fin. L. Rev.* 26 (No. 7, 1986)

Samtleben, Schiedsgerichtsbarkeit in den Andenpaktstaaten, 30 *RIW* 600 (1984)

Suarez, La clausula compromisoria y el compromiso como motivos de excepción previa, 2 *Revista de la Universidad Externado de Colombia* 79 (1983)

Suarez Melo, El arbitraje comercial en Colombia, in *El Arbitraje en el Derecho Latinoamericano y Español* 267 (L. Perret & U. Montoya Alberti eds. 1989)

COSTA RICA

Arguedas Salazar, El arbitraje en el proyecto de Código Procesal Civil de Costa Rica, in *El Arbitraje en el Derecho Latinoamericano y Español* 277 (L. Perrot & U. Montoya Alberti eds. 1989)

Dunshee de Abranches, C.A., ed., *El arbitraje comercial en Iberoamérica* (Madrid 1982)

Fournier, Costa Rica: National Report, 3 *Y.B. Com. Arb.* 70 (1978)

Garro, Costa Rica, in 2 *W.A.R.* 1373 (H. Smit & V. Pechota eds. 1987)

————, The UNCITRAL Model Law and the 1988 Spanish Arbitration Act: Models for Reform in Central America, 1 *Am. Rev. Int'l Arb.* 201 (1990)

————, The UNCITRAL Model Law and the 1988 Spanish Arbitration Act: Models for Reform in Central America, in *Commercial and Labor Arbitration in Central America* 23 (A. Garro ed. 1991)

Gómez Rodas, Commercial Arbitration in Costa Rica, in *Commercial and Labor Arbitration in Central America* 191 (A. Garro ed. 1991)

CUBA

Barclay, Arbitration in Latin America, 43 *Arbitration* 105 (1977)

Dahl, The Use of Arbitration in Cuba: International Solutions for the Resolution of Local Problems, 20 *U. Miami Inter-Am. L. Rev.* 681 (1989)

————, The Use of Arbitration in Cuba: International Solutions for the Resolution of Local Problems, in *Commercial and Labor Arbitration in Central America* 9 (A. Garro ed. 1991)

Dahl & Garro, Cuba's System of International Commercial Arbitration: A Convergence of Soviet and Latin American Trends, 15 *Law. Amer.* 441 (1984)

Fellhauer, H. & H. Strohbach, eds., *Handbuch der internationalen Handelsschiedsgerichtsbarkeit* (Berlin 1969)

Garcini, Cuba: National Report, 1 *Y.B. Com. Arb.* 27 (1976)

Garro, Cuba, in 2 *W.A.R.* 1389 (H. Smit & V. Pechota eds. 1987)

Lebedev, International Commercial Arbitration in the Socialist Countries Members of the CMEA, 158 *Recueil des Cours* 87 (1977-V)

Lebedev, S., ed., *Handbook on Foreign Trade Arbitration in the CMEA Member Countries* (Moscow 1983)

Perez Suarez, El arbitraje en las relaciones comerciales internacionales, 14 *Revista Cubana de Derecho* 225 (1978)

Pozdnyakov, Commercial Arbitration in CMEA Member Countries, 4 *Int'l Tax & Bus. Law.* 272 (1986)

Reyes Saila, El sistema del arbitraje estatal en Cuba, 20 *Revista Cubana de Derecho* 73 (1982)

Samtleben, Länderbericht Kuba, in *Die Aussenhandelsschiedsgerichts- barkeit der sozialistischen Länder* 274 (D. Pfaff ed. 1973)

Zorn & Mayerson, Cuba's Joint Venture Law: New Rules for Foreign Investment, 21 *Colum. J. Transn'l L.* 273 (1983)

CYPRUS

Shifman, Cyprus, in 2 *W.A.R.* 1399 (H. Smit & V. Pechota eds. 1987, 1988)

CZECHOSLOVAKIA

Blessing, Proper Law and Dispute Resolution Arising out of East-West Joint Ventures, in *Eastern Bloc Joint Ventures* 107 (D. Winter ed. 1990)

Bystricky, Les traits généraux de la codification tchécoslovaque en droit international privé. Chapitre IV: Loi sur l'arbitrage dans les relations commerciales internationales, 123 *Recueil des Cours* 407 (1968-I)

Cuth, The Arbitration Court of the Czechoslovak Chamber of Commerce and Industry, 21 *Bull. Czechoslovak L.* 94 (No. 2, 1982)

Donner, Czechoslovakia: National Report, 1 *Y.B. Com. Arb.* 30 (1976)

Hanak, Czechoslovakia, in *Int'l Handbook Com. Arb.* (A. van den Berg, gen. ed. 1984), Suppl. 5, May 1986

———, Some International Features of Arbitration in Czechoslovakia, in *Arbitration in Settlement of International Commercial Disputes Involving the Far East and Arbitration in Combined Transportation* 143 (P. Sanders ed. 1989)

Hrivnak, Czechoslovak Regulations Governing Arbitration in International Trade, 24 *Bull. Czechoslovak L.* 19 (1985)

Kasalova, E., T. Donner, J. Hrivnak & M. Stastny, *Thirty Years of the Arbitration Court of the Czechoslovak Chamber of Commerce and Industry in Prague* (Prague 1981)

Kos-Rabcewicz-Zubkowski, Central and East European Rules on the Form of International Arbitration Agreement, 3 *La Revue Juridique Themis* 415 (1969)

Kos-Rabcewicz-Zubkowski, L., *East European Rules on the Validity of International Arbitration Agreements* (Manchester and Dobbs Ferry, NY 1970)

Kotora, New Rules of Arbitration Proceedings and Recognition and Enforcement of Foreign Awards and Judicial Decisions in Czechoslovakia, 7 *Diritto negli Scambi Int'li* 225 (1968)

Kuss, Neuere Entwicklungen und Perspektiven der Ost-West-Schiedsgerichtsbarkeit, 33 *RIW* 584 (1987)

Majoros, Exécution de décisions étrangères et procédure d'exéquatur en Europe de l'Est: Tour d'horizon avec des références de droit comparé, in *Le Juriste Suisse Face au Droit et aux Jugements Etrangers: Ouverture ou Repli?* 135 (F. Knoepfler ed. 1988)

Melis, Austria as a Neutral Site for International Commercial Arbitration, 44 *Arb. J.* 31 (No. 4, 1989)

————, Enforcement of Arbitral Awards in Eastern Europe, in *Contemporary Problems in International Arbitration* 332 (J.D.M. Lew ed. 1986)

Pechota, Czechoslovakia, in 2 *W.A.R.* 1423 (H. Smit & V. Pechota eds. 1987)

————, International Economic Arbitration in the USSR and Eastern Europe, 8 *N.Y. L. Sch. J. Int'l & Comp. L.* 377 (1987)

Pfaff, Neuerungen der internationalen Schiedsgerichtsbarkeit im Ost-West-Handel vor den ständigen Aussenhandelsschiedsgerichten der RGW-Länder, 23 *RIW* 125 (1977)

Pisar, S., *Coexistence & Commerce,* Chapters 20-24 (New York 1970)

Pohunek, Principles of Proceedings Before the Arbitration Court of the Chamber of Commerce of Czechoslovakia in Prague, in *ICCA, Fifth Int'l Arb. Congress: Proceedings* C It 1-7 (1975)

Schütze, Die Neuordnung der Aussenhandelsschiedsgerichtsbarkeit in der Tschechoslowakei, 12 *Jahrbuch für Ostrecht* 95 (1975)

Sedlacek, V., *Arbitration in Czechoslovak Foreign Trade* (Prague 1982)

Stastny, La Cour d'Arbitrage près de la Chambre de Commerce de Tchéchoslovaquie à Prague et ses décisions, 13 *Rassegna dell'Arb.* 111 (1973)

Stastny, M. & S. Hanak, Act 98/1963 Relating to Arbitration in *International Trade and to Enforcement of Awards: A Commentary* (Prague 1984)

Steiner, V., *Solution of Disputes Arising out of International Trade in the Czechoslovak Socialist Republic* (Prague 1983)

Stumpf, Ost-West-Schiedsgerichtsbarkeit: Schiedsgerichte mit Sitz in dritten Ländern, 33 *RIW* 821 (1987)

Unger & Masilko, Das Schiedsverfahren in Handelssachen und die Vollstreckung von Schiedssprüchen in der Tschechoslowakei, 13 *AWD* 297 (1967)

Weiss, Arbitral Tribunals in the Czechoslovak Republic, 1 *Int'l Y.B. Civil & Com. Arb.* 161 (A. Nussbaum ed. 1928)

Zourek, New Rules of Arbitration Proceedings in Czechoslovakia, 1963 *Bull. Czechoslovak L.* 233

DENMARK

Blegvad, B.-M., P. Bolding & O. Lando, *Arbitration as a Means of Solving Conflicts* (Copenhagen 1973)

Eckstrom, L., *Licensing in Foreign and Domestic Operations.* Volume I, Chapter 7: Arbitration (by Steven Z. Szczepanski), (New York 1972, updated 1987)

Ehlers, L'arbitrage au Danemark, 1977 *Rev. Arb.* 327

————, Le consentement à une convention d'arbitrage en droit danois, 1978 *Rev. Arb.* 571

International Chamber of Commerce, *Arbitration Law in Europe* (Paris 1981)

————, Denmark/Danemark, in *Commercial Arbitration and the Law/ L'Arbitrage commercial et la Loi* (Basel 1949)

Jacobi, New Aspects of Arbitration Legislation in Scandinavia, in *ICCA, Third Int'l Arb. Congress: Proceedings* 475 (1969)

Klein, F.-E., *Considérations sur l'arbitrage en droit international privé* (Basel 1955)

Lando, Danisches Schiedsrecht nach dem Schiedsgerichtsbarkeitsgesetz von 1972, *Zeitschrift für das gesamte Handels- und Gesellschaftsrecht* 517 (1972)

MacLaren, Commercial Arbitration in the United States and Overseas, in *Arbitration and the Licensing Process* 5 (R. Goldscheider & M. de Haas eds. 1984-)

Pedersen, International Arbitration in Denmark, 14 *Case W. Res. J. Int'l L.* 357 (1982)

Philip, Arbitration in Denmark, 2 *Int'l Contr.* 97 (1981)

————, Arbitration in Denmark, 1 *Am. Rev. Int'l Arb.* 137 (1990)

————, Denmark, in *Int'l Handbook Com. Arb.* (A. van den Berg gen. ed. 1984), Suppl. 5, May 1986

Shifman, The Copenhagen Court of International Arbitration, in 4 *W.A.R.* 4387 (H. Smit & V. Pechota eds. 1989)

Trolle, Denmark: National Report, 5 *Y.B. Com. Arb.* 28 (1980)

DJIBOUTI

Bernini, Recent Legislations and International Unification of the Law on Arbitration, in *First International Commercial Arbitration Conference: Proceedings* 315 (N. Antaki & A. Prujiner eds. 1986)

Chatterjee, The Djibouti Code of International Arbitration, 4 *J. Int'l Arb.* 57 (No. 1, 1987)

Derains, Le code djiboutien de l'arbitrage international, 1984 *Rev. Arb.* 465

Dorman, Djibouti, in 2 *W.A.R.* 1499 (H. Smit & V. Pechota eds. 1987)

Ziadé, Selective Bibliography on Arbitration and Arab Countries, 3 *ICSID Rev. -Foreign Investment L.J.* 423 (1988)

DOMINICAN REPUBLIC

Campillo Perez, El arbitraje en Santo Domingo, in *El Arbitraje en el Derecho Latinoamericano y Español* 555 (L. Perret & U. Montoya Alberti eds. 1989)

Garro, Dominican Republic, in 2 *W.A.R.* 1515 (H. Smit & V. Pechota eds. 1987)

International Chamber of Commerce, Dominican Republic/Republique Dominicaine, in *Commercial Arbitration and the Law/L'Arbitrage commercial et la Loi* (Basel 1951)

ECUADOR

American Arbitration Association, *New Strategies for Peaceful Resolution of International Business Disputes* (Dobbs Ferry, NY 1971)

Aramburú Menchaca, International Commercial Arbitration in the Andean Pact (Observations for a Community Regime), in *The Art of Arbitration* 27 (J. Schultsz & A. van den Berg eds. 1982)

Dore, I., *Theory and Practice of Multiparty Commercial Arbitration, With Special Reference to the UNCITRAL Framework* (London 1990)

Dunshee de Abranches, C.A., ed., *El arbitraje comercial en Iberoamérica* (Madrid 1982)

Garro, Ecuador, in 2 *W.A.R.* 1525 (H. Smit & V. Pechota eds. 1987)

Goldman, Arbitration and Transfer of Technology in Latin America, in *Arbitration and the Licensing Process* 5-29 (R. Goldscheider & M. de Haas eds. 1984-)

Gomez de la Torre, Aspectos comerciales y procesuales del sistema ecuatoriano de derecho internacional privato, 6 *Anuario Ecuatoriano de Derecho Int'l* 83 (Nos. 8-9 y 10, Años 1976-1980)

Jimenez Salazar, Ecuador: National Report, 3 *Y.B. Com. Arb.* 76 (1978)

Paez, Ley de arbitraje comercial, *Revista de Derecho* 69 (No. 1, 1964)

Samtleben, Schiedsgerichtsbarkeit in den Andenpaktstaaten, 30 *RIW* 600 (1984)

EGYPT

Ballantyne, European Experience and Perception of Arbitration with Arab Countries, in *First Euro-Arab Arb. Conference: Proceedings* 160 (F. Kemicha ed. 1987)

Buchanan, Public Policy and International Commercial Arbitration, 26 *Am. Bus. L.J.* 511 (1988)

Chafic, L'impact de la Loi-type dans le monde arabe: le projet égyptien, in *Euro-Arab Arbitration III* 186 (F. Kemicha ed. 1991)

Chafik, Egypt: National Report, 4 *Y.B. Com. Arb.* 44 (1979)

Davies, Arbitration in Egyptian Contracts: Watch the Pyramid Oasis Case, 7 *Middle E. Exec. Rep.* 11 (No. 1, Jan. 1984)

———, The Draft Arbitration Law in Egypt, 3 *Arab L.Q.* 119 (1988)

Davies, M., *Business Law in Egypt* (chapter on Arbitration), (Deventer 1984)

Dilger, Arbitration, Enforcement of Foreign Judgments and Arbitration Awards, Clauses on the Choice of Law, and Agreements on Jurisdiction of the Court in Egypt, Saudi Arabia and the Gulf States, in *International Bar Association: Proceedings of the Seminar on Middle East Law* 35 (1981)

El-Ahdab, A. H., *Arbitration with the Arab Countries* (Deventer 1990)

———, *L'arbitrage dans les pays arabes* (Paris 1988)

El-Kosheri, Egypt, 15 *Y.B. Com. Arb.* 305 (1990)

———, Egypt, in *Int'l Handbook Com. Arb.* (A. van den Berg, gen. ed. 1984), Supp. 11, Jan. 1990

———, Public Policy under Egyptian Law, in *Comparative Arbitration Practice and Public Policy in Arbitration* 321 (P. Sanders ed. 1987)

———, Settlement of Disputes through Arbitration: Arbitration in Egypt, in 1 *Arab Comp. & Com. Law: The Int'l Approach: Proc. I.B.A. Conf.* 169 (1987)

———, Some Particular Aspects of Egyptian Official Attitudes Towards International Commercial Arbitration, 76 *L'Egypte Contemporaine* 109 (1985)

El-Kosheri & Riad, The Changing Roles in the Arbitration Process (with Regard to the Applicable Law Governing the New Generation of the Petroleum Agreements), 1 *Arab Law Q.* 475 (1986); also in *First Euro-Arab Arb. Conference: Proceedings* 253 (F. Kemicha ed. 1987)

Fadlallah, Les pays arabes du Machrek, in *First Euro-Arab Arb. Conference: Proceedings* 26 (F. Kemicha ed. 1987)

Feuerle, Economic Arbitration in Egypt: The Influence of a Soviet Legal Institution, 7 *J. Int'l L. & Econ.* 61 (1972)

Hoyle, An Introductory View of Arbitration in Egypt, 50 *Arbitration* 166 (Nov. 1984)

Ibrahim, Enforcement of Foreign Arbitral Awards, 1981 *Rev. Egyptienne de Droit Int'l* 1 (1981)

International Bar Association, *Arab Comparative & Commercial Law: The International Approach: Proceedings of the I.B.A. First Arab Regional Conference, Cairo 15-19 February 1987* (London 1987)

International Chamber of Commerce, Egypt/Egypte, in *Commercial Arbitration and the Law/L'Arbitrage commercial et la Loi* (Basel 1949)

Jarvin, Choosing the Place of Arbitration: Where Do We Stand? 16 *Int'l Bus. Law.* 417 (1988)

Kassis, Particularités et problèmes de l'arbitrage dans les droits des pays arabes, 63 *Rev. Droit Int'l & Droit Comp.* 7 (1986)

Leboulanger, Etats, politique et arbitrage. L'affaire du Plateau des Pyramides, 1986 *Rev. Arb.* 3

Mostafa, The Applicable Law in Commerce Arbitration between American and Egyptian Parties, 32 *Rev. Egyptienne Droit Int'l* 179 (1976)

Note, Enforcing Foreign Judgments and Arbitration Awards, 5 *Int'l Fin. L. Rev.* 26 (No. 7, 1986)

Rached, S., *At-Takhim fi Al-llakat Ad-Dawliyat Al-Khassat [Arbitration in Private International Law Relations]* - Vol.1 [Arbitration Convention], (Cairo 1984)

Rashed, The UNCITRAL Model Law and Recent Developments in Egypt, 3 *ICSID Rev. - Foreign Investment L.J.* 126 (1988)

Saleh, The Recognition and Enforcement of Foreign Arbitral Awards in the States of the Arab Middle East, in *Contemporary Problems in International Arbitration* 340 (J.D.M. Lew ed. 1986)

————, The Settlement of Disputes in the Arab World: Arbitration and Other Methods, 1 *Arab L. Q.* 198 (1986); reprinted in 4 *Int'l Tax & Bus. Law.* 280 (1986)

Saleh, S., *Commercial Arbitration in the Arab Middle East* (London 1984)

Sefrioui, Pratique de l'arbitrage et tendances reformatrices nouvelles, in *Euro-Arab Arbitration III* 61 (F. Kemicha ed. 1991)

Seppala, The Pyramids of Egypt Case, 2 *Int'l Constr. L. Rev.* 180

Stumpf, Schiedsgerichtsbarkeit in arabischen Ländern, 1 *Jahrbuch Schiedsgerichtsbarkeit* 102 (1987)

Taliadoros & El-Shalakany, Arbitration in Egyptian Law, 8 *Int'l Trade L. & Prac.* 133 (1981)

Troller, Arbitration and Enforcement of Arbitration Awards in Arab Countries, 2 *Int'l Contr.* 397 (1981)

Ziadé, Selective Bibliography on Arbitration and Arab Countries, 3 *ICSID Rev. -Foreign Investment L.J.* 423 (1988)

EL SALVADOR

Bernal Silva, Arbitration in Salvadoran Commercial Legislation, 20 *U. Miami Inter-Am. L. Rev.* 765 (1989)

Garro, El Salvador, in 2 *W.A.R.* 1547 (H. Smit & V. Pechota eds. 1987)

————, The UNCITRAL Model Law and the 1988 Spanish Arbitration Act: Models for Reform in Central America, 1 *Am. Rev. Int'l Arb.* 201 (1990)

————, The UNCITRAL Model Law and the 1988 Spanish Arbitration Act: Models for Reform in Central America, in *Commercial and Labor Arbitration in Central America* 23 (A. Garro ed. 1991)

International Chamber of Commerce, Salvador, in *Commercial Arbitration and the Law/L'Arbitrage commercial et la Loi* (Basel 1949)

Segovia, Commercial Arbitration in El Salvador, 20 *U. Miami Inter-Am. L. Rev.* 775 (1989)

————, Commercial Arbitration in El Salvador, in *Commercial and Labor Arbitration in Central America* 237 (A. Garro ed. 1991)

Silva, Arbitration in Salvadoran Commercial Legislation, in *Commercial and Labor Arbitration in Central America* 243 (A. Garro ed. 1991)

ETHIOPIA

Arnold, Die Vollstreckung ausländischer Urteile und Schiedssprüche in Aethiopien, 1968 *AWD* 309

EUROPEAN COMMUNITIES

Arnold, Das Europäische Übereinkommen vom 20. Januar 1966 zur Einführung eines einheitlichen Gesetzes über die Schiedsgerichtsbarkeit, 1967 *NJW* 142

Bebr, Arbitration Tribunals and Article 177 of the EEC Treaty, 22 *Common Mkt L. Rev.* 489 (1985)

Brown, Commercial Arbitration and the European Economic Community, 2 *J. Int'l Arb.* 21 (1985)

de Mello, Arbitrage et droit communautaire, 1982 *Rev. Arb.* 349

Goffin, Arbitrage et droit communautaire, in *L'Arbitrage* 159 (L. Matray & G. de Leval eds. 1989)

———, L'arbitrage et le droit européen, 67 *Rev. Droit Int'l & Droit Comp.* 315 (1990)

Hahn, D., *L'arbitrage commercial international en Suisse face aux règles de concurrence de la CEE* (Geneva 1985)

Jenard, L'arbitrage et le conventions C.E.E. en matière de droit international prive, in *Festschrift für Arthur Bülow* 79 (K.-H. Böckstiegel & O. Glossner eds. 1981)

Lew, EEC Restrictions on Arbitration, 47 *Arbitration* 117 (1981)

McClellan, Le rôle de l'arbitrage commercial et le droit communautaire dans la perspective de 1992, 67 *Rev. Droit Int'l & Droit Comp.* 301 (1990)

McClelland, Commercial Arbitration and European Community Law, 5 *Arb. Int'l* 68 (1989)

Marriott, Arbitration in a Single Unified Market, 56 *Arbitration* 88

Schlosser, The 1968 Brussels Convention and Arbitration, 25 *Riv. Dir. Int'le Priv. & Proc.* 545 (1989); also in 7 *Arb. Int'l* 227 (1991)

Schmitthoff, Arbitration and EEC Law, 24 *Common Mkt. L. Rev.* 143 (1987)

Spedding, Interpretation of Art. 132 of the Lome II Convention. Arbitration or Court Proceeding, 12 *Int'l Bus. Law.* 382 (1984)

ter Kuile, Internationale arbitrage en Gemeenschapsrecht, in *Iustitia et Amicitia. Geschillenbeslechting in en Buiten Rechte* 33 (Arnheim 1985)

von Zumbusch, Arbitrability of Antitrust Claims Under U.S., German, and EEC Law: The 'International Transaction' Criterion and Public Policy, 22 *Tex. Int'l L.J.* 291 (1987)

————, Die Schiedsfähigkeit privatrechtlicher Kartellrechtsstreitigkeiten nach US-, deutschem und EG-Recht, 1988 *GRUR Int'l* 541

Young, Arbitration and the European Communities' Judgments Convention, in *International Commercial and Maritime Arbitration* 77 (F.D. Rose ed. 1988)

FIJI

Speight, Resolution of Disputes in Some Smaller Pacific Countries, Paper presented to International Conference Growth of Arbitration in the Pacific, Auckland, NZ, Sept. 1985

FINLAND

Eckstrom, L., *Licensing in Foreign and Domestic Operations.* Volume I, Chapter 7: Arbitration (by Steven Z. Szczepanski), (New York 1972, updated 1987)

International Chamber of Commerce, *Arbitration Law in Europe* (Paris 1981)

————, Finland/Finlande, in *Commercial Arbitration and the Law/ L'Arbitrage commercial et la Loi* (Basel 1951)

Jacobi, New Aspects of Arbitration Legislation in Scandinavia, in *ICCA, Third Int'l Arb. Congress: Proceedings* 475 (1969)

Jokela, Finland: National Report, 5 *Y.B. Com. Arb.* 41 (1980)

Klein, F.-E., *Considérations sur l'arbitrage en droit international privé* (Basel 1955)

MacLaren, Commercial Arbitration in the United States and Overseas, in *Arbitration and the Licensing Process* 5 (R. Goldscheider & M. de Haas eds. 1984-)

Saario, The Principle of Party Autonomy in Arbitration of International Commercial Disputes, 1985 *Tidskrift, utgiven av Juridiska Foreningen i Finland* 500

FRANCE

Ancel, Arbitrage et procédures collectives après la loi du 26 janvier 1985, 1987 *Rev. Arb.* 128

Audit, A National Codification of International Commercial Arbitration: The French Decree of May 12, 1981, in *Resolving Transnational Disputes through International Arbitration* 117 (T. Carbonneau ed. 1984)

Batiffol, Arbitration Clauses Concluded Between French Government-Owned Enterprises and Foreign Private Parties, 7 *Colum. J. Transnat'l L.* 32 (1968)

Béguin, Le droit français de l'arbitrage international et la Convention de New York du 10 juin 1958, in *First International Commercial Arbitration Conference: Proceedings* 218 (N. Antaki & A. Prujiner eds. 1986)

Bellet, Paris, ville d'arbitrage? 33 *Revue de Jurisprudence Commerciale* 193 (1989); reprinted in 5 *Int'l Arb. Rep.* H-4 (No. 6, 1990)

————, The Evolution of French Judicial Views on International Arbitration, 34 *Arb. J.* 28 (No. 1, 1979)

Bellet & Mezger, L'arbitrage international dans le nouveau code de procédure civile, 70 *Rev. Crit. Droit Int'l Privé* 611 (1981)

Berger, Die Regelung der gerichtlichen Anfechtbarkeit internationaler Schiedssprüche in europäischen Schiedsgerichtsgesetzen, 35 *RIW* 850 (1989)

————, The Modern Trend Towards Exclusion of Recourse Against Transnational Arbitral Awards: A European Perspective, 12 *Fordham Int'l L. J.* 605 (1989)

Bernini, Recent Legislations and International Unification of the Law on Arbitration, in *First International Commercial Arbitration Conference: Proceedings* 315 (N. Antaki & A. Prujiner eds. 1986)

Böckstiegel, K.-H., ed., *Schiedsgerichtsbarkeit in Frankreich* (Cologne 1983)

Bösch, A., *Einstweiliger Rechtsschutz in der internationalen Handelsschiedsgerichtsbarkeit* (Berne 1989)

Bourdin, La convention d'arbitrage international en droit français depuis le Décret du 12 mai 1981, in *Droit et pratique de l'arbitrage international en France* 11 (Y. Derains ed. 1984)

Buchanan, Public Policy and International Commercial Arbitration, 26 *Am. Bus. L.J.* 511 (1988)

Buhart, Attachments and Other Interim Court Remedies in Support of Arbitration: French Law, in *Interim Court Remedies in Support of Arbitration* 163 (D. Shenton & W. Kühn eds. 1987)

————, Interim Court Remedies in Support of Arbitration, 12 *Int'l Bus. Law.* 107 (1984)

Carbonneau, American and Other National Variations on the Theme of International Commercial Arbitration, 18 *Ga. J. Int'l & Comp. L.* 143 (1988)

————, Etude historique et comparée de l'arbitrage: vers un droit materiel de l'arbitrage commercial international fondé sur la motivation des sentences, 36 *Rev. Int'l Droit Comp.* 727 (1984)

————, The Elaboration of a French Court Doctrine on International Commercial Arbitration: A Study in Liberal Civilian Judicial Creativity, 55 *Tul. L. Rev.* 1 (1980)

————, The French Jurisprudence on International Commercial Arbitration, in *Resolving Transnational Disputes Through International Arbitration* 146 (T. Carbonneau ed. 1984)

————, The Reform of the French Procedural Law on Arbitration: An Analytical Commentary on the Decree of May 14, 1980, 4 *Hastings Int'l & Comp. L. Rev.* 273 (1981)

Chapelle, L'arbitrage et les tiers: le droit des personnes morales (groupes de sociétés; interventions d'Etat), 1988 *Rev. Arb.* 475

Chartier, Centre d'Arbitrage de la Chambre Officielle Franco-Allemande de Commerce et d'Industrie, 1986 *Rev. Arb.* 291

Cohen, La soumission de l'arbitrage international à la loi française (Commentaire de l'article 1495 NCPC), 1991 *Rev. Arb.* 155

Courteault & Flécheux, La notion de l'ordre public international dans la jurisprudence de la Cour de Cassation française, in *ICCA, Sixth Int'l Arb. Congress: Proceedings* 257 (1978)

Craig, Park & Paulsson, French Codification of a Legal Framework for International Commercial Arbitration, 13 *L. & Pol'y Int'l Bus.* 727 (1981)

————, French Codification of Legal Framework for International Arbitration, 7 *Y.B. Com. Arb.* 407 (1982)

Cremades, La reconnaissance en Espagne des décisions judiciaires et des actes authentiques français, 1975 *Rev. Crit. Droit Int'l Privé* 355 and 595

David, R., *Arbitration in International Trade* (Deventer 1985)

————, *L'arbitrage dans le commerce international* (Paris 1982)

de Boisséson, La constitution de tribunal arbitral dans l'arbitrage institutionnel, 1990 *Rev. Arb.* 337

de Boisséson, M., *Le droit français de l'arbitrage* (Paris 1983)

de Grandcourt, Les interférences du contentieux arbitral et des contentieux adjacents, in *First Euro-Arab Arb. Conference: Proceedings* 224 (F. Kemicha ed. 1987)

de Hauteclocque, French Judicial Expertise Procedure and International Arbitration, 4 *J. Int'l Arb.* 77 (No. 2, 1987)

Delalande, Les honoraires dans l'arbitrage institutionnel, 1990 *Rev. Arb.* 367

Delaume, International Arbitration Under French Law: The Decree of May 12, 1981, 37 *Arb. J.* 38 (No. 3, 1982); reprinted in *Arbitration and the Licensing Process* 5 (R. Goldscheider & M. de Haas eds. 1984-)

————, Judicial Decisions Related to Sovereign Immunity and Transnational Arbitration, 2 *ICSID Rev. - Foreign Investment L.J.* 403 (1987)

————, SEEE v. Yugoslavia: Epitaph or Interlude? 4 *J. Int'l Arb.* 25 (No. 3, 1987)

Delvolvé, Immunity of Arbitrators under French Law, in *The Immunity of Arbitrators* 29 (J.D.M. Lew ed. 1990)

————, La reforme du droit de l'arbitrage: l'intervention du juge, 1980 *Rev. Arb.* 607

Delvolvé, J.-L., ed., *Arbitration in France. The French Law of National and International Arbitration.* Trilingual edition: French, English, German (Deventer 1982)

de Mello, Arbitration and Domestic Public Policy Resulting from Regulations on Competition, in *Arbitration and the Licensing Process* 6-109 (R. Goldscheider & M. de Haas eds. 1984-)

Derains, Clauses et procédures d'arbitrage internationales dans le pays arabes, in *First Euro-Arab Arb. Conference: Proceedings* 150 (F. Kemicha ed. 1987)

————, France, in *Int'l Handbook Com. Arb.* (P. Sanders ed. 1984)

————, France as a Place for International Arbitration, in *The Art of Arbitration* 111 (J. Schultsz & A. van den Berg eds. 1982)

————, France: National Report, 6 *Y.B. Com. Arb.* 1 (1981) and 7 *Y.B. Com. Arb.* 35 (1982)

Derains, Y., ed., *Droit et pratique de l'arbitrage international en France* (Paris 1984)

du Pontavice, Un centre spécialisé: La Chambre Arbitrale Maritime de Paris, 1990 *Rev. Arb.* 239

Eckstrom, L., *Licensing in Foreign and Domestic Operations.* Volume I, Chapter 7: Arbitration (by Steven Z. Szczepanski), (New York 1972, updated 1987)

Flécheux, Les difficultés d'exécution en France des sentences rendues contre les Etats ou leur émanations, 1985 *Rev. Arb.* 675

Fouchard, L'arbitrage commercial et la législation, *in Mélanges P. Roblot* 63 (1983)

————, L'arbitrage international après le décret du 12 mai 1981, 109 *J. Droit Int'l (Clunet)* 374 (1982)

————, La coopération du Président du Tribunal de Grande Instance à l'arbitrage, 1985 *Rev. Arb.* 5

————, Typologie des institutions d'arbitrage, 1990 *Rev. Arb.* 281

Foussard, Le juge administratif et l'arbitrage (Remarques à propos de l'arrêt A.R.E.A. du Conseil d'Etat du 3 mars 1989), 1989 *Rev. Arb.* 167

Friedland, Provisional Measures in ICSID Arbitration, 2 *Arb. Int'l* 335 (1986)

Gaillard, L'affaire SOFIDIF ou les difficultés de l'arbitrage multipartite (à propos de l'arrêt rendu par la Cour d'Appel de Paris le 19 décembre 1986), 1987 *Rev. Arb.* 275

————, The Enforcement of ICSID Awards in France: The Decision of the Paris Court of Appeal in the SOABI Case, 5 *ICSID Rev. - Foreign Investment L.J.* 69 (1990)

Gastambide, International Arbitration Under the French Decree of 12 May 1981, 48 *Arbitration* 45 (1982)

Goldman, International Arbitration in Europe, in *IBA, Soviet Foreign Trade Reforms & East/West Arbitration* 217 (1988)

————, La nouvelle réglementation française de l'arbitrage international, in *The Art of Arbitration* 153 (J. Schultsz & A. van den Berg eds. 1982)

————, La volonté des parties et le rôle de l'arbitrage dans l'arbitrage international, 1981 *Rev. Arb.* 469

————, Les problèmes spécifiques de l'arbitrage international, 1980 *Rev. Arb.* 323

Gomez, International Arbitration: A Case for Delocalization, 3 *Sri Lanka J. Int'l L.* 61 (1991)

Gonzalez Campos, El Convenio entre España y Francia de 28 de mayo de 1969 sobre reconocimiento y ejecución de decisiones extranjeras, in 2 *Estudios de Derecho internacional publico y privado. Homenaje al Profesor Sela* 993 (1970)

Goutal, L'arbitrage et les tiers: le droit des contrats, 1988 *Rev. Arb.* 439

Groos, L'arbitrage de la Chambre Officielle Franco-Allemande de Commerce et d'Industrie, 1986 *Int'l Bus. L.J.* 205

————, Schiedsgerichtsbarkeit im deutsch-französischen Wirtschaftsverkehr, 33 *RIW* 343 (1987)

Groos, Langer & Sandrock, Die Schiedsgerichtsbarkeit der Offiziellen Deutsch-Französischen Industrie-und Handelskammer, 40 *BB, Annex* 14 (No. 32, 1985)

Groos, Langer, Sandrock & Dorman, Rules of the Official Franco-German Chamber of Commerce and Industry, in 3 *W.A.R.* 3742 (H. Smit & V. Pechota eds. 1987)

Habscheid, L'expertise-arbitrage. Etude de droit comparé, in *Liber Amicorum for Martin Domke* 103 (P. Sanders ed. 1967)

Hahn, Die Anerkennung und Vollstreckung von ICSID-Schiedssprüchen in Frankreich, 37 *RIW* 459 (1991)

Huet, Les procedures de reconnaissance et d'exécution des jugements étrangers et de sentences arbitrales, en droit international privé français, 115 *J. Droit Int'l (Clunet)* 5 (1988)

International Chamber of Commerce, *Arbitration Law in Europe* (Paris 1981)

Jambu-Merlin, The New French Arbitration Act, in 1 *Fifth Int'l Congress of Maritime Arbitrators* (New York 1981)

Jarrosson, Le rôle respectif de l'institution, de l'arbitre et des parties dans l'instance arbitrale, 1990 *Rev. Arb.* 381

Jarrosson, C., *La notion d'arbitrage* (Paris 1987)

Jarvin, Choosing the Place of Arbitration: Where Do We Stand? 16 *Int'l Bus. Law.* 417 (1988)

Jeantet, L'accueil des sentences étrangères or internationales dans l'ordre juridique français, 1981 *Rev. Arb.* 503

Jestaedt, T., *Schiedsverfahren und Konkurs* (Berlin 1985)

Julliard, Les conventions bilatérales d'investissement conclues par la France, 106 *J. Droit Int'l (Clunet)* 274 (1979)

Kaplan, L'arbitrabilité des litiges commerciaux en matière de droit de la concurrence, 14 *Droit et Pratique du Com. Int'l* 403 (1988)

Kassis, A., *Problèmes de base de l'arbitrage en droit comparé et en droit international. Vol. 1: Arbitrage juridictionnel et arbitrage contractuel* (Paris 1987)

Klein, La nouvelle règlementation française de l'arbitrage international et le lois suisses, in *Recueil de Travaux Suisses* 57 (C. Reymond & E. Bucher eds. 1984)

Klein, F.-E., *Considérations sur l'arbitrage en droit international privé* (Basel 1955)

Kolkey, Attacking Arbitral Awards: Rights of Appeal and Review in International Arbitrations, 22 *Int'l Law.* 693 (1988)

Kühl, S. G., *Schiedsgerichtsbarkeit im Seehandel* (Kehl am Rhein 1990)

Langeveld, Iets over getuigen in internationale arbitrages, 1988 *Tijdschrift voor Arbitrage* 156

Laschet, Erneut zur Frage der Ablehnung von Schiedsrichtern in Frankreich - Beschluss der Cour d'Appel de Paris vom 15.1.1985, 1985 *KTS* 627

Lécuyer-Thieffry, C. & P. Thieffry, *Le règlement des litiges civils et commerciaux avec les Etats-Unis* (Paris 1986)

Le Fur, Un centre professionnel: La Chambre Arbitrale des Cafés et Poivres du Havre, 1990 *Rev. Arb.* 245

Legras de Grandcourt, Evolution contemporaine des législations européennes, in *Euro-Arab Arbitration III* 119 (F. Kemicha ed. 1991)

Lepp & Migeal, Powers of the Arbitrators, in *Fifth International Congress of Maritime Arbitrators* (New York 1981)

Level, La procédure arbitrale, in *Droit et pratique de l'arbitrage international en France* 51 (Y. Derains ed. Paris 1984)

Lorenzen, Commercial Arbitration — International and Interstate Aspects, 43 *Yale L.J.* 716 (1934)

Loussouarn, La réforme du droit de l'arbitrage: les voies de recours, 1980 *Rev. Arb.* 671

———, Les arbitres, in *Droit et pratique de l'arbitrage international en France* 37 (Y. Derains ed. Paris 1984)

MacLaren, Commercial Arbitration in the United States and Overseas, in *Arbitration and the Licensing Process* 5 (R. Goldscheider & M. de Haas eds. 1984-)

Marriott, Evidence in International Arbitration, 5 *Arb. Int'l* 280 (1989)

Matray, L'arbitre-partie en matière internationale, 53 *Rev. Droit Int'l & Droit Comp.* 152 (1976)

Mayer, L'insértion de la sentence dans l'ordre juridique français, in *Droit et pratique de l'arbitrage international en France* 81 (Y. Derains ed. Paris 1984)

Mebroukine, Le Règlement d'arbitrage algéro-français du 27 mars 1983, 1986 *Rev. Arb.* 191

Mezger, Das französische Dekret vom 14. Mai 1980 und die organisierte Schiedsgerichtsbarkeit, in *Festschrift für Arthur Bülow* 141 (K.-H. Böckstiegel & O. Glossner eds. 1981)

————, Kernpunkte der Reform des Rechts der internationalen Handelsschiedsgerichtsbarkeit in Frankreich, 27 *RIW* 511 (1981)

Moitry, Right to a Fair Trial and the European Convention on Human Rights, 6 *J. Int'l Arb.* 115 (No. 2, 1989)

Mok Young-Joon, The Principle of Reciprocity in the United Nations Convention on the Recognition and Enforcement of Foreign Arbitral Awards of 1958, 21 *Case W. Res. J. Int'l L.* 123 (1989)

Moreau, The Intervention of the Judge during the Arbitration in both French and Comparative law, in *ICCA, Sixth Int'l Arb. Congress: Proceedings* 287 (1978)

Moreau, B. & T. Bernard, *Droit interne et droit international de l'arbitrage* (2nd ed. 1985)

Note, Challenge of Arbitrators: Is an Institutional Decision Final? 2 *Arb. Int'l* 261 (1986)

————, Enforcing Foreign Judgments and Arbitration Awards, 5 *Int'l Fin. L. Rev.* 26 (No. 7, 1986)

Oppetit, Arbitrage juridictionnel et arbitrage contractuel: à propos d'une jurisprudence récente, 1977 *Rev. Arb.* 317

————, Arbitration in the Fields of Patents After the Law of July 13, 1978, in *Arbitration and the Licensing Process* 6-91 (R. Goldscheider & M. de Haas eds. 1984-)

————, Le refus d'exécution d'une sentence arbitrale étrangère dans le cadre de la Convention de New York, 1971 *Rev. Arb.* 97

Paclot, La réforme du droit de l'arbitrage: l'arbitrage institutionnel, 1980 *Rev. Arb.* 598

Padis, De la validité en droit français de le clause compromissoire inserée dans un contrat national ou international d'ingénieries (know-how), in *ICCA, Fourth Int'l Arb. Congress: Proceedings* 466 (1972)

Park, Judicial Controls in the Arbitral Process, 5 *Arb. Int'l* 230 (1989)

———, National Legal Systems and Private Dispute Resolution, 82 *Am. J. Int'l L.* 616 (1988)

———, Private Adjudicators and the Public Interest: The Expanding Scope of International Arbitration, 12 *Brooklyn J. Int'l L.* 629 (1986)

Parker School of Foreign and Comparative Law, *International Commercial Arbitration and the Courts* (Dobbs Ferry, NY 1990)

Pellerin, Les droits des parties dans l'instance arbitrale, 1990 *Rev. Arb.* 395

Perrot, Arbitrage interne et arbitrage international. Les recours devant la Cour d'appel empêchent-ils l'arbitre de poursuivre sa mission? 1987 *Rev. Arb.* 107

———, L'arbitrage international en droit français, 27 *Rassegna dell'Arb.* 1 (1987)

———, Le droit français de l'arbitrage, in *L'Arbitrage* 249 (L. Matray & G. de Leval eds. 1989)

———, La réforme du droit de l'arbitrage: l'application à l'arbitrage des règles de nouveau Code de procédure civile, 1980 *Rev. Arb.* 642

Petit, Le Règlement de la Chambre arbitrale de Paris et le décret du 14 mai 1980 relatif a l'arbitrage, 1981 *Rev. Arb.* 251

Peyre, Le juge de l'exéquatur: fantôme ou réalité? 1985 *Rev. Arb.* 231

Pfaff, Grenzbewegungen der Schiedsfähigkeit — Patentnichtigkeit im Schiedsverfahren, in *Beiträge zum internationalen Verfahrensrecht und zur Schiedsgerichtsbarkeit. Festschrift für Heinrich Nagel* 278 (W. Habscheid & K. Schwab eds. 1987)

Pluyette, Le point de vue du juge, 1990 *Rev. Arb.* 353

Poznanski, The Nature and Extent of an Arbitrator's Power in International Commercial Arbitration, 4 *J. Int'l Arb.* 71 (No. 3, 1987)

Real, G.K.L., *Der Schiedsrichtervertrag* (Cologne 1983)

Redfern, International Commercial Arbitration. Jurisdiction Denied: the Pyramid Collapses, 1986 *J. Bus. L.* 15

Reiner, Die internationale Schiedsgerichtsbarkeit nach österreichischem und französischem Recht. Ein Vergleich zweier Reformen jüngeren Datums, 27 *ZRV* 162 (1986)

Reymond, The Report of the Mustill Committee: A Foreign View, 106 *L.Q. Rev.* 431 (1990)

Riedberg, P., *Der amiable Compositeur im internationalen privaten Schiedsgerichtsverfahren* (Frankfurt 1962)

Rigault, Arbitrage de la Chambre Officielle Franco-Allemande de Commerce et d'Industrie, 1986 *Cah. Jurid. & Fisc.* 297

Robert, Arbitration in France, in 3 *The Law and Business of Licensing: Licensing in the 1980s* 2G-251 (R. Goldscheider & T. Arnold eds. 1987)

————, Arbitration in France, 23 *Les Nouvelles (J. Licencing Exec. Soc'y)* 26 (1988)

————, De la règle de conflit à la règle materielle en matière d'arbitrage international (spécialement en droit international privé français), in *The Art of Arbitration* 273 (J. Schultsz & A. van den Berg eds. 1982)

————, El arbitraje en los paises de la Comunidad Europea, in *El Arbitraje Comercial Internacional* 223 (Mexico 1983)

————, L'arbitrage en matière internationale. Commentaire du décret No. 81-500 du 12 mai 1981, 1981 *Recueil Dalloz Sirey* 209

————, Le rôle du juge pour la constitution du tribunal arbitral et pendant le deroulement de la procédure selon la récente législation française sur l'arbitrage, in *Festschrift für Arthur Büllow* 179 (K.-H. Böckstiegel & O. Glossner eds. 1981)

————, Un centre national: L'Association Française d'Arbitrage (A.F.A.), 1990 *Rev. Arb.* 233

Robert, J. & B. Morceau, *L'arbitrage— droit interne, droit international privé* (5th ed. Paris 1983)

Robert, J. & T. Carbonneau, *The French Law of Arbitration* (New York 1983)

Robine, Le choix des arbitres, 1990 *Rev. Arb.* 315

————, The Liability of Arbitrators and Arbitral Institutions in International Arbitrations under French Law, 5 *Arb. Int'l* 323 (1989)

Rubellin-Devichi, L'arbitrage et les tiers: le droit de l'arbitrage: les solutions juridictionnelles, 1988 *Rev. Arb.* 515

Ruiloba Santana, El Convenio hispano-francés de 28 de mayo de 1969 sobre reconocimiento y ejecución de sentencias extranjeras y actas autenticas en materia civil y mercantil, 23 *Rev. Esp. Der. Int'l* 42 (1970)

Sachs, Das bilaterale französisch-algerische Schiedsabkommen vom 27. März 1983— Ein Muster auch für andere Staaten? 6 *IPRax* 309 (1986)

Sage, Un centre régional: Le C.A.R.A. — Centre d'Arbitrage Rhône-Alps, 1990 *Rev. Arb.* 325

Samuel, A., *Jurisdictional Problems in International Commercial Arbitration: A Study of Belgian, Dutch, English, French, Swedish, Swiss, U.S. and West German Law* (Zurich 1989)

Sandrock, Die Entscheidung von Streitigkeiten durch Schiedsgerichte, in *Französisches Vertragsrecht für deutsche Exporteure* 54 (C. Witz & T.M. Bopp eds. 1989)

Schlosser, Deutsche und franzözische Rechtsprechung zur Schiedsgerichtbarkeit 1988, 2 *Jahrbuch Schiedsgerichtsbarkeit* 241 (1988)

————, Die lange Leine vom Gericht zum Schiedsgericht. Ein französisches Lehrstück für Deutschland, die Schweiz und manch'andere, in *Festschrift für Walther J. Habscheid* 273 (W. Lindacher, D. Pfaff et al. eds. 1989)

————, Party-Appointed Arbitrators and Multiple Defendants Having Conflicting Interests, in *Law in East and West/Recht in Ost und West* 739 (Tokyo 1988)

Schweyer, A., *Patentnichtigkeit und Patentverletzungund deren Beurteilung durch private Schiedsgerichte nach dem Recht der Schweiz, Deutsch-lands, Italiens und Frankreich* (St. Gallen 1981)

Seppala, French Domestic Arbitration Law, 16 *Int'l Law.* 749 (1982)

Shifman, France, in 2 *W.A.R.* 1641 (H. Smit & V. Pechota eds. 1987)

638

————, French Arbitration Association, in 4 *W.A.R.* 4545 (H. Smit & V. Pechota eds. 1989)

————, Maritime Arbitration Chamber of Paris, in 4 *W.A.R.* 4575 (H. Smit & V. Pechota eds. 1989)

Shifman, Paris Arbitral Chamber, in 4 *W.A.R.* 4557 (H. Smit & V. Pechota eds. 1989)

Smith, Impartiality of the Party-Appointed Arbitrator, 6 *Arb. Int'l* 320 (1990)

Stanton, The Court of Appeal of Paris and Lack of Arbitral Jurisdiction, 2 *Arb. Int'l* 220 (1986)

Stewart & Pechota, Franco-Algerian Agreement on the Settlement by Arbitration of Disputes Arising from Commercial Contracts, 1983, in 3 *W.A.R.* 3630 (H. Smit & V. Pechota eds. 1987)

Thompson, 'Detachment' from the National Law in International Commercial Arbitration, 48 *Arbitration* 105 (1982)

————, The Same Tribunal for Different Arbitrations, 4 *J. Int'l Arb.* 111 (No. 2, 1987)

Thuilleaux, La loi de 1986 sur l'arbitrage au Québec, au regard de la loi française sur l'arbitrage, 1988 *Int'l Bus. L.J.* 905

Tupman, Staying Enforcement of Arbitral Awards under the New York Convention, 3 *Arb. Int'l* 223 (1987)

von Breitenstein, Eine neue Arbitrage-Institution: Das COFACI-Schiedszentrum in Paris, 39 *NJW* 1402 (1986)

von Mehren, International Commercial Arbitration: The Contribution of the French Jurisprudence, 46 *La. L. Rev.* 1045 (1986)

Vulliemin, J.-M., *Jugement et sentence arbitrale* (2nd ed. Zurich 1990)

Zdravkovic, Certains cas de la jurisprudence yougoslave et étrangère sur l'exécution des sentences arbitrales étrangères, in *ICCA, Fifth Int'l Arb. Congress: Proceedings* C Izi 1-16 (1975)

GERMANY

A. FEDERAL REPUBLIC OF GERMANY

Aden, Der einstweilige Rechtsschutz im Schiedsgerichtsverfahren, 40 *B.B.* 2277 (1985)

Adlerstein, Zur Unabhängigkeit des Schiedsrichters, in *Studien zum Recht der internationalen Schiedsgerichtsbarkeit* 9 (K.-H. Böckstiegel ed. 1979)

Altenmüller, R., *Die schiedsrichterliche Entscheidung kartellrechtlicher Streitigkeiten* (Tübingen 1973)

Anderegg, Zum 'Doppelexequatur' ausländischer Schiedssprüche, 53 *Rabels Z.* 171 (1989)

Bartos, H., *Internationale Handelsschiedsgerichtsbarkeit: Verfahrensprinzipien* (Frankfurt 1984)

Basedow, Vertragsstatut und Arbitrage nach neuem IPR, 1 *Jahrbuch Schiedsgerichtsbarkeit* 3 (1987)

Baumbach, A. & K.H. Schwab, eds., *Schiedsgerichtsbarkeit. Systematischer Kommentar* (Munich 1960)

Baur, F., *Der Schiedsrichterliche Vergleich* (Munich 1971)

———, *Neuere Probleme der privaten Schiedsgerichtsbarkeit* (Berlin 1980)

Berger, The Modern Trend Towards Exclusion of Recourse Against Transnational Arbitral Awards: A European Perspective, 12 *Fordham Int'l L. J.* 605 (1989)

Bertram-Nothnagel, Enforcement of Foreign Judgments and Arbitral Awards in West Germany, 17 *Va. J. Int'l L.* 385 (1977)

Billings, International Standards for Automotive Arbitration, 28 *German Y.B. Int'l L.* 425 (1985)

Böshagen, Aus der Arbeit des Deutschen Ausschusses für Schiedsgerichtswesen, in *Festschrift für Arthur Bülow* 17 (K.-H. Böckstiegel & O. Glossner eds. 1981)

Böckstiegel, Abschluss von Schiedsvertragen durch konkludentes Handeln oder Stillschweigen, in *Festschrift für Arthur Bülow* 1 (K.-H. Böckstiegel & O. Glossner eds. 1981)

————, Schiedsgerichte und staatliche Gerichte, 25 *RIW* 161 (1979)

Böckstiegel, K.-H., ed., *Handelsschiedsgerichtsbarkeit in England und in der Bundesrepublik Deutschland/Commercial Arbitration in the Federal Republic of Germany and in England* (Cologne 1987)

————, *Rechtsfortbildung durch internationale Schiedsgerichtsbarkeit* (Cologne 1989)

————, *Schiedsgerichtsbarkeit im deutsch-amerikanischen Wirtschaftverkehr/Arbitration in U.S.-German Business Relations* (Cologne 1985)

Bork, Der Begriff der objektiven Schiedsfähigkeit (Par. 1025 Abs. 1 ZPO), 100 *ZZP* 249 (1987)

Bösch, A., *Einstweiliger Rechtsschutz in der internationalen Handelsschiedsgerichtsbarkeit* (Berne 1989)

Brinkmann, G., *Schiedsgerichtsbarkeit und Massnahmen des einstweiligen Rechtsschutzes* (Berlin 1977)

Brücher, Vollstreckung und Sicherung der Vollstreckung ausländischer Schiedssprüche, 13 *ADW* 337 (1967)

Carabiber, L'immunité de juridiction et d'exécution des Etats collectivités et établissements publics au regard de l'obligation assumée par une clause compromissoire insérée dans les contrats internationaux de droit privé, in *Liber Amicorum for Martin Domke* 23 (P. Sanders ed. 1967)

Chartier, Centre d'Arbitrage de la Chambre Officielle Franco-Allemande de Commerce et d'Industrie, 1986 *Rev. Arb.* 291

Chrocziel & Westin, Die Vollstreckbarkeit ausländischer Urteile und Schiedssprüche, 87 *Zeitschrift für vergleichende Rechtswissenschaft* 145 (1988)

Czimpiel & Kurth, Schiedsvereinbarung und Wechselforderung im deutschen und internationalen Privatrecht, 40 *NJW* 2118 (1987)

de Bruin, De 'affaire C,' 1989 *Tijdschrift voor Arbitrage* 1

Delaume, Judicial Decisions Related to Sovereign Immunity and Transnational Arbitration, 2 *ICSID Rev. - Foreign Investment L.J.* 403 (1987)

Deutsches Institut für Schiedsgerichtswesen e.V., *Übernahme des UNCITRAL Modellgesetz über die internationale Handelsschiedsgerichtsbarkeit in das deutsche Recht* (Cologne 1989)

Dobratz, Schiedsklausel und Vollstreckung im Aussenhandel, 8 *AWD* 188 (1962)

Eckstrom, L., *Licensing in Foreign and Domestic Operations.* Volume I, Chapter 7: Arbitration (by Steven Z. Szczepanski), (New York 1972, updated 1987)

Eisemann, Zur Rechtswahl in der Schiedsgerichtsbarkeit bei Kaufvertragen, in *Festschrift für Arthur Bülow* 59 (K.-H. Böckstiegel & O. Glossner eds. 1981)

Engelhardt, Aus der neueren Rechtsprechung zur Schiedsgerichtsbarkeit, 42 *JZ* 227 (1987)

Fischer-Zernin & Junker, Arbitration and Mediation: Synthesis or Antithesis? 5 *J. Int'l Arb.* 22 (No. 1, 1988)

————, Between Scylla and Charybdis: Fact Gathering in German Arbitration, 4 *J. Int'l Arb.* 9 (No. 2, 1987)

Gildeggen, R., *Internationale Schieds und Schiedsverfahrensverein- barungen in algemeinen Geschäftsbedingungen vor deutschen Gerichten* (Frankfurt 1991)

Glossner, Eine zentrale Gerichtsinstanz für internationale Schiedsver- fahren in der Bundesrepublik Deutschland? 32 *RIW* 214 (1986)

————, Federal Republic of Germany, in *Int'l Handbook Com. Arb.* (A. van den Berg gen. ed. 1984), Suppl. 7, April 1987

————, Federal Republic of Germany: National Report, 4 *Y.B. Com. Arb.* 60 (1979); 11 *Y.B. Com. Arb.* 67 (1986) and 12 *Y.B. Com. Arb.* 363 (1987)

————, Le droit allemand de l'arbitrage, in *L'Arbitrage* 199 (L. Matray & G. de Leval eds. 1989)

Glossner, O., *Commercial Arbitration in the Federal Republic of Germany* (Deventer 1984)

Glossner, O., J. Bredow & M. Bühler, *Das Schiedsgericht in der Praxis.* 3rd rev. ed. (Heidelberg 1990)

Groos, L'arbitrage de la Chambre Officielle Franco-Allemande de Commerce et d'Industrie, 1986 *Int'l Bus. L.J.* 205

————, Schiedsgerichtsbarkeit im deutsch-französischen Wirtschaftsverkehr, 33 *RIW* 343 (1987)

Groos, Langer & Sandrock, Die Schiedsgerichtsbarkeit der Offiziellen Deutsch-Französischen Industrie- und Handelskammer, 40 *BB, Annex* 14 (No. 32, 1985)

Groos, Langer, Sandrock & Dorman, Rules of the Official Franco-German Chamber of Commerce and Industry, in 3 *W.A.R.* 3742 (H. Smit & V. Pechota eds. 1987)

Grunsky, W., D. Leipold, W. Munzberg, P. Schlosser & E. Schumann, Stein-Jonas Kommentar zur Zivilprozessordnung. Paragraphs 1044 - 1048. *EG ZPO*, (20th rev. ed. Tübingen 1987)

Habscheid, L'expertise-arbitrage. Etude de droit comparé, in *Liber Amicorum for Martin Domke* 103 (P. Sanders ed. 1967)

————, Les jurisdictions et l'arbitage, in *ICCA, Sixth Int'l Arb. Congress: Proceedings* 261 (1978

Habscheid, Teil-, Zwischen- und Vorabschiedsprüche im schweizerischen und deutschen Recht, ihre Anfechtbarkeit und die Rechtsfolgen ihrer Aufhebung durch das Staatsgericht (unter besonderer Berücksichtigung, der Streitgenossenschaft) 106 *ZSR* 669 (1987)

Habscheid, W. & K. H. Schwab, eds., *Beiträge zum internationalen Verfahrensrecht und zur Schiedsgerichtsbarkeit. Festschrift für Heinrich Nagel zum 75. Geburtstag* (Münster 1987)

Hangarter, Die Schiedsgerichtsbarkeit der Handelskammer Deutschland-Schweiz, 1 *Jahrbuch Schiedsgerichtsbarkeit* 169 (1987)

————, Die Schiedsgerichtsbarkeit der Handelskammer Deutschland-Schweiz, in *Die Internationale Schiedsgerichtsbarkeit in der Schweiz* 189 (K.-H. Böckstiegel ed. 1989)

Hellwig, Nationale und internationale Schiedsgerichtsbarkeit, 30 *RIW* 421 (1984)

Henn, G., *Schiedsverfahrensrecht: ein Handbuch* (Heidelberg 1986)

Heyn, Parteivertretung durch Anwalte im Schiedsgerichtsverfahren, 11 *N.J.W.* 1667 (1958)

Hintz, Recht und Praxis der Streiterledigung im Ost-West-Handel am Beispiel des Handels zwischen der UdSSR und der Bundesrepublik Deutschland, 32 *RIW* 506 (1986)

Holland & Hantke, Beschränkung auf den Urkunden-Beweis im Schiedsverfahren, in *Festschrift für Arthur Bülow* 75 (K.-H. Böckstiegel & O. Glossner eds. 1981)

Hunter & Triebel, Awarding Interest in International Arbitration, 6 *J. Int'l Arb.* 7 (No. 1, 1989)

International Chamber of Commerce, *Arbitration Law in Europe* (Paris 1981)

————, Germany/Allemagne, in *Commercial Arbitration and the Law/ L'Arbitrage commercial et la Loi* (Basel 1949)

Jagenburg, Schiedsgerichtsbarkeit zwischen Wunsch and Wirklichkeit, in *Festschrift für Walter Oppenhoff zum 80. Geburtstag* 147 (W. Jagenburg, G. Maier-Reimer & T. Verhoeven eds. 1985)

Jannot, Überlegungen zu Bedeutung und Ausgestaltung von Schiedsgerichtsvereinbarungen in der Rückversicherung, in *Festschrift für Ernst C. Stiefel* 359 (M. Lutter, W. Oppenhoff, O. Sandrock & H. Winkhaus eds. 1987)

Jestaedt, T., *Schiedsverfahren und Konkurs* (Berlin 1985)

Junker, Discovery in deutsch-amerikanischen Rechtsverkehr - Entwicklungslinien und Perspektiven, 33 *RIW* 1 (1987)

————, Verjährungsunterbrechung beim Übergang vom Zivilprozess zum Schiedsverfahren, 48 *KTS* 37 (1987)

Jahrbuch für die Praxis der Schiedsgerichtsbarkeit (edited by O. Glossner). Vol. 1 (1987), (Heidelberg 1988-)

Kassis, A., *Problèmes de base de l'arbitrage en droit comparé et en droit international.* Vol. 1: Arbitrage juridictionnel et arbitrage contractuel (Paris 1987)

Kerr, Arbitration Law Relevant to English-German Business Relations, in *Handelsschiedsgerichtsbarkeit in England und in der Bundesrepublik Deutschland* 5 (K.-H. Böckstiegel ed. 1987)

Kessler, J., *Die Bindung des Schiedsgerichts an das materielle Recht* (Cologne 1964)

————, *Schiedsgerichtsvertrag und Schiedsverfahren* (Munich 1970)

Klein, F.-E., *Considérations sur l'arbitrage en droit international privé* (Basel 1955)

Kohl, Arbitrage en droit allemand, 67 *Rev. Droit Int'l & Droit Comp.* 7 (1990)

Kohl, B., *Vorläufiger Rechtsschutz in internationalen Handelsschieds-verfahren* (Berne 1990)

Kohler, K., *Die moderne Praxis des Schiedsgerichtswesens in der Wirtschaft* (Berlin 1967)

Kornblum, Ordre public transnational, ordre public international und ordre public interne im Recht der privaten Schiedsgerichtsbarkeit, in *Beiträge zum internationalen Verfahrensrecht und zur Schiedsgerichtsbarkeit. Festschrift für Heinrich Nagel* 140 (W. Habscheid & K. Schwab eds. 1987)

————, Das Gebot überparteilicher Rechtspflege und der deutsche schiedsrechtliche ordre public, 40 *NJW* 1105 (1987)

————, Nachprufbarkeit kartellrechtlicher Schiedssprüche durch die ordentliche Gerichte, 22 *NJW* 1793 (1969)

————, Übernahme des UNCITRAL-Modellgesetzes in das deutsche Schiedsverfahrensrecht, 1 *Jahrbuch Schiedsgerichtsbarkeit* 34 (1987)

Kornblum, U., *Probleme der schiedsrichterlichen Unabhängigkeit* (Munich 1968)

Kotzorel, A., *Private Gerichte als Alternative zur staatlichen Zivilgerichtsbarkeit: eine ökonomische Analyse* (Tübingen 1987)

Krafzik, B., *Die Spruchpraxis der Hanseatischen Schiedsgerichte* (Berlin 1974)

Krause, H., *Die geschichtliche Entwicklung des Schiedsgerichtswesens in Deutschland* (Berlin 1930)

Krause, H. & F. Bozenhardt, *Internationale Handelsschiedsgerichts-barkeit* (Stuttgart 1990)

Kropholler, J., ed., *Die deutsche Rechtsprechung auf dem Gebiete des Internationalen Privatrechts im Jahre 1981, 1982, 1983, 1984, 1985* (Tübingen 1984, 1985, 1986, 1987)

Krüger, Probleme des saudi-arabischen internationalen Vertrags- und Schiedsrecht, in *Vertragspraxis und Streiterledigung im Wirtschaftsverkehr mit arabischen Staaten* 61 (K.-H. Böckstiegel ed. 1981)

Kühl, S. G., *Schiedsgerichtsbarkeit im Seehandel* (Kehl am Rhein 1990)

Kühn, Arbitrability of Antitrust Disputes in the Federal Republic of Germany, 3 *Arb. Int'l* 226 (1987)

————, Die Anfechtung und Vollstreckung des Schiedsentscheides. Eine kritische Würdigung der neuen schweizerischen Regelung unter Berücksichtigung ihrer Auswirkungen im deutschen Vollstreckbarerklärungsverfahren, in *Die Internationale Schiedsgerichtsbarkeit in der Schweiz* 163 (K.-H. Böckstiegel ed. 1989)

————, Kartellrecht und Schiedsgerichtsbarkeit in der Bundesrepublik Deutschland, 1987 *BB* 621

————, The Liability of Arbitrators in West Germany, 8 *Int'l Bus. Law.* 345 (1980)

Kuner, The Public Policy Exception to the Enforcement of Foreign Arbitral Awards in the United States and West Germany under the New York Convention, 7 *J. Int'l Arb.* 71 (No. 4, 1990)

Laschet, Zur Anerkennung ausländischer Zwischenschiedssprüche, 4 *IPRax* 72 (1984)

Lau, Probleme der Niederlegung von Schiedssprüchen und von Schiedsvergleichen, 40 *Monatsschrift für das deutsche Recht* 545 (1986)

Lau & Lau, Die deutsche Schiedsgerichtbarkeit und der internationale Standard, 1990 *Transportrecht* 133 (No. 4)

Lionnet, The UNCITRAL Model Law: A German Perspective, 6 *Arb. Int'l* 343 (1990)

Lorcher, Kein Schiedsspruch ohne Unterschrift des Vorsitzenden? 43 *BB* 78 (1988)

————, Schiedsgerichtsbarkeit: Übernahme des UNCITRAL Modellgesetzes? 20 *Zeitschrift für Rechtspolitik* 230 (1987)

Lüer, German Court Decisions Interpreting and Implementing the New York Convention, 7 *J. Int'l Arb.* 127 (No. 1, 1990)

Luthge, J., *Die Kollisionsrechtliche Funktion der Schiedsgerichts-vereinbarung* (Bonn 1975)

MacLaren, Commercial Arbitration in the United States and Overseas, in *Arbitration and the Licensing Process* 5 (R. Goldscheider & M. de Haas eds. 1984-)

Maier, H. J., *Handbuch der Schiedsgerichtsbarkeit. Ein Handbuch der deutschen und internationalen Schiedsgerichtspraxis* (Berlin 1979)

Matray, L'arbitre-partie en matière internationale, 53 *Rev. Droit Int'l & Droit Comp.* 152 (1976)

Meckling, Arbitration, in 1 *Business Transactions in Germany* 6.1 (B. Rüster ed. 1983)

Mezger, Beschränkung des Geltungbereich von Par. 1044 ZPO durch internationale Übereinkommen, 17 *AWD* 322 (1971)

————, Die Anerkennung jugoslawischer und anderer osteuropäischer Schiedssprüche in der Bundesrepublik, 15 *NJW* 278 (1962)

————, Verstoss gegen die öffentliche Ordnung bei Beurteilung ausländischer Schiedssprüche, 23 *NJW* 368 (1970)

————, Vollstreckung ausländischer Schiedssprüche, 16 *AWD* 258 (1970)

Mittelstein, Law and Practice of Arbitral Tribunals in Germany, in 1 *Int'l Y.B. Civil & Com. Arb.* 33 (1928)

Mok Young-joon, The Principle of Reciprocity in the United Nations Convention on the Recognition and Enforcement of Foreign Arbitral Awards of 1958, 21 *Case W. Res. J. Int'l L.* 123 (1989)

Möller, Die neue Schiedsgerichtsordnung des Deutschen Ausschusses für Schiedsgerichtswesen, 34 *RIW* 605 (1988)

Nagel, Gedanken über die Beschleunigung des Schiedsverfahren, in *Festschrift für Karl Firsching* 191 (Munich 1985)

Nagel, H., *Internationales Zivilprozessrecht*, 2nd ed. (Münster 1984)

Nicklisch, Gutachter-, Schieds- und Schlichtungsstellen — rechtliche Einordnung und erforderliche Verfahrensgarantien, in *Festschrift für Arthur Bülow* 159 (K.-H. Böckstiegel & O. Glossner eds. 1981)

Nöcker, Gesetzgebungstechnische Aspekte bei einer Übernahme des UNCITRAL-Modellgesetzes, 36 *RIW* 28 (1990)

Nöcker, & French, Estoppel: What's the Government's Word Worth. An Analysis of German Law, Common Law Jurisdictions, and the Practice of International Arbitral Tribunals, 24 *Int'l Law.* 409 (1990)

Nolting, Empfielt es sich, das deutsche Schiedsrecht zu reformieren? 7 *IPRax* 387 (1987)

―――, Mangelnde Feststellung des für Formwirksamkeit der Schiedsklausel und Schiedsfähigkeit massgeblichen Rechts, 7 *IPRax* 349 (1987)

Parker School of Foreign and Comparative Law, *International Commercial Arbitration and the Courts* (Dobbs Ferry, NY 1990)

Pechota, Hamburg Friendly Arbitration, in 4 *W.A.R.* 4483 (H. Smit & V. Pechota eds. 1989)

―――, The German Arbitration Committee, in 4 *W.A.R.* 4451 (H. Smit & V. Pechota eds. 1989)

Pechota & Koerner, Federal Republic of Germany, in 2 *W.A.R.* 1565 (H. Smit & V. Pechota eds. 1987)

Pfaff, Grenzbewegungen der Schiedsfähigkeit — Patentnichtigkeit im Schiedsverfahren, in *Beiträge zum internationalen Verfahrensrecht und zur Schiedsgerichtsbarkeit. Festschrift für Heinrich Nagel* 278 (W. Habscheid & K. Schwab eds. 1987)

Pfaff, Zum Problem der Veröffentlichung von Schiedssprüchen der internationalen Handels-Schiedsgerichtsbarkeit, in *Um Recht und Freiheit, Festschrift für von der Heydte* 1127 (1977)

Pfaff, D., *Die Aussenhandelsschiedsgerichtsbarkeit der sozialistischen Länder im Handel mit der Bundesrepublik Deutschland* (Heidelberg 1973)

Raeschke-Kessler, Die neuere Rechtsprechung des Bundesgerichtshofs zur Schiedsgerichtsbarkeit, 1 *Jahrbuch Schiedsgerichtsbarkeit* 201 (1987)

―――, Die neuere Rechtsprechung zur Schiedsgerichtsbarkeit, 2 *Jahrbuch Schiedsgerichtsbarkeit* 225 (1988)

―――, Neuere Entwicklungen im Bereich der Internationalen Schiedsgerichtsbarkeit, 41 *NJW* 3041 (1988)

Raeschke-Kessler & Bühler, Aufsicht über den Schiedsrichter durch den ICC-Schiedsgerichtshof (Paris) und rechtliches Gehör der Parteien, 8 *ZIP* 1157 (1987)

Real, G.K.L., *Der Schiedsrichtervertrag* (Cologne 1983)

Reiner, A., *Handbuch der ICC Schiedsgerichtsbarkeit. Die Verfahrensordnung des Schiedsgerichtshofes der Internationalen Handelskammer* (Vienna 1989)

Riedberg, P., *Der amiable Compositeur im internationalen privaten Schiedsgerichtsverfahren* (Frankfurt 1962)

Rigault, Arbitrage de la Chambre Officielle Franco-Allemande de Commerce et d'Industrie, 1986 *Cah. Jurid. & Fisc.* 297

Robert, El arbitraje en los paises de la Comunidad Europea, in *El Arbitraje Comercial Internacional* 223 (Mexico 1983)

Rokison, The Practice of Arbitration in England Insofar as it Relates to Anglo-German Business Relations, in *Handelsschiedsgerichtsbarkeit in England und in der Bundesrepublik Deutschland* 19 (K.-H. Böckstiegel ed. 1987)

Roth, Schiedsklauseln in Gesellschaftsverträgen, in *Beiträge zum internationalen Verfahrensrecht und zur Schiedsgerichtsbarkeit. Festschrift für Heinrich Nagel* 318 (W. Habscheid & K. Schwab eds. 1987)

Samuel, A., *Jurisdictional Problems in International Commercial Arbitration: A Study of Belgian, Dutch, English, French, Swedish, Swiss, U.S. and West German Law* (Zurich 1989)

Sandrock, Arbitration between U.S. and West German Companies: An Example of Effective Dispute Resolution in International Business Transactions, 9 *U. Pa. J. Int'l Bus. L.* 27 (1987)

————, Das Gesetz zur Neuregelung des Internationalen Privatrechts und die internationale Schiedsgerichtsbarkeit, 33 *RIW Beilage 2 zu Heft* 5/1987 (1987)

————, Die Bedeutung des Gesetzes zur Neuregelung des Internationalen Privatrechts für die Unternehmenspraxis, 32 *RIW* 841 (1986)

————, Die Entscheidung von Streitigkeiten durch Schiedsgerichte, in *Französisches Vertragsrecht für deutsche Exporteure* 54 (C. Witz & T.M. Bopp eds. 1989)

649

————, Gerichtsstands- oder Schiedsklauseln in Verträgen zwischen U.S.-amerikanischen und deutschen Unternehmen: was ist zu empfehlen? in *Festschrift für Ernst C. Stiefel* 625 (M. Lutter, W. Oppenhoff, O. Sandrock & H. Winkhaus eds. 1987)

————, International Arbitration in the Federal Republic of Germany: A Hitherto Missed Opportunity, 1 *Am. Rev. Int'l Arb.* 49 (1990)

————, The German-German Merger: Changes in Arbitration Law and Practice, 1 *Am. Rev. Int'l Arb.* 272 (1990)

————, Zügigkeit und Leichtigkeit versus Grundlichkeit: Internationale Schiedsverfahren in der Bundesrepublik Deutschland, 41 *JZ* 370 (1986)

Sandrock & Hentzen, Enforcing Foreign Arbitral Awards in the Federal Republic of Germany: The Example of a United States Award, 2 *Transnat'l Law.* 49 (1989)

Sandrock & Nöcker, Einstweilige Massnahmen internationaler Schiedsgerichte: Blosse Papiertiger?, 1 *Jahrbuch Schiedsgerichtsbarkeit* 74 (1987)

Sareika, W., *Die Gültigkeit von Schiedsgerichtsvereinbarungen nach kanadischem und deutschem Recht* (Frankfurt 1978)

Schlosser, Deutsche und franzözische Rechtsprechung zur Schiedsgerichtbarkeit 1988, 2 *Jahrbuch Schiedsgerichtsbarkeit* 241 (1988)

————, Die lange Leine vom Gericht zum Schiedsgericht. Ein französisches Lehrstück für Deutschland, die Schweiz und manch'andere, in *Festschrift für Walther J. Habscheid* 273 (W. Lindacher, D. Pfaff et al. eds. 1989)

————, Notwendige Reformen des deutschen Rechts der Schiedsgerichtsbarkeit, 1987 *ZIP* 492

————, Party-Appointed Arbitrators and Multiple Defendants Having Conflicting Interests, in *Law in East and West/Recht in Ost und West* 739 (Tokyo 1988)

————, Probleme der internationalen Handelsschiedsgerichtsbarkeit (II), 24 *AktG* 278 (1979)

————, Quelles nouvelles de l'arbitrage Outre-Rhin? 1987 *Rev. Arb.* 293

————, Right and Remedy in Common Law Arbitration and in German Arbitration Law, 4 *J. Int'l Arb.* 27 (No. 1, 1987)

————, Schiedsgerichtsbarkeit und öffentlich-rechtlich beeinflusste Streitgegenstände, in *Festschrift für Arthur Bülow* 189 (K.-H. Böckstiegel & O. Glossner eds. 1981)

————, The German Law on Arbitration and its Relevance for the German-English Business Relations, in *Handelsschiedsgerichtsbarkeit in England und in der Bundesrepublik Deutschland* 59 (K.-H. Böckstiegel ed. 1987)

————, Verfahrensintegrität und Anerkennung von Schiedsprüchen im deutsch-amerikanischen Verhältnis, 31 *NJW* 455 (1978)

Schlosser, P., *Das Recht der internationalen privaten Schiedsgerichtsbarkeit* (2nd rev. ed. Tübingen 1989)

Schmidt, Präklusion und Einlassung auf die schiedsgerichtliche Verhandlung zur Hauptsache — Vertragsdenken und Prozessdenken in der jüngeren Praxis, in *Beiträge zum internationalen Verfahrensrecht und zur Schiedsgerichtsbarkeit. Festschrift für Heinrich Nagel* 373 (W. Habscheid & K. Schwab eds. 1987)

————, Statutarische Schiedsklauseln zwischen prozessualer und verbandsrechtlicher Legitimation: Ein Beitrag zum Anwendungsbereich des Par. 1048 *ZPO*, 44 *JZ* 1077 (1989)

Schönke, A., *Das Schiedsgerichtsverfahren nach dem heutigen deutschen Recht* (Berlin 1954)

Schottelius, Das Schiedsverfahren im Rahmen des DIN Deutsches Institut für Normung e.V., in *Festschrift für Arthur Bülow* 199 (K.-H. Böckstiegel & O. Glossner eds. 1981)

Schottelius, D.J., *Die internationale Schiedsgerichtsbarkeit: eine Studie über die Bildung eines internationalen Schiedsgerichtssystem* (Cologne 1957)

————, *Die kaufmannische Schiedsgerichtsbarkeit* (Bremen 1953)

Schütze, Anerkennung und Vollstreckbarerklärung von Zivilurteilen und Schiedssprüchen im deutsch-saudiarabischen Verhältnis, 30 *RIW* 261 (1984)

————, Die Anerkennung und Vollstreckbarerklärung von Zivilurteilen und Schiedssprüchen im deutsch-chinesischen Rechtsverkehr, 32 *RIW* 269 (1986)

————, Verbesserungen des Zivilgerichtsverfahrens aus Erfahrungen mit der Schiedsgerichtsbarkeit, in Effiziente Rechtsverfulgung. Efficiency in the Pursuit of Justice. Landesberichte zum VIII. Weltkongress für Prozessrecht in Utrecht 1987. *German National Reports* 65 (P. Gilles, ed. 1987)

————, Zur Wirksamkeit von internationalen Schiedsvereinbarungen und zur Wirkungserstreckung ausländischer Schiedsspruche über Ansprüche aus Börsentermingeschäften, 1 *Jahrbuch Schiedsgerichtsbarkeit* 94 (1987)

Schütze, R., D. Tscherning & W. Wais, *Handbuch des Schiedsverfahrens. Praxis der deutschen und internationalen Schiedsgerichtsbarkeit* (2nd ed. Berlin 1990)

Schütze, R. A., *Rechtsverfolgung im Ausland. Prozessführung vor ausländischer Gerichten und Schiedsgerichten* (Heidelberg 1986)

Schurmann, Plan eines zentralen Gerichtshofs für die Anerkennung von Schiedssprüchen, 33 *RIW* 415 (1987)

Schwab, Das UNCITRAL-Model Law und das deutsche Recht, in *Beiträge zum internationalen Verfahrensrecht und zur Schiedsgerichtsbarkeit. Festschrift für Heinrich Nagel* 427 (W. Habscheid & K. Schwab eds. 1987)

————, Die Entscheidung des Schiedsgerichts über seine eigene Zuständigkeit: Eine Stellungsnahme zum Verhältnis von Hauptvertrag und Schiedsvertrag und zur sog. Kompetenz-Kompetenz des Schiedsgerichts, 22 *KTS* 17 (1961)

————, Die Schiedsgerichtsbarkeit der Internationalen Handelskammer aus der Sicht des deutschen Rechts, in *Festschrift für Winfried Kralik* 317 (Vienna 1986)

————, Kollisionsrechtliche Fragen des deutschen internationalen Schiedsverfahrensrechts, in *Festschrift für Martin Luther* 163 (Munich 1976)

————, Schiedsrichterernennung und Schiedsrichtervertrag, in *Festschrift für Gerhard Schiedermair* 499 (Munich 1976)

————, The Legal Foundations and Limitations of Arbitration Procedure in the U.S. and Germany, in *International Arbitration: Liber Amicorum for Martin Domke* 301 (P. Sanders ed. 1967)

Schwab, K. H. & G. Walter, *Schiedsgerichtsbarkeit: Systematischer Kommentar zu den Vorschriftender Zivilprozessordnung, des Arbeitsgerichtsgesetzes, der Staatsverträge und der Kostengesetze über das privatrechtliche Schiedsgerichtsvefahren* (4th ed. Munich 1990)

Schweyer A., *Patentnichtigkeit und Patentverletzung und deren Beurteilung durch private Schiedsgerichte nach dem Recht der Schweiz, Deutschlands, Italiens und Frankreich* (St. Gallen 1981)

Sieg, Bindung des Haftpflichtversicherers an Schiedssprüche und Schiedsgutachten im Haftpflichtverhältniss, 35 *VersR* 501 (1984)

Steindorf, Kartellrecht und Schiedsgerichtsbarkeit, 34 *Wirtschaft und Wettbewerb* 189 (1984)

Straatmann, Bemerkungen zur Hamburger Freundschaftlichen Arbitrage, in *Festschrift für Reimers* 199 (1979)

————, Federal Republic of Germany: Hamburg Friendly Arbitration, in *Handbook of Institutional Arbitration* 45 (E. Cohn, M. Domke & F. Eisemann eds. 1977)

Straatmann, K. & P. Ulmer, eds., *Handelsrechtliche Schiedsgerichts-Praxis. Sammlung von Schiedssprüchen unter Einschuss von Urteilen und Texten zur Schiedsgerichtsbarkeit,* 2 vols. (Cologne 1975)

Strieder, J., *Rechtliche Einordnung und Behandlung des Schiedsrichtervertrages* (Cologne 1984)

Swoboda & Möller, Der Deutsche Ausschuss für Schiedsgerichtswesen und seine Verfahrensordnung, 1 *Jahrbuch Schiedsgerichtsbarkeit* 117 (1987)

Swoboda, M., *Fachleute als Richter — Schiedsgerichtsbarkeit in der Bundesrepublik Deutschland (Schriftreihe des Deutschen Industrie- und Handelstag)* (1984)

Timmermann, F.H., ed., *Rechtssprechung kaufmännischer Schieds-gerichte: Sammlung von Schiedssprüchen unter Einschluss von Urteilen und Texten zur Schiedsgerichtsbarkeit.* Vol. 4 (Baden-Baden 1988) [Continuation of K. Straatmann & P. Ulmer eds., *Handelsrechtliche Schiedsgerichts-Praxis*]

Trappe, Links Between Arbitrators and the Courts, 44 *Arbitration* 69 (1978)

————, Maritime Arbitration in Hamburg, 14 *Int'l Bus. Law* 12 (February 1986)

————, Progress and Future Improvements in Arbitration, 42 *Arbitration* 98 (1975)

————, The Law and Institutions of Arbitration in the Federal Republic of Germany and their Relevance for English-German Business Relations, in *Handelsschiedsgerichtsbarkeit in England und in der Bundesrepublik Deutschland* 77 (K.-H. Böckstiegel ed. 1987)

Triebel, The ICC Rules of Conciliation and Arbitration of 1988, 3 *Int'l Arb. Rep.* 19 (No. 4, 1988)

————, An Outline of the Swiss/German Rules of Civil Procedure and Practice Relating to Evidence, 47 *Arbitration* 221 (1982)

Triebel & Hyden, Immunity of Arbitrators under German Law, in *The Immunity of Arbitrators* 39 (J.D.M. Lew 1990)

Triebel & Viertel, Die Bundesrepublik Deutschland wird als Schiedsgerichtsort im internationalen Schiedsverfahren gemieden: Zur Reform bedürftigkeit des par. 1039 *ZPO*, 41 *BB* 1168 (1986)

Tueller, Problems of Arbitration of International Contract Disputes and Recognition and Enforcement of Foreign Judgments in the Federal Republic of Germany: A Recent Decision of the Bundesgerichtshof, 17 *Stan. J. Int'l L.* 207 (1981)

von Breitenstein, Eine neue Arbitrage-Institution: Das COFACI-Schiedszentrum in Paris, 39 *NJW* 1402 (1986)

von Hoffmann, Die Novellierung des deutschen Schiedsverfahrensrechts von 1986, 6 *IPRax* 337 (1986)

von Hoffmann, B., *Internationale Handelsschiedsgerichtsbarkeit. Die Bestimmung des massgeblichen Rechts* (Frankfurt 1970)

von Hülsen, H.-V., *Die Gültigkeit von internationalen Schiedsvereinbarungen* (Berlin 1973)

von Rhein, Zur Anerkennung und Vollstreckung von schweizerischen Gerichtsentscheidungen, Schiedssprüchen und Vergleichen in der Bundesrepublik Deutschland, 82 *SJZ* 141 (1986)

von Staff, A., *Das Schiedsgerichtsverfahren nach dem heutigen deutschen Recht* (Berlin 1926)

von Winterfeld, Noch einmal: Der deutsche ordre public in der internationalen Schiedsgerichtsbarkeit, 1987 *NJW* 3059

von Zumbusch, Arbitrability of Antitrust Claims Under U.S., German, and EEC Law: The "International Transaction" Criterion and Public Policy, 22 *Tex. Int'l L.J.* 291 (1987)

————, Die Schiedsfähigkeit privatrechtlicher Kartellrechtsstreitigkeiten nach U.S.-, deutschem und EG-Recht, 1988 *GRUR Int'l* 541

Wackenhuth, Die Einrede der Unzuständigkeit des Schiedsgerichts nach ausgewählten Schiedsgerichtsordnungen, 32 *RIW* 11 (1986)

————, Nochmals: Verletzung des rechtlichen Gehörs im schiedsgerichtlichen Verfahren, 7 *IPRax* 355 (1987)

Waehler, Internationale Schiedsgerichtsbarkeit in den Wirtschaftsbeziehungen zwischen der Bundesrepublik Deutschland und der Sowjetunion, in *Deutsches und sowjetisches Wirschaftsrecht* (1981)

Walter, Das Schiedsverfahren im deutsch-italienischen Rechtsverkehr, 28 *RIW* 693 (1982)

————, Der nicht niedergelegte Schiedsspruch (zu Par. 1039 Abs. 3 ZPO n.F.), 34 *RIW* 945 (1988)

Westermann, Gesellschaftsrechtliche Schiedsgerichte — Übersicht und Erfahrungsbericht, in *Festschrift für Robert Fischer* 853 (M. Lutter, W. Stimpel & H. Wiedermann eds. 1979)

Westin, Enforcing Foreign Commercial Judgments and Arbitral Awards in the United States, West Germany, and England, 19 *L. & Pol'y Int'l Bus.* 325 (1987)

Zdravkovic, Certains cas de la jurisprudence yougoslave et étrangère sur l'exécution des sentences arbitrales étrangères, in *ICCA, Fifth Int'l Arb. Congress: Proceedings* C Izi 1-16 (1975)

Zimmer, D., *Zulässigkeit und Grenzen schiedsgerichtlicher Entscheidung von Kartellrechtsstreitigkeiten* (Baden-Baden 1991)

B: FORMER GERMAN DEMOCRATIC REPUBLIC

Ackermann, Die Rechtsprechung des Schiedsgerichtes bei der Kammer für Aussenhandel der DDR, 33 *RIW* 499 (1987)

Fellhauer, H. & H. Strohbach, eds., *Handbuch der internationalen Handelsschiedsgerichtsbarkeit* (Berlin 1969)

Grzybowski, Arbitral Tribunals for Foreign Trade in Socialist Countries, 37 *Law & Contemp. Probs.* 592 (1972)

Haendcke-Hoppe & Mampel, Die Schiedsgerichtsbarkeit im Aussenhandel der DDR, *Recht in Ost und West* 75 (1976)

Koerner, German Democratic Republic, in 2 *W.A.R.* 1719 (H. Smit & V. Pechota eds. 1987)

Kos-Rabcewicz-Zubkowski, Central and East European Rules on the Form of International Arbitration Agreement, 3 *La Revue Juridique Themis* 415 (1969)

Kos-Rabcewicz-Zubkowski, L., *East European Rules on the Validity of International Arbitration Agreements* (Manchester and Dobbs Ferry, NY 1970)

Kudryashev & Kozhevnikov, Vneshnetorgovyi arbitrazh v stranakh-chlenakh SEV, *Vneshniaia torgovlia* 52 (No. 4, 1984)

Lebedev, International Commercial Arbitration in the Socialist Countries Members of the CMEA, 158 *Recueil des Cours* 87 (1977-V)

Lebedev, S., ed., *Handbook on Foreign Trade Arbitration in the CMEA Member Countries* (Moscow 1983)

Majoros, Exécution de décisions étrangères et procédure d'exéquatur en Europe de l'Est: Tour d'horizon avec des références de droit comparé, in *Le Juriste Suisse Face au Droit et aux Jugements Etrangers: Ouverture ou Repli?* 135 (F. Knoepfler ed. 1988)

Melis, Enforcement of Arbitral Awards in Eastern Europe, in *Contemporary Problems in International Arbitration* 332 (J.D.M. Lew ed. 1986)

Pechota, International Economic Arbitration in the USSR and Eastern Europe, 8 *N.Y. L. Sch. J. Int'l & Comp. L.* 377 (1987)

Pisar, S., *Coexistence & Commerce,* Chapters 20 - 24 (New York 1970)

Pozdnyakov, Commercial Arbitration in CMEA Member Countries, 4 *Int'l Tax & Bus. Law.* 272 (1986)

Sandrock, The German-German Merger: Changes in Arbitration Law and Practice, 1 *Am. Rev. Int'l Arb.* 272 (1990)

Stalev, The Continental Case of Eastern Europe, 41 *Arbitration* 95 (1974)

Strohbach, Arbitration Between Foreign Trade Organizations of Socialist Countries and Parties from the Capitalist Economic Sphere, 4 *Pace L. Rev.* 607 (1984)

————, Force Majeur and Hardship Clauses in International Commercial Contacts and Arbitration: The East German Approach, 1 *J. Int'l Arb.* 39 (1984)

————, German Democratic Republic, in *Int'l Handbook Com. Arb.* (P. Sanders ed. 1984)

————, German Democratic Republic: National Report, 1 *Y.B. Com. Arb.* 40 (1976)

————, German Democratic Republic: The Arbitration Court Attached to the Chamber of Foreign Trade, in *Handbook of Institutional Arbitration in International Trade* 59 (E. Cohn, M. Domke & F. Eisemann eds. 1977)

————, International Arbitration and Public Policy. Comment on the Legal Practice in the German Democratic Republic, in *Comparative Arbitration Practice and Public Policy in Arbitration* 358 (P. Sanders ed. 1987)

————, International Commercial Arbitration in the GDR, *Law and Legislation in the German Democratic Republic* 26 (Nos. 1-2, 1984)

————, On the Setting Aside of Arbitration Awards, in *ICC, Hommage à Frederic Eisemann* 77 (1978)

———— Schiedsgerichtsbarkeit in Ostdeutschland heute, 46 *BB* (Beilage 8) (1991)

————, The CMEA Countries, in *Arbitration in Settlement of International Commercial Disputes Involving the Far East and Arbitration in Combined Transportation* 133 (P. Sanders ed. 1989)

Strohbach, H., *Die Anerkennung und Vollstreckung schiedsgerichtlicher Entscheidungen in der Deutschen Demokratischen Republik* (Berlin 1977)

————, *Handbuch der internationalen Handelsschiedsgerichtsbarkeit* (Berlin 1990)

Stumpf, Ost-West-Schiedsgerichtsbarkeit: Schiedsgerichte mit Sitz in dritten Ländern, 33 *RIW* 821 (1987)

GHANA

Agbosu, Arbitration under the Customary Law, 15 *Rev. Ghana L.* 204 (1983-86)

Bannerman, Digging for Gold in Ghana, 6 *Int'l Fin. L. Rev.* 29 (No. 7, 1987)

Bimpong-Buta, The Legal Effect of Executive Confirmation of Findings or Awards by Quasi-Judicial Bodies in Ghana, 32 *J. Afr. L.* 95 (1988)

Parker School of Foreign and Comparative Law, *International Commercial Arbitration and the Courts* (Dobbs Ferry, NY 1990)

Tiewul, The Enforcement of Arbitration Agreements and Awards, 11 *U. Ghana L.J.* 143 (1974)

GREECE

Carabiber, L'immunité de juridiction et d'exécution des Etats collectivités et établissements publics au regard de l'obligation assumée par une clause compromissoire inserée dans les contrats internationaux de droit privé, in *Liber Amicorum for Martin Domke* 23 (P. Sanders ed. 1967)

Dimilitsa, Arbitration Agreements and Foreign Investments: The Greek State between Contractual Commitment and Sovereign Intervention, 5 *J. Int'l Arb.* 17 (No. 4, 1988)

Foustoucos, Greece, in *Int'l Handbook Com. Arb.* (A. van den Berg, gen. ed. 1984), Suppl. 4, 1985

———, Greece: National Report, 5 *Y.B. Com. Arb.* 57 (1980); 11 *Y.B. Com. Arb.* 69 (1986); 12 *Y.B. Com. Arb.* 367 (1987) and 13 *Y.B. Com. Arb.* 417 (1988)

———, L'arbitrage international en Grèce, 1987 *Rev. Arb.* 23

———, La reconnaissance et l'exécution en Grèce des sentences arbitrales étrangères après la récente réforme du droit de l'arbitrage, 1974 *Rev. Arb.* 265

———, Les institutions d'arbitrage commercial en Grèce, in *ICCA, Sixth Int'l Arb. Congress: Proceedings* 121 (1978)

———, Sentences arbitrales nationals et étrangères: exécution et voies de recours en Grèce, 1991 *Int'l Bus. L.J.* 285

———, Une novelle institution permanente d'arbitrage en Grèce, 1978 *Rev. Arb.* 418

Foustoucos, A.C., *L'arbitrage (interne et international) en droit privé hellénique* (Paris 1976)

Fragistas, L'exécution en Grèce des sentences arbitrales étrangères, 1957 *Rev. Arb.* 74

Horomides, The Enforcement of Foreign Arbitral Awards in Greece, 3 *Arb. Int'l* 240 (1987)

International Chamber of Commerce, *Arbitration Law in Europe* (Paris 1981)

————, Greece/Grèce, in *Commercial Arbitration and the Law/L'Arbitrage commercial et la Loi* (Basel 1949)

Kassis, A., *Problèmes de base de l'arbitrage en droit comparé et en droit international.* Vol. 1: *Arbitrage juridictionnel et arbitrage contractuel* (Paris 1987)

Kerameus, Arbitrage international et ordre juridique hellénique, 1987 *Rev. Arb.* 35

————, Probleme des griechischen Schiedsverfahrensrechts aus rechtsvergleichender Sicht, 1979 *ZZP* 413

Klein, F.-E., *Considérations sur l'arbitrage en droit international privé* (Basel 1955)

Parker School of Foreign and Comparative Law, *International Commercial Arbitration and the Courts* (Dobbs Ferry, NY 1990)

Patkos, The United Nations Convention of 1958 on the Recognition and Enforcement of Foreign Arbitral Awards in the Light of the Greek Civil Procedure Code of 1971, 25 *Rev. Hellénique Droit Int'l* 295 (1972)

Real, G.K.L., *Der Schiedsrichtervertrag* (Cologne 1983)

Shifman, Greece, in 2A *W.A.R.* 1787 (H. Smit & V. Pechota eds. 1987)

Taliadoros, Arbitral Award Given in Athens: SA Industrielle et Commerciale Aluminium de Grece v. The Public Enterprise for Electricity of Greece, 15 *Int'l Bus. Law.* 360 (1987)

————, Arbitration Between Private Persons in Greek Law, 9 *Int'l Trade L. & Prac.* 604 (1983)

————, Comment deux sentences arbitrales rendues dans le cadre de la législation hellénique relative à la protection des investissements étrangères et portant toutes deux sur un objet identique, 1984 *Droit et Pratique du Com. Int'l* 603

Timagenis, Admissibility and Enforcement of Foreign Court Decisions and Arbitration Awards in Greece, 1984 *Lloyd's Mar. & Com. L.Q.* 488

————, Arbitration in Piraeus—a Growing Trend, 1977 *Lloyd's Mar. & Com. L.Q.* 319

GUATEMALA

Chacón Corado, La conciliación y el arbitraje como instrumentos para la solución de conflictos en Guatemala, in *El Arbitraje en el Derecho Latinoamericano y Español* 331 (L. Perret & U. Montoya Alberti eds. 1989)

Garro, Guatemala, in 2A *W.A.R.* 1805 (H. Smit & V. Pechota eds. 1987)

————, The UNCITRAL Model Law and the 1988 Spanish Arbitration Act: Models for Reform in Central America, 1 *Am. Rev. Int'l Arb.* 201 (1990)

————, The UNCITRAL Model Law and the 1988 Spanish Arbitration Act: Models for Reform in Central America, in *Commercial and Labor Arbitration in Central America* 23 (A. Garro ed. 1991)

Rohrmoser, Status of International Commercial Arbitration in Guatemala, in *Commercial and Labor Arbitration in Central America* 265 (A. Garro ed. 1991)

Umaña Aragón, Arbitration in Guatemala: Difficulties in Its Application, in *Commercial and Labor Arbitration in Central America* 268 (A. Garro ed. 1991)

Vasquez Martinez, La ejecución de sentencias y laudos extranjeros en el derecho guatelmalteco, 2 *Boletin de la Asociación de Abogados de Guatemala* 3 (March-April 1960)

HONDURAS

Casco Zelaya, Arbitration as a Means to Improve the Administration of Justice in Honduras, in *Commercial and Labor Arbitration in Central America* 277 (A. Garro ed. 1991)

Garro, Honduras, in 2A *W.A.R.* 1821 (H. Smit & V. Pechota eds. 1987)

—————, The UNCITRAL Model Law and the 1988 Spanish Arbitration Act: Models for Reform in Central America, 1 *Am. Rev. Int'l Arb.* 201 (1990)

—————, The UNCITRAL Model Law and the 1988 Spanish Arbitration Act: Models for Reform in Central America, in *Commercial and Labor Arbitration in Central America* 23 (A. Garro ed. 1991)

Gutierrez Falla, Informal Commercial Arbitration in Honduras, in *Commercial and Labor Arbitration in Central America* 285 (A. Garro ed. 1991)

International Chamber of Commerce, Honduras, in *Commercial Arbitration and the Law/L'Arbitrage commercial et la Loi* (Basel 1949)

León Gomez, Ejecución de la sentencia arbitral en Honduras, in *El Arbitraje en el Derecho Latinoamericano y Español* 349 (L. Perrot & U. Montoya Alberti eds. 1989)

HONG KONG

Bernini, Recent Legislations and International Unification of the Law on Arbitration, in *First International Commercial Arbitration Conference: Proceedings* 315 (N. Antaki & A. Prujiner eds. 1986)

Brazil, Resolution of Trade Disputes in the Asian Pacific Region, 10 *Adel. L. Rev.* 49 (1985)

Caldwell, A Practitioner's Guide to the New Hong Kong Arbitration Ordinance, 6 *Int'l Arb. Rep.* 22 (No. 2, 1991)

de Speville, Arbitration in Hong Kong: The Arbitration Ordinance 1963—1982, 1 *Arb. Int'l* 109 (1985)

Dore, I., *Theory and Practice of Multiparty Commercial Arbitration, With Special Reference to the UNCITRAL Framework* (London 1990)

Grieg & Kaplan, Hong Kong, in *Int'l Handbook Com. Arb.* (A. van den Berg gen. ed. 1984), Suppl. 4, Nov. 1985

————, Hong Kong: National Report, 11 *Y.B. Comm. Arb.* 3 (1986)

Hunter, Arbitration in Hong Kong, in *Arbitration in Settlement of International Commercial Disputes Involving the Far East and Arbitration in Combined Transportation* 73 (P. Sanders ed. 1989)

Jarvin, Is Exclusion of Concurrent Courts' Jurisdiction over Conservatory Measures to Be Introduced by a Revision of the Convention? 6 *J. Int'l Arb.* 171 (No. 1, 1989)

Kaplan, Arbitration in Hong Kong, 3 *J. Int'l Arb.* 7 (No. 4, 1986); also 52 *Arbitration* 12 (Feb. 1986)

————, Hong Kong and the UNCITRAL Model Law, 54 *Arbitration* 173 (1988)

————, Hong Kong's Development in Law, Rules and Facilities, *Paper presented to Int'l Conf Growth of Arb. in the Pacific, Auckland, NZ, Sept. 1985*

————, Modern International Arbitration: A Hong Kong Viewpoint, 53 *Arbitration* 225 (1987)

————, The Hong Kong Arbitration Ordinance: Some Features and Recent Developments, 1 *Am. Rev. Int'l Arb.* 25 (1990)

————, The Hong Kong Arbitration Ordinance and UNCITRAL Model Law, 57 *Arbitration* 110 (1991)

Kaplan, N., J. Spruce & T. Cheng, *Hong Kong Arbitration: Cases and Materials* (Singapore/Hong Kong 1991)

Leung, The Arbitration (Amendment) Ordinance (1982) of Hong Kong, 48 *Arbitration* 92 (1982)

————, The Hong Kong Arbitration Ordinance 1982, 1985 *J. Bus. L.* 423 (1985)

McClelland, A Survey of Pacific Rim Commercial Arbitration, 40 *Arb. J.* 3 (No. 1, 1985)

MacNaughton, The Practical Aspects of Arbitrating Commercial Disputes in Hong Kong, 0 *World Arb. & Med.* 13 (1989)

Miller, Consolidation in Hong Kong — the Shui On Case, 3 *Arb. Int'l* 87 (No. 1, 1987)

Pacific Rim Advisory Council, *Pacific Rim: Commercial Arbitration Procedures* (San Diego, CA 1985)

Parker School of Foreign and Comparative Law, *International Commercial Arbitration and the Courts* (Dobbs Ferry 1990)

Paulsson, La réforme de la loi de l'arbitrage de Hong Kong, 1984 *Rev. Arb.* 325

Rhodes, Judicial Review of Commercial Arbitration, 14 *Hong Kong L.J.* 159 (1984)

Roberts, The Development of Arbitration in Hong Kong, 50 *Arbitration* 27 (1984)

Simmonds, K., B. Hill & S. Jarvin, eds., *Commercial Arbitration Law in Asia and the Pacific* (Paris & Dobbs Ferry, NY 1987)

Strellet, Hong Kong, 3 *Int'l Commercial Arbitration: A World Handbook* 20 (1965)

Stucken, Hong Kong als internationaler Schiedsgerichtsstand, 37 *RIW* 394 (1991)

Surrey & Kellner, International Arbitration in Hong Kong, in *Legal Aspects of Doing Business with China* 1986 (Practising Law Institute, New York 1986)

Sutton, Hong Kong Enacts the UNCITRAL Model Law, 6 *Arb. Int'l* 358 (1990)

Thomas, Arbitration in Hong Kong, 14 *Int'l Bus. Law.* 142 (1986)

Tisdall, The Hong Kong International Arbitration Centre, in *UNCITRAL Arbitration Model in Canada* 31 (R. Paterson & B. Thompson eds. 1987)

Voûte, Een partij-arbiter in Hong Kong, 1988 *Tijdschrift voor Arbitrage* 184

Williams, Law Reform, Hong Kong Arbitration, 10 *Int'l Bus.L.* 317 (1982)

HUNGARY

Blessing, Proper Law and Dispute Resolution Arising out of East-West Joint Ventures, in *Eastern Bloc Joint Ventures* 107 (D. Winter ed. 1990)

Dietz, Foreign Trade Arbitration in Hungary, 5 *N.Y.U. J. Int'l L. & Pol.* 251 (1972)

Farago, Decisions of the Hungarian Chamber of Commerce in COMECON Arbitrations, 14 *Int'l & Comp. L.Q.* 1124 (1965)

Farkas, Einige theoretische Fragen des Schiedsgerichtsverfahrens in Ungarn, in *Festschrift für Karl Heinz Schwab* 85 (P. Gottwald & H. Prütting eds. 1990)

Grzybowski, Arbitral Tribunals for Foreign Trade in Socialist Countries, 37 *Law & Contemp. Probs.* 592 (1972)

Harmathy, Arbitrage en Hongrie (Contrat de commission), 27 *Acta Juridica Academiae Sci. Hungaricae* 295 (1985)

————, Trends in Hungarian Arbitration: Disputes Arising from Ongoing Economic Relations, 4 *Questions of Int'l Law* 73 (H. Bokor-Szegö ed. 1988)

International Chamber of Commerce, Hungary/Hongrie, in *Commercial Arbitration and the Law/L'Arbitrage commercial et la Loi* (Basel 1949)

Katona, Problems of Arbitration in International Trade, 23 *Acta Juridica (Budapest)* 57 (Nos. 1-2, 1981)

Kos-Rabcewicz-Zubkowski, Central and East European Rules on the Form of International Arbitration Agreement, 3 *La Revue Juridique Themis* 415 (1969)

Kos-Rabcewicz-Zubkowski, L., *East European Rules on the Validity of International Arbitration Agreements* (Manchester and Dobbs Ferry, NY 1970)

Kudryashev & Kozhevnikov, Vneshnetorgovyi arbitrazh v stranakh-chlenakh SEV, *Vneshniaia torgovlia* 52 (No. 4, 1984)

Kuss, Neuere Entwicklungen und Perspektiven der Ost-West-Schiedsgerichtsbarkeit, 33 *RIW* 584 (1987)

Lebedev, International Commercial Arbitration in the Socialist Countries Members of the CMEA, 158 *Recueil des Cours* 87 (1977-V)

Lebedev, S., ed., *Handbook on Foreign Trade Arbitration in the CMEA Member Countries* (Moscow 1983)

Leloczky, East-West Arbitration: A Practitioner's Viewpoint from Hungary, 4 *Arb. Int'l* 266 (1988)

Majoros, Exécution de décisions étrangères et procédure d'exéquatur en Europe de l'Est: Tour d'horizon avec des références de droit comparé, in *Le Juriste Suisse Face au Droit et aux Jugements Etrangers: Ouverture ou Repli?* 135 (F. Knoepfler ed. 1988)

Melis, Enforcement of Arbitral Awards in Eastern Europe, in *Contemporary Problems in International Arbitration* 332 (J.D.M. Lew ed. 1986)

Minakov, A.I., *Arbitrazhnye soglashenia i praktika rassmotreniya vneshneekonomicheskikh sporov* (Moscow 1985)

Pechota, International Economic Arbitration in the USSR and Eastern Europe, 8 *N.Y. L. Sch. J. Int'l & Comp. L.* 377 (1987)

Pfaff, Neuerungen der internationalen Schiedsgerichtsbarkeit im Ost-West-Handel vor den ständigen Aussenhandelsschiedsgerichten der RGW-Länder, 23 *RIW* 125 (1977)

Pisar, S., *Coexistence & Commerce*, Chapters 20-24 (New York 1970)

Pozdnyakov, Commercial Arbitration in CMEA Member Countries, 4 *Int'l Tax & Bus. Law.* 272 (1986)

Przetacznik, The Court of Arbitration Attached to the Hungarian Chamber of Commerce, in 4 *W.A.R.* 4641 (H. Smit & V. Pechota eds. 1989)

Révai, Quelques caractéristiques de l'organisation de la Cour d'Arbitrage auprès de la Chambre de Commerce de Hongrie et ses relations avec les Cours d'Arbitrage à l'étranger, in *ICCA, Third Int'l Arb. Congress: Proceedings* 541 (1969)

Sebestyen, Hungary: National Report, 1 *Y.B. Com. Arb.* 53 (1976)

Stalev, The Continental Case of Eastern Europe, 41 *Arbitration* 95 (1974)

Strohbach, The CMEA Countries, in *Arbitration in Settlement of International Commercial Disputes Involving the Far East and Arbitration in Combined Transportation* 133 (P. Sanders ed. 1989)

Stumpf, Ost-West-Schiedsgerichtsbarkeit: Schiedsgerichte mit Sitz in dritten Ländern, 33 *RIW* 821 (1987)

ICELAND

Miller, Avoiding Legal Judgment: The Submission of Disputes to Arbitration in Medieval Iceland, 28 *Am. J. Leg. History* 95 (1984)

INDIA

Agarwal, R.G., ed., *S.C. Das's The Arbitration Act: Act X of 1940.* 4th ed. (Allahabad 1978)

American Arbitration Association, *New Strategies for Peaceful Resolution of International Business Disputes* (Dobbs Ferry, NY 1971)

Anand, Arbitration in the Context of Technology Transfer Agreements: The Case of India, 7 *J. Int'l Arb.* 87 (No. 2, 1990)

Bachawat, R.S., *Law of Arbitration* (Calcutta 1983)

Bakshi, Arbitration Agreement: A Very Important Judgment, 1985(1) *Company L.J.* 195

―――, Arbitration Law: Foreign Awards, 3 *The Lawyers* 33 (No. 4, 1988)

―――, The Arbitrator and His Norms of Conduct, 3 *The Lawyers* 41 (No. 5, 1988)

―――, Foreign Forum for Enforcing Awards, 1987(1) *Company L.J.* 16

―――, Misconduct by the Arbitrator, 1989(2) *Company L.J.* 49

―――, Time Limits in Arbitration: Reform Needed, 1987(1) *Company L.J.* 13

Bansal, Arbitration Proceedings — A Farcical Drama, 75(12) *A.I.R. Journal* 181 (1988)

Basu, N.D., *The Arbitration Act, 1940* (8th. ed.) (Calcutta 1982)

Baxi, Goodbye to Unification? The Indian Supreme Court and the United Nations Arbitration Convention, 15 *J. Ind. L. Inst.* 353 (1973)

Chowdhuri, S.K.R. & H.K. Saharay, *Arbitration Law.* 2nd ed. (Calcutta 1986)

Desai, India, 3 *Int'l Commercial Arbitration: A World Handbook* 26 (P. Sanders ed. 1965)

Deshpande, Arbitration in India, 52 *Arbitration* 200 (1986)

671

————, Court, Contract and Arbitration, 26 *J. Ind. L. Inst.* 378 (1984)

————, Enforcement of Foreign Awards in India, U.K. and U.S.A., 4 *J. Int'l Arb.* 41 (No. 1, 1987)

————, International Commercial Arbitration and Domestic Courts in India, 2 *J. Int'l Arb.* 45 (No. 1, 1985)

————, Judicial Interpretation of Commercial Arbitration, 16 *I.C.A. Arb. Q.* 3 (No. 1, April-March 1981)

————, Jurisdiction over 'Foreign' and 'Domestic' Awards in the New York Convention 1958, 7 *Arb. Int'l* 123 (1991)

————, Law of Arbitration, 20 *Annual Survey of Indian Law* 1 (1984)

————, Law of Arbitration, 21 *Annual Survey of Indian Law* 1 (1985)

————, Law of Arbitration, 22 *Annual Survey of Indian Law* 1 (1986)

————, Law of Arbitration, 23 *Annual Survey of Indian Law* 1 (1987)

————, Law of Arbitration, 24 *Annual Survey of Indian Law* 339 (1988)

Ebb, At the End of a Long Trail: How the Bombay High Court Strengthened International Arbitration in India, 44 *Arb. J.* 28 (No. 2, 1989)

————, Developing Views on What Constitutes a 'Foreign Arbitration Agreement' and a 'Foreign Award' under the New York Convention, 1 *Am. Rev. Int'l Arb.* 364 (1990)

Hariani, Enforcement of Foreign Arbitration Agreements and Awards in India, 7 *Indian J. Int'l L.* 31 (1967)

Hossain, International Commercial Arbitration, State Succession and the Commonwealth, 36 *Brit. Y.B. Int'l L.* 370 (1960)

International Chamber of Commerce, India/Inde, in *Commercial Arbitration and the Law/L'Arbitrage commercial et la Loi* (Basel 1964)

Jambholkar, Enforcement of Foreign Awards in India: A Critique of Judicial Practice, 12 *Indian J. Int'l L.* 109 (1972)

Karmali, A.E., *International Commercial Arbitration* (Bombay 1974)

Krishnamurthi, India, in *Int'l Handbook Com. Arb.* (A. van den Berg, gen. ed. 1984), Suppl. 4, Nov. 1985

———, India: The Indian Council of Arbitration, in *Handbook of Institutional Arbitration in International Trade* 83 (E. Cohn, M. Domke & F. Eisemann eds. 1977)

———, Training Facilities at the Indian Council of Arbitration, 5 *Y.B. Com. Arb.* 305 (1980)

———, India: National Report, 2 *Y.B. Com. Arb.* 31 (1977); 11 *Y.B. Com. Arb.* 73 (1986)

Malik, Arbitration Clause in an International Contract: Whether a Bar to Local Civil Jurisdiction, 8 *Indian J. Leg. Studies* 160 (1988)

Merchant & Merchant, The Law Relating to Recognition and Enforcement of Foreign Arbitral Agreements and Awards in the United States of America and India, in *ICCA, Fifth Int'l Arb. Congress: Proceedings* C Im 1-10 (1975)

Nariman, Foreign Arbitral Awards in India: Problems, Pitfalls, and Progress, 6 *J. Int'l Arb.* 25 (No. 1, 1989)

———, Problems of Public Policy — the Indian Perspective, in *Comparative Arbitration Practice and Public Policy in Arbitration* 336 (P. Sanders ed. 1987)

———, Standards of Behaviour of Arbitrators, 4 *Arb. Int'l* 311 (1988)

Nirwani, S.C., *Guide to Arbitration in India* (New Delhi 1981)

Parker School of Foreign and Comparative Law, *International Commercial Arbitration and the Courts* (Dobbs Ferry, NY 1990)

———, *The 1989 Guide to International Arbitration and Arbitrators* (Dobbs Ferry, NY 1989)

Pechota, The Indian Council of Arbitration, in 4 *W.A.R.* 4719 (H. Smit & V. Pechota eds. 1989)

Rao, Indian Experience of International Commercial Arbitration: Some Problems and Pitfalls, in *ICCA, Fifth Arb. Congress: Proceedings* C Ip 1 (1975)

———, Proper Law of Contract with Arbitration Clauses, 29 *J. Ind. L. Inst.* 60 (1987)

————, Some Recent Developments and Non-Developments in Indian Private International Law, 27 *J. Ind. L. Inst.* 555 (1985)

Rogers, Forum Non Conveniens in Arbitration, 4 *Arb. Int'l* 240 (1988)

Santhanam, Arbitration Award Without Reasons: Validity, 1989(2) *Company L.J.* 8

Shroff, Enforcement in India of Foreign Commercial Awards, 21 *J. Indian L. Inst.* 31 (1979)

Simmonds, K., B. Hill & S. Jarvin, eds., *Commercial Arbitration Law in Asia and the Pacific* (Paris & Dobbs Ferry, NY 1987)

Singh, Arbitration in India, in 2 *Studi in Onore di Giorgio Balladore Palieri* 557 (Milan 1978)

Singh, M., ed., *Nathuni Lal's Law of Arbitration in India* (4th ed. Lucknow 1983)

Singh, S.D., *The Law of Arbitration* (8th ed. Lucknow 1980)

Singhania, Arbitrating State Contracts, 2 *Lex et Juris - The Law Magazine* 43 (No. 6, 1987)

————, Arbitration in the Construction Industry in India, 7 *J. Int'l Arb.* 49 (No. 2, 1990)

————, Attachments and Other Court Remedies in Support of Arbitration Available in India, in *Interim Court Remedies in Support of Arbitration* 153 (D. Shenton & W. Kühn eds. 1987)

Singhania & Co. (New Delhi), *International Commercial Arbitration Law, Procedures and Facilities in India* (New Delhi 1985)

Sujan, M.A., *The Law Relating to Government Arbitration* (New Delhi 1985)

Sundaraswamy, Law of Arbitration in India, 20 *Arbitration* Q. 3 (1985)

Taylor, India, in 2A *W.A.R.* 1837 (H. Smit & V. Pechota eds. 1987, 1988)

Tupman, Staying Enforcement of Arbitral Awards under the New York Convention, 3 *Arb. Int'l* 223 (1987)

INDONESIA

Gautama, Indonesia, in *Int'l Handbook Com. Arb.* (A. van den Berg, gen. ed. 1984), Suppl. 6, Nov. 1986

————, Some Legal Aspects of International Commercial Arbitration in Indonesia, 7 *J. Int'l Arb.* 93 (No. 4, 1990)

Gingerich, Indonesia to Enforce Foreign Arbitral Awards, 12 *East Asian Exec. Rep.* 9 (No. 6, 1990)

Hornick, Indonesia — Foreign Arbitral Awards Not Enforceable, 7 *East Asian Exec. Rep.* 11 (No. 11, 1985)

————, The Recognition and Enforcement of Foreign Judgments in Indonesia, 18 *Harv. Int'l L.J.* 97 (1977)

Indonesian Board of Arbitration, *Arbitration in Indonesia and International Conventions on Arbitration* (Jakarta 1978)

McClelland, A Survey of Pacific Rim Commercial Arbitration, 40 *Arb. J.* 3 (No. 1, 1985)

Pacific Rim Advisory Council, *Pacific Rim: Commercial Arbitration Procedures* (San Diego, CA 1985)

Ricafrente, Commercial Arbitration in ASEAN Countries, in *Commercial Arbitration* 39 (J. Ricalde ed. 1983)

Simmonds, K., B. Hill & S. Jarvin, eds., *Commercial Arbitration Law in Asia and the Pacific* (Paris & Dobbs Ferry, NY 1987)

Subekti, Indonesia: National Report, 5 *Y.B. Com. Arb.* 84 (1980) and 7 *Y.B. Com. Arb.* 63 (1982)

IRAN

Abhod, Iran: National Report, 4 *Y.B. Com. Arb.* 81 (1979)

Amin, Arbitration Law in Iran: Post-revolutionary Changes, 11 *Middle E. Exec. Rep.* (August 1988 and September 1988)

————, Changes in the Law of Arbitration in Iran, 8 *Islamic & Comp. L.Q.* 21 (1988)

Amin, S.H., *Commercial Arbitration in Islamic and Iranian Law* (Tehran and Glasgow 1988)

————, *Middle East Legal Systems* (Glasgow 1985)

Audit, Les 'Accords' d'Alger du 19 janvier 1981 tendant au règlement des différends entre les Etats-Unis et l'Iran, 108 *J. Droit Int'l (Clunet)* 713 (1981)

Barclay, Rules for the Settlement of International Disputes, 42 *Arbitration* 31 (1975)

Bernini, Recent Legislations and International Unification of the Law on Arbitration, in *First International Commercial Arbitration Conference: Proceedings* 315 (N. Antaki & A. Prujiner eds. 1986)

Böckstiegel, Schwierigkeiten bei Gerichtsstansvereinbarungen und Schiedsklauseln im Wirtschaftsverkehr mit dem Iran, 1974 *AWD* 117

Fouchard, L'arbitrage ELF Aquitaine Iran c/ National Iranian Oil Company: une nouvelle contribution au droit international de l'arbitrage, 1984 *Rev. Arb.* 333

International Chamber of Commerce, Iran, in *Commercial Arbitration and the Law/L'Arbitrage commercial et la Loi* (Basel 1949)

Lewis, What Goes Around Comes Around: Can Iran Enforce Awards of the Iran-U.S. Claims Tribunal in the United States?, 26 *Colum. J. Transnat'l L.* 515 (1988)

Liemen, Schiedsgerichtsbarkeit und Vollstreckung von Schiedssprüchen im Iran, 24 *RIW* 780 (1978)

Malloy, The Iran Crisis: Law under Pressure, 1984 *Wis. Int'l L.J.* 15 (Symposium)

Rouhani, Iran, 3 *Int'l Commercial Arbitration: A World Handbook* 46 (P. Sanders ed. 1965)

Suratgar, Arbitration in the Iranian Legal System, 20 *Arb. J.* 143 (1965)

Taylor, National Iranian Oil Co. v. Ashland Oil, Inc.: All Dressed Up and Nowhere to Arbitrate, 63 *N.Y.U.L. Rev.* 1142 (1988)

IRAQ

Al-Mukhtar, Arbitration in Iraq — Its Practical Problems — Opinions and Suggestions, 50 *Arbitration* 171 (Nov. 1984)

Al-Tabachkali, Settlement of Disputes through Arbitration: Iraq, in 1 *Arab Comparative & Commercial Law: The International Approach: Proceedings I.B.A. Conference* 279 (1987)

Amin, S.H., *Middle East Legal Systems* (Glasgow 1985)

El-Ahdab, A. H., *Arbitration with the Arab Countries* (Deventer 1990)

⸻, *L'arbitrage dans les pays arabes* (Paris 1988)

International Bar Association, *Arab Comparative & Commercial Law: The International Approach: Proceedings of the I.B.A. First Arab Regional Conference, Cairo 15-19 February 1987* (London 1987)

International Chamber of Commerce, Iraq, in *Commercial Arbitration and the Law/L'Arbitrage commercial et la Loi* (Basel 1964)

Jalili, International Arbitration in Iraq, 4 *J. Int'l Arb.* 109 (No. 3, 1987)

Kassis, Particularités et problèmes de l'arbitrage dans les droits des pays arabes, 63 *Rev. Droit Int'l & Droit Comp.* 7 (1986)

Lew, The Recognition and Enforcement of Arbitration Agreements and Awards in the Middle East, 1 *Arb. Int'l* 161 (1985)

Rovine, An Iraq Claims Process: Where and How? 1 *Am. Rev. Int'l Arb.* 411 (1990)

⸻, An Iraq Claims Process: Where and How? Part II, 2 *Am. Rev. Int'l Arb.* 102 (1991)

Saleh, The Recognition and Enforcement of Foreign Arbitral Awards in the States of the Arab Middle East, in *Contemporary Problems in International Arbitration* 340 (J.D.M. Lew ed. 1986)

Saleh, S., *Commercial Arbitration in the Arab Middle East* (London 1984)

Stumpf, Schiedsgerichtsbarkeit in arabischen Ländern, 1 *Jahrbuch Schiedsgerichtsbarkeit* 102 (1987)

Taha, Arbitration Clauses in Iraqi Contracts, 13 *Middle E. Exec. Rep.* 15 (No. 6, 1990)

Troller, Arbitration and Enforcement of Arbitration Awards in Arab Countries, 2 *Int'l Contr.* 397 (1981)

Yamulki, Iraq: National Report, 4 *Y.B. Com. Arb.* 104 (1979)

Ziadé, Selective Bibliography on Arbitration and Arab Countries, 3 *ICSID Rev. -Foreign Investment L.J.* 423 (1988)

IRELAND

Abrahamson, Ireland, in *Int'l Handbook Com. Arb.* (A. van den Berg, gen. ed. 1984), Suppl. 2, August 1984

————, Ireland: National Report, 9 *Y.B. Com. Arb.* 3 (1984)

International Chamber of Commerce, Ireland/Irlande, in *Commercial Arbitration and the Law/L'Arbitrage commercial et la Loi* (Basel 1949)

ISRAEL

Domke, The Israeli-Soviet Oil Arbitration, 53 *Am. J. Int'l L.* 787 (1959)

International Chamber of Commerce, Israel, in *Commercial Arbitration and the Law/L'Arbitrage commercial et la Loi* (Basel 1949)

Manheim, Arbitrator's Power to Grant Injunction and Temporary Attachment (in Hebrew), 36 *Hapraklit (Israel)* 233 (1985)

Ottolenghi, Arbitration Institutions in Israel, 38 *Arb. J.* 53 (No. 3, 1983)

————, Israel, in *Int'l Handbook Com. Arb.* (A. van den Berg gen. ed. 1984), Suppl. 2, Aug. 1984

————, Israel: National Report, 2 *Y.B. Com. Arb.* 47 (1977); 11 *Y.B. Com. Arb.* 79 (1986)

ITALY

Addamo, La funzione della Camera Arbitrale Italiana per il Commercio delle Pelle, 25 *Rassegna dell'Arb.* 145 (1985)

――――, I cinquant'anni della Camera Arbitrale Italiana delle Pelli, 26 *Rassegna dell'Arb.* 128 (1986)

Addamo, R. R., *Manuale dell'arbitrate commerciale e dell'arbitro* (Milan 1987)

Ascarelli, Arbitration under Italian Law, 1 *Int'l Y. B. Civil & Com. Arb.* 79 (1928)

Azzali, Chamber of Arbitration of Milan, 8 *Int'l Constr. L. Rev.*

Bernardini, P., *L'arbitrato internazionale* (Milan 1987)

Bernardini, P. & A. Giardina, *Il Codice dell'arbitrato* (Milan 1990)

Bernini, Domestic and International Arbitration in Italy After the Legislative Reform, 5 *Pace L. Rev.* 543 (1985)

――――, Esecuzione del lodo arbitrale, in *Arbitrato nazionale e internazionale: interpretazione ed esecuzione del lodo* 13 (G. Carli ed. 1989)

――――, Il riconoscimento all'estero del lodo arbitrale irrituale, 45 *Riv. Trim. Dir. & Proc. Civ.* 357 (1991)

――――, Italy, in *Int'l Handbook Com. Arb.* (A. van den Berg gen. ed. 1984), Suppl. 3, Jan. 1985

――――, Italy: National Report, 6 *Y.B. Com. Arb.* 24 (1981); 12 *Y.B. Com. Arb.* 369 (1987) and 13 *Y.B. Com. Arb.* 420 (1988)

――――, La legge 9 Febbraio 1983 N.28 e la modifica dell'arbitrato: prospettive internazionali, 24 *Rassegna dell'Arb.* 193 (1984)

――――, Observations Regarding Recognition and Enforcement of Foreign Arbitral Awards in Italy, in *A.I.A., Essays in Memoriam Eugenio Minoli* 39 (Turin 1974)

――――, Recent Legislations and International Unification of the Law on Arbitration, in *First International Commercial Arbitration Conference: Proceedings* 315 (N. Antaki & A. Prujiner eds. 1986)

Bin, Il compromesso e la clausola compromissoria in arbitrato irrituale, 45 *Riv. Trim. Dir. & Proc. Civ.* 373 (1991)

Briguglio, Die Schiedsrichterablehnung im italianischen Recht und nach den Regeln der ICC-Schiedsordnung, 2 *Jahrbuch Schiedsgerichtsbarkeit* 23 (1988)

————, La riforma dell'arbitrato, 35 *Giustizia Civile* 415 (1985)

Bronzini, Arbitrato, recenti innovazione legislative. Problemi e soluzione, 61 *Nuovo Diritto* 161 (1984)

Cafani Panico, Clausola compromissoria e capacita delle persone giuridiche, 24 *Diritto Comunitario e degli Scambi Internazionali* 480 (1985)

Carabiber, L'immunité de juridiction et d'exécution des Etats collectivités et établissements publics au regard de l'obligation assumée par une clause compromissoire inserée dans les contrats internationaux de droit privé, in *Liber Amicorum for Martin Domke* 23 (P. Sanders ed. 1967)

Carli, G., ed., *Arbitrato nazionale e internazionale: interpretazione ed esecuzione del lodo* (Milan 1989)

Carpi, Gli aspetti processuali della riforma dell'arbitrato, 38 *Riv. Trim. Dir. & Proc. Civ.* 47 (1984)

————, Il procedimento nell'arbitrato irrituale, 45 *Riv. Trim. Dir. & Proc. Civ.* 389 (1991)

Costabel, Fundamental Changes in Italian Arbitration Law, 1983 *Lloyd's Mar. & Com. L.Q.* 440

————, Non-Domestic Arbitration Clauses, Stay of Proceedings and Recognition of Foreign Awards in Italy, 2 *Fifth Int'l Congress of Maritime Arbitrators* (New York 1981)

Dalla Verita, Note sull'impugnazione del lodo arbitrale, 42 *Riv. Trim. Dir. & Proc. Civ.* 614 (1988)

de Berti, Arbitration and Technology: The Italian Experience, in *ICCA, Sixth Int'l Arb. Congress: Proceedings* 347 (1978)

de Nova, Nullità del contratto e arbitrato irrituale, 45 *Riv. Trim. Dir. & Proc. Civ.* 401 (1991)

Deodato, G. & G. Migliorisi, eds., *Codice dell'arbitrato* (Milan 1989)

di Blase, Gli ammodernamienti alla disciplina italiana dell'arbitrato e le convenzioni internazionali, 66 *Riv. Dir. Int'le* 859 (1983)

Di Cagno, Sull'interpretazione della nuova disciplina dell'arbitrato, in *Arbitrato nazionale e internazionale: interpretazione ed esecuzione del lodo* 41 (G. Carli ed. 1989)

Donnini, Su alcuni aspetti della riforma dell'arbitrato: in particolare la riconoscibilita del lodo all'estero, 25 *Rassegna dell'Arb.* 283 (1985)

Dorman, Italy, in 2A *W.A.R.* 1855 (H. Smit & V. Pechota eds. 1987)

Eckstrom, L., *Licensing in Foreign and Domestic Operations.* Volume I, Chapter 7: Arbitration (by Steven Z. Szczepanski) (New York 1972, updated 1987)

Ferrante, Enforcement of Foreign Arbitral Awards in Italy and Public Policy, in *ICC, Hommage à Frederic Eisemann* 83 (1978)

————, Profili pratici della formazione del lodo, 26 *Rassegna dell'Arb.* 1 (1986)

————, Sull'indivisibilità del lodo arbitrale, 30 *Rassegna dell'Arb.* 155 (1930)

Fiammenghi, Brevetti ed arbitrato: una penalizzazione che andrebbe eliminata, 30 *Rassegna dell'Arb.* 150 (1990)

————, Motivi che impendiscono la definizione arbitrale delle controversie in materia di brevetti di invenzioni, 25 *Rassegna dell'Arb.* 123 (1985)

Fois, Primi orientamenti giurisprudenziali in Italia circa l'interpretazione della Convenzione di New York sull'Arbitrato, 12 *Riv. Dir. Int'le Priv. & Proc.* 299 (1976)

Franchi, Le contenu necessaire de la clause compromissoire selon le droit italien, in *A.I.A., Essays in Memoriam Eugenio Mineli* 179 (1974)

Fumagalli, La legge applicabile al merito della controversia nell'arbitrato commerciale internazionale, 21 *Riv. Dir. Int'le Priv. & Proc.* 465 (1985)

Galgano, L'equità degli arbitri, 45 *Riv. Trim. Dir. & Proc. Civ.* 409 (1991)

Gambardella & Carbone, Développement de l'arbitrage commercial en Italie: le rôle des Chambres de Commerce et la coopération entre organismes d'arbitrage au niveau national, in *ICCA, Third Int'l Arb. Congress: Proceedings* 431(1969)

Garbagnati, Ancora in tema d'impugnazione per nullità del lodo arbitrale rituale, 45 *Riv. Dir. Proc.* 1 (1990)

———, Sull'efficacia di cosa giudicata del lodo arbitrale rituale, 40 *Riv. Dir. Proc.* 425(1985)

Giardina, Arbitrato transnazionale e lex mercatoria di fronte alla Corte di Cassazione, 18 *Riv. Dir. Int'le Priv. & Proc.* 754 (1982)

———, L'applicazione in Italia della Convenzione di New York sull'Arbitrato, 7 *Riv. Dir. Int'le Priv. & Proc.* 268 (1971)

Grasso, La nuova disciplina dell'arbitrato alla luce della legge 9 febbraio 1983, N.28, 25 *Rassegna dell'Arb.* 27 (1985)

Habscheid, L'expertise-arbitrage. Etude de droit comparé, in *Liber Amicorum for Martin Domke* 103 (P. Sanders ed. 1967)

Impallomeni, Une modification au Code de procedure civile en Italie: les nouvelles règles sur l'arbitrage, 9 *Int'l Trade L. & Prac.* 599 (1983)

International Chamber of Commerce, *Arbitration Law in Europe* (Paris 1981)

———, Italy/Italie, in *Commercial Arbitration and the Law/L'Arbitrage commercial et la Loi* (Basel 1949)

Irti, L'interpretazione del lodo arbitrale, in *Arbitrato nazionale e internazionale: interpretazione ed esecuzione del lodo* 3 (G. Carli ed. 1989)

Kassis, A., *Problèmes de base de l'arbitrage en droit comparé et en droit international. Vol. 1: Arbitrage juridictionnel et arbitrage contractuel* (Paris 1987)

Klein, F.-E., *Considérations sur l'arbitrage en droit international privé* (Basel 1955)

La China, L'arbitrato interno e internazionale, 42 *Riv. Trim. Dir. & Proc. Civ.* 1387 (1988)

Legras de Grandcourt, Evolution contemporaine des législations européennes, in *Euro-Arab Arbitration III* 119 (F. Kemicha ed. 1991)

Levoni, A., *L'arbitrato dopo la riforma* (Milano 1985)

Lodigiani, La Camera Arbitrale Cotoni sodi dell'Associazione Cotoniera Italiana, 19 *Rassegna dell'Arb.* 89 (1978)

Longo, Arbitres et Cour d'Arbitrage dans les procédures de l'Association Italienne pour l'Arbitrage, in *A.I.A., Essays in Memoriam Eugenio Minoli* 293 (Turin 1974)

Lotti, Sull'impugnabilità del lodo rituale non reso esecutivo, 43 *Riv. Dir. Proc.* 646 (1988)

Lucchesi, Zur Frage der Anerkennung und Vollstreckung des 'lodo irrituale' (=formfreien Schiedsspruches) ausserhalb Italiens, 24 *ZRV* 1 (1983)

Luzzatto, Arbitrato irrituale italiano e Convenzione di New York, 21 *Rassegna dell'Arb.* 105 (1981)

MacLaren, Commercial Arbitration in the United States and Overseas, in *Arbitration and the Licensing Process* 5 (R. Goldscheider & M. de Haas eds. 1984-)

Malagu, Natura giuridica del lodo arbitrale non depositato ed imposta di registro, 38 *Riv. Trim. Dir. & Proc. Civ.* 259 (1984)

Minoli, L'Italia et la Convenzione di New York per il ricinoscimento e l'esecuzione delle sentenze arbitrali straniere, 42 *Riv. Dir. Int'le* 102 (1959)

———, L'Italie et la Convention de New York pour la reconnaissance et l'exécution des sentences arbitrales étrangères, in *Liber Amicorum for Martin Domke* 199 (P. Sanders ed. 1967)

———, L'esecuzione delle sentenze arbitrali straniere in Italia, 12 *Rassegna dell'Arb.* 66 (1972)

Mirabelli, The Application of the New York Convention by the Italian Courts, 4 *Y.B. Com. Arb.* 362 (1979)

Mirabelli, Recchia & Galli Fonseca, Les juges italiens et l'arbitrage commercial international, in *ICCA, Sixth Int'l Arb. Congress: Proceedings* 273 (1978)

Monteleone, Il nuovo regime giuridico dei lodi arbitrali rituali, 40 *Riv. Dir. Proc.* 552 (1985)

Montesano, Aspetti problematici dell'arbitrato irrituale dopo la riforma del 1983, 45 *Riv. Trim. Dir. & Proc. Civ.* 214 (1991)

———, Negozio e processo nel nuovo arbitrato, 39 *Riv. Dir. Proc.* 214 (1984)

Mordiglia, Enforcement of Foreign Arbitration Awards in Italy, in 2 *Fifth Int'l Congress of Maritime Arbitrators* (New York 1981)

Morera, Consequences de l'entrée en vigueur en Italie de la Convention de New York du 10 juin 1958 sur le régime des arbitrages étrangères, in *A.I.A., Essays in Memoriam Eugenio Minoli* 337 (Turin 1974)

Nicotina, Il regime dell'arbitrato in Italia dopo la legge 9 febbraio 1983 No. 28, 25 *Rassegna dell'Arb.* 291 (1985)

———, Oggetto e limiti dell'accertamento giudiciale nel giudicio do delibazione di lodo estero secondo la Convenzione di New York, 25 *Rassegna dell'Arb.* 129 (1985)

Nicotina, G., *La dichiarazione di esecutività del lodo arbitrale* (aggiornato con le innovazione legislative del 9-2-1983 n.28), (Padova 1983)

Nobili, I costi fiscali dell'arbitrato in Italia: sviluppi recenti, 26 *Rassegna dell'Arb.* 13 (1986)

Pajardi, P., *L'arbitrato. Col massimario completo comentato della giurisprudenza di legittimità e di merito dal 1980 al 1988,* (Milan 1990)

Parker School of Foreign and Comparative Law, *International Commercial Arbitration and the Courts* (Dobbs Ferry, NY 1990)

Pechota, Chamber of National and International Arbitration of Milan, in 4 *W.A.R.* 4839 (H. Smit & V. Pechota eds. 1989)

Piergrossi, Problems of Arbitrability of Patent and Licensing Controversies in Italian and United States Law, in *ICCA, Fourth Int'l Arb. Congress: Proceedings* 752 (1972); 6 *N.Y.U.J. Int'l L. & Pol.* 85 (1973)

Plenteda, Arbitrato e società, 29 *Rassegna dell'Arb.* 1 (1989)

Punzi, L'arbitrato di fronte alla riforma generale ed alle riforme parziali del processo civile, 26 *Rassegna dell'Arb.* 23 (1986)

————, La riforma dell'arbitrato (osservazione a margine della legge 9 febbraio 1983, n.28), 38 *Riv. Dir. Proc.* 78 (1983); also in II/2 *Studi in Onore di Tito Carnacini* 1755 (Milan 1984)

————, Le clausole arbitrali nell'ordinamento sportivo, 26 *Rassegna dell'Arb.* 165 (1986)

————, Sull'inammissibilità dell'impugnazione immediata con le azioni c.d. negoziali del lodo arbitrale non dichiarato esecutivo, 26 *Rassegna dell'Arb.* 183 (1986)

Recchia, An Italian Approach to International Conventions on Arbitration, in *A.I.A., Essays in Memoriam Eugenio Minoli* 393 (Turin 1974)

————, Enforcement of American Arbitration Awards in Italy, 2 *N.Y.U. J. Int'l L. & Pol.* 219 (1969)

————, Italy: Associazione Italiana per l'Arbitrato, in *Handbook of Institutional Arbitration in International Trade* 101 (E. Cohn, M. Domke & F. Eisemann eds. 1977)

————, La nouvelle loi italienne sur l'arbitrage, 1984 *Rev. Arb.* 65

————, Le nouveau Règlement d'arbitrage de l'Association italienne pour l'arbitrage, 1979 *Rev. Arb.* 217

————, Nouvelles questions constitutionnelles sur les droits de propriété industrielle et l'arbitrage en Italie, 1977 *Rev. Arb.* 93

————, Nuove prospettive dell'arbitrato commerciale in Italia, 23 *Rassegna dell'Arb.* 41 (1983)

————, Questions actuelles de l'arbitrage international en Italie, 1978 *Rev. Arb.* 3

Recchia, G., *Enforcement of Foreign Arbitration Agreements and Awards in Italy and the United States: A Comparative Study* (Naples 1970)

Ricci, Modificazioni della disciplina dell'Arbitrato (Legge 9 febbraio 1983, n.28), 1983 *Nuove Leggi Civili Commentate* 733

————, Problemi sulla recezione all'estero dei lodi rituali italiani, 41 *Riv. Dir. Proc.* 117 (1986)

————, Disciplina dell'arbitrato e riforme dell'ordinario processo civile, 41 *Riv. Dir. Proc.* 913 (1986)

————, Sul contradditorio nell'arbitrato irrituale, 27 *Rassegna dell'Arb.* 13 (1987)

Riccomagno, Recognition and Enforcement of Foreign Arbitral Awards in Italy under the New York Convention of 1958, 1 *Y.B. Mar. L.* 119 (1984)

Robert, El arbitraje en los paises de la Comunidad Europea, in *El Arbitraje Comercial Internacional* 223 (Mexico 1983)

Rubino-Sammartano, M., *L'arbitrato internazionale* (Padua 1989)

Rubino-Sammartano & Abbatescianni, Italy: Arbitration, in *B2 World Litigation Law & Practice ITA* 14-2 (R. Myrick ed. 1986)

Sacerdoti, Italian Arbitration Association, in 4 *W.A.R.* 4807 (H. Smit & V. Pechota eds. 1980)

Savarese, Arbitration and Contracts for the Transfer of Technology in the Experience of Some Italian State-owned Companies, in *ICCA, Sixth Int'l Arb. Congress: Proceedings* 405 (1978)

Schizzerotto, G., *Dell'arbitrato* (Milan 3rd ed. 1988)

Schlesinger, L'esecuzione del lodo arbitrale rituale, 43 *Riv. Dir. Proc.* 751 (1988); also in *Arbitrato nazionale e internazionale: interpretazione ed esecuzione del lodo* 55 (G. Carli ed. 1989)

Schweyer, A., *Patentnichtigkeit und Patentverletzung und deren Beurteilung durch private Schiedsgerichte nach dem Recht der Schweiz, Deutschlands, Italiens und Frankreich* (St. Gallen 1981)

Selvaggi, Legge 9 febbraio 1983 n.28 e l'efficacia del lodo arbitrale, 23 *Rassegna dell'Arb.* 69 (1983)

Solveni, Dichiarazione di efficacia in Italia di lodi arbitrali inglesi convertiti in sentenze della High Court of Justice ai sensi della Sez. 26 dell'Arbitration Act, 1950, 88 *Dir. Mar.* 451 (1986)

Sutti, Giurisdizione italiana ed arbitrato estero: problemi di connessione, 26 *Riv. Dir. Int'le Priv. & Proc.* 631 (1990)

Tarzia, Dichiarazione di esecutività e attuazione del lodo, 27 *Rassegna dell'Arb.* 195 (1987); also in *Arbitrato nazionale e internazionale: interpretazione ed esecuzione del lodo* 59 (G. Carli ed. 1989)

————, Efficacia del lodo e impugnazione nell'arbitrato rituale e irrituale, 42 *Riv. Dir. Proc.* 14 (1987)

————, Efficacia ed impugnabilità del lodo nell'arbitrato rituale, 25 *Rassegna dell'Arb.* 1 (1985)

————, Le droit italien de l'arbitrage, in *L'Arbitrage* 255 (L. Matray & G. de Leval eds. 1989)

————, Nullità e annullamento del lodo arbitrale irrituale, 45 *Riv. Trim. Dir. & Proc. Civ.* 451 (1991)

Traverso, The Liability of Arbitrators in Italy, 8 *Int'l Bus. Law.* 339 (1980)

Ughi, Attachments and Other Interim Court Remedies in Support of Arbitration: Italy, in *Interim Court Remedies in Support of Arbitration* 99 (D. Shenton & W. Kühn eds. 1987)

————, Interim Court Remedies in Support of Arbitration, 12 *Int'l Bus. Law.* 115 (1984)

Verde, G., ed., *L'arbitrato secondo la legge* 28/1983 (Naples 1985)

Vigoriti, Corte d'Appello Firenze e l'impugnazione del lodo arbitrale (1987-1989), 30 *Rassegna dell'Arb.* 33 (1990)

————, International Arbitration in Italy, 1 *Am. Rev. Int'l Arb.* 77 (1990)

————, Recent Developments in the Recognition and Execution of Foreign Judgments and Arbitral Awards in Italy, 6 *Civil Just. Q.* 248 (1987)

Walter, Das Schiedsverfahren im deutsch-italienischen Rechtsverkehr, 28 *RIW* 693 (1982)

Wenger, Zur Anwendbarkeit des New Yorker Übereinkommen über die Anerkennung und Vollstreckung ausländischer Schiedssprüche auf einem 'freien' Schiedsspruch (lodo irrituale) des italienischen Rechts, 2 *IPRax* 135 (1982)

Zaccheo, Contratto e clausola compromissoria, 41 *Riv. Trim. Dir. & Proc. Civ.* 423 (1987)

Zdravkovic, Certains cas de la jurisprudence yougoslave et étrangère sur l'exécution des sentences arbitrales étrangères, in *ICCA, Fifth Int'l Arb. Congress: Proceedings* C Izi 1-16 (1975)

IVORY COAST

Idot, Talal Massih c/ Omais: une note, 1989 *Rev. Arb.* 536

JAPAN

Akroyd, The Role of Arbitration in Japanese Foreign Trade, 44 *Arbitration* 136 (1978)

Auchter, L'arbitrage maritime dans la pratique japonaise, 25 *Droit Mar. Français* 181 (1973)

Brazil, Resolution of Trade Disputes in the Asian Pacific Region, 10 *Adel. L. Rev.* 49 (1985)

Chave, Profile: The Japan Commercial Arbitration Association, 2 *Int'l Arb. Rep.* 96 (1987)

Coleman, A Preliminary Investigation of Possible Areas of Discrimination Against Foreign Litigants in Japanese Courts on Arbitration Practice, in *Business Transactions with China, Japan and South Korea* 9-1 (P. Saney & H. Smit eds. 1983)

Coulson, Aspects of Pacific Arbitration - The U.S.A. View, *Paper presented to Int'l Conf. Growth of Arb. in the Pacific, Auckland, NZ, Sept. 1985*

Doi, International Commercial Arbitration in Japan, in *Liber Amicorum for Martin Domke* 65 (P. Sanders ed. 1967)

————, Japan, in *Int'l Handbook Com. Arb.* (A. van den Berg, gen. ed. 1984), Suppl. 6, 1986

————, Japan: National Report, 4 *Y.B. Com. Arb.* 115 (1979)

————, *Recognition and Enforcement of Foreign Judgments and Arbitral Awards in Japan, Quarterly of the Japan Commercial Arbitration Association* 1 (Nos. 13/14, 1963)

————, Role of Arbitration in the 'Amicable' Settlement of Contractual Disputes, in *Ninth Lawasia Conference* (New Delhi, Oct. 7-12, 1985): *Working Papers* at 267

————, The Effect of an Arbitration Clause in a Voidable Contract: Separability Doctrine Adopted by the Supreme Court of Japan, in *Law in East and West/Recht in Ost und West* 609 (Tokyo 1988)

Gardiner, Japanese Arbitration Law, 8 *Arb. J.* 89 (1953)

Goldring J., *Commercial Arbitration in Japan-Australia Trade Disputes* (Sydney 1973)

Grieg, International Commercial Arbitration in Japan — A User's Report, 6 *J. Int'l Arb.* 21 (No. 4, 1989)

Hanamizu, Attachments and Other Interim Court Remedies in Support of Arbitration: Japan, in *Interim Court Remedies in Support of Arbitration* 127 (D. Shenton & W. Kühn eds. 1987)

Hattori, International Commercial Arbitration Practiced by the Japan Commercial Arbitration Association, in *ICCA, Third Int'l Arb. Congress: Proceedings* 459 (1969)

Holtzmann & Bernini, Hypothetical Case for Use in a Comparative Study of Arbitration Practice in Various Legal Systems, in *Comparative Arbitration Practice and Public Policy in Arbitration* 19 (P. Sanders ed. 1987)

Hosoi, Matters of Comity and Enforcement of Foreign Judgments and Awards in Japan, 15 *Bull. Japan Shipping Exch.* 34 (1987)

―――, Practical Aspects of the Recognition and Enforcement in Japan of Foreign Arbitration Awards Under the 1958 New York Convention, 10 *Bull. Japan Shipping Exch.* 31 (No. 10, March 1984)

―――, Recent Developments in Arbitration Schemes in Japan, 13 *Bull. Japan Shipping Exch.* 12 (1986)

―――, The Role of Japanese and American Lawyers in Maritime Dispute Settlement: Foreign Judgments and Awards in Japan, 3 *Y.B. Mar. L.* 105 (1986-1987)

International Chamber of Commerce, Japan/Japon, in *Commercial Arbitration and the Law/L'Arbitrage commercial et la Loi* (Basel 1958)

Iwasaki, Application of New York Convention by Japanese Courts, 10 *Bull. Japan Shipping Exch.* 1 (1984)

―――, Drafting Arbitration Clauses Designating Tokyo As Arbitration Site, 11 *Bull. Japan Shipping Exch.* 1 (1985)

―――, Immunity of Arbitrators under Japanese Law, in *The Immunity of Arbitrators* 53 (J.D.M. Lew ed. 1990)

―――, International Arbitration in Japan in the 1990s, 21 *Bull. Japan Shipping Exch.* 1 (1991)

Kakinuki, Dispute Resolution in Japan: Choosing the Right Alternative, 9 *East Asian Exec. Rep.* 7 (No. 11, 1987)

Kawakami & Henderson, Arbitration in U.S./Japanese Sales Disputes, 42 *Wash. L. Rev.* 541 (1967)

Kitagawa, Commercial Arbitration Law and Practice in Japan, 12 *Japanese Ann. Int'l L.* 59 (1968)

————, Contractual Autonomy in International Commercial Arbitration Including a Japanese Perspective, in *Liber Amicorum for Martin Domke* 133 (P. Sanders ed. 1967)

Kitagawa, Z., ed., *Doing Business in Japan*, Volume 7, Ch.4, Arbitration (New York 1984)

Kitagawa & Fukushima, Japan: The Japan Commercial Arbitration Association, in *Handbook of Institutional Arbitration in International Trade* 115 (E. Cohn, M. Domke & F. Eisemann eds. 1977)

Kono & Trunk, Anerkennung und Vollstreckung ausländischer Urteile in Japan, 102 *ZZP* 319 (1989)

Lubic, International Commercial Arbitration in Japan: Background and Suggestions, 2 *Am. Rev. Int'l Arb.* 87 (1991)

McClelland, A Survey of Pacific Rim Commercial Arbitration, 40 *Arb. J.* 3 (No. 1, 1985)

Nakata, Japan, 3 *International Commercial Arbitration: A World Handbook* 72 (P. Sanders ed. 1965)

Nomura, Some Aspects of the Use of Commercial Arbitration by Japanese Corporations, 33 *Osaka U. L. Rev.* 47 (March 1986); also in *East and West: Legal Philosophies in Japan* 50 (M. Yasaki ed. 1987)

Note, Enforcing Foreign Judgments and Arbitration Awards, 5 *Int'l Fin. L. Rev.* 26 (No. 7, 1986)

Ogawa, Proposed Draft of Japan's New Arbitration Law, 7 *J. Int'l Arb.* 33 (No. 2, 1990)

Ohashi, M., *Maritime Arbitration in Tokyo: Its Legal Aspects* (Tokyo 1979)

Pacific Rim Advisory Council, *Pacific Rim: Commercial Arbitration Procedures* (San Diego, CA 1985)

Parker School of Foreign and Comparative Law, *International Commercial Arbitration and the Courts* (Dobbs Ferry, NY 1990)

Pryles, M. & K. Iwasaki, *Dispute Resolution in Australia-Japan Transactions* (Sydney 1983)

Ragan, Arbitration in Japan: Caveat Foreign Drafter and Other Lessons, 7 *Arb. Int'l* 93 (1991)

———, Preparing for the Pitfalls of Arbitration in Japan, 13 *East Asian Exec. Rep.* 9 (No. 1, 1991)

Sawada, International Commercial Arbitration — Practice of Arbitral Institutions in Japan, 30 *Japanese Ann. Int'l L.* 69 (1987)

———, On Mr. Ragan's Lessons on Arbitration in Japan: A Response, 7 *Arb. Int'l* 121 (1991)

———, Practice of Arbitral Institutions in Japan, 4 *Arb. Int'l* 120 (1988)

Shifman, Japan, in 2A *W.A.R.* 1933 (H. Smit & V. Pechota eds. 1987)

———, Japan Commercial Arbitration Association, in 4 *W.A.R.* 4913 (H. Smit & V. Pechota eds. 1989)

Simmonds, K., B. Hill & S. Jarvin, eds., *Commercial Arbitration Law in Asia and the Pacific* (Paris & Dobbs Ferry, NY 1987)

Sono, The Japanese Experience, in *UNCITRAL Arbitration Model in Canada* 25 (R. Paterson & B. Thompson eds. 1987)

Stevens & Takahashi, The East Asian Preference for Conciliation: An Example in a Kabuki Play, in *Arbitration in Settlement of International Commercial Disputes Involving the Far East and Arbitration in Combined Transportation* 69 (P. Sanders ed. 1989). Reproduced in 5 *Arb. Int'l* 43 (1989)

Tajiri, Possibility of Arbitration in International Combined Transport, in *Arbitration and Settlement of International Commercial Disputes Involving the Far East and Arbitration in Combined Transportation* 377 (P. Sanders ed. 1989)

Tanaka, Enforcement of American Awards in Japan, 10 *Arb. J.* 88 (1955)

Taniguchi, Commercial Arbitration in Japan, in *Arbitration in Settlement of International Commercial Disputes Involving the Far East and Arbitration in Combined Transportation* 29 (P. Sanders ed. 1989)

————, Internationalizing Commercial Arbitration in Japan, 2 *Asia L. & Prac.* 22 (No. 3, 1990)

Tanimoto, Arbitration by the Tokyo Maritime Arbitration Commission, 16 *Bull. Japan Shipping Exch.* 1 (Dec. 1987)

————, How to Make Use of Tokyo Maritime Arbitration, 13 *Bull. Japan Shipping Exch.* 1 (1986)

von Preuschen, Die Vollstreckung ausländischer Schiedssprüche in Japan nach dem Inkrafttreten des UN-Übereinkommens, 10 *AWD* 112 (1964)

Yamane, Resolving Disputes in U.S.-Japan Trade: The Japanese Perspective, 39 *Arb. J.* 3 (No. 4, 1984)

JORDAN

Amin, S.H., *Middle East Legal Systems* (Glasgow 1985)

Dallal, Appointment of an Arbitrator under ICC Rules in Jordan, 2 *Int'l Constr. L. Rev.* 177 (1985)

———, Arbitration: Jordan, 13 *Int'l Bus. Law.* 243 (1985)

El-Ahdab, A. H., *Arbitration with the Arab Countries* (Deventer 1990)

———, *L'arbitrage dans les pays arabes* (Paris 1988)

Fadlallah, Les pays arabes du Machrek, in *First Euro-Arab Arb. Conference: Proceedings* 26 (F. Kemicha ed. 1987)

International Bar Association, *Arab Comparative & Commercial Law: The International Approach: Proceedings of the I.B.A. First Arab Regional Conference, Cairo 15-19 February 1987* (London 1987)

Kassis, Particularités et problèmes de l'arbitrage dans les droits des pays arabes, 63 *Rev. Droit Int'l & Droit Comp.* 7 (1986)

Nabulsi, Settlement of Disputes through Arbitration: Jordan, in 1 *Arab Comparative & Commercial Law: The International Approach: Proceedings I.B.A. Conference* 223 (1987)

Peter, Settlement of Investment Disputes, 5 *J. Int'l Arb.* 131 (No. 1, 1988)

Saleh, The Recognition and Enforcement of Foreign Arbitral Awards in the States of the Arab Middle East, in *Contemporary Problems in International Arbitration* 340 (J.D.M. Lew ed. 1986)

———, The Settlement of Disputes in the Arab World: Arbitration and Other Methods, 1 *Arab L. Q.* 198 (1986); reprinted in 4 *Int'l Tax & Bus. Law.* 280 (1986)

Saleh, S., *Commercial Arbitration in the Arab Middle East* (London 1984)

Troller, Arbitration and Enforcement of Arbitration Awards in Arab Countries, 2 *Int'l Contr.* 397 (1981)

Ziadé, Selective Bibliography on Arbitration and Arab Countries, 3 *ICSID Rev. -Foreign Investment L.J.* 423 (1988)

KENYA

O'Connor, The Law Is a Suit to Be Worn, Not a Strait-Jacket, 54 *Arbitration* 226 (1988)

————, The Rise (or Is It Demise) of Arbitration in Kenya, 53 *Arbitration* 61 (1987)

Parker School of Foreign and Comparative Law, *International Commercial Arbitration and the Courts* (Dobbs Ferry, NY 1990)

Peter, Settlement of Investment Disputes, 5 *J. Int'l Arb.* 131 (No. 1, 1988)

KOREA

Byoung Kook Min, Practical Observations on Transnational Commercial Arbitration in Korea, 14 *Korean J. Comp. L.* 1 (1986)

Cho Dong-Won, Republic of Korea: National Report, 7 *Y.B. Com. Arb.* 16 (1982)

Coulson, *Aspects of Pacific Arbitration — The U.S.A. View*, Paper presented to Int'l Conf. Growth of Arb. in the Pacific, Auckland, NZ, Sept. 1985

Glossner, Schiedsverfahren oder Zivilprozessverfahren: Der Macao Sardine Case. The Rt. Hon. Lord Justice Kerr, 1 *Jahrbuch Schiedsgerichtsbarkeit* 251 (1987)

Kang Seok Jeon, Non-Judicial Dispute Resolution Procedures in the Republic of Korea with an Emphasis on Arbitration, 14 *Korean J. Comp. L.* 31 (1986)

Kerr, Arbitration v. Litigation. The Macao Sardine Case, 15 *Int'l Bus. Law.* 152 (1987); 3 *Arb. Int'l* 79 (No. 1, 1987).

Kim, Arbitration in Korea, in *Private Investments and International Transactions in Asian and South Pacific Countries* (New York 1975)

Korean Commercial Arbitration Board, *Guide to Arbitration Practice in Korea* (Seoul 1990)

Lee Tae Hee, Arbitration in the Republic of Korea, 0 *World Arb. & Med.* 18 (1989)

———, Arbitration of International Commercial Disputes in Korea, 3 *Arb. Int'l* 14 (No. 1, 1987)

———, The Development of International Commercial Arbitration in Korea, in *Selected Problems in Contemporary Comparative Law: Festschrift for Professor Chin Kim's Sixtieth Birthday* 242 (Seoul 1987)

Liew Song-kun, Commercial Arbitration in Korea with Special Reference to the UNCITRAL Rules, 5 *Korean J. Comp. L.* 69 (1977)

———, Commercial Arbitration in Korea with Special Reference to the UNCITRAL Rules, in *Business Laws in Korea* 905 (Kim Chan-Jin ed., 2nd ed. 1988)

————, The Republic of Korea, in *Int'l Handbook Com. Arb.* (A. van den Berg gen. ed. 1984), Suppl. 6, Nov. 1986

McClelland, A Survey of Pacific Rim Commercial Arbitration, 40 *Arb. J.* 3 (No. 1, 1985)

Min Byoung-Kook, Practical Observations on Transnational Commercial Arbitration in Korea, in *Business Laws in Korea* 925 (Kim Chan-Jin ed., 2nd ed. 1988)

Mok Young-Joon, The Principle of Reciprocity in the United Nations Convention on the Recognition and Enforcement of Foreign Arbitral Awards of 1958, 21 *Case W. Res. J. Int'l L.* 123 (1989)

Pacific Rim Advisory Council, *Pacific Rim: Commercial Arbitration Procedures* (San Diego, CA 1985)

Shifman, Korea, in 2A *W.A.R.* 1997 (H. Smit & V. Pechota eds. 1987)

Simmonds, K., B. Hill & S. Jarvin, eds., *Commercial Arbitration Law in Asia and the Pacific* (Paris & Dobbs Ferry, NY 1987)

Song Sang-Hyun, Commercial Arbitration Procedures in the Republic of Korea, in *Selected Problems in Contemporary Comparative Law: Festschrift for Professor Chin Kim's Sixtieth Birthday* 262 (Seoul 1987)

————, Commercial Arbitration: A Dimensional Concept of Mediation — Korean Experience (I), 26 *Seoul L.J.* 69 (No. 4, 1985)

————, Commercial Arbitration: A Dimensional Concept of Mediation — Korean Experience (II), 27 *Seoul L.J.* 101 (No. 1, 1986)

————, Recent Trends in Commercial Arbitration in Korea, in *Arbitration in Settlement of International Commercial Disputes Involving the Far East and Arbitration in Combined Transportation* 63 (P. Sanders ed. 1989)

————, Recent Trends in Commercial Arbitration in Korea, 3 *Int'l Arb. Rep.* 21 (No. 9, 1988)

KUWAIT

Abdulredha, Commentary, in *First Int'l Com. Arb. Conference: Proceedings* 27 (N. Antaki & A. Prujiner eds. 1986)

―――, The Practice of International Arbitration in Kuwait, in *First Euro-Arab Arb. Conference: Proceedings* 110 (F. Kemicha ed. 1987)

Abu Zayyad, Kuwait: National Report, 4 *Y.B. Com. Arb.* 139 (1979)

Al-Ayoub, The Legal System of Kuwait: 1.6 Arbitration, in *Modern Legal Systems Cyclopedia, Supplement One* 110.7 (K.R. Redden ed. 1987)

Amin, S.H., *Middle East Legal Systems* (Glasgow 1985)

Asa'ad, *Commercial Arbitration and Legal System in Kuwait* (Kuwait 1978)

Ballantyne, Arbitration in the Gulf States: Delocalisation: A Short Comparative Study, 1 *Arab L. Q.* 205 (1986)

―――, European Experience and Perception of Arbitration with Arab Countries, in *First Euro-Arab Arb. Conference: Proceedings* 160 (F. Kemicha ed. 1987)

Bernardini, Les arbitrages petroliers et le droit applique par les arbitres, in *First Euro-Arab Arb. Conference: Proceedings* 282 (F. Kemicha ed. 1987)

Chaudhri & Sifri, Arbitration in Kuwait: Procedures and Options, 8 *Middle E. Exec. Rep.* 14 (No. 9, 1985)

Dilger, Schiedsgerichtsbarkeit und Volstreckung ausländischer Entscheidungen in den Golfstaaten, in *Vetragspraxis und Streiterledigung im Wirtschaftverkehr mit arabischen Staaten* 101 (K.-H. Böckstiegel ed. 1981)

El-Ahdab, A. H., *Arbitration with the Arab Countries* (Deventer 1990)

―――, *L'arbitrage dans les pays arabes* (Paris 1988)

El-Kosheri & Riad, The Changing Roles in the Arbitration Process (with Regard to the Applicable Law Governing the New Generation of the Petroleum Agreements), 1 *Arab L. Q.* 475 (1986); also in *First Euro-Arab Arb. Conference: Proceedings* 253 (F. Kemicha ed. 1987)

Huneidi, Arbitration under Kuwaiti Law, 6 *J. Int'l Arb.* 77 (No. 3, 1989)

————, Arbitration under Kuwaiti Law, 55 *Arbitration* 203 (1989)

International Bar Association, *Arab Comparative & Commercial Law: The International Approach: Proceedings of the I.B.A. First Arab Regional Conference, Cairo 15-19 February 1987,* (London 1987)

Kassim, Settlement of Disputes through Arbitration: Arbitration in Kuwait, in 1 *Arab Comp. & Com. Law: The Int'l Approach: Proc. I.B.A. Conf.* 269 (1987)

Kassis, Particularités et problèmes de l'arbitrage dans les droits des pays arabes, 63 *Rev. Droit Int'l & Droit Comp.* 7 (1986)

Krüger, The State of Arbitration in Kuwait and Dubai, 4 *Int'l Arb. Rep.* 15 (No. 2, 1989)

Lew, The Recognition and Enforcement of Arbitration Agreements and Awards in the Middle East, 1 *Arb. Int'l* 161 (1985)

Marston, The Aminoil-Kuwait Arbitration, 17 *J. World Trade L.* 177 (1983)

Mulhim, Proper Law and Arbitration — Kuwait, 41 *Arbitration* 183 (1974)

Redfern, The Arbitration Between the Government of Kuwait and Aminoil, 55 *Brit. Y.B. Int'l L.* 65 (1984)

Saleh, The Recognition and Enforcement of Foreign Arbitral Awards in the States of the Arab Middle East, in *Contemporary Problems in International Arbitration* 340 (J.D.M. Lew ed. 1986)

————, The Settlement of Disputes in the Arab World: Arbitration and Other Methods, 1 *Arab L. Q.* 198 (1986); reprinted in 4 *Int'l Tax & Bus. Law.* 280 (1986)

Saleh, S., *Commercial Arbitration in the Arab Middle East* (London 1984)

Stumpf, Schiedsgerichtsbarkeit in arabischen Ländern, 1 *Jahrbuch Schiedsgerichtsbarkeit* 102 (1987)

Tesón, State Contracts and Oil Expropriations: The Aminoil-Kuwait Arbitration, 24 *Va. J. Int'l L.* 323 (1984)

Troller, Arbitration and Enforcement of Arbitration Awards in Arab Countries, 2 *Int'l Contr.* 397 (1981)

Tschanz, Contributions of the Aminoil Award to the Law of State Contract, 18 *Int'l Law.* 245 (1984)

Ziadé, Selective Bibliography on Arbitration and Arab Countries, 3 *ICSID Rev. -Foreign Investment L.J.* 423 (1988)

LATIN AMERICA

Abbot, Latin America and International Arbitration Conventions: The Quandary of Non-Ratification, 17 *Harv. Int'l L.J.* 131 (1976)

Aksen, Commercial Arbitration with Latin America: A Practical Necessity, in *Reference Manual on Doing Business in Latin America* 112 (D. Shea, F. Swacker, R. Radway & S. Stairs eds. 1979)

Aramburú Menchaca, Reflexiones sobre el arbitraje comercial internacional, in 2 *Estudios de Derecho internacional en homenaje a Miaja de la Muela,* 981 (1972)

Barclay, Arbitration in Latin America, 43 *Arbitration* 105 (1977)

Barrios de Angelis, Sistema y estructura del arbitraje comercial internacional, in E*l Arbitraje en el Derecho Latinoamericano y Español* 569 (L. Perret & U. Montoya Alberti eds. 1989)

Cabanas Rodriguez, La ley-tipo de arbitraje para Iberoamérica, 1 *Rev. Corte Esp. Arb.* 29 (1984)

Caminos, The Inter-American Convention on International Commercial Arbitration, 3 *ICSID Rev. - Foreign Investment L.J.* 107 (1988)

Domke & Keller, Western Hemisphere System of Commercial Arbitration, 6 *Univ. Toronto L.J.* 308 (1946)

Eyzaguirre Echeverria, Arbitration in Latin America: The Experience of the Inter-American Commercial Arbitration Commission, 4 *Int'l Tax & Bus. Law.* 288 (1986)

———, Ventajas del arbitraje. Eficacia y validez en el Derecho Iberoamericano, in *Alternativas a la justicia institucional: arbitraje, conciliación* 111 (Bogota 1988)

Eyzaguirre Echeverria & Siqueiros, Arbitration in Latin America, in *Arbitration in Settlement of International Commercial Disputes Involving the Far East and Arbitration in Combined Transportation* 81 (P. Sanders ed. 1989)

Fouchard, La Convention interamericain sur l'arbitrage commercial international (Panama, 20 janvier 1975), 1977 *Rev. Arb.* 203

Garro, El arbitraje en America Central y la Ley modelo propuesta por la Comision de las Naciones Unidas para el Derecho Mercantil Internacional (UNCITRAL), in *A.B.A., Conferencia sobre Arbitraje Comercial y Laboral, San Salvador, 7-12 Diciembre 1987*

————, Enforcement of Arbitration Agreements and Jurisdiction of Arbitral Tribunals in Latin America, 1 *J. Int'l Arb*. 293 (No. 4, 1984)

————, Inter-American Convention on International Commercial Arbitration, 1975, in 1 *W.A.R.* 255.1 (H. Smit & V. Pechota eds. 1986, 1987)

————, Introduction: Commercial Arbitration in Central America, 20 *U. Miami Inter-Am. L. Rev.* 679 (1989)

————, The Inter-American Convention on Extraterritorial Validity of Foreign Judgments and Arbitral Awards, 1979, in 1 *W.A.R.* 265.0 (H. Smit & V. Pechota eds. 1986, 1987)

Goldman, Arbitration and Transfer of Technology in Latin America, in *Arbitration and the Licensing Process* 5-29 (R. Goldscheider & M. de Haas eds. 1984-)

Grigera Naón, El arbitraje comercial internacional en América Latina, *Revista de Derecho Industrial* 1 (No. 4, Jan-Feb. 1980)

Holtzmann & Bernini, Hypothetical Case for Use in a Comparative Study of Arbitration Practice in Various Legal Systems, in *Comparative Arbitration Practice and Public Policy in Arbitration* 19 (P. Sanders ed. 1987)

Kellor, F., *American Arbitration* (New York 1948)

Kos-Rabcewicz-Zubkowski, Les conventions interaméricaines sur l'arbitrage commercial et la Commission interaméricaine d'arbitrage commercial, 1983 *Rev. Arb.* 411

————, Panamerykanskie konwencje dotyczace arbitrazu handlowego, 44 *Panstwo i Prawo* 84 (No. 3, 1989)

Larsen, Enforcement of Foreign Judgments in Latin America: Trends and Individual Differences, 17 *Tex. Int'l L.J.* 213 (1982)

Leich, The Inter-American Convention on International Commercial Arbitration, 75 *Am. J. Int'l L.* 982 (1981)

706

Montoya Alberti, Arbitration, Foreign Law and Jurisdiction in International Loan Agreements in Some Countries of Latin America, in *Arbitration in Settlement of International Commercial Disputes Involving the Far East and Arbitration in Combined Transportation* 99 (P. Sanders ed. 1989)

Nattier, International Commercial Arbitration in Latin America: Enforcement of Arbitral Agreements and Awards, 21 *Tex. Int'l L. J.* 397 (1986)

Norberg, General Introduction to Inter-American Commercial Arbitration, in *Int'l Handbook Com. Arb.* (A. van den Berg, gen. ed. 1984), Suppl. 12, January 1991

————, General Introduction to Inter-American Commercial Arbitration, 3 *Y.B. Com. Arb.* 1 (1978) and 8 *Y.B. Com. Arb.* 77 (1983)

————, Inter-American Commercial Arbitration, 1 *Law. Am.* 25 (1969)

————, Inter-American Commercial Arbitration Revisited, 7 *Law. Am.* 275 (1975)

————, Inter-American Commercial Arbitration: Unicorn or Beast of Burden? 5 *Pace L. Rev.* 607 (1985)

————, Inter-American Convention on International Commercial Arbitration, in *ICCA, Sixth Int'l Arb. Congress: Proceedings* 451 (1978)

————, Recent Developments in Inter-American Commercial Arbitration, 13 *Case W. Res. J. Int'l L.* 107 (1981)

————, Recent Developments in Inter-American Commercial Arbitration, 12 *Nw. J. Int'l L. & Bus.* 86 (1991)

Norberg, C., *Inter-American Commercial Arbitration* (Dobbs Ferry and Paris 1989)

Note, International Commercial Arbitration: Domestic Recognition and Enforcement of the Inter-American Convention on International Commercial Arbitration, 10 *Syracuse J. Int'l L. & Com.* 169 (1983)

————, The Future of Arbitration in Latin America: A Study of Its Regional Development, 8 *Case W. Res. U. J. Int'l L.* 480 (1976)

————, The Inter-American Convention on International Commercial Arbitration, 9 *Law. Am..* 43 (1977)

Perret, L. & U. Montoya Alberti, eds., *El Arbitraje en el Derecho Latinoamericano y Español: Liber Amicorum en Homenaje a Ludwik Kos Rabcewicz Zubkowski* (Lima 1989)

Rinker, The Future of Arbitration in Latin America: A Study of its Regional Development, 8 *Case W. Res. J. Int'l L.* 480 (1976)

Siqueiros, Arbitral Autonomy and National Sovereign Authority in Latin America, in *Lex Mercatoria and Arbitration* 183 (T. Carbonneau ed. 1990)

―――, Panórama actual del arbitraje comercial internacional, in *El Arbitraje Comercial Internacional* 135 (Mexico 1983)

Sprague, A Courageous Course for Latin America: Urging the Ratification of the ICSID, 5 *Houston J. Int'l L.* 157 (1982)

Sterling, Draft Uniform Law on Inter-American Commercial Arbitration, 1956, in 1 *W.A.R.* 249.9 (H. Smit & V. Pechota eds. 1986, 1987)

Straus, Co-operation amongst Arbitration Organizations of the Americas, in *ICCA, Third Int'l Arb. Congress: Proceedings* 199 (1969)

―――, Why International Commercial Arbitration Is Lagging in Latin America: Problems and Cures, 33 *Arb. J.* 21 (1978)

Summers, Arbitration and Latin America, 3 *Cal. W. Int'l L. J.* 1 (1972)

―――, Private Versus State Arbitration in Latin America, 4 *Cal. W. Int'l L.J.* 121 (1973)

Szasz, The Investment Disputes Convention and Latin America, 11 *Va. J. Int'l L.* 256 (1971)

van den Berg, L'arbitrage commercial en Amérique latine, 1979 *Rev. Arb.* 128

van den Berg, The New York Arbitration Convention 1958 and the Panama Convention of 1975, 5 *Arb. Int'l* 214 (1989)

Vita, *Comparative Study of American Legislation Governing Commercial Arbitration* (Washington 1928)

LEBANON

Bernini, Recent Legislations and International Unification of the Law on Arbitration, in *First International Commercial Arbitration Conference: Proceedings* 315 (N. Antaki & A. Prujiner eds. 1986)

El-Ahdab, A.H., *Arbitration with the Arab Countries* (Deventer 1990)

———, *L'arbitrage dans les pays arabes* (Paris 1988)

Fadlallah, Les pays arabes du Machrek, in *First Euro-Arab Arb. Conference: Proceedings* 26 (F. Kemicha ed. 1987)

International Chamber of Commerce, Lebanon/Liban, in *Commercial Arbitration and the Law/L'Arbitrage commercial et la Loi* (Basel 1949)

Kassis, Particularités et problèmes de l'arbitrage dans les droits des pays arabes, 63 *Rev. Droit Int'l & Droit Comp.* 7 (1986)

Parker School of Foreign and Comparative Law, *International Commercial Arbitration and the Courts* (Dobbs Ferry, NY 1990)

Saleh, The Recognition and Enforcement of Foreign Arbitral Awards in the States of the Arab Middle East, in *Contemporary Problems in International Arbitration* 340 (J.D.M. Lew ed. 1986)

———, The Settlement of Disputes in the Arab World: Arbitration and Other Methods, 1 *Arab L. Q.* 198 (1986); reprinted in 4 *Int'l Tax & Bus. Law.* 280 (1986)

Saleh, S., *Commercial Arbitration in the Arab Middle East* (London 1984)

Troller, Arbitration and Enforcement of Arbitration Awards in Arab Countries, 2 *Int'l Contr.* 397 (1981)

Tyan, E., *Le droit de l'arbitrage* (Beyrouth 1972)

Ziadé, Lebanon: International Arbitration Provisions of the Code of Civil Procedure, 27 *I.L.M.* 1022 (1988)

———, Selective Bibliography on Arbitration and Arab Countries, 3 *ICSID Rev. -Foreign Investment L.J.* 423 (1988)

LIBERIA

Schütze, Die Anerkennung und Vollstreckbarerklärung ausländischer
Zivilurteile und Schiedssprüche in Liberia, 33 *RIW* 598 (1987)

LIBYA

Aksen, Arbitration Under International Commercial Contracts. Current Issues and Practical Problems: Enforcement of Awards against Governments — The Libyan Awards, in *Essays on International Law* 104 (New Delhi 1981)

Bernardini, Les arbitrages petroliers et le droit applique par les arbitres, in *First Euro-Arab Arb. Conference: Proceedings* 282 (F. Kemicha ed. 1987)

Buzghaia, Libya: National Report, 4 *Y.B. Com. Arb.* 148 (1979)

Catranis, Probleme der Nationalisierung ausländischer Unternehmen vor internationalen Schiedsgerichten: die Libyschen Schiedsfälle, 28 *RIW* 19 (1982)

Cohen-Jonathan, L'arbitrage Texaco-Calasiatic contre le gouvernement Libyen: sentence au fond du 19 janvier 1977, 23 *Ann. Français Droit Int'l.* 452 (1977)

Derains, Clauses et procédures d'arbitrage internationales dans le pays arabes, in *First Euro-Arab Arb. Conference: Proceedings* 150 (F. Kemicha ed. 1987)

El-Ahdab, A. H., *Arbitration with the Arab Countries* (Deventer 1990)

―――, *L'arbitrage dans les pays arabes* (Paris 1988)

El-Alem, Arbitration in Disputes Relating to Libyan Administrative Contracts, 3 *Int'l Constr. L. Rev.* 21 (1985)

―――, L'arbitrage dans les litiges relatifs aux contrats administratifs libyens, 1983 *Rev. Arb.* 295

Gruss, Enteignung und Aufhebung von Erdölkonzessionen: der Schiedsspruch im libyschen Erdölstreit, 39 *Zeitschrift f. ausl. öffentl. Recht & Völkerrecht* 782 (1979)

Kadiki, The Reality of Commercial Arbitration in the Arab Countries and Firms, in *First Euro-Arab Arb. Conference: Proceedings* 122 (F. Kemicha ed. 1987)

Kassis, Particularités et problèmes de l'arbitrage dans les droits des pays arabes, 63 *Rev. Droit Int'l & Droit Comp.* 7 (1986)

Krüger, Schiedsklauseln im Libyen-Geschäft — ein hoffnungsloser Fall,

Saleh, The Recognition and Enforcement of Foreign Arbitral Awards in the States of the Arab Middle East, in *Contemporary Problems in International Arbitration* 340 (J.D.M. Lew ed. 1986)

————, The Settlement of Disputes in the Arab World: Arbitration and Other Methods, 1 *Arab L. Q.* 198 (1986); reprinted in 4 *Int'l Tax & Bus. Law.* 280 (1986)

Saleh, S., *Commercial Arbitration in the Arab Middle East* (London 1984)

Sefrioui, Pratique de l'arbitrage et tendances reformatrices nouvelles, in *Euro-Arab Arbitration III* 61 (F. Kemicha ed. 1991)

Stumpf, Schiedsgerichtsbarkeit in arabischen Ländern, 1 *Jahrbuch Schiedsgerichtsbarkeit* 102 (1987)

Varma, Petroleum Concessions in International Arbitration: Texaco Overseas Petroleum Company v. Libyan Arab Republic, 18 *Colum. J. Transnat'l L.* 259 (1979)

von Mehren & Kourides, International Arbitration between States and Foreign Private Parties: The Libyan Nationalization Case, 75 *Am. J. Int'l L.* 476 (1981)

————, The Libyan Nationalizations: TOPCO/CALASIATIC v. Libyan Arbitration, 12 *Natural Resources Law.* 419 (1979)

White, Expropriation of the Libyan Oil Concessions: Two Conflicting International Arbitrations, 30 *Int'l & Comp. L.Q.* 1 (1981)

Ziadé, Selective Bibliography on Arbitration and Arab Countries, 3 *ICSID*

LIECHTENSTEIN

Rechberger, Das Anerkennungs- und Vollstreckungsabkommen zwischen Österreich und dem Fürstentum Liechtenstein, 16 *ZRV* 122 (1975)

LUXEMBOURG

International Chamber of Commerce, *Arbitration Law in Europe* (Paris 1981)

————, Luxembourg, in *Commercial Arbitration and the Law/L'Arbitrage commercial et la Loi* (Basel 1949)

Sauvepanne, Die Schiedsgerichtsbarkeit in der Benelux, 7 *Jahrbuch für internationales Recht* 86 (1956)

MADAGASCAR

International Chamber of Commerce, Madagascar, in *Commercial Arbitration and the Law/L'Arbitrage commercial et la Loi* (Basel 1964)

MALAYSIA

Bernini, Recent Legislations and International Unification of the Law on Arbitration, in *First International Commercial Arbitration Conference: Proceedings* 315 (N. Antaki & A. Prujiner eds. 1986)

Brazil, Resolution of Trade Disputes in the Asian Pacific Region, 10 *Adel. L. Rev.* 49 (1985)

Holmes, Malaysian Newsletter No. 1, July 1989, 55 *Arbitration* 292 (1989)

McClelland, A Survey of Pacific Rim Commercial Arbitration, 40 *Arb. J.* 3 (No. 1, 1985)

Mooney, Representation in Arbitrations in Malaysia and Singapore, 1989 *Malayan L.J.* cvii

Pacific Rim Advisory Council, *Pacific Rim: Commercial Arbitration Procedures* (San Diego, CA 1985)

Ricafrente, Commercial Arbitration in ASEAN Countries, in *Commercial Arbitration* 39 (J. Ricalde ed. 1983)

Simmonds, K., B. Hill & S. Jarvin, eds., *Commercial Arbitration Law in Asia and the Pacific* (Paris & Dobbs Ferry, NY 1987)

Tan, Unmeritorious Claims and Defences in Arbitration Proceedings, [1987] 2 *Malayan L.J.* cxvii

MEXICO

Alcala Zamora, La ejecución de sentencias arbitrales en México, 11 *Boletín del Instituto de Derecho Comparado de México* 45 (1958)

Alcantara Gonzales, Enforcement of Awards, in 2 *Fifth Int'l Congress of Maritime Arbitrators* (New York 1981)

Alvarez Soberanis, El arbitraje en los contratos de asistencia de tecnologia, in *El Arbitraje Comercial Internacional* 341 (Mexico 1983)

Barclay, Arbitration in Latin America, 43 *Arbitration* 105 (1977)

Briseño Sierra, Arbitration and Technical Checking of Due Performance of Contracts, in *ICCA, Fourth Int'l Arb. Congress: Proceedings* 98 (1972)

———, El arbitraje comercial y su funcionamento en México, in *Memoria del Segundo Simposio Sobre Arbitraje Mercantil Internacional* 127 (Mexico 1975)

———, Mexico: National Report, 3 *Y.B. Com. Arb.* 94 (1978)

———, El arbitraje comercial en México, in *El Arbitraje en el Derecho Latinoamericano y Espanol* 361 (L. Perret & U. Montoya Alberti eds. 1989)

———, El arbitraje comercial en México y las leyes-tipo internacionales, 1 *Rev. Corte Esp. Arb.* 67 (1984)

———, El arbitraje comercial y su funcionamento en México, in *El Arbitraje Comercial Internacional* 261 (Mexico 1983)

Briseño Sierra, H., *El arbitraje en el derecho privado* (Mexico 1963)

———, *El arbitraje comercial: doctrina y legislación* (Mexico 1979)

Carrillo Ramirez, Arbitraje comercial international, 11 *Revista de la Facultad de Derecho de México* 478 (1961)

Dunshee de Abranches, C.A., ed., *El arbitraje comercial en Iberoamérica* (Madrid 1982)

Fernandez del Castillo, El arbitraje comercial en la legislación de México, 9 *Boletin del Instituto de Derecho Comparado de México* 55 (1956)

Garro, Mexico, in 2A *W.A.R.* 2059 (H. Smit & V. Pechota eds. 1987)

Goldman, Arbitration and Transfer of Technology in Latin America, in *Arbitration and the Licensing Process* 5-29 (R. Goldscheider & M. de Haas eds. 1984-)

Gomez Lara, Arbitraje e inversiones extranjeras, in *El Arbitraje Comercial Internacional* 363 (Mexico 1983)

Hoagland, Modification of Mexican Arbitration Law, 7 *J. Int'l Arb.* 91 (No. 1, 1990)

Holtzmann & Bernini, Hypothetical Case for Use in a Comparative Study of Arbitration Practice in Various Legal Systems, in *Comparative Arbitration Practice and Public Policy in Arbitration* 19 (P. Sanders ed. 1987)

International Chamber of Commerce, Mexico/Mexique, in *Commercial Arbitration and the Law/L'Arbitrage commercial et la Loi* (Basel 1964)

Nattier, International Commercial Arbitration in Latin America: Enforcement of Arbitral Agreements and Awards, 21 *Tex. Int'l L. J.* 397 (1986)

Ochoa Bunsow, A., *El derecho applicable en el arbitraje comercial international* (Mexico 1980)

Orrico, International Commercial Arbitration in Mexico, in *ICCA, Fifth Int'l Arb. Congress: Proceedings* C Izd 1-5 (1975)

Pacific Rim Advisory Council, *Pacific Rim: Commercial Arbitration Procedures* (San Diego, CA 1985)

Parker School of Foreign and Comparative Law, *International Commercial Arbitration and the Courts* (Dobbs Ferry, NY 1990)

Pereznieto Castro, Arbitraje privado en México, in *El Arbitraje en el Derecho Latinoamericano y Español* 407 (L. Perret & U. Montoya Alberti eds. 1989)

Rangel Medina, El arbitraje en los contratos sobre usos de marcas y explotación de patentes, in *El Arbitraje Comercial Internacional* 323 (Mexico 1983)

Ray, La responsibilidad de transportistas en las reglas de Hamburgo y la solución arbitral de controversias, in *El Arbitraje Comercial Internacional* 461 (Mexico 1983)

Rendon Graniel & Zivy, Jurisprudence méxicaine: la validité de la clause arbitrale internationale, 1987 *Int'l Bus. L.J.* 629

Schrameyer, Die Anerkennung ausländischer Entscheidungen in Mexico, 1966 *AWD* 253

Siqueiros, El arbitraje comercial en México, 15 *Revista de la Facultad de Derecho de México* 703 (1965)

————, Mexico, in *Int'l Handbook Commercial Arbitration* (A.J. van den Berg gen. ed. 1984), Suppl. 12, January 1991

————, Mexico, 15 *Y.B. Com. Arb.* 307 (1990)

————, Reconocimiento y ejecución de laudos extranjeros en la República Mexicana, in *El Arbitraje Comercial Internacional* 285 (Mexico 1983)

————, Resolution of Commercial Disputes: Enforcement of Foreign Arbitral Awards in Mexico, in *Doing Business in Mexico* 18-1 (S. Lefler ed. 1980)

Toral Moreno, Procede el amparo contra laudos de arbitros nombrados por particulares? 1-3 *Revista de Derecho Procesal* 5 (1975)

Trigueros & Vasquez Pando, La Convención Interamericana sobre Arbitraje Comercial Internacional, 8 *Revista de Investigaciones Juridicas* 289 (1984)

Universidad Nacional Autónoma de México, *El Arbitraje Comercial Internacional: Selección de Lecturas* (Mexico 1983)

Witker, El derecho económico internacional y el arbitraje comercial, in *El Arbitraje Comercial Internacional* 15 (Mexico 1983)

Zamora Sanchez, El arbitraje comercial internacional en México, in *El Arbitraje en el Derecho Latinoamericano y Español* 427 (L. Perret & U. Montoya Alberti eds. 1989)

Zepeda, Fideicomiso y arbitraje, in *El Arbitraje Comercial Internacional*

MIDDLE EAST

Al-Baharna, International Commercial Arbitration in Perspective, 3 *Arab L.Q.* 3 (1988)

Al-Hejailan, Arab Middle East and the New York Convention, in *First International Commercial Arbitration Conference: Proceedings* 262 (N. Antaki & A. Prujiner eds. 1986)

Beaumont, The Rules of Conciliation, Arbitration and Expertise of the Euro-Arab Chambers of Commerce, 2 *Int'l Constr. L. Rev.* 392 (1985)

Böckstiegel, K.-H., ed., *Vertragspraxis und Streiterledigung im Wirtschaftverkehr mit arabischen Staaten* (Cologne 1981)

Budin, Experience et perception de l'arbitrage international entre l'Europe et les pays arabes, in *First Euro-Arab Arb. Conference: Proceedings* 166 (F. Kemicha ed. 1987)

Dilger, Arbitration, Enforcement of Foreign Judgments and Arbitration Awards, Clauses on the Choice of Law, and Agreements on Jurisdiction of the Court in Egypt, Saudi Arabia and the Gulf States, in *International Bar Association: Proceedings of the Seminar on Middle East Law* 35 (1981)

El-Ahbar, Le Centre arabe d'arbitrage commercial à Rabat, 1989 *Rev. Arb.* 631

―――――, The Moslem Arbitration Law, in 1 *Arab Compartive & Commercial Law: The International Approach: Proceedings I.B.A. Conference* 323 (1987)

El-Ahdab, General Introduction on Arbitration in Arab Countries, in *Int'l Handbook Com. Arb.* (A. van den Berg, gen. ed. 1984), Suppl. 11, Jan. 1990

El-Ahdab, A. H., *Arbitration with the Arab Countries* (Deventer 1990)

―――――, *L'arbitrage dans les pays arabes* (Paris 1988)

El-Hakim, Conditions de validité dans le droit et la pratique des pays arabes, in *Euro-Arab Arbitration II* 131 (F. Kemicha ed. 1989)

Fadlallah, Les règles de procédure internes des pays arabes et la procédure arbitrale, in *Euro-Arab Arbitration II* 79 (F. Kemicha ed. 1989)

Gaillard, Euro-Arab Chambers of Commerce: Rules of Conciliation, Arbitration and Expertise, Introductory Note, 24 *I.L.M.* 1119 (1985)

Haddad, The Amman Convention of 1987 on Commercial Arbitration, 1 *Am. Rev. Int'l Arb.* 132 (1990)

————, Inter-Arab Conventions on Commercial Arbitration, in *Euro-Arab Arbitration III* 48 (F. Kemicha ed. 1991)

Holtzmann & Bernini, Hypothetical Case for Use in a Comparative Study of Arbitration Practice in Various Legal Systems, in *Comparative Arbitration Practice and Public Policy in Arbitration* 19 (P. Sanders ed. 1987)

International Bar Association, *Arab Comparative & Commercial Law: The International Approach: Proceedings of the I.B.A. First Arab Regional Conference, Cairo 15-19 February 1987* (London 1987)

Jalili, Amman Arab Convention on Commercial Arbitration, 7 *J. Int'l Arb.* 139 (No. 1, 1990)

Kadiki, The Reality of Commercial Arbitration in the Arab Countries and Firms, in *First Euro-Arab Arb. Conference: Proceedings* 122 (F. Kemicha ed. 1987)

Kassis, Particularités et problèmes de l'arbitrage dans les droits des pays arabes, 63 *Rev. Droit Int'l & Droit Comp.* 7 (1986)

Kemicha, F., ed., *Euro-Arab Arbitration II/Arbitrage Euro-Arabe II* (London 1989)

————, *Euro-Arab Arbitration III/Arbitrage Euro-Arabe III* (London 1991)

————, *Proceedings of the First Euro-Arab Arbitration Conference* (Port El Kantaoui, Tunisia, 24-27 September 1985), (London 1987)

Layton, Is International Arbitration a Viable Remedy for disputes in the Middle East? *Middle E. Exec. Rep.* 14 (June 1983)

Level, Caractères particuliers de l'arbitrage dans les contracts industriels et de grands travaux, in *First Euro-Arab Arb. Conference: Proceedings* 193 (F. Kemicha ed. 1987)

Maktouf, Euro-Arab Arbitration Rules, 6 *Middle E. Exec. Rep.* 15 (No. 1, 1983)

Rycx, L'accord sur le règlement des litiges entre Etats hôtes d'investissements arabes et ressortissants des autres Etats arabes et ses perspectives, 1981 *Rev. Arb.* 259

Sefrioui, Pratique de l'arbitrage et tendances reformatrices nouvelles, in *Euro-Arab Arbitration III* 61 (F. Kemicha ed. 1991)

Shihata, Le CIRDI et les pays en voie de développement et plus particulièrement les pays arabes, in *First Euro-Arab Arb. Conference: Proceedings* 89 (F. Kemicha ed. 1987)

Stumpf, Schiedsgerichtsbarkeit in arabischen Ländern, 1 *Jahrbuch Schiedsgerichtsbarkeit* 102 (1987)

van den Berg, The New York Arbitration Convention of 1958 and the Arab Countries, in *First Euro-Arab Arb. Conference: Proceedings* 54 (F. Kemicha ed. 1987)

van Houtte & Hudson, Les conventions d'arbitrage conclues entre partenaires commerciaux arabes et européens, 1990 *Int'l Bus. L.J.* 65

Ziadé, Selective Bibliography on Arbitration and Arab Countries, 3 *ICSID Rev. -Foreign Investment L.J.* 423 (1988)

MONGOLIA

Dashdondog, Mongolia: National Report, 1 *Y.B. Com. Arb.* 63 (1976)

Fellhauer, H. & H. Strohbach, eds., *Handbuch der internationalen Handelsschiedsgerichtsbarkeit* (Berlin 1969)

Lebedev, S., ed., *Handbook on Foreign Trade Arbitration in the CMEA Member Countries* (Moscow 1983)

Pozdnyakov, Commercial Arbitration in CMEA Member Countries, 4 *Int'l Tax & Bus. Law.* 272 (1986)

MOROCCO

American Arbitration Association, *New Strategies for Peaceful Resolution of International Business Disputes* (Dobbs Ferry, NY 1971)

El-Ahdab, A. H., *Arbitration with the Arab Countries* (Deventer 1990)

————, *L'arbitrage dans les pays arabes* (Paris 1988)

Friedland, Provisional Measures in ICSID Arbitration, 2 *Arb. Int'l* 335 (1986)

Haddad, The Amman Convention of 1987 on Commercial Arbitration, 1 *Am. Rev. Int'l Arb.* 132 (1990)

————, Inter-Arab Conventions on Commercial Arbitration, in *Euro-Arab Arbitration III* 48 (F. Kemicha ed. 1991)

International Chamber of Commerce, Morocco/Maroc, in *Commercial Arbitration and the Law/L'Arbitrage commercial et la Loi* (Basel 1949)

Mezghani, Les pays arabes du Maghreb, in *First Euro-Arab Arb. Conference: Proceedings* 39 (F. Kemicha ed. 1987)

Razon, L'arbitrage en droit marocain, 1 *Rev. Marocaine Droit* 9 (No. 1, 1985)

Sefrioui, Pratique de l'arbitrage et tendances reformatrices nouvelles, in *Euro-Arab Arbitration III* 61 (F. Kemicha ed. 1991)

Terki, L'arbitrage et l'entreprise publique en Afrique du Nord, 66 *Rev. Droit Int'l & Droit Comp.* 124 (1989)

Troller, Arbitration and Enforcement of Arbitration Awards in Arab Countries, 2 *Int'l Contr.* 397 (1981)

Ziadé, Selective Bibliography on Arbitration and Arab Countries, 3 *ICSID Rev. -Foreign Investment L.J.* 423 (1988)

NETHERLANDS

Berger, Die Regelung der gerichtlichen Anfechtbarkeit internationaler Schiedssprüche in europäischen Schiedsgerichtsgesetzen, 35 *RIW* 850 (1989)

Bühler, Das neue niederlandische Gesetz für Schiedsgerichtsbarkeit, 33 *RIW* 901 (1987)

Carabiber, L'immunité de juridiction et d'exécution des Etats collectivités et établissements publics au regard de l'obligation assumée par une clause compromissoire inserée dans les contrats internationaux de droit privé, in *Liber Amicorum for Martin Domke* 23 (P. Sanders ed. 1967)

de Bruin, De 'affaire C,' 1989 *Tijdschrift voor Arbitrage* 1

de Groot, Arbitration in the Netherlands: Background to the Arbitration Act 1986, 1 *Int'l Company & Com. L. Rev.* 191 (1990)

Delaume, SEEE v. Yugoslavia: Epitaph or Interlude? 4 *J. Int'l Arb.* 25 (No. 3, 1987)

Dore, I., *Theory and Practice of Multiparty Commercial Arbitration, With Special Reference to the UNCITRAL Framework* (London 1990)

Duintjer Tebbens, A Facelift for Dutch Arbitration Law, 34 *Neth. Int'l L. Rev.* 141 (1987)

Eckstrom, L., *Licensing in Foreign and Domestic Operations*. Volume I, Chapter 7: Arbitration (by Steven Z. Szczepanski), (New York 1972, updated 1987)

Gaillard, L'affaire SOFIDIF ou les difficultés de l'arbitrage multipartite (à propos de l'arrêt rendu par la Cour d'Appel de Paris le 19 décembre 1986), 1987 *Rev. Arb.* 275

————, The UNCITRAL Model Law and Recent Statutes on International Arbitration in Europe and North America, 2 *ICSID Rev. - Foreign Investment L.J.* 424 (1987)

Gomez, International Arbitration: A Case for Delocalization, 3 *Sri Lanka J. Int'l L.* 61 (1991)

Goudsmit, Arbitration in Construction Contracts in the Netherlands, 2 *Int'l Constr. L. Rev.* 185 (1985)

Hardenberg, The Awards of the Iran-U.S. Claims Tribunal Seen in Connection with the Law of the Netherlands, 12 *Int'l Bus. Law.* 337 (1984)

International Chamber of Commerce, *Arbitration Law in Europe* (Paris 1981)

Klein, F.-E., *Considérations sur l'arbitrage en droit international privé* (Basel 1955)

Langeveld, Iets over getuigen in internationale arbitrages, 1988 *Tijdschrift voor Arbitrage* 156

Legras de Grandcourt, Evolution contemporaine des législations européennes, in *Euro-Arab Arbitration III* 119 (F. Kemicha ed. 1991)

MacLaren, Commercial Arbitration in the United States and Overseas, in *Arbitration and the Licensing Process* 5 (R. Goldscheider & M. de Haas eds. 1984-)

Marriott, Evidence in International Arbitration, 5 *Arb. Int'l* 280 (1989)

Mok Young-Joon, The Principle of Reciprocity in the United Nations Convention on the Recognition and Enforcement of Foreign Arbitral Awards of 1958, 21 *Case W. Res. J. Int'l L.* 123 (1989)

Netherlands Arbitration Institute (adapted by Bette E. Shifman), in 4A *W.A.R.* 4989 (H. Smit & V. Pechota eds. 1989)

Parker School of Foreign and Comparative Law, *International Commercial Arbitration and the Courts* (Dobbs Ferry, NY 1990)

Samuel, A., *Jurisdictional Problems in International Commercial Arbitration: A Study of Belgian, Dutch, English, French, Swedish, Swiss, U.S. and West German Law* (Zurich 1989)

Sanders, A New Arbitration Law for the Netherlands, 4 *Pace L. Rev.* 581 (1984)

———, Netherlands: National Report, 6 *Y.B. Com. Arb.* 60 (1981)

———, The Dutch Arbitration Act of 1986, 1987 *J. Bus. L.* 321 & 403

———, The New Dutch Arbitration Act, 3 *Arb. Int'l* 194 (1987)

———, The New Dutch Arbitration Act, 27 *Rassegna dell'Arb.* 27 (1987)

————, The New Dutch Arbitration Act, 14 *N. Ky. L. Rev.* 41 (1987)

————, The New Dutch Arbitration Act, 1987 *Int'l Bus. L.J.* 539

————, The New Dutch Arbitration Act, in *AAA, Arbitration & the Law, 1986* 162 (1987)

Sanders, P., *Het nieuwe arbitragerecht* (Deventer 1987)

Sanders, P. & A. van den Berg, eds., *The Netherlands Arbitration Act 1986: Text and Notes, English, Français, Deutsch* (Deventer 1987)

Sauvepanne, Die Schiedsgerichtsbarkeit in der Benelux, 7 *Jahrbuch für internationales Recht* 86 (1956)

Schaafsma, Recognition and Enforcement of Foreign Country Judgments and Arbitral Awards in the Netherlands, in *Enforcement of Foreign Country Judgments* (Commercial Law & Practice Course Handbook Series, No. 104) 151 (New York: Practicing Law Institute 1974)

Schultsz, Ein neues Schiedsgerichtsgesetz für die Nederlande, 7 *IPRax* 383 (1987)

————, Les nouvelles dispositions de la législation néederlandaise en matière d'arbitage, 1988 *Rev. Arb.* 209

————, The Bill on Applicability of Dutch Law to Awards Rendered by the Iran-United States Claims Tribunal, in *Legislation in the Netherlands and International Arbitration* 32 (1986)

Schultsz, J.C. & S.L. Buruma, eds., *Legislation in the Netherlands and International Arbitration./Internationale Arbitrage* (Deventer 1986)

Shifman, The Netherlands, in 2A *W.A.R.* 2077 (H. Smit & V. Pechota eds. 1987)

Sillevis Smitt, Arbitrage, bemiddeling en conciliatie, in *Iustitia et Amicitia. Geschillenbeslechting in en Buiten Rechte* 93 (Arnheim 1985)

Smit, De eerste ICC-arbitrage in Venezuela, 1988 *Tijdschrift voor Arbitrage* 173

Tupman, Staying Enforcement of Arbitral Awards under the New York Convention, 3 *Arb. Int'l* 223 (1987)

van den Berg, Aan de Balie van het Scheidsgerecht: De Nieuwe Arbitragewet, 1984 *Tijdschrift voor Arbitrage* 171

————, Consolidated Arbitrations and the 1958 New York Arbitration Convention, 2 *Arb. Int'l* 367 (1986)

————, Immunity of Arbitrators under Netherlands Law, in *The Immunity of Arbitrators* 59 (J.D.M. Lew ed. 1990)

————, Le droit néerlandais de l'arbitrage, in *L'Arbitrage* 265 (L. Matray & G. de Leval eds. 1989)

————, Proposed Dutch Law on the Iran-U.S. Claims Settlement Declaration, 12 *Int'l Bus. Law.* 341 (1984)

————, The Draft Dutch Arbitration Law, 49 *Arbitration* 158 (1983)

————, The Netherlands, in *Int'l Handbook Com. Arb.* (A. van den Berg, gen. ed. 1984), Suppl. 7, April 1987

————, The Netherlands Arbitration Act 1986, 15 *Int'l Bus. Law.* 356 (1987)

————, The Netherlands: National Report, 12 *Y.B. Com. Arb.* 3 (1987)

van den Berg, A.J., R. van Delden & H.J. Snijders, *Arbitragerecht* (Zwolle 1988)

van Marwijk Kooy, Multi-Party Arbitration, in 5 *Hague-Zagreb Essays* 139 (C. Voskuil & J. Wade, eds. 1985)

————, The Netherlands: The Netherlands Arbitration Institute, in *Handbook of Institutional Arbitration in International Trade* 133 (E. Cohn, M. Domke & F. Eisemann eds. 1977)

van Praag, Arbitral Tribunals for Civil and Commercial Disputes Under the Law of the Netherlands, 1 *Int'l Y.B. Civil & Com. Arb.* 99 (1928)

van Rooij, R. & M. Polak, *Private International Law in the Netherlands.* Chapter 4: Arbitration (Deventer 1987)

Vellekoop, The New Arbitration Law in the Netherlands, 6 *Int'l Fin. L. Rev.* 16 (No. 5, May 1987)

Voskuil & Freedberg-Swartzburg, Composition of the Arbitral Tribunal, in *Essays on International Commercial Arbitration* 64 (P. Sarcevic ed. 1989)

Voûte, Een partij-arbiter in Hong Kong, 1988 *Tijdschrift voor Arbitrage* 184

NEW ZEALAND

Bull, S., *The Arbitral Process and the Courts* (Wellington 1983)

Coulson, *Aspects of Pacific Arbitration — The U.S.A. View,* Paper presented to Int'l Conf. Growth of Arb. in the Pacific, Auckland, NZ, Sept. 1985

Kennedy-Grant, Attachments and Other Interim Court Remedies in Support of Arbitration — The New Zealand Position, in *Interim Court Remedies in Support of Arbitration* 261 (D. Shenton & W. Kühn eds. 1987)

―――, New Zealand, in *Int'l Handbook Com. Arb.* (A. van den Berg gen. ed. 1984), Suppl. 2, Aug. 1984

―――, New Zealand: National Report, 8 *Y.B. Com. Arb.* 34 (1983); 11 *Y.B. Com. Arb.* 83 (1986)

Kerr, Growth of Arbitration in the Pacific: A View from the United Kingdom, 52 *Arbitration* 84 (1986); Paper presented to Int'l Conf. Growth of Arb. in the Pacific, Auckland, NZ, Sept. 1985

Neill, New Zealand and the UNCITRAL Model Law, 6 *Arb. Int'l* 271 (1990)

New Zealand Law Commission, Preliminary Paper No. 7. *Arbitration: A Discussion Paper* (Wellington 1988)

―――, *Arbitration: Report No. 20* (Wellington 1991)

Pacific Rim Advisory Council, *Pacific Rim: Commercial Arbitration Procedures* (San Diego, CA 1985)

Simmonds, K., B. Hill & S. Jarvin, eds., *Commercial Arbitration Law in Asia and the Pacific* (Paris & Dobbs Ferry, NY 1987)

Sprott, A., *Judicial Control of Arbitration* (Auckland 1988)

Thomas, *A Commercial List for the Auckland High Court.* Paper presented to Int'l Conf. Growth of Arb. in the Pacific, Auckland, NZ, Sept. 1985

NICARAGUA

Arauz, Arbitration in Nicaragua: A Comparison with the UNCITRAL Model Law, in *Commercial and Labor Arbitration in Central America* 295 (A. Garro ed. 1991)

Dunshee de Abranches, C.A., ed., *El arbitraje comercial en Iberoamérica* (Madrid 1982)

Garro, Nicaragua, in 2A *W.A.R.* 2109 (H. Smit & V. Pechota eds. 1987)

International Chamber of Commerce, Nicaragua, in *Commercial Arbitration and the Law/L'Arbitrage commercial et la Loi* (Basel 1951)

NIGERIA

Achebe, The United Nations Convention on the Recognition and Enforcement of Foreign Arbitral Awards of June 10, 1958: Implications for United States Investors in Nigeria, 9 *Tex. Int'l L.J.* 157 (1974)

————, United Nations Arbitration Convention: Implications for Nigeria, 8 *J. World Trade L.* 240 (1974)

American Arbitration Association, *New Strategies for Peaceful Resolution of International Business Disputes* (Dobbs Ferry, NY 1971)

Amoussou-Guenou, La réforme de l'arbitrage en République fédérale du Nigéria, 1989 *Rev. Arb.* 445

Atanda, Review of Arbitration Law and Practice in Sub-Saharan Africa, 1 *Am. Rev. Int'l Arb.* 123 (1990)

————, The Nigerian Arbitration and Conciliation Decree, 1988, 1 *Am. Rev. Int'l Arb.* 452 (1990)

Ezejiofor, Enforcement of Arbitration Awards in Nigeria, 1981 *J. Bus. L.* 319 (1981)

Holtzmann & Bernini, Hypothetical Case for Use in a Comparative Study of Arbitration Practice in Various Legal Systems, in *Comparative Arbitration Practice and Public Policy in Arbitration* 19 (P. Sanders ed. 1987)

Orojo, J.O., *Nigerian Commercial Law and Practice*, Chapter 4: Arbitration (London 1983)

Oti, Nigeria, in 2A *W.A.R.* 2127 (H. Smit & V. Pechota eds. 1987)

Oyekunle, The Federal Republic of Nigeria, *Int'l Handbook Com. Arb.* (A. van den Berg gen. ed. 1984), Suppl. 11, Jan. 1990

————, Nigeria: National Report, 2 *Y.B. Com. Arb.* 66 (1977)

Parker School of Foreign and Comparative Law, *International Commercial Arbitration and the Courts* (Dobbs Ferry, NY 1990)

Tiewul & Tsegah, Arbitration and the Settlement of Commercial Disputes: A Selective Survey of African Practice, 24 *Int'l & Comp. L.Q.* 393 (1975)

NORWAY

Brauer, Schiedsgerichtsbarkeit in Norwegen, 35 *RIW* 611 (1989)

Eckhoff, Norway, in *Int'l Handbook Com. Arb.* (P. Sanders ed. 1984)

———, Norway: National Report, 5 *Y.B. Com. Arb.* 97 (1980); 7 *Y.B. Com. Arb.* 64 (1982); 11 *Y.B. Com. Arb.* 87 (1986)

Eckstrom, L., *Licensing in Foreign and Domestic Operations.* Volume I, Chapter 7: Arbitration (by Steven Z. Szczepanski), (New York 1972, updated 1987)

Haug, Immunity of Arbitrators under Norwegian Law, in *The Immunity of Arbitrators* 65 (J.D.M. Lew ed. 1990)

———, Internasjonal Kommersiell Voldgift, *Rett og Rettssal (Oslo)* 603 (1984)

———, Norway, 15 *Y.B. Com. Arb.* 309 (1990)

———, Norway, in *Int'l Handbook Com. Arb.* (A. van den Berg gen. ed. 1984), Suppl. 10, June 1989

International Chamber of Commerce, *Arbitration Law in Europe* (Paris 1981)

———, Norway/Norvege, in *Commercial Arbitration and the Law/ L'Arbitrage commercial et la Loi* (Basel 1949)

Jacobi, New Aspects of Arbitration Legislation in Scandinavia, in *ICCA, Third Int'l Arb. Congress: Proceedings* 475 (1969)

Klein, F.-E., *Considérations sur l'arbitrage en droit international privé* (Basel 1955)

Lindboe, A., *Privat Rettergang* (Oslo 1974)

MacLaren, Commercial Arbitration in the United States and Overseas, in *Arbitration and the Licensing Process* 5 (R. Goldscheider & M. de Haas eds. 1984-)

Norwegian Group of the International Bar Association, *International Commercial Arbitration in Action: Papers from a Conference in Oslo in 1982* (Oslo 1983)

Ringdal, Special Features of International Arbitration in Norway, 49 *Arbitration* 91 (Aug. 1983)

OMAN

Ballantyne, Arbitration in the Gulf States: Delocalisation: A Short Comparative Study, 1 *Arab L. Q.* 205 (1986)

Dilger, Schiedsgerichtsbarkeit und Volstreckung ausländischer Entscheidungen in den Golfstaaten, in *Vetragspraxis und Streiterledigung im Wirtschaftverkehr mit arabischen Staaten* 101 (K.-H. Böckstiegel ed. 1981)

El-Ahdab, A. H., *Arbitration with the Arab Countries* (Deventer 1990)

———, *L'arbitrage dans les pays arabes* (Paris 1988)

Hirst, Settlement of Disputes through Arbitration: Sultanate of Oman, in 1 *Arab Comparative & Commercial Law: The International Approach: Proceedings of I.B.A. Conference* 135 (1987)

Jarvin, Enforcement of an Arbitration Award in Oman, 2 *J. Int. Arb.* 81 (No. 4, 1985)

Lane & Morton, Enforcement of a Foreign Award in Oman, 2 *Arb. Int'l* 75 (No. 1, Jan 1986); 1 *Int'l Arb. Report* 28 (1986)

Lew, The Recognition and Enforcement of Arbitration Agreements and Awards in the Middle East, 1 *Arb. Int'l* 161 (1985)

Pechota, Oman, in 2A *W.A.R.* 2193 (H. Smit & V. Pechota eds. 1987)

Saleh, The Recognition and Enforcement of Foreign Arbitral Awards in the States of the Arab Middle East, in *Contemporary Problems in International Arbitration* 340 (J.D.M. Lew ed. 1986)

———, The Settlement of Disputes in the Arab World: Arbitration and Other Methods, 1 *Arab L. Q.* 198 (1986); reprinted in 4 *Int'l Tax & Bus. Law.* 280 (1986)

Saleh, S., *Commercial Arbitration in the Arab Middle East* (London 1984)

Sefrioui, Pratique de l'arbitrage et tendances reformatrices nouvelles, in *Euro-Arab Arbitration* III 61 (F. Kemicha ed. 1991)

Troller, Arbitration and Enforcement of Arbitration Awards in Arab Countries, 2 *Int'l Contr.* 397 (1981)

Ziadé, Selective Bibliography on Arbitration and Arab Countries, 3 *ICSID Rev. -Foreign Investment L.J.* 423 (1988)

PACIFIC RIM

Bernini, Arbitration in Settlement of International Commercial Disputes Involving the Far East. Synthesis Report, in *Arbitration in Settlement of International Commercial Disputes Involving the Far East and Arbitration in Combined Transportation* 313 (P. Sanders ed. 1989)

Fine, Continuum or Chasm? Can West Meet East? 6 *J. Int'l Arb.* 27 (No. 4, 1989)

McDermott, A Survey of Methods for the Enforcement of Foreign Judgments and Foreign Arbitral Awards in the Asia-Pacific Region, 12 *Loy. L.A. Int'l & Comp. L.J.* 114 (1989)

————, Enforcement of Arbitration Agreements in the United States and in the Asia-Pacific Region, 10 *Loy. L.A. Int'l & Comp. L.J.* 615 (1988)

Sanders, P., ed., *Arbitration in Settlement of International Commercial Disputes Involving the Far East and Arbitration in Combined Transportation: ICCA Ninth Int'l Arb. Congress* (Tokyo, 31 May - 3 June 1988), (Deventer 1989)

PAKISTAN

Bernini, Recent Legislations and International Unification of the Law on Arbitration, in *First International Commercial Arbitration Conference: Proceedings* 315 (N. Antaki & A. Prujiner eds. 1986)

Burton, Pakistan, 3 *Int'l Commercial Arbitration: A World Handbook* 98 (P. Sanders ed. 1965)

Chaudhri, Arbitral procedure, 37 *Pakistan Horizon* 22 (No. 2 1984)

Chaudri, M.A., ed., *Prospects of International Arbitration* (Karachi 1966)

Dias, Pakistan, in 2A *W.A.R.* 2259 (H. Smit & V. Pechota eds. 1987)

Farani, M., *Law of Arbitration* (Lahore 1979)

————, *The Arbitration Laws* (3rd ed. Lahore 1977)

Hassan & Samie, International Commercial Arbitration in Pakistan, 33 *Arb. J.* 41 (1978)

Hossain, International Commercial Arbitration, State Succession and the Commonwealth, 36 *Brit. Y.B. Int'l L.* 370 (1960)

International Chamber of Commerce, Pakistan, in *Commercial Arbitration and the Law/L'Arbitrage commercial et la Loi* (Basel 1958)

Jaffer & Osmany, Pakistan: National Report, 5 *Y.B. Com. Arb.* 114 (1980) and 7 *Y.B. Com. Arb.* 66 (1982)

Jillani, Recognition and Enforcement of Foreign Arbitral Awards in Pakistan, 37 *Int'l & Comp. L.Q.* 926 (1988)

Mokal, S. M. I. K., *The Arbitration Act, 1940 (X of 1940): With Commentary* (4th ed., Lahore 1986)

Parker School of Foreign and Comparative Law, *International Commercial Arbitration and the Courts* (Dobbs Ferry, NY 1990)

Simmonds, K., B. Hill & S. Jarvin, eds., *Commercial Arbitration Law in Asia and the Pacific* (Paris & Dobbs Ferry, NY 1987)

PANAMA

Boutin, De la teoria de la doble personalidad del Estado y el arbitraje internacional en el nuevo Código Judicial Panameño, in *El Arbitraje en el Derecho Latinoamericano y Español* 459 (L. Perret & U. Montoya Alberti eds. 1989)

de la Guardia, Panama: National Report, 3 *Y.B. Com. Arb.* 106 (1978)

Garro, Panama, in 2A *W.A.R.* 2283 (H. Smit & V. Pechota eds. 1987)

Goldman, Arbitration and Transfer of Technology in Latin America, in *Arbitration and the Licensing Process* 5-29 (R. Goldscheider & M. de Haas eds. 1984-)

Illueca, La ejecución de las sentencias arbitrales extranjeras en Panamá, 11 *Anuario de Derecho (Panama)* 77 (1981)

PAPUA NEW GUINEA

Koiri, Dispute Settlement in International Commercial Agreements: The Law and National Interest in Papua New Guinea, 10 *Melanesian L.J.* 71 (1982)

Simmonds, K., B. Hill & S. Jarvin, eds., *Commercial Arbitration Law in Asia and the Pacific* (Paris & Dobbs Ferry, NY 1987)

PARAGUAY

Ahrens & Samtleben, Schiedsgerichtsbarkeit in Paraguay, 36 *RIW* 721 (1990)

Alvarado, The Legal System of Paraguay, in 10 *Modern Legal Systems Cyclopedia* 171 (K.R. Redden gen. ed. 1985)

Dunshee de Abranches, C.A., ed., *El arbitraje comercial en Iberoamérica* (Madrid 1982)

Garro, Paraguay, in 2A *W.A.R.* 2297 (H. Smit & V. Pechota eds. 1987)

International Chamber of Commerce, Paraguay, in *Commercial Arbitration and the Law/L'Arbitrage commercial et la Loi* (Basel 1951)

Mallmann, Das paraguayische Schiedsverfahrensrecht, 32 *ZRF* 246 (1991)

PERU

Aramburú Menchaca, Commercial Arbitration in Peru, in *Arbitration in Settlement of International Commercial Disputes Involving the Far East and Arbitration in Combined Transportation* 111 (P. Sanders ed. 1989)

————, International Commercial Arbitration in the Andean Pact (Observations for a Community Regime), in *The Art of Arbitration* 27 (J. Schultsz & A. van den Berg eds. 1982)

————, Peru: National Report, 3 *Y.B. Com. Arb.* 116 (1978)

Barclay, Arbitration in Latin America, 43 *Arbitration* 105 (1977)

Diez-Canseco, El juicio arbitral, 34 *Revista jurídica del Perú* 289 (1983)

Dunshee de Abranches, C.A., ed., *El arbitraje comercial en Iberoamérica* (Madrid 1982)

Garro, Peru, in 2A *W.A.R.* 2309 (H. Smit & V. Pechota eds. 1987)

Goldman, Arbitration and Transfer of Technology in Latin America, in *Arbitration and the Licensing Process* 5-29 (R. Goldscheider & M. de Haas eds. 1984-)

International Chamber of Commerce, Peru/Perou, in *Commercial Arbitration and the Law/L'Arbitrage commercial et la Loi* (Basel 1949)

Lohmann Luca de Tena, J. G., *El arbitraje*. 2nd ed. (Lima 1988)

Montoya Alberti, Arbitration, Foreign Law and Jurisdiction in International Loan Agreements in Some Countries of Latin America, in *Arbitration in Settlement of International Commercial Disputes Involving the Far East and Arbitration in Combined Transportation* 99 (P. Sanders ed. 1989)

————, El arbitraje en los contratos de prestamo internacionales, in *El Arbitraje en el Derecho Latinoamericano y Español* 481 (L. Perret & U. Montoya Alberti eds. 1989)

————, Peru, in *Int'l Handbook of Com. Arb.* (A. van den Berg, gen. ed. 1984), Suppl. 10, June 1989

————, Peru, 15 *Y.B. Com. Arb.* 312 (1990)

Montoya Alberti, U., *El arbitraje comercial* (Lima 1988)

Parodi Remon, El arbitraje en el Perú, in *El Arbitraje en el Derecho Latinoamericano y Español* 513 (L. Perret & U. Montoya Alberti eds. 1989)

Samtleben, Schiedsgerichtsbarkeit in den Andenpaktstaaten, 30 *RIW* 600 (1984)

————, Schiedsklauseln in Peru and Venezuela, 33 *RIW* 20 (1987)

Sanchez Dominguez, Arbitraje y conciliación en el comercio internacional, in *El Arbitraje en el Derecho Latinoamericano y Español* 527 (L. Perret & U. Montoya Alberti eds. 1989)

de Trazegniez, Los conceptos y las cosas: vicisitudes peruanas de la clausula compromisoria y del compromiso arbitral, in *El Arbitraje en el Derecho Latinoamericano y Español* 543 (L. Perret & U. Montoya Alberti eds. 1989)

PHILIPPINES

American Arbitration Association, *New Strategies for Peaceful Resolution of International Business Disputes* (Dobbs Ferry, NY 1971)

Bongco, The Enforcement of Foreign Arbitration Agreements and Awards in the Philippines, 21 *Arb. J.* 34 (1966)

Eckstrom, L., *Licensing in Foreign and Domestic Operations.* Volume I, Chapter 7: Arbitration (by Steven Z. Szczepanski), (New York 1972, updated 1987)

Gonzalez & Padilla, The International Centre for the Settlement of Investment Disputes: An Assessment from the Philippine Perspective, 59 *Philippine L.J.* 222 (1984)

Lazatin, Mechanics and Procedural Aspects of Commercial Arbitration, in *Commercial Arbitration* 14 (J. Ricalde ed. 1983)

McClelland, A Survey of Pacific Rim Commercial Arbitration, 40 *Arb. J.* 3 (No. 1, 1985)

MacLaren, Commercial Arbitration in the United States and Overseas, in *Arbitration and the Licensing Process* 5 (R. Goldscheider & M. de Haas eds. 1984-)

Marcos, Concept, Legal Basis and Scope of Commercial Arbitration, in *Commercial Arbitration* 1 (J. Ricalde ed. 1983)

Parlade, Remedies after Arbitration Award, in *Commercial Arbitration* 75 (J. Ricalde ed. 1983)

Ricalde, J., ed., *Commercial Arbitration: Proceedings of the Symposium on Commercial Arbitration - 1981* (Quezon City 1983)

Simmonds, K., B. Hill & S. Jarvin, eds., *Commercial Arbitration Law in Asia and the Pacific* (Paris & Dobbs Ferry, NY 1987)

POLAND

American Arbitration Association, *New Strategies for Peaceful Resolution of International Business Disputes* (Dobbs Ferry, NY 1971)

Blessing, Proper Law and Dispute Resolution Arising out of East-West Joint Ventures, in *Eastern Bloc Joint Ventures* 107 (D. Winter ed. 1990)

Erecinski, Evidence in Polish International Commercial Arbitration, 1987 *Y.B. Socialist Legal Systems* 331

Gola, Die Aussenhandelsschiedsgerichtsbarkeit in Polen, 19 *ZRV* 18 (1978)

Golob, Arbitral Tribunals According to the Draft of the Polish Code of Civil Procedure, 1 *Int'l Y.B. Civil & Com. Arb.* 128 (A. Nussbaum ed. 1928)

Grzybowski, Arbitral Tribunals for Foreign Trade in Socialist Countries, 37 *Law & Contemp. Probs.* 592 (1972)

Holtzmann & Bernini, Hypothetical Case for Use in a Comparative Study of Arbitration Practice in Various Legal Systems, in *Comparative Arbitration Practice and Public Policy in Arbitration* 19 (P. Sanders ed. 1987)

Jakubowski, The Continental Case in Eastern Europe, 41 *Arbitration* 106 (1974)

————, The Recognition and Enforcement of Foreign Arbitral Awards in Poland, *Polish Y.B. Int'l L.* 65 (1975)

————, The Settlement of Foreign Trade Disputes in Poland, 11 *Int'l & Comp. L.Q.* 806 (1962)

Jakubowski, J., *Permanent Arbitration Courts for Foreign Trade in Poland* (Warsaw 1962)

Jakubowski & Wisniewski, Poland: National Report, 1 *Y.B. Com. Arb.* 64 (1976)

————, Poland: The Court of Arbitration at the Polish Chamber of Foreign Trade, in *Handbook of Institutional Arbitration in International Trade* 147 (E. Cohn, M. Domke & F. Eisemann eds., 1977)

745

Kos-Rabcewicz-Zubkowski, Central and East European Rules on the Form of International Arbitration Agreement, 3 *La Revue Juridique Themis* 415 (1969)

————, Polish Law on International Commercial Arbitration, 23 *Jahrbuch für Ostrecht* 305 (1981)

Kos-Rabcewicz-Zubkowski, L., *East European Rules on the Validity of International Arbitration Agreements* (Manchester and Dobbs Ferry, NY 1970)

Kuss, Neuere Entwicklungen und Perspektiven der Ost-West-Schiedsgerichtsbarkeit, 33 *RIW* 584 (1987)

Lebedev, International Commercial Arbitration in the Socialist Countries Members of the CMEA, 158 *Recueil des Cours* 87 (1977-V)

Lebedev, S., ed., *Handbook on Foreign Trade Arbitration in the CMEA Member Countries* (Moscow 1983)

Lisowski, Establishing a New Permanent Court of Arbitration in International Wool Commerce at Gdynia Wool Federation, 10 *Rassegna dell'Arb.* 31 (1970)

————, Selected Problems Concerning International Commercial Arbitration in Poland, 13 *Rassegna dell'Arb.* 171 (1973)

————, Specialist Arbitration Courts in Poland and Their Role in the International Cotton and Wool Trade, in *ICCA, Fourth Int'l Arb. Congress: Proceedings* 738 (1972)

Majoros, Exécution de décisions étrangères et procédure d'exéquatur en Europe de l'Est: Tour d'horizon avec des références de droit comparé, in *Le Juriste Suisse Face au Droit et aux Jugements Etrangers: Ouverture ou Repli?* 135 (F. Knoepfler ed. 1988)

Melis, Enforcement of Arbitral Awards in Eastern Europe, in *Contemporary Problems in International Arbitration* 332 (J.D.M. Lew ed. 1986)

Nanowski, International Commercial Arbitration Practices in Poland, in *ICCA, Third Int'l Arb. Congress: Proceedings* 511 (1969)

————, L'arbitrage commercial international en Pologne, 1966 *Rev. Arb.* 78

Nanowski, Z., *Z problematyki miedzynarodowego arbitrazu handlowego v Polsce* (Warsaw 1982?)

Niemotko, International Commercial Arbitration in Poland, 29 *Arb. J.* 247 (1974)

Pechota, International Economic Arbitration in the USSR and Eastern Europe, 8 *N.Y. L. Sch. J. Int'l & Comp. L.* 377 (1987)

Pisar, S., *Coexistence & Commerce*, Chapters 20—24 (New York 1970)

Pozdnyakov, Commercial Arbitration in CMEA Member Countries, 4 *Int'l Tax & Bus. Law.* 272 (1986)

Przetacznik, The Court of Arbitration Attached to the Polish Chamber of Foreign Trade, in 4A *W.A.R.* 5081 (H. Smit & V. Pechota eds. 1989)

――――, The Court of Arbitration at the Gdynia Wool Federation, in 4A *W.A.R.* 5123 (H. Smit & V. Pechota eds. 1989)

Sawczuk, M., ed., *Odrebnosci krajowe miedzynarodowego arbitrazu handlowego — Les particularités nationales de l'arbitrage commercial international* (Lublin 1987)

Sobkowski, Die Zulässigkeit der Nebenintervention im polnischen Schiedsverfahren, 102 *ZZP* 358 (1989)

Stalev, The Continental Case of Eastern Europe, 41 *Arbitration* 95 (1974)

Strohbach, The CMEA Countries, in *Arbitration in Settlement of International Commercial Disputes Involving the Far East and Arbitration in Combined Transportation* 133 (P. Sanders ed. 1989)

Stumpf, Ost-West-Schiedsgerichtsbarkeit: Schiedsgerichte mit Sitz in dritten Ländern, 33 *RIW* 821 (1987)

Szurski, Basic Information on Polish Law and Practice Concerning International Commercial Arbitration, in *Arbitration in Settlement of International Commercial Disputes Involving the Far East and Arbitration in Combined Transportation* 149 (P. Sanders ed. 1989)

――――, Comments on 'Comparative Arbitration Practice' as Presented in Four Reports, in *Comparative Arbitration Practice and Public Policy in Arbitration* 169 (P. Sanders ed. 1987)

――――, Commercial Arbitration, in *Prospects of International Arbitration* 21 (M.A. Chaudri ed. 1966)

————, Schiedsordnung des Schiedsrichterkollegiums der Polnischen Kammer für Aussenhandel, Warschau, 2 *Jahrbuch Schiedsgerichtsbarkeit* 213 (1988)

Szurski & Wisniewski, Polish People's Republic, in *Int'l Handbook Com. Arb.* (A. van den Berg gen. ed. 1984), Suppl. 7, April 1987

Trammer, Poland, in 2 *Int'l Commercial Arbitration: A World Handbook* 136 (P. Sanders ed. 1960)

Tyczka, M., *Arbitraz i postepowanie arbitrazove*, 3rd ed. (Warsaw 1985)

Wisniewski, Awards of the Court of Arbitration at the Polish Chamber of Foreign Trade, 15 *Polish Y.B. Int'l L.* 301 (1986)

————, Awards of the Court of Arbitration at the Polish Chamber of Foreign Trade, 16 *Polish Y.B. Int'l L.* 191 (1987)

————, Awards of the Court of Arbitration at the Polish Chamber of Foreign Trade in Warsaw, 10 *Polish Y.B. Int'l L.* 269 (1980)

————, Awards of the Court of Arbitration at the Polish Chamber of Foreign Trade in Warsaw, 17 *Polish Y.B. Int'l L.* 251 (1988)

————, The Practice of the Court of Arbitration at the Polish Chamber of Foreign Trade: Major Trends and Problems as Illustrated by Chosen Awards, 1989 *Int'l Bus. L.J.* 1011

Wysocka, B., *Uznawanie i wykonywanie zagranicznych orzeczen arbitrazowych w Polsce* (Warsaw 1987)

PORTUGAL

Coelho Bento Suares & Moura Ramos, Arbitragem comercial internacional: analise da lei-modelo da CNUDCI de 1985, 1985 *Documentaçao e Direito Comparado* 231 (No. 21)

―――――, Arbitragem comercial internacional: analise da lei-modelo da CNUDCI de 1985 e das disposicoes pertinentes do direito portugues, in *Contratos internacionais: compra e venda, clausulas penais, arbitragem* 315 (Coimbra 1986)

Cruz, *La posición de Portugal en relación el arbitraje internacional,* A paper presented at the conference on Spain, Portugal and International Arbitration (Barcelona, 27 May 1986)

Cruz & Moura Vicente, Portugal, in *Int'l Handbook on Commercial Arbitration* (A.J. van den Berg gen. ed. 1984), Suppl. 12, January 1991

Garro, Portugal, in 2A *W.A.R.* 2333 (H. Smit & V. Pechota eds. 1987)

Glossner, Schiedsverfahren oder Zivilprozessverfahren: Der Macao Sardine Case. The Rt. Hon. Lord Justice Kerr, 1 *Jahrbuch Schiedsgerichtsbarkeit* 251 (1987)

International Chamber of Commerce, *Arbitration Law in Europe* (Paris 1981)

―――――, Portugal, in *Commercial Arbitration and the Law/L'Arbitrage commercial et la Loi* (Basel 1951)

Kerr, Arbitration v. Litigation. The Macao Sardine Case., 15 *Int'l Bus. Law.* 152 (1987); 3 *Arb. Int'l* 79 (No. 1, 1987)

Klein, F.-E., *Considérations sur l'arbitrage en droit international privé* (Basel 1955)

Mallmann, Schiedsvertragsregelungen in Portugal, 35 *RIW* 691 (1989)

Moura Vicente, L'évolution récente du droit de l'arbitrage au Portugal, 1991 *Rev. Arb.* 419

Pereira Barrocas, Necessidade de uma nova ordem judicial a arbitragem, 45 *Revista da Ordem dos Advogados* 433 (1985)

Pessoa Vaz & Alvaro Dias, La reconnaissance et l'exécution des jugements étrangers judiciaires et arbitraux en matière civile et commerciale au Portugal, 33-34 *Documentaçao e Direito Comparado* 513 (1988)

Ventura, Convençao de arbitragem, 46 *Revista da Ordem dos Advogados* 289 (1986)

————, Convençao de arbitragem e clausulas contratuais gerais, 46 *Revista da Ordem dos Advogados* 5 (1986)

QATAR

Amin, S.H., *Middle East Legal Systems* (Glasgow 1985)

Ballantyne, Arbitration in the Gulf States: Delocalisation: A Short Comparative Study, 1 *Arab L. Q.* 205 (1986)

————, European Experience and Perception of Arbitration with Arab Countries, in *First Euro-Arab Arb. Conference: Proceedings* 160 (F. Kemicha ed. 1987)

Bernardini, Les arbitrages pétroliers et le droit appliqué par les arbitres, in *First Euro-Arab Arb. Conference: Proceedings* 282 (F. Kemicha ed. 1987)

Dilger, Schiedsgerichtsbarkeit und Volstreckung ausländischer Entscheidungen in den Golfstaaten, in *Vetragspraxis und Streiterledigung im Wirtschaftverkehr mit arabischen Staaten* 101 (K.-H. Böckstiegel ed. 1981)

El-Ahdab, A. H., *Arbitration with the Arab Countries* (Deventer 1990)

————, *L'arbitrage dans les pays arabes* (Paris 1988)

International Bar Association, *Arab Comparative & Commercial Law: The International Approach: Proceedings of the I.B.A. First Arab Regional Conference, Cairo 15-19 February 1987* (London 1987)

Krüger, Zur Vollstreckung ausländischer Entscheidungen in Qatar, 37 *RIW* 1007 (1991)

Majdalany, Settlement of Disputes through Arbitration: Qatar, in 1 *Arab Comparative & Commercial Law: The International Approach: Proceedings I.B.A. Conference 151* (1987)

Saleh, The Recognition and Enforcement of Foreign Arbitral Awards in the States of the Arab Middle East, in *Contemporary Problems in International Arbitration* 340 (J.D.M. Lew ed. 1986)

————, The Settlement of Disputes in the Arab World: Arbitration and Other Methods, 1 *Arab L. Q.* 198 (1986); reprinted in 4 *Int'l Tax & Bus. Law.* 280 (1986)

Saleh, S., *Commercial Arbitration in the Arab Middle East* (London 1984)

Sefrioui, Pratique de l'arbitrage et tendances reformatrices nouvelles, in *Euro-Arab Arbitration III* 61 (F. Kemicha ed. 1991)

Troller, Arbitration and Enforcement of Arbitration Awards in Arab Countries, 2 *Int'l Contr.* 397 (1981)

Ziadé, Selective Bibliography on Arbitration and Arab Countries, 3 *ICSID Rev. -Foreign Investment L.J.* 423 (1988)

ROMANIA

Blessing, Proper Law and Dispute Resolution Arising out of East-West Joint Ventures, in *Eastern Bloc Joint Ventures* 107 (D. Winter ed. 1990)

Capatina, Admissibilité de l'arbitrage occasionnel de commerce exterieur en droit roumain, *Revue roumain d'études internationales* 411 (No. 4, 1981)

―――――, L'arbitrage commercial international en Roumanie/International Commercial Arbitration in Romania, 1990 *Int'l Bus. L.J.* 591

―――――, Les charactéristiques de la Commission d'arbitrage pour les litiges de commerce extèrieur de Bucarest, *Annuaire de l'URSS et des pays socialistes européens* 89 (Strasbourg 1974)

―――――, Limites du droit de contrôle exercé par l'instance roumaine d'exéquatur en matière de regularité internationale des sentences arbitrales étrangères, 1973 *Revue Roumaine d'Etudes Internationales* 250 (No. 4)

―――――, Nouvelles tendances dans la réglementation des effets des sentences arbitrales étrangères, [1977] 1 *Revue Roumaine des Sciences Sociales, Série de Sciences Juridiques* 63

Capatina, O., *Litigio arbitral de comercio exterior* (Havana 1985)

Capatina & Zilberstein, La reconnaissance et l'exécution des décisions judiciares civiles et des sentences arbitrales étrangères dans le droit de la République Socialiste de Roumanie, 16 *Revue Roumaine des Sciences Sociales, Série de Sciences Juridiques* 285 (1972

Deak, Repartizarea intre parti a taxei arbitrale in litigiile solutionate de Comisia de Arbitraj de pe linga Camera de Comert si Industrie, 40 *Revista Romana de Drept* 20 (No. 3, 1984)

Filip & Capatina, Les effets des sentences arbitrales étrangères en matière de rapports de commerce extérieur, conformément au droit de la République socialiste de Roumanie, 1967 *Revue Roumaine d'Etudes Internationales* 105

Filipescu, I. & A. Dragos Sitaru, *Dreptul international privat. Spete si solutii din practica judiciara arbitrala pentru comertul exterior* (Bucharest 1986)

Grzybowski, Arbitral Tribunals for Foreign Trade in Socialist Countries, 37 *Law & Contemp. Probs.* 592 (1972)

Kleckner, Foreign Trade Arbitration in Romania, 5 *N.Y.U. J. Int'l L. & Pol.* 233 (1972)

Kos-Rabcewicz-Zubkowski, Central and East European Rules on the Form of International Arbitration Agreement, 3 *La Revue Juridique Themis* 415 (1969)

Kos-Rabcewicz-Zubkowski, L., *East European Rules on the Validity of International Arbitration Agreements* (Manchester and Dobbs Ferry, NY 1970)

Kuss, Neuere Entwicklungen und Perspektiven der Ost-West-Schiedsgerichtsbarkeit, 33 *RIW* 584 (1987)

Lebedev, International Commercial Arbitration in the Socialist Countries Members of the CMEA, 158 *Recueil des Cours* 87 (1977-V)

Lebedev, S., ed., *Handbook on Foreign Trade Arbitration in the CMEA Member Countries* (Moscow 1983)

Majoros, Exécution de décisions étrangères et procédure d'exéquatur en Europe de l'Est: Tour d'horizon avec des références de droit comparé, in *Le Juriste Suisse Face au Droit et aux Jugements Étrangères: Ouverture ou Repli?* 135 (F. Knoepfler ed. 1988)

Melis, Enforcement of Arbitral Awards in Eastern Europe, in *Contemporary Problems in International Arbitration* 332 (J.D.M. Lew ed. 1986)

Nestor, Romania: National Report, 1 *Y.B. Com. Arb.* 77 (1976)

Nestor & Capatina, Applicabilité des réglementations du droit commun roumain pour l'autorisation de l'exécution des sentences arbitrales provenant d'un autre pays socialiste membre du CAEM, [1973] 4 *Revue Roumaine d'Etudes Internationales* 246

————, Règlements bilateraux de conciliation conclus par les chambres de commerce ou des associations professionnelles, in *The Art of Arbitration* 261 (J. Schultsz & A. van den Berg eds. 1982)

————, Rumania: The Foreign Trade Arbitration Commission, in *Handbook of Institutional Arbitration in International Trade* 165 (E. Cohn, M. Domke & F. Eisemann eds. 1977)

Parker School of Foreign and Comparative Law, *International Commercial Arbitration and the Courts* (Dobbs Ferry, NY 1990)

Pechota, International Economic Arbitration in the USSR and Eastern Europe, 8 *N.Y. L. Sch. J. Int'l & Comp. L.* 377 (1987)

Pisar, S., *Coexistence & Commerce*, Chapters 20 - 24 (New York 1970)

Popescu, Romania, 15 *Y.B. Com. Arb.* 320 (1990)

————, Socialist Republic of Romania, in *Int'l Handbook Com. Arb.* (A. van den Berg gen. ed. 1984), Suppl. 10, June 1989

Popescu, T. & C. Birsan, *Dreptul comertului international.* Vol IV: *Arbitrajul comertial international* (Bucharest 1983)

Pozdnyakov, Commercial Arbitration in CMEA Member Countries, 4 *Int'l Tax & Bus. Law.* 272 (1986)

————, The Arbitration Commission of the Chamber of Commerce and Industry of the Socialist Republic of Romania, in 4A *W.A.R.* 5195 (H. Smit & V. Pechota eds. 1989)

Sitaru, Aspects nouveaux concernant la compétence de l'arbitrage commercial international dans le domaine des contrats conclus avec l'extérieur, 1981 *Analele Universitatii Bururesti: Drept* 51

————, Reglementari procedurale si de fond privind arbitrajul comercial international in acordurile bilaterale incheiate de Republica Socialista Romania, 40 *Revista Romana de Drept* 19 (August 1984)

Stalev, The Continental Case of Eastern Europe, 41 *Arbitration* 95 (1974)

Strohbach, The CMEA Countries, in *Arbitration in Settlement of International Commercial Disputes Involving the Far East and Arbitration in Combined Transportation* 133 (P. Sanders ed. 1989)

Stumpf, Ost-West-Schiedsgerichtsbarkeit: Schiedsgerichte mit Sitz in dritten Ländern, 33 *RIW* 821 (1987)

Zilberstein, Die Zwangsvollstreckung von ausländischen gerichtlichen und schiedsgerichtlichen Entscheidungen in Rumänien, 40 *Rabels Z.* 56 (1976)

RUSSIA

Abova, T.E., *Arbitrazhny i protsess v SSSR: poniatie, osnovnye printsipy* (Moscow 1985)

American Arbitration Association, *New Strategies for Peaceful Resolution of International Business Disputes* (Dobbs Ferry, NY 1971)

Barinova, I.I., *Kommentarii sudebnoi i arbitrazhnoi praktiki po morskim delam* (Moscow 1988)

Bell, Resolution of International Trade Disputes: An Analysis of the Soviet Foreign Trade Arbitration Commission's Decisions Concerning the Doctrine of Force Majeure as an Excuse to the Performance of Private International Trade Agreements, 10 *Md. J. Int'l L. & Trade* 135 (1986)

Berman, Force Majeur and the Denial of an Export License under Soviet Law: A Comment on Jordan Investments Ltd. v. Soiuznefteksport, 73 *Harv. L. Rev.* 1128 (1960)

Blessing, Proper Law and Dispute Resolution Arising out of East-West Joint Ventures, in *Eastern Bloc Joint Ventures* 107 (D. Winter ed. 1990)

Buchanan, Public Policy and International Commercial Arbitration, 26 *Am. Bus. L.J.* 511 (1988)

Butler, Soviet Maritime Arbitration, in *International Commercial and Maritime Arbitration* 37 (F.D. Rose ed. 1988)

Butler, W., *Arbitration in the Soviet Union* (Dobbs Ferry, NY 1989)

———, *Soviet Commercial Arbitration* (Dobbs Ferry and Paris 1989)

———, *Soviet Commercial and Maritime Arbitration* (Dobbs Ferry, NY 1980-)

Chew, A Procedural and Substantive Analysis of Fairness of Chinese and Soviet Foreign Trade Arbitrations, 21 *Tex. Int'l L.J.* 291 (1986)

Coulson, Soviet-American Contract Arbitration, 1983 *Y.B. Swed. & Int'l Arb.* 20

Crespi-Reghizzi & Hascher, La reconnaissance et l'exécution des jugements étrangers et des sentences arbitrales étrangères. Le nouveau droit soviétique de l'Ordonnance du 21 juin 1988, 118 *J. Droit Int'l (Clunet)* 90 (1991)

Domke, The Israeli-Soviet Oil Arbitration, 53 *Am. J. Int'l L.* 787 (1959)

Feldman, Soviet Joint Ventures: Providing for Appropriate Dispute Resolution, 23 *Cornell Int'l L.J.* 107 (1990)

Gardner, The Doctrine of Separability in Soviet Arbitration Law: An Analysis of Sojuzneftexport v. JOC Oil Co., 28 *Colum. J. Transnat'l L.* 301 (1990)

Garnefsky, Das Europäische Übereinkommen über die internationale Handelsschiedsgerichtsbarkeit und das Sowjetrecht, 9 *Osteuroparecht* 14 (1963)

Ginsburgs, Execution of Foreign Arbitration Awards: The Heritage of Domestic Legislation, Bilateral Treaties, and Intra-COMECON Ententes, in *The Impact of Perestroika on Soviet Law* 457 (A.J. Schmidt ed. 1990)

————, Execution of Foreign Commercial Awards in Post-war Soviet Bilateral Treaty Practice, 9 *Can. Y.B. Int'l L.* 59 (1971)

————, Recognition of Arbitration Agreements in Post-war Soviet Bilateral Treaty Practice, 11 *Rev. Soc. L.* 13 (1985)

————, Soviet International Trade Contracts and the Execution of Foreign Commercial Arbitral Awards, in *Contemporary Soviet Law. Essays in Honor of John N. Hazard* 195 (D. Barry, W. Butler & G. Ginsburgs eds. 1974)

Ginsburgs, G., *The Soviet Union and International Cooperation in Legal Matters.* Part I: Recognition of Arbitral Agreements and Execution of Foreign Commercial Arbitral Awards (Dordrecht 1988)

Grzybowski, Arbitral Tribunals for Foreign Trade in Socialist Countries, 37 *Law & Contemp. Probs.* 592 (1972)

Hanotiau, L'arbitrage commercial dans les relations belgo-soviétiques, 1983 *JT* 462

Hascher, Actualité de l'arbitrage international en U.R.S.S., 1988 *Rev. Arb.* 237

Heifets, Jurisdictions of Permanent USSR Arbitration Courts Distinguished, in *ICCA, Fifth Int'l Arb. Congress: Proceedings* C Izb 1-4 (1975)

Hertzfeld, Applicable Law and Dispute Settlement in Soviet Joint Ventures, 3 *ICSID Rev. - Foreign Investment L.J.* 249 (1988)

Hines, Dispute Resolution and Choice of Law in United States-Soviet Trade, 15 *Brooklyn J. Int'l L.* 591 (1989)

Hintz, Recht und Praxis der Streiterledigung im Ost-West-Handel am Beispiel des Handels zwischen der UdSSR und der Bundesrepublik Deutschland, 32 *RIW* 506 (1986)

Hobér, Arbitration in Moscow, 3 *Arb. Int'l* 119 (1987)

———, The Doctrine of Separability Under Swedish Arbitration Law, Including Comments on the Position of American and Soviet Law, 68 *Svensk Juristtidning* 257 (1983)

Hobér, K., *Joint Ventures in the Soviet Union.* Chapter XII: Dispute Resolution and Applicable Law (Dobbs Ferry, NY 1989)

Holtzmann, Dispute Resolution Procedures in East-West Trade, 13 *Int'l Law.* 233 (1979)

———, Five Ways the American Arbitration Association Can Assist in Resolving Disputes in Trade with the Soviet Union, in *IBA, Soviet Foreign Trade Reforms & East/West Arbitration* 155 (1988)

———, New Uses for Arbitration in Soviet-American Contracts for Industrial, Scientific, and Technical Development, 5 *Den. J. Int'l L. & Pol'y,* spec. issue 357 (1975)

Holtzmann & Bernini, Hypothetical Case for Use in a Comparative Study of Arbitration Practice in Various Legal Systems, in *Comparative Arbitration Practice and Public Policy in Arbitration* 19 (P. Sanders ed. 1987)

International Bar Association, *Soviet Foreign Trade Reforms & East/West Arbitration.* Papers Presented at the IBA Moscow Seminar in Conjunction with the Assciation of Soviet Lawyers, 5-7 June 1988 (Moscow 1988)

Istomin, Maritime Arbitration and Sources of International Legal Adjustment of Merchant Marine Fleet Commercial Operation Issues, in *ICCA, Fourth Int'l Arb. Congress: Proceedings* 725 (1972)

Jarvis, The Soviet Maritime Arbitration Commission: A Practitioner's Perspective, 21 *Tex. Int'l L.J.* 341 (1986)

Kabatov, Arbitration in the USSR: New Statute and Rules of the Arbitration Court at the USSR Chamber of Commerce and Industry, in *IBA, Soviet Foreign Trade Reforms & East/West Arbitration* 119 (1988). Also in 5 *Arb. Int'l* 45 (1989)

————, Kompetentsia Vneshnetorgovoi Arbitrazhnoi Kommissii, 1983 *S.G.P.* 55 (No. 2)

Kalpin, A. G., *Spory, svyazannye s torgovym moreplavaniem. Nauchno-prakticheskii komentarii arbitrazhnoi praktiki* (Moscow 1971)

Kelmann, Arbitration Under Soviet Law, in *Int'l Y.B. Civil & Com. Arb.* 145 (A. Nussbaum ed. 1928)

Keviczky, U.S.-USSR International Arbitration, 25 *Les Nouvelles* 21 (1990)

Kheifets, O pravilakh proizvodstva del v Morskoi arbitrazhnoi komissii, 1988 *Khozaistvo i Pravo* 60 (No. 3)

————, On the Changes in the Procedure of the Hearing of Cases in the Maritime Arbitration Commission at the USSR Chamber of Commerce and Industry, 1984 *Soviet Y.B. Mar. L.* 113

————, Recognition and Enforcement of Foreign Court Judgements and Arbitral Awards in Maritime Disputes, 1985 *Soviet Y.B. Mar. L.* 87

King-Smith, Communist Foreign-Trade Arbitration, 10 *Harv. Int'l L.J.* 34 (1969)

Kos-Rabcewicz-Zubkowski, Central and East European Rules on the Form of International Arbitration Agreement, 3 *La Revue Juridique Themis* 415 (1969)

Kos-Rabcewicz-Zubkowski, L., *East European Rules on the Validity of International Arbitration Agreements* (Manchester and Dobbs Ferry, NY 1970)

Kotlarchuk, Has the U.S.S.R. Foreign Trade Commission Reached the Age of Aquarius with the Newly Revised Arbitration Statute of 1975? 11 *Int'l Law.* 467 (1977)

Kudryashev & Kozhevnikov, Vneshnetorgovyi arbitrazh v stranakh-chlenakh SEV, *Vneshniaia torgovlia* 52 (No. 4, 1984)

Kuss, Neuere Entwicklungen und Perspektiven der Ost-West-Schiedsgerichtsbarkeit, 33 *RIW* 584 (1987)

Larkin, The Effect of the Commission on International Trade Arbitration in the Soviet Union, 33 *Geo. Wash. L. Rev.* 728 (1965)

Lebedev, 'Combined Transport' Disputes in Soviet Arbitration Practice, in *Arbitration in Settlement of International Commercial Disputes Involving the Far East and Arbitration in Combined Transportation* 347 (P. Sanders ed. 1989)

————, Application of Law by the Maritime Arbitration Commission in Settling Disputes, 6 *Ga. J. Int'l & Comp. L.* 519 (1976)

————, Application of Law by the Maritime Arbitration Commission in Settling Disputes, 44 *Arbitration* 18 (1977)

————, Arbitration in Soviet-American Trade Relations, 5 *Den. J. Int'l L. & Pol'y* 337 (1975)

————, Commentary on the Statute of the Maritime Arbitration Commission at the USSR Chamber of Commerce and Industry, 7 *Y.B. Com. Arb.* 249 (1982)

————, International Commercial Arbitration in the Socialist Countries Members of the CMEA, 158 *Recueil des Cours* 87 (1977-V)

————, La Commission d'arbitrage maritime près de la Chambre de commerce de l'URSS, 1971 *Rev. Arb.* 137

————, Morskoi Arbitrazh v SSSR, 1971 *Soviet Y.B. Int'l L.* 226

————, The 1977 Optional Clause for Soviet-American Contracts, 27 *Am. J. Comp. L.* 469 (1979)

————, U.S.S.R., in *Int'l Handbook Com. Arb.* (P. Sanders ed. 1984)

————, Union of Soviet Socialist Republics: The Foreign Trade Arbitration Commission of the U.S.S.R. Chamber of Commerce and Industry, in *Handbook of Institutional Arbitration in International Trade* 273 (E. Cohn, M. Domke & F. Eisemann eds. 1977)

Lebedev, S., *Mezdunarodnoe sotrudnichestvo v oblasti kommercheskogo arbitrazha* (Moscow 1980)

————, *Mezhdunarodnyi kommercheskii arbitrazh: kompetentsia arbitrov i soglashenie stran* (Moscow 1988)

————, *Mezhdunarodnyi torgovyi arbitrazh* (Moscow 1965)

————, *Morskaia Arbitrazhnaia Komissia* (Moscow 1972)

Lebedev, S., ed., *Handbook on Foreign Trade Arbitration in the CMEA Member Countries* (Moscow 1983)

Lebedev & Pozdnyakov, USSR: National Report, 1 *Y.B. Com. Arb.* 91 (1976) and 12 *Y.B. Com. Arb.* 397 (1987)

Leff, The Foreign Trade Arbitration Commission of the USSR and the West, 24 *Arb. J.* 1 (1969); also in *A.A.A., New Strategies* 143 (1971)

Lunts, Arbitrazh po sporam sovetskich khozaistvennykh organizatsii s kapitalisticheskimi predpriatiami, 1979 *S.G.P.* 50 (No. 2)

Lux, MAC in Moscow, 19 *Int'l Bus. Law.* 212 (1991)

Majoros, Exécution de décisions étrangères et procédure d'exéquatur en Europe de l'Est: Tour d'horizon avec des références de droit comparé, in *Le Juriste Suisse Face au Droit et aux Jugements Etrangers: Ouverture ou Repli?* 135 (F. Knoepfler ed. 1988)

Makowski, Disputes Concerning Lay Days (A Practical Point of View of the Maritime Arbitration Commission), 1 *Y.B. Mar. L.* 135 (1984)

Maslov, Awards of the Maritime Arbitration Commission, 6 *Ga. J. Int'l & Comp. L.* 529 (1976)

—————, Settlement of Shipping Disputes by the Maritime Arbitration Commission at the USSR Chamber of Commerce and Industry, in *IBA, Soviet Foreign Trade Reforms & East/West Arbitration* 271 (1988)

Melis, Enforcement of Arbitral Awards in Eastern Europe, in *Contemporary Problems in International Arbitration* 332 (J.D.M. Lew ed. 1986)

Minakov, K voprosu ob opredelenii prava, primenimogo k soglasheniu ob arbitrazhe (arbitrazhnoi ogovorke), 1976 *Soviet Y.B. Int'l L.* 136

—————, Practice of the Foreign Trade Arbitration Commission of the USSR Chamber of Commerce and Industry, 24 *Soviet Stat. & Dec.* 63 (No. 4, 1988)

Minakov, A.I., *Arbitrazhnye soglashenia i praktika rassmotreniya vneshneekonomicheskikh sporov* (Moscow 1985)

Morton, United States-Soviet Commercial Arbitration Under the 1972 Trade Agreement, 7 *Case W. Res. J. Int'l L.* 121 (1974)

Orban, The Challenge to the Enforcement of Socialist Arbitral Awards, 17 *Va. J. Int'l L.* 375 (1977)

Orlov, Arbitration Procedure in East-West Trade, 55 *Nordic J. Int'l L.* 310 (1986)

Osakwe, A Soviet Perspective on Foreign Sovereign Immunity: Law and Practice, 23 *Va. J. Int'l L.* 13 (1982)

————, The Soviet Position on International Commercial Arbitration as a Method of Resolving Transnational Disputes, in *Resolving Transnational Disputes Through International Arbitration* 184 (T. Carbonneau ed. 1984)

Pechota, An Outline of Recent Changes in Soviet Domestic and International Arbitration, 1 *Am. Rev. Int'l Arb.* 154 (1990)

————, International Economic Arbitration in the USSR and Eastern Europe, 8 *N.Y. L. Sch. J. Int'l & Comp. L.* 377 (1987)

————, The Court of Arbitration at the USSR Chamber of Commerce and Industry, in 4A *W.A.R.* 5439 (H. Smit & V. Pechota eds. 1989)

————, The Maritime Arbitration Commission at the USSR Chamber of Commerce and Industry, in 4A *W.A.R.* 5485 (H. Smit & V. Pechota eds. 1989)

————, UNCITRAL Rules as Applied in Arbitrations under the Optional Clause for Use in Contracts in USSR-United States Trade, 1977, in 3 *W.A.R.* 3313 (H. Smit & V. Pechota eds. 1987)

————, U.S.S.R. Creates High Arbitration Court and Arbitral Procedures, 2 *Soviet & East European Law* 6 (No. 4, 1991)

————, Union of Soviet Socialist Republics, in 2A *W.A.R.* 2625 (H. Smit & V. Pechota eds. 1987)

Pfaff, Neuerungen der internationalen Schiedsgerichtsbarkeit im Ost-West-Handel vor den ständigen Aussenhandelsschiedsgerichten der RGW-Länder, 23 *RIW* 125 (1977)

Pisar, The Communist System of Foreign Trade Adjudication, 72 *Harv. L. Rev.* 1409 (1959)

Pisar, S., *Coexistence & Commerce,* Chapters 20 - 24 (New York 1970)

Power, A Comparison of Soviet and American Maritime Arbitration, 21 *Vand. J. Transnat'l L.* 127 (1988)

Pozdnyakov, 50 let Vneshnetorgovoi arbitrazhnoi komissii, *Vneshniaya Torgovlya* 39 (No. 7, 1982)

————, Commercial Arbitration in CMEA Member Countries, 4 *Int'l Tax & Bus. Law.* 272 (1986)

————, Commercial Arbitration in Relations of Soviet FTOs with Firms of Capitalist Countries, in *USSR Contract Law* (V. Pozdnyakov ed. 1982)

————, Decree of the Presidium of the USSR Supreme Soviet, December 14, 1987 on Arbitration Court at the USSR Chamber of Commerce and Industry, Moscow, 2 *Jahrbuch Schiedsgerichtsbarkeit* 181 (1988)

————, Dispute Resolution in Commercial Contracts and Joint Ventures, in *The Moscow Conference on Law and Bilateral Economic Relations* 239 (Washington 1991)

————, The Foreign Trade Corporation as a Side in an Arbitration Dispute, in *ICCA, Fourth Int'l Arb. Congress: Proceedings* 129 (1974)

Pozdnyakov, V.S., ed., *USSR Contract Law* (Helsinki 1982)

Rabinovich, The Procedure for Signing Transactions with Soviet Foreign Trade Organizations, 22 *Int'l Law.* 143 (1988)

Ramzaitsev, Deiatel'nost' Vneshnetorgovoi Arbitrazhnoi Komissii v Moskve v 1957 godu, 1958 *Soviet Y.B. Int'l L.* 463

————, Deiatel'nost' Vneshnetorgovoi Arbitrazhnoi Komissii v Moskve v 1958 i 1959 gg., 1960 *Soviet Y.B. Int'l L.* 346

————, La jurisprudence en matière de droit international privé de la Commission arbitrale soviétique pour le commerce extérieur, 1958 *Rev. Crit. Droit Int'l Privé* 459

————, Primenenie mezhdunarodnykh obychaev v kommercheskom arbitrazhe v SSSR (The Application of International Custom in Commercial Arbitration in the Soviet Union), 1961 *Soviet Y.B. Int'l L.* 387

————, The Law Applied by Arbitral Tribunals, in *The Sources of the Law of International Trade* 138 (C. Schmitthoff ed. 1964)

Ramzaitsev, D.F., *Arbitrazh v torgovom moreplavanii* (Moscow 1960)

————, *Vneshnetorgovyi arbitrazh v SSSR* (Moscow 1952)

Razumov, Arbitration Treaties between the USSR and Countries in the Far East, in *Arbitration in Settlement of International Commercial Disputes Involving the Far East and Arbitration in Combined Transportation* 145 (P. Sanders ed. 1989)

————, Public Policy as a Condition for Recognition and Enforcement of Foreign Court Judgments and Arbitral Awards in the USSR, in *Comparative Arbitration Practice and Public Policy in Arbitration* 348 (P. Sanders ed. 1987)

Samuels, The Soviet Position on International Arbitration: A Wealth of Choices or Choices for the Wealthy, 26 *Va. J. Int'l L.* 417 (1986)

Sanders, Arbitration Clause for Optional Use in USA-USSR Trade, 3 *Y.B. Com. Arb.* 299 (1978)

Sanoff, SNE v. JOC Oil Ltd.: A Recent Development in the Theory of the Separability of the Arbitration Clause, 1 *Am. Rev. Int'l Arb.* 157 (1990)

Schmidt, L'interprétation des contrats internationaux par la Commission Arbitrale du Commerce Extérieur de l'URSS, 1985 *Int'l Bus. L.J.* 239

Semmler, The Case for FTAC Arbitration of Disputes Between Soviet Enterprises and American Firms, 14 *Colum. J. Transnat'l L.* 302 (1975)

Stalev, The Continental Case of Eastern Europe, 41 *Arbitration* 95 (1974)

Strohbach, The CMEA Countries, in *Arbitration in Settlement of International Commercial Disputes Involving the Far East and Arbitration in Combined Transportation* 133 (P. Sanders ed. 1989)

Stumpf, Ost-West-Schiedsgerichtsbarkeit: Schiedsgerichte mit Sitz in dritten Ländern, 33 *RIW* 821 (1987)

Timmermans, The New Statute on the Arbitration Court at the USSR Chamber of Commerce and Industry, 5 *J. Int'l Arb.* 97 (No. 3, 1988)

Timmermans, The USSR Maritime Arbitration Commission, 1987 *Lloyd's Mar. & Com. L.Q.* 350 and 468

Timmermans, W. A., *Carriage of Goods by Sea in the Practice of the USSR Maritime Arbitration Commision* (Dordrecht 1990)

Waehler, Internationale Schiedsgerichtsbarkeit in den Wirtschaftsbeziehungen zwischen der Bundesrepublik Deutschland und der Sowjetunion, in *Deutsches und sowjetisches Wirtschaftsrecht* (1981)

Waehler, J.P., *Die Aussenhandels- und Seeschiedsgerichtsbarkeit in der UdSSR* (Berlin 1974)

SAUDI ARABIA

Ahdab, L'arbitrage en Arabie Saoudite, 1981 *Rev. Arb.* 234

Amin, S.H., *Middle East Legal Systems* (Glasgow 1985)

Ballantyne, Arbitration in the Gulf States: Delocalisation: A Short Comparative Study, 1 *Arab L. Q.* 205 (1986)

————, European Experience and Perception of Arbitration with Arab Countries, in *First Euro-Arab Arb. Conference: Proceedings* 160 (F. Kemicha ed. 1987)

Bernardini, Les arbitrages pétroliers et le droit appliqué par les arbitres, in *First Euro-Arab Arb. Conference: Proceedings* 282 (F. Kemicha ed. 1987)

Bernini, Recent Legislations and International Unification of the Law on Arbitration, in *First International Commercial Arbitration Conference: Proceedings* 315 (N. Antaki & A. Prujiner eds. 1986)

Blumereau, L'adhésion de l'Arabie Saoudite à la Convention CIRDI: ouverture à l'arbitrage international, 7 *Droit et Pratique du Com. Int'l* 726 (1981)

Boshoff, Saudi Arabia: Arbitration vs Litigation, 1 *Arab L. Q.* 299 (1986)

Dilger, Arbitration, Enforcement of Foreign Judgments and Arbitration Awards, Clauses on the Choice of Law, and Agreements on Jurisdiction of the Court in Egypt, Saudi Arabia and the Gulf States, in *International Bar Association: Proceedings of the Seminar on Middle East Law* 35 (1981)

El-Ahbar, L'arbitrage en Arabie saoudite sous le régime de la nouvelle loi de 1983 et de son décret d'application de 1985, 1986 *Rev. Arb.* 541

————, Arbitration in Saudi Arabia under the New Arbitration Act, 1983 and Its Implementation Rules of 1985 — Part One, 3 *J.Int'l Arb.* 27 (No. 3, 1986) and 3 *J. Int'l Arb.* 23 (No. 4, 1986)

El-Ahdab, A. H., *Arbitration with the Arab Countries* (Deventer 1990)

————, *L'arbitrage dans les pays arabes* (Paris 1988)

El-Hakim, Litiges commerciaux multilatéraux dans le cadre des projets en Moyen-Orient, 1981 *Rev. Arb.* 86

Hejailan, Saudi Arabia: National Report, 4 *Y.B. Com. Arb.* 162 (1979)

Hoshan, The Arab Gulf Countries, in *First Euro-Arab Arb. Conference: Proceedings* 22 (F. Kemicha ed. 1987)

International Bar Association, *Arab Comparative & Commercial Law: The International Approach: Proceedings of the I.B.A. First Arab Regional Conference, Cairo 15-19 February 1987* (London 1987)

Jalili, Arbitration in Saudi Arabia, 50 *Arbitration* 163 (Nov. 1984)

Kassis, Particularités et problèmes de l'arbitrage dans les droits des pays arabes, 63 *Rev. Droit Int'l & Droit Comp.* 7 (1986)

Klingmüller, Zu den Grundlagen von Schiedsgeichtsvereinbarungen in Saudisch-Arabien, in *Vertragspraxis und Streiterledigung im Wirtschaftsverkehr mit arabischen Staaten* 5 (K.-H. Böckstiegel ed. 1981)

Krüger, Probleme des saudi-arabischen internationalen Vertrags- und Schiedsrecht, in *Vertragspraxis und Streiterledigung im Wirtschaftsverkehr mit arabischen Staaten* 61 (K.-H. Böckstiegel ed. 1981)

Lerrick, A. & Q.J. Mian, *Saudi Arabia Business and Labour Law: Its Interpretation and Application*, Chapter 3 - Arbitration (2nd ed., London 1987)

Lew, The Recognition and Enforcement of Arbitration Agreements and Awards in the Middle East, 1 *Arb. Int'l* 161 (1985)

Moore & Lott, Arbitration under the Saudi Legal System, 4 *Middle E. Exec. Rep.* 11 (No. 2, 1981)

Nader, Settlement of Disputes through Arbitration: The Kingdom of Saudi Arabia, in 1 *Arab Comparative & Commercial Law: The International Approach: Proceedings I.B.A Conference* 145 (1987)

Nerz, Abfassen von Schiedsklauseln in Verträgen mit saudiarabischen Parteien, 33 *RIW* 23 (1987)

⸺, Die Schiedsfähigkeit von Rechtsstreitigkeiten zwischen einem Agenten und seinem Prinzipal in Saudi-Arabien, 31 *RIW* 465 (1985)

⸺, Saudi Arabian qadi-Gerichtsbarkeit und The Commission for the Settlement of Commercial Disputes, 30 *RIW* 33 (1984)

⸺, The Structuring of an Arbitration Clause in a Contract with a Saudi Party, 1 *Arab L. Q.* 380 (1986)

————, Vollstreckbarkeit ausländischer Schiedssprüche im Königreich Saudi-Arabien, 29 *RIW* 811 (1983)

Note, Saudi Arabia: Arbitration Rules Introduced, *Int'l Fin. L. Rev.* 42 (Nov. 1985)

O'Neill, Recent Developments in International Commercial Arbitration: an American Perspective, 4 *J. Int'l Arb.* 7 (No. 1, 1987); also in 53 *Arbitration* 177 (1987)

Saleh, The Recognition and Enforcement of Foreign Arbitral Awards in the States of the Arab Middle East, in *Contemporary Problems in International Arbitration* 340 (J.D.M. Lew ed. 1986)

————, The Settlement of Disputes in the Arab World: Arbitration and Other Methods, 1 *Arab L. Q.* 198 (1986); reprinted in 4 *Int'l Tax & Bus. Law.* 280 (1986)

Saleh, S., *Commercial Arbitration in the Arab Middle East* (London 1984)

Sayen, Arbitration, Conciliation and the Islamic Legal Tradition in Saudi Arabia, 9 *U. Pa. J. Int'l Bus. L.* 211 (1987)

Schütze, Anerkennung und Vollstreckbarerklärung von Zivilurteilen und Schiedssprüchen im deutsch-saudiarabischen Verhältnis, 30 *RIW* 261 (1984)

Stumpf, Schiedsgerichtsbarkeit in arabischen Ländern, 1 *Jahrbuch Schiedsgerichtsbarkeit* 102 (1987)

Troller, Arbitration and Enforcement of Arbitration Awards in Arab Countries, 2 *Int'l Contr.* 397 (1981)

Turck, Arbitration in Saudi Arabia, 6 *Arb. Int'l* 281 (1990)

————, Dispute Resolution in Saudi Arabia, 22 *Int'l Law.* 415 (1988)

van den Berg, Saudi Arabia, in *Int'l Handbook Com. Arb.* (P. Sanders ed. 1984)

————, Saudi Arabia: National Report, 9 *Y.B. Com. Arb.* 7 (1984)

Ziadé, Selective Bibliography on Arbitration and Arab Countries, 3 *ICSID Rev. -Foreign Investment L.J.* 423 (1988)

SENEGAL

Gaillard, The Enforcement of ICSID Awards in France: The Decision of the Paris Court of Appeal in the SOABI Case, 5 *ICSID Rev. - Foreign Investment L.J.* 69 (1990)

SINGAPORE

Bellhouse, Singapore: International Arbitration Center Established, 3 *Asia Law & Practice* 31 (No. 9, 1991)

Karthigesu, The Settlement of Commercial Disputes in Singapore, 1981 *Malayan L.J.* xi

Kimbrough, Singapore, in *Int'l Handbook Com. Arb.* (A. van den Berg gen. ed. 1984), Suppl. 7, April 1987

―――, Singapore: National Report, 11 *Y.B. Com. Arb.* 29 (1986)

―――, Viabilité générale de l'arbitrage a Singapour: l'accession a la Convention de New York comble la dernière lacune, 1986 *Int'l Bus. L.J.* 783

Lowenfeld, Singapore and the Local Bar: Aberration or Ill Omen?, 5 *J. Int'l Arb.* 71 (No. 3, 1988)

McClelland, A Survey of Pacific Rim Commercial Arbitration, 40 *Arb. J.* 3 (No. 1, 1985)

Mooney, Representation in Arbitrations in Malaysia and Singapore, 1989 *Malayan L.J.* cvii

Ng, Singapore, in *Interim Court Remedies in Support of Arbitration* 89 (D. Shenton & W. Kühn eds. 1987)

Pacific Rim Advisory Council, *Pacific Rim: Commercial Arbitration Procedures* (San Diego, CA 1985)

Polkinghorne, The Right of Representation in a Foreign Venue, 4 *Arb. Int'l* 333 (1988)

Ricafrente, Commercial Arbitration in ASEAN Countries, in *Commercial Arbitration* 39 (J. Ricalde ed. 1983)

Simmonds, K., B. Hill & S. Jarvin, eds., *Commercial Arbitration Law in Asia and the Pacific* (Paris & Dobbs Ferry, NY 1987)

Sornarajah, The Enforcement of Foreign Arbitral Awards in Singapore, *Malayan L.J.* lxxxvi

Sornarajah, M., *International Commercial Arbitration: The Problem of State Contracts* (Singapore 1990)

SOUTH AFRICA

Cowen, Expropriation and the Arbitration Process, 35 *Comp. & Int'l L. J. Southern Afr.* 146 (1972)

Forsyth, Enforcement of Arbitral Awards, Choice of Law in Contract, Characterization and a New Attitude to Private International Law, 104 *South Afr. L.J.* 4 (1987)

International Chamber of Commerce, Union of South Africa/Union Sud Africaine, in *Commercial Arbitration and the Law/L'Arbitrage commercial et la Loi* (Basel 1949)

Jacobs, South Africa, in *Int'l Handbook Com. Arb.* (A. van den Berg gen. ed. 1984), Suppl. 1, May 1984

————, South Africa: National Report II, 9 *Y.B. Com. Arb.* 50 (1984)

Jacobs, M.S., *The Law of Arbitration in South Africa* (Capetown 1977)

Parker School of Foreign and Comparative Law, *International Commercial Arbitration and the Courts* (Dobbs Ferry, NY 1990)

Rouse, Arbitration in South Africa, 48 *Arbitration* 314 (1983)

Schaeffer, South Africa: National Report I, 2 *Y.B. Com. Arb.* 76 (1977)

van Niekerk, Aspects of Proper Law, Curial Law and International Commercial Arbitration, 2 *SA Mercantile L.J.* 117 (1990)

Williams, Attachments and Other Interim Court Remedies in Support of Arbitration: South Africa, in *Interim Court Remedies in Support of Arbitration* 281 (D. Shenton & W. Kühn eds. 1987)

SPAIN

Alcántara Gonzales, Enforcement of Awards, in 2 *Fifth Int'l Congress of Maritime Arbitrators* (New York 1981)

Alvarez Gonzalez, Arbitraje y derecho aplicable (Anotaciones al Título X de la Ley 36/1988 de Arbitraje), 5 *Rev. Corte Esp. Arb.* 171 (1988-89)

Alvarez Rodriguez, Formación, contenido y efectos del laudo arbitral en la Ley española de Arbitraje, 5 *Rev. Corte Esp. Arb.* 95 (1988-89)

Angell, Spain's Attitude to Arbitration, *Int'l Fin. L. Rev.* 23 (June 1984)

Armenta Deu, Perspectivas de futuro de la cláusula compromisoria arbitral, 2 *Revista Juridica de Cataluña* 49 (1984)

Arroyo, Recognition and Enforcement of Foreign Arbitral Awards in Spanish Law, 6 *Bus. L.J.* 763 (1985)

Arroyo Martinez, I., *Legislación arbitral* (Madrid 1989)

Barona Vilar, El recurso de anulación del laudo arbitral, 5 *Rev. Corte Esp. Arb.* 111 (1988-89)

Barrios de Angelis, Naturaleza juridica del arbitraje privado. Su proyección en la practica, 1 *Rev. Corte Esp. Arb.* 53 (1984)

Briguglio, La disciplina spagnola dell'arbitrato e le recenti modifiche introdotte dalla Ley del 6 agosto 1984 — qualche riflessione comparatistica, 25 *Rassegna dell'Arb.* 259 (1985)

Bühring-Uhle, Das neue spanische Schiedsgerichtsbarkeit-Gesetz, *88 Zeitschrift für vergleichende Rechtswissenschaft* 287 (1989)

Calvo Caracava, A.-L. & L. Fernandez de la Gándara, *El arbitraje comercial internacional* (Madrid 1989)

Chillón Medina & Merino Merchán, International Arbitration of Transfer of Technology Contracts in Spanish Law, in *ICCA, Sixth Int'l Arb. Congress: Proceedings* 339 (1978)

————, The Arbitration Object in Spanish Law, in *ICCA, Sixth Int'l Arb. Congress: Proceedings* 249 (1978)

Chillón Medina, J. M. & J. F. Merino Merchán, *Tratado de arbitraje privado interno e internacional* (Madrid 1978)

Cobos, L'arbitrage en Espagne et le Règlement du Centre espagnol d'arbitrage, 1980 *Rev. Arb.* 64

Cremades, Arbitration in Spain, in *Arbitration in Settlement of International Commercial Disputes Involving the Far East and Arbitration in Combined Transportation* 255 (P. Sanders ed. 1989)

————, Attachments and Other Interim Court Remedies in Support of Arbitration: The Spanish Courts, in *Interim Court Remedies in Support of Arbitration* 215 (D. Shenton & W. Kühn eds. 1987)

————, España estrena nueva Ley de arbitraje, 5 *Rev. Corte Esp. Arb.* 9 (1988-89)

————, Evolution récente du droit espagnol en matière d'arbitrage, 1988 *Rev. Arb.* 223

————, Immunity of Arbitrators under Spanish Law, in *The Immunity of Arbitrators* 71 (J.D.M. Lew ed. 1990)

————, Handelsschiedsgerichtsbarkeit in Spanien, 2 *Jahrbuch Schiedsgerichtsbarkeit* 28 (1988)

————, L'arbitrage dans les contrats internationaux de transfert de technologie passés par les entreprises espagnoles, 1972 *Rev. Arb.* 72

————, L'Espagne étrenne une nouvelle loi sur l'arbitrage, 1989 *Rev. Arb.* 189

————, La reconnaissance en Espagne des decisions judiciaires et des actes authentiques français, 1975 *Rev. Crit. Droit Int'l Privé* 355 and 595

————, Le caractère prejudiciel de la procédure pénal et la procédure d'arbitrage, in *Festschrift für Arthur Bülow* 25 (K.-H. Böckstiegel & O. Glossner eds. 1981)

————, Les effets de la clause d'arbitrage dans la jurisprudence espagnole récente, in *The Art of Arbitration* 83 (J. Schultsz & A. van den Berg eds. 1982)

————, Spain, in *Int'l Handbook Com. Arb.* (A. van den Berg gen. ed. 1984), Suppl. 6, Nov. 1986

————, Spain, 12 *Y.B. Com. Arb.* 39 (1987); 15 *Y.B.* 325 (1990)

————, The Enforcement of British Arbitral Awards in Spain, 45 *Arbitration* 30 and 97 (1979)

————, The New Spanish Law of Arbitration, 6 *J. Int'l Arb.* 35 (No. 2, 1989)

Cremades, B. M., *Arbitraje Comercial Internacional* (2nd ed. 1984)

————, *Arbitration in Spain* (London/Madrid/Cologne 1991)

————, *Estudios sobre arbitraje* (Madrid 1977)

————, *Panorámica Española del Arbitraje Comercial Internacional* (Madrid 1975)

Cremades, B. M. & E. G. Cabiedes, *Litigating in Spain. Considerations for Foreign Practitioners, including International Judicial Assistance, Enforcement of Foreign Judgments, Bankruptcy, Arbitration and Other Civil Proceedings in Spain* (Deventer 1989)

Dunshee de Abranches, C.A., ed., *El arbitraje comercial en Iberoamérica* (Madrid 1982)

Eckstrom, L., *Licensing in Foreign and Domestic Operations.* Volume I, Chapter 7: Arbitration (by Steven Z. Szczepanski), (New York 1972, updated 1987)

Esplugues Mota, Reflexiones en torno a una frustración: El Título IX de la nueva Ley española de Arbitraje relativo a la ejecución en España de los laudos arbitrales extranjeros, 5 *Rev. Corte Esp. Arb.* 143 (1988-89)

Estudios sobre arbitraje comercial internacional, Madrid (1978)

Fernández Rozas, El largo camino hacia la Ley 36/1988 de Arbitraje, 5 *Rev. Corte Esp. Arb.* 29 (1988-89)

Fernández Rozas, La situación del arbitraje comercial en España, 3 *Rev. Corte Esp. Arb.* 29 (1986)

Fernández Rozas, J., *Legislación sobre Arbitraje Interno e Internacional* (Madrid 1990)

Fröhlingsdorf, Das neue spanische Gesetz über Schiedsgerichtsbarkeit, 35 *RIW* 686 (1989)

García de Enterría, The Role of Public Policy in International Commercial Arbitration, 21 *L. & Pol'y Int'l Bus.* 389 (1990)

García Rubio, El Convenio arbitral en la Ley de Arbitraje de 5 de diciembre de 1988, 5 *Rev. Corte Esp. Arb.* 71 (1988-89)

Garro, Spain, in 2A *W.A.R.* 2405 (H. Smit & V. Pechota eds. 1987)

————, The UNCITRAL Model Law and the 1988 Spanish Arbitration Act: Models for Reform in Central America, 1 *Am. Rev. Int'l Arb.* 201 (1990)

————, The UNCITRAL Model Law and the 1988 Spanish Arbitration Act: Models for Reform in Central America, in *Commercial and Labor Arbitration in Central America* 23 (A. Garro ed. 1991)

Goni, La nouvelle politique d'exécution des sentences arbitrales étrangères en Espagne, 35 *Droit Mar. Français* 55 (1983)

Gonzales Soria, Ventajas del arbitraje para resolver los litigios de caracter comercial, in *El Arbitraje en el Derecho Latinoamericano y Español* 315 (L. Peret & U. Montoya Alberti eds. 1989)

Gonzales Soria, J., *La intervención judicial en el arbitraje. Recursos jurisdiccionales y ejecución judicial del laudo arbitral* (Madrid 1988)

Gonzalez Campos, El Convenio entre España y Francia de 28 de mayo de 1969 sobre reconocimiento y ejecución de decisiones extranjeras, in 2 *Estudios de Derecho internacional publico y privado. Homenaje al Profesor Sela* 993 (1970)

————, Sobre el convenio de arbitraje en el derecho internacional privado español, 2 *Anuario Der. Int'l* 13 (1975)

Guasp, J., *El arbitraje en el derecho español* (Barcelona 1956)

Hamilton, 1988 Law Makes Spain Well-Positioned to Be Commercial Arbitration Center, 1 *World Arb. & Med. Rep.* 163 (1990)

International Chamber of Commerce, *Arbitration Law in Europe* (Paris 1981)

————, Spain/Espagne, in *Commercial Arbitration and the Law/L'Arbitrage commercial et la Loi* (Basel 1964)

Klein, F.-E., *Considérations sur l'arbitrage en droit international privé* (Basel 1955)

Legras de Grandcourt, Evolution contemporaine des législations européennes, in *Euro-Arab Arbitration III* 119 (F. Kemicha ed. 1991)

Löber, Spanischer Schiedsgerichtshof errichtet: Corte Española de Arbitraje, 4 *IPRax* 112 (1984)

Lois Caballe, Comentarios a la Ley 36/1988, de 5 de diciembre, de Arbitraje, 46 *Revista General de Derecho* 7789 (1989)

Lopez Anton, Spain and Commercial Arbitration, 20 *U. Miami Inter-Am. L. Rev.* 697 (1989)

————, Spain and Commercial Arbitration, in *Commercial and Labor Arbitration in Central America* 113 (A. Garro ed. 1991)

MacLaren, Commercial Arbitration in the United States and Overseas, in *Arbitration and the Licensing Process* 5 (R. Goldscheider & M. de Haas eds. 1984-)

Marin Lopez, La Ley aplicable al convenio arbitral, 5 *Rev. Corte Esp. Arb.* 191 (1988-89)

Menchaca, Reflexiones sobre el arbitraje commercial internacional, in 2 *Estudios de derecho internacional: Homenaje al Profesor Miaja de la Muela* 995 (Madrid 1979)

Meneu, La legislación y la práctica española del arbitraje mercantil, in *ICCA, Third Int'l Arb. Congress: Proceedings* 501 (1969)

Merino Merchán, La exepción de sumisión de la cuestión litigiosa a arbitraje, 5 *Rev. Corte Esp. Arb.* 235 (1988-89)

Note, Enforcing Foreign Judgments and Arbitration Awards, 5 *Int'l Fin. L. Rev. 26* (No. 7, 1986)

Parker School of Foreign and Comparative Law, *International Commercial Arbitration and the Courts* (Dobbs Ferry, NY 1990)

Pechota, Spanish Court of Arbitration, in 4A *W.A.R.* 5275 (H. Smit & V. Pechota eds. 1989)

Perez Bevia, Sobre la ley aplicable por el árbitro al fondo de la controversia en el derecho internacional privado español, 5 *Rev. Corte Esp. Arb.* 213 (1988-89)

Plehn, International Arbitration in Spain: A New Institution versus an Old Law, 20 *Int'l Law.* 247 (1986)

Ramos Mendez, First Applications by the Spanish Supreme Court of the New York Convention of June 10, 1958 to the Exequatur of Foreign Arbitral Awards, 10 *Int'l Trade L. & Prac.* 95 (1984)

————, La nuova disciplina dell'arbitrato in Spagna, 44 *Riv. Trim. Dir. & Proc. Civ.* 241 (1990)

————, Les clauses d'arbitrage international et leur validité selon le droit espagnol, 1982 *Rev. Arb.* 147

Ramos Mendez, The Relationship between Civil and Criminal Actions and Arbitration Agreements in Maritime Disaster Cases under Spanish Law, 2 *Y.B. Mar. L.* 125 (1985-1986)

————, Vereinbarkeit eines Schiedsverfahrens nach der VglSchO der IHK mit einem Schiedsverfahren nach dem spanischen Gesetz von 1953, in *Festschrift für Walther J. Habscheid* 239 (W. Lindacher, D. Pfaff et al. eds. 1989)

Ramos Mendez, F., *Arbitraje y Proceso Internacional* (Barcelona 1987)

Remiro Brotons, A., *Ejecución de sentencias arbitrales extranjeras. Los convenios internacionales y su aplicación en España* (Madrid 1980)

Requejo Pages, La nueva configuración del Arbitraje en España (consideraciones en torno al Titulo I de la Ley 36/1988 de 5 de diciembre), 5 *Rev. Corte Esp. Arb.* 51 (1988-89)

Revoredo de Debakey, La selección de las leyes aplicables a la validez del acuerdo arbitral y al fondo de la controversia en el arbitraje comercial international, 7 *Anuario Hispano-Luso-Americano de Derecho Internacional* 329 (1984)

Roca Aymar, La Corte Española de Arbitraje y el comercio exterior, 1 *Rev. Corte Esp. Arb.* 265 (1984)

Ruiloba Santana, El Convenio hispano-francés de 28 de mayo de 1969 sobre reconocimiento y ejecución de sentencias extranjeras y actas autenticas en materia civil y mercantil, 23 *Rev. Esp. Der. Int'l* 42 (1970)

Ruiz, Spain: New Arbitration Law, 55 *Arbitration* 281 (1989)

Verdera y Tuells, International Commercial Arbitration and the Spanish Court of Arbitration, 3 *J. Int'l Arb.* 47 (No. 1, 1986)

Vulliemin, J.-M., *Jugement et sentence arbitrale* (2nd ed. Zurich 1990)

SRI LANKA

American Arbitration Association, *New Strategies for Peaceful Resolution of International Business Disputes* (Dobbs Ferry, NY 1971)

Cooray, International Commercial Arbitration— Facilities and Impediments in Sri Lanka, in *9th Lawasia Conference* (New Delhi, Oct. 7-12, 1985): *Working Papers* at 272

Gomez, International Arbitration: A Case for Delocalization, 3 *Sri Lanka J. Int'l L.* 61 (1991)

Simmonds, K., B. Hill & S. Jarvin, eds., *Commercial Arbitration Law in Asia and the Pacific* (Paris & Dobbs Ferry, NY 1987)

Weeraratna, The Enforcement of Arbitral Awards in Sri Lanka, [1988] 2 *Bar Association Law Journal* 4

Wickremesinghe, K.D.P., *Civil Procedure in Ceylon* (Ch. 24 - Reference to Arbitration), (Colombo 1971)

SUDAN

El-Ahdab, A. H., *Arbitration with the Arab Countries* (Deventer 1990)

————, L'arbitrage dans les pays arabes (Paris 1988)

Troller, Arbitration and Enforcement of Arbitration Awards in Arab Countries, 2 *Int'l Contr.* 397 (1981)

Ziadé, Selective Bibliography on Arbitration and Arab Countries, 3 *ICSID Rev. -Foreign Investment L.J.* 423 (1988)

SWEDEN

Aden, M., *Internationale Handelsschiedsgerichtsbarkeit. Kommentar zu den Verfahrensordnungen* (Heidelberg 1988)

Alley, International Arbitration: The Alternative of the Stockholm Chamber of Commerce, 22 *Int'l Law.* 837 (1988)

Arbitration Institute of the Stockholm Chamber of Commerce, *Arbitration in Sweden* (2nd rev. ed. 1984)

Bagner, Attachments and Other Interim Court Remedies in Support of Arbitration in Sweden, 1985 *Y.B. Swed. & Int'l Arb.* 24

———, Attachments and Other Interim Court Remedies in Support of Arbitration: Sweden, in *Interim Court Remedies in Support of Arbitration* 143 (D. Shenton & W. Kühn eds. 1987)

Bagner & Franke, International Commercial Arbitration in Sweden, 82 *L. Soc'y Gazette* 3274 (1985)

Barclay, The Arbitration Award, 45 *Arbitration* 118 (1979)

Berger, Die Regelung der gerichtlichen Anfechtbarkeit internationaler Schiedssprüche in europäischen Schiedsgerichtsgesetzen, 35 *RIW* 850 (1989)

———, The Modern Trend Towards Exclusion of Recourse Against Transnational Arbitral Awards: A European Perspective, 12 *Fordham Int'l L. J.* 605 (1989)

Bernini, Recent Legislations and International Unification of the Law on Arbitration, in *First International Commercial Arbitration Conference: Proceedings* 315 (N. Antaki & A. Prujiner eds. 1986)

Billings, International Standards for Automotive Arbitration, 28 *German Y.B. Int'l L.* 425 (1985)

Blegvad, B.-M., P. Bolding & O. Lando, *Arbitration as a Means of Solving Conflicts* (Copenhagen 1973)

Bogdan, Some Arbitration-Related Problems of Swedish Private International Law, 1990 *Y.B. Swed. & Int'l Arb.* 70

Carabiber, L'immunité de juridiction et d'exécution des Etats collectivités et établissements publics au regard de l'obligation assumée par une clause compromissoire insérée dans les contrats internationaux de droit privé, in *Liber Amicorum for Martin Domke* 23 (P. Sanders ed. 1967)

Chiu, Consolidation of Arbitral Proceedings and International Commercial Arbitration, 7 *J. Int'l Arb.* 53 (No. 2, 1990)

Eckstrom, L., *Licensing in Foreign and Domestic Operations.* Volume I, Chapter 7: Arbitration (by Steven Z. Szczepanski), (New York 1972, updated 1987)

Franke, The Arbitration Institute of the Stockholm Chamber of Commerce, 1982 *Y.B. Swed. & Int'l Arb.* 6

————, The Arbitration Institute of the Stockholm Chamber of Commerce, 1990 *Y.B. Swed. & Int'l Arb.* 14

————, International Arbitration in Sweden, 2 *Int'l Const. L. Rev.* 159 (1985)

————, International Arbitration in Sweden, 76 *Am. Soc. Int'l L. Proc.* 166 (1982)

————, SCC Arbitration Goes Further International, 3 *Int'l Arb. Rep.* 22 (No. 3, 1988)

————, Special Features of Arbitration in Stockholm, 49 *Arbitration* 99 (Aug. 1983)

Gomez, International Arbitration: A Case for Delocalization, 3 *Sri Lanka J. Int'l L.* 61 (1991)

Gothberg, Coercive Measures for Obtaining Production of Documentary Evidence in Arbitration Proceedings, 8 *Int'l Arb. Gazette* 361 (1986)

Hagberg, Evidence in Swedish Arbitral Procedure, 1982 *Y.B. Swed. & Int'l Arb.* 29

————, Salient Features of the Swedish Arbitral Procedure, 1990 *Y.B. Swed. & Int'l Arb.* 34

Heuman, Transplanting Arbitral Processes into Civil Procedure — A Swedish Perspective, 7 *Civil Just. Q.* 156 (1988)

Heuman, L., *Current Issues in Swedish Arbitration* (Deventer and Stockholm 1990)

Hjerner, Awarding Interest in Swedish Arbitration, 1985 *Y.B. Swed. & Int'l Arb.* 29

————, Choice of Law Problems in International Arbitration with Particular Reference to Arbitration in Sweden, 1982 *Y.B. Swed. & Int'l Arb.* 18

————, The Immunity of Arbitrators under Swedish Law, in *The Immunity of Arbitrators* 81 (J.D.M. Lew ed. 1990)

————, On Partial Awards, Orders and Other Decisions in Arbitral Proceedings, in Particular with Respect to Arbitration in Sweden, 1984 *Y.B. Swed. & Int'l Arb.* 31

————, Recourse to Law Courts in International Arbitration in Sweden, in *ICC, Hommage à Fréderic Eisemann* 61 (1978)

————, Sweden: The Stockholm Arbitration Institute, in *Handbook of Institutional Arbitration* 187 (E. Cohn, M. Domke & F. Eisemann eds. 1977)

Hobér, Arbitration and the Swedish Courts, 1990 *Y.B. Swed. & Int'l Arb.* 53

————, Das anzuwendende Recht beim internationalen Schiedsverfahren in Schweden, 32 *RIW* 685 (1986)

————, The Doctrine of Separability Under Swedish Arbitration Law, Including Comments on the Position of American and Soviet Law, 68 *Svensk Juristtidning* 257 (1983)

————, Finality of Swedish Awards: the Nordic Saga in the Laczay Estate v. AGAAB, 2 *Arb. Int'l* 77 (1986)

————, Judicial Review in International Arbitration: The Swedish Supreme Court Decision in the Uganda Case, 1 *Am. Rev. Int'l Arb.* 596 (1990)

————, Party Substitution Under Swedish Arbitration Law, 1983 *Y.B. Swed. & Int'l Arb.* 43

————, Schiedsort Stockholm: Verjährung und das anzuwendende Recht, 2 *Jahrbuch Schiedsgerichtsbarkeit* 80 (1988)

Holmback, Commercial Arbitration in Sweden, 6 *Int'l Trade L. & Prac.* 491 (1980)

Holmbäck & Mangård, Sweden, in *Int'l Handbook Com. Arb.* (A. van den Berg gen. ed. 1984), Suppl. 10, June 1989

781

————, Sweden, 3 *Y.B. Com. Arb.* 161 (1978); 7 *Y.B.* 68 (1982); 11 Y.B. 91 (1986); 15 *Y.B.* 326 (1990) (by U. Holmbäck)

International Chamber of Commerce, *Arbitration Law in Europe* (Paris 1981)

————, Sweden/Suede, in *Commercial Arbitration and the Law/ L'Arbitrage commercial et la Loi* (Basel 1949)

Jacobi, New Aspects of Arbitration Legislation in Scandinavia, in *ICCA, Third Int'l Arb. Congress: Proceedings* 475 (1969)

Klein, F.-E., *Considérations sur l'arbitrage en droit international privé* (Basel 1955)

Kolkey, Attacking Arbitral Awards: Rights of Appeal and Review in International Arbitrations, 22 *Int'l Law.* 693 (1988)

Lee, E., *Encyclopedia of International Commercial Arbitration* (London 1986)

MacLaren, Commercial Arbitration in the United States and Overseas, in *Arbitration and the Licensing Process* 5 (R. Goldscheider & M. de Haas eds. 1984-)

Nilsson, Problems of Sovereign Immunity under the Swedish Law of Arbitration, 1982 *Y.B. Swed. & Int'l Arb.* 41

————, Arbitration and Anti-trust — Enforcing Treble Damages from a Swedish Point of View, 1987 *J. Bus. L.* 227

Nordenson, The Arbitral Proceedings in International Arbitration in Sweden, 1984 *Y.B. Swed. & Int'l Arb.* 6

————, The Arbitral Tribunal, 1990 *Y.B. Swed. & Int'l Arb.* 19

Norwegian Group of the International Bar Association, *International Commercial Arbitration in Action: Papers from a Conference in Oslo in 1982* (Oslo 1983)

Paulsson, Arbitrage international et voies de recours: La Cour suprême de Suède dans le sillage des solutions belge et helvétique, 117 *J. Droit Int'l (Clunet)* 588 (1990)

————, Arbitre et juge en Suède: exposé générale et réflexions sur la délocalisation des sentences arbitrales, 1980 *Rev. Arb.* 441

————, Rights of Recourse in Sweden, 5 *Arb. Int'l* 291 (1989)

————, The Role of Swedish Court in Transnational Commercial Arbitration, 21 *Va. J. Int'l L.* 211 (1981)

Pechota, UNCITRAL Rules as Applied in Arbitrations under the Optional Clause for Use in Contracts in USSR-United States Trade, 1977, in 3 *W.A.R.* 3313 (H. Smit & V. Pechota eds. 1987)

Riedberg, P., *Der amiable Compositeur im internationalen privaten Schiedsgerichtsverfahren* (Frankfurt 1962)

Samuel, A., *Jurisdictional Problems in International Commercial Arbitration: A Study of Belgian, Dutch, English, French, Swedish, Swiss, U.S. and West German Law* (Zurich 1989)

Schlosser, Party-Appointed Arbitrators and Multiple Defendants Having Conflicting Interests, in *Law in East and West/Recht in Ost und West* 739 (Tokyo 1988)

Shifman, Sweden, in 2A *W.A.R.* 2471 (H. Smit & V. Pechota eds. 1987)

Tupman, Staying Enforcement of Arbitral Awards under the New York Convention, 3 *Arb. Int'l* 223 (1987)

Westerling, Publishing of Arbitral Awards, 1983 *Y.B. Swed. & Int'l Arb.* 59

————, Void and Challengeable Awards in Swedish Arbitral Procedure, 1984 *Y.B. Swed. & Int'l Arb.* 45

Wetter, Choice of Law in International Arbitration Proceedings in Sweden, 2 *Arb. Int'l* 294 (1986)

————, Choice of Law in International Arbitration Proceedings in Sweden, 1984 *Y.B. Swed. & Int'l Arb.* 16

————, Institutional Arbitration in Sweden: A Guide to the 1988 Rules of the Arbitration Institute of the Stockholm Chamber of Commerce, 43 *Arb. J.* 5 (No. 2, 1988)

————, Salient Features of Swedish Arbitration Clauses, 1983 *Y.B. Swed. & Int'l Arb.* 33

————, Sweden as the Location of International Arbitration Proceedings, in *Private Investors Abroad: Problems and Solutions in International Business* 223 (New York 1977)

Wetter & Shifman, The Arbitration Institute of the Stockholm Chamber of Commerce, in 4A *W.A.R.* 5339 (H. Smit & V. Pechota eds. 1989)

SWITZERLAND

Bachmann, Switzerland: The Court of Arbitration of the Zurich Chamber of Commerce, in *Handbook of Institutional Arbitration in International Trade* 203 (E. Cohn, M. Domke & F. Eisemann eds. 1977)

Baum, Arbitration and Court Intervention: Recent Swiss, U.S. Examples, 1 *Int'l Arb. Rep.* 449 (1986)

Baumgartner, P., *Die Kosten des Schiedsgerichtsprozesses* (Zurich 1982)

Berger, Die Regelung der gerichtlichen Anfechtbarkeit internationaler Schiedssprüche in europäischen Schiedsgerichtsgesetzen, 35 *RIW* 850 (1989)

————, The Modern Trend Towards Exclusion of Recourse Against Transnational Arbitral Awards: A European Perspective, 12 *Fordham Int'l L. J.* 605 (1989)

Bernini, Recent Legislations and International Unification of the Law on Arbitration, in *First International Commercial Arbitration Conference: Proceedings* 315 (N. Antaki & A. Prujiner eds. 1986)

Blessing, Das neue Internationale Schiedsgerichtsrecht der Schweiz — Ein Fortschritt oder ein Rückschritt?, in *Die Internationale Schiedsgerichtsbarkeit in der Schweiz* 13 (K.-H. Böckstiegel ed. 1989)

————, The New International Arbitration Law in Switzerland: A Significant Step towards Liberalism, 5 *J. Int'l Arb.* 9 (No. 2, 1988)

Böckstiegel, K.-H., ed., *Die Internationale Schiedsgerichtsbarkeit in der Schweiz. Das neue Recht ab 1. Januar 1989* (Cologne 1989)

Bond, The New Swiss Law on International Arbitration and the Arbitral Institutions, 1989 *Int'l Bus. L.J.* 785

Briner, Die Anfechtung und Vollstreckung des Schiedsentscheides, in *Die Internationale Schiedsgerichtsbarkeit in der Schweiz* 99 (K.-H. Böckstiegel ed. 1989)

————, La révision des sentences arbitrales dans les cantons faisant partie du Concordat intercantonal sur l'arbitrage, in *Recueil de Travaux Suisses* 285 (C. Reymond & E. Bucher 1984)

————, Switzerland, in *Int'l Handbook Com. Arb.* (A. van den Berg gen. ed. 1984), Suppl. 9, Sept. 1988

————, Switzerland: National Report, 3 *Y.B. Com. Arb.* 181 (1978); 7 *Y.B. Com. Arb.* 70 (1982); 9 *Y.B. Com. Arb.* 55 (1984); 12 *Y.B. Com. Arb.* 393 (1987) and 14 *Y.B. Com. Arb.* 1 (1989)

Bucher, Das Kapitel 11 des IPR-Gesetzes über die internationale Schiedsgerichtsbarkeit, in *Beiträge zum neuen IPR des Sachen-, Schuld- und Gesellschaftsrechts. Festschrift für Professor Rudolf Moser* 193 (Zurich 1987)

————, Les voies de recours, 1989 *Int'l Bus. L.J.* 771

————, Arbitration under the ICC-Rules in Switzerland and the Concordat, in *Recueil de Travaux Suisses* 127 (C. Reymond & E. Bucher 1984)

————, Die Regeln betreffend Schiedsgerichtsbarkeit im neuen IPRG und deren verfassungsrechtlicher Hintergrund, in *Die schweizerische Rechtsordnung in ihren internationalen Bezügen* 265 (G. Jenni & W. Kälin eds. 1988)

————, Die Schweiz als traditioneller Sitzort internationaler Schiedsgerichte, in *Die Internationale Schiedsgerichtsbarkeit in der Schweiz* 119 (K.-H. Böckstiegel ed. 1989)

————, Unabdingbarkeit der Nichtigheitsbeschwerde nach schweizerischem Konkordat über die Schiedsgerichtsbarkeit, 6 *IPRax* 187 (1986)

Bucher, A., *Die neue internationale Schiedsgerichtsbarkeit in der Schweiz* (Basel 1989)

————, *Le nouvel arbitrage international en Suisse. Théorie et pratique de droit* (Basel 1988)

Bucher, A. & P.-Y. Tschanz, *International Arbitration in Switzerland* (Basel 1989)

Budin, Arbitration in Switzerland, in *Arbitration and the Licensing Process* 5-107 (R. Goldscheider & M. de Haas eds. 1984)

————, L'exécution des sentences arbitrales étrangères en Suisse et les limites de l'ordre public, 1977 *Rev. Arb.* 107

————, La nouvelle loi suisse sur l'arbitrage international, 1988 *Rev. Arb.* 51

————, La suspension dans l'arbitrage international, 1986 *Rev. Arb.* 415

————, Nature et cessibilité d'une convention d'arbitrage en droit suisse, 1979 *Rev. Arb.* 435

Burckhardt, Zum gegenwärtigen Stand der Revision des Rechtes der internationalen Schiedsgerichte, 81 *SJZ* 297 (1985)

Burckhardt, T., *Zum Anwendungsbereich des interkantonalen Konkordats über die Schiedsgerichtsbarkeit vom 27. März 1969* (Basel 1982)

Carabiber, L'immunité de juridiction et d'exécution des Etats collectivités et établissements publics au regard de l'obligation assumée par une clause compromissoire inserée dans les contrats internationaux de droit privé, in *Liber Amicorum for Martin Domke* 23 (P. Sanders ed. 1967)

Cohen, De la validité formelle des clauses compromissoires conclues par télex, 75 *SJZ* 259 (1979)

Delaume, Judicial Decisions Related to Sovereign Immunity and Transnational Arbitration, 2 *ICSID Rev. - Foreign Investment L.J.* 403 (1987)

————, New Swiss Arbitration Statute Emphasizes Party Autonomy and Restricts Judicial Review, in *The New Swiss Law on International Arbitration* 21 (Swiss Arbitration Association 1990)

Dutois, B., F. Knoepfler, P. Lalive & P. Mercier, eds., *Répertoire de droit international privé suisse*. Volume I: *Le contrat international/L'arbitrage international* (Berne 1982)

Eckstrom, L., *Licensing in Foreign and Domestic Operations*. Volume I, Chapter 7: Arbitration (by Steven Z. Szczepanski), (New York 1972, updated 1987)

Forni, Il potere dell'arbitro di statuire sulla propia competenza e l'arbitrabilità del litigio, in *Recueil de Travaux Suisses* 191 (C. Reymond & E. Bucher eds. 1984)

Freimüller, Attachments in Switzerland and Their Validation in International Commercial Arbitration, 2 *Bull. Swiss Arb. A.* 72 (1984)

————, Interim Court Remedies in Support of Arbitration, 12 *Int'l Bus. Law.* 119 (March 1984)

————, Attachments and Other Interim Court Remedies in Support of Arbitration: Switzerland, in *Interim Court Remedies in Support of Arbitration* 245 (D. Shenton & W. Kühn eds. 1987)

Friedland, Provisional Measures in ICSID Arbitration, 2 *Arb. Int'l* 335 (1986)

Gaillard, A Foreign View of the New Swiss Law on International Arbitration, 4 *Arb. Int'l* 25 (1988)

————, Le point de vue d'un utilisateur étranger, 1989 *Int'l Bus. L.J.* 793

————, The UNCITRAL Model Law and Recent Statutes on International Arbitration in Europe and North America, 2 *ICSID Rev. - Foreign Investment L.J.* 424 (1987)

Geisinger & Renold, Arbitrage international, ordre public et reconnaissance en Suisse de sentences arbitrales étrangères, in *Le Juriste Suisse Face au Droit et aux Jugements Etrangers: Ouverture ou Repli?* 89 (F. Knoepfler ed. 1988)

Guyet, La propriété industrielle et l'arbitrage en Suisse, in *Recueil de Travaux Suisses* 45 (C. Reymond & E. Bucher eds. 1984)

Habscheid, Das neue schweizerische Recht der internationalen Schiedsgerichtsbarkeit nach dem Bundesgesetz über das Internationale Privatrecht, 34 *RIW* 766 (1988)

————, Das neue schweizerische Recht der internationalen Schiedsgerichtsbarkeit nach dem Bundesgesetz über das Internationale Privatrecht, 23 *Revue de Droit Comparé/Comparative Law Revue* (Tokyo) (No. 3, 1989)

————, Das neue schweizerische Recht des internationalen Schiedsverfahrens, 48 *KTS* 177 (1987)

————, Das schweizerische Schiedskonkordat, der Entwurf zu einem Bundesgesetz über das Internationale Privatrecht und die internationale Schiedsgerichtsbarkeit, in *Beiträge zum internationalen Verfahrensrecht und zur Schiedsgerichtsbarkeit. Festschrift für Heinrich Nagel* 70 (W. Habscheid & K. Schwab eds. 1987)

————, Einstweiliger Rechtsschutz durch Schiedsgericht nach dem schweizerischen Gesetz über das Internationale Privatrecht (IPRG), 9 *IPRax* 134 (1989)

————, Il concordato svizzero sull'arbitrato e l'arbitrato internazionale, 40 *Riv. Trim. Dir. & Proc. Civ.* 1197 (1986)

————, L'expertise-arbitrage. Etude de droit comparé, in *Liber Amicorum for Martin Domke* 103 (P. Sanders ed. 1967)

————, Statutarische Schiedsgerichte und Schiedskonkordat: Einige grundsätzliche Fragen, 57 *Schweizerische Aktiengesellschaft/La societé anonyme suisse* 157 (1985)

————, Teil-, Zwischen- und Vorabschiedsprüche im schweizerischen und deutschen Recht, ihre Anfechtbarkeit und die Rechtsfolgen ihrer Aufhebung durch das Staatsgericht (unter besonderer Berücksichtigung, der Streitgenossenschaft), 106 *ZSR* 669 (1987)

————, Zur internationalen Schiedsgerichtsbarkeit in der Schweiz, 43 *KTZ* 177

Hahn, D., *L'arbitrage commercial international en Suisse face aux règles de concurrence de la CEE* (Geneva 1985)

Hangarter, Die Schiedsgerichtsbarkeit der Handelskammer Deutschland-Schweiz, 1 *Jahrbuch Schiedsgerichtsbarkeit* 169 (1987)

————, Die Schiedsgerichtsbarkeit der Handelskammer Deutschland-Schweiz, in *Die Internationale Schiedsgerichtsbarkeit in der Schweiz* 189 (K.-H. Böckstiegel ed. 1989)

Heini, Der materiellrechtliche Ordre public im neuen schweizerischen Recht der internationalen Schiedsgerichtsbarkeit, in *Festschrift für Walther J. Habscheid* 153 (W. Lindacher, D. Pfaff et al. eds. 1989)

International Chamber of Commerce, *Arbitration Law in Europe* (Paris 1981)
————, Switzerland/ Suisse, in *Commercial Arbitration and the Law/ L'Arbitrage commercial et la Loi* (Basel 1949)

Jarvin, Choosing the Place of Arbitration: Where Do We Stand? 16 *Int'l Bus. Law.* 417 (1988)

————, Is Exclusion of Concurrent Courts' Jurisdiction over Conservatory Measures to Be Introduced by a Revision of the Convention? 6 *J. Int'l Arb.* 171 (No. 1, 1989)

Jolidon, La sentence en equité dans le Concordat suisse sur l'arbitrage, in *Recueil de Travaux Suisses* 259 (C. Reymond & E. Bucher eds. 1984)

Jolidon, P., *Commentaire du Concordat suisse sur l'arbitrage* (Berne 1984)

Karrer, Arbitration Procedure in Switzerland: Zurich and Geneva Compared, 2 *Int'l Contr.* 49 (1981)

———, International Arbitration in Switzerland, 6 *Int'l Fin. L. Rev.* 24 (No. 11, 1987)

———, Les rapports entre le tribunal arbitral, les tribunaux étatiques et l'institution arbitrale, 1989 *Int'l Bus. L.J.* 761

———, Switzerland's New Law is Modern, Liberal and Pragmatic, 3 *Int'l Arb. Rep.* 21 (1988)

Karrer, P. & K.W. Arnold, *Switzerland's Private International Law Statute 1987: The Swiss Code on Conflict of Laws and Related Legislation* (Deventer 1989)

Kassis, A., *Problèmes de base de l'arbitrage en droit comparé et en droit international*. Vol. 1: *Arbitrage juridictionnel et arbitrage contractuel* (Paris 1987)

Kaufmann-Kohler, Specificity of International Arbitration — Its Increasing Role in Case Law Illustrated by Geneva Court Practice on Application for Stays Imposed on Arbitral Awards, in *Recueil de Travaux Suisses* 297 (C. Reymond & E. Bucher eds. 1984)

Klein, A propos de l'exécution en Suisse des sentences arbitrales étrangères, in *Festgabe zum Schweizerischen Juristentag* 157 (Basel 1985)

———, Internationales Schiedsverfahren und nationale Rechtsordnungen, 24 *Schweiz. Jahrbuch Int'les Recht* 87 (1967)

———, L'arbitrage international de droit privé: réalités et perspectives, 20 *Ann. Suisse Droit Int'l* 41 (1963)

———, La nouvelle règlementation française de l'arbitrage international et le lois suisses, in *Recueil de Travaux Suisses* 57 (C. Reymond & E. Bucher eds. 1984)

———, Zur Anwendung der neuen schweizerischen Regelung über die internazionale Schiedsgerichtsbarkeit, 2 *Jahrbuch Schiedsgerichtsbarkeit* 92 (1988)

Klein, F.-E., *Considérations sur l'arbitrage en droit international privé* (Basel 1955)

Knoepfler & Schweizer, L'arbitrage international et des voies de recours: à propos du projet de Loi fédérale sur le DIP, in *Mélanges Guy Flattet* 491 (Lausanne 1985)

Kolkey, Attacking Arbitral Awards: Rights of Appeal and Review in International Arbitrations, 22 *Int'l Law.* 693 (1988)

Kornblum, "Ordre public transnational", "ordre public international" und "ordre public interne" im Recht der privaten Schiedsgerichtsbarkeit, in *Beiträge zum internationalen Verfahrensrecht und zur Schiedsgerichtsbarkeit. Festschrift für Heinrich Nagel* 140 (W. Habscheid & K. Schwab eds. 1987)

Kühn, Die Anfechtung und Vollstreckung des Schiedsentscheides. Eine kritische Würdigung der neuen schweizerischen Regelung unter Berücksichtigung ihrer Auswirkungen im deutschen Vollstreckbarerklärungsverfahren, in *Die Internationale Schiedsgerichtsbarkeit in der Schweiz* 163 (K.-H. Böckstiegel ed. 1989)

Kuster, Zurich, siège d'arbitrage international, 1982 *Rev. Arb.* 3

Lalive, Immunity of Arbitrators under Swiss Law, in *The Immunity of Arbitrators* 117 (J.D.M. Lew ed. 1990)

———, Arbitrage international et ordre public suisse, *Revue de Droit Suisse* 529 (1978)

———, Le droit suisse de l'arbitrage, in *L'Arbitrage* 279 (L. Matray & G. de Leval eds. 1989)

———, Les règles de conflit de lois appliqués au fond du litige par l'arbitrage international siégeant en Suisse, 1976 *Rev. Arb.* 135

———, Problèmes specifique de l'arbitrage international, 1980 *Rev. Arb.* 341

———, The New Swiss Law on International Arbitration, 4 *Arb. Int'l* 2 (1988)

Lalive & Gaillard, Le nouveau droit de l'arbitrage international en Suisse, 116 *J. Droit Int'l (Clunet)* 905 (1989)

Lalive, P., J.-F. Poudret & C. Reymond, *Le droit de l'arbitrage interne et international en Suisse* (Lausanne 1989)

Lanz, R., *Das Konkordat über die Schiedsgerichtsbarkeit vom 27. März 1969*, (Zurich 1971)

Lee, E., *Encyclopedia of International Commercial Arbitration* (London 1986)

Legras de Grandcourt, Evolution contemporaine des législations européennes, in *Euro-Arab Arbitration* III 119 (F. Kemicha ed. 1991)

Levy, Dissenting Opinions in International Arbitration in Switzerland, 5 *Arb. Int'l* 35 (1989)

MacLaren, Commercial Arbitration in the United States and Overseas, in *Arbitration and the Licensing Process* 5 (R. Goldscheider & M. de Haas eds. 1984-)

Majoros, Das Kollisionsrecht der Konventionskonflikte etabliert sich: Die Regel der maximalen Wirksamkeit in der doctrine des schweizerischen Bundesgerichts (Entscheidung Denysiana v. 14 Marz 1984), in *Festschrift für Karl H. Neumayer* 431 (W. Barfuss; B. Dutois, H. Forkel, U. Immenga & F. Majoros eds. 1985)

Marriott, Evidence in International Arbitration, 5 *Arb. Int'l* 280 (1989)

Marti & Kohler, La récusation des arbitres en droit suisse, in *Mélanges offerts à Raymond Vander Elst* 595 (Brussels 1986)

Mirimanoff, Objection to Arbitrators Following the Annulment of a Partial Award: A Potential Jeopardy of Arbitration in Switzerland? 3 *J. Int'l Arb.* 101 (No. 2, 1986)

Monnier, Le rôle de la Suisse dans l'histoire de l'arbitrage de droit international privé, in *Recueil de Travaux Suisses* 3 (C. Reymond & E. Bucher, eds. 1984)

Neumann, Limiting Judicial Review in International Commercial Arbitration: The New Swiss and Belgian Laws Offer Less Than They Promise, 1 *Am. Rev. Int'l Arb.* 435 (1990)

Neuroud & Park, Predestination and Swiss Arbitration Law: Geneva's Application of the Intercantonal Concordat, 2 *B. U. Int'l L.J.* 1 (1983)

Nuber J., *Die objektive Schiedsfähigkeit im Zusammenhang mit der Gültigkeit der Schiedsvereinbarung (anwendbares Recht) und mit der Vollstreckung* (ordre public), (Zurich 1986)

Note, Challenge of Arbitrators: Is an Institutional Decision Final? 2 *Arb. Int'l* 261 (1986)

—————, Enforcing Foreign Judgments and Arbitration Awards, 5 *Int'l Fin. L. Rev.* 26 (No. 7, 1986)

O'Neill, Has Switzerland Solved Its Problems as a Site for Arbitration? 45 *Arb. J.* 16 (No. 4, 1990)

Panchaud, Le siège de l'arbitrage international de droit privé, 61 *SJZ* 369 (1965)

—————, Le siège de l'arbitrage international en droit privé, 1966 *Rev. Arb.* 2

—————, Une législation en matière d'arbitrage: le projet de Concordat des Cantons suisses, 1969, in *ICCA, Third Int'l Arb. Congress: Proceedings* 539 (1969)

Park, Judicial Controls in the Arbitral Process, 5 *Arb. Int'l* 230 (1989)

—————, Private Adjudicators and the Public Interest: The Expanding Scope of International Arbitration, 12 *Brooklyn J. Int'l L.* 629 (1986)

Parker School of Foreign and Comparative Law, *International Commercial Arbitration and the Courts* (Dobbs Ferry, NY 1990)

—————, *The 1989 Guide to International Arbitration and Arbitrators* (Dobbs Ferry, NY 1989)

Paulsson, Arbitrage international et voies de recours: La Cour suprême de Suède dans le sillage des solutions belge et helvétique, 117 *J. Droit Int'l (Clunet)* 588 (1990)

Pechota, Switzerland, in 2A *W.A.R.* 2543 (H. Smit & V. Pechota eds. 1987)

Pedrazzini, Arbitration and Technology: Some Remarks on Swiss Law, in *ICCA, Sixth Int'l Arb. Congress: Proceedings* 385 (1978)

Pestalozzi, Die Schiedsgerichtsbarkeit der Zürcher Handelskammer, in *Die Internationale Schiedsgerichtsbarkeit in der Schweiz* 183 (K.-H. Böckstiegel ed. 1989)

Pfaff, Grenzbewegungen der Schiedsfähigkeit — Patentnichtigkeit im Schiedsverfahren, in *Beiträge zum internationalen Verfahrensrecht und zur Schiedsgerichtsbarkeit. Festschrift für Heinrich Nagel* 278 (W. Habscheid & K. Schwab eds. 1987)

Poncet, Challenges to the Jurisdiction of International Arbitrators: An Important Decision of the Swiss Supreme Court, 50 *Arbitration* 156 (1984)

Poudret, Challenge and Enforcement of Arbitral Awards in Switzerland, 4 *Arb. Int'l* 278 (1988)

————, Jurisprudence du Tribunal cantonal vaudois en matière d'arbitrage interne et international (1980-1987), 136 *JdT* 1 (No. 1, 1988)

————, L'interprétation des sentences arbitrales (étude de droit suisse et de droit comparé), in *Recueil de Travaux Suisses* 269 (C. Reymond & E. Bucher eds. 1984)

————, La clause arbitrale par référence selon la Convention de New York et l'art. 6 du Concordat sur l'arbitrage, in *Mélanges Guy Flattet* 523 (Lausanne 1985)

————, Le recours au Tribunal fédéral en matière d'arbitrage interne et international, 6 *ASA Bulletin* 33 (1988)

————, Les voies de recours en matière d'arbitrage international en Suisse selon le Concordat et la nouvelle loi fédérale, 1988 *Rev. Arb.* 595

————, Réflexions à propos de la recevabilité du recours en réforme ou en nulité au Tribunal fédérale en matière d'arbitrage, 106 *ZSR* 765 (1987)

Poudret, Reymond & Würzburger, L'application du concordat inter-cantonal sur l'arbitrage par le tribunal cantonal vaudois, 1981 *JdT* 67 (1981)

Poudret, J.-F. & A. Würzburger, *Code de procédure civile vaudois et concordat sur l'arbitrage, annoté et commenté* (2nd ed. Lausanne 1980)

Real, G.K.L., *Der Schiedsrichtervertrag* (Cologne 1983)

Reiner, A., *Handbuch der ICC-Schiedsgerichtsbarkeit. Die Verfahrensordnung des Schiedsgerichtshofes der Internationalen Handelskammer* (Vienna 1989)

Reymond, Das Zusammenwirken von Kapitel XII des Bundesgesetzes über das Internationale Privatrecht mit dem kantonalen Recht, in *Die Internationale Schiedsgerichtsbarkeit in der Schweiz* 113 (K.-H. Böckstiegel ed. 1989)

————, International Arbitration in Switzerland: First Experiences with the New Act, 1 *Am. Rev. Int'l Arb.* 303 (1990)

————, La nouvelle loi suisse et le droit de l'arbitrage international. Réflexions de droit comparé, 1989 *Rev. Arb.* 385

————, Le nouveau droit suisse de l'arbitrage international, 1989 *Int'l Bus. L.J.* 741

————, The New Swiss Uniform Arbitration Act and International Commercial Arbitration, 7 *Ga. J. Int'l & Comp. L.* 85 (1977)

Reymond, C. & E. Bucher, eds., *Recueil de Travaux Suisses sur l'Arbitrage International/Swiss Essays on International Arbitration* (Zurich 1984)

Ruede, T. & R. Hadenfeldt, *Schweizerisches Schiedsgerichtsrecht* (Zurich 1980)

Samuel, A Critical Look at the Reform of Swiss Arbitration Law, 7 *Arb. Int'l* 27 (1991)

————, The New Swiss Private International Law Act, 37 *Int'l & Comp. L.Q.* 681 (1988)

Samuel, A., *Jurisdictional Problems in International Commercial Arbitration: A Study of Belgian, Dutch, English, French, Swedish, Swiss, U.S. and West German Law* (Zurich 1989)

Schlosser, Die lange Leine vom Gericht zum Schiedsgericht. Ein französisches Lehrstück für Deutschland, die Schweiz und manch'andere, in *Festschrift für Walther J. Habscheid* 273 (W. Lindacher, D. Pfaff et al. eds. 1989)

————, Party-Appointed Arbitrators and Multiple Defendants Having Conflicting Interests, in *Law in East and West/Recht in Ost und West* 739 (Tokyo 1988)

Schneider, Internationale Schiedsverfahren in der Schweiz: Das Übergangsrecht zum Bundesgesetz über das Internationale Privatrecht (IPRG), 2 *Jahrbuch Schiedsgerichtsbarkeit* 141 (1988)

Schneider & Patocchi, The New Swiss Law on International Arbitration, 55 *Arbitration* 268 (1989)

Schnyder, Intertemporalrecht und internationale Schiedsgerichtsbarkeit im neuen IPR-Gesetz in der Schweiz, 10 *IPRax* 60 (1990)

Schnyder, A. K., Das neue IPR-Gesetz (Zurich 1988)

Schulthess, H. K., *Der verfahrensrechtliche Ordre public in der internationalen Schiedsgerichtsbarkeit in der Schweiz* (Zurich 1981)

Schweizer & Guillod, L'exception de litispendance et l'arbitrage international: quelques refléxions sur le pour et le contre, in *Le Juriste Suisse Face au Droit et aux Jugements Etrangers: Ouverture ou Repli?* 71 (F. Knoepfler ed. 1988)

Schweyer, A., *Patentnichtigkeit und Patentverletzung und deren Beurteilung durch private Schiedsgerichte nach dem Recht der Schweiz, Deutschlands, Italiens und Frankreich* (St. Gallen 1981)

Tackaberry, Elementary Economics and the Construction Dispute. An Outsider's Look at Swiss Law Remedies Available to the Unpaid Contractor, 7 *J. Int'l Arb.* 73 (No. 3, 1990)

Toller, Rechtsschutz durch ständige Schiedsgerichte. Eine Nachlese zum Schweizerischen Juristentag 1988, 85 *SJZ* 312 (1989)

Triebel, An Outline of the Swiss/German Rules of Civil Procedure and Practice Relating to Evidence, 47 *Arbitration* 221 (1982)

Tschanz, A Breakthrough in International Arbitration: Switzerland's New Act, 24 *Int'l Law.* 1107 (1990)

———, La convention d'arbitrage, 1989 *Int'l Bus. L.J.* 749

———, Le nouveau droit suisse de l'arbitrage international, 1988 *Int'l Bus. L.J.* 437

Uzan-Spira, Appointment of Arbitrators by the Geneva Chamber of Commerce and Industry (GCCI), 1 *J. Int'l Arb.* 73 (No. 1, 1984)

von Hoffmann, Anmerkungen zum neuen Internationalen Schiedsrecht der Schweiz, in *Die Internationale Schiedsgerichtsbarkeit in der Schweiz* 147 (K.-H. Böckstiegel ed. 1989)

von Rhein, Zur Anerkennung und Vollstreckung von schweizerischen Gerichtsentscheidungen, Schiedssprüchen und Vergleichen in der Bundesrepublik Deutschland, 82 *SJZ* 141 (1986)

Vulliemin, Jurisprudenzia suiza en materia de arbitraje comercial internacional, 5 *Rev. Corte Esp. Arb.* 255 (1986)

Vulliemin, J.-M., *Jugement et sentence arbitrale: étude de droit international privé et de droit comparé* (2nd ed., Lausanne 1990)

Walder-Bohner, Das UNCITRAL-Model Law und die Bestimmungen über die Internationale Schiedsbarkeit im schweizerischen IPR-Gesetz: Vergleich anhand einiger Beispiele, in *Law in East and West: On the Occasion of the 30th Anniversary of the Institute of Comparative Law, Waseda University* 727 (Tokyo 1988)

————, Die neuen Zürcher Bestimmungen über die Schiedsgerichtsbarkeit im Lichte des Konkordats, 72 *SJZ* 249 (1976)

————, Frage der Anfechtung von Schiedsgerichtsentscheiden durch Rechtsmittel (Ein Gegenvorschlag zum Entwurf des Bundesrates über das Internationale Privatrecht), 79 *SJZ* 356 (1983)

Walder-Bohner, H. U., *Das schweizerische Konkordat über die Schiedsgerichtsbarkeit* (Zurich 1982)

————, *Die Einführung in das internationale Zivilprozessrecht der Schweiz: Anerkennung und Vollstreckung ausländischer Entscheidungen, Zuständigkeit der schweizerischen Gerichte, Schiedsgerichtsbarkeit und weitere Fragen nach IPRG und Staatsverträgen* (Zurich 1989)

Walter, Die internationale Schiedsgerichtsbarkeit in der Schweiz - Offene Fragen zu Kap. 12 des IPR-Gesetzes, 1990 *Zeitschrift des Berner Juristenvereins* 161 (No. 4)

————, L'arbitrato internazionale in Svizzera, 43 *Riv. Trim. Dir. & Proc. Civ.* 517 (1989)

Wehrli, D., *Rechtsprechung zum Schweizerischen Konkordat über die Schiedsgerichtsbarkeit* (Zurich 1985)

Wenger, Internationale Schiedsverfahren in der Schweiz. Beständigkeit und Fortentwicklung in der neueren Rechtssprechung (zu Cour de Justice de Genève vom 6.5.1983 und 3.6.1983), 1985 *Praxis des int'len Privat- und Verfahrensrechts* 54 (No. 1)

————, Zur Ablehnung von Schiedsrichtern im schweizerischen Schiedsverfahrensrecht, 8 *IPRax* 116 (1988)

Wenger & Huber, Neue Enscheide des schweizerischen Bundesgericht zum Recht der internationalen Schiedsgerichtsbarkeit gemäss IPR-Gesetz, 11 *IPRax* 87 (1991)

Wenger, W., *Zum obligationenrechtlichen Schiedsverfahren im schweizerischen Recht: Eine rechtsvergleichende und historische Studie* (Basel 1968)

Wenner, Swiss Judges as Arbitrators or as Nominators for Arbitrators, 35 *Arb. J.* 22 (No. 4, 1980)

Wiget, Über das Verhältniss der Schiedsgerichtsordnungen ICC, UNCITRAL, ECE zum Zürcher Schiedsgerichtsrecht, 75 *SJZ* 17 (1979)

TAIWAN

Glossner, Schiedsverfahren oder Zivilprozessverfahren: Der Macao Sardine Case. The Rt. Hon. Lord Justice Kerr, 1 *Jahrbuch Schiedsgerichtsbarkeit* 251 (1987)

Kerr, Arbitration v. Litigation. The Macao Sardine Case., 15 *Int'l Bus. Law.* 152 (1987); 3 *Arb. Int'l* 79 (No. 1, 1987).

———, The Enforcement of a Taiwanese Arbitration Award, 6 *Arb. Int'l* 167 (1990)

McClelland, A Survey of Pacific Rim Commercial Arbitration, 40 *Arb. J.* 3 (No. 1, 1985)

Pacific Rim Advisory Council, *Pacific Rim: Commercial Arbitration Procedures* (San Diego, CA 1985)

TANZANIA

Peter, *Foreign Private Investments in Tanzania.* Chapter 7: Settlement of Investment Disputes (Konstanz 1989)

―――, Settlement of Investment Disputes, 5 *J. Int'l Arb.* 131 (No. 1, 1988)

THAILAND

Asawaroj, Thailand, in *Int'l Handbook Com. Arb.* (A. van den Berg, gen. ed. 1984), Suppl. 9, Sept. 1988

Athueck, Asvanund, *Introduction to Arbitration under Thai Laws, Bangkok* (1981). (A paper presented at the Seventh Lawasia Conference)

Chantikul, The Convention on the Settlement of Investment Disputes between States and Nationals of Other States, 1 *Chulalongkorn L. Rev.* 48 (1982)

International Chamber of Commerce, Thailand/Thailande, in *Commercial Arbitration and the Law/L'Arbitrage commercial et la Loi* (Basel 1958)

McClelland, A Survey of Pacific Rim Commercial Arbitration, 40 *Arb. J.* 3 (No. 1, 1985)

Note, Arbitration in Thailand, 4 *L.J. of The Marut Bunnang Int'l Office* 8 (1975)

Ogawa, The New Thai Arbitration Act of 1987, 6 *J. Int'l Arb.* 97 (No. 3, 1989)

Pacific Rim Advisory Council, *Pacific Rim: Commercial Arbitration Procedures* (San Diego, CA 1985)

Ricafrente, Commercial Arbitration in ASEAN Countries, in *Commercial Arbitration* 39 (J. Ricalde ed. 1983)

Simmonds, K., B. Hill & S. Jarvin, eds., *Commercial Arbitration Law in Asia and the Pacific* (Paris & Dobbs Ferry, NY 1987)

Suwit Suwan, International Commercial Arbitration and Enforcement of Foreign Judgements, 8 *Law J. of Marut Bunnag Int'l L.Office* 7 (No. 2, 1981)

Uwanno & Sathirathai, Introduction to the Thai Legal System. [Section c) International Commercial Arbitration], 4 *Chulalongkorn L. Rev.* 39, 105 (1985-1986)

TUNISIA

Centre d'Etudes de Recherches, *Les Entreprises Tunisiennes et l'Arbitrage Commercial International.* Colloque: 2, 3, 4 Novembre 1981 (Tunis 1983)

Charfi, L'expérience tunisienne en matière d'arbitrage international, in *Centre d'Etudes, Les Entreprises Tunisiennes et l'Arbitrage Commercial International* 209 (1983)

Derains, Clauses et procédures d'arbitrage internationales dans le pays arabes, in *First Euro-Arab Arb. Conference: Proceedings* 150 (F. Kemicha ed. 1987)

El-Ahdab, A. H., *Arbitration with the Arab Countries* (Deventer 1990)

———, *L'arbitrage dans les pays arabes* (Paris 1988)

Kassis, Particularités et problèmes de l'arbitrage dans les droits des pays arabes, 63 *Rev. Droit Int'l & Droit Comp.* 7 (1986)

Malouche, Les entreprises public et l'arbitrage en droit tunisien, 1989 *Rev. Arb.* 374

Mechri, L'arbitrage en Tunisie, 16 *Rassegna dell'Arb.* 3 (1976)

———, La procédure de l'arbitrage en Tunisie. Première partie, 1976 *Revue Tunisienne de Droit* 15 (No. 1)

———, La procédure de l'arbitrage en Tunisie. Deuzième partie, 1976 *Revue Tunisienne de Droit* 15 (No. 2)

———, Les insuffisances du Code de Procédure civile et Commerciale et les modifications qui s'imposent, in *Centre d'Etudes, Les Entreprises Tunisiennes et l'Arbitrage Commercial International* 365 (1983)

Mestre, Les établissements publics industriels et commerciaux et le recours a l'arbitrage, 1976 *Rev. Arb.* 4

Mezghani, Convergence et harmonization du droit et de la pratique de l'arbitrage commercial international (A propos de 35 clauses compromissoires contenues dans les contrats commerciaux internationaux tunisiens), 1981 *Revue tunisienne de droit* 35

———, Les pays arabes du Maghreb, in *First Euro-Arab Arb. Conference: Proceedings* 39 (F. Kemicha ed. 1987)

Sefrioui, Pratique de l'arbitrage et tendances reformatrices nouvelles, in *Euro-Arab Arbitration III* 61 (F. Kemicha ed. 1991)

Terki, L'arbitrage et l'entreprise publique en Afrique du Nord, 66 *Rev. Droit Int'l & Droit Comp.* 124 (1989)

Troller, Arbitration and Enforcement of Arbitration Awards in Arab Countries, 2 *Int'l Contr.* 397 (1981)

Ziadé, Selective Bibliography on Arbitration and Arab Countries, 3 *ICSID Rev. -Foreign Investment L.J.* 423 (1988)

TURKEY

Alangoya, Die Vollstreckung ausländischer Schiedsprüche nach türkischem Recht, in *Festschrift für Karl Heinz Schwab* 1 (P. Gottwald & H. Prütting eds. 1990)

Ansay, Commercial Arbitration in Turkey, 12 *Arb. J.* 31 (1957)

Ayiter, Vollstreckbarkeit ausländischer Schiedssprüche in der Türkei, in *Konflikt und Ordnung, Festschrift für Murad Ferid* 15 (Munich 1978)

Bernini, Recent Legislations and International Unification of the Law on Arbitration, in *First International Commercial Arbitration Conference: Proceedings* 315 (N. Antaki & A. Prujiner eds. 1986)

International Chamber of Commerce, Turkey/Turquie, in *Commercial Arbitration and the Law/L'Arbitrage commercial et la Loi* (Basel 1949)

Koral, L'action en exécution dans l'arbitrage international et nouveau projet de loi turc sur le droit international de procédure civile, 28 *Annales de la Faculté de Droit d'Istanbul* 3 (1981)

————, La nouvelle loi turque sur le droit international privé et la procédure internationale et le principe de la reciprocité dans l'arbitrage, 1983 *Rev. Arb.* 47

————, L'exécution des sentences arbitrales étrangères en Turquie. A propos des progrès jurisprudentiels récents, 1989 *Rev. Arb.* 467

————, Turkey, in *Int'l Handbook Com. Arb.* (A. van den Berg, gen. ed. 1984), Suppl. 10, June 1989

Krüger, Neues internationales Privatrecht in der Turkei, 23 *ZRV* 169 (1982)

Ozbakan, La reconnaissance et l'exécution des jugements étrangers en Turquie, 70 *SJZ* 353 (1983)

Rubino-Sammartano, The Keban arbitration (a report on the judgment of the Supreme Court of Turkey), 46 *Arbitration* 241 (1980)

Tekinay, The Turkish Situation in the Field of International Commercial Arbitration, 1989 *Int'l Bus. L.J.* 161

Ünal, The New York Convention and the Recognition and Enforcement of Foreign Arbitral Awards in Turkish Law, 7 *J. Int'l Arb.* 55 (No. 4, 1990)

Yegengil, R., *Tahkim (L'arbitrage),* (Istanbul 1974)

UNITED ARAB EMIRATES

Angell & Feulner, Settlement of Disputes through Arbitration: Arbitration of Disputes in the United Arab Emirates, in 1 *Arab Comparative & Commercial Law: The International Approach: Proceedings I.B.A. Conference* 233

Ballantyne, Arbitration in the Gulf States: Delocalisation: A Short Comparative Study, 1 *Arab L. Q.* 205 (1986)

―――, European Experience and Perception of Arbitration with Arab Countries, in *First Euro-Arab Arb. Conference: Proceedings* 160 (F. Kemicha ed. 1987)

Bernardini, Les arbitrages pétroliers et le droit appliqué par les arbitres, in *First Euro-Arab Arb. Conference: Proceedings* 282 (F. Kemicha ed. 1987)

Dilger, Schiedsgerichtsbarkeit und Volstreckung ausländischer Entscheidungen in den Golfstaaten, in *Vetragspraxis und Streiterledigung im Wirtschaftsverkehr mit arabischen Staaten* 101 (K.-H. Böckstiegel ed. 1981)

El-Ahdab, A. H., *Arbitration with the Arab Countries* (Deventer 1990)

―――, *L'arbitrage dans les pays arabes* (Paris 1988)

Feulner & Khan, Dispute Resolution in the UAE, 1 *Arab L. Q.* 312 (1986)

International Bar Association, *Arab Comparative & Commercial Law: The International Approach: Proceedings of the I.B.A. First Arab Regional Conference, Cairo 15-19 February 1987* (London 1987)

Krüger, The State of Arbitration in Kuwait and Dubai, 4 *Int'l Arb. Rep.* 15 (No .2, 1989)

Saleh, The Recognition and Enforcement of Foreign Arbitral Awards in the States of the Arab Middle East, in *Contemporary Problems in International Arbitration* 340 (J.D.M. Lew ed. 1986)

―――, The Settlement of Disputes in the Arab World: Arbitration and Other Methods, 1 *Arab L. Q.* 198 (1986); reprinted in 4 *Int'l Tax & Bus. Law.* 280 (1986)

Saleh, S., *Commercial Arbitration in the Arab Middle East* (London 1984)

Troller, Arbitration and Enforcement of Arbitration Awards in Arab Countries, 2 *Int'l Contr.* 397 (1981)

Ziadé, Selective Bibliography on Arbitration and Arab Countries, 3 *ICSID Rev. -Foreign Investment L.J.* 423 (1988)

UNITED KINGDOM

Abrahams, The Origins of Arbitration in Britain, 54 *Arbitration* 263 (1988)

Abromson, The English Arbitration Act of 1979: A Symbiotic Relationship Between the Courts and Arbitration Tribunals, 5 *Suff. Transnat'l L.J.* 7 (1980)

Adams, Arbitration, 1985 *All ER Ann. Rev.* 13

———, Arbitration, 1986 *All ER Ann. Rev.* 11

Anton, Arbitration: International Aspects, 1986 *The Scots Law Times* 45 and 53

Barclay, Enforcement of Arbitration Awards, 41 *Arbitration* 194 (1974)

———, The Arbitration Award, 45 *Arbitration* 118 (1979)

Barker, Judicial Review of English Arbitration in the Wake of the Nema and Evia, 23 *Va. J. Int'l L.* 432 (1983)

Bentil, Judicial Intervention and International Commercial Arbitration, 130 *Solicitors' J.* 191 (1986)

———, Making England a More Attractive Venue for International Commercial Arbitration by Less Judicial Oversight, 5 *J. Int'l Arb.* 49 (No. 1, 1988)

Berger, Die Regelung der gerichtlichen Anfechtbarkeit internationaler Schiedssprüche in europäischen Schiedsgerichtsgesetzen, 35 *RIW* 850 (1989)

———, The Modern Trend Towards Exclusion of Recourse Against Transnational Arbitral Awards: A European Perspective, 12 *Fordham Int'l L. J.* 605 (1989)

Bernini, Recent Legislations and International Unification of the Law on Arbitration, in *First International Commercial Arbitration Conference: Proceedings* 315 (N. Antaki & A. Prujiner eds. 1986)

Bernstein, R., ed., *Handbook of Arbitration Practice* (London 1987)

Billings, International Standards for Automotive Arbitration, 28 *German Y.B. Int'l L.* 425 (1985)

Bingham, Reasons and Reasons for Reasons: Differences Between a Court Judgment and an Arbitration Award, 4 *Arb. Int'l* 141 (1988)

————, The Problem of Delay in Arbitration, 5 *Arb. Int'l* 333 (1989); also in 56 *Arbitration* 164 (1990)

Bischoff, Arbitration Act 1979: cinq ans après, 37 *Droit Mar. Français* 179 (1985)

————, Amiables Compositeurs in English Arbitration Law, 44 *Arbitration* 60 (1978)

Borrie, The Use and Abuse of Arbitration, 55 *Arbitration* 234 (1989)

Boyd, The Role of National Law and the National Courts in England, In *Contemporary Problems in International Arbitration* 149 (J.D.M. Lew ed. 1986)

Boyd & Veeder, Le développement du droit anglais de l'arbitrage depuis la loi de 1979, 1991 *Rev. Arb.* 209

Carabiber, L'immunité de juridiction et d'exécution des Etats collectivités et établissements publics au regard de l'obligation assumée par une clause compromissoire inserée dans les contrats internationaux de droit privé, in *Liber Amicorum for Martin Domke* 23 (P. Sanders ed. 1967)

Carbonneau, American and Other National Variations on the Theme of International Commercial Arbitration, 18 *Ga. J. Int'l & Comp. L.* 143 (1988)

————, Etude historique et comparée de l'arbitrage: vers un droit materiel de l'arbitrage commercial international fondé sur la motivation des sentences, 36 *Rev. Int'le Droit Comp.* 727 (1984)

Chapman, FOSFA International Arbitration, 2 *Arb. Int'l* 323 (1986)

Clark & Lange, Recent Changes in English Arbitration Practice Widen Opportunities for More Effective International Arbitrations, 35 *Bus. Law.* 1621 (1980)

Cohen, A New Yorker Looks at London Maritime Arbitration, 1986 *Lloyd's Mar. & Com. L.Q.* 57 (No. 1)

————, England & Wales: Arbitration, in B1 *World Litigation Law & Practice E&W* 13-2 (R. Myrick ed. 1986)

Collins, The Law Governing the Agreement and Procedure in International Commercial Arbitration in England, in *Contemporary Problems in International Arbitration* 126 (J.D.M. Lew ed. 1986)

Collins, L. A., gen. ed., *Dicey and Morris on the Conflict of Laws. Vol. 1, Chapter 16: Arbitration and Foreign Awards* (11th ed. London 1987)

Colman, A.D., *The Practice and Procedure of the Commercial Court* (2nd ed. London 1986)

Comish, Arbitration at Common Law before the First (English) Arbitration Act 1698, 56 *Arbitration* 194 (1990)

Conrick, Where the Kings Writ Does Not Run: The Origins and Effect of the Arbitration Act 1979, 1 *Queensl. Inst. Tech. L.J.* 1 (1985)

Crawford, Les Etats et l'exécution des sentences arbitrales dans les droits américain et anglais, 1985 *Rev. Arb.* 689

Crawford & Feldman, American Perceptions of London as a Situs for International Commercial Arbitration, 2 *Arb. Int'l* 232 (1986)

Cremades, The Enforcement of British Arbitral Awards in Spain, 45 *Arbitration* 30 and 97 (1979)

Croal, Misconception about Discovery in English Arbitration, 51 *Arbitration* 532 (Nov. 1985)

Comment, Judicial Implementation of the United Kingdom Arbitration Act, 1979: Pioneer Shipping v. B.T.P. Tioxide (The Nema), 24 *Harv. Int'l L.J.* 103 (1983)

Darling, Salvage Arbitration, in *International Commercial and Maritime Arbitration* 95 (F.D. Rose ed. 1988)

Davenport, Stale Arbitrations—Again, 104 *L.Q. Rev.* 493 (1988)

Davies, Immunity of the Arbitrator, 43 *Arbitration* 3 (Summer 1976)

———, Some Powers of the Arbitrator Under English Law, in 1 *Fifth Int'l Congress of Maritime Arbitrators* (New York 1981)

———, A View of London Maritime Arbitration, 52 *Arbitration* 150 (1986)

Delaume, Judicial Decisions Related to Sovereign Immunity and Transnational Arbitration, 2 *ICSID Rev. - Foreign Investment L.J.* 403 (1987)

Dervaird, Lord, Scotland and the UNCITRAL Model Law. The Report to the Lord Advocate of the Scottish Advisory Committee on Arbitration Law, 6 *Arb. Int'l* 63 (1990)

Deshpande, Enforcement of Foreign Awards in India, U.K. and U.S.A., 4 *J. Int'l Arb.* 41 (No. 1, 1987)

————, Practice Versus the Law in Arbitration, 6 *J. Int'l Arb.* 55 (No. 4, 1989)

————, The Applicable Law in International Commercial Arbitration, 31 *J. Ind. L. Inst.* 127 (1989)

Diplock, The Alexander Lecture (The Case Stated — Its Use and Abuse), 44 *Arbitration* 107 (1978)

Donaldson, Commercial Arbitration — 1979 and After, 11 *Int'l Bus. Law.* 189 (1983); 48 *Arbitration* 259 (1983)

————, Commercial Arbitration — 1979 and After, in *International Commercial and Maritime Arbitration* 1 (F.D. Rose ed. 1988)

————, The 1979 Arbitration Act, 45 *Arbitration* 147 (1979)

Dore, I., *Theory and Practice of Multiparty Commercial Arbitration, With Special Reference to the UNCITRAL Framework* (London 1990)

Eckstrom, L., *Licensing in Foreign and Domestic Operations.* Volume I, Chapter 7: Arbitration (by Steven Z. Szczepanski), (New York 1972, updated 1987)

Elland & Goldsmith, The Arbitration Act 1979, 6 *Int'l L. & Prac.* 63 (1980)

Ellison & Ellison, Arbitration in Pensions, 46 *Arbitration* 234 (1980)

Evans, Some Thoughts on Adoption of the UNCITRAL Model Law, 53 *Arbitration* 121 (1987)

Forsyth, Enforcement of Arbitral Awards, Choice of Law in Contract, Characterization and a New Attitude to Private International Law, 104 *South Afr. L.J.* 4 (1987)

811

Fox, States and the Undertaking to Arbitrate, 37 *Int'l & Comp. L.Q.* 1 (1988)

Gardner, The Doctrine of Separability in Soviet Arbitration Law: An Analysis of Sojuzneftexport v. JOC Oil Co., 28 *Colum. J. Transnat'l L.* 301 (1990)

Gibson-Jarvie, R. & G. Hawker, *A Guide to Commercial Arbitration under the 1979 Act* (London 1980)

Gill, W.H., *Evidence and Procedure in Arbitration* (London 1965)

Gimson, Scottish Law and Arbitration, 42 *Arbitration* 62 (1975)

Ginnings, A.T., *Arbitration: A Practical Guide* (Aldershot, England 1984)

Gomez, International Arbitration: A Case for Delocalization, 3 *Sri Lanka J. Int'l L.* 61 (1991)

Goode, The Proposed London School of International Arbitration, 47 *Arbitration* 279 (1982)

Goodman, UNCITRAL Model Law on International and Commercial Arbitration: Divergent Approaches in England and Scotland: A Question of Appeal? 18 *Int'l Bus. Law.* 250 (1990)

Habscheid, L'expertise-arbitrage. Etude de droit comparé, in *Liber Amicorum for Martin Domke* 103 (P. Sanders ed. 1967)

Hacking, Where We Are Now: Trends and Developments since the Arbitration Act, 2 *J. Int. Arb.* 7 (No. 4, 1985)

Hall, Arbitrations and the New Supreme Court Costs Rules, 52 *Arbitration* 174 (1986)

Hallgarten, International Commercial Arbitration in London, in *IBA, Soviet Foreign Trade Reforms & East/West Arbitration* 181 (1988)

Herrmann, For an UNCITRAL Model Restatement of Arbitration Law in the United Kingdom, 4 *Arb. Int'l* 62 (1988)

Holland & Hantke, Beschränkung auf den Urkunden-Beweis im Schiedsverfahren, in *Festschrift für Arthur Bülow* 75 (K.-H. Böckstiegel & O. Glossner eds. 1981)

Holtzmann & Bernini, Hypothetical Case for Use in a Comparative Study of Arbitration Practice in Various Legal Systems, in *Comparative Arbitration Practice and Public Policy in Arbitration* 19 (P. Sanders ed. 1987)

Hunter, Arbitration Procedure in England: Past, Present and Future, 1 *Arb. Int'l* 82 (1985)

————, Impact of the UNCITRAL Model Law in the Non-Arab World, in *Euro-Arab Arbitration III* 180 (F. Kemicha ed. 1991)

————, Judicial Assistance for the Arbitrator, in *Contemporary Problems in International Arbitration* 195 (J.D.M. Lew ed. 1986)

Hunter & Paulsson, A Commentary on the 1985 Rules of the London Court of International Arbitration, 50 *Arbitration* 333 (May 1985); also in 10 *Y.B. Com. Arb.* 167 (1985)

Hunter & Triebel, Awarding Interest in International Arbitration, 6 *J. Int'l Arb.* 7 (No. 1, 1989)

Hunter, R.L.C., *The Law of Arbitration in Scotland* (Edinburgh 1987)

Inglis, Some Points of Difference Between the Scots and English Laws of Arbitration, 43 *Arbitration* 72 (1977)

International Chamber of Commerce, *Arbitration Law in Europe* (Paris 1981)

————, Scotland/Ecosse, in *Commercial Arbitration and the Law/ L'Arbitrage commercial et la Loi* (Basel 1958)

Irons, J., *Treatise on the Law of Arbitration in Scotland: With An Appendix of Forms and Excerpts from Statutes Relating to Arbitration* (Edinburgh 1903)

Jaffe, Judicial Supervision of Commercial Arbitration in England, 55 *Arbitration* 184 (1989)

————, The Judicial Trend Toward Finality of Commercial Arbitral Awards in England, 24 *Tex. Int'l L.J.* 67 (1989)

Jarvin, London As a Place for International Arbitration: Some Observations in Light of the Arbitration Act 1979 and the Bank Mellat v. Helleniki Techniki case, 1 *J. Int'l Arb.* 59 (1984)

Johnson, Commodity Trade Arbitration, in *Handbook of Arbitration Practice* 189 (R. Bernstein ed. 1987)

Johnson, D., *International Commodity Arbitration* (London 1991)

Jones, History of Commercial Arbitration in England and the United States, in *Int'l Trade Arbitration* 127 (M. Domke ed. 1958)

Kassis, A., *Problèmes de base de l'arbitrage en droit comparé et en droit international.* Vol. 1: *Arbitrage juridictionnel et arbitrage contractuel* (Paris 1987)

Kerr, Commercial Dispute Resolution: The Changing Scene, in *Liber Amicorum for The Rt. Hon. Lord Wilberforce* 111 (M. Bos & I. Brownlie eds. 1987)

——, Arbitration Law Relevant to English-German Business Relations, in *Handelsschiedsgerichtsbarkeit in England und in der Bundesrepublik Deutschland* 5 (K.-H. Böckstiegel ed. 1987)

——, Growth of Arbitration in the Pacific: A View from the United Kingdom, 52 *Arbitration* 84 (1986); Paper presented to Int'l Conf. 'Growth of Arb. in the Pacific, Auckland, NZ, Sept. 1985

——, The Arbitration Act 1979, 43 *Mod. L. Rev.* 45 (1980)

Klein, F.-E., *Considérations sur l'arbitrage en droit international privé* (Basel 1955)

Kolkey, Attacking Arbitral Awards: Rights of Appeal and Review in International Arbitrations, 22 *Int'l Law.* 693 (1988)

Kühl, S. G., *Schiedsgerichtsbarkeit im Seehandel* (Kehl am Rhein 1990)

Kühn, Practical Experiences with English Arbitration Proceedings, in *Handelsschiedsgerichtsbarkeit in England und in der Bundesrepublik Deutschland* 121 (K.-H. Böckstiegel ed. 1987)

Langeveld, Iets over getuigen in internationale arbitrages, 1988 *Tijdschrift voor Arbitrage* 156

Laschet, Anordnung gemeinsamer Verhandlung zweier getrennter Schiedsverfahren durch ein Schiedsgericht in England — Aufhebung durch den High Court, 6 *IPRax* 182 (1986)

Lebedev, Reglament Mezhdunarodnogo kommercheskogo arbitrazha: angliiskaia model', 1991 *S.G.P.* 84 (No. 5, 1991)

⸻, Sudebnyi kontrol za pravoprimenitelnoi deyatelnostiu arbitrov (Angliiskii zakon 1979 goda), 29 *Pravovedenie* 88 (January-February 1985)

Lee, E., *Encyclopedia of Arbitration Law* (London 1984)

⸻, *Encyclopedia of International Commercial Arbitration* (London 1986)

Lepp, Arbitration Appeals: A Comparison of Certain English and American Trade Associations, 39 *Arbitration* 125 (1972)

⸻, Arbitration Appeals: A Comparison of Certain English and American Trade Associations, 28 *Rassegna dell'Arb.* 57 (1988)

Lew, The Recognition and Enforcement of Arbitration Awards in England, 10 *Int'l Law.* 425 (1976)

⸻, The School of International Arbitration, London, 5 *J. Int'l Arb.* 127 (No. 3, 1988)

Lew, J., ed., *Contemporary Problems in International Arbitration* (London 1986)

Lewis, Leave of Appeal Under the Arbitration Act 1979, 1982 *Lloyd's Mar. & Com. L.Q.* 271

Littman, The Common Law Countries: United Kingdom, in *Arbitration in Settlement of International Commercial Disputes Involving the Far East and Arbitration in Combined Transportation* 171 (P. Sanders ed. 1989)

Lloyd, Arbitration and the Commercial Court, 49 *Arbitration* 13 (Aug. 1983)

Lorenzen, Commercial Arbitration — International and Interstate Aspects, 43 *Yale L.J.* 716 (1934)

MacLaren, Commercial Arbitration in the United States and Overseas, in *Arbitration and the Licensing Process* 5 (R. Goldscheider & M. de Haas eds. 1984-)

McCrindell, Arbitration in the Insurance Industry in the United Kingdom, in ICCA, *Sixth Int'l Arb. Congress: Proceedings* 149 (1978)

————, Arbitration in the English Insurance Industry, 45 Arbitration 229 (1979)

Mackie, Integration of Arbitration Systems as Regards the Commodity Trades, 44 *Arbitration* 89 (1978)

————, GAFTA Arbitration Procedures, 56 *Arbitration* 150 (1990)

————, The Grain and Feed Trade Association and Immunity of Arbitrators, in *The Immunity of Arbitrators* 111 (J.D.M. Lew ed. 1990)

McIntosh, The Practice of Maritime Arbitration in London: Recent Developments in the Law, 1983 *Lloyd's Mar. & Com. Q.* 235

McLachlan, Transnational Applications of Mareva Injunctions and Anton Piller Orders, 36 *Int'l & Comp. L.Q.* 669 (1987)

McLaughlin, Arbitral Immunity, in *International Commercial and Maritime Arbitration* 55 (F.D. Rose ed. 1988)

Mankabady, Arbitration in Shipping Disputes Under English Law, 14 *N. Ky. L. Rev.* 13 (1987)

Mann, An 'Agreement in Writing' to Arbitrate, 3 *Arb. Int'l* 171 (1987)

————, British Treaties for the Promotion and Protection of Investments, 52 *Brit. Y.B. Int'l L.* 241 (1981)

————, England Rejects Delocalised Contracts and Arbitration, 33 *Int'l & Comp. L.Q.* 193 (1984)

————, English Procedural Law and Foreign Arbitrations, 19 *Int'l & Comp. L.Q.* 693 (1970)

————, Private Arbitration and Public Policy, 10 *Holdsworth L. Rev.* 11 (1985)

————, Private Arbitration and Public Policy, 4 *Civil Just. Q.* 257 (1985)

————, Some Recent Developments in English Law of Arbitration, in *Inter Nationes. Festschrift für Stefan Riesenfeld* (E. Jayme, G. Kegel & M. Lutter eds. 1983)

Marriott, Arbitrating International Commercial Disputes in the United Kingdom, 44 *Arb. J.* 3 (No. 3, 1989)

————, Evidence in International Arbitration, 5 *Arb. Int'l* 280 (1989)

Marshall, The Law of Arbitration — A Difference between Scotts and English, 15 *Juridical Review* 115 (1970)

Marshall, E., *Gill: The Law of Arbitration* (3rd ed., London 1983)

Meisel, The Changing Role of the High Court in Relation to Supervision of Commercial Arbitrations, 25 *Les Cahiers de Droit* 653 (1984)

Morgan & Redmont, Arbitration in the Channel Islands, *Int'l Bus.Law.* 275(1985)

Murray, Claims for Damage and Submission to Arbitration Clauses as Traps for Lethargic Businessmen in the United States and England, 87 *Com. L.J.* 359(1982)

Mustill, A New Arbitration Act for the United Kingdom? The Response of the Departmental Advisory Committee to the UNCITRAL Model Law, 6 *Arb. Int'l* 3 (1990)

————, Delays in Arbitration: the Role of the Court, 52 *Arbitration* 163 (1986)

————, Distinctive Features of English Commercial Arbitration, 14 *Arkiv for Sjorett (NOR)* 321 (1976-77)

————, Domestic Arbitration Law — Proposals for Consolidation Amendment and Development, 56 *Arbitration* 82 (1990)

————, The New Lex Mercatoria: The First Twenty-five Years, in *Liber Amicorum for the Rt. Hon. Lord Wilberforce* 149 (M. Bos & I. Brownlie eds. 1987)

————, Transnational Arbitration and English Law, in *International Commercial and Maritime Arbitration* 15 (F.D. Rose ed. 1988)

————, Transnational Arbitration in English Law, 37 *Current Legal Problems* 133 (1984)

————, Vers une nouvelle loi anglaise sur l'arbitrage, 1991 *Rev. Arb.* 383

Nathan, Arbitrate or Litigate — Powers of the Court, 55 *Arbitration* 285 (1989)

Note, Enforcing Foreign Judgments and Arbitration Awards, 5 *Int'l Fin. L. Rev.* 26 (No. 7, 1986)

Note, The Use of Pre-Judgment Attachments and Temporary Injunctions in International Commercial Arbitration Proceedings: A Comparative Analysis of the British and American Approaches, 50 *U. Pitt. L. Rev.* 667 (1989)

Oparil, Waiver of Sovereign Immunity in the United States and Great Britain by an Arbitration Agreement, 3 *J. Int'l Arb.* 61 (No. 4, 1986)

Park, El arbitraje comercial internacional y la lex loci arbitri: perspectiva de la Ley de Arbitraje inglesa, 2 *Rev. Corte Esp. Arb.* 57 (1957)

――――, Judicial Controls in the Arbitral Process, 5 *Arb. Int'l* 230 (1989)

――――, Judicial Supervision of Transnational Commercial Arbitration: The English Arbitration Act of 1979, 21 *Harv. Int'l L.J.* 87 (1980)

――――, National Legal Systems and Private Dispute Resolution, 82 *Am. J. Int'l L.* 616 (1988)

――――, Private Adjudicators and the Public Interest: The Expanding Scope of International Arbitration, 12 *Brooklyn J. Int'l L.* 629 (1986)

――――, The Influence of National Legal Systems on International Commercial Arbitration: Recent Developments in English Arbitration Law, in *Resolving Transnational Disputes Through International Arbitration* 80 (T. Carbonneau ed. 1980)

Park & Paulsson, The Binding Force of International Arbitral Awards, 23 *Va. J. Int'l L.* 253 (1983)

Parker School of Foreign and Comparative Law, *International Commercial Arbitration and the Courts* (Dobbs Ferry, NY 1990)

Parker School of Foreign and Comparative Law, *The 1989 Guide to International Arbitration and Arbitrators* (Dobbs Ferry, NY 1989)

Parris, J., *Casebook of Arbitration Law* (London 1976)

Paulsson, The Contribution of English and American Legislation, in *Euro-Arab Arbitration III* 104 (F. Kemicha ed. 1991)

Pestel-Debord, La procédure d'arbitrage en droit anglais, 41 *Droit Mar. Français* 291 (1989)

Phillips, J.F., *Arbitration: Law, Practice and Precedents* (Cambridge 1988)

Powell, Settlement of Disputes by Arbitration in Fifteenth-Century England, 2 *Law & Hist. Rev.* 21 (1984)

Poznanski, The Nature and Extent of an Arbitrator's Power in International Commercial Arbitration, 4 *J. Int'l Arb.* 71 (No. 3, 1987)

Ray, La responsibilidad de transportistas en las reglas de Hamburgo y la solución arbitral de controversias, in *El Arbitraje Comercial Internacional* 461 (Mexico 1983)

Real, G.K.L., *Der Schiedsrichtervertrag* (Cologne 1983)

Redfern, England as a Forum for the Arbitration of International Construction Disputes, 2 *Int'l Constr. L. Rev.* 258 (1985)

Redmond, Arbitration in the Channel Islands, 2 *J. Int'l Arb.* 45 (No. 4, 1985)

——, Arbitration in the Channel Islands, 52 *Arbitration* 181 (1986)

Reymond, The Report of the Mustill Committee: A Foreign View, 106 *L.Q. Rev.* 431 (1990)

Riedberg, P., *Der amiable Compositeur im internationalen privaten Schiedsgerichtsverfahren* (Frankfurt 1962)

Robert, El arbitraje en los paises de la Comunidad Europea, in *El Arbitraje Comercial Internacional* 223 (Mexico 1983)

Rogers, Contemporary Problems in International Commercial Arbitration, 17 *Int'l Bus. L.* 154 (1989)

——, Forum Non Conveniens in Arbitration, 4 *Arb. Int'l* 240 (1988)

Rokison, The Practice of Arbitration in England Insofar as it Relates to Anglo-German Business Relations, in *Handelsschiedsgerichtsbarkeit in England und in der Bundesrepublik Deutschland* 19 (K.-H. Böckstiegel ed. 1987)

——, The Sources and Limits of the Arbitrator's Powers in England, in *Contemporary Problems of International Arbitration* 86 (J.D.M. Lew ed. 1986); also 52 *Arbitration* 219 (1986)

Rose, F.D., ed., *International Commercial and Maritime Arbitration* (London 1988)

Russell, F., *Russell on the Law of Arbitration* (20th ed. by A. Walton & M. Vitoria 20th ed. 1982)

Rutherford, Arbitration: Be There Dragons? 84 *L. Soc'y Gazette* 2422 (1987)

Samuel, Developments in English Arbitration Law since the 1984 Antaios Decision, 5 *J. Int'l Arb.* 9 (No. 3, 1988)

———, Pre-Award Interest: England and Scotland, 5 *Arb. Int'l* 310 (1989)

———, Separability in English Law — Should an Arbitration Clause Be Regarded as an Agreement Separate and Collateral to a Contract in Which It Is Contained? 3 *J. Int'l Arb.* 95 (No. 3, 1986)

———, The 1979 Arbitration Act — Judicial Review of Arbitration Awards on the Merits in England, 2 *J. Int. Arb.* 53 (No. 4, 1985)

———, The Recognition and Enforcement of Foreign Judgments and Arbitral Awards in England with a Comparative Look at the United States of America, in *Le Juriste Suisse Face au Droit et aux Jugements Etrangers: Ouverture ou Repli?* 105 (F. Knoepfler ed. 1988)

———, Tribunal of Two, 53 *Arbitration* 141 (1987)

Samuel, A., *Jurisdictional Problems in International Commercial Arbitration: A Study of Belgian, Dutch, English, French, Swedish, Swiss, U.S. and West German Law* (Zurich 1989)

Sanders, International Commercial Arbitration — How to Improve Its Functioning? 46 *Arbitration* 9 (1980)

———, Observations sur la loi britannique sur l'arbitrage ('Arbitration Act 1979'), *Rassegna dell'Arb.* 155 (1979)

Sanoff, SNE v. JOC Oil Ltd.: A Recent Development in the Theory of the Separability of the Arbitration Clause, 1 *Am. Rev. Int'l Arb.* 157 (1990)

Schlosser, The German Law on Arbitration and Its Relevance for the German-English Business Relations, in *Handelsschiedsgerichtsbarkeit in England und in der Bundesrepublik Deutschland* 59 (K.-H. Böckstiegel ed. 1987)

Schmitthoff, Arbitration — the Next Step in the United Kingdom, 4 *Arb. Int'l* 67 (1988)

————, Arbitration and EEC Law, 24 *Common Mkt L. Rev.* 143 (1987)

————, The Supervisory Jurisdiction of the English Courts, in *Liber Amicorum for Martin Domke* 289 (P. Sanders ed. 1967)

Semple, New Scottish Arbitration Rules, 57 *Arbitration* 79 (1991)

————, The UNCITRAL Model Law and the United Kingdom, 56 *Arbitration* 95 (1990)

Sethu, Abandonment in Contract, 1987 *Malayan L.J.* xli

Shenton, Arbitral Impartiality: The Attitude of the English Courts, 8 *Int'l Bus. Law.* 76 (1980)

————, Attachments and Interim Court Remedies in Support of Arbitration: The English Courts, in *Interim Court Remedies in Support of Arbitration* 53 (D. Shenton & W. Kühn eds. 1987)

————, Interim Court Remedies in Support of Arbitration, 12 *Int'l Bus. Law.* 101 (1984)

————, The Enforcement of International Commercial Arbitral Awards in English Courts, 8 *Int'l Bus. Law.* 35 (1980)

————, The Liability of Arbitrators, England, 8 *Int'l Bus. Law.* 335 (1980)

Shenton & Toland, London as a Venue for International Arbitration: The Arbitration Act, 1979, 12 *L. & Pol. Int'l Bus.* 643 (1980)

Shifman, The London Court of International Arbitration, in 4A *W.A.R.* 5561 (H. Smit & V. Pechota eds. 1989)

Shilston, Milestone in the Evolution of Modern Commercial Arbitration, 53 *Arbitration* 26 (1987)

Shilston, The Evolution of Modern Commercial Arbitration, 4 *J. Int'l Arb.* 44 (No. 2, 1987)

Simpson, Licensing Disputes in England and Scotland — Arbitration or Litigation? in *Arbitration and the Licensing Process* 5-97 (R. Goldscheider & M. de Haas eds. 1984-)

Sims, Trust Your Arbitrator? 137 *New L.J.* 855 (1987)

Slade, London Court of International Arbitration, in *First International Commercial Arbitration Conference: Proceedings* 75 (N. Antaki & A. Prujiner, eds. 1986)

————, The Arbitration Rules (1988) of the Chartered Institute of Arbitration, 54 *Arbitration* 265 (1988)

Smedresman, The Arbitration Act, 1979, 11 *J. Mar. L. & Com.* 319 (1980)

Smith, Impartiality of the Party-Appointed Arbitrator, 6 *Arb. Int'l* 320 (1990)

Solveni, Dichiarazione di efficacia in Italia di lodi arbitrali inglesi convertiti in sentenze della High Court of Justice ai sensi della Sez. 26 dell'Arbitration Act, 1950, 88 *Dir. Mar.* 451 (1986)

Soper, Authority and the English Arbitrator, 46 *Arbitration* 195 (1980)

————, The Importance of the Preliminary Proceedings, 41 *Arbitration* 17 (1974)

Spiro, England Rejects Delocalized Contracts and Arbitration, 33 *Int'l & Comp. L.Q.* 193 (1984)

Sterling, United Kingdom, in 2A *W.A.R.* 2701 (H. Smit & V. Pechota eds. 1987)

Steyn, Remedies Against the Reluctant Respondent: The Position Under English Law, 5 *Arb. Int'l* 294 (1989)

————, Arbitration Law Reform: Towards a New Arbitration Act, 6 *Int'l Arb. Rep.* 27 (No. 4, 1991)

————, Arbitration and the Courts: Arbitration Systems in England and Wales and Recent Changes in Arbitration Law, 46 *Arbitration* 146 (1980)

————, Arbitration in England: The Current Issues, 15 *Int'l Bus. Law.* 432 (1987); also in 54 *Arbitration* 221 (1988)

————, England, in *Int'l Handbook Com. Arb.* (P. Sanders ed. 1984)

————, England: National Report, 8 *Y.B. Com. Arb.* 3 (1983)

————, Methods of Conducting International Commercial Arbitrations: A Re-Examination, in *Second Bermuda Int'l Arb. Conference: A Collection of Papers* (Hamilton, Bermuda, April 19-22, 1983)

————, Reasoned Awards Under the Arbitration Act 1979, 47 *Arbitration* 264 (1982)

————, Towards a New English Arbitration Act, 7 *Arb. Int'l* 17 (1991)

Steyn & Marriott, Towards a New Arbitration Act, 57 *Arbitration* 14 (1991)

Steyn & Veeder, England, in *Int'l Handbook Com. Arb.* (A. van den Berg, gen. ed. 1984), Suppl. 9, Sept. 1988

————, England: National Report, 14 *Y.B. Com. Arb.* 499 (1989)

Summerskill, Maritime Arbitrations, in *Handbook of Arbitration Practice* 265 (R. Bernstein ed. 1987)

Sutton, Choosing a Forum for International Commercial Arbitration in London, 76 *Am. Soc. Int'l L. Proc.* 178 (1982)

————, Discovery and Production of Evidence in Arbitral Proceedings: the U.S. and England Distinguished, in *ICC, Taking of Evidence in International Proceedings* 57 (1990)

Tackaberry, The Conduct of Arbitration Proceedings Under English Law, in *Contemporary Problems in International Arbitration* 216 (J.D.M. Lew ed. 1986); also 52 *Arbitration* 227 (1986)

Tan, Multiple Parties and Causes of Action in Arbitration Proceedings, 1988 *Malayan L.J.* li

————, Unmeritorious Claims and Defences in Arbitration Proceedings, 1987 *Malayan L.J.* cxvii

Thomas, Admiralty Security and the Arbitral Process, 1983 *Lloyd's Mar. & Com. L.Q.* 493

————, An Appraisal of the Arbitration Act 1979, 1981 *Lloyd's Mar. & Com. L.Q.* 199

————, Arbitration: The Basis and Validity of a Restricted Reasons Agreement, 1986 *Lloyd's Mar. & Com. L.Q.* 235

————, Commercial Arbitration: The Curial Law of Arbitration Proceedings, 1984 *Lloyd's Mar. & Com. L.Q.* 491

————, International Commercial Arbitration Agreements and the Enforcement of Foreign Arbitral Awards — A Commentary on the Arbitration Act 1975, 1981 *Lloyd's Mar. & Com. L.Q.* 17

————, Power of the Court to Extend Time for Commencing Arbitration Proceedings, 1981 *Lloyd's Mar. Com. L.Q.* 529

————, The Availability of a Security Obtained in Rem to the Arbitral Process Under English Law, in 2 *Fifth Int'l Congress of Maritime Arbitrators* (New York 1981)

————, The Injunctive Jurisdiction of the Commercial Court with Regard to Consensual Commercial Arbitration, 1981 *Lloyd's Mar. Com. L.Q.* 389

————, Arbitration in England: The Current Issues, 4 *Arb. Int'l* 75 (1988)

————, Right to Remuneration under the Arbitration Rules of 1988 of the Chartered Institute of Arbitrators, 55 *Arbitrator* 179 (1989)

————, The Antaios: The Nema Guidelines Reconsidered, 1985 *J. Bus. L.* 200

Thompson, The Same Tribunal for Different Arbitrations, 4 *J. Int'l Arb.* 111 (No. 2, 1987)

Triebel & Lange, Reform des englischen Schiedsgerichtsrechts, 26 *RIW* 616 (1980)

Turner, The Powers of an Arbitrator under English Law and the English Legal System, 47 *Arbitrator* 33 (1981)

van Delden, English Commodity Arbitrations: A Foreigner Looking Around in London, in *The Art of Arbitration* 95 (J. Schultsz & A. van den Berg eds. 1982)

Veeder, Multi-Party Disputes: Consolidation under English Law, 2 *Arb. Int'l* 310 (1986)

Vigrass, Arbitration Services in the United Kingdom Relevant to Anglo-German Business Relations, in *Handelsschiedsgerichtsbarkeit in England und in der Bundesrepublik Deutschland* 143 (K.-H. Böckstiegel ed. 1987)

————, Arbitration in London, 45 *Arbitration* 104 (1979)

————, The Role of Institutions in Arbitration, in *Handbook of Arbitration Practice* 367 (R. Bernstein ed. 1987)

Vis, Want of Prosecution in English Commercial Arbitration, in *The Art of Arbitration* 311 (J. Schultsz & A. van den Berg eds. 1982)

von Mehren, From Vynior's Case to Mitsubishi: The Future of Arbitration and Public Law, 12 *Brooklyn J. Int'l L.* 583 (1986)

Wall, United Kingdom: The London Court of Arbitration, in *Handbook of Institutional Arbitration in International Trade* 225 (E. Cohn, M. Domke & F. Eisemann eds. 1977)

Wallace, Control by the Courts: A Plea for More, Not Less, 6 *Arb. Int'l* 253 (1990)

Weir, Arbitration in Scotland, 4 *J. Int'l Arb.* 35 (No. 4, 1987)

————, Scotland, in *Int'l Handbook Com. Arb.* (A. van den Berg gen. ed. 1984), Suppl. 2, April 1984

————, Scotland as a Centre for International Commercial Arbitration, 6 *J. Int'l Arb.* 83 (No. 4, 1989)

Westin, Enforcing Foreign Commercial Judgments and Arbitral Awards in the United States, West Germany, and England, 19 *L. & Pol'y Int'l Bus.* 325 (1987)

Wetter, The Importance of Having a Connection, 3 *Arb. Int'l* 329 (1987)

————, The Mustill Committee Report on the UNCITRAL Model Law, 6 *Arb. Int'l* 268 (1990)

UNITED STATES

Aksen, American Arbitration Accession Arrives in the Age of Aquarius: United States Implements United Nations Convention on the Recognition and Enforcement of Foreign Arbitral Awards, 3 *Sw. U. L. Rev.* 1 (1971); also in *A.A.A., New Strategies for Peaceful Resolution of Int'l Business Disputes* 37 (1971)

————, International Arbitration Received Favorably in U.S., *N.Y.U. L.J.* 1 (1976)

————, Les arbitrages multiparties aux Etats-Unis, 1981 *Rev. Arb.* 98

————, Multi-party Arbitrations in the United States, in *Arbitration and the Licensing Process* 5-3 (R. Goldscheider & M. de Haas eds. 1984-)

————, The Application of the New York Convention by the United States, 4 *Y.B. Com. Arb.* 341 (1979)

Aksen & Dorman, Application of the New York Convention by United States Courts: A Twenty-Year Review, 2 *Am. Rev. Int'l Arb.* 65 (1991)

Allison, Arbitration of Private Antitrust Claims in International Trade: A Study in the Subordination of National Interests to the Demands of a World Market, 18 *N.Y.U. J. Int'l L. & Pol.* 361 (1986)

American Arbitration Association, *New Strategies for Peaceful Resolution of International Business Disputes* (Dobbs Ferry, NY 1971)

Anderson & Rugman, The Canada-U.S. Free Trade Agreement: A Legal and Economic Analysis of the Dispute Settlement Mechanism, 6 *J. Int'l Arb.* 65 (No. 4, 1989)

Apuzzo & Kerr, International Arbitration — The Dispute Settlement Procedures Chosen for the Canada-U.S. Free Trade Agreement, 5 *J. Int'l Arb.* 7 (No. 4, 1988)

Atkeson & Ramsey, Proposed Amendment of the Foreign Sovereign Immunities Act, 79 *Am. J. Int'l L.* 770 (1985)

Atwood, Issues in Federal - State Relations Under the Federal Arbitration Act, 37 *U. Fla. L. Rev.* 61 (1985)

Audit, Les 'Accords' d'Alger du 19 janvier 1981 tendant au règlement des différends entre les Etats-Unis et l'Iran, 108 *J. Droit Int'l (Clunet)* 713 (1981)

Azrieli, Dispute Resolution Under Chapter 18 of the Canada-United States Free Trade Agreement, 1 *Am. Rev. Int'l Arb.* 419 (1990)

Baker & Yoder, ICSID Arbitration and the U.S. Multilateral Corporation: An Alternative Dispute Resolution Method in International Business, 5 *J. Int'l Arb.* 81 (No. 4, 1988)

Barclay, The Arbitration Award, 45 *Arbitration* 118 (1979)

Barron, Court-Ordered Consolidation of Arbitration Proceedings in the United States, 4 *J. Int'l Arb.* 81 (No. 1, 1987)

Bauer, Maritime Arbitration in New York, 8 *Int'l Bus. Law.* 306 (1980)

————, Some Suggested Changes to the U.S. Arbitration Act, in 1 *Fifth International Congress of Maritime Arbitrators* (New York 1981)

Baum, Arbitration and Court Intervention: Recent Swiss, U.S. Examples, 1 *Int'l Arb. Rep.* 449 (1986)

Becker, Attachments and International Arbitration — An Addendum, 2 *Arb. Int'l* 365 (1986)

————, Attachments in Aid of International Arbitration — The American Position, 1 *Arb. Int'l* 40 (1985)

————, Antitrust and International Arbitration — The New American Synthesis, 13 *Int'l Bus. Law.* 445 (1985)

————, Choice of Law and the Federal Arbitration Act: The Shock of Volt, 45 *Arb. J.* 32 (No. 2, 1990)

————, The Supervisory and Adjunctive Jurisdiction of American Courts in Arbitration Cases, in *Contemporary Problems in International Arbitration* 207 (J.D.M. Lew ed. 1986)

Becker & Kleyn, Public Policy and Arbitration — The 'Unruly Horse' and the Arbitrability of Claims in America, 17 *Int'l Bus. Law* 422 (1989)

Bedell, Punitive Damages in Arbitration, 21 *J. Marshall L. Rev.* 21 (1987)

Bedell, Harrison & Harvey, The McMahon Mandate: Compulsory Arbitration of Securities and RICO Claims, 19 *Loy. U. Chi. L.J.* 1 (1987)

827

Behre, Arbitration: A Permissible or Desirable Method of Resolving Disputes Involving Federal Acquisition and Assistance Contracts? 16 *Pub. Cont. L.J.* 66 (1986)

Berg, Punitive Damages: Are They Properly Awarded in Arbitration? 1 *Int'l Arb. Rep.* 248 (1986)

————, Maritime RICO as Seen by an Arbitrator, 12 *Tul. Mar. L.J.* 85 (1987)

————, Internationale Schiedsgerichtsbarkeit und Staatsimmunität: Die Revision des U.S. Foreign Sovereign Immunities Act, 35 *RIW* 956 (1989)

Berglin, The Application in United States Courts of the Public Policy Provisions of the Convention on the Recognition and Enforcement of Foreign Arbitral Awards, 4 *Dick. J. Int'l L.* 167 (1986)

Bernardini, Stati Uniti: arbitrabilità di controversie in materia de legislazione antitrust, 25 *Rassegna dell'Arb.* 109 (1985)

Bernini, Recent Legislations and International Unification of the Law on Arbitration, in *First International Commercial Arbitration Conference: Proceedings* 315 (N. Antaki & A. Prujiner eds. 1986)

Billings, International Standards for Automotive Arbitration, 28 *German Y.B. Int'l L.* 425 (1985)

Böckstiegel, K.-H., ed., *Schiedsgerichtsbarkeit im deutsch-amerikanischen Wirtschaftverkehr/Arbitration in U.S.-German Business Relations* (Cologne 1985)

Borris, C., *Die internationale Handelsschiedsgerichtsbarkeit in den USA* (Cologne 1987)

Bösch, A., *Einstweiliger Rechtsschutz in der internationalen Handelsschiedsgerichtsbarkeit* (Berne 1989)

Boyd, The UNCITRAL Model Law on International Commercial Arbitration: Commentary, in *First International Commercial Arbitration Conference: Proceedings* 393 (N. Antaki & A. Prujiner eds. 1986)

Branson, Neuere Entwicklungen auf dem Gebiet der Schiedsgerichtsbarkeit in den USA, 1 *Jahrbuch Schiedsgerichtsbarkeit* 227 (1987)

Branson & Wallace, Choosing the Substantive Law to Apply in International Commercial Arbitration, 27 *Va. J. Int'l L.* 39 (1986)

————, Court-Ordered Consolidated Arbitrations in the United States: Recent Authority Assures Parties the Choice, 5 *J. Int'l Arb.* 89 (No. 1, 1988)

————, Immunity of Arbitrators under United States Law, in *The Immunity of Arbitrators* 85 (J.D.M. Lew ed. 1990)

————, Neuere Entwicklungen auf dem Gebiet der Schiedsgerichtsbarkeit in den USA, 2 *Jahrbuch Schiedsgerichtsbarkeit* 268 (1988)

Brower, Discovery and Production of Evidence in the U.S.: Theory and Practice, in ICC, *Taking of Evidence in International Arbitral Proceedings* 7 (1990)

Brown, An Introduction to Arbitration for Idaho Lawyers, 20 *Idaho L. Rev.* 303 (1984)

Brunelli, L'arbitrato commerciale negli Stati Uniti e i metodi di risoluzione alternativa delle controversie, 41 *Riv. Trim. Dir. & Proc. Civ.* 1015 (1987) and 42 *Riv. Trim. Dir. & Proc. Civ.* 235 (1988)

Buchanan, Public Policy and International Commercial Arbitration, 26 *Am. Bus. L.J.* 511 (1988)

Byrne, The Effect of RICO on Maritime Arbitration, 12 *Tul. Mar. L.J.* 77 (1987)

Campbell & Vollmer, U.S. Supreme Court's Mitsubishi Decision Boosts International Arbitrations, 82 *L. Soc'y Gazette* 2830 (1985)

Carabiber, L'immunité de juridiction et d'exécution des Etats collectivités et établissements publics au regard de l'obligation assumée par une clause compromissoire inserée dans les contrats internationaux de droit privé, in *Liber Amicorum for Martin Domke* 23 (P. Sanders ed. 1967)

Carbonneau, American and Other National Variations on the Theme of International Commercial Arbitration, 18 *Ga. J. Int'l & Comp. L.* 143 (1988)

————, Etude historique et comparée de l'arbitrage: vers un droit matériel de l'arbitrage commercial international fondé sur la motivation des sentences, 36 *Rev. Int'le Droit Comp.* 727 (1984)

————, L'arbitrage en droit américain, 1988 *Rev. Arb.* 3

————, Le droit américain de l'arbitrage, in *L'Arbitrage* 205 (L. Matray & G. de Leval eds. 1989)

————, Mitsubishi: The Folly of Quixotic Internationalism, 2 *Arb. Int'l* 116 (1986)

————, The Exuberant Pathway to Quixotic Internationalism: Assessing the Folly of Mitsubishi, 19 *Vand. J. Transnat'l L.* 265 (1986)

Carper, Remedies in Business Arbitration, 46 *Arb. J.* 49 (No. 3, 1991)

Chapman, Comment, The Case for Domestic Arbitration of Federal Securities Claims: Is the Wilko Doctrine Still Valid? 16 *Sw. U.L. Rev.* 619 (1986)

Chiu, Consolidation of Arbitral Proceedings and International Commercial Arbitration, 7 *J. Int'l Arb.* 53 (No. 2, 1990)

Cleveland, How to Save Maritime Arbitration in New York (A Modest Proposal), in 2 *Fifth International Congress of Maritime Arbitrators* (New York 1981)

Cloud, Mitsubishi and the Arbitrability of Antitrust Claims: Did the Supreme Court Throw the Baby Out with the Bathwater? 18 *L. & Pol. Int'l Bus.* 341 (1986)

Cohen, El arbitraje maritimo. La experiencia norteamericana, in *El Arbitraje Comercial Internacional* 501 (Mexico 1983)

————, International Commercial Arbitration: A Comparative Analysis of the United States System and the UNCITRAL Model Law, 12 *Brooklyn J. Int'l L.* 703 (1986)

Cohen, M.M., ed., *Index and Digest of the Award Service of the Society of Maritime Arbitrators*, Volumes 3A & 3B (New York 1986)

Cohen & Dayton, The New Federal Arbitration Law, 12 *Va. L. Rev.* 265 (1926)

Cole, Public Policy Exception to the New York Convention on the Recognition and Enforcement of Arbitral Awards, 1 *Ohio St. J. Disp. Res.* 365 (1986)

Coll, United States Enforcement of Arbitral Awards Against Sovereign States: Implications of the ICSID Convention, 17 *Harv. J. Int'l L.* 401 (1976)

Connell, The Federal Arbitration Act: The Expanding Impediment of State Law upon Rigorous Enforcement, 20 *J. Mar. L. & Com.* 327 (1989)

Coulson, An American Critique of the IBA's Ethics for International Arbitrators, 4 *J. Int'l Arb.* 103 (No. 2, 1987)

————, Commercial Arbitration in the United States, 51 *Arbitration* 367 (May 1985)

————, International Commercial Arbitration in the United States of America, in *Arbitration in Settlement of International Commercial Disputes Involving the Far East and Arbitration in Combined Transportation* 161 (P. Sanders ed. 1989)

————, Soviet-American Contract Arbitration, 1983 *Y.B. Swed. & Int'l Arb.* 20

Crawford, Les Etats et l'exécution des sentences arbitrales dans les droits américain et anglais, 1985 *Rev. Arb.* 689

Comment, Arbitration and Antitrust: A Leg Up for International Arbitration [Mitsubishi Motors Corp. v. Soler Chrysler-Plymouth, Inc., 105 S. Ct. 3346 (1985)], 25 *Washburn L.J.* 536 (1986)

————, Arbitration and Intellectual Property: A Survey of Arbitration in Patent, Trademark and Copyright Cases, 48 *Alb. L. Rev.* 797 (1984)

————, Enforcement of Interim Awards, 3 *Forum New York* 4 (No. 2, 1986)

————, Enforcing International Commercial Arbitration Agreements — Post-Mitsubishi Motors Corp. v. Soler Chrysler-Plymouth, Inc., 36 *Am. U.L. Rev.* 57 (1986)

————, Preemption of State Law under the Federal Arbitration Act, 15 *U. Balt. L. Rev.* 129 (1985)

————, Transnational Contractual Disputes: Antitrust Joins Securities Law Claims as Arbitrable Subject Matter, 12 *Brooklyn J. Int'l L.* 731 (1986)

————, United Nations Foreign Arbitral Awards Convention: United States Accession, 2 *Cal. W. Int'l L.J.* 69 (1971)

Daughtrey, Enforcement of Arbitration Clauses Against Deceived Franchisees, 21 *U. Rich. L. Rev.* 391 (1987)

De Seife, R., *Solving Disputes through Commercial Arbitration* (Wilmette, IL 1987)

Deitrick, The Conflicting Policies Between Arbitration and Bankruptcy, 40 *Bus. Law.* 33 (1984)

Delaume, Judicial Decisions Related to Sovereign Immunity and Transnational Arbitration, 2 *ICSID Rev. - Foreign Investment L.J.* 403 (1987)

———, L'arbitrage transnational et les tribunaux américains, 108 *J. Droit Int'l (Clunet)* 788 (1981)

Deshpande, Enforcement of Foreign Awards in India, U.K. and U.S.A., 4 *J. Int'l Arb.* 41 (No. 1, 1987)

Devow, Commercial Dispute Resolution Between the United States and the People's Republic of China: Problems and Prospects, 7 *Suff. Transnat'l L.J.* 329 (1983)

Diamond, 1983 California Court of Appeal Survey: Arbitration, 6 *Whittier L. Rev.* 207 (1984)

DiBenedetto, Arbitration under the C.P.L.R., 16 *Trial Lawyers Q.* 39 (1984)

———, An Outline for Arbitration under the Civil Practice Law and Rules, 48 *Alb. L. Rev.* 763 (1984)

Dietrich, Internationale Schiedsvereinbarungen vor amerikanischen Gerichten, 40 *Rabels Z.* 1 (1976)

Dobkin, Arbitration of Patent Disputes under the U.S. Arbitration Act, 23 *Arb. J.* 1 (1968)

Domke, The United States Implementation of the United Nations Arbitral Convention, 19 *Am. J. Comp. L.* 575 (1971)

Donaldson, Mitsubishi and Antitrust Arbitration — It's All the Japanese You Need to Know, 1986 *B. Y. U. L. Rev.* 219 (1986)

Dore, I., *Theory and Practice of Multiparty Commercial Arbitration, With Special Reference to the UNCITRAL Framework* (London 1990)

Dreyer, Arbitration Agreements after Volt and Browning-Ferris, 38 *U. Kan. L. Rev.* 667 (1990)

Ebb, Flight of Assets from the Jurisdiction 'In the Twinkling of a Telex': Pre- and Post-Award Conservatory Relief in International Commercial Arbitration, 7 *J. Int'l Arb.* 9 (No. 1, 1990)

————, Developing Views on What Constitutes a 'Foreign Arbitration Agreement' and a 'Foreign Award' under the New York Convention, 1 *Am. Rev. Int'l Arb.* 364 (1990)

Ebke & Parker, Foreign-Country Money Judgments and Arbitral Awards and the Restatement (Third) of the Foreign Relations Law of the United States: A Conventional Approach, 24 *Int'l Law.* 21 (1990)

Eckstrom, L., *Licensing in Foreign and Domestic Operations*. Volume I, Chapter 7: Arbitration (by Steven Z. Szczepanski), (New York 1972, updated 1987)

Eisemann, L'arbitrage commercial international et le juge américain, 1 *Droit et Pratique du Com. Int'l* 653 (1975)

Escudero, The Enforceability of Predispute Arbitration Agreements under 10(b) and 10b-5 Claims, 43 *Wash. & Lee L. Rev.* 923 (1986)

Ettinger, The Public Relations Value of Arbitration, 2 *Arb. J.* 304 (1947)

Evans, The Nonarbitrability of Subject Matter Defense to Enforcement of Foreign Arbitral Awards in United States Federal Courts, 21 *N.Y.U. J. Int'l L. & Pol.* 329 (1989)

Everard Goodman, Choosing a Place for International Arbitration: The New York Option, 2 *J. Int'l Arb.* 39 (No. 2, 1985)

Farrug & McHugh, What's New in Arbitration? 34 *Federation of Insurance Counsel Q.* 347 (1984)

Feldman, Enforcement of Foreign Arbitral Awards in the U.S. Courts, 3 *Int'l Arb. Rep.* 15 (No. 11, 1988)

Feldman, Waiver of Foreign Sovereign Immunity by Agreement to Arbitrate: Legislation Proposed by the American Bar Associatiom, 40 *Arb. J.* 24 (No. 1, 1985)

Fiotto, The United States Arbitration Act and Preliminary Injunctions: A New Interpretation of an Old Statute, 66 *B. U. L. Rev.* 1041 (1986)

Fletcher, Privatizing Securities Disputes through the Enforcement of Arbitration Agreements, 71 *Minn. L. Rev.* 393 (1987)

Fletcher, C.E., *Arbitrating Securities Disputes* (New York 1990)

Foster, C.A., *The Law and Practice of Commercial Arbitration in North Carolina* (Durham 1986)

Fox, Mitsubishi v. Soler and Its Impact on International Commercial Arbitration, 19 *J. World Trade L.* 579 (1985)

——, Preemption of State Law under the Federal Arbitration Act, 15 *Baltimore L. Rev.* 129 (1985)

Friedland, Provisional Measures in ICSID Arbitration, 2 *Arb. Int'l* 335 (1986)

Furnish, Commercial Arbitration Agreements and the Uniform Commercial Code, 67 *Calif. L. Rev.* 317 (1979)

Gaillard, The UNCITRAL Model Law and Recent Statutes on International Arbitration in Europe and North America, 2 *ICSID Rev. - Foreign Investment L.J.* 424 (1987)

Gann, The U.S. Bilateral Investment Treaty Program, 21 *Stan. J. Int'l L.* 373 (1985)

García de Enterría, The Role of Public Policy in International Commercial Arbitration, 21 *L. & Pol'y Int'l Bus.* 389 (1990)

Garvey & Heffelfinger, Towards Federalizing U.S. International Commercial Arbitration Law, 25 *Int'l Law.* 209 (1991)

Golbert, International Arbitration Law Proposed for California, in *Arbitration & the Law: AAA General Counsel's Annual Report 1987-88* 262 (1988)

Golbert & Kolkey, California — A More Attractive Venue for Dispute Resolution, 4 *Int'l Arb. Rep.* 13 (1989)

——, California's Adoption of a Code for International Commercial Arbitration and Conciliation, 10 *Loy. L.A. Int'l & Comp. L.J.* 583 (1988)

——, California's New International Arbitration and Conciliation Code, 11 *L.A. Law.* 46 (No. 8, 1988)

Gomez, International Arbitration: A Case for Delocalization, 3 *Sri Lanka J. Int'l L.* 61 (1991)

Goodman, Arbitrability and Antitrust: Mitsubishi Motors Corp. v. Soler Chrysler-Plymouth, 23 *Colum. J. Transnat'l L.* 655 (1986)

Gray, Arbitration Under Section 294 and Patent Licensing, in 2 *The Law and Business of Licensing: Licensing in the 1980s* 2C-213 (R. Goldscheider & T. Arnold eds. 1987)

Gudgeon, Arbitration Provisions of U.S. Bilateral Investment Treaties, in *International Investment Disputes: Avoidance and Settlement* 41 (S. Rubin & R. Nelson eds. 1985)

Hascher, Consolidation of Arbitration by American Courts: Fostering or Hampering International Commercial Arbitration? 1 *J. Int'l Arb.* 127 (No. 2, 1984)

Hennington, Computer Arbitration: Taking the Byte Out of Data Processing Disputes, 19 *Cumb. L. Rev.* 279 (1989)

Herzel & Harris, Contracting out of Jury Trials, 6 *J. Int'l Arb.* 41 (No. 1, 1989)

Hines, Dispute Resolution and Choice of Law in United States-Soviet Trade, 15 *Brooklyn J. Int'l L.* 591 (1989)

Hinman, China, Modernization, and Sino-United States Trade: Will China Submit to Arbitration? 10 *Cal. W. Int'l L.J.* 53 (1980)

Hiramoto, A Path to Resources on International Commercial Arbitration 1980-1986, 4 *Int'l Tax & Bus. Law.* 297 (1986)

Hirschman, The Second Arbitration Trilogy: The Federalization of Arbitration Law, 71 *Va. L. Rev.* 1305 (1985)

Hobér, Defenses to Recognition and Enforcement of Foreign Arbitral Awards in the United States, 48 *Nordisk Tidsskrift for International Ret* 38 (1978)

Hoellering, Arbitrability in the Wake of Byrd and Mitsubishi, in *Arbitration & the Law: AAA General Counsel's Annual Report 1986* 59 (1987)

————, Arbitration in the United States, in *Arbitration & the Law: AAA General Counsel's Annual Report 1986* 101 (1987)

————, Arbitration in the United States, 76 *Am. Soc. Int'l L. Proc.* 175 (1982)

————, Interim Measures and Arbitration: The Situation in the United States, 46 *Arb. J.* 22 (No. 2, 1991)

————, Interim Relief in Aid of International Commercial Arbitration, 1984 *Wis. Int'l L.J.* 1 (Symposium)

————, International Arbitration: A U.S. View, 13 *Can. Bus. L.J.* 86 (1987)

————, International Commercial Arbitration: A Peaceful Method of Dispute Settlement, 40 *Arb. J.* 19 (No. 4, 1985)

————, International Commercial Arbitration in the United States, 1 *Am. Rev. Int'l Arb.* 14 (1990)

————, International Commercial Arbitration: United States Perspective, in *UNCITRAL Arbitration Model in Canada* 17 (R. Paterson & B. Thompson eds. 1987)

————, Is a New Practice Emerging from the Experience of the American Arbitration Association? 4 *Int'l Tax & Bus Law.* 230 (1986)

————, Neuere Entwicklungen im U.S.-Recht, 2 *Jahrbuch Schiedsgerichtsbarkeit* 265 (1988)

————, New Opportunities for Patent Arbitration in the United States, in *Arbitration and the Licensing Process* 5-28.1 (R. Goldscheider & M. de Haas, eds. 1984); reprinted from *N.Y.L.J.*, Dec. 16, 1982

————, Provisions of U.S. Law on Arbitration Agreements, in *Arbitration & the Law: AAA General Counsel's Annual Report 1987-88* 170 (1988)

————, Remedies in Arbitration, 20 *The Forum* 516 (1984-85)

————, Shearson/American Express v. McMahon: Broadened Domain of Arbitration in U.S.A., 4 *J. Int'l Arb.* 153 (No. 3, 1987)

————, The American Arbitration Association, in *First International Commercial Arbitration Conference: Proceedings* 81 (N. Antaki & A. Prujiner eds. 1986)

————, Training and Development of Commercial Arbitrators (U.S.A.), 10 *Y.B. Com. Arb.* 551 (1985)

Hoellering & Shifman, American Arbitration Association, in 4A *W.A.R.* 5647 (H. Smit & V. Pechota eds. 1989)

Hoeniger, B., *Commercial Arbitration Handbook* (Carlsbad, CA 1990)

Holtzmann, Dispute Resolution Procedures in East-West Trade, 13 *Int'l Law*. 233 (1979)

————, New Uses for Arbitration in Soviet-American Contracts for Industrial, Scientific, and Technical Development, 5 *Den. J. Int'l L. & Po'y, Spec. Issue* 357 (1975)

————, Powers of Arbitrators Under United States Law to Fill "Gaps" Arising under Long-Term Commercial Contracts, in *ICCA, Fifth Int'l Arb. Congress: Proceedings* C IVh 1-17 (1975)

————, The Importance of Choosing the Right Place to Arbitrate an International Case, in *Private Investors Abroad: Problems and Solutions in International Business* 183 (New York 1977)

————, United States, in *Int'l Handbook Com. Arb.* (P. Sanders ed. 1984)

————, United States of America: The American Arbitration Association, in *Handbook of Institutional Arbitration in International Trade* 249 (E. Cohn, M. Domke & F. Eisemann eds. 1977)

————, United States, 2 *Y.B. Com. Arb.* 116 (1977); 9 *Y.B.* 60 (1984); 15 *Y.B.* 329 (1990)

Holtzmann & Bernini, Hypothetical Case for Use in a Comparative Study of Arbitration Practice in Various Legal Systems, in *Comparative Arbitration Practice and Public Policy in Arbitration* 19 (P. Sanders ed. 1987)

Ishizumi, International Commercial Arbitration and Federal Securities Regulations: Reconciling Two Conflicting Policies, 6 *J. Comp. Bus. & Cap. Mkt. L.* 81 (1984)

Iwasaki, Survey of Maritime Arbitration in New York, 15 *J. Mar. L. & Com.* 69 (1984)

Janicke & Borovoy, Resolving Patent Disputes by Arbitration: An Alternative to Litigation, 62 *J. Pat. Off. Soc'y* 337 (1980)

Jarvin, Arbitrability of Anti-Trust Disputes: the Mitsubishi v. Soler Case, 2 *J. Int'l Arb.* 69 (1985)

————, Arbitrability of Antitrust Disputes: The Mitsubishi v. Soler Case, 25 *Swiss Rev. Int'l Competition L.* 53 (Oct. 1985)

————, Is Exclusion of Concurrent Courts' Jurisdiction over Conservatory Measures to Be Introduced by a Revision of the Convention? 6 *J. Int'l Arb.* 171 (No. 1, 1989)

————, Skiljeforfarande och konkurrenslagstiftning; nagra anmarkningar till Mitsubishimalet [Arbitration and antitrust law: some remarks on the Mitsubishi case], 1986 *Tidskrift utgiven av Juridiska Foreningen i Finland* 219

Jarvis, Problems with and Solutions for New York Maritime Arbitration, 1986 *Lloyd's Mar. & Com. L.Q.* 535

Jarvis & Mellman, A Comment of the Rules of the Maritime Arbitration Board of Miami, 19 *J. Mar. L. & Com.* 463 (1988)

Jones, Punitive Damages as an Arbitration Remedy, 4 *J. Int'l Arb.* 35 (No. 2, 1987)

————, Punitive Damages in Arbitration in the USA, 14 *Int'l Bus. Law.* 188 (1986)

————, Win Punitive Damages in Arbitration, 1987 *ABA Journal* 86

————, Arbitration from the Viewpoint of the Practicing Attorney: An Analysis of Arbitration Cases Decided by the New York State Court of Appeals from January, 1973 to September, 1985, 14 *Fordham Urb. L.J.* 523 (1985-86)

————, History of Commercial Arbitration in England and the United States, in *International Trade Arbitration* 127 (M. Domke ed. 1958)

————, Three Centuries of Commercial Arbitration in New York: A Brief Survey, 1956 *Wash. U. L.Q.* 193

Juliano, Hawaii's Bid to Be an International Alternative Dispute Resolution Forum, 22 *Hawaii Bar J.* 67 (1989)

Junker, Discovery in deutsch-amerikanischen Rechtsverkehr — Entwicklungslinien und Perspektiven, 33 *RIW* 1 (1987)

Kahale, New Legislation in the United States Facilitates Enforcement of Arbitral Agreements and Awards Against Foreign States, 6 *J. Int'l Arb.* 57 (No. 2, 1989)

Kanowitz, Alternative Dispute Resolution and the Public Interest: The Arbitration Experience, 38 *Hastings L.J.* 239 (1987)

Kaplan, L'arbitrabilité des litiges commerciaux en matière de droit de la concurrence, 14 *Droit et Pratique du Com. Int'l* 403 (1988)

―――, The Use of Arbitration to Resolve Market Access Disputes, 22 *Cornell Int'l L.J.* 469 (1989)

Kassis, A., *Problèmes de base de l'arbitrage en droit comparé et en droit international.* Vol. 1: *Arbitrage juridictionnel et arbitrage contractuel* (Paris 1987)

Kawakami & Henderson, Arbitration in U.S./Japanese Sales Disputes, 42 *Wash. L. Rev.* 541 (1967)

Kellor, F., *American Arbitration* (New York 1948)

Keviczky, U.S.-USSR International Arbitration, 25 *Les Nouvelles* 21 (1990)

Kochery, The Enforcement of Arbitration Agreements in the Federal Courts: Erie v. Tompkins, 39 *Cornell L. Q.* 74 (1953)

Kolkey, Attacking Arbitral Awards: Rights of Appeal and Review in International Arbitrations, 22 *Int'l Law.* 693 (1988)

―――, Towards Adoption of the UNCITRAL Model Law: Reflections on the U.S. Statutory Framework for International Commercial Arbitration, 1 *Am. Rev. Int'l Arb.* 491 (1990)

Koslow, The Arbitrator's Power to Award Punitive Damages in International Contract Actions, 19 *N.Y.U. J. Int'l L. & Pol.* 203 (1986)

Kühl, S. G., *Schiedsgerichtsbarkeit im Seehandel* (Kehl am Rhein 1990)

Kuner, The Public Policy Exception to the Enforcement of Foreign Arbitral Awards in the United States and West Germany under the New York Convention, 7 *J. Int'l Arb.* 71 (No. 4, 1990)

Lange & Wiessner, Die Schiedsfähigkeit internationaler Antitrust-Streitigkeiten: zur Mitsubishi-Entscheidung des U.S. Supreme Court, 31 *RIW* 757 (1985)

Langeveld, Iets over getuigen in internationale arbitrages, 1988 *Tijdschrift voor Arbitrage* 156

Leacock, American Public Policy and International Arbitration, 1988 *J. Bus. L.* 518

Lécuyer-Thieffry, Les nouvelles lois des Etats américans sur l'arbitrage international, 1989 *Rev. Arb.* 43

―――, Un nouveau domaine pour l'arbitrage aux Etats-Unis: la validité et la contrefaçon des brevets, 1985 *Rev. Arb.* 405

Lécuyer-Thieffry, C. & P. Thieffry, *Le règlement des litiges civils et commerciaux avec les Etats-Unis* (Paris 1986)

Leahy & Pierce, Sanctions to Control Party Misbehavior in International Arbitration, 26 *Va. J. Int'l L.* 291 (1986)

Lebedev, Arbitration in Soviet-American Trade Relations, 5 *Den. J. Int'l L. & Pol'y* 337 (1975)

―――, The 1977 Optional Clause for Soviet-American Contracts, 27 *Am. J. Comp. L.* 469 (1979)

Lee, Antitrust and Commercial Arbitration: An Economic Analysis, 62 *St. John's L. Rev.* 1 (1987)

Lefkowitz, The Trademark Forum: A Place for Arbitration in Proceedings Before the Trademark Trial and Appeal Board, 72 *Trademark Rep.* 275 (1982); reprinted in *Arbitration and the Licensing Process* 5-28.33 (R. Goldscheider & M. de Haas eds. 1984-)

Lepp, Arbitration Appeals: A Comparison of Certain English and American Trade Associations, 39 *Arbitration* 125 (1972)

―――, Arbitration Appeals: A Comparison of Certain English and American Trade Associations, 28 *Rassegna dell'Arb.* 57 (1988)

Lepp & Migeal, Powers of the Arbitrators, in 1 *Fifth International Congress of Maritime Arbitrators* (New York 1981)

Less, Late Arbitration Awards Enforceable Where Party Fails to Make Timely Objection, 21 *Suff. U.L. Rev.* 447 (1987)

Lessing, Sauer-Getriebe K.G. v. White Hydraulics, Inc.― Applicability of the Federal Arbitration Act to International Commercial Arbitration, 2 *Int'l Tax & Bus. Law.* 331 (1984)

―――, Schiedsgerichtsbarkeit und Massnahmen des provisorischen Rechtsschutzes: Jüngste Entwicklungen in den Vereinigten Staaten, 25 *ZRV* 26 (1984)

Lewis, What Goes Around Comes Around: Can Iran Enforce Awards of the Iran-U.S. Claims Tribunal in the United States? 26 *Colum. J. Transnat'l L.* 515 (1988)

Lindsay, 'Public' Rights and Private Forums: Predispute Arbitration Agreements and Securities Litigation, 20 *Loy. L.A. L. Rev.* 643 (1987)

Lipner, International Antitrust Law: To Arbitrate or Not to Arbitrate, 19 *Geo. Wash. J. Int'l L. & Econ.* 395 (1985)

Loftis, Securing Arbitral Awards: Waiving Immunity Under the Foreign Sovereign Immunities Act and Ensuring Equitable Remedy by Pre-Award Attachment Under the New York Convention, 9 *Suff. Transnat'l L.J.* 235 (1985)

Lombard, Arbitration Has Worked at Exxon, 42 *Arb. J.* 3 (No. 1, 1987)

Lord, Arbitration in the United States, 9 *Mar. Law.* 227 (1984)

Lorenzen, Commercial Arbitration — International and Interstate Aspects, 43 *Yale L.J.* 716 (1934)

Loumiet, United States: Florida International Arbitration Act. Introductory Note, 26 *I.L.M.* 949 (1987)

Loumiet, O'Naghten & Swan, Proposed Florida International Arbitration Act, 16 *U. Miami Inter-Am. L. Rev.* 591 (1985)

Love, Arbitration: the Convention on the Recognition and Enforcement of Foreign Arbitral Awards, as Implemented by U.S. Law, Applies to Arbitration Awards Involving Wholly Foreign Interests and Rendered in the United States, 15 *J. Mar. L. & Com.* 134 (1984)

Lowenfeld, The Mitsubishi Case: Another View, 2 *Arb. Int'l* 178 (1986)

Lowry, The United States Joins the Inter-American Arbitration Convention, 7 *J. Int'l Arb.* 84 (No. 3, 1990)

Lutz, International Arbitration and Judicial Intervention, 10 *Loy. L.A. Int'l & Comp. L.J.* 621 (1988)

MacLaren, Commercial Arbitration in the United States and Overseas, in *Arbitration and the Licensing Process* 5 (R. Goldscheider & M. de Haas eds. 1984-)

McClendon, Enforcement of Foreign Arbitral Awards in the United States, 4 *Nw. J. Int'l L. & Bus.* 58 (1982)

————, State International Arbitration Laws: Are They Needed or Desirable? 1 *Am. Rev. Int'l Arb.* 245 (1990)

————, Subject-Matter Arbitrability in International Cases: Mitsubishi Motors Closes the Circle, 11 *N.C. J. Int'l L. & Com. Reg.* 81 (1986)

————, The World Arbitration Institute: Attracting International Arbitration to the United States, in *Private Investors Abroad - Problems and Solutions in International Business* 145 (New York 1985)

————, Arbitrability of Statutory Claims, in *AAA, Arbitration & the Law 1986* 63 (1987)

McClendon, J.S. & R.E. Everard Goodman, *International Commercial Arbitration in New York* (Ardsley-on-Hudson, NY 1986)

McCormack, A Lawyer's View of Arbitration Proceedings and Composition of the Arbitration Panel, 1984 *Y.B. Mar. L.* 55

————, Arbitration in Combined Transportation — A Rare Bird, in *Arbitration in Settlement of International Commercial Disputes Involving the Far East and Arbitration in Combined Transportation* 325 (P. Sanders ed. 1989)

McDermott, Enforcement of Arbitration Agreements in the United States and in the Asia-Pacific Region, 10 *Loy. L.A. Int'l & Comp. L.J.* 615 (1988)

————, Significant Developments in the United States Law Governing International Commercial Arbitration, 1 *Conn. J. Int'l L.* 111 (1985-86)

McGovan, Arbitration Clauses as Waivers of Immunity from Jurisdiction and Execution under the Foreign Sovereign Immunity Act of 1976, 5 *N.Y. L. Sch. J. Int'l & Comp.L.* 409 (1984)

McGrath, Son of Mitsubishi — Arbitration of Domestic Antitrust Disputes, 12 *Brooklyn J. Int'l L.* 693 (1986)

McKellar, To Consolidate or Not to Consolidate: A Study of Federal Court Decisions, 44 *Arb. J.* 15 (No. 4, 1989)

McLaughlin & Genevro, Enforcement of Arbitral Awards Under the New York Convention — Practice in U.S.Courts, 3 *Int'l Tax & Bus. Law.* 249 (1986)

McMahon, Implementation of U.N. Convention on Foreign Arbitral Awards in the U.S., in *A.A.A., New Strategies for Peaceful Resolution of Int'l Business Disputes* 75 (1971); also in 2 *J. Mar. L. & Com.* 735 (1971)

Malcolm & Segall, The Arbitrability of Claims Arising under Section 10(b) of the Securities Exchange Act: Should Wilko Be Extended? 50 *Alb. L. Rev.* 725 (1986)

Malloy, The Iran Crisis: Law under Pressure, 1984 *Wis. Int'l L.J.* 15 (Symposium)

Manbeck, Voluntary Arbitration of Patent Disputes — Background to 35 U.S.C. 294, in *Arbitration and the Licensing Process* 5-28.25 (R. Goldscheider & M. de Haas eds. 1984-)

Martinez, Recognition and Enforcement on International Arbitral Awards under the United Nations Convention of 1958: The 'Refusal' Provisions, 24 *Int'l Law.* 487 (1990)

Massoff, Authority of United States Bankruptcy Courts to Stay International Arbitral Proceedings, 11 *Fordham Int'l L.J.* 148 (1987)

Medalie, R., ed., *Commercial Arbitration for the 1990s* (Chicago 1991)

Meier, Provisional Judicial Remedies in Arbitration: The United States Position, in *Interim Court Remedies in Support of Arbitration* 31 (D. Shenton & W. Kühn eds. 1987)

Mellman, Seeking Its Place in the Sun: Florida's Emerging Role in International Commercial Arbitration, 19 *U. Miami Inter-Am. L. Rev.* 363 (1987-88)

Merchant & Merchant, The Law Relating to Recognition and Enforcement of Foreign Arbitral Agreements and Awards in the United States of America and India, in *ICCA, Fifth Int'l Arb. Congr.: Proceedings* C Im 1-10 (1975)

Miller, Consolidated Arbitrations in New York Maritime Disputes, 14 *Int'l Bus. Law.* 58 (1986)

Mills, State International Arbitration Statutes and the U.S. Arbitration Act: Unifying the Availability of Interim Relief, 13 *Fordham Int'l L.J.* 604 (1989-1990)

Moglen, Commercial Arbitration in the Eighteenth Century: Searching for the Transformation of American Law, 93 *Yale L.J.* 135 (1983)

Mok Young-Joon, The Principle of Reciprocity in the United Nations Convention on the Recognition and Enforcement of Foreign Arbitral Awards of 1958, 21 *Case W. Res. J. Int'l L.* 123 (1989)

Mooney, Interim Awards — Their Usage and Enforceability in the United States, in 2 *Fifth International Congress of Maritime Arbitrators* (New York 1981)

843

Morgan, Contract Theory and the Sources of Rights: An Approach to the Arbitrability Question, 60 *S. Cal.. L. Rev.* 1059 (1987)

Morris, Schiedsgerichtsbarkeit in den USA, 35 *RIW* 857 (1987)

Morton, United States-Soviet Commercial Arbitration Under the 1972 Trade Agreement, 7 *Case W. Res. J. Int'l L.* 121 (1974)

Mosk, Enforcement of International Arbitral Awards, 2 *Calif. Int'l Practitioner* 9 (1990-91)

Mostafa, The Applicable Law in Commerce Arbitration between American and Egyptian Parties, 32 *Rev. Egyptienne Droit Int'l* 179 (1976)

Murray, Claims for Damage and Submission to Arbitration Clauses as Traps for Lethargic Businessmen in the United States and England, 87 *Com. L.J.* 359 (1982)

Nelson, The Arbitrability of Securities Disputes between Brokers and Customers — Phillips v. Merrill Lynch, Pierce, Fenner & Smith, Inc., 20 *Creighton L. Rev.* 1009 (1987)

Newman & Burrows, New York Law Revision Changes Attachment Picture, 1 *Int'l Arb. Rep.* 301 (1986)

Newton, Arbitration and Antitrust: A Leg Up for International Arbitration, 25 *Washburn L.J.* 536 (1986)

Norberg, U.S. Ratification and Implementation of the Inter-American Convention: A Commentary, 1 *Am. Rev. Int'l Arb.* 588 (1990)

————, United States Implements Inter-American Convention on Commercial Arbitration? 45 *Arb. J.* 23 (No. 4, 1990)

Note, Appealability of District Court Orders Granting or Denying Stays of Arbitration under 28 U.S.C. 1291(a)(1), 36 *Case W. Res. L. Rev.* 1 (1985-86)

————, Application of the Convention on the Recognition and Enforcement of Foreign Arbitral Awards: Mitsubishi Motor Corp. v. Soler Chrysler-Plymouth, Inc., 8 *Fordham Int'l L.J.* 194 (1984)

————, Arbitrability of Implied Rights of Action under Section 10(b) of the Securities Exchange Act, 61 *N.Y.U. L. Rev.* 506 (1986)

————, Arbitrability of Claims Arising under the Securities Exchange Act of 1934, 1986 *Duke L.J.* 548

—, Arbitration: Public Policy Exception to Arbitration of Anti-trust Issues: Mitsubishi Motors Corp. v. Soler Chrysler Plymouth, Inc. 723 F.2d 155 (1st Cir. 1983), 25 *Harv. Int'l L.J.* 427 (1984)

—, Authority of United States Bankruptcy Courts to Stay International Arbitral Proceedings, 11 *Fordham Int'l L.J.* 148 (1987)

—, Commercial Dispute Resolution between the United States and the People's Republic of China: Problems and Prospects, 7 *Suff. Transnat'l L.J.* 329 (1983)

—, Enforcement of Foreign Arbitral Awards under the United Nations Convention of 1958: A Survey of Recent Federal Case Law. Notes and Comments, 11 *Md. J. Int'l L. & Trade* 13 (1987)

—, Enforcing Foreign Judgments and Arbitration Awards, 5 *Int'l Fin. L. Rev.* 26 (No. 7, 1986)

—, Enforcing International Commercial Arbitration Agreements and Awards Not Subject to the New York Convention, 23 *Va. J. Int'l L.* 75 (1982)

—, Predispute Arrangements to Arbitrate Claims Arising under the Commodity Exchange Act, 42 *Wash. & Lee L. Rev.* 939 (1985)

—, Resolving the Conflict between Arbitration Clauses and Claims under Unfair and Deceptive Practices Acts, 64 *B. U. L. Rev.* 377 (1984)

—, The Effectiveness of Arbitration for the Resolution of Consumer Disputes, 6 *N.Y.U. Rev. L. & Soc. Change* 175 (1977)

—, The Recognition and Enforcement of Foreign Arbitral Awards: Defenses to Arbitrability, 37 *S.C. L. Rev.* 719 (1986)

—, The Use of Pre-Judgment Attachments and Temporary Injunctions in International Commercial Arbitration Proceedings: A Comparative Analysis of the British and American Approaches, 50 *U. Pitt. L. Rev.* 667 (1989)

—, The Validity of the Foreign Sovereign Immunity Defense in Suits Under the Convention on the Recognition and Enforcement of Foreign Arbitral Awards, 7 *Fordham Int'l L. J.* 321 (1983-84)

—, Transnational Antitrust Claims are Nonarbitrable under the Federal Arbitration Act and Art. II(1) of the Convention on the Recognition & Enforcement of Foreign Arbitral Awards: Mitsubishi v. Soler Chrysler-Plymonth, 17 *Vand. J. Transnat'l L.* 741 (1984)

O'Connell, Arbitration and Forum Selection Clauses in International Business: The Supreme Court Takes on Internationalist View, 43 *Fordham L. Rev.* 424 (1974)

O'Neill, American Legal Developments in Commercial Arbitration Involving Foreign States and State Enterprises, 6 *J. Int'l Arb.* 117 (No. 1, 1989)

————, Recent Developments in International Commercial Arbitration: an American Perspective, 4 *J. Int'l Arb.* 7 (No. 1, 1987); also in 53 *Arbitration* 177 (1987)

Oehmke, T., *Commercial Arbitration* (Rochester 1989)

————, *International Arbitration* (Rochester 1990)

Olson, International Arbitration and Securities Laws, 1976 *Sec. L. Rev.* 747 (1976)

Oparil, Waiver of Sovereign Immunity in the United States and Great Britain by an Arbitration Agreement, 3 *J. Int'l Arb.* 61 (No. 4, 1986)

Overby, Arbitrability of Disputes under the Federal Arbitration Act, 71 *Iowa L. Rev.* 1137 (1986)

Ovington, Arbitration and U.S. Antitrust Law: A Conflict of Policies, 2 *J. Int'l Arb.* 53 (No. 2, 1985)

Palmer, Mitsubishi: the Erosion of the New York Convention and International Arbitration, 1984 *Wis. Int'l L.J.* 151 (Symposium)

Park, National Legal Systems and Private Dispute Resolution, 82 *Am. J. Int'l L.* 616 (1988)

————, Private Adjudicators and the Public Interest: The Expanding Scope of International Arbitration, 12 *Brooklyn J. Int'l L.* 629 (1986)

Park & Hill, International Arbitration, in *Modern Legal Systems Cyclopedia* 873 (K.R. Redden gen. ed. 1984)

Parker School of Foreign and Comparative Law, *International Commercial Arbitration and the Courts* (Dobbs Ferry, NY 1990)

————, *The 1989 Guide to International Arbitration and Arbitrators* (Dobbs Ferry, NY 1989)

Parlade, Remedies after Arbitration Award, in *Commercial Arbitration* 75 (J. Ricalde ed. 1983)

Parnass, International Arbitration and the Comity of Error: Mitsubishi Motors Corp. v. Soler Chrysler-Plymouth, Inc., 19 *Conn. L. Rev.* 435 (1987)

Paulsson, Means of Recourse Against Arbitral Awards Under U.S. Law, 6 *J. Int'l Arb.* 101 (No.2, 1989)

—————, The Contribution of English and American Legislation, in *Euro-Arab Arbitration III* 104 (F. Kemicha ed. 1991)

Pechota, UNCITRAL Rules as Applied in Arbitrations under the Optional Clause for Use in Contracts in USSR-United States Trade, 1977, in 3 *W.A.R.* 3313 (H. Smit & V. Pechota eds. 1987)

Penna, Partial Final Awards, in *AAA, Arbitration & the Law, 1986* 67 (1987)

Pestalozzi, The Validity of Arbitration Clauses under N.Y. UCC 2-207 (The Battle of Forms), in *Dr. Lee Jaechul, in Celebration of His 60th Birthday,* 2 *Studies on Modern Civil & Commercial Law* 615 (1984)

Peterson, The Arbitrability of Claims Under the Federal Securities Laws, 12 *J. Corp. L.* 535 (1987)

Peterson, C. & C. McCarthy, *Arbitration Strategy and Technique* (Charlottesville, VA 1986)

Pew & Jarvis, Pre-Award Attachment in International Arbitration: The Law in New York, 7 *J. Int'l Arb.* 31 (No. 3, 1990)

Pfaff, Grenzbewegungen der Schiedsfähigkeit — Patentnichtigkeit im Schiedsverfahren, in *Beiträge zum internationalen Verfahrensrecht und zur Schiedsgerichtsbarkeit. Festschrift für Heinrich Nagel* 278 (W. Habscheid & K. Schwab eds. 1987)

Piergrossi, Problems of Arbitrability of Patent and Licensing Controversies in Italian and United States Law, in *ICCA, Fourth Int'l Arb. Congress: Proceedings* 752 (1972); 6 *N.Y.U. J. Int'l L. & Pol.* 85 (1973)

Polebaum & Conlan, U.S. Rules on Proper Venue in Which to Petition to Vacate a Foreign Arbitration Award, 19 *Int'l Bus. Law.* 219 (1991)

Poser, Arbitrability of International Securities Disputes, 12 *Brooklyn J. Int'l L.* 675 (1986)

Potter, International Commercial Arbitration in the United States: Considering Whether to Adopt UNCITRAL's Model Law, 10 *Mich. J. Int'l L.* 912 (1989)

Power, A Comparison of Soviet and American Maritime Arbitration, 21 *Vand. J. Transnat'l L.* 127 (1988)

Poznanski, The Nature and Extent of an Arbitrator's Power in International Commercial Arbitration, 4 *J. Int'l Arb.* 71 (No. 3, 1987)

Quigley, Accession by the United States to the United Nations Convention on the Recognition and Enforcement of Foreign Arbitral Awards, 70 *Yale L.J.* 1049 (1961)

Rabbino, International Commercial Arbitration — The Relationship between Arbitration and the Federal Securities Laws. Alberto-Culver Co. v. Scherk, 7 *N.Y.U. J. Int'l L. & Pol.* 383 (1974)

Recchia, Enforcement of American Arbitration Awards in Italy, 2 *N.Y.U. J. Int'l L. & Pol.* 219 (1969)

Recchia, G., *Enforcement of Foreign Arbitration Agreements and Awards in Italy and the United States: A Comparative Study* (Naples 1970)

Recent Developments: The Federal Arbitration Act, 1986 *Mo. J. Disp. Res.* 143

Recent Developments: The Uniform Arbitration Act, 1986 *Mo. J. Disp. Res.* 169

Recent Developments: The Uniform Arbitration Act, 1987 *Mo. J. Disp. Res.* 177

Reder, Securities Law and Arbitration: The Enforceability of Predispute Arbitration Clauses in Broker-Customer Agreements, 1990 *Colum. Bus. L. Rev.* 91

Reichert, Provisional Remedies in the Context of International Commercial Arbitration, 3 *Int'l Tax & Bus. Law.* 368 (1986)

Renold, Arbitrage international et droit antitrust: l'arrêt Mitsubishi v. Soler de la Cour suprême des Etats-Unis, 105(127) *ZSR* 545 (1986)

Richard, Enforcement of Foreign Arbitral Awards under the United Nations Convention of 1958: A Survey of Recent Federal Case Law, 11 *Md. J. Int'l L. & Trade* 13 (1987)

Richards, Enforceability of Arbitration Provisions in Construction Contracts, 34 *Federation of Insurance Counsel Q*. 95 (1983)

Rivkin & Kellner, In Support of the F.A.A.: An Argument Against U.S. Adoption of the UNCITRAL Model Law, 1 *Am. Rev. Int'l Arb*. 535 (1990)

Robert, Une date dans l'extension de l'arbitrage international: l'arrêt Mitsubishi c/ Soler, 1986 *Rev. Arb*. 173

Rodman, R.M., *Commercial Arbitration* (With Forms), (St.Paul, Minn. 1984)

Rogers, Forum Non Conveniens in Arbitration, 4 *Arb. Int'l* 240 (1988)

Romeu-Matta, New Developments in International Commercial Arbitration: A Comparative Survey of New State Statutes and the UNCITRAL Model Law, 1 *Am. Rev. Int'l Arb*. 140 (1990)

Rothstein, Recognizing and Enforcing Arbitral Agreements and Awards Against Foreign States: The Mathias Amendments to the Foreign Sovereign Immunities Act and Title 9, 1 *Emory J. Int'l Disp. Res*. 101 (1986)

Rotunda, Cautionary Lessons from American Securities Arbitration: Litigation v. Arbitration, 5 *Arb. Int'l* 199 (1989)

Rovine, U.S. Public Policy on Recognition, Enforcement of Foreign Awards, 1 *Int'l Arb. Rep*. 41 (1986)

Ruga, An Argument Against the Availability of Punitive Damages in Commercial Arbitration, 62 *St. John's L. Rev*. 270 (1988)

Sachs, The New U.S. Bilateral Investment Treaties, 2 *Int'l Tax & Bus. Law*. 192 (1984)

Sacks, Arbitration in Connecticut: Issues in Judicial Intervention Under the Connecticut Arbitration Statutes, 17 *Conn. L. Rev*. 387 (1985)

――――, Arbitration of Disputes Between the People's Republic of China and U.S. Corporations, in *Arbitration and the Licensing Process* 5-83 (R. Goldscheider & M. de Haas eds. 1984-)

Samuel, The Recognition and Enforcement of Foreign Judgments and Arbitral Awards in England with a Comparative Look at the United States of America, in *Le Juriste Suisse Face au Droit et aux Jugements Etrangers: Ouverture ou Repli?* 105 (F. Knoepfler ed. 1988)

849

Sanchez, Should Claims Involving Public Customers Arising Under the Securities Exchange Act of 1934 Be Subject to Compulsory Arbitration? 10 *Harv. J. L. & Pub. Pol'y* 173 (1987)

Sanders, Arbitration Clause for Optional Use in USA-USSR Trade, 3 *Y.B. Com. Arb.* 299 (1978)

Sandrock, Arbitration between U.S. and West German Companies: An Example of Effective Dispute Resolution in International Business Transactions, 9 *U. Pa. J. Int'l Bus. L.* 27 (1987)

―――, Gerichtsstands- oder Schiedsklauseln in Verträgen zwischen U.S.-amerikanischen und deutschen Unternehmen: was ist zu empfehlen?, in *Festschrift für Ernst C. Stiefel* 625 (M. Lutter, W. Oppenhoff, O. Sandrock & H. Winkhaus eds. 1987)

Sandrock & Hentzen, Enforcing Foreign Arbitral Awards in the Federal Republic of Germany: The Example of a United States Award, 2 *Transnat'l Law.* 49 (1989)

Saravalle, Arbitrato internazionale e leggi antitrust: il caso Mitsubishi, 22 *Riv. Dir. Int'le Priv. & Proc.* 597 (1986)

Sayre, Development of Commercial Arbitration Law, 37 *Yale L.J.* 595 (1927)

Schlicher, The Patent Arbitration Law: A New Procedure for Resolving Patent Infringement Disputes, 40 *Arb. J.* 7 (No. 4, 1985)

Schlosser, Party-Appointed Arbitrators and Multiple Defendants Having Conflicting Interests, in *Law in East and West/Recht in Ost und West* 739 (Tokyo 1988)

―――, Verfahrensintegrität und Anerkennung von Schiedssprüchen im deutsch-amerikanischen Verhältnis, 31 *NJW* 455 (1978)

Schwab, The Legal Foundations and Limitations of Arbitration Procedure in the U.S. and Germany, in *International Arbitration: Liber Amicorum for Martin Domke* 301 (P. Sanders ed. 1967)

Schwartz, Multiparty Disputes and Consolidated Arbitrations: An Oxymoron or the Solution to a Continuing Dilemma? 22 *Case W. Res. J. Int'l L.* 341 (1990)

Semmler, The Case for FTAC Arbitration of Disputes Between Soviet Enterprises and American Firms, 14 *Colum. J. Transnat'l L.* 302 (1975)

Shifman, Maritime International Nominees Establishment v. Republic of Guinea: Effect on U.S. Jurisdiction of an Agreement by a Foreign Sovereign to Arbitrate before the ICSID, 16 *J. Int'l L. & Econ.* 451 (1982)

————, United States, in 2A *W.A.R.* 2813 (H. Smit & V. Pechota eds. 1987)

Smit, Elements of International Arbitration in the United States, 1 *Am. Rev. Int'l Arb.* 64 (1990)

————, Mitsubishi: It Is Not What It Seems to Be, 4 *J. Int'l Arb.* 7 (No. 3, 1987)

————, The Carte Blanche Case, 1 *Am. Rev. Int'l Arb.* 172 (1990)

Smith, Determining the Arbitrability of International Antitrust Disputes, 8 *J. Comp. Bus. & Cap. Market L.* 197 (1986)

————, Impartiality of the Party-Appointed Arbitrator, 6 *Arb. Int'l* 320 (1990)

Sommer, Maritime Arbitration — Some of the Legal Aspects, 49 *Tul. L. Rev.* 1035 (1975)

Sopata, Mitsubishi Motors Corp. v. Soler Chrysler-Plymouth, Inc.: International Arbitration and Antitrust Claims, 7 *Nw. J. Int'l L. & Bus.* 595 (1986)

Stein, Pre-hearing Discovery in International Arbitrations in the U.S., 2 *Forum New York* (No. 1, 1985)

Stipanowich, Punitive Damages in Arbitration: Garrity v. Lyle Stuart, Inc. Reconsidered, 66 *B. U. L. Rev.* 953 (1986)

Sturges, Commercial Arbitration in the United States of America, in 1 *Int'l Y.B. Civil & Com. Arb.* 165 (A. Nussbaum ed. 1928)

Sultan, The United Nations Arbitration Convention and United States Policy, 53 *Am. J. Int'l L.* 807 (1959)

Sutton, Discovery and Production of Evidence in Arbitral Proceedings: the U.S. and England Distinguished, in *ICC, Taking of Evidence in International Proceedings* 57 (1990)

Sweeney, Judicial Review of Arbitral Proceedings, in 2 *Fifth International Congress of Maritime Arbitrators* (New York 1981)

851

Swisher, International Commercial Arbitration under the United Nations Convention and the Amended Federal Arbitration Statute, 47 *Wash. L. Rev.* 441 (1972)

Tanaka, Enforcement of American Awards in Japan, 10 *Arb. J.* 88 (1955)

Taylor, National Iranian Oil Co. v. Ashland Oil, Inc.: All Dressed Up and Nowhere to Arbitrate, 63 *N.Y.U. L. Rev.* 1142 (1988)

————, The Arbitrability of Federal Securities Claims: Wilko's Swan Song, 42 *U. Miami L. Rev.* 203 (1987)

Thieffry, P. & C. Lecuyer-Thieffry, *Le règlement des litiges civils et commerciaux avec les Etats-Unis* (Paris 1986)

Tindall, International Commercial Arbitration, 7 *Am. Bus. L. J.* 65 (1969)

Tolson, Conflicts Presented by Arbitral Awards of Punitive Damages, 4 *Arb. Int'l* 255 (1988)

Tschanz, International Arbitration in the United States: The Need for a New Act, 3 *Arb. Int'l* 309 (1987)

Tschanz, Le droit américain et la Convention de New York, in *First International Commercial Arbitration Conference: Proceedings* 249 (N. Antaki & A. Prujiner eds. 1986)

Tupman, Arbitration of Intellectual Property Disputes under U.S. Law, 42 *Arb. J.* 3 (No. 4, 1987)

————, Discovery and Evidence in U.S. Arbitration: The Prevailing Views, 44 *Arb. J.* 27 (No. 1, 1989)

————, Staying Enforcement of Arbitral Awards under the New York Convention, 3 *Arb. Int'l* 223 (1987)

Vaca, Arbitrating Civil RICO and Implied Causes of Action Arising under Section 10(b) of the Securities Exchange Act of 1934, 36 *Cath. U.L. Rev.* 455 (1987)

Victor & Bialos, The Arbitration of International Antitrust Claims: A Bold Supreme Court Experiment in Alternative Dispute Resolution, in *Fordham Corporate Law Institute: Annual Proceedings: Antitrust & Trade Policy in the U.S. and the European Community* 184 (New York 1986)

852

Volk, Discovery in Arbitration in the United States, in *Second Bermuda Int'l Arb. Conference: Collection of Papers* (Hamilton, Bermuda, April 19-22, 1983)

von Mehren, From Vynior's Case to Mitsubishi: The Future of Arbitration and Public Law, 12 *Brooklyn J. Int'l L.* 583 (1986)

———, The Enforcement of Arbitral Awards under Conventions and United States Law, 9 *Yale J. World Pub. Ord.* 343 (1983)

von Zumbusch, Arbitrability of Antitrust Claims Under U.S., German, and EEC Law: The 'International Transaction' Criterion and Public Policy, 22 *Tex. Int'l L.J.* 291 (1987)

———, Die Schiedsfähigkeit privatrechtlicher Kartellrechtsstreitigkeiten nach US-, deutschem und EG-Recht, 1988 *GRUR Int'l* 541

Vorhees, International Commercial Arbitration and the Arbitrability of Antitrust Claims: Mitsubishi Motors Corp. v. Soler Chrysler Plymouth, 14 *N. Ky. L. Rev.* 65 (1987)

Walker, Commercial Arbitration in United States Treaties, 11 *Arb. J.* 68 (1956)

Walsh, Arbitration in International Commercial Transactions: Mitsubishi Motors Corp. v. Soler Chrysler-Plymouth, Inc. and Its Aftermath, 13 *Syracuse J. Int'l L. & Com.* 200 (1986)

Weitbrecht, U.S.-Antitrustrecht vor internationalen Handelsschiedsgerichten (zu Mitsubishi Motors Corp. v. Soler Chrysler-Plymouth, Inc., U.S. Supreme Court, Entscheidung von 2 Juli 1985, -U.S.-, 105 S.Ct.3346), 6 *IPRax* 313 (1986)

Werner, A Swiss Comment on Mitsubishi, 3 *J. Int'l Arb.* 81 (No. 4, 1986)

Westin, Enforcing Foreign Commercial Judgments and Arbitral Awards in the United States, West Germany, and England, 19 *L. & Pol'y Int'l Bus.* 325 (1987)

Wilkinson, Judicial Review of Foreign Arbitral Awards on Antitrust Matters After Mitsubishi Motors, 26 *Colum. J. Transnat'l L.* 407 (1988)

Wills, Is Court Enforced Discovery Proper in Aid of an Arbitration Governed by the U.S. Arbitration Act? in 1 *Fifth International Congress of Maritime Arbitrators* (New York 1981)

Wodehouse, New York Arbitration As Seen by a Londoner, 1986 *Lloyd's Mar. & Com. L.Q.* 43

Wright, California's International Commercial Arbitration Act: New Procedures for the Arbitration and Conciliation of International Commercial Disputes, 17 *Int'l Bus. Law.* 45 (1989)

Yamane, Resolving Disputes in U.S.-Japan Trade: The Japanese Perspective, 39 *Arb. J.* 3 (No. 4, 1984)

Zimmer, D., *Zulässigkeit und Grenzen schiedsgerichtlicher Entscheidung von Kartellrechtsstreitigkeiten* (Baden-Baden 1991)

Zubrod, A History of Appeal of Arbitration Awards in the United States, in 2 *Fifth Int'l Congress of Maritime Arbitrators* (New York 1981)

————, Interim Decisions and Partial Final Awards in United States Arbitrations, in *Second Bermuda Int'l Arb. Conference: A Collection of Papers* (Hamilton, Bermuda, April 19-22, 1983)

————, Maritime Arbitration in New York, 39 *Arb. J.* 16 (No. 4, 1984)

URUGUAY

Barclay, Arbitration in Latin America, 43 *Arbitration* 105 (1977)

Dunshee de Abranches, C.A., ed., *El arbitraje comercial en Ibero-américa* (Madrid 1982)

Garro, Uruguay, in 2A *W.A.R.* 2861 (H. Smit & V. Pechota eds. 1987)

Holz & Samtleben, Schiedsgerichtsbarkeit in Uruguay, 34 *RIW* 107 (1988)

International Chamber of Commerce, Uruguay, in *Commercial Arbitration and the Law/L'Arbitrage commercial et la Loi* (Basel 1949)

Rodriguez Sanguinetti, Uruguay: un arbitrio imprescindible: la dilucidación arbitral de controversias entre partes, 1 *Rev. Corte Esp. Arb.* 274 (1984)

Santos Belandro, R., *Arbitraje comercial internacional: tendencias y perspectivas* (Montevideo 1988)

VENEZUELA

Aramburú Menchaca, International Commercial Arbitration in the Andean Pact (Observations for a Community Regime), in *The Art of Arbitration* 27 (J. Schultsz & A. van den Berg eds. 1982)

Dunshee de Abranches, C.A., ed., *El arbitraje comercial en Ibero-américa* (Madrid 1982)

Gabaldon, F., *El arbitraje en el Código de procedimiento civil* (Caracas 1987)

Garro, Venezuela, in 2A *W.A.R.* 2911 (H. Smit & V. Pechota eds. 1987)

Goldman, Arbitration and Transfer of Technology in Latin America, in *Arbitration and the Licensing Process* 5-29 (R. Goldscheider & M. de Haas eds. 1984-)

International Chamber of Commerce, Venezuela, in *Commercial Arbitration and the Law/L'Arbitrage commercial et la Loi* (Basel 1949)

Mantellini Gonzales, El proceso arbitral en el Código de Procedimientos Civil Venezolano de 1987, in *El Arbitraje en el Derecho Latinoamericano y Español* 619 (L. Perret & U. Montoya Alberti eds. 1989)

Montoya Alberti, Arbitration, Foreign Law and Jurisdiction in International Loan Agreements in Some Countries of Latin America, in *Arbitration in Settlement of International Commercial Disputes Involving the Far East and Arbitration in Combined Transportation* 99 (P. Sanders ed. 1989)

———, El arbitraje en los contratos de prestamo internacionales, in *El Arbitraje en el Derecho Latinoamericano y Español* 481 (L. Perret & U. Montoya Alberti eds. 1989)

Parra Aranguren, Venezuela: National Report, 3 *Y.B. Com. Arb.* 133 (1978)

Samtleben, Schiedsgerichtsbarkeit in den Andenpaktstaaten, 30 *RIW* 600 (1984)

———, Schiedsklauseln in Peru and Venezuela, 33 *RIW* 20 (1987)

Smit, De eerste ICC-arbitrage in Venezuela, 1988 *Tijdschrift voor Arbitrage* 173

VIETNAM

Fellhauer, H. & H. Strohbach, eds., *Handbuch der internationalen Handelsschiedsgerichtsbarkeit* (Berlin 1969)

Lebedev, S., ed., *Handbook on Foreign Trade Arbitration in the CMEA Member Countries* (Moscow 1983)

Pozdnyakov, Commercial Arbitration in CMEA Member Countries, 4 *Int'l Tax & Bus. Law.* 272 (1986)

WESTERN SAMOA

Speight, Resolution of Disputes in Some Smaller Pacific Countries, *paper presented to International Conference "Growth of Arbitration" in the Pacific, Auckland, NZ, Sept. 1985*

YEMEN

El-Ahdab, A.H., *Arbitration with the Arab Countries* (Deventer 1990)

————, *L'arbitrage dans les pays arabes* (Paris 1988)

Ghanem, The Enforcement of Arbitral Awards and Foreign Judgments in the Yemen Arab Republic, 3 *Arab. L.Q.* 81 (1988)

Saleh, The Recognition and Enforcement of Foreign Arbitral Awards in the States of the Arab Middle East, in *Contemporary Problems in International Arbitration* 340 (J.D.M. Lew ed. 1986)

————, The Settlement of Disputes in the Arab World: Arbitration and Other Methods, 1 *Arab L. Q.* 198 (1986); reprinted in 4 *Int'l Tax & Bus. Law.* 280 (1986)

Saleh, S., *Commercial Arbitration in the Arab Middle East* (London 1984)

Sohbi, Settlement of Disputes through Arbitration: Arbitration in the Yemen Arab Republic, in *Arab Comparative & Commercial Law: The International Approach: Proceedings I.B.A. Conference* 207 (1987)

Troller, Arbitration and Enforcement of Arbitration Awards in Arab Countries, 2 *Int'l Contr.* 397 (1981)

Ziadé, Selective Bibliography on Arbitration and Arab Countries, 3 *ICSID Rev. - Foreign Investment L.J.* 423 (1988)

YUGOSLAVIA

Bernini, Recent Legislations and International Unification of the Law on Arbitration, in *First International Commercial Arbitration Conference: Proceedings* 315 (N. Antaki & A. Prujiner eds. 1986)

Cicin-Sajn, A. & M. Ellis, eds., *Doing Business with Yugoslavia: Economic and Legal Aspects*. Chapter XII: Arbitration in International Commerce (Belgrade/Zagreb 1986)

Dika, The Problem of Multiparty Arbitration from the Standpoint of Yugoslav Law, in 5 *Hague-Zagreb Essays* 125 (C. Voskuil & J. Wade eds. 1985)

Djurovic, Foreign Trade Court of Arbitration at the Economic Chamber of Yougoslavia: An Institution of Self-Management Judiciary, 10 *Yugoslav L.* 25 (1983)

Goldstajn, Arbitration and Arbitral Procedure in Yugoslavia, 7 *Am. J. Comp. L.* 588 (1958)

―――, Yugoslavia, in *Int'l Handbook Com. Arb.* (A. van den Berg gen. ed. 1984), Suppl. 4, Nov. 1985

―――, Yugoslavia: National Report, 1 *Y.B. Com. Arb.* 106 (1976); 8 *Y.B. Com. Arb.* 81 (1983); 10 *Y.B. Com. Arb.* 3 (1985)

Goldstajn, A. & S. Triva, *Medunarodna trgovacka arbitraza* (Zagreb 1987)

Heller, Zur Vollstreckung eines jugoslawischen Schiedsspruches in Österreich, 9 *IPRax* 315 (1989)

Kuss, Neuere Entwicklungen und Perspektiven der Ost West Schiedsgerichtsbarkeit, 33 *RIW* 584 (1987)

Lew, Commercial Arbitration in the Socialist Federal Republic of Yugoslavia, 28 *Arb. J.* 34 (March 1973)

―――, Commercial Arbitration in the Socialist Federal Republic of Yugoslavia, 13 *Rassegna dell'Arb.* 97 (1973)

Mezger, Die Anerkennung jugoslawischer und anderer osteuropäischer Schiedssprüche in der Bundesrepublik, 15 *NJW* 278 (1962)

Pisar, S., *Coexistence & Commerce*, Chapters 20 - 24 (New York 1970)

Przetacznik, The Foreign Trade Court of Arbitration Attached to the Yugoslav Chamber of Economy, in 4A *W.A.R.* 5797 (H. Smit & V. Pechota eds. 1989)

Sajko, Die jugoslawische Aussenhandelsschiedsgerichtsbarkeit, 29 *RIW* 916 (1983)

————, The New York Arbitration Convention of 1958 from the Yugoslav Point of View: Selected Issues, in *Essays on International Commercial Arbitration* 199 (P. Sarcevic ed. 1989)

Stalev, The Continental Case of Eastern Europe, 41 *Arbitration* 95 (1974)

Stojkovic, Anerkennung und Vollstreckung ausländischer Schiedssprüche in Jugoslawien, 30 *Rabels Z.* 685 (1966)

Stumpf, Ost-West-Schiedsgerichtsbarkeit: Schiedsgerichte mit Sitz in dritten Ländern, 33 *RIW* 821 (1987)

Triva, Pocetak arbitraznog postupka. Uoci prihvacanja UNCITRAL-ovog model-zakona o medunarodnoj trgovackoj arbitrazi i mogucnosti da ga SFR Jugoslavija inkorporira u svoj pravni system, 35 *Zbornik Pravnog Fakulteta u Zagrebu* 195 (1985)

Varady, Les développements nouveaux concernant la reconnaissance et l'exécution des sentences arbitrales étrangères en Yougoslavie, 1983 *Rev. Arb.* 163

————, Règlement de la Cour d'arbitrage du commerce extérieur auprès de la Chambre Economique de Yugoslavie, texte et commentarire, 1984 *Rev. Arb.* 151

Vilius, J., ed., *Spoljnotrgovinska arbitraza* (Beograd 1982)

Zdravkovic, Certains cas de la jurisprudence yougoslave et étrangère sur l'exécution des sentences arbitrales étrangères, in *ICCA, Fifth Int'l Arb. Congress: Proceedings* C Izi 1-16 (1975)

ZAIRE

Phanzu-Nianga di Mazanza, *Introduction à l'arbitrage commercial* (Kinshasa 1981)

ZIMBABWE

Christie, R.H., *Business Law in Zimbabwe* (Cape Town 1985)